Maryland Casualties in the War of 1812

by

Christos Christou, Jr.

Maryland State President, 2012–2015
Society of the War of 1812 in the State of Maryland
National Registrar General, 2008–2017
General Society of the War of 1812

and

Henry C. Peden, Jr.

Maryland State Genealogist, 1990–2020
Society of the War of 1812 in the State of Maryland
National Genealogist General, 2008–2020
General Society of the War of 1812

HERITAGE BOOKS
2019

...wrong to mourn the men who died.
Rather we should thank God that such men lived."
Gen. George S. Patton, *American soldier*

HERITAGE BOOKS
AN IMPRINT OF HERITAGE BOOKS, INC.

Books, CDs, and more—Worldwide

For our listing of thousands of titles see our website
at
www.HeritageBooks.com

Published 2019 by
HERITAGE BOOKS, INC.
Publishing Division
5810 Ruatan Street
Berwyn Heights, Md. 20740

Copyright © 2019 Christos Christou, Jr.
and Henry C. Peden, Jr.

International Standard Book Number
Paperbound: 978-0-7884-5815-6

"It is foolish and wrong to mourn the men who died.
Rather we should thank God that such men lived."
Gen. George S. Patton, *American soldier*

Table of Contents

"A soldier doesn't fight because he hates what is in front of him;
he fights because he loves what he left behind."
G. K. Chesterton, *English poet*

Acknowledgements

As with any publication, many people have helped in various ways from research of original records, secondary sources, providing and sharing their discoveries, and obtaining copies from distant places. We also live off the backs of those historians and writers who have gone before us such as William M. Marine's great 1914 work and F. Edward Wright's many volumes published in the 1980s. The authors appreciate the cooperation and help of all of them.

Both authors have donated their time freely to the War of 1812 Society and put in numerous hours of research to ensure that future generations remember and venerate the sacrifices of these men listed within these pages.

The War of 1812 Society has through the last century published many works of importance, as have others, which will help researchers with their ancestry and we encourage the use of numerous publications prepared by members outside our organization as well. Some of these known resources are noted below. Also see "Additional Sources" listed at the back of this book.

A Chronicle of War of 1812 Soldiers, Seamen, and Mariners, by Dennis F. Blizzard and Thomas L. Hollowak (1993, 2000)

American Prisoners of War Held at Halifax during the War of 1812, by Harrison Scott Baker II (2 volumes) (2004)

American Prisoners of War Held in Quebec during the War of 1812, by Eric Eugene Johnson (2011)

American Prisoners of War Paroled at Dartmouth, Halifax, Jamaica and Odiham during the War of 1812, by Eric Eugene Johnson (2016)

Register of the General Society of the War of 1812 (3 volumes), by Frederick I. Ordway, Jr. (1972), Robert G. Thurtle (1976), and Dennis F. Blizzard (1989)

The Citizen Soldiers at North Point and Fort McHenry, by Nathaniel Hickman (1858)

Maryland Militia in the War of 1812, by F. Edward Wright, 11 volumes (1986-2006)

Maryland Regulars in the War of 1812, by Eric Eugene Johnson & Christos Christou, Jr.

North Point, War of 1812, Maryland War of 1812 Privateers, and Dartmoor War of 1812 Prison, by Thomas Vincent Huntsberry and Joanne M. Huntsberry (1983)

Society of the War of 1812 in Maryland Roster, by C. Louis Raborg, Jr. (2011)

About the Authors

"The legacy of heroes is the memory of a great name and the inheritance of a great example."
Benjamin Disraeli, *English politician*

The authors are distantly related through their direct descent from John Peden (1734-1815), a Revolutionary War soldier who served in western Virginia and they are both very active in the State and National Societies of the War of 1812. Their interest in gathering years of research about the heroes of 1812 led to the publication of this book.

Christos Christou, Jr., of Baltimore, MD, Past President of the Maryland Society 2012-2015, has served in many roles in the War of 1812 Society and published several books and articles, newsletters, etc., for numerous hereditary societies. In the General Society he served nine years as the National Registrar General, 2008-2017. He served as State President of the Maryland Society during the great Bicentennial 2012-2015 (the state bylaws were modified to allow him to serve 3 consecutive years) and served as Vice President, and Corresponding Secretary, and various Committee Chairmen. Christos is an expert genealogist and has published many genealogical works and helped hundreds of people join various hereditary societies. He is also a past President of the Maryland Society Sons of the American Revolution and served as its youngest State President in the 125+ year history of the Society and the only Greek-American President.

He has documented his ancestors **Captain *Alexander Anderson, Private James Beckett, Private John S. Berry, Private Andrew Fleming, Private William Davis Hill, and Teter Null*** in the War of 1812 and his children's ancestors **Colonel James Almony, Corporal Richard Barnhouse, Private Isaac Fowler** and **Corporal Philip R. Rasin**. He thanks his children John, Guy, and Kay for their long-time support of his passion and love of history. It is his birth in Maryland and their birth and ancestry in Maryland that started him on the path of Maryland history studies.

Henry C. Peden, Jr., of Bel Air, MD, renowned genealogist, local historian and award-winning author, has written 180 genealogical and historical books. One of these is *The Delaware Militia in the War of 1812* that he published in 2003. "Hank" has served as Genealogist of the Maryland Society of the War of 1812 since 1990, the longest serving officer in that position, and has served as National Genealogist General of the General Society of the War of 1812 since 2008. At the time of the bicentennial of the War of 1812 he compiled listings of War of 1812 soldiers in Harford County and Cecil County for an on-line project coordinated with the Maryland State Archives and Fort McHenry. He has been a member of the Historical Society of Harford County for 40 years, has served as its President and as chairman of the Library and Genealogy Departments for 20 years. "Hank" is a Fellow and Past President of the Maryland Genealogical Society. In 2007 he was honored as an Archer Fellow of the Historical Society of Harford County. In 2009 he received the prestigious Historical Preservationist Award from the Harford County Historical District Commission. In 2016 he played an instrumental role in returning the Sgt. John Clemm trunk to Fort McHenry. The Library of the Historical Society of Harford County was named *"The Henry C. Peden, Jr. Research Library"* in his honor in September 2017. He continues to write books, assists others in genealogical research and co-directs the "Harford's Heritage" history series on Harford Cable Network that was first aired in 2017.

His War of 1812 ancestors are **Capt. John Bagby,** of Virginia, and **Pvt. George Frank,** of Maryland. Hank served as a Staff Sergeant, U.S. Air Force, 1966-1970, Vietnam Veteran, and received his degrees from Towson University, Bachelor of Science in 1973 and Master of Arts in 1980. He is the husband of the former Veronica Ann Clarke (married 1970) and father of one son Henry Clint Peden III.

This modification to our War of 1812 Society Emblem was designed by President Christos Christou Jr. only to be used during the Bicentennial years.

We have received great support from the Society of the War of 1812 in the State of Maryland in which we are both officers and from the 1812 Community and well-known historians who provided some information found within these pages. Special thanks to the following contributors:

Eric E. Johnson for his extraordinary War of 1812 publications and his database of prisoners of war in England that made our book's coverage more comprehensive.

Christopher T. George for background and details on the Baltimore battle.

John McCavitt for assistance in deciphering the British soldiers' lists.

Scott S. Sheads for background and corrections for the individual soldiers.

Christopher T. Smithson for ordering materials about those named on the Battle Monument from the National Archives and supplementing data.

8

Introduction

The objective of this work is to identify those Maryland heroes who became casualties during the War of 1812. By definition, **a casualty is a military person lost by death, wounds, injury, sickness, internment, or capture or through being missing in action**. This book is based on available records and it is not a complete list because many men who were wounded in battle in 1814 treated themselves and fought on; thus, many were not recorded as such on company muster rolls. Still others would be recorded if they were unable to serve for a period of time and would be listed as sick or absent in hospital and even more men reported their wounds only when they were in the process of applying for government assistance in their old age, such as for bounty land or a pension.

The names of those who died also may never be fully known either as some did not die immediately from their wounds, but lingered for years after the war, eventually succumbing to the wounds. Such was the case with Commodore Joshua Barney injured in 1814 and eventually dying in 1818 from the wound. Deaths of privates, for that period of history, were not valued more than a financial obligation by the government authorities; therefore, the soldiers listed on the Baltimore Battle Monument are understandably incomplete as well.

There are 2,890 soldiers and seamen in this book and many with biographical data. Documented corrections and additions may be sent to Christos Christou, Jr., 303 Nicholson Road, Essex MD 21221-6609 (cchristousoc@gmail.com).

Some abbreviations used:
BLW# – Bounty Land Warrant Number
CMSR – Compiled Military Service Record
NARA – National Archives Records Administration

Authors'cited within this book (also see Additional Sources):
Huntsberry – Thomas V. and Joanne M. Huntsberry
Johnson – Eric E. Johnson
Johnson and Christou – Eric E. Johnson and Christos Christou, Jr.
Mallick and Wright – Sallie A. Mallick and F. Edward Wright
Marine – William M. Marine
Peterson – Clarence S. Peterson
Sheads – Scott S. Sheads
Shomette – Donald G. Shomette
Wright – F. Edward Wright

Maryland Casualties in the War of 1812
A

Abbott, John, of Maryland, served as a Seaman on the ship *LaHogue* and was reported by Capt. Jeduthan Upton, Jr. in 1814 as having been impressed into service and was being held as a Prisoner of War on the prison ship *San Antonio* at Chatham, England (*Niles Weekly Register*, 26 Feb 1814)

Abercrombie, James, served as a Private in Capt. John Rothrock's Co. of the 38th U.S. Infantry, enlisted on 2 Jun 1813, died at Baltimore on 31 Jul 1814 and his widow Syrena Abercrombie received a pension. (Johnson and Christou, p. 18; Pension WO-40106; *Index to War of 1812 Pension Files*, by Virgil D. White, 1992, p. 3, listed his name, company and widow and stated "no other data")

Abick, John, served as a Marine and was taken from the barracks and admitted to the Naval Hospital in Washington, DC as Patient No. 170 as of 1 June 1814, but his injury or illness was not stated (Sharp's Database, 2018)

Ackerman, Mr., served as Sail Maker on the privateer *Surprise* of Baltimore and drowned in a shipwreck on 5 Apr 1815 (Marine p. 199; *Niles Weekly Register*, 15 Apr 1815)

Ackley, William, served as a Private of the 14th U.S. Infantry, enlisted 20 Apr 1812 in Baltimore for 5 years at the age of 40, 5' 5½" tall, was born in Boston. Prisoner of War #3752 (Halifax), captured at Beaver Dams, Upper Canada, ten miles west of Niagara Falls, on 24 Jun 1813, exchanged on 15 Apr 1814 and discharged on 20 Apr 1815 at Greenbush, NY, for wounds, old age and inability (Johnson and Christou, p. 19; Baker, Vol. 1, p. 2, stated he was "discharged for exchange" on 3 Feb 1814)

Adams, Isaac, served as a Ship's Carpenter and was born in Maryland. Age: 27. Prison Depot: Dartmoor, Prison of War #4865. Captured by HM Frigate *Acasta* on 16 Oct 1814. Where Taken: Chesapeake Bay. Prize Name: *Olive Branch*. Ship Type: Merchant Vessel. Date Received: 9 Oct 1814. From what ship: HMT *Freya* from Halifax, NS. Discharged on 21 Jun 1815. (Johnson's Database, 2019)

Adams, John C., served as a Private in Capt. George Flautt's Rifle Co., Frederick Co., from 29 Apr 1813 and died on 11 May 1813 (Wright Vol. 8, p. 333; Mallick and Wright, p. 30)

Adams, Robert, served as a Private in Capt. James Haslett's Co. of the 38th U.S. Infantry, enlisted 4 Jun 1813 for 1 year and either died or was discharged on 15 Jul 1813 (Johnson and Christou, p. 19)

Addison, William H., served as an Ensign in the 38th U.S Infantry from 20 Sep 1813 (date of commission), born in Maryland, commissioned a Captain in U.S. Sea Fencibles on 27 Apr 1814 and died on 9 Dec 1814; his wife Anna Addison received a widow's pension (Old War WF-15507; Johnson and Christou, p. 20)

Agnew, Patrick, served as a Private in Capt. Thomas Montgomery's Co., 14th U.S. Infantry, enlisted 27 Apr 1812 at Baltimore for 5 years at age of 30, 5' 5" tall, born in Montgomery Co., and was discharged at Greenbush, NY because of a rupture (BLW# 11825-160-12; Johnson and Christou, p. 20)

Aikman, Thomas (1791-1815), served as a Private in Capt. Joseph Hook's Co., 36th U.S. Infantry, enlisted 16 Aug 1813 in Snow Hill, MD at age 22, 5' 7½" tall, born in Somerset Co., MD, re-enlisted at Sandy Point, VA on 18 Mar 1814 for 1 year and died on 1 Mar 1815; bounty land issued to brother William Aikman and other heirs at law (BLW# 23224-160-12; Johnson and Christou, p. 20)

Aisquith, Edward, served as Captain of Sharp Shooters, 1st Rifle Battalion, and died in April 1815 (Marine, p. 200)

Aisquith, George, served as a Midshipman of the U.S. Chesapeake Flotilla, entered service on 16 Jun 1814 and was killedat St. Leonard's Creek, 2nd Battle, on 26 Jun 1814 (Shomette, p. 296, spelled his name Asquith; Sheads, p. 22) Later in life Naval Capt. John Adams Webster recalled in his 1853 memoirs that Midshipman Aisquith was "killed on my barge." (Marine, p. 177) A newspaper article at the time stated Midshipman Aisquith, who recently joined the service, was killed in the engagement under Commodore Barney on the Patuxent River on 26 Jun 1814. (*Niles Weekly Register*, 2 Jul 1814)

Albert, Jacob (c1780-1813), served as a Captain in the Extra Battalion, Harford Co. Militia, from 26 Apr to 3 May 1813 and died on 19 Aug 1813, but place and cause of death not stated. (Wright Vol. 3, p. 33; Marine, p. 201, mistakenly stated he died in 1814; *Maryland Bible Records, Volume 2: Baltimore and Harford Counties*, by Henry C. Peden, Jr., 2003, p. 145) Final distribution of his estate was made on 24 Oct 1815 to his widow Elizabeth Albert and their four children Joseph, Sarah, Hannah and Elizabeth Albert. (*Heirs and Legatees of Harford County, Maryland, 1802-1846*, by Henry C. Peden, Jr., 1988, p. 20)

Alexander, George (Mulatto), served as a Seaman and was born in Maryland. Age: 32. Prison Depot: Dartmoor, Prisoner of War #6547. How Taken: Gave himself up off HMS *Theodoria*. When Taken: 22 Feb 1815. Date Received: 7 Mar 1815. From what ship: HMT *Ganges* from Plymouth. Discharged on 11 Jul 1815. (Johnson's Database, 2019)

Alexander, James, served as a Seaman and was born in Baltimore. Age: 23. Prison Depot: Dartmoor, Prisoner of War #5080. Captured by HM Ship-of-the-

Line *Newcastle*. When Taken: 9 Aug 1814. Where Taken: At sea. Prize Name: *Ida*. Home Port: Boston. Ship Type: Letter of Marque. Date Received: 28 Oct 1814. From what ship: HMT *Alkbar* from Halifax, NS. Discharged on 29 Jun 1815. (Johnson's Database, 2019)

Alexander, Pedro, served as a Seaman and was born in Havre de Grace, MD. Age: 36. Prison Depot: Dartmoor, Prisoner of War #5129. Captured by HM Brig *Castilian*. When Taken: 29 Sep 1814. Where Taken: off Ireland. Prize Name: *Calabria*. Ship Type: Merchant Vessel. Date Received: 31 Oct 1814. From what ship: HMT *Castilian*. Discharged on 29 Jun 1815. (Johnson's Database, 2019); see Pedro Alexander Mahu, q.v.

Alexander, William, served as a Private in Capt. Philip B. Sadtler's Co., 39th Regiment, Baltimore Militia, from 16 Aug to 23 Aug 1813 and served at Camp Lookout for 8 days, and then served as a Private in Capt. William Roney's Co., 39th Regiment, from 19 Aug 1814 and was killed in battle at North Point on 12 Sep 1814. His name is on the Baltimore Battle Monument. (NARA; Wright Vol. 2, p. 24; *Baltimore American*, 12 Jun 1819)

Alexander, William, served as a Marine and was taken from the barracks and admitted to the Naval Hospital in Washington, DC as Patient No. 65 on 31 Jul 1814 (injury or illness was not specified) and was discharged on 3 Aug 1814 and sent to the barracks (Sharp's Database, 2018)

Allen, Barnes, served as a Seaman and was born in Baltimore. Age: 33. Prison Depot: Portsmouth, Prisoner of War #163. Captured by HM Transport *Diadem*. When Taken: 7 Oct 1812. Where Taken: S. Andera (St. Andrews, Scotland). Prize Name: *Baltimore*. Home Port: Baltimore. Ship Type: Privateer. Date Received: 3 Nov 1812 San Antonio. From what ship: HMS *Diadem*. Discharged on 19 Feb 1813 and sent to Chatham on HM Store Ship *Dromedary*. Prison Depot: Chatham, Prisoner of War #532. Date Received: 23 Feb 1813 from Portsmouth on HMS *Dromedary*. Discharged on 8 Jun 1813 and released to the Cartel *Rodrigo*. (Johnson's Database, 2019)

Allen, Bryan, served as a Private and was captured at North Point on 12 Sep 1814; Dr. James H. McCulloh, Jr. wrote this soon after the battle to the British commander: "In consequence of the humanity shown the following American prisoners of war, I do promise upon honor that they shall not directly or indirectly serve against the British until regularly exchanged." (Marine, p. 171)

Allen, John (1795-1815), served as a Private in Capt. Samuel Raisin's Co., 36th U.S. Infantry, enlisted 31 Mar 1814 in Westmoreland or Sandy Point, Kinsale, VA for 1 year at the age of 19, 5' 6½" tall, born in Annapolis and died on 4 Feb 1815 (Johnson and Christou, p. 22)

Allen, John, served as a Private in Capt. John R. Brown's Co., 2nd Regiment, 11th Brigade, Baltimore Militia, from 26 Jul 1814 and was wounded on 24 Aug 1814 at Bladensburg (Wright Vol. 2, p. 87)

Allen, John M., served as a Private in Capt. Horatio C. McElderry's Co., 17th Regiment, Prince George's Co. Militia, from 18 Jul to 2 Aug 1814 and was stationed at Port Tobacco, Blennum and Nottingham. On 22 Apr 1878, age 83, in Summerfield, Noble Co., OH he applied for a pension, stating he was called out at Piscataway in 1813, marched to Nottingham, from thence to the Tanyard Springs, took sick on the last tour and we got home a few days before the Battle of Bladensburg. When he enlisted he was age 18, 5' 4" tall, black hair, grey eyes and dark complexion and he was born in Prince George's Co. John M. Allen appears to be the John Allen who was a Private in Capt. Gavin Hamilton's Co., with Horatio C. McElderry as Lieutenant, from 18 to 28 Jul 1813 and was stationed at Accokeek Church. (Wright Vol. 6, pp. 4, 10, 26; Pension SO-32380)

Allen, Noah, served as Prize-master of the privateer *Globe* and was severely wounded in action on 1 Nov 1813 (Marine p. 202)

Allen, Philip (African American), served as a Seaman and was born in Maryland. Age: 28. Prison Depot: Plymouth 1, Prisoner of War #1936. Captured by HM Frigate *President*. When Taken: 14 Aug 1813. Where Taken: off Nantes, France. Prize Name: *Marmion*. Ship Type: Merchant Vessel. Received: 27 Aug 1813. From what ship: HMS *Urgent*. Discharged on 8 Sep 1813 and sent to Dartmoor. Prison Depot: Dartmoor, Prisoner of War #652. Received: 8 Sep 1813 from Plymouth. Discharged on 26 Apr 1815. (Johnson's Database, 2019)

Alman, John (African American), served as a Seaman and was born in Baltimore. Age: 25. Prison Depot: Plymouth 1, Prisoner of War #1426. Captured by HM Frigate *Leonidas* on 23 May 1813 off Cape Clear, Ireland. Prize Name: *Paul Jones*. Home Port: New York. Ship Type: Privateer. Received: 26 May 1813. From what ship: HMS *Leonidas*. Discharged on 3 Jul 1813 and sent to Stapleton Prison. Prison Depot: Stapleton, Prisoner of War #401. Date Received: 11 Jul 1813 from Plymouth. Discharged on 16 Jun 1814 and sent to Dartmoor. Prison Depot: Dartmoor, Prisoner of War #1645. Date Received: 23 Jun 1814 from Stapleton. Discharged on 1 May 1815. (Johnson's Database, 2019)

Almeda, Joseph, served as Captain of the privateer *Caroline* in Oct 1813, which was captured by the ship *Medusa*, and he was later Captain of the privateer *Kemp* in Nov 1814 (Marine p. 203)

Allnut, James N. (c1790-1854), served as 4th Sgt. in Capt. Thomas F. W. Vinson's Co., Extra Battalion, Montgomery Co. Militia, from 1 Aug 1814 and engaged in the Battle of Bladensburg, but not in actual service after the retreat from said Battle, as he was wholly disabled there from by disease contracted in said service which disability continued until after his company was discharged. After retreating from Bladensburg to Rockville James was brought to his father's farm "sick of disease." Dr. William Brewer was the Allnut family physician and he visited James on 28 Aug 1814. On 12 Sep 1855 Barbara Ann Allnut, age 43, of Montgomery Co., widow of James N. Allnut, stated they were married on 4 Dec 1832 by Rev. Gilmore and her former name was Dawson. James died on 1 Jun 1854 in Montgomery Co. (Wright Vol. 7, pp. 5, 12; BLW# 55-160-14055)

Amich (Amick, Ammick), George, served as a Private in the Frederick Co. Militia and was captured at the Battle of Bladensburg on 24 Aug 1814 and returned to service under Capt. George Washington Magee from 14 Oct 1814 to 10 Jan 1815 (Marine, p. 174; Mallick and Wright, p. 32)

Amoss, Thomas, served as a Private in Capt. Peter Pinney's Co., 27th Regiment, Baltimore Militia, from 19 Aug 1814, allegedly killed on 12 Sep 1814 at North Point, but was reported as "missing" on the muster roll dated 19 Aug – 18 Nov 1814 (Wright Vol. 2, p. 20) His name is on the Baltimore Battle Monument)

Anderson, Alexander, served as a Seaman and was born in Maryland. Age: 29. Prison Depot: Dartmoor, Prisoner of War #5067. Captured by HM Ship-of-the-Line *Newcastle* on 9 Aug 1814 at sea. Prize Name: *Ida*. Home Port: Boston. Ship Type: Letter of Marque. Date Received: 28 Oct 1814. From what ship: HMT *Alkbar* from Halifax, NS. Discharged on 29 Jun 1815. (Johnson's Database, 2019)

Anderson, David (African American), served as a Seaman and was born in Maryland. Age: 30. Prison Depot: Plymouth 1, Prisoner of War #1256. Captured by HM Frigate *Medusa*. When Taken: 12 Apr 1813. Where Taken: Bay of Biscayne. Prize Name: *Caroline*. Ship Type: Merchant Vessel. Date Received: 10 May 1813. From what ship: HMS *Medusa*. Discharged on 3 Jul 1813 and sent to Stapleton Prison. Prison Depot: Stapleton, Prisoner of War #273. Date Received: 11 Jul 1813 from Plymouth. Discharged on 16 Jun 1814 and sent to Dartmoor. Dartmoor, Prisoner of War #1557. Date Received: 23 Jun 1814 from Stapleton. Discharged on 1 May 1815. (Johnson's Database, 2019)

Anderson, Edward, served as a Seaman and was born in Baltimore. Age: 26. Prison Depot: Plymouth 1, Prisoner of War #2340. Captured by HM Brig *Castilian* on 27 Jan 1814 off Ushant, France. Prize Name: *Apparencen*, prize of the Privateer *Bunker Hill*. Ship Type: Privateer. Date Received: 30 Jan 1814. From what ship: Cardian. Discharged on 31 Jan 1814 and sent to Dartmoor. Prison Depot: Dartmoor, Prisoner of War #992. Date Received: 31 Jan 1814 from Plymouth. Discharged on 27 Apr 1815. (Johnson's Database, 2019)

Anderson, James (African American), served as a Seaman and was born in Maryland. Age: 21. Prison Depot: Chatham, Prisoner of War #2292. How Taken:

Gave himself up off HM Brig *Scorpion* on 20 Oct 1812. Received: 17 Sep 1813 on HMS *Raisonable*. Discharged on 16 Feb 1814. (Johnson's Database, 2019)

Anderson, James (African American), served as a Cook and was born in Maryland. Age: 25. Prison Depot: Plymouth 1, Prisoner of War #1452. Captured by HM Frigate *Leonidas*. When Taken: 23 May 1813. Where Taken: off Cape Clear, Ireland. Prize Name: *Paul Jones*. Home Port: New York. Ship Type: Privateer. Received: 26 May 1813. From what ship: HMS *Leonidas*. Discharged on 30 Jun 1813 and sent to Stapleton. Prison Depot: Stapleton, Prisoner of War #34. Date Received: 8 Jul 1813 from Plymouth. Discharged on 13 Jun 1814 and sent to Dartmoor. (Johnson's Database, 2019)

Anderson, John (African American), served as a Seaman and was born in Maryland. Age: 24. Prison Depot: Portsmouth, Prisoner of War #1384. Captured by *Vittoria*, Guernsey Privateer. When Taken: 28 Jan 1814. Where Taken: off Bordeaux, France. Prize Name: *Pilot*. Home Port: Baltimore. Ship Type: Letter of Marque. Date Received: 7 Feb 1814. From what ship: *Mary* from Guernsey. Discharged on 13 Feb 1814 and sent to Chatham on HMT *Malabar No. 352*. Prison Depot: Chatham, Prisoner of War #3513. Date Received: 23 Feb 1814 from Portsmouth on HMT *Malabar*. Discharged on 25 Sep 1814 and sent to Dartmoor on HMS *Leyden*. Prison Depot: Dartmoor, Prisoner of War #4553. Received: 8 Oct 1814. From what ship: HMT *Leyden* from Chatham. Discharged on 15 Jun 1815. (Johnson's Database, 2019)

Anderson, Joseph, served as a Seaman and was born in Baltimore. Age: 33. Prison Depot: Portsmouth, Prisoner of War #505. How Taken: Gave himself up off HM Ship-of-the-Line *Diomed* on 16 Jan 1813 on HMS *Diomede*. Discharged on 11 Mar 1813 and sent to Chatham on HM Store Ship *Abundance*. Prison Depot: Chatham, Prisoner of War #1184. Date Received: 16 Mar 1813 on HMS *Abundance*. Discharged on 11 Aug 1814 and sent to Dartmoor. Prison Depot: Dartmoor, Prisoner of War #2607. Date Received: 21 Aug 1814 on HMT *Freya* from Chatham. Discharged on 26 Apr 1815. (Johnson's Database, 2019)

Anderson, Jos., of Maryland, served as a Seaman on the ship *Rodney* and was reported by Capt. Jeduthan Upton, Jr. in 1814 as having been impressed into service and was being held a Prisoner of War on the prison ship *San Antonio* at Chatham, England. (*Niles Weekly Register*, 26 Feb 1814)

Anderson, Joseph (African American), served as a Seaman and was born in Maryland. Age: 26. Prison Depot: Dartmoor, Prisoner of War #1341. Captured by HM Frigate *Leonidas*. When Taken: 23 May 1813. Where Taken: off Cape Clear, Ireland. Prize Name: *Paul Jones*. Home Port: New York. Ship Type: Privateer. Date Received: 19 Jun 1814 from Stapleton. Discharged on 28 Apr 1815. (Johnson's Database, 2019)

Anderson, Joseph, served as a Private in Capt. William Roney's Co., 39th Regt., Baltimore Militia, from 16 Aug 1814 and was "discharged sick on 20 Aug" 1814 (Wright Vol. 2, p. 24)

Anderson, Joshua, of Maryland, served as a Seaman on the ship *Salvador* and was reported by Capt. Jeduthan Upton, Jr. in 1814 as having been impressed into service and was being held as a Prisoner of War on the prison ship *San Antonio* at Chatham, England (*Niles Weekly Register*, 26 Feb 1814)

Andre, Gregorius (1787-1814) served as 1st Lieutenant in Capt. Dominic Bader's Co. of Rifleman, 1st Rifle Bttn., Maryland Militia, from 19 Aug 1814, served 25 days and was killed in Battle of Long Log Lane [North Point] on 12 Sep 1814. Name is on Baltimore Battle Monument. (NARA; Wright Vol. 2, p. 53; *Baltimore American*, 12 Jun 1819) Mary Andre, administratrix of Gregorius, on 19 Nov 1814, was ordered to place a notice in the *Baltimore American* informing creditors to exhibit their claims against his estate. Caroline and John Gregory Andre, orphans of Gregorius Andre, came to Court in Dec 1815. Peter Benson was appointed their guardian. (Baltimore Orphans Court Proceedings Book 9, pp. 66, 69, 81; Baltimore Administration Accounts Book 20, p. 8) His tombstone is inscribed: "Gregorius Andre, Lieut., 1st Rifles, a native of Bremen, who fell at the Battle of North Point 12th of Sept. 1814" (Green Mount Cemetery)

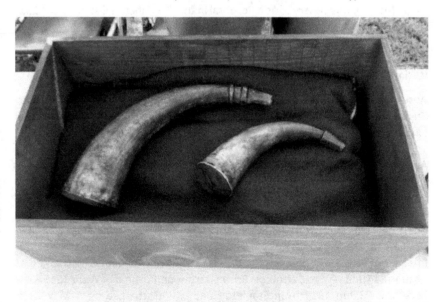

Gregorius Andre powder flasks owned by 1812 member Robert T. Cummins, Jr.

16

Andrew, Edward, served as a Private in the 14th U.S. Infantry, enlisted 26 Jan 1813 for 18 months and was later captured. Prisoner of War, sent to England , returned and was discharged on 31 Mar 1815 (Johnson and Christou, p. 24)

Andrew, Philip, served as a Private in Capt. Thomas Montgomery's Co., 14th U.S. Infantry, enlisted 21 May 1812 for 5 years and died on 13 Jan 1813; bounty land issued to brother Michael Andrew and other heirs (BLW# 20267-160-12; Johnson and Christou, p. 24)

Andrews, Luke (1788-1814), served as a Private in Capt. Reuben Gilder's Co., 14th U.S. Infantry, enlisted 14 Nov 1812 for 18 months, age 24, 5' 5½" tall, born in Sussex Co., DE, re-enlisted on 1 Mar 1814 for the war and died on 24 Apr 1814 at Plattsburgh, NY from sickness; bounty land issued to John Andrews and other heirs at law (BLW# 27782-160-42; Johnson and Christou, p. 24)

Andrey, Alexander, served as a Seaman and was born in Baltimore. Age: 23. Prison Depot: Chatham, Prisoner of War #553. Captured by HM Transport *Diadem*. When Taken: 7 Oct 1812. Where Taken: S. Andera (St. Andrews, Scotland). Prize Name: *Baltimore*. Home Port: Baltimore. Ship Type: Privateer. Date Received: 23 Feb 1813 on Portsmouth on HMS *Dromedary*. Discharged on 8 Jun 1813 and released to the Cartel *Rodrigo* (Johnson's Database, 2019)

Angel (Angle), David, served as a Corporal in the U.S. Rifles, enlisted 26 Oct 1813 for 5 years at Hanover, PA, born in Frederick Co., MD, age 23, 5' 8" tall, grey eyes, sandy hair, light complexion, served at Province Island Barracks in 1813, mustered at Sackett's Harbor, NY and reported "absent sick at Buffalo or Williamsville," but no date was given (Mallick and Wright, p. 34)

Ansel, Philip, served as a Private in 14th U.S. Infantry and was later captured. Prisoner of War #3966 at Halifax, NS, interned 24 Jun 1813 and discharged for exchange on 3 Feb 1814 (Johnson and Christou, p. 25; Baker Vol. 1, p. 10)

Anthony, Stephen (African American), served as a Seaman and was born in Maryland. Age: 28. Prison Depot: Plymouth 1, Prisoner of War #1561. Captured by HM Frigate *Andromache*. When Taken: 14 Mar 1813. Where Taken: off Nantes, France. Prize Name: *Courier*. Home Port: Baltimore. Ship Type: Letter of Marque. Date Received: 29 May 1813. From what ship: HMS *Hannibal*. Discharged on 30 Jun 1813 and sent to Stapleton. Prison Depot: Stapleton, Prisoner of War #123. Date Received: 8 Jul 1813 from Plymouth. Discharged on 13 Jun 1814 and sent to Dartmoor. Prison Dartmoor, Prisoner of War #1515. Date Received: 23 Jun 1814 from Stapleton and was discharged on 1 May 1815. (Johnson's Database, 2019)

Arell, Richard, served as a Captain in the 14th U.S. Infantry; commissioned a 1st Lieutenant on 12 Mar 1812, age 24, born in Pennsylvania, promoted to Captain on 14 Nov 1813. Prisoner of War #4201 at Dartmouth, released on 31 May 1814, discharged on 15 Jun 1815 (Johnson and Christou, p. 25; Johnson, p. 23)

Arkwright, Isaac, served as a Private in Capt. Stanton Sholes' Co., 2nd U.S. Artillery, enlisted 15 Feb 1813 at Greensburg, Beaver Co., PA at the age of 24, 5' 8" tall, born in Harford Co., MD and was discharged on 16 Oct 1815 on a Surgeon's Certificate, reason not stated (Johnson and Christou, p. 25; Society of the War of 1812 Application National No. 3849 in 1977 stated "Isaac Akright" was born circa 1789 in Harford Co., MD and died before 1864 in Brown Co., IL)

Armstrong, Archibald, served as a Corporal in Capt. Daniel Cushing's Co., 2nd U.S. Artillery, enlisted 16 Dec 1812 for 5 years, transferred to Captain Cushing's Co., 2nd U.S. Artillery, and died on 3 Dec 1813; widow Nancy Dayton received pension Old War File 9831; bounty land issued to his son David Armstrong and other heirs at law (BLW# 26335-160-12; Johnson and Christou, p. 26)

Armstrong, Daniel or David, served as a Seaman and was born in Baltimore. Age: 19. Prison Depot: Plymouth 1, Prisoner of War #2703. Captured by HM Brig *Foxhound*. When Taken: 27 May 1814. Where Taken: off Isles of Scilly, England. Prize Name: *Margaret*, prize of the Privateer *Surprise*. Home Port: Baltimore. Ship Type: Privateer. Date Received: 16 Jun 1814. From what ship: HMS *Foxhound*. Discharged on 20 Jun 1814 and sent to Dartmoor. Prison Depot: Dartmoor, Prisoner of War #1498. Captured by HM Brig *Foxhound*. When Taken: 27 May 1814. Received: 20 Jun 1814 from Mill Prison. Discharged on 1 May 1815. (Johnson's Database, 2019)

Armstrong, Elijah, of Harford Co., served as a Seaman and was a Prisoner of War in England. "Apparently many Yankee seamen preferred to be prisoners in the miserable conditions of the British prisons than to fight against their own nation. One such man was Harford-born Elijah Armstrong, a seaman from naval hero Admiral Nelson's own flagship H.M.S. *Victory*, no less. Armstrong is described as a white man, five foot five inches tall, and age 22 when he 'delivered himself up' on December 14, 1812. He was first confined in that Chatham prison depot and the transferred to Dartmoor [in Devon, England] on July 25, 1814. He was eventually released on April 26, 1815. British records indicate that Armstrong and a number of other Harford-born mariners spent much of the war languishing as prisoners of war in British depots." ("Harford County in the War of 1812," by Christopher T. George, *Harford Historical Bulletin* No. 76, Spring 1998, pp. 20-21) Elijah Armstrong served as a Seaman and was born in Harford Co., MD. Prison Depot: Portsmouth, Prisoner of War #214. Age 22. How Taken: Gave himself up off HM Ship-of-the-Line *Victory*. Date Received: 23 Dec 1812. From what ship: HM Guard Ship *Royal William*. Discharged on 19 Feb 1813 and sent to Chatham on HM Store Ship *Dromedary*. Prison Depot: Chatham, Prisoner of War #578. Date Received: 23 Feb 1813 from Portsmouth on HMS *Dromedary*. Discharged on 26 Jul 1814 and sent to Dartmoor on HMS *Raven*. Prison Depot: Dartmoor, Prisoner of War #2143. Date Received: 8 Aug 1814. From what ship: HMT *Raven* from Chatham. Discharged on 26 Apr 1815. (Johnson's Database, 2019)

Armstrong, Joshua (1779-1815), served as a Private in Capt. Thomas Warner's Co., 39th Regt., Baltimore Militia, from 19 Aug 1814 and was wounded in action on 12 Sep 1814 at North Point. His name is on the Baltimore Battle Monument. Ann Armstrong, widow of Joshua Armstrong, stated he volunteered on 19 Aug 1814 and served 14 days and was later discharged on 18 Nov 1814. She was married to him as Ann White by Rev. Mr. Richards, a Baptist Minister. Her husband died 2nd of February 1815 of wounds received in the Battle of North Point. She had obtained 40 acres previously. Witnesses were Charles Ferguson and Catharine Ferguson. Records of the Third Auditor's Office states he is on list 11 Sep to 18 Nov as discharged, "wounded in action 12 Sep." Nancy Armstrong, age 70, a resident of Baltimore, declares Joshua Armstrong, deceased, was a private under Capt. Thomas Warner, 39th Regiment, commanded by Lt. Col. Benjamin Fowler in the War with Great Britain. He enlisted from 19th August 1814 to unlimited term, that he was wounded at Battle of North Point on 12 Sep 1814 and her said husband died several months afterwards in consequence of said wound, as well as muster rolls of said Co. and pensions list. She married in Baltimore on 12th of July 1795 by Rev. Lewis Richards and one Stephen Hill, Pastor of the First Baptist; her said husband died 3rd day of February 1815 in consequence of wounds received at the Battle of North Point 12 Sep 1814 (by Dr. Jammison's Voucher) Her Mark. Letter dated in Baltimore on 24 Oct 1836: This may certify that the subscriber officiated as one of the Surgeons at the Maryland Hospital during the War with England in 1814 and was called upon to the care of Joshua Armstrong who had been wounded at the Battle of North Point. The wound being severe occasioned by a musket ball entering into one of his hips, it passed deep into the flesh and could not be found. He remained some weeks in the hospital was taken to his own house where I attended him for several months where he received every attention on the part of his wife that could possibly be rendered by her. He gradually sank lower and lower in general health. The ball having taken a downward direction eventually discovered itself pretty near the knee at which place I cut for and removed it. Cessions discharge continued and in the court of treatment some pieces of his clothing that had been carried into the wound by the ball made their escape in the opening though the bullet had been extracted. What with the copious discharges, fever and high constitutional irritation arising from the wound, the excision bodies lodged there and Mr. Armstrong died under his affliction after long and severe suffering. Horatio G. Jameson. I hereby certify that having examined the records of my predecessor Rev. Lewis Richards and find that Joshua Armstrong and Nancy White were married by him on July 12, 1795. Signed Stephen P. Hill, Pastor of the first Baptist Church. Baltimore Oct. 25, 1835. Joshua Armstrong wounded in action 12 Sep 1814 and the 18 Nov 1814 roll states he was "absent, sick." (BLW# 55-rej-150886, reason for rejection not stated; NARA; CMSR; Wright Vol. 2, p. 27; *Baltimore American*, 12 Jun 1819)

Armstrong, William, served as a Private in Capt. William McIlvane's Co., 14th U.S. Infantry, enlisted 22 Sep 1812 for 5 years and was captured at Beaver Dams, Upper Canada on 24 Jun 1813. Prisoner of War #3762 at Halifax until discharged on 3 Feb 1814 and exchanged on 15 Apr 1814; deserted at Fort Severn, MD on 14 Jul 1815 (Johnson and Christou, p. 26; Baker Vol. 1, p. 12)

Arnold, Richard, served as a Marine and was taken from the barracks and admitted to the Naval Hospital in Washington, DC as Patient No. 58 on 7 Jul 1814 (injury or illness was not specified) and was discharged on 10 Jul 1814 and sent to the barracks (Sharp's Database, 2018)

Arnold, William, served as a Seaman and was born in Baltimore. Age: 16. Prison Depot: Portsmouth, Prisoner of War #709. Captured by *Lion*, British Privateer. When Taken: 15 Feb 1813. Where Taken: Bay of Biscayne. Prize Name: *Tom Thumb*. Ship Type: Merchant Vessel. Date Received: 24 Feb 1813. From what ship: HM Brig *Escort*. Discharged on 6 Mar 1813 and sent to Chatham on HMS *Cornwall*. Prison Depot: Chatham, Prisoner of War #1111. Date Received: 14 Mar 1813 from Portsmouth on HMS *Beagle*. Discharged on 23 Jul 1814 and sent to Dartmoor. Prison Depot: Dartmoor, Prisoner of War #1906. Age 18. Date Received: 3 Aug 1814. From what ship: HMS *Alceste* from Chatham Depot. Discharged on 2 May 1815. (Johnson's Database, 2019)

Arthur, James, served as a Private in Capt. Henry Fleming's Co., 14th U.S. Inf., enlisted 15 Feb 1813 for 5 years. Prisoner of War, captured at Beaver Dams, Upper Canada [on 24 Jun 1813], ten miles west of Niagara Falls, and died at Halifax, NS, date not given, but probably in 1813; bounty land was issued to his brother Daniel Arthur and other heirs at law(BLW# 22563-160-12; Johnson and Christou, p. 27; Baker, Vol. 1, p. 12, did not mention him)

Aseburg, Philip, served as a Private in the 14th U.S. Infantry and was captured. Prisoner of War until released on 15 Apr 1814 (Johnson and Christou, p. 27)

Ascom, John, served as a Seaman of the U.S. Chesapeake Flotilla, entered service on 7 May 1814, was on board on 7 Apr 1814, reported sick (date not stated) and died on 7 Oct 1814 (Shomette, p. 391)

Ash, Sampson (African American), served as a Boy onboard a ship and was born in Baltimore. Age: 19. Prison Depot: Dartmoor, Prisoner of War #645. Captured by HM Brig *Pelican*. When Taken: 14 Aug 1813. Where Taken: off St. David's Head, Wales. Prize Name: U.S. Brig *Argus*. Ship Type: Warship. Date Received: 8

Sep 1813 from Plymouth. Discharged and was sent to Dartmouth on 30 Jul 1813. (Johnson's Database, 2019)

Asher, Frederick (c1790-1813), served as a Private in the 14th U.S. Infantry and was captured [at Beaver Dams, Upper Canada, ten miles west of Niagara Falls], and sent to Halifax, NS. Prisoner of War #4123 and died in prison on 7 Oct 1813 of dysentery (Johnson and Christou, p. 27; Baker, Vol. 1, p. 12)

Ashton, Erasmus (1780-1852), served as a Private in Capt. Robert T. Dade's Co., Cramer's Regt., Montgomery Co. Militia, from 3 Aug 1814 and reported as "discharged after 3 Oct" on the muster roll dated 3 Aug – 10 Nov 1814. On 29 Oct 1850, Erasmus "Rozi" Ashton, age 70, if Georgetown, DC, stated he was a substitute for John Cammel, drafted at Seneca, 1813-1814, and was discharged by furlough at Bladensburg "being sick" around 23 Aug 1814. On 21 Mar 1855 Jemima Ashton, age 67, of Washington, DC, widow of Erasmus Ashton, stated her former name was Etcheson and they were married at Georgetown on 1 Sep 1811. He died on 26 Dec 1852. (Wright Vol. 7, pp. 8, 12; BLW# 55-120-2671)

Askew, William, served as a Private in Samuel Archer's Co., 2nd U.S. Artillery, enlisted 25 Jun 1812, age 34, 5' 10" tall, born in Baltimore, and discharged at Sackett's Harbor, NY on 19 Jul 1814 for debility (Johnson and Christou, p. 27)

Atkins, Hezekiah W., served as a Private in Capt. Henry Lowery's Co., Allegany Co. Militia, and was "furloughed 11 – 19 Oct sick" 1814 (Wright Vol. 9, p. 5)

Atkins, John, served as a Private in Capt. Reuben Gilder's Co., 14th U.S. Infantry, enlisted on 18 Feb 1813 for the duration of the war and died at Plattsburgh, NY on 31 Mar 1814; bounty land issued to brother William Atkins and other heirs (BLW# 20522-160-12; Johnson and Christou, p. 27)

Atkins, John C. (1796-1814), served as a Private in 14th U.S. Infantry (company and captain not stated), enlisted 17 Aug 1814 at the age of 18, 5' 3" tall, born in Baltimore and died there in Oct 1814; bounty land issued to brother William Atkins and other heirs (BLW# 20522-160-12; Johnson and Christou, p. 28)

Atkins, Samuel, served as a Private in the 17th U.S. Infantry (company and captain not stated) and served at Fort Meigs and in New York in 1813, was reported as "absent sick, sent to Lower Sandusky" and then enlisted in March 1814 by Lt. McDonald at Charlestown, VA, age 20 or 22, born in Frederick Co., MD, dark eyes, dark hair and fair or sallow complexion, served in the 12th U.S. Infantry under Col. Cole and at Fort Washington from 31 Dec 1814 to 28 Feb 1815; he lost four days because of desertion, but returned to duty and later was reported to be an invalid and unfit for service (Mallick and Wright, p. 36)

Atkinson, Henry, served as a Seaman and was born in Baltimore. Age: 32. Prison Depot: Dartmoor, Prisoner of War #2154. Captured by HM Frigate *Hyperion*.

When Taken: 26 Jun 1814. Where Taken: off Cape Finisterre, Spain. Prize Name: *Rattlesnake*. Home Port: Philadelphia. Ship Type: Privateer. Date Received: 16 Aug 1814 on HMS *Dublin* from Halifax, NS. Discharged on 2 May 1815. (Johnson's Database, 2019)

Atkinson, John (African American), served as a Seaman and was born in Baltimore. Age: 29. Prison Depot: Chatham, Prisoner of War #1578. How Taken: Gave himself up off HM Ship-of-the-Line *Braham*. When Taken: 10 Dec 1812. Date Received: 16 Apr 1813 from HMS *Namur*, an admiral's tender. Discharged on 3 Aug 1813 and released to HMS *Ceres*. (Johnson's Database, 2019)

Atkinson, William, served as a Seaman and was born in Harford Co., MD. Age: 36. Prison Depot: Plymouth 1, Prisoner of War #1025. Captured by *Bootle of Liverpool*, letter of marque. When Taken: 18 Mar 1813. Where Taken: off Western Islands, Scotland. Prize Name: *Two Brothers*. Ship Type: Merchant Vessel. Date Received: 21 Apr 1813. From what ship: HMS *Bittern*. Sent to Dartmoor on 1 Jul 1813. Prison Depot: Dartmoor, Prisoner of War #361. Date Received: 1 Jul 1813 from Plymouth. Discharged on 20 Apr 1815. (Johnson's Database, 2019)

Attix, William, served as a Corporal in the U.S. Marine Corps, enlisted 1 Oct 1810 and was taken from the barracks and admitted to the Naval Hospital in Washington, DC as Patient No. 63 on 18 Nov 1814 with erysipelas (severe skin infection) and was discharged on 14 Dec 1814 and sent to the barracks (Sharp's Database, 2018)

Atwell, Austin, served as a Private in 1st Lt. Richard H. Battee's Co., Watkins' Regt., Anne Arundel Co. Militia, from 8 Jun 1813 and reported sick on furlough on 26 Aug 1813 on muster roll dated 16 Apr – 31 Jul 1813 (Wright Col. 4, p. 41)

Atwell, James, served as a Private in Capt. James Haslett's Co. of the 38th U.S. Infantry, enlisted 3 Jul 1813 for 1 year and died on 29 Mar 1814; heirs received half pay for five years in lieu of bounty land (Johnson and Christou, p. 28)

Auld, James, served as a 2nd Sergeant in Capt. Stephen H. Moore's Co. of U.S. Volunteers, enlisted 8 Sep 1812 for 1 year and died on 3 Jan 1813 (Johnson and Christou, p. 28; Wright Vol. 2, p. 57)

Aulajo, Thomas, served as a Seaman and was born in Baltimore. Age: 23. Prison Depot: Plymouth 1, Prisoner of War #222. Captured by HM Frigate *Phoebe*. When Taken: 1 Jan 1813. Where Taken: Lat. 44.4N Long. 23W. Prize Name: *Vengeance*. Ship Type: Letter of Marque. Date Received: 9 Jan 1813. From what ship: HMS *Phoebe*. Discharged and sent to Portsmouth on 8 Feb 1813 on HMS *Colossus*. Prison Depot: Chatham, Prisoner of War #837. Age 28. Date Received:

1 Mar 1813 from Plymouth on HMS *Namur*. Discharged on 24 Jul 1813 and released to the Cartel *Hoffning*. (Johnson's Database, 2019)

Austin, Benjamin (1787-1815), served as a Private in Capt. Reuben Gilder's Co., 14th U.S. Infantry, enlisted on 15 Jan 1813, at the age of 26, 5' 10" tall, born in England and died at hospital in Cheektowaga, NY on 18 Jan 1815 of dysentery (Johnson and Christou, p. 28; https://wnyroots.tripod.com/Index-1812.html)

Ausunt, William, served as a Private in Capt. Earle's Co., 14th U.S. Infantry, and died in the hospital in Cheektowaga, NY on 10 Jan 1815 of dysentery (Johnson and Christou, p. 28; https://wnyroots.tripod.com/Index-1812.html)

Avis, Jarvis, served as a Private in 14th U.S. Infantry and was born in Maryland. Age: 31. Prison Depot: Chatham, Prisoner of War #3072. When Taken: 24 Jun 1813. Where Taken: Beaver Dams, Upper Canada. Date Received: 7 Jan 1814 from Halifax, NS. Discharged on 10 Oct 1814 and sent to U.S. on the Cartel *St. Philip*. (Johnson's Database, 2019)

Ayres, Henry, served as a Seaman and was born in Maryland. Age: 30. Prison Depot: Chatham, Prisoner of War #2302. Captured by HM Brig *Curlew*. When Taken: 1 Feb 1813. Where Taken: off Barbados. Prize Name: *Dolphin*. Ship Type: Privateer. Date Received: 29 Sep 1813. From what ship: HMS *Raisonable*. Discharged on 4 Sep 1814 and sent to Dartmoor on HMS *Freya*. Prison Depot: Dartmoor, Prisoner of War #3144. Date Received: 11 Sep 1814. From what ship: HMT *Freya* from Chatham. Discharged on 28 May 1815. (Johnson's Database, 2019)

B

Babb, Charles (1775-1815), served as a Private in Capt. Bracham's Co., 2nd U.S. Infantry, enlisted 23 Dec 1807 at Staunton, VA, born in Frederick Co., MD, age 32, 5' 11" tall, blue eyes, light hair, fair complexion, was tried three times for various offenses and was discharged on 22 Dec 1812, yet re-enlisted on 29 Dec 1812 at Mt. Vernon, was appointed Corporal on 15 Jan 1815 and died at New Orleans on 16 Apr 1815 (Mallick and Wright, p. 38)

Bacon, James, served as a Seaman and was born in Baltimore. Age: 28. Prison Depot: Dartmoor, Prisoner of War #6193. Captured by HM Ship-of-the-Line *Leander*, HM Ship-of-the-Line *Newcastle* & HM Frigate *Acasta*. When Taken: 28 Dec 1814. Where Taken: Lat. 35N Long. 52W. Prize Name: *Prince de Neufchatel*. Home Port: New York. Ship Type: Privateer. Received: 30 Jan 1815. From what ship: HMT *Pheasant*. Discharged 5 Jul 1815. (Johnson's Database, 2019)

Bader, Dominic (c1780-1832), served as a Captain in the 1st Rifle Bttn., Union Yagers, from 19 Aug 1814 and was captured during the Battle of Bladensburg on 24 Aug 1814 (Marine p. 174; Wright Vol. 2, p. 53, did not mention his capture, but stated he participated in the Battle of Long Log Lane [North Point] near Baltimore on 12 Sep 1814) Bader married Eve Hennewalt in 1802 at St. Peter's Catholic Church and died in 1832 in Baltimore, but a review of their burial records indicates he was not buried there. A daughter was baptized at St. Alphonsus Catholic Church so Dominic was probably buried in that cemetery at Saratoga Street and Park Avenue, but burials were since removed to another location in 1834 and again in 1873. Some time after 1961 "the City did acquire the land and now has offices on what was once a scared place. Though the cemetery is shown on maps dated as late as 1989, it no longer exists and has not for many years." (Jane B. Wilson's *The Very Quiet Baltimoreans*, p. 46)

Bailey, Daniel, served as a Private in Capt. John T. Randall's Rifle Co., Baltimore Co., from 26 Jul 1814, wounded in action at Bladensburg on 24 Aug 1814 and later listed as a Private in Capt. Benjamin Gorsuch's Co., 2nd Regt. 11th Brigade, Baltimore Co., stationed at Camp Hampstead in Baltimore, from 14 Oct 1814 and noted on muster roll as wounded in action (Wright Vol. 2, pp. 73, 88). In Baltimore on 11 Mar 1826 Daniel Bailey, former private in the late war in Capt. John T. Randall's Co. of Foot, 2nd Maryland Militia, a resident of Anne Arundel Co. for almost two years and previously of Baltimore Co., collected his own $24.00 pension due from 4 Sep 1825 to 4 Mar 1826. (Pierce, p. 8)

Bailey, Isaac (Mulatto), served as a Seaman and was born in Baltimore. Age: 29. Prison Depot: Chatham, Prisoner of War #3269. Captured by HM Ship-of-the-Line *Valiant* & HM Brig *Curlew*. When Taken: 26 Mar 1813. Where Taken: Georges Bank. Prize Name: *Volant*. Ship Type: Letter of Marque. Date Received: 23 Feb 1814 from Halifax, NS on HMT *Malabar*. Discharged on 10 Oct 1814 and sent to Dartmoor on HMS *Mermaid*. Prison Depot: Dartmoor, Prisoner of War #5164. Date Received: 31 Oct 1814. From what ship: HMT *Mermaid* from Chatham. Discharged on 29 Jun 1815. (Johnson's Database, 2019)

Bailey, Joseph, served as a Private in a Marine Battery under Sailing Master Rodman and was wounded on 13 Sep 1814 at Fort McHenry (Marine p. 173)

Bailey, Samuel, served as a Passenger and was born in Baltimore. Age: 18. Prison Depot: Dartmoor, Prisoner of War #6497. Captured by HM Ship-of-the-Line *Abercrombie*. When Taken: 23 Oct 1814. Where Taken: St. Jago. Prize Name: *Dolores*. Ship Type: Merchant Vessel. Date Received: 3 Mar 1815. From what ship: HMT *Ganges* from Plymouth. Discharged on 11 Jul 1815. (Johnson's Database, 2019)

Baker, Jacob, served as a Private in Capt. Matthew Murray's Co., Middletown Blues, Frederick Co. Militia, from 25 Aug 1814, was in Montgomery Co. at the time of the Battle of Bladensburg and marched to Baltimore; he was reported as "sick present," but no date or place were given (Mallick and Wright, p. 355)

Baker, Jesse, served as a Seaman and was born in Baltimore. Age: 30. Prison Depot: Dartmoor, Prisoner of War #6166. Captured by HM Frigate *Grancius*. When Taken: 2 Dec 1814. Where Taken: off Lisbon, Portugal. Prize Name: *Leo*. Home Port: Baltimore. Ship Type: Privateer. Received: 18 Jan 1815. From what ship: HMT *Impregnable*. Discharged on 5 Jul 1815. (Johnson's Database, 2019)

Baker, John, served as a Seaman and was born in Baltimore. Age: 25. Prison Depot: Plymouth 1, Prisoner of War #726. Captured by HM Ship-of-the-Line *Warspite*. When Taken: 26 Feb 1813. Where Taken: Bay of Biscayne. Prize Name: *Mars*. Ship Type: Merchant Vessel. Date Received: 19 Mar 1813. From what ship: HMS *Warspite*. Discharged and sent to Dartmoor on 2 Apr 1813. Prison Depot: Dartmoor, Prisoner of War #214. Date Received: 2 Apr 1813 from Plymouth. Discharged on 20 Apr 1815. (Johnson's Database, 2019)

Baker, John, served as a Seaman and was born in Baltimore. Age: 32. Prison Depot: Dartmoor, Prisoner of War #1199. Captured by HM Brig Achates. When Taken: 14 Jun 1810. Where Taken: English Channel. Prize Name: *Ocean*. Ship Type: Privateer. Date Received: 4 Jun 1814 from Dartmouth. Discharged on 28 Apr 1815. (Johnson's Database, 2019)

Baker, John (1796-1815), served as a Private in Capt. John O'Fallon's Co., 2nd U.S. Rifles, enlisted 16 Apr 1814 for 5 years in Lexington, KY at the age of 18, 5'1½" tall, born in Worcester Co., MD and died at Amherstburg, Upper Canada on 27 Feb 1815 (BLW# 26211-160-12; Johnson and Christou, pp. 29-30)

Baker, Peter, served as a Private in Capt. Charles Gore's Co., Nace's Regiment, Baltimore Co. Militia, from 26 Aug 1814 and was cleared by certificate of a surgeon (Wright Vol. 2, p. 39)

Baldwin, Charles E. (1788-1851), served as 1st Sgt. in Capt. .John Ridgely's Co., Calvert Co., under Lt. Col. Frisby Tilghman's Cavalry Troops, from 22 Aug 1814 and was furloughed sick (no date or cause given) as reported on the muster roll dated 22 Aug – 24 Sep 1814. On 1 Apr 1857 Elizabeth Baldwin, age 57, of Morgan Co., OH, widow of Charles E. Baldwin, stated he was an officer in a company of light horse, the name of the captain not remembered. She stated he enrolled at or near Ellicotts Mills around August 1814 and participated in the Battle of Bladensburg. She stated he died on 8 Aug 1851, but his tombstone in McConnelsville Cemetery is inscribed 8 Dec 1851, age 63 years and 8 months. Charles E. Baldwin, second son of Joseph and Rebecca Baldwin of Chester Co., PA, married Elizabeth White, daughter of Thomas and Elizabeth White, formerly of Derbyshire, England, on 31 Aug 1817 (information in family Bible). Elizabeth Baldwin stated they were married in Maryland by Parson Richards of the Baptist Church. (Wright Vol. 4, pp. 48, 61; www.findagrave.com)

Baldwin, John, served as a Private and was listed as deserted 28 Sep and since dead on 28 Sep – 17 Oct 1814 list of Capt. Thomas T. Simmons (with 1st Lt. John Thomas) of the 2nd Regt. of Anne Arundel Co. and on 2 Aug – 27 Oct 1814 list of 1st Lt. John Thomas 3rd of 32nd Regt. of same county states John Baldwin has been 8 days absent without leave and since dead. (Wright Vol. 4, pp. 28, 43)

Ball, Adam A. (1794-1815), served as a Corporal in Capt. David Holt's Co., 19th U.S. Infantry, enlisted 7 Apr 1814 for the war in Marietta, OH, age 20, 5′ 5½″ tall, born in Maryland, died at Williamsville, NY on 7 Jan 1815 and was buried in the War of 1812 Cemetery in Cheektowaga, Erie Co., NY; bounty land issued to Dinah Bryan, his only heir (BLW# 24687-160-12; Johnson and Christou, p. 30)

Ballard, Martin, served as a Private in the 14th U.S. Infantry and was captured at Beaver Dams, Upper Canada on 24 Jun 1813, sent to England as a Prisoner of War, but place of imprisonment not indicated (Johnson and Christou, p. 30)

Baltzell, Lewis, served as a Private in Capt. Archibald Dobbins' Co., 39th Regt., Baltimore Militia, and was reported as "prisoner on parole" on the muster roll of 19 Aug – 18 Nov 1814 (Wright Vol. 2, p. 26)

Banks, Perry (Mulatto), served as a Seaman and was born in Baltimore. Age: 29. Prison Depot: Plymouth 1, Prisoner of War #2705. Captured by HM Brig *Foxhound*. When Taken: 27 May 1814. Where Taken: off Isles of Scilly, England. Prize Name: *Margaret*, prize of the Privateer *Surprise*. Home Port: Baltimore. Ship Type: Privateer. Date Received: 16 Jun 1814. Discharged on 20 Jun 1814 and sent to Dartmoor. Prison Depot: Dartmoor, Prisoner of War #1500. Date Received: 20 Jun 1814 from Mill Prison. Discharged on 1 May 1815. (Johnson's Database, 2019)

Banning, Peter (African American), served as a Seaman and was born in Talbot Co., MD. Age: 32. Prison Depot: Dartmoor, Prisoner of War #6289. How Taken: Gave himself up off HM Brig *Beaver*. Date Received: 17 Feb 1815. From what ship: HMT *Ganges* from Plymouth. Discharged on 5 Jul 1815. (Johnson's Database, 2019)

Banser (Bauser?), Perry (1786-1813), served as a Seaman and was born in Maryland. Age: 27. Prison Depot: Halifax, Prisoner of War #3666. Captured by HM Ship-of-the-Line *Majestic*. When Taken: 30 Jun 1813. Where Taken: off Western Islands, Scotland. Prize Name: *Ulysses*. Ship Type: Letter of Marque. Died on 13 Oct 1813 from inflammation of lungs. (Johnson's Database, 2019)

Baptist, John, was a Seaman who was wounded in the neck on 24 Aug 1814 on the field of battle at Bladensburg, was admitted to the Naval Hospital in Washington, DC as Patient No. 11, and reportedly deserted on 28 Sep 1814 (Sharp's Database, 2018)

Barkdoll, Christian, served as a Private in Capt. John Galt's Co., joined 31 Aug 1814 and deserted on 13 Sep 1814, but he stated he "was in service for 15 days and sent home from the camp at Oldtown near Baltimore because of sickness (rheumatism) from which he did not recover until sometime in the following spring and has been a cripple ever since" (BLW# 177303 in 1855 was rejected; Mallick and Wright, p. 42)

Barker, Thomas, served as a Seaman of the U.S. Chesapeake Flotilla, entered service on 14 Sep 1813, was on board on 7 Apr 1814 and discharged sick on 6 Oct 1814 (Shomette p. 362)

Barnard, William, served as a Seaman of the U.S. Chesapeake Flotilla, entered service on 12 Oct 1813 and died on 19 Dec 1813 (Shomette p. 366)

Barnes, Hosea, served as a Captain in the Harford Co. Militia (dates not stated), but when the British attacked and burned Havre de Grace on 3 May 1813 it is known that "The elder, Mr. Levy, was taken about this time, as was also Capt. Barnes, and one or two men … Most of the Prisoners they released while on shore." (*Narrative Respecting the Conduct of the British From the First Landing on Spesutie Island Till Their Progress to Havre de Grace*, by James Jones Wilmer, 1814, pp. 12-13; Wright Vol. 3 does not list Capt. Hosea Barnes, but their was a Hosea Barnes, aged 64 and upwards, who was living in Harford County in 1828, as documented in Historical Society of Harford County Court Records 90.29.67)

Barnett, John (African American), served as a Seaman and was born in Baltimore. Age: 53. Prison Depot: Chatham, Prisoner of War #1599. How Taken: Gave himself up. When Taken: 13 Feb 1813. Where Taken: Gravesend, UK. Date Received: 19 Apr 1813. From what ship: HMS *Raisonable*. Discharged on 7 Aug 1813 and released to HMS *Ceres*. (Johnson's Database, 2019)

Barney, Joshua (1759-1818), served as a Commodore in 1814 and defended the National Capitol with 360 sailors and 120 marines, fighting against the enemy hand-to-hand with cutlasses and pikes. The battle raged for four hours, but the British eventually defeated the Americans. The defenders were forced to fall back after nearly being cut off and the British went on to burn the Capitol and White House. Barney was severely wounded, receiving a bullet deep in his thigh that could never be removed. He eventually died in Pittsburgh, PA on 10 Dec 1818 en route to Kentucky from complications related to the wounds he received at the Battle of Bladensburg 4 years earlier. He lies at rest in Allegheny Cemetery in Pittsburgh. "Com. Barney and Col. Ragan, having been exchanged for Colonels Thornton and Wood and Major ----, taken at Bladensburg they will resume their commands. The Commodore has so far recovered his wounds as

to be able to walk his chamber." (North Point Dead and Wounded Article, 4 Oct 1814, Columbian Register CT Vol. III 97, p. 4; Marine, p. 174; *Niles Weekly Register*, 5 Dec 1818) Joshua Barney married Anne Bedford. (*1812 Ancestor Index Volume I, 1892-1970*, National Society United States Daughters of 1812, 2005, p. 31) In 1959 Frederick Arthur Winsor Bryan, a descendant of Joshua Barney, wrote: "It is well known how, at Bladensburg, the British General Ross said 'Barney and his Flotilla Men have given us the only real fighting we have encountered today.'" In 2012 the Regent Julia Williams of the Commodore Joshua Barney – John Eager Howard Chapter of the Maryland D.A.R., the President Guy Almony of the Thomas Johnson Society of the Maryland C.A.R., and the President Christos Christou of the Society of the War of 1812 in the State of Maryland traveled to Pittsburgh to dedicate a new marker in his honor – see the pictures that follow.

Barnhouse, Joseph, served as a Private in the U.S. Dragoons in Capt. Nelson Luckett's Co., 1st Regiment, enlisted 18 Jun 1812 for 3 to 5 years at Baltimore, commanded by Col. Covington, and marched to Carlisle, PA, thence to Sackett's Harbor, NY and was in the Battle of Sackett's Harbor and Battle of Crestler's Fields and while on a charge in the latter, he was wounded in the knee by a musket ball. Col. Covington was mortally wounded and Col. Walback assumed command; they then marched to Sackett's Harbor from thence to Buffalo, thence to Fort Erie and Chippewa Plains and then finally to Governor's Island where he was discharged on surgeon's certificate of disability on 3 Sep 1815. Surgeon's Affidavit by Th. Bond and R. H. Edwards dated 31 Mar 1853 stated during Nov 1813 in charging the enemy at Cristers (sic) Field in Lower Canada Joseph Barnhouse, private in the Co. of Capt. Nelson Luckett's 1st Regt. of U.S. Light Dragoons, received a wound from a musket ball in his left knee, fracturing his bones and at the Battle of Lundy's Lane received a wound on the left side of the head, fracturing his skull and in falling over a British gun carriage received considerable injury in his left hip; these injuries left him lame and produced frequent headaches and he is one-half disabled. Pension Application #12241 was rejected due to lack of record of injury in military records, but eventually a bounty land warrant was approved (BLW# 2690-180-12) and he was issued 160 acres. BLW# 101099 granted for Richard Barnhouse, private and then corporal in Capt. Samuel Duvall's Co., 29th Maryland Regiment, mentioned that Richard's widow Margaret Jane Barnhouse married Joseph Barnhouse after Richard's death on 14 Dec 1845, that the widow Margaret Jane Barnhouse intermarried with Joseph Barnhouse, her deceased's husband's brother on or about 19 Nov 1849. The children of Richard and Margaret, viz., Jonas P. Barnhouse, age 19 on or about 30th day of Feb last, Sarah Jane May, age 21 on or about 29 Mar last, John Barnhouse born 14 Sep 1819, Randolph Barnhouse born 12 Feb 1827, Sidney Barnhouse born 17 Feb 1831 (information from Family Bible). Jonas served in the Rebel service in Capt. Meads' Cavalry Co. near Leesburg, VA. The widow Margaret was given bounty land of 160 acres in 1855. (BLW# 55-160-101099; Johnson and Christou, p. 31; Old War Pension File IF-#12241)

Barnover, George, served as a Private in the 14th U.S. Infantry and was born in Frederick Co. circa 1774, enlisted on 12 May 1812, hazel eyes, dark hair, dark complexion; mustered under Capt. F. Montgomery at Lewiston on 31 Jul 1813, was reported "absent sick" at Williamsville, NY, was wounded at Brownstown and discharged at Chillicothe, OH on 22 Dec 1814. (Mallick and Wright p. 43)

Barr, David, served as a Private in Capt. William McLaughlin's Co., 50th Regt., Allegany Co. Militia, called into service to serve in the defense of Baltimore, was reported as "sick in hospital" on 7 Sep 1814 on the muster roll dated 11 Aug – 13 Oct 1814 and was discharged by a surgeon on 26 Nov 1814 ("Allegany County Militia (Including Garrett Co.), 1794-1815," by F. Edward Wright and Marlene S. Bates, *Maryland Genealogical Society Bulletin,* Vol. 32, No. 2, Spring 1991, p. 173; Wright Vol. 9, p. 6, stated he served in Capt. Henry Lowrey's Co., while Wright Vol. 10, p. 2, stated he served in Capt. William McLaughlin's Co.)

Barrett, Thomas, served as a Private in Capt. Bedington Hands' Co., 21st Regt., Kent Co. Militia, for 18 days and reported as "volunteer having a certificate of inability" on the muster roll dated 15 Apr – 23 May 1813 (Wright Vol. 1, p. 12)

Barrick, John (c1783-1844), served as a Private in Capt. Jacob Creager's Co., Washington County Militia, joined 1 Aug 1814, leg was broken, on furlough 21 days, was wounded [again?] at Annapolis en route to Bladensburg and taken home. He married Esther Kurtz on 29 Jan 1818 in Fredericktown and died at Woodsboro on 13 Oct 1844. (BLW# 55-40-83499; Mallick and Wright p. 44)

Barrington, John (1786-1813), served as a Private in the 14th U.S. Infantry at the age of 27, was captured at Beaver Dams, Upper Canada, ten miles west of Niagara Falls, on 24 Jun 1813, and sent to Halifax, NS. Prisoner of War #4079 and died at Halifax on 3 Sep or 4 Sep 1813 of dysentery (Johnson and Christou, p. 32, stated he died on 3 Sep 1813 and Johnson's Database, 2019, stated he died on 3 Sep 1813, but Baker Vol. 1, p. 23, stated he died on 4 Sep 1813)

Barry, Garrett, served as a Surgeon's Mate, 38th U.S. Infantry, commissioned 8 Apr 1814, born in Maryland and died 22 Apr 1815 (Johnson and Christou, p. 32)

Barry, James, served as a Seaman and was born in Annapolis. Age: 29. Prison Depot: Plymouth 1, Prisoner of War #1875. Captured by HM Brig *Pelican*. When Taken: 14 Aug 1813. Where Taken: off St. David's Head, Wales. Prize Name: U.S. Brig *Argus*. Ship Type: Warship. Date Received: 23 Aug 1813. From what ship: HMS *Pelican*. Discharged on 8 Sep 1813 and sent to Dartmoor. Prison Depot: Dartmoor, Prisoner of War #603. Received: 8 Sep 1813 from Plymouth. Discharged and sent to Dartmouth on 2 Nov 1814. (Johnson's Database, 2019)

Bartlett, James, served as a Private in the 14th U.S. Infantry and was captured at Beaver Dams, Upper Canada on 24 Jun 1813. Prisoner of War #3978 at Halifax, NS, interned 24 Jun 1813 and discharged for exchange on 3 Feb 1814 (Johnson and Christou, p. 32; Baker Vol. 1, p. 27)

Barton, Aquilla, served as a Private in Capt. William Brown, Jr.'s Co., 6th Regt., Baltimore Militia, joined 22 Aug 1814 and was discharged on 3 Sep 1814 by the Surgeon, but the medical reason was not stated (Wright Vol. 2, p. 9)

Barton, Nathan (Mulatto), served as a Seaman and was born in Baltimore. Age: 26. Prison Depot: Plymouth 1, Prisoner of War #292. Captured by HM Frigate *Britton*. When Taken: 17 Dec 1812. Where Taken: off Bordeaux, France. Prize Name: *Columbia*. Ship Type: Merchant Vessel. Date Received: 21 Jan 1813. From what ship: HMS *Abercrombie*. Discharged and sent to Portsmouth on 8 Feb 1813 on HMS *Colossus*. Prison Depot: Chatham, Prisoner of War #867. Date Received: 1 Mar 1813 from Plymouth on HMS *Namur*. Discharged in Jul 1813 and released to the Cartel *Moses Brown*. (Johnson's Database, 2019)

Baseman (Bausman, Bousman), John (1784-1827), served as a Private in Capt. Jeremiah Ducker's Co., 2nd Regt., 11th Brigade, Baltimore Co., stationed in Baltimore from 14 Oct 1814 and was reported "absent – sick on furlough since Sep 30" 1814; bounty land issued to Elias A. White on 1 Jul 1859 (BLW# 55-80-9067; Wright Vol. 2, p. 88, spelled his name Bousman and other privates listed on the muster roll dated 14 Oct – 1 Dec 1814 in the same company were Herbert Bousman, William Baseman and Thomas Baseman). John Baseman was born on 6 May 1784, died on 25 Sep 1827 and was buried in Baseman Family Cemetery in Reisterstown, Baltimore Co., MD (Smith's Database, 2019). Images of the cemetery and his gravestone are posted online at www.findagrave.com.

Bassett, David (African American), served as a Seaman and was born in Baltimore. Age: 43. Prison Depot: Plymouth 1, Prisoner of War #1693. Captured by HM Brig *Royalist*. When Taken: 31 May 1813. Where Taken: Bay of Biscayne. Prize Name: *Governor Gerry*. Home Port: New Haven. Ship Type: Merchant Vessel. Received: 26 Jun 1813. From what ship: HMS *Duncan*. Discharged on 30 Jun 1813 and sent to Stapleton. Prison Depot: Stapleton, Prisoner of War #199. Date Received: 8 Jul 1813 from Plymouth. Discharged on 13 Jun 1814 and sent to Dartmoor. Prison Depot: Dartmoor, Prisoner of War #1470. Received: 19 Jun 1814 from Stapleton. Discharged on 28 Apr 1815. (Johnson's Database, 2019)

Bateman, Charles, served as a Mate and was born in Baltimore. Age: 28. Prison Depot: Plymouth 1, Prisoner of War #18. How Taken: Gave himself up off MV *Jenny*. When Taken: 18 Oct 1812. Where Taken: Liverpool, UK. Date Received: 21 Nov 1812. From what ship: HMS *Salvador del Mundo*. Discharged and sent on 8 Dec 1812 to Ashburton on parole. (Johnson's Database, 2019)

Bateman, John (1786-1814), served as a Seaman and was born in Baltimore. Age: 18. Prison Depot: Dartmoor, Prisoner of War #3459. Captured by HM Sloop *Tartarus*. When Taken: 1 Sep 1814. Where Taken: in the Atlantic. Prize Name: *Chasseur*. Home Port: Baltimore. Ship Type: Privateer. Date Received: 19 Sep 1814. From what ship: HMT *Salvador del Mundo*. Died on 23 Nov 1814. (Johnson's Database, 2019; Centennial Trails, United States Daughters of 1812, online at www.war1812trails.com/Dartmoor)

Batman, John, served as a Seaman and was born in Maryland. Age: 38. Prison Depot: Plymouth 1, Prisoner of War #1381. Captured by HM Frigate *Surveillante*. When Taken: 27 Apr 1813. Where Taken: Bay of Biscayne. Prize Name: *Tom*. Home Port: Baltimore. Ship Type: Letter of Marque. Date Received: 15 May 1813 on HMS *Foxhound*. Discharged on 3 Jul 1813 and sent to Stapleton Prison. (Johnson's Database, 2019)

Battle, Timothy, served as a Private (company not stated) and enlisted in the U.S. Marine Corps on 11 Dec 1810, was wounded in his brain on 24 Aug 1814 on the field of battle at Bladensburg, was admitted to the Naval Hospital in Washington, DC as Patient No. 24 on 26 Aug 1814 and was discharged on 26 Oct 1814 and sent to barracks (Sharp's Database, 2018)

Bausman, John, see John Baseman (Bausman, Bousman), q.v.

Bay, John, served as a Private in the 14th U.S. Infantry and was captured at Beaver Dams, Upper Canada on 24 Jun 1813. Prisoner of War #4083 at Halifax, NS, interned 24 Jun 1813 and was discharged for exchange on 3 Feb 1814 (Johnson and Christou, p. 33; Baker Vol. 1, p. 24)

Bay, John, served as a Seaman with the U.S. Chesapeake Flotilla under Comm. Barney, was wounded in the head and admitted to the Naval Hospital in Washington, DC as Patient No. 7 on 24 Aug 1814, but reportedly deserted that same day and went to Baltimore (Sharp's Database, 2018)

Bayce, Nelson, served as a Private in the 14th U.S. Infantry and was captured. Prisoner of War #3831 at Halifax, NS, interned 6 Jun 1813 and was discharged for exchange on 3 Feb 1814 (Johnson and Christou, p. 33; Baker Vol. 1, p. 24)

Baynard, Nathan, served as a Captain in the 35th Regiment, Queen Anne's Co. Militia, in 1813 and was reported "sick and returned home" on the muster roll dated 7 May – 14 May 1813 (Wright Vol. 1, p. 36)

Baynes, Thomas, served as a Private in the 14th U.S. Infantry and was captured at Beaver Dams, Upper Canada on 24 Jun 1813. Prisoner of War #3950 at Halifax, NS, was discharged for exchange on 3 Feb 1814 (Johnson and Christou, p. 33; Baker Vol. 1, p. 27)

Beachman, George, served as a ship's Carpenter and was born in Baltimore. Age: 32. Prison Depot: Plymouth 1, Prisoner of War #55. Captured by HM Frigate *Medusa*. When Taken: 9 Nov 1812. Where Taken: off San Sebastian, Spain. Prize Name: *Independence*. Ship Type: Merchant Vessel. Date Received: 27 Nov 1812. From what ship: HMS *Wasp*. Discharged and sent to Portsmouth on 29 Dec 1812 on HMS *Northumberland*. Prison Depot: Portsmouth, Prisoner of War #323. Date Received: 31 Dec 1812. From what ship: HM Ship-of-the-Line *Northumberland*. Discharged on 4 Mar 1813 and sent to Chatham on HMS *Queen*. (Johnson's Database, 2019)

Beadley, Daniel, served as a Marine and was taken from the barracks and admitted to the Naval Hospital in Washington, DC as Patient No. 63 on 25 Jul 1814 (injury or illness was not specified) and was discharged on 3 Aug 1814 and sent to the barracks (Sharp's Database, 2018)

Beal, David, served as a Private in Capt. John Fonsten's Co., Frederick County Militia, from 2 Sep 1814, marched to Baltimore, engaged in the defense of the city and discharged by certificate on 24 Sep 1814 (Mallick and Wright, p. 363)

Beales, John, served as a Private in 14th U.S. Infantry and was captured at Beaver Dams, Upper Canada on 24 Jun 1813. Prisoner of War #3766 at Halifax, NS, was discharged on 9 Nov 1813 and was sent to England on HMS *Success*(Johnson and Christou, p. 33; Baker Vol. 1, p. 29) John Beals served as a Private in 14th U.S. Inf. and was born in Maryland. Prison Depot: Chatham, Prisoner of War #3109. Age: 23. When Taken: 24 Jun 1813. Where Taken: Beaver Dams, Upper Canada. Date Received: 7 Jan 1814 from Halifax, NS. Discharged on 10 Oct 1814 and sent to U.S. on the Cartel *St. Philip*. (Johnson's Database, 2019)

Bean, Amos, served as a Seaman and was born in Brentwood, MD. Age: 22. Prison Depot: Portsmouth, Prisoner of War #595. How Taken: Gave himself up off HM Ship-of-the-Line *Mars*. Received: 31 Jan 1813 on HMS *Mars*. Discharged on 11 Mar 1813 and sent to Chatham on HM Store Ship *Abundance*. Prison Depot: Chatham, Prisoner of War #1264. How Taken: Gave himself up off HM Ship-of-the-Line *Mars*. When Taken: 9 Dec 1812. Received: 16 Mar 1813 from Portsmouth on HMS *Abundance*. Discharged on 23 Jul 1814 and was sent to Dartmoor. (Johnson's Database, 2019)

Beanes, William (1749-1828), a highly esteemed physician of Upper Marlboro, was "compelled to give rise from his bed, and hurried off to the British camp [on 8 Sep 1814], hardly allowing him time to put his clothes on; that he was treated with great harshness, and closely guarded; and that as soon as his friends were apprised of his situation, they hastened to the headquarters of the English army to solicit his release." (Marine, p. 183) Dr. Beanes was held prisoner on board the British ship *Surprise* [military historian Scott S. Sheads stated Beanes was on board the *Tonnant*] during the attack on Fort McHenry on 12-14 Sep 1814. (J. Thomas Scharf's *The Chronicles of Baltimore*, Vol. 1, p. 351) This information, and more, can be found online in further detail, as well as in Marine, pp. 183-187; also see Francis Scott Key, q.v.

Beard, John, served as a Private in the 14th U.S. Infantry (company not stated) and was captured on 24 Jun 1813 [at Beaver Dams, Upper Canada] and sent to England as a Prisoner of War (Johnson and Christou, p. 34)

Beard, Richard, served as a Private in 14th U.S. Infantry (company not stated) and was born in Maryland. Age: 19. Prison Depot: Chatham, Prisoner of War #3098. When Taken: 24 Jun 1813. Where Taken: Beaver Dams, Upper Canada. Date Received: 7 Jan 1814 from Halifax, NS. Discharged on 10 Oct 1814 and sent to U.S. on the Cartel *St. Philip*. (Johnson's Database, 2019)

Beasley, Edward, served as a Seaman and was born in Maryland. Age: 22. Prison Depot: Chatham, Prisoner of War #1201. Captured by HM Frigate *Briton* & HM Frigate *Andromache*. When Taken: 20 Dec 1812. Where Taken: off Bordeaux, France. Prize Name: *Exception*. Ship Type: Merchant Vessel. Date Received: 16 Mar 1813 from Portsmouth on HMS *Abundance*. Discharged on 2 Jul 1813 and released to the Cartel *Moses Brown*. (Johnson's Database, 2019)

Beatty, J., served as a Seaman on the privateer *Globe* and was wounded in action on 1 Nov 1813 (Marine p. 215)

Beauty, Edmund, served as a Seaman and was born in Baltimore. Age: 17. Prison Depot: Chatham, Prisoner of War #3630. Captured by HM Frigate *Pomone* & HM Frigate *Cydnus*. When Taken: 4 Mar 1814. Where Taken: Bay of Biscayne. Prize Name: *Bunker Hill*. Ship Type: Privateer. Date Received: 31 Mar 1814 on HMS *Raisonable*. Discharged on 22 Oct 1814 and sent to Dartmoor on HMS *Leyden*. (Johnson's Database, 2019)

Beavin, Charles, served as a Private in a detachment of Charles Co.'s 43rd Regt. and was wounded in the arm by a bayonet on 24 Jul 1814 when Cedar Point warehouse was burnt and confined him for nearly 16 days (Wright Vol. 5, p. 42)

Bechm, Joseph, served as a Private in the 14th U.S. Infantry and was captured on 24 Jun 1813 at Beaver Dams, Upper Canada. Prisoner of War #3772 at Halifax, NS and was discharged for exchange on 3 Feb 1814 (Johnson and Christou, p. 34; Baker Vol. 1, p. 29)

Beck (Beek), Steward or Stewart, served as a Seaman and was born in Maryland. Age: 18. Prison Depot: Plymouth 1, Prisoner of War #1396. Captured by HM Brig *Orestes*. When Taken: 13 Apr 1813. Where Taken: Bay of Biscayne. Prize Name: *Henry Clements*. Ship Type: Merchant Vessel. Date Received: 15 May 1813. From what ship: HMS *Orestes*. Discharged on 3 Jul 1813 and sent to Stapleton Prison. Prison Depot: Stapleton, Prisoner of War #391. Received: 11 Jul 1813 from Plymouth. Discharged on 16 Jun 1814 and sent to Dartmoor. Prison Depot: Dartmoor, Prisoner of War #1638. Age 19. Date Received: 23 Jun 1814 from Stapleton. Discharged on 1 May 1815. (Johnson's Database, 2019)

Beckett, John (1791-1850), served as a Captain at the Battle of York and bore General Pike from the field when he was mortally wounded; also participated in the capture of Fort George and the affair at Stoney Creek in June 1813. He went aboard our fleet at the invitation of Capt. Woolsey and Gen. Williamson and was in the fight that took place on Lake Ontario. He was also at the Battle of Chrystler's field and Lyon's Creek where he received a wound. He served in both branches of the State Legislature. (*National Intelligencer*, May 25, 1850) DEATH OF A VETERAN MARYLANDER. Capt. John Beckett, for many years a member of the Maryland Legislature, and a prominent officer in the War of 1812, died suddenly on the 20th instant, at his residence at Locust Grove, Calvert county, in the 59th year of his age. He was at the battle of York, and bore from the field Gen. Pike, who was mortally wounded. He also participated in the capture of Fort George, and in the affair at Stoney Creek, and was on board the fleet in the hardest fight that took place on Lake Ontario. He was in the battle of Chrystler's Field, where Covington fell, and in the battle of Lyon's Creek he received a severe wound. (*The [Baltimore] Sun*, May 28, 1850) Other heroes of the War of 1812 were Capt. John Beckett and Col. William Lawrence. Captain Beckett served in the American Army throughout the war and was severely wounded in the final Montreal Campaign. (*A History of Calvert County, Maryland* by Charles F. Stein, 1976, p. 154) Son of John Beckett and Elizabeth Heighe Blake, buried at Beckett Family Cemetery at Selby Cliffs on Dares Road, John served in 14th U.S. Infantry, commissioned 2nd Lieutenant on 12 Mar 1812, promoted to 1st Lieutenant on 13 Mar 1813 and discharged on 15 Jun 1815; bounty land was issued to his widow Susan N. Beckett (BLW# 21922-160-50; Johnson and Christou, pp. 34-35, did not mention his wound)

Beckwith, Charles, served as a Private in Capt. Benjamin Thomas' Co., 49th Regt., Cecil Co. Militia, for 3 days between 18 Apr 1813 and 16 May 1813 and was "discharged on account of sickness" (Wright Vol. 3, p. 13)

Beckwith, James, served as a Seaman and was born in Maryland. Age: 25. Prison Depot: Portsmouth, Prisoner of War #1323. How Taken: Gave himself up off HM Transport *Leopard*. Date Received: 25 Dec 1813. From what ship: HMS *Leopard*. Discharged on 26 Dec 1813 and sent to Chatham on HMS *Nemesis*. Prison Depot: Chatham, Prisoner of War #3203. Date Received: 7 Jan 1813 from Portsmouth. Discharged on 26 Sep 1814 and sent to Dartmoor on HMS *Leyden*. Prison Depot: Dartmoor, Prisoner of War #4701. How Taken: Gave himself up off HM Transport *Leopard*. When Taken: 25 Dec 1813. Date Received: 9 Oct 1814. From what ship: HMT *Leyden* from Chatham. Discharged on 15 Jun 1815. (Johnson's Database, 2019)

Beckwith (Beckworth), Lenox, served as 1st Sergeant in Capt. Jacob Alexander's Co., Frederick Co. Militia, from 22 Jul to 19 Sep 1814 and "sick on furlough" (Mallick and Wright, p. 49, also stating Lenox married Rebecca Ridgely in 1812)

Beeson, Thomas Vandever (1785-1814), served as a Private in Capt. John Berry's Co., 1st Artillery Regt., MD Militia, from 19 Aug 1814 and was killed in action at Fort McHenry on 13 Sep 1814. His name is on the Baltimore Battle Monument. (NARA; Wright Vol. 2, p. 49; Marine, p. 173; *Baltimore American*, 12 Jun 1819, reported his name as Thomas V. Beeston). Notice: WASHINGTON ARTILLERISTS: You are ordered to assemble in Water street head of Cheapside, on Sunday morning next, the 25th inst., at 7 o'clock, to pay the last tribute of respect due to the late Thomas V. Beeson, who so nobly fell in defense of his country at the siege of Fort McHenry. The Independent Artillerists are particularly requested to attend, and also the relatives and friends of the deceased. Order by John Mackey, Jr. Secty. (*Baltimore American*, 23 Sep 1814) An Old Defender Re-interred: In December 1872, Jacob Cobb, one of the Old Defenders' of Baltimore in 1814, discovered while walking in South Baltimore within an old burying ground near Fort Ave. and Webster St., a crumbling tombstone, upon which was deciphered the name of Thomas V. Beeson. The Association of Old Defenders of 1814 at once made arrangements for the re-interment of the remains to Mount Olivet Cemetery on Frederick Road west of the city. The remains were transferred to a handsome casket and were re-interred with appropriate ceremonies. One of the speakers and the Old Defenders' who attended the ceremony referred to the debt of gratitude due to the deceased by those whom he had defended and thought no more beautiful expression of that obligation could be made than the erection of a monument over his remains. Several of the Old Defenders were present to act as pallbearers. A search of Mount Olivet Cemetery has yet to find his grave, perhaps on the many gravestones that lie flat upon the ground covered by grass. (*The [Baltimore] Sun*, 25 Dec 1872). In March 2019, primarily through the efforts of Christos Christou, Jr., the Society of the War of 1812 in the State of Maryland restored the grave marker of Pvt. Beeson. In 1872 the original grave marker was found by a Society member broken in pieces so the Society at that time paid to have a new one made and his grave moved to Mt. Olivet where it has since been; however, the stone had fallen over and became buried in the last 147 years until Christou was able to poke around the lot it was supposed to be in and find it. Digging out part of it revealed the name. Tegeler Monument Co. was hired to dig it out completely and stand it erect again for all to see. It is inscribed as follows, with his last name misspelled: "In Memory of Thomas V. Beason a member of Capt. Berry's Artillery Co. who nobly fell in the defence of *Fort McHenry* on the 13th day of Sept 1814 in the 30th year of his Age." Beeson is interred in Lot 147-A. (*Mt. Olivet Cemetery, Baltimore, Maryland, Caretaker Records*, compiled by John J. Winterbottom, 1989, p. 23, transcribed his burial information incorrectly as "Thomas M. Beason … Sept. 15, 1811, 50 years old")

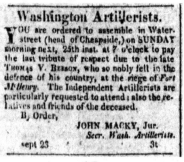

In Memory of
THOMAS V. BEASON
a member of Capt. Berry
Artillery company
who nobly fell in
the defence of
FORT MCHENRY
on the 13th day of Sept 1814
in the 30th year of his Age

Belfield, Henry, served as a Marine and was taken from the barracks and admitted to the Naval Hospital in Washington, DC as Patient No. 171 as of 1 Jun 1814, but his injury or illness was not stated (Sharp's Database, 2018)

Bell, Archibald E., served as a Private in Capt. Robert T. Dade's Co., Cramer's Regt., Montgomery Co., and reported "sick absent 28 days" on the muster roll dated 3 Aug – 10 Nov 1814 (Wright Vol. 7, p. 8)

Bell, Brooks, served as a Private (company not stated) and was captured at the Battle of Bladensburg on 24 Aug 1814 (Marine, p. 174)

Bell, Cecelius (1792-1814), served as a Private in Capt. Michael Haubert's Co., 51st Regiment, Baltimore Militia, under command of Lt. F. Maynard (name also written and filed incorrectly as Cornelius Bell). Cecelius joined on 7 Sep 1814 and was killed in the Battle of North Point on 12 Sep 1814. His name is on the Baltimore Battle Monument. (NARA; Wright Vol. 2, p. 35; *Baltimore American*, 12 Jun 1819, spelled his name Cecilius and stated he died defending Baltimore)

Bell, John, served as a Private in 14th U.S. Infantry (company and captain not stated) and died on 24 Jun 1813; heirs received half pay for 5 years in lieu of bounty land (Johnson and Christou, p. 35)

Belt, James, served as a Passenger and was born in Montgomery Co., MD. Age and Race not stated. Prison Depot: Jamaica, Prisoner of War #25. Captured by HM Frigate Gar*land*. When Taken: 3 Aug 1812. Where Taken: at sea. Prize Name: *Madisonia*. Ship Type: Merchant Vessel. Date Received: 22 Aug 1812. From what ship: HMS Gar*land*. Discharged on 11 Nov 1812 and sent to U.S. on the Cartel *Medosa*. (Johnson's Database, 2019)

Benner, Lewis (Mulatto), served as a Seaman and was born in Baltimore. Age: 22. Prison Depot: Plymouth 1, Prisoner of War #94. Captured by HM Brig *Rover*. When Taken: 21 Oct 1812. Where Taken: off Bordeaux, France. Prize Name: *Experiment*. Ship Type: Merchant Vessel. Date Received: 25 Dec 1812. From what ship: HMS *Northumberland*. Discharged and sent to Portsmouth on 29 Dec 1812 on HMS *Northumberland*. Prison Depot: Portsmouth, Prisoner of War #348. Date Received: 31 Dec 1812. From what ship: HM Ship-of-the-Line *Northumberland*. Discharged on 4 Mar 1813 and sent to Chatham on HMS *Queen*. Prison Depot: Chatham, Prisoner of War #925. Date Received: 10 Mar 1813. From what ship: HMS *Tigress*. Discharged on 8 Jun 1813 and released to the Cartel *Rodrigo*. (Johnson's Database, 2019)

Bennett, Frederick F., served as a Private in Capt. Joseph H. Nicholson's Artillery Co., Baltimore City, from 19 Aug 1814 and was "taken prisoner," but the date and place were not given (Wright Vol. 2, p. 51)

Bennett, George, served as a Private in Capt. Christian Adreon's Co., 5th Regt., Baltimore Militia, was wounded on 12 Sep 1814 at North Point and listed as prisoner of war who was later exchanged. Dr. James H. McCulloh, Jr. wrote this note soon after the battle to the British commander: "In consequence of the humanity shown the following American prisoners of war, I do promise upon honor that they shall not directly or indirectly serve against the British until regularly exchanged." (Wright Vol. 2, p. 3; Marine p. 171)

Bennett, Joseph, served as a Private in Capt. Adam Shower's Co., Baltimore Co., 2nd Regiment, 11th Brigade, stationed in Baltimore on 26 Jul 1814 and was "taken prisoner Aug 24, paroled Aug 27" (Wright Vol. 2, p. 84; Marine pp. 174, 217, stated he served as a Private in Capt. Moale's Co. of Columbian Artillery when he was captured at Bladensburg on 24 Aug 1814)

Bennett, Rezin J. (1795-1875), served as a Private in Capt. Thomas F. W. Vinson's Co., Extra Battalion, 42nd Regt., Montgomery Co. Militia, volunteered at Long Old Fields near Barnesville around 27 Jul 1814, served from 1 Aug 1814 until 27 Sep 1814 "then went home on account of sickness on a furlough from Baltimore" and a few days later the company was discharged. On 31 Jul 1871 Rezin J. Bennett, age 76, of Felicity, Clermont Co., OH, stated his wife's name was Mary Lenhart and they married at Ripley, Brown Co., OH on 18 Aug 1847. On 16 Apr 1878 Mary Bennett, widow, stated Rezin was born about 1795, was of medium height and died at Felicity, OH in January 1875. (Wright Vol. 7, pp. 5, 16; Pensions SO-22838, WO-17474; BLW# 52-40-63049; BLW# 55-120-65900)

Bennington, Henry (1776-1814), of Harford Co., served as a Private in the 35th U.S. Infantry on 27 Apr 1814, age 38, and died at Norfolk, VA on 23 Oct 1814 of unspecified causes ("Harford County in the War of 1812," by Christopher T. George, *Harford Historical Bulletin* No. 76, Spring 1998, p. 7 footnote)

Benskin, Solomon (1787-1813), enlisted 11 May 1812 for five years as a Private in the 2nd Regt., Light Dragoons, age 25, born in Allegany Co. and died on 20 May or 1 Jun 1813 at Utica, NY. (Wright Vol. 10, p. 9)

Benson, Jonas, served as a Seaman and was born in Maryland. Age: 23. Prison Depot: Portsmouth, Prisoner of War #829. How Taken: Gave himself up off HM Frigate *North Star*. Date Received: 26 May 1813. From what ship: HMS *North Star*. Discharged on 10 Jun 1813 and sent to Chatham on HMS *Arathursa*. Prison Depot: Chatham, Prisoner of War #1768. Date Received: 14 Jun 1813. From what ship: HMS *Arathursa*. Discharged on 24 Jul 1814. Sent to Dartmoor on HMS *Lyffey*. (Johnson's Database, 2019)

Bergen, Leven (Mulatto), served as a Seaman and was born in Baltimore. Age: 33 or 36. Prison Depot: Portsmouth, Prisoner of War #831. How Taken: Gave himself up off HM Ship-of-the-Line *Sterling Castle*. Date Received: 5 Jun 1813. From what ship: HM Guard Ship *Royal William*. Discharged on 10 Jun 1813 and sent to Chatham on HMS *Arethus*.Prison Depot: Chatham, Prisoner of War #1763. Date Received: 14 Jun 1813 from HMS *Arathursa*. Discharged on 24 Jul 1814 and sent to Dartmoor on HMS *Lyffey*. Prison Depot: Dartmoor, Prisoner of War #2042. Date Received: 3 Aug 1814. From what ship: HMS *Lyffey* from Chatham Depot. Discharged on 26 Apr 1815. (Johnson's Database, 2019)

Berry, Bayne L. (1788-1821), served as a Private in Capt. Reuben Gilder's Co., 14th U.S. Infantry, enlisted 31 Dec 1812 in Alexandria, DC for 5 years at the age of 24, 5' 4" tall, born at Port Tobacco, MD, was wounded at Cook's Mills, Upper Canada and was discharged on 19 Oct 1814 at Greenbush, NY due to wound in his right thigh; he died on 24 Sep 1821. (Johnson and Christou, p. 36, also listed him as Bayne S. Berry)

Berry, Benjamin, served as a Private in Capt. Jasper M. Jackson's Co., 34th Regt., Prince George's Co. Militia, from 21 Aug 1814 and was furloughed on 9 Sep 1814 for indisposition (Wright Vol. 6, p. 22)

Berry, Brook, served as a Seaman and was born in Prince George's Co., MD. Age: 20. Prison Depot: Plymouth 1, Prisoner of War #518. How Taken: Gave himself up off MV *Allegany*. When Taken: 8 Aug 1812. Where Taken: Gibraltar. Date Received: 15 Feb 1813. From what ship: HMS *Andromeda*. Discharged and sent to Dartmoor on 2 Apr 1813. Prison Depot: Dartmoor, Prisoner of War #30. Date Received: 2 Apr 1813 from Plymouth. Discharged and sent to Dartmouth on 30 Jul 1813. (Johnson's Database, 2019)

Berry, Joseph, served as a Seaman and was born in Baltimore. Age: 18. Prison Depot: Portsmouth, Prisoner of War #557. Captured by HM Frigate *Dryad*. When Taken: 7 Jan 1813. Where Taken: at sea. Prize Name: *Rossie*. Ship Type: Merchant Vessel. Date Received: 25 Jan 1813. From what ship: HM Ship-of-the-Line *Queen*. Discharged on 11 Mar 1813 and sent to Chatham on HM Store Ship *Abundance*. Prison Depot: Chatham, Prisoner of War #1230. Received: 16 Mar 1813 from Portsmouth on HMS *Abundance*. Discharged on 24 Jul 1813 and released to the Cartel *Hoffning*. (Johnson's Database, 2019)

Berryman, John (African American), served as a Seaman and was born in Maryland. Age: 25. Prison Depot: Plymouth 1, Prisoner of War #1560. Captured by HM Frigate *Andromache*. When Taken: 14 Mar 1813. Where Taken: off Nantes, France. Prize Name: *Courier*. Home Port: Baltimore. Ship Type: Letter of Marque. Date Received: 29 May 1813. From what ship: HMS *Hannibal*. Discharged on 30 Jun 1813 and sent to Stapleton. Prison Depot: Stapleton, Prisoner of War #122. Date Received: 8 Jul 1813 from Plymouth. Discharged on 13 Jun 1814 and sent to Dartmoor. Prison Depot: Dartmoor, Prisoner of War #1406. Date Received: 19 Jun 1814 from Stapleton. Discharged on 28 Apr 1815. (Johnson's Database, 2019)

Bevers, Clement, served as a Seaman and was born in Baltimore. Age: 43. Prison Depot: Chatham, Prisoner of War #841. Captured by HM Frigate *Phoebe*. When Taken: 1 Jan 1813. Where Taken: Lat 44.4 Long 23. Prize Name: *Vengeance*. Ship Type: Letter of Marque. Date Received: 1 Mar 1813 from Plymouth on HMS *Namur*. Prison Depot: Plymouth 1, Prisoner of War #226. Date Received: 9 Jan (sic) 1813. From what ship: HMS *Phoebe*.Discharged on 24 Jul 1813 and released to the Cartel *Hoffning*. (Johnson's Database, 2019)

Bhare, Charles, served as a Seaman under Sailing Master Simmones Bunbury, U. S. Sea Fencibles, and was dangerously wounded on 13 Sep 1814 at Fort McHenry (Marine pp. 173, 219)

Biays, Joseph Jr. (1789-1814), served as a Private in Capt. Thomas Sheppard's Co., 6th Regiment, Baltimore Militia, from 19 Aug 1814, probably wounded at North Point on 13 Sep 1814 and died on 30 Sep 1814. His name is <u>not</u> on the Baltimore Battle Monument. (Wright Vol. 2, p. 14; Marine p. 219) He was buried in Green Mount Cemetery.

Bilson, William (1780-1827), served as 2nd Sergeant in Capt. Henry Fowler's Co., Randall's Rifle Bttn., Baltimore Co., from 26 Aug 1814 and "in captivity from Sep 13" 1814 (Wright Vol. 2, p. 74; Family Bible; Baltimore County Will 12:417)

Birch, Andrew, served as a Seaman and was born in Baltimore. Age: 19. Prison Depot: Plymouth 1, Prisoner of War #493. Captured by HM Brig *Reindeer*. When Taken: 3 Feb 1813. Where Taken: Bay of Biscayne. Prize Name: *Cashiere*. Home

Port: Baltimore. Ship Type: Letter of Marque. Date Received: 12 Feb 1813. From what ship: HMS *Reindeer*. Discharged and sent to Dartmoor on 2 Apr 1813. Prison Depot: Dartmoor, Prisoner of War #10. Date Received: 2 Apr 1813 from Plymouth. Discharged and sent to Dartmouth on 30 Jul 1813. (Johnson's Database, 2019)

Birkhead, Hugh, served as a Private in Capt. Samuel Sterett's Co., 5th Regiment, Baltimore Militia, from 19 Aug 1814, promoted to 4th Corporal on 12 Sep 1814, was taken prisoner the same day at North Point and was exchanged on 8 Nov 1814 (Wright Vol. 2, p. 6)

Bisbee, John, from the *Ontario*, served as an Armourer of the U.S. Chesapeake Flotilla, entered service 17 Mar 1814 and died 28 Aug 1814 (Shomette p. 377)

Bishop, ----, served as a Marine, taken from the barracks and admitted to Naval Hospital in Washington, DC as Patient No. 84 on 26 Dec 1814 with typhoid fever, discharged on 16 Jan 1815 and sent to barracks (Sharp's Database, 2018)

Bishop, Henry, served as a Private in Capt. Stephen Moore's Co., Baltimore Volunteers Infantry Co., enlisted 8 Sep 1812 for 1 year and died on 6 Aug 1813; bounty land issued to James Legg, John Henry Legg, William E. Legg and Charles M. Legg, his nephews and only heirs at law (BLW# 27388-160-12; Johnson and Christou, p. 37; Wright Vol. 2, p. 57)

Bishop, Jesse, served as a Private in the 14th U.S. Infantry and was captured at Beaver Dams, Upper Canada on 24 Jun 1813. Prisoner of War #3851 at Halifax, NS, interned 24 Jun 1813, but date of discharge was not recorded (Johnson and Christou, p. 35; Baker Vol. 1, p. 35)

Bishop, William, served as a Private in Capt. Richard Bell's Co., 5th U.S. infantry, enlisted 3 Apr 1813 at Baltimore, age 25, 5' 5" tall, born in New Haven, CT and discharged at Greenbush, NY on 15 Apr 1815 on Surgeon's Certificate, medical reason not stated (Johnson and Christou, p. 37)

Bivens, Timothy, served as a Private in Capt. Robert C. Gallaway's Co., 46th Regiment, Baltimore County Militia, was stationed at Carroll's Island on the lower end of Middle River Neck at the mouth of Gunpowder River and reported "dead., left a wife and children," but the date of death was not given on the muster roll dated 19 Apr – 22 Apr 1813 (Wright Vol. 2, p. 71)

Black, Isaac, served as a Private in Capt. George Washington Magee's Co., Frederick Co. Militia in the 1st Regiment, New Windsor area, from 22 Jul 1814 and was reported "missing" on 22 Aug 1814 (Mallick and Wright, p. 341)

Black, John, served as a Private in the 14th U.S. Infantry and captured at Beaver Dams, Upper Canada on 24 Jun 1813. Prisoner of War #3794 at Halifax, NS, interned on 24 Jun 1813 and sent to England on 9 Nov 1813 on HMS *Success* (Johnson and Christou, p. 37; Baker Vol. 1, p. 35) John Black served as a Private in 14th U.S. Infantry and was born in Maryland. Age: 24. Prison Depot: Chatham, Prisoner of War #3123. When Taken: 24 Jun 1813. Where Taken: Beaver Dams, Upper Canada. Date Received: 7 Jan 1814 from Halifax, NS. Discharged on 10 Oct 1814 and sent to U.S. on the Cartel *St. Philip*. (Johnson's Database, 2019)

Blackburn, William, served as a Seaman and was born in Frederick Town, MD. Age: 26. Prison Depot: Chatham, Prisoner of War #44. Captured by HM Brig *Recruit*. When Taken: 11 Jun 1812. Where Taken: off Rhode Island. Prize Name: *General Blake*. Ship Type: Merchant Vessel. Date Received: 3 Nov 1812. From what ship: HMS *Plover*. Discharged on 23 Mar 1813 and released to the Cartel *Robinson Potter*. (Johnson's Database, 2019)

Blackston, William (Mulatto), served as a Seaman and was born in Baltimore. Age: 26. Prison Depot: Dartmoor, Prisoner of War #6397. Captured by HM Brig *Onyx*. When Taken: 25 Dec 1814. Where Taken: off San Domingo (Haiti). Prize Name: *Netterville*. Ship Type: Merchant Vessel. Date Received: 3 Mar 1815. From what ship: HMT *Ganges* from Plymouth. Discharged on 11 Jul 1815. (Johnson's Database, 2019)

Blades, Elijah, served as a Private in Capt. Peter Willis' Co., 19th Regiment, Caroline Co. Militia, for 10 days and was reported "went beside himself and ... mad" (sic) on the muster roll dated 15 Aug – 30 Aug 1813 (Wright Vol. 1, p. 82)

Blagcon, Stephen, served as a Seaman and was born in Baltimore. Age: 23. Prison Depot: Dartmoor, Prisoner of War #2598. Captured by *Lion*, British Privateer. When Taken: 15 Feb 1813. Where Taken: Bay of Biscayne. Prize Name: *Tom Thumb*. Ship Type: Merchant Vessel. Date Received: 21 Aug 1814. From what ship: HMT *Freya* from Chatham. Discharged on 3 May 1815. (Johnson's Database, 2019)

Blair, Richard, served as a Seaman on the privateer *Globe* and was killed in action on 1 Nov 1813 (*Niles Weekly Register*, 19 Feb 1814)

Blaze, William, served as a Private in the 12th U.S. Infantry, enlisted at Fincastle by Lt. Houston on 29 Dec 1814 for 5 years, age 31, 5' 10" tall, born in Frederick County, gray eyes, dark hair and dark complexion, mustered 16 Feb 1815 in Capt. Page's Co., served at Carlisle Barracks, PA on 30 Apr 1815 and was discharged at Camp Jefferson on 1 Mar 1819 in consequence of a stiff ankle joint (Mallick and Wright, p. 53)

Blazon, Stephen, served as a Seaman and was born in Baltimore. Age: 23. Prison Depot: Portsmouth, Prisoner of War #707. Captured by *Lion*, British Privateer. When Taken: 15 Feb 1813. Where Taken: Bay of Biscayne. Prize Name: *Tom*

Thumb. Ship Type: Merchant Vessel. Date Received: 24 Feb 1813. From what ship: HM Brig *Escort*. Discharged on 6 Mar 1813 and sent to Chatham on HMS *Cornwall*. Prison Depot: Chatham, Prisoner of War #1109. Date Received: 14 Mar 1813 from Portsmouth on HMS *Beagle*. Discharged on 11 Aug 1814 and sent to Dartmoor on HMS *Freya*. (Johnson's Database, 2019)

Bloise, Zachariah, served as a Private in Capt. Henry Grindage's Co., 14th U.S. Infantry, enlisted 10 Sep 1812 for 5 years, was captured on 24 Jun 1813 at Beaver Dams, Upper Canada and was interned as Prisoner of War #3779 at Halifax, NS until discharged on 3 Feb 1814; bounty land was issued to his son Morecai (sic) Bloise and other heirs at law (Johnson and Christou, p. 37; Baker Vol. 1, p. 38, listed the soldier's name as Mordecaiah Blois)

Blossom, Seth, served as a Seaman and was born in Baltimore. Age: 45. Prison Depot: Dartmoor, Prisoner of War #1882. How Taken: Gave himself up off HM Frigate *Belvidera*. When Taken: 15 Nov 1813. Date Received: 29 Jul 1814. From what ship: HMS *Ville de Paris* from Chatham Depot. Discharged on 2 May 1815. (Johnson's Database, 2019)

Blufford, Henry, served as a Private in Capt. George Washington Magee's Co., Frederick County Militia, 1st Regiment, New Windsor area, from 22 Jul 1814, engaged in the Battle of Bladensburg and was reported "sick absent" on 24 Aug 1814 (Mallick and Wright, p. 341)

Blunt, Benjamin, served as an Ensign in Capt. McConcking's Co., 38th U.S. Regiment, and died in 1814 (Marine p. 221)

Boardby, Samuel, of Baltimore, served as a Seaman on the ship *Fiere Facia* and was captured, but date was not given. Prisoner of War #4356 at Dartmoor and died on 29 Mar 1815 (Centennial Trails, United States Daughters of 1812, online at www.war1812trails.com/Dartmoor; Johnson's Database, 2019, did not list him)

Boater, Alexander, served as a Seaman in Commodore Barney's Flotilla and was wounded on 24 Aug 1814 on the field of battle at Bladensburg, was admitted to the Naval Hospital in Washington, DC as Patient No. 46 on 24 Aug 1814 and was discharged on 28 Sep 1814 and sent to the Navy Yard (Sharp's Database, 2018)

Boatman, John, served as a Private from Maryland and died on 23 Nov 1813 in Dartmoor Prison in England (Peterson p. 7; Johnson's Database, 2019, did not list this man)

Boivie, James, served as a Seaman and was born in Maryland. Age: 27. Prison Depot: Dartmoor, Prisoner of War #372. Captured by HM Ship-of-the-Line *Superb*. When Taken: 16 Mar 1813. Where Taken: Bay of Biscayne. Prize Name:

Independence. Ship Type: Merchant Vessel. Date Received: 1 Jul 1813 from Plymouth. Discharged on 20 Apr 1815. (Johnson's Database, 2019)

Boldine, Alexander, served as a Private in Capt. Samuel Hopkins' Co., 2nd U.S. Light Dragoons, enlisted 29 Mar 1814 in Philadelphia, age 17, 5' 6" tall, born in Baltimore, discharged on 6 Sep 1815 as an invalid (Johnson and Christou, p. 38)

Bond, Benjamin, served as a Private in Capt. Michael Haubert's Co., 51st Regt., Baltimore Militia, under command of Lt. F. Maynard, from 18 Aug 1814 and was killed on 12 Sep 1814 at the Battle of North Point. His name is on the Baltimore Battle Monument. (NARA; Wright Vol. 2, p. 35; Marine p. 222, did not mention his death; *Baltimore American*, 12 Jun 1819) October Term 1814: Mary Bond, administratix of Benjamin Bond, was ordered to place a notice in the *Baltimore American* informing creditors, to exhibit their claims against Benjamin Bond's estate. (Baltimore Orphans Court Proceedings, Book 9, p. 64) On 15 Jan 1816 the final account of Mary Bond, administratrix of Benjamin Bond, listed a frame house and lot on Union Street for his wife Mary (her one-third share) and two brick houses and lots on Biddle Street to his orphaned children, Samuel, Elizabeth and William Bond (two-thirds share). (Baltimore County Administration Accounts Book 20, p. 233)

Bond, Henry, served as a Private in Capt. Joseph H. Nicholson's Artillery Co. and was slightly wounded on 13 Sep 1814 at Fort McHenry (Marine pp. 173, 223)

Bond, Samuel (African American), served as a Seaman and was born in Baltimore. Age: 40. Prison Depot: Chatham, Prisoner of War #2126. How Taken: Gave himself up off HM Ship-of-the-Line *Ocean*. When Taken: 28 May 1813. Date Received: 9 Aug 1813. From what ship: HMS *Thames*. Discharged on 12 Aug 1814 and sent to Dartmoor on HMS *Alpheus*. Prison Depot: Dartmoor, Prisoner of War #2899. Date Received: 24 Aug 1814. From what ship: HMT *Alpheus* from Chatham. Discharged 19 May 1815. (Johnson's Database, 2019)

Bonie, James, served as a Seaman and was born in Maryland. Age: 26. Prison Depot: Plymouth 1, Prisoner of War #1046. Captured by HM Ship-of-the-Line *Superb*. When Taken: 16 Mar 1813. Where Taken: Bay of Biscayne. Prize Name: *Independence*. Ship Type: Merchant Vessel. Date Received: 22 Apr 1813. From what ship: HMS *Superb*. Discharged and sent to Dartmoor on 1 Jul 1813. (Johnson's Database, 2019)

Boone, James (1773-1813), served as a Seaman and was born in Maryland. Age: 40. Prison Depot: Bermuda, Prisoner of War #1335. Captured by HM Frigate *Loire*. When Taken: 10 Dec 1813. Where Taken: off Block Island, Rhode island. Prize Name: *Rolla*. Home Port: Baltimore. Ship Type: Privateer. Died on 22 Mar 1813 from pneumonia. (Johnson's Database, 2019)

Booth, George, served as a Private in the 14th U.S. Infantry and was captured at Beaver Dams, Upper Canada on 24 Jun 1813. Prisoner of War #3787 at Halifax, NS, and was discharged on 9 Nov 1813 and sent to England on HMS *Success* (Johnson and Christou, p. 39; Baker Vol. 1, p. 40) George Booth served as a Private in 14th U.S. Infantry and was born in Maryland. Age: 21. Prison Depot: Chatham, Prisoner of War #3117. When Taken: 24 Jun 1813. Where Taken: Beaver Dams, Upper Canada. Received: 7 Jan 1814 from Halifax, NS. Discharged 10 Oct 1814 and sent to U.S. on the Cartel *St. Philip*. (Johnson's Database, 2019)

Booth, John, served as a Private in the 14th U.S. Infantry and was captured at Beaver Dams, Upper Canada on 24 Jun 1813. Prisoner of War #3980 at Halifax, NS, and was discharged for exchange on 3 Feb 1814 (Johnson and Christou, p. 39; Baker Vol. 1, p. 40)

Booth, Joseph (African American), served as a Seaman and was born in Herring Bay, MD. Age: 30. Prison Depot: Chatham, Prisoner of War #329. How Taken: Gave himself up off MV *Thomas* on 4 Jan 1813. Where Taken: London, UK. Date Received: 11 Jan 1813. From what ship: HMS *Raisonable*. Discharged on 12 Apr 1813 and released to HMS *Carnatic*. (Johnson's Database, 2019)

Booth, Thomas (African American), served as a Seaman and was born in Maryland. Age: 27 or 30. Prison Depot: Portsmouth, Prisoner of War #631. How Taken: Gave himself up off, HM Guard Ship *Royal William*. Date Received: 3 Feb 1813. From what ship: HMS *Royal William*. Discharged on 11 Mar 1813 and sent to Chatham on HM Store Ship *Abundance*. Prison Depot: Chatham, Prisoner of War #1297. Date Received: 16 Mar 1813 from Portsmouth on HMS *Abundance*. Discharged on 23 Jul 1814 and sent to Dartmoor. Prison Depot: Dartmoor, Prisoner of War #1927. Received: 3 Aug 1814. From what ship: HMS *Alceste* from Chatham. Discharged on 2 May 1815. (Johnson's Database, 2019)

Booth, Thomas, of Maryland, served as a Seaman on the ship *LaHogue* and was reported by Capt. Jeduthan Upton, Jr. in 1814 as having been impressed into service and was being held as a Prisoner of War on the prison ship *San Antonio* at Chatham, England (*Niles Weekly Register*, 26 Feb 1814)

Boran, John, served as a Private in the 5th U.S. Infantry and died in 1813; heirs received half pay for 5 years in lieu of bounty land (Johnson and Christou, p. 39)

Borgea, John, served as a Private in the 14th U.S. Infantry and was captured at Beaver Dams, Upper Canada on 24 Jun 1813. Prisoner of War at Halifax, NS, and discharged on 3 Feb 1814 (Johnson and Christou, p. 39, but Baker Vol. 1, p. 40, did not mention him)

Boriesa, John Pierre (African American), served as a Seaman and was born in Maryland. Age: 23. Prison Depot: Plymouth 1, Prisoner of War #1552. Captured by HM Frigate *Andromache*. When Taken: 2 Apr 1813. Where Taken: Bay of Biscayne. Prize Name: *Good Friends*. Ship Type: Merchant Vessel. Date Received: 29 May 1813. From what ship: HMS *Hannibal*. Discharged on 30 Jun 1813 and sent to Stapleton. Prison Depot: Stapleton, Prisoner of War #116. Captured by HM Frigate *Andromache*. When Taken: 2 Apr 1813. Date Received: 8 Jul 1813 from Plymouth. Discharged on 13 Jun 1814 and sent to Dartmoor. Prison Depot: Dartmoor, Prisoner of War #1402. Date Received: 19 Jun 1814 from Stapleton. Discharged on 28 Apr 1815. (Johnson's Database, 2019)

Boroughs, Isaac, served as a Private in Capt. Samuel Dawson's Co., Frederick Co. Militia, from 26 Jul 1814, engaged in the Battle of Bladensburg and in the defense of Baltimore City and was reported sick in Baltimore on 12 Oct 1814 (Mallick and Wright, p. 338)

Bosely, Thomas, served as a Private in the 14th U.S. Infantry (company not stated) and was captured at Beaver Dams, Upper Canada on 24 Jun 1813. Prisoner of War #3972 at Halifax, NS and was discharged for exchange on 3 Feb 1814 (Johnson and Christou, p. 39; Baker Vol. 1, p. 40)

Bostell, James, served as a Seaman and was born in Baltimore. Age: 31. Prison Depot: Dartmoor, Prisoner of War #2479. Captured by HM Frigate *Orpheus*. When Taken: 20 Apr 1814. Where Taken: off Matanzas, Cuba. Prize Name: U.S. Sloop-of-War *Frolic*. Ship Type: Warship. Received: 16 Aug 1814 from HMT *Queen* from Halifax, NS. Discharged on 3 May 1815. (Johnson's Database, 2019)

Boswell, John, served as a Private in 1st Lt. John Thomas 3rd Co., 32nd Regt., Anne Arundel Co. Militia, from 24 Aug 1814 and reported "sick at home since Sep 22" on the muster roll dated 24 Aug – 27 Sep 1814 (Wright Vol. 4, p. 43)

Boulder, James, served as a Private in the 14th U.S. Infantry (company not stated) and died on 19 Oct 1814; heirs received half pay for 5 years in lieu of bounty land (Johnson and Christou, p. 39)

Bourdon, John, served as a Seaman and was born in Maryland. Age: 39. Prison Depot: Dartmoor, Prisoner of War #1627. Captured by HM Frigate *Surveillante*. When Taken: 27 Apr 1813. Where Taken: Bay of Biscayne. Prize Name: *Tom*. Home Port: Baltimore. Ship Type: Letter of Marque. Date Received: 23 Jun 1814 from Stapleton. Discharged on 1 May 1815. (Johnson's Database, 2019)

Bousman, John, see John Baseman (Bausman, Bousman), q.v.

Bowan, Benjamin, served as a Private in the 28th U.S. Infantry (company not stated) and died in June 1814; heirs received half pay for 5 years in lieu of bounty land (Johnson and Christou, p.39)

Bowen, Artemus, served as a Sergeant in Capt. David Cummings' Co., 14th U.S. Infantry, enlisted on 20 Mar 1813 for 5 years, was captured at Beaver Dams, Upper Canada on 24 Jun 1813. Prisoner of War #4778 at Halifax, NS, interned 15 Nov 1813, discharged on 19 Nov 1813 (Johnson and Christou, p. 39; Baker Vol. 1, p. 42, spelled his name Artimus Bowen)

Bowen, Nathan, served as a Private in Capt. Conrad Hook's Co., Baltimore County, 2nd Regt., 11th Brigade, stationed at Camp Hampstead in Baltimore from 25 Jul 1814 and was listed as dead, but no date was given on the muster roll dated 25 Jul – 1 Dec 1814 (Wright Vol. 2, p. 81)

Bowen, Thomas, served as a Private in Capt. Nathan Towson's Co., 2nd U.S. Artillery, was captured at the Battle of Stoney Creek in June 1813 and taken prisoner (Johnson and Christou, pp. 39-40)

Bowen, William, served as a Private in Capt. Clement Sullivan's Co., 14th U.S. Infantry, enlisted 22 May 1812 for 18 months, captured at Beaver Dams, Upper Canada. Prisoner of War, sent to England and was discharged on 31 Mar 1815 (Johnson and Christou, p. 39) William Bowen served as a Private in 14th U.S. Infantry and was born in Maryland. Age: 23. Prison Depot: Chatham, Prisoner of War #3096. When Taken: 24 Jun 1813. Where Taken: Beaver Dams, Upper Canada. Date Received: 7 Jan 1814 from Halifax, NS. Discharged on 10 Oct 1814 and sent to U.S. on the Cartel *St. Philip*. (Johnson's Database, 2019)

Bowermaster, Henry, served as a Private in Capt. Nathan Towson's 2nd U.S Artillery at the age of 18, was captured at the Battle of Stoney Creek in June 1813 and taken as a prisoner of war (Johnson and Christou, p. 40)

Bowers, Jacob (1776-1812), served as a Private in the 14th U.S. Infantry under Capt. Samuel Lane, enlisted 25 May 1812 at Westminster by Lt. Gist; born in Frederick MD, age 36, 5' 8½ " tall, dark eyes, black hair, dark complexion, and killed in action on Niagara River 28 Nov 1812 (Mallick and Wright, pp. 57-58)

Bowers (Bower, Boyer), Joseph, served as a Seaman and was born in Maryland. Captured by HM Frigate *Andromache*. When Taken: 14 Mar 1813. Where Taken: off Nantes, France. Prize Name: *Courier*. Home Port: Baltimore. Ship Type: Letter of Marque (Privateer). Prison Depot: Plymouth 1, Prisoner of War #1538. Age 26. Date Received: 29 May 1813. From what ship: HMS *Hannibal*. Discharged on 30 Jun 1813 and sent to Stapleton. Prison Depot: Stapleton, Prisoner of War #102. Date Received: 8 Jul 1813 from Plymouth. Discharged on 13 Jun 1814 and sent to Dartmoor as Joseph Bowers and received there from Stapleton as Joseph Boyer, age 28, on 19 Jun 1814 as Prisoner of War #1392. Discharged and sent to Mill Prison on 26 Jun 1814. (Johnson's Database, 2019)

Bowing, John, served as a Private in Capt. Adam Shower's Co., Baltimore Co., 2nd Regiment, 11th Brigade, stationed in Baltimore from 26 Jul 1814 and was discharged by a doctor on 4 Sep 1814 (Wright Vol. 2, p. 84)

Bowstred, Samuel, served as a Private in Capt. Stephen Moore's Co. of the U.S. Volunteers, Baltimore, enlisted on 8 Sep 1812 for 1 year and died at Buffalo, NY on 6 Dec 1812 (Johnson and Christou, p. 40; Wright Vol. 2, p. 57)

Boyce, Joseph, served as a Drummer in the 14th U.S. Infantry and was captured and interned on 6 Jun 1813 at Halifax, NS. Prisoner of War #4015, discharged for exchange on 3 Feb 1814 (Johnson and Christou, p. 40; Baker Vol. 1, p. 42)

Boyd, Andrew, served as a Seaman and was born in Maryland. Age: 22. Prison Depot: Portsmouth, Prisoner of War #1139. Captured by HM Brig *Zenobia*. When Taken: 22 Jun 1813. Where Taken: off Lisbon, Portugal. Prize Name: *Hepsey*. Ship Type: Merchant Vessel. Date Received: 6 Oct 1813. From what ship: HM Sloop *Kingfisher*. Discharged on 17 Oct 1813 and sent to Chatham on HMT *Malabar No. 352*. Prison Depot: Chatham, Prisoner of War #2430. Date Received: 21 Oct 1813 from Portsmouth on HMT *Malabar*. Discharged on 4 Sep 1814 and sent to Dartmoor on HMS *Freya*. Prison Depot: Dartmoor, Prisoner of War #3239. Received: 11 Sep 1814 on HMT *Freya* from Chatham. Discharged on 28 May 1815. (Johnson's Database, 2019)

Boyd, David, served as a Private in Capt. Henry Steiner's Co., Frederick Co. Militia, from 25 Aug 1814 and was reported sick on furlough, but no date was given (Mallick and Wright, p. 353)

Boyd, Francis, served as a Private in the 2nd U.S. Rifles, enlisted 25 May 1814 for 5 years in Chillicothe, OH at the age of 27, 5' 8¾" tall, was born in Cecil Co., MD and was discharged at Detroit, MI on 22 Sep 1815 for inability and abscess in the jaw (Johnson and Christou, p. 39)

Boyd, John, served as a Master and was born in Havre de Grace, MD. Age: 31. Prison Depot: Plymouth 1, Prisoner of War #1571. Captured by HM Brig *Lyra*. When Taken: 29 May 1813. Where Taken: off north coast of Spain. Prize Name: *Hannah & Eliza*. Ship Type: Merchant Vessel. Date Received: 10 May 1813. From what ship: MV *Hannah & Eliza*. Discharged on 11 May 1813 and sent to Ashburton on parole. (Johnson's Database, 2019)

Boyd, Samuel, served as a Private in Capt. Clement Sullivan's Co., 14th U.S. Infantry, and was captured during the Battle of Stoney Creek on 12 Jun 1813. Prisoner of War #5079, interned at Halifax, NS on 12 Dec 1813 and discharged on 31 May 1814 (Johnson and Christou, p. 41; Baker Vol. 1, p. 43)

Boyd, William, served as a Private in Capt. Nathan Towson's Co., 2nd U.S. Artillery and was killed during the Battle of Chippewa, Upper Canada, in July 1814; bounty land issued to Elizabeth Boyd, sister and only heir (BLW# 21735-160-12; Johnson and Christou, p. 40)

Boyer (Byer), George, served as 4th Corporal in the company of Capt. Thomas Contee Washington, Frederick Co. Militia, on 22 Sep 1812 and died on 31 Dec 1812 (Mallick and Wright, p. 332)

Boyer, Joseph, see Joseph Bowers (Bower, Boyer), q.v.

Boyle, George S., served as 1st Corporal in Capt. Edward Aisquith's Co., 1st Rifle Bttn., Baltimore City, from 19 Aug 1814 and was taken prisoner on 12 Sep 1814 at North Point (Wright Vol. 2, p. 53)

Boyle, John, served as a Seaman and was born in Baltimore. Age: 34. Prison Depot: Dartmoor, Prisoner of War #4079. Captured by HM Frigate *Belvidera*. When Taken: 21 Apr 1813. Where Taken: off Delaware. Prize Name: New Zealander (whaler), prize of the U.S. Frigate *Essex*. Ship Type: Warship. Date Received: 6 Oct 1814 on HMT *Chesapeake* from Halifax, NS. Discharged on 13 Jun 1815. (Johnson's Database, 2019)

Boyle, Thomas (1776-1825), was a Captain and the most famous and successful of Maryland's privateers. He was born in Marblehead, MA and commanded a ship when only 16 years old in 1792, later married and moved to Baltimore in 1794. "First in the *Comet* [July 1812] and later in the *Chasseur* [in 1814] he destroyed thousands of tons of shipping, the value of which ran into millions, sent in hundreds of prisoners and on more than one occasion attacked the lighter vessels of the British regular navy." (Marine, pp. 19, 226) As commander of the privateer (armed brigantine) *Chausseur* of Baltimore, he was wounded in action on 26 Feb 1815. (*Niles Weekly Register*, 25 Mar 1815) He was born on 29 Jun 1776 and died at sea on 12 Oct 1825. (Marine, p. 226)

Boyton, Thomas, served as a Quarter Gunner on the privateer *Surprise* of Baltimore and drowned in a shipwreck on 5 Apr 1815 (Marine p. 226; *Niles Weekly Register*, 15 Apr 1815)

Brachgood, James, served as a Private in Capt. Roderick Burgess' Co., 32nd Regt., Anne Arundel Co. Militia, from 22 Jul 1814 and reported sick on furlough in Aug 1814 on muster roll dated 22 Jul – 19 Sep 1814 (Wright Vol. 4, p. 42)

Bradford, James (African American), served as a Cook and was born in Maryland. Age: 22. Prison Depot: Plymouth 1, Prisoner of War #1978. Captured by HM Frigate *Tenedos*. When Taken: 12 Sep 1813. Where Taken: Western Ocean. Prize Name: *Hero*. Ship Type: Merchant Vessel. Date Received: 19 Sep 1813. From what ship: HMS *Bittern*. Discharged on 27 Sep 1813 and sent to Dartmoor. Prison Depot: Dartmoor, Prisoner of War #699. Date Received: 27 Sep 1813 from Plymouth. Discharged 26 Apr 1815. (Johnson's Database, 2019)

Bradford, James, served as a Sergeant in Capt. James Paxton's Co., 12th U.S. Infantry, and died on 23 Feb 1814; bounty land issued to Joseph Bradford, his father and only heir (BLW# 24548-160-12; Johnson and Christou, p. 40)

Bradley, Daniel, served as a Private (company not stated) and was captured at the Battle of Bladensburg on 24 Aug 1814 (Marine, p. 174)

Bradly, Samuel (African American) served as a Seaman and was born in Baltimore. Age: 29. Prison Depot: Dartmoor, Prisoner of War #4356. Captured by HM Ship-of-the-Line *Ramillies*. When Taken: 26 Feb 1814. Where Taken: off New York. Prize Name: *Fieri Facias*. Ship Type: Privateer. Date Received: 7 Oct 1814. From what ship: HMT *Salvador del Mundo* from Halifax, NS. Died on 29 Mar 1814 from variola (smallpox). (Johnson's Database, 2019)

Brady, James, served as a Seaman and was born in Baltimore. Age: 23. Prison Depot: Chatham, Prisoner of War #1217. Captured at sea by HM Frigate *Dryad* on 7 Jan 1813. Prize Name: *Rossie*. Ship Type: Merchant Vessel. Received: 16 Mar 1813 from Portsmouth on HMS *Abundance*. Discharged on 24 Jul 1813 and released to the Cartel *Hoffning*. (Johnson's Database, 2019)

Brady, Jason, served as a Seaman and was born in Baltimore. Age: 23. Prison Depot: Portsmouth, Prisoner of War #544. Captured by HM Frigate *Dryad*. When Taken: 7 Jan 1813. Where Taken: at sea. Prize Name: *Rossie*. Ship Type: Merchant Vessel. Date Received: 25 Jan 1813. From what ship: HM Ship-of-the-Line *Queen*. Discharged on 11 Mar 1813 and sent to Chatham on HM Store Ship *Abundance*. (Johnson's Database, 2019)

Branard, George (1789-1815), served as a Private in the 39th U.S. Infantry, enlisted 28 Oct 1814 in Knoxville, TN for 5 years at the age of 25, 5'8" tall, born in Frederick Co., MD and died on 17 Feb 1815 (Johnson and Christou, p. 41)

Brannen, Alexander, served as a Seaman and was born in Baltimore. Age: 22. Prison Depot: Dartmoor, Prisoner of War #2162. Captured by HM Frigate *Hyperion*. When Taken: 26 Jun 1814. Where Taken: off Cape Finisterre, Spain. Prize Name: *Rattlesnake*. Home Port: Philadelphia. Ship Type: Privateer. Date Received: 16 Aug 1814 on HMS *Dublin* from Halifax, NS. Discharged on 2 May 1815. (Johnson's Database, 2019)

Brawner, William, of Edward, served as a Private in Capt. John F. Gray's Co., 43rd Regiment, Charles Co. Militia, from 24 June 1814 and discharged on 3 Jul 1814 on account of sickness (Wright Vol. 5, pp. 39, 40)

Bray, George, served as a ship's Carpenter and was born in Baltimore. Age: 29. Prison Depot: Chatham, Prisoner of War #377. How Taken: Gave himself up off MV *Union* American. When Taken: 25 Jan 1813. Where Taken: London, UK. Date

Received: 31 Jan 1813. From what ship: HMS *Raisonable*. Discharged on 24 Jul 1813 and released to the Cartel *Hoffning*. (Johnson's Database, 2019)

Brazier, Thomas, served as a Private in Capt. Joseph Marshall's Co., 14th U.S. Infantry, and died at Cheektowaga Hospital, NY on 10 Jan 1815; bounty land was issued to his brother William Brazier and other heirs (BLW# 21483-160-12; Johnson and Christou, p. 41; https://wnyroots.tripod.com/Index-1812.html)

Brengman, Thomas, served as a Private (command unknown) and was captured at North Point on 12 Sep 1814. Dr. James H. McCulloh, Jr. wrote this note after the battle to the British commander: "In consequence of the humanity shown the following American prisoners of war, I do promise upon honor that they shall not directly or indirectly serve against the British until regularly exchanged." (Marine, pp. 171, 227)

Brice, Henry, served as a Private in Capt. David Warfield's Co., 5th Regiment, Baltimore Militia, United Volunteers, was wounded on 12 Sep 1814 at North Point, and was on the list of prisoners of war exchanged with the British. Dr. James H. McCulloh, Jr. wrote this note soon after the battle to the British commander: "In consequence of the humanity shown the following American prisoners of war, I do promise upon honor that they shall not directly or indirectly serve against the British until regularly exchanged." (Wright Vol. 2, p. 8; Marine pp. 171, 172, 228)

Briers, John R., served as a Private in Capt. Stephen H. Moore's Co., Baltimore Volunteers Infantry Co., from 8 Sep 1812 for 1 year and died at Buffalo, NY on 25 Jan 1813 (Johnson and Christou, p. 42; Wright Vol. 2, p. 57)

Brightwell, Peter, served as a Private in Capt. Joshua Naylor's Co., 17th Regt., Prince George's Co. Militia, between 17 Jul and 2 Aug 1814, was stationed at Mill Town and was taken ill on the march from Mill Town to Port Tobacco, but no date was given (Wright Vol. 6, p. 9)

Brison, James, served as a Private in 14th U.S. Infantry and was born in Baltimore. Age: 22. Prison Depot: Chatham, Prisoner of War #3097. When Taken: 24 Jun 1813. Where Taken: Beaver Dams, Upper Canada. Date Received: 7 Jan 1814 from Halifax, NS. Discharged on 10 Oct 1814 and sent to U.S. on the Cartel *St. Philip*. (Johnson's Database, 2019)

Brisons, John (1783-1815) (African American), served as a Seaman and was born in Baltimore. Age: 32. Prison Depot: Chatham, Prisoner of War #3648. Captured by HM Frigate *Pomone* & HM Frigate *Cydnus*. When Taken: 4 Mar 1814. Where Taken: Bay of Biscayne. Prize Name: *Bunker Hill*. Ship Type: Privateer. Date Received: 31 Mar 1814. From what ship: HMS *Raisonable*. Discharged on 25 Sep 1814 and sent to Dartmoor on HMS *Niobe*. Prison Depot: Dartmoor, Prisoner of

War #4231. Captured by HM Frigate *Pomone* & HM Frigate *Cydnus*. Date Received: 7 Oct 1814. From what ship: HMT *Niobe* from Chatham. Died on 24 Jan 1815 from phthisis pulmonalis (tuberculosis). (Johnson's Database, 2019; Centennial Trails, United States Daughters of 1812, online at www.war1812trails.com/Dartmoor spelled his name Brissons)

Broadest, Moses, served as a Private in 14th U.S. Infantry and was born in Maryland. Age: 20. Prison Depot: Chatham, Prisoner of War #3101. When Taken: 24 Jun 1813. Where Taken: Beaver Dams, Upper Canada. Date Received: 7 Jan 1814 from Halifax, NS. Discharged on 10 Oct 1814 and sent to U.S. on the Cartel *St. Philip*. (Johnson's Database, 2019)

Broadwater, Samuel, served as a Seaman and was born in Maryland. Age: 21. Prison Depot: Plymouth 1, Prisoner of War #1270. Captured by HM Frigate *Medusa*. When Taken: 12 Apr 1813. Where Taken: Bay of Biscayne. Prize Name: *Caroline*. Ship Type: Merchant Vessel. Received: 10 May 1813. From what ship: HMS *Medusa*. Discharged on 3 Jul 1813 and sent to Stapleton Prison. Prison Depot: Stapleton, Prisoner of War #287. Received: 11 Jul 1813 from Plymouth. Discharged on 16 Jun 1814 and sent to Dartmoor. Prison Depot: Dartmoor, Prisoner of War #1568. Received: 23 Jun 1814 from Stapleton. Discharged on 1 May 1815. (Johnson's Database, 2019)

Brooks, Benjamin (c1790-1814), served as an Ordinary Seaman with the U.S. Chesapeake Flotilla, entered the service on 19 Feb 1814, was on board on 7 Apr 1814 and killed at St. Leonards Creek, 2nd Battle, on 26 Jun 1814 (Shomette, p. 373; Sheads, p. 22)

Brooks, Edward (African American), served as a Seaman and was born in Baltimore. Age: 22. Prison Depot: Portsmouth, Prisoner of War #141. Captured by HM Sloop *Goree*. When Taken: 15 Aug 1812. Where Taken: off Bermuda. Prize Name: Gossypium. Ship Type: Merchant Vessel. Date Received: 29 Oct 1812. From what ship: HM Ship-of-the-Line *Ardent*. Discharged on 19 Feb 1813 and sent to Chatham on HM Store Ship *Dromedary*. Prison Depot: Chatham, Prisoner of War #512. Date Received: 23 Feb 1813 from Portsmouth on HMS *Dromedary*. Discharged on 10 May 1813 and released to the Cartel *Admittance*. (Johnson's Database, 2019)

Brooks, Joseph R. (1778-1852), served as 2nd Lieutenant under Capt. John Montgomery in the 1st Artillery Co., Baltimore Union Artillery, from 25 Mar 1814 and was wounded on 12 Sep 1814 at North Point (Wright Vol. 2, p. 46; Marine p. 170 spelled his name Brookes and p. 229 spelled it Brooks)

Brooks, Philip (African American), served as a Seaman and was born in Maryland. Age: 28. Prison Depot: Dartmoor, Prisoner of War #6159. Captured by HM Frigate *Grancius*. When Taken: 2 Dec 1814. Where Taken: off Lisbon, Portugal.

Prize Name: *Leo*. Home Port: Baltimore. Ship Type: Privateer. Date Received: 18 Jan 1815. From what ship: HMT *Impregnable*. Discharged on 5 Jul 1815. (Johnson's Database, 2019)

Broudent, Moses, served as a Private in the 14th U.S. Infantry and was captured at Beaver Dams, Upper Canada on 24 Jun 1813. Prisoner of War #3746 at Halifax, NS, and discharged on 9 Nov 1813 and sent to England on HMS *Success* (Johnson and Christou, p. 43; Baker Vol. 1, p. 50)

Brown, Abel, served as a Private in Capt. Reuben Gilder's Co., 14th U.S. Infantry, enlisted 2 Dec 1812 for 18 months, age 42, 5' 9" tall, born in Maryland and discharged at Burlington, VT on 29 Mar 1814 because of old age and inability (Johnson and Christou, p. 43)

Brown, Benjamin G., served as a Seaman of the U.S. Chesapeake Flotilla, entered service on 18 Mar 1814 and was killed at St. Leonards Creek, 2nd Battle, on 26 Jun 1814 (Shomette, p. 380; Sheads, p. 22)

Brown, Charles, served as a Private from Maryland (company not stated) and died on 17 Feb 1815 in Dartmoor Prison (Peterson p. 9)

Brown, Christian, served as a Private in the 38th U.S. Infantry, enlisted 7 Feb 1814 at Hagerstown by Lt. Fletcher, age 27, 5' 8" tall, blue eyes, brown or sandy hair, fair complexion, born in Frederick Co., mustered in Capt. H. H. Hook's Co., on 1 Jun 1814, mustered near Fort Covington on 31 Dec 1814 and discharged on 24 Nov 1814 (sic) at Baltimore on a Surgeon's Certificate for a rupture (Mallick and Wright, p. 62)

Brown, David, served as a Private in Capt. Thomas T. Timmons' Co., 2nd Regt., Anne Arundel Co. Militia, from 28 Sep 1814 and was discharged from duty "on account of inability" on 10 Nov 1814 (Wright Vol. 4, pp. 28, 29)

Brown, David (African American), served as a Seaman and was born in Maryland. Age: 35. Prison Depot: Plymouth 1, Prisoner of War #2226. Captured by HM Frigate *Pyramus*. When Taken: 30 Nov 1813. Where Taken: off Lorient, France. Prize Name: *Zephyr*. Ship Type: Merchant Vessel. Received: 3 Jan 1814. From what ship: HMS *Warspite*. Discharged on 10 May 1814 and sent to Dartmoor. Prison Depot: Dartmoor, Prisoner of War #1172. Received: 10 May 1814 from Plymouth. Discharged on 28 Apr 1815. (Johnson's Database, 2019)

Brown, Francis, served as a Private in Capt. Thomas Contee Washington, of the Frederick Co. Militia, and was reported sick at Fort Severn some time between 17 Aug and 31 Dec 1812 (Mallick and Wright, p. 332)

Brown, Frederick, served as a Corporal in Capt. Denton Darby's Co., Frederick Co. Militia, New Market area, from 3 Aug to 8 Nov 1814 and reported "sick," but no place or date were stated (Mallick and Wright, p. 620)

Brown, George, served as a Seaman and was born in Baltimore. Age: 34. Prison Depot: Dartmoor, Prisoner of War #5612. How Taken: Gave himself up off the Cape. When Taken: 8 May 1812. Date Received: 24 Dec 1814. From what ship: HMT *Tay*. Discharged and released on 27 Mar 1815. (Johnson's Database, 2019)

Brown, George, served as a Seaman and was born in Baltimore. Age: 31. Prison Depot: Chatham, Prisoner of War #1610. How Taken: Gave himself up off HM Frigate *President*. When Taken: 27 Apr 1813. Where Taken: Chatham, UK. Date Received: 1 May 1813. From what ship: HMS *President*. Discharged on 24 Jul 1814 and sent to Dartmoor. Prison Depot: Dartmoor, Prisoner of War #1992. Received: 3 Aug 1814. From what ship: HMS *Lyffey* from Chatham. Discharged on 3 Jul 1815. (Johnson's Database, 2019)

Brown, Isaac N. (c1793-1833), served as a Private in Capt. Samuel Coe's Rifle Co., 17th Regiment, Prince George's Co. Militia, from 18 to 24 Jun 1814, from 19 Aug to 13 Sep 1814, was wounded in the leg and discharged at Ft. Washington in Sep 1814. On 19 Nov 1851 Mary Brown, age 51, of Anne Arundel Co., widow of Isaac N. Brown, confirmed his service and stated they were married on 31 Mar 1818 in Prince George's Co. and her maiden name was Mangun. Isaac died on 26 Nov 1833. (BLW# 55-rej-126495; Wright Vol. 6, pp. 7, 13, 31)

Brown, James, served as a Private in Capt. Kenneth McKenzie's Co., 14th U.S. Infantry, and was captured at Beaver Dams, Upper Canada on 24 Jun 1813. Prisoner of War #4067 at Halifax, NS, and was discharged for exchange on 3 Feb 1814 (Johnson and Christou, p. 43; Baker Vol. 1, p. 51)

Brown, James (Mulatto), served as a Seaman and was born in Maryland. Age: 40. Prison Depot: Plymouth 2, Prisoner of War #530. Captured by HM Frigate *Barbadoes*. When Taken: 6 Dec 1815. Where Taken: off St. Bartholomew, West Indies. Prize Name: *Gallant*. Ship Type: Merchant Vessel. Date Received: 16 Apr 1815. From what ship: HMS *Swiftsure*. Discharged on 2 Jun 1815 and released to the Cartel *Soverign*. (Johnson's Database, 2019)

Brown, James, served as a Seaman and was born in Maryland. Age: 30. Prison Depot: Portsmouth, Prisoner of War #974. How Taken: Gave himself up off HM Ship-of-the-Line *Caledonia*. Date Received: 31 Jul 1813. From what ship: HMS *Leviathan*. Discharged on 13 Aug 1813 and sent to Chatham on HMS Cadmus. Prison Depot: Chatham, Prisoner of War #2196. Date Received: 18 Aug 1813. From what ship: French Account. Discharged on 11 Aug 1814 and sent to Dartmoor on HMS *Freya*. Prison Depot: Dartmoor, Prisoner of War #2644. Date

Received: 21 Aug 1814. From what ship: HMT *Freya* from Chatham. Discharged on 26 Apr 1815. (Johnson's Database, 2019)

Brown, John, served as a Private in the 14th U.S. Infantry (company not stated) and was captured at Beaver Dams, Upper Canada on 24 Jun 1813. Prisoner of War #4154 at Halifax, NS, interned on 24 Jun 1813 and was discharged on 27 Aug 1813 and sent to England on HMS *Regulus* (Johnson and Christou, p. 44; Baker Vol. 1, p. 52, but Johnson's Database, 2019, did not list him)

Brown, John, served as a Seaman and was born in Maryland. Age: 25. Prison Depot: Plymouth 2, Prisoner of War #532. Captured by HM Frigate *Barbadoes*. When Taken: 6 Dec 1815. Where Taken: off St. Bartholomew, West Indies. Prize Name: *Gallant*. Ship Type: Merchant Vessel. Date Received: 16 Apr 1815. From what ship: HMS *Swiftsure*. Discharged on 2 Jun 1815 and released to the Cartel *Soverign*. (Johnson's Database, 2019)

Brown, John Riggs (1775-1814), served as 2nd Lieutenant In Capt. Charles S. Ridgely's 3rd Regiment of Cavalry Division, and was in the battle of North Point on 12 Sep 1814; he was born on 27 Oct 1775 and died on 3 Oct 1814; his wife Sarah Gassaway Brown died on 7 Feb 1858, age 82. (Brown Family Cemetery at Good Fellowship, Woodstock, Howard Co., MD; Peterson, p. 9) John Riggs Brown married Sarah Gassaway on 14 Dec 1797 and Lieut, Brown "died three weeks after the battle of North Point, probably of injuries received in the service." (*Side-Lights of Maryland History*, by Hester Dorsey Richardson, 1967, Volume 2, pp. 299-301; *1812 Ancestor Index Volume I, 1892-1970*, National Society United States Daughters of 1812, 2005, p. 31)

Brown, Joshua, served as a Seaman on the privateer *Globe* and was killed in action on 1 Nov 1813 (Marine, p. 231; *Niles Weekly Register*, 19 Feb 1814)

Brown, Mark, served as a Seaman and was born in Maryland. Age: 28. Prison Depot: Portsmouth, Prisoner of War #963. How Taken: Gave himself up off HM Ship-of-the-Line *Leviathan*. Date Received: 31 Jul 1813. From what ship: HMS *Leviathan*. Discharged on 7 Aug 1813 and sent to Chatham on HMS *Rinaldo*. Prison Depot: Chatham, Prisoner of War #2178. Date Received: 16 Aug 1813 from Portsmouth on an admiral's tender. Discharged on 11 Aug 1814 and sent to Dartmoor on HMS *Freya*. Prison Depot: Dartmoor, Prisoner of War #2633. Date Received: 21 Aug 1814 on HMT *Freya* from Chatham. Discharged on 3 May 1815. (Johnson's Database, 2019)

Brown, Michael, served as a Private in the 14th U.S. Infantry and captured at Beaver Dams, Upper Canada on 24 Jun 1813. Prisoner of War #3977 at Halifax, NS, interned on 24 Jun 1813, discharged on 19 Nov 1813 and sent to England per order of Sir J. B. Warren (Johnson and Christou, p. 44; Baker Vol. 1, p. 53)

Brown, Perry, served as a Private in the 14th U.S. Infantry and was captured at Beaver Dams, Upper Canada on 24 Jun 1813. Prisoner of War #3969 at Halifax, NS, interned 24 Jun 1813 and discharged for exchange on 3 Feb 1814 (Johnson and Christou, p. 44; Baker Vol. 1, p. 53)

Brown, Richard (African American), served as a Cook and was born in Baltimore. Age: 38. Prison Depot: Plymouth 1, Prisoner of War #2093. How Taken: Gave himself up off MV *Indian*. When Taken: 14 Sep 1813. Where Taken: Liverpool, UK. Date Received: 3 Nov 1813. From what ship: HMS *Bittern*. Discharged on 29 Nov 1813 and sent to Dartmoor. Prison Depot: Dartmoor, Prisoner of War #821. Date Received: 29 Nov 1813 from Plymouth. Discharged on 26 Apr 1815. (Johnson's Database, 2019)

Brown, Robert, served as a Seaman and was born in Baltimore. Age: 30. Prison Depot: Chatham, Prisoner of War #2508. Captured by HM Ship-of-the-Line *Victorious* on 8 Jun 1813. Where Taken: Chesapeake Bay. Prize Name: *Globe*. Ship Type: Privateer. Date Received: 22 Oct 1813 from Portsmouth on HMT *Malabar*. Discharged on 8 Sep 1814 and sent to Dartmoor on HMS *Niobe*. Prison Depot: Dartmoor, Prisoner of War #3313. Date Received: 13 Sep 1814. From what ship: HMT *Niobe* from Chatham. Discharged on 25 Mar 1815. (Johnson's Database, 2019)

Brown, Thomas (African American), served as a Seaman and was born in Baltimore. Age: 15. Prison Depot: Chatham, Prisoner of War #3407. Captured by HM Frigate *Crescent*. When Taken: 16 Sep 1813. Where Taken: off Cape Cod, MA. Prize Name: *Elbridge Gerry*. Home Port: NY & RI. Ship Type: Privateer. Date Received: 23 Feb 1814 from Halifax, NS on HMT *Malabar*. Discharged on 22 Oct 1814 and sent to Dartmoor on HMS *Leyden*. (Johnson's Database, 2019)

Brown, Thomas, served as an Ordinary Seaman with the U.S. Chesapeake Flotilla, entered service on 22 Jan 1814, was on board on 7 Apr 1814 and died on 29 Sep 1814 (Shomette, p. 401, listed him as "Thomas Brown 2nd on Ont" and commented "Files for him Captured")

Brown, William, served as a Seaman and was born in Baltimore. Age: 25. Prison Depot: Dartmoor, Prisoner of War #2480. Captured by HM Frigate *Orpheus*. When Taken: 20 Apr 1814. Where Taken: off Matanzas, Cuba. Prize Name: U.S. Sloop-of-War *Frolic*. Ship Type: Warship. Date Received: 16 Aug 1814. From what ship: HMT *Queen* from Halifax, NS. Discharged on 3 May 1815. (Johnson's Database, 2019)

Brown, William, served as a Seaman and was born in Baltimore. Age: 34. Prison Depot: Chatham, Prisoner of War #105. How Taken: Gave himself up off MV *Earl St. Vincent*. When Taken: 26 Oct 1812. Where Taken: London, UK. Date Received:

4 Nov 1812. From what ship: HMS *Namur*. Discharged on 28 Apr 1813 and released to the *David Scott*. (Johnson's Database, 2019)

Brown, William, served as a Private in Capt. Isaac Aldridge's Co., 38th U.S. Inf., enlisted on 22 Jun 1813 and died on 21 Feb 1814 (Johnson and Christou, p. 45)

Brown, William, served as a Private in Capt. Thomas Montgomery's Co., 14th U.S. Infantry, enlisted 10 Mar 1813, discharged at Plattsburgh, NY on 25 May 1814 on Surgeon's Certificate (BLW# 5259-160-12; Johnson and Christou, p. 44)

Brown, William, served as 2nd Lieutenant and Adjutant in Maj. Beale Randall's Rifle Bttn., Baltimore Co., joined 10 Sep 1814 and reported "sick-absent with leave on Oct 12" 1814 (Wright Vol. 2, p. 72)

Brown, William, served as a Private in Capt. James McCulten's Co., 41st U.S. Infantry, enlisted 9 Aug 1814 in New York City at the age of 35, 5' 9" tall, born in Baltimore and discharged on 13 Jul 1815 on Surgeon's Certificate (Johnson and Christou, p. 44)

Brown, Zachariah, served as a Corporal in Capt. Thomas Montgomery's Co., 14th U.S. Infantry, enlisted 6 Apr 1813, wounded at LaCole Mill, Lower Canada and died 13 May 1814 at Plattsburgh, NY (Johnson and Christou, p. 45)

Brownell, John, served as a Seaman on 24 Aug 1814, was on the field of battle at Bladensburg, admitted to the Naval Hospital, Washington, DC, as Patient No. 30 with erysipelas [skin disease] on 28 Aug 1814, was discharged on 2 Oct 1814 and sent to barracks (Sharp's Database, 2018)

Bryan, John, served as a Private in Capt. William Curtis' Co., Washington Co. Militia, joined 26 Jul 1814, was wounded (date and place were not stated) and was discharged on 3 Dec 1814 (Wright Vol. 9, p. 3)

Bryant, James, served as a Private in Capt. Jacob Alexander's Co. of Volunteers that left Middletown Valley for Annapolis and arrived 15 minutes before the British in Aug 1814. Their service covered 22 Jul 1814 to 19 Sep 1814 and they participated in the Battle of Bladensburg on 24 Aug 1814 where James Bryant died on the field. (Wright Vol. 8, pp. 11, 12, 340; Mallick and Wright, p. 63)

Buchanan, William B., served as 3rd Sergeant in Capt. James Sterett's Co., 5th Cavalry Regiment, Baltimore, joined 26 Aug 1814 and while serving on picket guard duty on 12 Sep 1814 at North Point he, along with two others, became separated, with the British army in between them. They were ordered to surrender, but refused, leaped on their horses and escaped. They offered to pay for directions to Baltimore from a Negro man who said he would as he performed a service for some gentlemen and soon returned followed by British soldiers who forced them to surrender. The prisoners were taken to General Ross and gave an exaggerated account of the strength of the American forces. (Wright Vol. 2, p. 56; Marine, p. 150, citing *Oration by H. Clay Dallam, 1878*)

Buckley, Joseph, served as a Seaman and was born in Maryland. Age: 23. Prison Depot: Dartmoor, Prisoner of War #3996. Captured by HM Ship-of-the-Line *Leander* on 22 Jun 1814 off Cape Sable, NS. Prize Name: U.S. Brig *Rattlesnake*. Ship Type: Warship. Received: 6 Oct 1814. From what ship: HMT *Chesapeake* from Halifax, NS. Discharged on 9 Jun 1815. (Johnson's Database, 2019)

Buckley, William, served as a Lieutenant and was born in Maryland. Age: 54. Prison Depot: Dartmoor, Prisoner of War #3558. Captured by HM Frigate *Piqua* on 26 Apr 1814 near Mona Passage, West Indies. Prize Name: *Hawk*. Home Port: Wilmington. Ship Type: Privateer. Date Received: 30 Sep 1814. From what ship: HMT *Sybella*. Discharged on 4 Jun 1815. (Johnson's Database, 2019)

Bucklin, John C., served as a Private in Capt. Joseph H. Nicholson's Artillery Co., Baltimore, from 19 Aug 1814 and was "sick absent in the country on Oct 31" 1814 (Wright Vol. 2, p. 51)

Bull, John, served as a Private in Capt. Lawson Cuddy's Co., 41st Regiment, Baltimore Co. Militia, from 25 Aug 1814 and was reported as "sick-absent since Sep 27" 1814 (Wright Vol. 2, p. 67)

Bull, Nicholas, served as a Private in Capt. Lawson Cuddy's Co., 41st Regiment, Baltimore Co. Militia, from 25 Aug 1814 and was reported as "sick-absent since Sep 10" 1814 (Wright Vol. 2, p. 67)

Bullman, John, served as a Seaman and was born in Maryland. Age: 38. Prison Depot: Stapleton, Prisoner of War #376. Captured by HM Frigate *Surveillante*. When Taken: 27 Apr 1813. Where Taken: Bay of Biscayne. Prize Name: *Tom*. Home Port: Baltimore. Ship Type: Letter of Marque (Privateer). Date Received: 11 Jul 1813 from Plymouth. Discharged on 16 Jun 1814 and sent to Dartmoor. (Johnson's Database, 2019)

Burgess, John (c1778-1813), served as a Private in Capt. Edward Hughes' Co., Montgomery Co. Militia, on 30 Jul 1808 and in Capt. James Wallace's Co., Extra Battalion of Militia, having been drafted on 29 Apr 1813. He was sick while on duty at Annapolis (date was not given nor reported on the muster roll dated 29 Apr – 15 May 1813), was discharged and brought home in one of the baggage wagons and died about 5 days later. John Burgess and Hellen Maccubbin were married on 20 Mar 1800 by Rev. Aaron Trueman and she was granted Letters of Administration on his estate on 13 Jul 1813. On 9 Jun 1855 Helen Burgess, age 78, widow of John Burgess, applied for bounty land, but her claim was rejected. (Wright Vol. 7, pp. 3, 7, 18; BLW# 55-rej-163857; *Anne Arundel Gentry*, by Harry Wright Newman, 1970, Vol. 1, p. 44)

Burk, Greenbury, served as a Seaman on the privateer *High Flyer* and was wounded in action in December 1812 (Marine p. 234)

Burk, Jacob, served as a ship's Carpenter on the privateer (armed brigantine) *Chausseur* of Baltimore commanded by Capt. Thomas Boyle and was reported as killed in action on 26 Feb 1815 (*Niles Weekly Register*, 25 Mar 1815)

Burk, Malchijah (Malkijah), served as a Private in Capt. John T. Randall's Rifle Co., Baltimore Co., from 26 Jul 1814, and "Malkijah" was wounded in action at Bladensburg on 24 Aug 1814 and "Milkijah" was later listed as a Private in Capt. Benjamin Gorsuch's Co., 2nd Regt. 11th Brigade, Baltimore Co., stationed at Camp Hampstead in Baltimore from 14 Oct 1814 and was noted on muster roll as wounded in action (Wright Vol. 2, pp. 73, 88). In Hampshire Co., VA on 4 Mar 1843 "Malchijah" Burk, former private in Capt. Gorsuch's Co., 2nd Maryland Militia, U.S. Service, a resident of this county for five years and previously of Baltimore Co., appointed John Falconar as his attorney to collect the $24.00 pension due from 4 Sep 1842 to 4 Mar 1843. (Pierce, p. 25)

Burlue, Gilbert, served as a Private in the 14th U.S. Infantry and was captured at Beaver Dams, Upper Canada on 24 Jun 1813. Prisoner of War #3975 at Halifax, NS, interned on 24 Jun 1813 and was discharged on 9 Nov 1813 and sent to England (Johnson and Christou, p. 47; Baker Vol. 1, p. 60)

Burnell, John, served as a Private in the 14th U.S. Infantry and was captured at Beaver Dams, Upper Canada on 24 Jun 1813. Prisoner of War #3753 at Halifax, NS, interned on 24 Jun 1813 and was discharged for exchange on 3 Feb 1814 (Johnson and Christou, p. 46; Baker Vol. 1, p. 60)

Burneston, Joseph Jr. (1764-1814), served as a Private in Capt. John McKane's Co., 27th Regiment, Baltimore Militia, from 19 Aug 1814 and was killed on 12 Sep 1814 at North Point. Name is on the Baltimore Battle Monument. (NARA; CMSR; *Baltimore American*, 12 Jun 1819; Wright Vol. 2, p. 18, mistakenly stated he was discharged on 12 Sep 1814)

Burnham, Edward (1777-1878), served as a Private in Capt. John Bond's Co., 41st Regiment, Baltimore Co., joined 30 Aug 1814, stationed at Kelley's Field in Baltimore and was discharged by a Surgeon on 8 Sep 1814 (Wright Vol. 2, p. 67) He died at age 100 years, 6 months, 18 days and his wife Elizabeth died on 9 Feb 1843 in her 60th year. They were buried in Sater's Baptist Church Cemetery in northern Baltimore County. (Smith's Database, 2019; *Baltimore Cemeteries, Volume 1*, by Baltimore County Genealogical Society, 1985, p. 16)

Burns, John, served as a Private in the 38th U.S. Infantry and died 4 May 1814, place and cause not stated; heirs received half pay for 5 years in lieu of bounty land (Johnson and Christou, p. 46)

Burroughs, Isaac, see Isaac Boroughs, q.v.

Bush, Abraham (1766-1814), served as a Private in the 1st U.S. Artillery at the age of 48, born in Maryland. Prisoner of War #9[?] at Quebec and died there on 22 Mar 1814 (Johnson and Christou, p. 47; Johnson's Database, 2019)

Bush, William S., served as a Lieutenant in U.S. Marine Corps and was killed in action in battle between the *Constitution* and the *Guerrierre*. (Marine p. 236)

Bushell, William, served as a Seaman and was born in Baltimore. Age: 40. Prison Depot: Chatham, Prisoner of War #3869. Captured by HM Frigate *Rhin*. When Taken: 17 Mar 1814. Where Taken: off Bermuda. Prize Name: *Rattlesnake*. Ship Type: Letter of Marque. Date Received: 26 Aug 1814 from London. Discharged on 26 Sep 1814 and sent to Dartmoor on HMS *Leyden*. Prison Depot: Dartmoor, Prisoner of War #5384. Date Received: 31 Oct 1814. From what ship: HMT *Leyden* from Chatham. Discharged and released on 1 Jul 1815. (Johnson's Database, 2019)

Busson, John, served as a Seaman and was born in Baltimore. Age: 21. Prison Depot: Portsmouth, Prisoner of War #788. Captured by HM Brig *Dispatch*. When Taken: 17 Mar 1813. Where Taken: at sea. Prize Name: *Dick*. Ship Type: Merchant Vessel. Date Received: 3 Apr 1813. From what ship: Prussian Ship *Argo*. Discharged on 3 Apr 1813 and sent to Chatham on HM Transport *Chatham*. Prison Depot: Chatham, Prisoner of War #1537. Date Received: 8 Apr 1813 from Portsmouth on an admiral's tender. Discharged on 11 Jul 1814. (Johnson's Database, 2019)

Butler, Benjamin (African American), served as a Seaman and was born in Baltimore. Age: 25. Prison Depot: Dartmoor, Prisoner of War #2530. Captured by HM Ship-of-the-Line *Saturn*. When Taken: 25 May 1814. Where Taken: off Sandy Hook, NJ. Prize Name: *Hussar*. Home Port: New York. Ship Type: Privateer. Date Received: 16 Aug 1814. From what ship: HMT *Queen* from Halifax, NS. Discharged on 3 May 1815. (Johnson's Database, 2019)

Butler, George, of Maryland, served as a Seaman on the ship *Cresy* and was reported by Capt. Jeduthan Upton, Jr. in 1814 as having been impressed into service and was being held as a Prisoner of War on the prison ship *San Antonio* at Chatham, England (*Niles Weekly Register*, 26 Feb 1814)

Butler, James, served as a Private in Capt. George Washington Magee's Co., Frederick Co. Militia in the 1st Regiment, New Windsor area, from 22 Jul 1814, engaged in the Battle of Bladensburg and in the defense of Baltimore and was "discharged by surgeon" on 1 Sep 1814 (Mallick & Wright, p. 341, and this source on p. 68 mistakenly stated he was in service from 22 Jul to 1 Sep 1813)

Butler, John (African American), served as a Steward and was born in Leonards, MD. Age: 29. Prison Depot: Chatham, Prisoner of War #188. How Taken: Gave himself up off MV *Arabella*. When Taken: 27 Oct 1812. Where Taken: London, UK. Date Received: 5 Nov 1812. From what ship: HMS *Namur*. Discharged in Jul 1813 and released to the Cartel *Moses Brown*. (Johnson's Database, 2019)

Butler, Thomas, served as a Seaman and was born in Maryland. Age: 37. Prison Depot: Portsmouth, Prisoner of War #1357. How Taken: Gave himself up off HM Ship-of-the-Line *Bulwark*. Date Received: 28 Jan 1814. From what ship: HMS *Bulwark*. Discharged on 13 Feb 1814 and sent to Chatham on HMT *Malabar No. 352*. Prison Depot: Chatham, Prisoner of War #3491. Date Received: 23 Feb 1814 from Portsmouth on HMT *Malabar*. Discharged on 26 Sep 1814 and sent to Dartmoor on HMS *Leyden*. Prison Depot: Dartmoor, Prisoner of War #4274. Date Received: 7 Oct 1814. From what ship: HMT *Niobe* from Chatham. Discharged on 13 Jun 1815. (Johnson's Database, 2019)

Butler, William, served as a Seaman and was born in Baltimore. Age: 40. Prison Depot: Chatham, Prisoner of War #1641. Captured by HM Brig *Castilian*. When Taken: 12 Mar 1813. Where Taken: off Cape Ortegal, Spain. Prize Name: *Kergettos*. Ship Type: Merchant Vessel. Received: 9 May 1813. From what ship: HMS *Raisonable*. Discharged on 24 Jul 1814 and sent to Dartmoor. Prison Depot: Dartmoor, Prisoner of War #1995. Captured by HM Brig *Castilian*. When Taken: 12 Mar 1813. Where Taken: off Cape Ortegal, Spain. Prize Name: *Kergettos*. Ship Type: Merchant Vessel. Received: 3 Aug 1814. From what ship: HMS *Lyffey* from Chatham. Discharged 2 May 1815. (Johnson's Database, 2019)

Butler, William (1763-1814) (African American), served as a Seaman at the advanced age of 51. Born in Maryland. Prison Depot: Chatham, Prisoner of War #2078. How Taken: Gave himself up off HM Ship-of-the-Line *Armada*. When Taken: 8 Jun 1813. Date Received: 9 Aug 1813 from HMS *Thames*. Died on 29 Apr 1814 from phthisis pulmonalis (tuberculosis). (Johnson's Database, 2019)

Butler, William, served as a Private in Capt. William Littlejohn's Co., 2nd U.S. Light Dragoons, enlisted 4 Dec 1813 in Baltimore at the young age of 15, 5' 1" tall, born in Pennsylvania and was discharged on 6 Sep 1815 on a Surgeon's Certificate (Johnson and Christou, p. 47)

Byard, Peter, served as a private in Capt. William Roney's Co., 39th Regiment, Baltimore Militia, from 22 Aug 1814 and was killed in battle on 12 Sep 1814 at North Point. His name is on the Baltimore Battle Monument. (Wright Vol. 2, p. 20; Marine p. 236) Cassandra Byard, widow of Peter Bayard, was granted letters of administration of his estate on 31 Dec 1814. (NARA; CMSR; Wright Vol. 2, p. 24; *Baltimore American*, 12 Jun 1819)

Byer, George, see George Boyer (Byer), q.v.

Byrd, John Carter (1789-1814), served as a private in Capt. David Warfield's Co., 5th Regiment, Baltimore Militia, from Aug 19 1814 and was killed on 12 Sep 1814 at North Point. "John C. Bird (a young gentleman from Virginia), private in the 5th Regiment, killed" (North Point dead and wounded Article 4 Oct 1814 Columbian Register CT Vol. III 97, p. 4) John Carter Byrd was killed on 12 Sep at North Point. His name is on the Baltimore Battle Monument. (NARA; Wright Vol. 2, p. 8; Marine, pp. 172, 236; *Baltimore American*, 12 Jun 1819, spelled his name John Carter Bird)

C

Cable, Henry (1757-1817), served as a Private in Capt. James Hook's Co., 38th U.S. Infantry, enlisted 28 Feb 1814 in Alexandria, DC at the advanced age of 57, 5' 4" or 6" tall, grey or blue eyes, dark hair, dark or ruddy complexion, born in Frederick or Anne Arundel Co., discharged at Fort Covington, MD, on 31 Mar 1815, for disability, placed on pension rolls on 1 Oct 1816 and died 3 Dec 1817 (BLW# 7097-160-12; Johnson and Christou, p. 47; Mallick and Wright, p. 70)

Cabristal, Matthew, see Matthew Copasses, q.v.

Cadell, William, served as a Corporal in the U.S. Corps of Artillery and died in Dec 1814; his heirs received half pay for 5 years in lieu of bounty land (Johnson and Christou, p. 48)

Caernt (Caent), Levie, served as a Private in the 14th U.S. Infantry and was captured at Beaver Dams, Upper Canada on 24 Jun 1813. Prisoner of War #3745 at Halifax, NS, interned 24 Jun 1813 and discharged for exchange on 3 Feb 1814 (Johnson and Christou, p. 44, spelled his name Caent, and Baker, Vol. 1, p. 52, spelled it Caernt)

Cafferty, William, served as a Private Capt. William McIlvane's Co., 14th U.S. Infantry, enlisted 13 Jul 1812 for 5 years and was captured at Beaver Dams, Upper Canada on 24 Jun 1813. Prisoner of War #3799 at Halifax, NS, interned on 27 Aug 1813 and discharged on 3 Feb 1813 (Johnson and Christou, p. 48; Baker, Vol. 1, p. 64)

Caheve, Patrick, served as a Private in the 14th U.S. Infantry and was captured at Beaver Dams, Upper Canada on 24 Jun 1813. Prisoner of War #4147 at Halifax, NS, interned 24 Jun 1813 and was discharged on 27 Aug 1813 and sent to England (Johnson and Christou, p. 48; Baker, Vol. 1, p. 64)

Cain, John, served as a Private in Capt. Kenneth McKenzie's Co., 14th U.S. Infantry, enlisted 18 Dec 1812, age 29, 5' 9" tall, and captured at Beaver Dams, Upper Canada on 24 Jun 1813. Prisoner of War at Halifax, NS and discharged on 27 Aug 1814 (Johnson and Christou, p. 48; Baker, Vol. 1, p. 64, did not list him)

Cairns, Thomas, served as a Seaman and was born in Baltimore. Age: 20. Prison Depot: Dartmoor, Prisoner of War #5780. Captured by HM Sloop *Acorn*. When Taken: 27 Oct 1812. Where Taken: Lat 14. Prize Name: *William Penn*. Ship Type: Merchant Vessel. Date Received: 26 Dec 1814. From what ship: HMT *Argo*. Discharged on 27 Apr 1815. (Johnson's Database, 2019)

Caldwell, William, served as a Major in the 42nd Regiment and died in Dec 1814 (Marine p. 237)

Cammel, John R., served as a Lieutenant in Capt. Litton's Co., 44th Regiment, and died in 1814. (Marine p. 238)

Campbell, Frederick, served as a Private in the 14th U.S. Infantry, was captured at Beaver Dams, Upper Canada on 24 Jun 1813. Prisoner of War #3994 at Halifax, NS, and discharged for exchange on 3 Feb 1814 (Johnson and Christou, p. 50; Baker Vol. 2, p. 66)

Campbell, John, served as a Seaman and was born in Maryland. Age: 26. Prison Depot: Chatham, Prisoner of War #3218. Captured by *Vittoria*, Guernsey Privateer. When Taken: 26 Dec 1813. Where Taken: Bay of Biscayne. Prize Name: *Volunteer*. Ship Type: Merchant Vessel. Date Received: 13 Jan 1814 from Portsmouth on HMS *Poictiers*. Discharged on 25 Sep 1814. Sent to Dartmoor on HMS *Leyden*. Prison Depot: Dartmoor, Prisoner of War #4547. Date Received: 8 Oct 1814. From what ship: HMT *Leyden* from Chatham. Discharged on 15 Jun 1815. (Johnson's Database, 2019)

Campbell, Matthew, served as a Private in the 14th U.S. Infantry, was captured at Beaver Dams, Upper Canada on 24 Jun 1813. Prisoner of War #4180 at Halifax, NS, and was discharged on 27 Aug 1814 and sent to England (Johnson and Christou, p. 50; Baker Vol. 2, p. 67)

Campbell, Neil, served as a Private in the U.S. Marine Corps, enlisted 29 Dec 1810 and was taken from the barracks and admitted to the Naval Hospital in Washington, DC as Patient No. 80 on 21 Dec 1814 with typhoid fever and died on 24 Dec 1814 (Sharp's Database, 2018)

Cannon, Dominick, served as a Private in Capt. David Cummings' Co. of the 14th U.S. Infantry, enlisted 19 Sep 1812 for 5 years in Baltimore at the age of 30, 5' 7½" tall, born in Ireland. Prisoner of War, sent to England, apparently exchanged and discharged at Baltimore on 20 Apr 1815 due to a wound in his left shoulder that he received at York, Upper Canada on 27 Apr 1813 (Johnson and Christou, p. 51)

Carden, John (Mulatto), served as a Seaman and was born in Maryland. Age: 28. Prison Depot: Dartmoor, Prisoner of War #6041. Captured by HM Frigate *Forth*. When Taken: 19 Sep 1814. Where Taken: off Egg Harbor, NJ. Prize Name: *Regent*.

Home Port: New York. Ship Type: Letter of Marque. Date Received: 28 Dec 1814. From what ship: HMT *Penelope*. Discharged on 3 Jul 1815. (Johnson's Database, 2019)

Carlisle, James, served as a Marine, was taken from the barracks and admitted to the Naval Hospital in Washington, DC as Patient No. 69 on 27 Jul 1814 (injury or illness was not specified) and was discharged on 11 Aug 1814 and sent to the barracks (Sharp's Database, 2018)

Carlo, William, served as a Seaman and was born in Maryland. Age: 22. Prison Depot: Plymouth 2, Prisoner of War #464. Captured by HM Brig *Barbadoes*. When Taken: 11 Jan 1815. Where Taken: off St. Bartholomew, West Indies. Prize Name: *Fox*. Home Port: Baltimore. Ship Type: Privateer. Date Received: 16 Apr 1815. From what ship: HMS *Swiftsure*. Discharged on 2 Jun 1815 and released to the Cartel *Soverign*. (Johnson's Database, 2019)

Carmickle, James (1790-1814), served as a Private in Capt. Simon Owens' Co., 1st U.S. Infantry, enlisted 2 Aug 1809 for 5 years in Winchester at the age of 19, 5' 7¾" tall, born in Frederick, MD and died at Fort Clark, IL on 30 Jan 1814 (Johnson and Christou, p. 52)

Carnacombe, George (1791-1814), served as a Private in Capt. James Dorman's Co., 5th U.S. Infantry, enlisted 7 Jan 1812 for 5 years in Hagerstown, MD at the age of 21, 5' 5" tall, born in Harristown, Washington Co., MD and died at Buffalo, NY on 13 Nov or 22 Dec 1814 (Johnson and Christou, p. 52)

Carnass, William, served as a Seaman and was born in Baltimore. Age: 24. Prison Depot: Dartmoor, Prisoner of War #5029. Captured by HM Brig *Wasp*. When Taken: 27 Jul 1814. Where Taken: Georges Bank. Prize Name: HM Schooner *Landrail*, prize of the Privateer *Syren*. Home Port: Baltimore. Ship Type: Privateer. Date Received: 28 Oct 1814. From what ship: HMT *Alkbar* from Halifax, NS. Escaped on 27 Jun 1815. (Johnson's Database, 2019)

Carnes, Jacob, served as a Private in Capts. Huston/Green's Co., Frederick Co. Militia, joined 23 Jul 1814 and was discharged in Baltimore on 6 Dec 1814 by the regimental surgeon, cause was not stated (Mallick and Wright, pp. 73, 346)

Carnes, Thomas, served as a Private in Capt. Samuel Dawson's Co., Frederick Co. Militia, joined 21 Jul 1814 and died 30 Dec 1814 (Mallick and Wright, p. 73)

Carney, John, served as a Seaman and was born in Maryland. Age: 22. Prison Depot: Plymouth 2, Prisoner of War #484. Captured by HM Brig *Barbadoes*. When Taken: 11 Jan 1815. Where Taken: off St. Bartholomew, West Indies. Prize Name: *Fox*. Home Port: Baltimore. Ship Type: Privateer. Date Received: 16 Apr 1815. From what ship: HMS *Swiftsure*. Discharged on 2 Jun 1815 and released to the Cartel *Soverign*. (Johnson's Database, 2019)

Carpenter, John, served as a Private in Capt. Samuel Lane's Co., 14th U.S. Infantry, enlisted 28 May 1812 at Cumberland, MD, at the age of 16, 5' 4" tall, born in Frederick, MD, was captured at Beaver Dams, Upper Canada on 24 Jun 1813. Prisoner of War #3750 at Halifax, NS, was discharged on 3 Feb 1814 and deserted at Fort Severn, MD on 16 Jul 1815 (Johnson and Christou, p. 53; Baker Vol. 2, p. 69)

Carpenter, John, served as a Seaman on board the privateer (armed brigantine) *Chasseur* of Baltimore commanded by Capt. Thomas Boyle and was reported killed in action on 26 Feb 1815 (*Niles Weekly Register*, 25 Mar 1815)

Carr, James, served as a Private in the 14th U.S. Infantry, enlisted 3 Jun 1812 at Baltimore, at the age of 27, 5' 5" tall, born in Baltimore, and was captured at Beaver Dams, Upper Canada on 24 Jun 1813. Prisoner of War #4086 at Halifax, NS, was discharged for exchange on 3 Feb 1814, returned to service and deserted at Fort Severn, MD on 16 Jul 1815 (Johnson and Christou, p. 53; Baker Vol. 2, p. 70)

Carr, John, served as a Private in 14th U.S. Infantry and was born in Maryland. Age: 26. Prison Depot: Chatham, Prisoner of War #3060. When Taken: 24 Jun 1813. Where Taken: Beaver Dams, Upper Canada. Date Received: 7 Jan 1814 from Halifax, NS. Discharged on 10 Oct 1814 and sent to U.S. on the Cartel *St. Philip*. (Johnson's Database, 2019)

Carroll, Henry James, served as Lieutenant Colonel in the 11th Cavalry District, Worcester & Somerset Counties, commissioned on 28 Feb 1812 and Major in the 23rd Regiment, Somerset Co. Militia, in 1814 and died in December 1814 (Marine p. 240; Wright Vol. 1, p. v) Henry James Carroll married Elizabeth Barnes King, daughter of Sir Thomas King, baronet of England. (*Sketches of Maryland Eastern Shoreman*, by F. Edward Wright, 1985, p. 21)

Carroll, Isaac, served as a Private in Capt. William McIlvane's Co., 14th U.S. Infantry, enlisted 27 Aug 1812 and was captured, date and place not stated. Prisoner of War, exchanged on 15 Apr 1814 and discharged on 3 Aug 1814; placed on pension rolls on 15 Aug 1816 (Johnson and Christou, p. 53)

Carroll, Patrick, served as a Private in Capt. John Hanna's Co., 5th Cavalry Regt., Baltimore City, from 19 Aug 1814 and was "dismissed for being drunk at North Point on 12 Sep" (Wright Vol. 2, p. 57)

Carroll, William, served as a Seaman and was born in Baltimore. Age: 28. Prison Depot: Dartmoor, Prisoner of War #5603. Captured by HM Brig *Wasp*. When Taken: 14 Sep 1814. Where Taken: off Cape Sable, NS. Prize Name: *Alexander*, prize of the Privateer *Monmouth*. Ship Type: Privateer. Date Received: 17 Dec

1814. From what ship: HMT *Loire* from Halifax. Discharged on 5 Jul 1815. (Johnson's Database, 2019)

Carson, Morgan, served as a Private in Capt. Michael Peters' Co., 51st Regt., Baltimore Militia, from 19 Aug 1814, was reported "in captivity," but no date was given, most probably at North Point on 12 Sep 1814 (Wright Vol. 2, p. 36)

Carson, Robert, served as a Seaman and was born in Cherry Hill, MD. Age: 23. Prison Depot: Plymouth 1, Prisoner of War #236. How Taken: Gave himself up off MV *John Barnes*. When Taken: 17 Nov 1812. Where Taken: Liverpool, UK. Date Received: 12 Jan 1813. From what ship: HMS *Bittern*. Discharged and sent to Portsmouth on 8 Feb 1813 on HMS *Colossus*. (Johnson's Database, 2019)

Carter, Jesse (African American), served as a Seaman and was born in Baltimore. Age: 23. Prison Depot: Dartmoor, Prisoner of War #1685. How Taken: Gave himself up. When Taken: 18 Apr 1814. Where Taken: Greenock, Scotland. Date Received: 2 Jul 1814 from Plymouth. Discharged on 1 May 1815. (Johnson's Database, 2019)

Carter, John, served as a Private in Capt. Richard Bell's Co., 5th U.S. Infantry, enlisted at Towsontown, MD on 19 May 1813 at the age of 40, 5' 11" tall, born in New York or Ireland and was discharged on 21 Jun 1815 as unfit for service (Johnson and Christou, p. 54)

Carter, Joseph, served as a Private in Capt. Thomas Sangster's Co., 12th U.S. Infantry, enlisted 13 Jun 1812 in Baltimore at the age of 21, 5' 7½" tall, born in Baltimore and was captured, place and date not stated. Prisoner of War #4132 at Halifax, NS, interned 24 Jun 1813 and discharged 3 Feb 1814 (Johnson and Christou, p. 54; Baker Vol. 1, p. 71)

Carter, Nathaniel, served as a Private in the 14th U.S. Infantry and was Prisoner of War #3823 at Halifax, NS, interned on 6 Jun 1813, discharged on 30 Oct 1813 and died from disease of lungs (Johnson and Christou, p. 54; Baker Vol. 1, p. 71)

Cary, James, served as a Private in Capt. David Cummings' Co., 14th U.S. Inf., enlisted 29 May 1812 for 5 years and was captured, place and date not stated. Prisoner of War, sent to England, was apparently exchanged later and died at Sackett's Harbor, NY in Oct 1814; bounty land issued to Moses Cary and other heirs at law (BLW# 15767-160-12; Johnson and Christou, p. 55)

Cassaday, Michael, served as a Private in Capt. Sheppard Leakin's Co., 38th U.S. Infantry, enlisted on 21 Jun 1813 for 1 year and died on 20 Mar or 26 Mar 1814 (Johnson and Christou, p. 55)

Casteel, Jeremiah (1788-1812), served as a Private in the 14th U.S. Infantry, enlisted 21 May 1812 by Lt. Nelson at the age of 24, 6' 1" tall, born in Allegany

Co., MD and died at Carlisle Barracks, PA, on 31 Jul or 31 Aug 1812 (Johnson and Christou, p. 55; Wright Vol. 10, p. 9)

Caster, James M. (1790-1812), served as a Private in Capt. John Stanard's Co. of the 20ᵗʰ U.S. Infantry, enlisted 12 Aug 1812 for 5 years at age 22, 5' 5½" tall, born in Maryland and died at Buffalo, NY on 1 Dec 1812; bounty land issued to Elizabeth Meyers and others (BLW# 26642-160-12; Johnson and Christou, p. 55)

Cateret, James (1792-1814) (Mulatto), served as a Seaman and was born in Talbot Co., MD. Age: 22. Prison Depot: Dartmoor, Prisoner of War #3901. Captured by HM Frigate *Loire*. When Taken: 9 Jul 1814. Where Taken: Chesapeake Bay. Prize Name: *Mary*. Ship Type: Merchant Vessel. Date Received: 5 Oct 1814. From what ship: HMT *Orpheus* from Halifax, NS. Died on 11 Nov 1814. (Johnson's Database, 2019; Centennial Trails, United States Daughters of 1812, online at www.war1812trails.com/Dartmoor)

Cathcart, Robert (1786-1814), served as a Private in Capt. Andrew Smith's Co., 51ˢᵗ Regt., Baltimore Militia, from 19 Aug 1814 and died 24 Sep 1814 (Wright Vol. 2, p. 38, spelled his name Kithcart; Society of the War of 1812 Application National No. 1023 in 1909 spelled it Cathcart as did National No. 1498 in 1925 and which stated Robert Cathcart married Anne Maxwell on 6 May 1813)

Catley, William, served as a Gunner and was born in Maryland. Age: 24. Prison Depot: Chatham, Prisoner of War #3933. Captured by HM Frigate *Piqua*. When Taken: 26 Apr 1814. Where Taken: near Mona Passage, West Indies. Prize Name: *Hawk*. Home Port: Wilmington. Ship Type: Privateer. Date Received: 25 Sep 1814 from London. Discharged on 22 Oct 1814 and sent to Dartmoor on HMS *Leyden*. Prison Depot: Dartmoor, Prisoner of War #5394. Date Received: 31 Oct 1814. From what ship: HMT *Leyden* from Chatham. Escaped on 27 Jun 1815. (Johnson's Database, 2019)

Cator, John, served as a Private in Capt. John Montgomery's 1ˢᵗ Artillery Co., Baltimore Union Artillery, and was wounded on 12 Sep 1814 at North Point (Wright Vol. 2, p. 46; Marine p. 241, but did not list his name on p. 170)

Cease, John (1792-1814), served as a Private in Capt. Andrew Madison's Co., 12ᵗʰ U.S. Infantry, enlisted 19 May 1812 for 5 years by Lt. Morgan in Middle Town, MD, age 20, 5' 5½" tall, grey eyes, black hair, dark complexion, born in Frederick Co., mustered at Burlington, VT on 28 Feb 1814 and was captured, date not given. Prisoner of War at Halifax, NS, later released, returned to service and died on 1 Dec 1814 at Buffalo, NY from an accident (Johnson and Christou, p. 56; Mallick and Wright, p. 75; Baker, Vol. 1, p. 73, did not list him)

Chain, John, served as a Seaman and was born in Maryland. Age: 23. Prison Depot: Plymouth 1, Prisoner of War #2210. Captured by HM Frigate *Belle Poule*.

When Taken: 14 Dec 1813. Where Taken: Bay of Biscayne. Prize Name: *Squirrel*. Ship Type: Merchant Vessel. Date Received: 27 Dec 1813. From what ship: HMS *Protector*. Discharged on 31 Jan 1814 and sent to Dartmoor. Prison Depot: Dartmoor, Prisoner of War #900. Date Received: 31 Jan 1814 from Plymouth. Discharged on 27 Apr 1815. (Johnson's Database, 2019)

Chalk, John, served as a Private in Capt. John T. Randall's Rifle Co., Baltimore Co.,joined 8 Aug 1814 and wounded in action on 24 Aug 1814 at Bladensburg (Wright Vol. 2, p. 73)

Chalmers, James, served as a Private in Capt. John Montgomery's 1st Artillery Co., Baltimore, from 19 Aug 1814 and was wounded on 12 Sep 1814 at North Point (Wright Vol. 2, p. 46; Marine p. 170 did not give his name)

Chamberlain, Walter, served as a Private in Capt. John Fonsten's Co., Frederick Co. Militia, from 2 Sep 1814 and marched to Baltimore in defense of the city and was reported "sick-absent Oct 3" 1814 (Mallick and Wright, pp. 75 363)

Chambers, Henry, served as a Private in 14th U.S. Infantry and was born in Maryland. Age: 29. Prison Depot: Chatham, Prisoner of War #3070. When Taken: 24 Jun 1813. Where Taken: Beaver Dams, Upper Canada. Date Received: 7 Jan 1814 from Halifax, NS. Discharged on 10 Oct 1814 and sent to U.S. on the Cartel *St. Philip*. (Johnson's Database, 2019)

Chambers, Richard, served as a Private in Capt. Joseph Talbott's Co., 19th Regt., Caroline Co., having been drafted at Denton, served 8 days between 15 Aug and 30 Aug 1813, stationed as St. Michaels and was "honorably discharged in consequence of disability incurred by the service on or about 24 Aug 1813 but was subject to duty until 2 Sep 1813;" in 1855 Rachel Green testified that she was well acquainted with Richard Chambers and during the war he "went home sick caused as I then understood and now am sure by the hard service and long march in the hot weather. I was not at the seat of war but well know that said Chambers came home sick and understood his services were suspended solely on that account." (Wright Vol. 1, pp. 81, 108)

Chaplain, Thoma, served as a Passenger and was born in Baltimore. Age: 48. Prison Depot: Chatham, Prisoner of War #3354. Captured by HM Ship-of-the-Line *Victorious*. When Taken: 8 Jan 1813. Where Taken: off Halifax, NS. Prize Name: *Rolla*. Ship Type: Privateer. Date Received: 23 Feb 1814 from Halifax, NS on HMT *Malabar*. Discharged on 10 Oct 1814 and sent to Dartmoor on HMS *Mermaid*. Prison Depot: Dartmoor, Prisoner of War #5219. Date Received: 31 Oct 1814. From what ship: HMT *Mermaid* from Chatham. Discharged on 29 Jun 1815. (Johnson's Database, 2019)

Chapman, Eliphalet, served as a Private in Capt. William McIlvane's Co., 14th U.S. Inf., enlisted 18 Mar 1813 and was captured, place and date not stated. Prisoner of War #3832 at Halifax, NS, interned 6 Jun 1813 and discharged for exchange on 3 Feb 1814 per order of Rear Adm. Griffith (Johnson and Christou, p. 58; Baker Vol. 1, p. 75 spelled his name Elephelia Chapman)

Chapman, William, served as a Seaman on the privateer *Surprise* of Baltimore and drowned in a shipwreck on 5 Apr 1815 (Marine p. 243; *Niles Weekly Register*, 15 Apr 1815)

Charter, James, served as a Passenger and was born in Maryland. Age: 30. Prison Depot: Dartmoor, Prisoner of War #503. Captured by HM Brig *Royalist*. When Taken: 31 May 1813. Where Taken: Bay of Biscayne. Prize Name: *Governor Gerry*. Home Port: New Haven. Ship Type: Merchant Vessel. Date Received: 8 Sep 1813 from Plymouth. Discharged and sent to Dartmouth on 16 Jun 1814. (Johnson's Database, 2019)

Charter, Samuel, served as a Passenger and was born in Maryland. Age: 30. Prison Depot: Plymouth 1, Prisoner of War #1599. Captured by HM Brig *Royalist*. When Taken: 31 May 1813. Where Taken: Bay of Biscayne. Prize Name: *Governor Gerry*. Home Port: New Haven. Ship Type: Merchant Vessel. Date Received: 14 Jun 1813. From what ship: HMS *Royalist*. Discharged on 3 Jun 1813 and sent to Dartmoor. (Johnson's Database, 2019)

Charlton, Armstrong, served as a Private in U.S. Light Dragoons, also in Corps of Artillery, enlisted on 9 Jun 1812 in Baltimore at the age of 34, 5' 7½" tall, and was discharged on 21 Jul 1815 as an invalid (Johnson and Christou, p. 58)

Chase, Joseph, served as a Private (company not stated) and was captured at the Battle of Bladensburg on 24 Aug 1814 (Marine, p. 174)

Chase, Joshua (African American), served as a servant at age 21, company unknown, born in Baltimore and captured during the Battle of Stoney Creek in June 1813. Prisoner of War #263 at Quebec, interned 24 Jun 1813 and was discharged, but date not given (Johnson and Christou, p. 58; Baker Vol. 1, p. 26)

Chase, Samuel (African American), served as a Seaman and was born in Maryland. Age: 45. Prison Depot: Dartmoor, Prisoner of War #6162. Captured by HM Frigate *Grancius*. When Taken: 2 Dec 1814. Where Taken: off Lisbon, Portugal. Prize Name: *Leo*. Home Port: Baltimore. Ship Type: Privateer. Date Received: 18 Jan 1815. From what ship: HMT *Impregnable*. Discharged on 5 Jul 1815. (Johnson's Database, 2019)

Chattles, John, served as a Seaman and was born in Baltimore. Age: 26. Prison Depot: Portsmouth, Prisoner of War #171. Captured by HM Transport *Diadem*. When Taken: 7 Oct 1812. Where Taken: S. Andera (St. Andrews, Scotland). Prize

Name: Baltimore. Home Port: Baltimore. Ship Type: Privateer. Date Received: 3 Nov 1812 San Antonio. From what ship: HMS *Diadem*. Discharged on 19 Feb 1813 and sent to Chatham on HM Store Ship *Dromedary*. Prison Depot: Chatham, Prisoner of War #540. Date Received: 23 Feb 1813 from Portsmouth on HMS *Dromedary*. Discharged on 8 Jun 1813 and released to the Cartel *Rodrigo*. (Johnson's Database, 2019)

Chesney, Thomas E., served as a Private in Capt. Thomas Montgomery's Co., 14th U.S. Infantry, enlisted 16 Jun 1812 for 5 years in Baltimore at the advanced age of 55, 5' 5" tall, born in Harford Co., MD and was discharged at Greenbush, NY on 4 May 1815 due to rupture (Johnson and Christou, p. 59; Pension Old War IF-12459; BLW# 4360-160-12)

Cheston, James, served as Adjutant in Capt. Samuel Sterett's Co., 5th Regt., Baltimore Militia. "James H. Cheston, merchant, Adj., 5th Rgt. – Wounded" at North Point on 12 Sep 1814 (North Point dead and wounded Article 4 Oct 1814 Columbian Register CT Vol. III 97, p. 4; Marine p. 165, stated slightly wounded)

Childers, Joseph, served as a Private in the 14th U.S. Infantry and was captured. Prisoner of War #4019 at Halifax, NS, interned 24 Jun 1813, discharged on 9 Nov 1813 and sent to England (Johnson and Christou, p. 59; Baker Vol. 1, p. 77)

Chrise, John (1789-1815), served as a Private in Capt. James Dorman's Co., 5th U.S. Infantry, enlisted 5 Jun 1812 in Creagerstown, MD, age 23, 5' 8½" tall, born in Maryland. Prisoner of War #4088 at Halifax, NS, exchanged on 15 Apr 1814 and died at Pittsburgh, PA on 24 Jul 1815 by drowning; bounty land issued to Henry Chrise, father and only heir (BLW# 10617-160-12; Johnson and Christou, p. 59; Baker, Vol. 1, p. 78, stated he was discharged on 3 Feb 1814)

Chrisman, Powel (1777-1813), served as a Private in Capt. David Cummings' Co., 14th U.S. Infantry, enlisted 21 May 1812 for 5 years in Cumberland, MD at the age of 35, 5' 7" tall, born in Washington Co., MD and was killed at Beaver Dams, Upper Canada, ten miles west of Niagara Falls, on 24 Jun 1813; bounty land issued to his son Powel (BLW# 27243-160-42; Johnson and Christou, p. 60)

Christian, Samuel, served as a Seaman on the privateer *Nonsuch* of Baltimore under Capt. Levely and was killed in action on 28 Sep 1812 during a battle with a British schooner off Martinique (*Niles Weekly Register*, 14 Nov 1812; J. Thomas Scharf's *The Chronicles of Baltimore*, Vol. 1, p. 359)

Christopher, Samuel, served as a Private in the 14th U.S. Infantry, enlisted 27 Apr 1812 at Salisbury, MD for 5 years, age 19, 5' 6½" tall, born in Worcester Co., MD, captured at Beaver Dams, Upper Canada on 24 Jun 1813. Prisoner of War #3742 at Halifax, NS, discharged for exchange on 3 Feb 1814, exchanged on 15 Apr 1814 and discharged from the service on 27 Aug 1817 (Johnson and Christou, p. 60; Baker Vol. 1, p.79)

Chunn, Zachariah (1784-1815), served as a Sergeant in Capt. Reuben Gilder's Co., 14th U.S. Infantry, enlisted 1 May 1813 for 5 years at the age of 29, 6' 2" tall, born in Maryland and died at Burlington, VT in April 1815 (Johnson and Christou, p. 60)

Church, Richard, served as a Seaman and was born in Baltimore. Age: 32. Prison Depot: Chatham, Prisoner of War #1066. How Taken: Gave himself up off HM Frigate *Ulysses*. When Taken: 13 Jan 1813. Date Received: 14 Mar 1813 from Portsmouth on HMS *Cornwell*. Discharged on 11 Aug 1814 and sent to Dartmoor. Prison Depot: Dartmoor, Prisoner of War #2585. Date Received: 21 Aug 1814. From what ship: HMT *Freya* from Chatham. Discharged 3 May 1815. (Johnson's Database, 2019)

Clagett, Elie (1781-1848), served as a Private in Capt. David Warfield's Co., 5th Regiment, Baltimore United Volunteers, from 19 Aug 1814 and was wounded on 12 Sep 1814 at North Point. "Eli Claggett" married Mary Grant on 21 Jan 1816 at the First Methodist Episcopal Church in Baltimore. In 1818 he bought Brown's Brewery which was the site used to sew the huge Star Spangled Banner by Mary Pickersgill when her little home down the street was getting too small to complete this flag. He was the brother of Levi Clagett who died at North Point. Elie was buried in Green Mount Cemetery. (Marine p. 245; Wright Vol. 2, p. 8; *Across the Years in Prince George's County*, by Effie Gwynn Bowie, 1947, p. 126; Society of the War of 1812 Application National No. 1527 in 1925 stated Elie died on 17 Aug 1848 and his wife Mary was born on 5 Mar 1790 and died on 4 Sep 1872; *Maryland Marriages, 1801-1820*, by Robert Barnes, p. 33)

Clagett, Levi, served as 3rd Lieutenant in Capt. Joseph H. Nicholson's Artillery Co. from 19 Aug 1814 and was killed on 13 Sep 1814 at Fort McHenry. Name is on the Baltimore Battle Monument (CMSR; Wright Vol. 2, p. 51; *Baltimore American*, 12 Jun 1819) On 27 Sep 1814 Letters of Administration granted to Eli Clagett. Signed 19 Feb 1820, William Buchanan, to the Estate of Levi Claggett, late third Lieut. of the Artillery Co., Elie Clagett, Administrator. Eli was his brother, both being sons of Alexander Clagett, a patriot of the American Revolution (1742-1821), who was buried at Old St. Paul's Cemetery. (Scharf, p. 95; NARA; CMSR) *"This afternoon, at 4 o'clock, the Baltimore Artillery Co. of Fencibles, under the command of Captain (Joseph Hooper) NICHOLSON, will parade for the purpose of rendering the last tribute of respect to Lieutenant LEVI CLAGGETT, & Sergeant JOHN CLEMM, who fell in defense of this city and their country's rights, at Fort M'Henry, during the bombardment of that fortress by the enemy. To have fallen in such a cause, would have, of itself, entitled the memory of the dead to respect and sympathy. But they needed no such adventitious* *circumstances to excite the most poignant regret at their untimely departure. They formed a prominent part of the rich price, which was paid for victory and safety. In civil life, they were men of the most amiable manners, honorable principles, and respectable standing in society. In the hour of danger, they evinced ardent and collected courage. Their friends lament their loss, with sorrow not loud but deep. May the reflection, that they died in a cause and at a time, when every tongue was eloquent in their praise; that they departed in the path of honor; that the gratitude of their countrymen will embalm their names in every heart, afford to the bereaved of their connections and friends, the only alleviations for such a loss. Their brethren in arms will cherish their memory; with affectionate care. They sleep on the soldier's bed, the bed of honor; and while their loss may call forth the manly tear of fraternal regret, their example will animate to deeds, such as living, they would have approved and aided."* (*Baltimore Patriot,* 21 Sep 1814*)* October Term 1814: Elie Clagett, admin. of Levi Clagett, was ordered to place a notice in the *Baltimore American* informing creditors to exhibit their claims against his estate. (Baltimore Orphans Court Proceedings, Book 9, p. 66) April Term 1815: Eli Clagett was ordered by the Court to sell the personal estate of Levi Clagett. (Baltimore Orphans Court Proceedings Book 9, p. 127) 29 Nov 1815: First Account of Elie Clagett, admin. of Levi, contained lists of debts and payments including Thomas Griffin for opening his grave and G. Wall for a coffin. (Baltimore County Administration Accounts Book 20, pp. 203-205) On 30 Mar 1816: the final account of Elie Clagett, admin. of Levi Clagett, mentioned only that the balance of Levi's estate was "paid to A. Clagett the father and heir of the deceased." (Baltimore County Administration Accounts Book 20, p. 308) The death of "Lt. Claggett of Capt. Nicholson's Co." was reported in the *Niles Weekly Register.* (1 Oct 1814)

Clark, Abraham (1787-1839), served as a 2nd Lieutenant in 14th U.S. Infantry at age 25; commissioned an Ensign on 12 Mar 1812, promoted to 3rd Lieutenant on 13 Mar 1813 and promoted to 2nd Lieutenant on 1 Oct 1813. Prisoner of War (Dartmouth), released on 31 May 1814 and was discharged on 15 Jun 1815. Abraham Clarke (sic) married Maria Clarke (sic) on 14 Oct 1818 (license dated 12 Oct) in Bladensburg, MD and died on 4 Sep 1839 (Johnson and Christou, pp. 60-61; BLW# 10217-160-50; WO-15768; Prince George's Co. Marriage License)

Clark, Charles G. (1785-1814), served as a Private in Capt. James McDonald's Co., 14th U.S. Infantry, enlisted on 15 Jan 1815 for 5 years at age 30, 5' 9" tall, born in Connecticut and died at Burlington, VT on 7 Oct 1814 (Johnson and Christou, p. 61)

Clark, George W., served as a Private in Capt. David Warfield's Co., 5th Regt., Baltimore Militia, and was wounded on 12 Sep 1814 at North Point. (Wright Vol. 2, p. 8)

Clark, James, served as a Private in Capt. Reuben Gilder's Co., 14th U.S. Infantry, enlisted 18 Apr 1813, age 42, 5' 5½" tall, born in England and captured at Beaver Dams, Upper Canada on 24 Jun 1813. Prisoner of War #3761 at Halifax, NS, interned 24 Jun 1813 and discharged for exchange on 3 Feb 1814 per order of Rear Adm. Griffith (Johnson and Christou, p. 61; Baker Vol. 1, p. 80)

Clark, John, served as a Private in Capt. Benjamin Gorsuch's Co., 2nd Regt., 11th Brigade, Baltimore Co., wounded in action in 1814 [probably at Bladensburg] and was discharged at Camp Hampstead in Baltimore, 22 miles from home (Wright Vol. 2, p. 88)

Clark, John, served as a Private in Capt. Robert Conway's Co., 6th Regiment, Baltimore Militia, from 19 Aug 1814 and was discharged by the Surgeon on 29 Sep 1814, but the medical cause was not stated (Wright Vol. 2, p. 13)

Clark, John, served as a Seaman and was born in Maryland. Age: 27. Prison Depot: Dartmoor, Prisoner of War #2394. Captured by HM Frigate *Orpheus*. When Taken: 20 Apr 1814. Where Taken: off Matanzas, Cuba. Prize Name: U.S. Sloop-of-War *Frolic*. Ship Type: Warship. Date Received: 16 Aug 1814. From what ship: HMT *Queen* from Halifax, NS. Discharged and sent to Dartmouth on 19 Oct 1814. (Johnson's Database, 2019)

Clark, Mathias, served as a Private in Capt. Thomas Biddle's Co., 2nd U.S. Artillery, enlisted 8 Jan 1813 for 5 years at the age of 22, 5' 6" tall, born in Baltimore, transferred to Capt. Nathan Towson's Co. and died on 12 Dec 1815 by drowning; bounty land issued to daughter Catherine Clark and other heirs at law (Johnson and Christou, p. 62)

Clark, Sheldon, served as a Private in the 14th U.S. Infantry and was captured. Prisoner of War #4063 at Halifax, NS, interned 24 Jun 1813 and discharged for exchange on 3 Feb 1814 per order of Rear Adm. Griffith (Johnson and Christou, p. 62; Baker Vol. 1, p. 81 spelled his name Sheldren Clark)

Clark, Stephen, served as a Private in Capt. David Cummings' Co., 14th U.S. Infantry, enlisted 25 Jan 1813 and was captured at Beaver Dams, Upper Canada on 24 Jun 1813. Prisoner of War #4790 at Halifax, NS, interned 15 Nov 1813 and discharged 19 Nov 1813 per order of Sir J. B. Warren and sent to England (Johnson and Christou, p. 62; Baker Vol. 1, p. 81)

Clark, Thomas S., served as a Corporal in the 22nd U.S. Infantry under Col. Hugh Brady, enlisted 23 Mar 1814 at Chambersburg, age 25, 5' 8" tall, 5' 8" tall, blue eyes, sandy hair, fair complexion, born in Franklin Co., PA or Frederick Co., MD, mustered at Pittsburgh on 30 Apr 1814, wounded at Williamsville, left sick at Williamsville since 26 Oct 1814, was discharged from the hospital on 8 Nov 1814 and reported as deserted, but returned to service at Sackett's Harbor, NY by 30 Dec 1814 (Mallick and Wright, p. 78)

Clark, William, served as a Private in Capt. John T. Randall's Rifle Co., Baltimore Co., joined on 8 Aug 1814 and was wounded in action on 24 Aug 1814 at Bladensburg; later served in Capt. Benjamin Gorsuch's Co., 2nd Regiment, from 14 Oct 1814 and discharged on 1 Dec 1814 at Camp Hampstead in Baltimore City, 12 miles from his residence (Wright Vol. 2, pp. 73, 88)

Clarke, George W., served as a Private in Capt. David Warfield's Co., 5th Regt., Baltimore Militia, and was wounded at Bladensburg on 24 Aug 1814 (Marine p. 246; Wright Vol. 2, p. 8)

Clarke, John, served as a Private in the 14th U.S. Infantry and was captured. Prisoner of War #4040 at Halifax, NS, interned 24 Jun 1813 and discharged for exchange on 3 Feb 1813 (Johnson and Christou, pp. 62-63; Baker Vol. 1, p. 82)

Clary, Nathaniel, served as a Private in Capt. James Hook's Co., 38th U.S. Inf., enlisted 7 Feb 1814 for 1 year, re-enlisted on 14 Jun 1814 for the duration of the war and died on 3 Sep 1814; bounty land issued to John Clary, brother and only heir (BLW# 21508-160-12; Johnson and Christou, p. 63)

Clary, Samuel, served as a Private in Capt. John Fonsten's Co., Frederick Co. Militia, from 2 Sep 1814, marched to Baltimore, engaged in the defense of the city and reported "sick absent 16 Sep" 1814 (Mallick and Wright, p. 363)

Claude, Abraham, served as a Corporal in Capt. Pinkney's Artillery Co. and in Ensign Brewer's Detachment, 36th Regiment, and was captured at the Battle of Bladensburg on 24 Aug 1814 (Marine, pp. 174, 247)

Clay, Walter, served as a Private in the 14th U.S. Infantry and was captured. Prisoner of War #3822 at Halifax, NS, interned 6 Jun 1813 and discharged for exchange on 3 Feb 1814 per order of Rear Adm. Griffith (Johnson and Christou, p. 63; Baker Vol. 1, p. 82)

Clayton, Thomas, served as a Private in the 14th U.S. Infantry (company not stated) and was captured, probably at Beaver Dams, Upper Canada, ten miles west of Niagara Falls, on 24 Jun 1813. Prisoner of War #4176 at Halifax, NS, interned 24 Jun 1813 and was sent to England on 27 Aug 1813 (Johnson and Christou, p. 63; Baker Vol. 1, p. 83)

Cleat, Cawsford, served as a Seaman of the U.S. Chesapeake Flotilla, entered service on 6 May 1814 and died on 1 Apr 1815 (Shomette, p. 388)

Cleaver, Seth (c1793-1813), served as a Corporal in 14th U.S. Infantry (company not stated) and was captured at Beaver Dams, Upper Canada, ten miles west of

Niagara Falls, on 24 Jun 1813. Prisoner of War #3805 at Halifax, NS and died there on 16 Oct 1813 (Johnson and Christou, p. 63; Baker, Vol. 1, p. 83)

Clement, David (1769-1813), served as a Sergeant and was born in Maryland. Age: 44. Prison Depot: Quebec, Prisoner of War #693. When Taken: 26 Jun 1813. Where Taken: Beaver Dams, Upper Canada. Date Received: 7 Jul 1813. From what ship: Steamboat. Died on 3 Aug 1813. (Johnson's Database, 2019)

Clements, Caleb, served as a Private in Capt. Nathan Baynard's Co., 35th Regt., Queen Anne's Co. Militia, from 7 May 1813 and was reported "absent by leave 4 days on account of indigestion" (Wright Vol. 1, p. 36)

Clements, Samuel (1775-1815), served as a Private in Capt. John Rothrock's Co., 38th U.S. Infantry, enlisted 6 Apr 1814 in Richmond, VA at the age of 39, 5' 2" tall, born in Maryland and died 8 Feb 1815; bounty land issued to James A. Clements, son and others (BLW# 26853-160-12; Johnson and Christou, p. 64)

Clements, Thomas (1788-1868), served as a Private in Capt. David Crawford's Co., 17th Regiment, Prince George's Co. Militia, for five days between 18 Jul and 2 Aug 1814 and was reported sick, but no date was given (Wright Vol. 6, p. 11). On 1 Nov 1850 Thomas Clements, age 62, of Bladensburg, Prince George's Co., stated he had engaged in the Battle of Bladensburg. On 22 Jun 1855, age about 66, he stated he wished to correct the statement regarding Capt. Crawford who he now says did not command his company at Bladensburg, but now recalls his company was commanded by Lieut. Carter. On 12 Mar 1878 Sarah Clements, age 64, widow of Thomas Clements, stated he was discharged at Bladensburg around 18 Sep 1814, they were married on 25 Nov 1856 [actually they obtained a marriage license in Washington, DC on 25 Nov 1857], her former name was Pumphrey and he died 16 Jan 1868. (Pension WO-12501; BLW# 55-160-2736)

Clements, William (1757-1814), served as a Private in Capt. John Whistler's Co., 1st Infantry, enlisted 28 Nov 1805 in Fort Dearborn, IL at the age of 48, 5' 8" tall, was born in Charles Co., MD, re-enlisted at Detroit, MI on 22 Aug 1810 and died on 9 Jan 1814 at Fort Wayne, IN of typhus fever (Johnson and Christou, p. 64)

Clemm, John (1780-1814), served as 1st Corporal in Capt. Joseph H. Nicholson's Artillery Co., 1st Volunteer Artillerists, from 4 Aug to 24 Aug 1813, then as 2nd Sergeant from 19 Aug 1814 and was killed on 13 Sep 1814 at Fort McHenry. Letter dated 12 Feb 1819 to Robert Brent, Esq., from L. Eichelberger stated as follow: "I have furnished herewith the evidence required to establish the claim of Mrs. Clemm, I have been told by Col. Benjamin c. Howard that it is the same which was transmitted to by him to provide a pension for the widow of one of his men. On 3rd of Feb 1819 before a Justice of the Peace of Baltimore County came Thomas Russell and Louis Eichelberger of the City of Baltimore and severally made oath that they were stationed at Fort McHenry at the time of the death of Mr. John Clemm which happened on Tuesday the 14th day of Sep 1814 and that he was at that time a sergeant in Capt. Nicholson's Artillery Co. Sworn before John F. Harris. On 11 Feb 1819 before a justice of the peace personally appeared Maria Clemm, widow of the above mentioned John Clemm, and Elizabeth Eichelberger, the mother of the said Maria Clemm, and made witness that Maria was lawfully married to John Clemm and has remained a widow since his decease and that Maria Clemm has a daughter named Elizabeth who was about 3 years old at that period. It appears (from roll of B. Hodges Accounts Abs C V 62) that John Clemm, a Sgt. of Capt. Nicholson's Co., was paid from the 19 Aug 18 to 13 Sep 1814 which payment was made to Louis Eichelberger, his administrator. John Clemm, merchant, killed in Fort M'Henry by a shell." (North Point dead and wounded Article 4 Oct 1814 Columbian Register CT Vol. III 97, page 4). Clemm's name is on Baltimore Battle Monument. John Clemm, 2nd Sgt., killed on 13 Sep 1814 in Capt. Joseph H. Nicholson's Co. of Volunteer Artillerists under the command of Lt. Col. George Armistead. (CMSR; Wright Vol. 2, p. 51; *Baltimore American*, 12 Jun 1819) John Clemm married Maria Eichelberger in August 1810 (*Baltimore Scourge*, 11 Aug 1810). He was the son of Col. William Clemm (of Revolutionary War) and Anna Catherine Shultz who married in York Co., PA, and their 3 children were: Joseph Clemm, John Clemm and William Clemm, Jr. The latter Clemm, John's brother, married into the Poe family, first to Harriet Poe and second to Maria Poe (daughter of Gen. David Poe, of Baltimore) and their daughter Virginia Clemm married first cousin Edgar Alan Poe, which makes him the nephew of Sgt. Clemm. {The Green Book Appendix 1, and documented research by Francis B. Culver, renowned genealogist and registrar for several patriotic organizations in the early 1900s}. The death of Sgt. John Clemm was reported in *Niles Weekly Register* on 1 Oct 1814 as well: "Lt. Claggett of Capt. Nicholson's Company was killed in battle of Fort McHenry. Also Sgt. Clemm and James Lowry Donaldson, Adj. of 27th Regt."

See image of Sgt. Clemm's trunk on the next page.

The Clemm trunk in the foreground was donated by the Historical Society of Harford County to the Ft. McHenry National Monument and Historic Shrine in 2016. Pictured above during that event are: Maryanna Skowronski, Executive Director, Historical Society of Harford County; Carol Deibel, Vice President, Historical Society of Harford County; Anne Longanecker, Assistant to the Curator, Fort McHenry and Hampton Mansion; Gregory Weidman, Curator, Fort McHenry; Henry C. Peden, Jr., Genealogist General, General Society of the War of 1812 and Genealogist, Society of the War of 1812 in State of Maryland; and, Jacob Bensen, Administrative Assistant, Historical Society of Harford County.

Cleveland, Ebenezer (African American), served as a Seaman and was born in Maryland. Age: 25. Prison Depot: Chatham, Prisoner of War #3326. Captured by HM Frigate *Acasta* & HM Brig *Wasp*. When Taken: 17 Jun 1813. Where Taken: off Cape Sable, NS. Prize Name: *Porcupine*. Home Port: Boston. Ship Type: Letter of Marque. Date Received: 23 Feb 1814 from Halifax, NS on HMT *Malabar*. Discharged on 21 Jul 1814 and sent to Dartmoor on HMS *Portia*. Prison Depot: Dartmoor, Prisoner of War #1865. Date Received: 29 Jul 1814. From what ship: HMS *Ville de Paris* from Chatham Depot. Discharged on 2 May 1815. (Johnson's Database, 2019)

Cline, Lewis, served as a Seaman and was born in Baltimore. Age: 26. Prison Depot: Dartmoor, Prisoner of War #4138. Captured by HM Frigate *Niemen*. When Taken: 28 Jun 1814. Where Taken: off Delaware. Prize Name: *Bordeaux Packet*. Home Port: Baltimore. Ship Type: Letter of Marque. Date Received: 6 Oct 1814. From what ship: HMT *Chesapeake* from Halifax, NS. Discharged on 13 Jun 1815. (Johnson's Database, 2019)

Coak, Jeremiah, served as a Private in Capt. Jeremiah Ducker's Co., 2nd Regt., 11th Brigade, Baltimore Co., stationed in Baltimore from 14 Oct 1814 and was reported "absent – sick on furlough since Sep 30" 1814 (Wright Vol. 2, p. 88)

Coates, Daniel, served as a Private in Capt. Stephen H. Moore's Co., Baltimore Volunteers Infantry Co., from 8 Sep 1812 for 1 year and was discharged on 10 Dec 1812 as unfit for service (Wright Vol. 2, p. 57)

Coates, S. Murray, served as a Seaman and was born in Baltimore or Harford Co., MD. Age: 30. Prison Depot: Portsmouth, Prisoner of War #182. Captured by HM Transport *Diadem*. When Taken: 7 Oct 1812. Where Taken: S. Andera (St. Andrews, Scotland). Prize Name: *Baltimore*. Home Port: Baltimore. Ship Type: Privateer. Date Received: 3 Nov 1812 San Antonio. From what ship: HMS *Diadem*. Discharged on 19 Feb 1813, age 33, and sent to Chatham on HM Store Ship *Dromedary*. Samuel M. Coates, age 33, served as a Boatswain and was born in Baltimore. Prison Depot: Plymouth 2, Prisoner of War #142. Captured by HM Ship-of-the-Line *Medway*. When Taken: 12 Jul 1814. Where Taken: coast of Africa. Prize Name: U.S. Brig *Syren*. Ship Type: Warship. Date Received: 21 Feb 1815. From what ship: HMS *Slaney*. Discharged on 24 Feb 1815 and sent to Dartmoor. Prison Depot: Dartmoor, Prisoner of War #6367. Date Received: 24 Feb 1815. From what ship: HMT *Ganges* from Plymouth. Escaped on 1 Jun 1815. (Johnson's Database, 2019)

Coblentz, Jacob, served as a Private in Capt. William Knox's Rifle Co., Frederick Co. Militia, Taneytown area, joined 26 Aug 1814 and discharged by a doctor on 8 Sep 1814, but the cause was not stated, probably in Baltimore (Mallick and Wright, pp. 79, 356)

Cochran, David, served as a Private in Capt. Samuel Lane's Co., 14th U.S. Infantry, enlisted 22 May 1812 in "W. M., MD" at the age of 36, 5' 5" tall, born in Ireland and was wounded in his left arm at Beaver Dams, Upper Canada, ten miles west of Niagara Falls, on 24 Jun 1813 (Johnson and Christou, p. 66)

Cockey, Samuel (1792-1859), served as a Private in Capt. Walter S. Hunt's, 41st Regiment, Baltimore Co. Militia, from 25 Aug 1814 and reported as "sick-absent since Sep 15" 1814 (Wright Vol. 2, p. 68). He was born on 18 Oct 1792, died on 12 Jul 1859 and was buried in Sater's Baptist Church Cemetery. His gravesite is enclosed within an iron fence. (Smith's Database, 2019; *Baltimore Cemeteries, Volume 1*, by Baltimore County Genealogical Society, 1985, p. 14)

Cohen, Philip J., served as a Private in Capt. Joseph H. Nicholson's Artillery Co., Baltimore City, from 19 Aug 1814 and was reported "sick-absent in Philadelphia on Oct 31" 1814 (Wright Vol. 2, p. 51)

Cole, Abraham (1786-1845), served as a Private in Capt. Joshua Taylor's Co., 41st Regiment, Baltimore Co. Militia, from 25 Aug 1814 and was reported "sick-absent since Sep 4" 1814 (Wright Vol. 2, p. 71). He was born 25 Jan 1786, died 8 Oct 1845 and was buried in Jessop United Methodist Church Cemetery at Sparks in Baltimore County. (Smith's Database, 2019; www.findagrave.com)

Cole, Andrew, served as a Private in the 14th U.S. Infantry and was captured. Prisoner of War #4191 at Halifax, NS, interned 24 Jun 1813, discharged on 27 Aug 1813 and sent to England (Johnson and Christou, p. 63; Baker Vol. 1, p. 86)

Cole, John, served as a Private in Capt. Aaron R. Levering's Co., 5th Regiment, Baltimore Militia, from 19 Aug 1814 and listed on muster roll as "prisoner on parole," but no date was given (Wright Vol. 2, p. 5)

Cole, John, of Baltimore, served as a Seaman on the ship *Adeline* and was captured, but the date was not given. Prisoner of War #4201253 at Dartmoor and died on 26 Nov 1814 (Centennial Trails, United States Daughters of 1812, online at www.war1812trails.com/Dartmoor)

Cole, John (1776-1814) (African American), served as a Seaman and was born in Baltimore. Age: 38. Prison Depot: Plymouth 1, Prisoner of War #2627. Captured by HM Frigate *Magiciene*. When Taken: 14 Mar 1814. Where Taken: off Cape Finisterre, Spain. Prize Name: *Adeline*. Ship Type: Letter of Marque. Received: 17 May 1814. From what ship: HMS *Tortois*. Discharged on 14 Jun 1814. Sent to Dartmoor. Prisoner of War #1253 at Dartmoor. Died on 26 Nov 1814 of pneumonia. (Johnson's Database, 2019)

Cole, Perry (Mulatto), served as a Seaman and was born in Baltimore. Age: 23. Prison Depot: Dartmoor, Prisoner of War #3104. How Taken: Gave himself up by *Pilot* boat. When Taken: 27 Aug 1814. Where Taken: Bristol, UK. Prize Name: *Mary*, prize of the Privateer *Mammouth*. Ship Type: Privateer. Date Received: 9 Sep 1814. From what ship: HMS *Abercrombie*. Discharged on 28 May 1815. (Johnson's Database, 2019)

Cole, Thomas D. (1787-1814), served as a Private in Capt. John Pentland's Co., 22nd U.S. Infantry, enlisted 5 Feb 1813 in Harrisburg, PA, age 26, 5' 11" tall, born in Maryland and died on 7 Jan 1814 near Ogdensburgh, NY from diarrhea (Johnson and Christou, p. 67)

Cole, Zachariah (African American), served as a Seaman and was born in Annapolis. Age: 23. Prison Depot: Chatham, Prisoner of War #3362. Captured by HM Frigate *Narcissus*. When Taken: 12 Jun 1813. Where Taken: York River, Virginia. Prize Name: U.S.R.M. *Cutter Surveyor*. Ship Type: Warship. Date Received: 23 Feb 1814 from Halifax, NS on HMT *Malabar*. Discharged on 10 Oct 1814 and sent to U.S. on the Cartel *St. Philip*. (Johnson's Database, 2019)

Coleman, Joseph, served as a Seaman and was born in Baltimore. Age: 19. Prison Depot: Dartmoor, Prisoner of War #4984. Captured by HM Frigate *Armide*. When Taken: 16 Aug 1814. Where Taken: off Nantucket, MA. Prize Name: *Invincible*. Home Port: Salem. Ship Type: Letter of Marque. Received: 28 Oct 1814. From what ship: HMT *Alkbar* from Halifax, NS. Discharged on 21 Jun 1815. (Johnson's Database, 2019)

Coleman, Perre (Peregrine), served as a Private in Capt. William Copper's Artillery Co., 21st Regiment, Kent Co., in 1813 and was reported as "excused on inability" on the muster roll dated 15 Apr – 12 May 1813 (Wright Vol. 1, p. 13)

Collins, Andrew, served as a Seaman and was born in Annapolis. Age: 29. Prison Depot: Plymouth 1, Prisoner of War #1919. Captured by HM Brig *Pelican*. When Taken: 14 Aug 1813. Where Taken: off St. David's Head, Wales. Prize Name: U.S. Brig *Argus*. Ship Type: Warship. Received: 23 Aug 1813. From what ship: HMS *Pelican*. Discharged on 8 Sep 1813 and sent to Dartmoor. Prison Depot: Dartmoor, Prisoner of War #621. Received: 8 Sep 1813 from Plymouth. Discharged and sent to Dartmouth on 2 Nov 1814. (Johnson's Database, 2019)

Collins, Cornelius, served as a Private in Capt. Berry's Washington Artillery Co. and slightly wounded at Fort McHenry on 13 Sep 1814 (Marine pp. 173, 250)

Collins, George, served as a Private and was promoted to Corporal in Capt. Christian Adreon's Co., 5th Regiment, Baltimore Militia, on 10 Sep 1814 and was reported "in captivity – wounded as of Nov 18" (Wright Vol. 2, p. 3; Marine, p. 250, did not mention his wound)

Collins, John, served as a Seaman and was born in Baltimore. Age: 35. Prison Depot: Dartmoor, Prisoner of War #6026. Captured by HM Frigate *Forth*. When Taken: 19 Sep 1814. Where Taken: off Egg Harbor, NJ. Prize Name: *Regent*. Home Port: New York. Ship Type: Letter of Marque (Privateer). Date Received: 28 Dec 1814. From what ship: HMT *Penelope*. Discharged on 3 Jul 1815. (Johnson's Database, 2019)

Collins, William (African American), served as a Seaman and was born in Annapolis. Age: 25. Prison Depot: Plymouth 1, Prisoner of War #1896. Captured by HM Brig *Pelican*. When Taken: 14 Aug 1813. Where Taken: off St. David's Head, Wales. Prize Name: U.S. Brig *Argus*. Ship Type: Warship. Date Received: 23 Aug 1813. From what ship: HMS *Pelican*. Discharged on 8 Sep 1813 and sent to Dartmoor. (Johnson's Database, 2019)

Collins (Collings), William, served as a Private in Capt. James McConkey's Co., 27th Regiment, Baltimore Militia, from 19 Aug 1814 and was wounded on 12 Sep 1814 at North Point. Marine (Wright Vol. 2, p. 19; Marine p. 250 mentioned two men with this name: one in Capt. McConkey's Co., 27th Regt., and the other in Capt. John McKane's Co., 27th Regt., captured at North Point; Huntsberry, pp. 91, 92, states both were wounded). Dr. James H. McCulloh, Jr. wrote this note soon after the battle to the British commander: "In consequence of the humanity shown the following American prisoners of war, I do promise upon honor that they shall not directly or indirectly serve against the British until regularly exchanged." (Marine, p. 171)

Collison, Elliott, served as a Seaman and was born in Baltimore. Age: 24. Prison Depot: Dartmoor, Prisoner of War #3853. Captured by HM Ship-of-the-Line *Majestic* & HM Brig Dotterell. When Taken: 22 May 1814. Where Taken: off Charleston, SC. Prize Name: *Dominica*. Ship Type: Merchant Vessel. Date Received: 5 Oct 1814. From what ship: HMT *Orpheus* from Halifax, NS. Discharged on 9 Jun 1815. (Johnson's Database, 2019)

Columbia, John, served as a Seaman and was born in Maryland. Age: 19. Prison Depot: Dartmoor, Prisoner of War #2254. Captured by HM Brig *Curlew*. When Taken: 25 May 1814. Where Taken: off Halifax, NS. Prize Name: *Ontario*, prize of Privateer *Lawrence*. Home Port: Baltimore. Ship Type: Privateer. Date Received: 16 Aug 1814. From what ship: HMS *Dublin* from Halifax. Discharged on 3 May 1815. (Johnson's Database, 2019)

Combs, Thomas, served as a Seaman and was born in Maryland. Age: 37. Prison Depot: Portsmouth, Prisoner of War #562. Captured by HM Frigate *Dryad*. When Taken: 7 Jan 1813. Where Taken: at sea. Prize Name: *Rossie*. Ship Type: Merchant Vessel. Date Received: 25 Jan 1813. From what ship: HM Ship-of-the-Line *Queen*. Discharged on 11 Mar 1813 and sent to Chatham on HM Store Ship *Abundance*. Prison Depot: Chatham, Prisoner of War #1235. Date Received: 16 Mar 1813 from Portsmouth on HMS *Abundance*. Discharged on 24 Jul 1813 and released to the Cartel *Hoffning*. (Johnson's Database, 2019)

Comegys, Cornelius Jr. (1792-1815), served as a Lieutenant in the 14th U.S. Infantry, born in Maryland, commissioned a 3rd Lieutenant on 10 May 1813, promoted to 2nd Lieutenant on 14 Nov 1813 and died on 31 Mar 1815 (Johnson and Christou, p. 69) Cornelius Comegys, of Kent Co., wrote his will on 22 Feb 1807 and stated at that time he was lieutenant in the U.S. Army and wished "to be buried in the family burying ground on the farm now held by John Wallis provided I died in Maryland." He also bequeathed his military clothes to said John Wallis, his sword and belt to Capt. Nathaniel Comegys, Jr. and his horseman's pistols and holster to Capt. Samuel Rasin. His will was proved on 21 Sep 1815 in Washington Co., MD and a copy filed in Kent Co. on 10 Nov 1815. (*Abstracts of Kent County, Maryland Wills, Volume I, 1777-1816*, by Christos Christou, Jr. and John Anthony Barnhouser, 1997, pp. 254-255)

Conahy, Benjamin M., served as a Private in the 14th U.S. Infantry and was captured, probably at Beaver Dams, Upper Canada. Prisoner of War #3955 at Halifax, NS, interned 24 Jun 1813 and was discharged on 27 Aug 1813 and sent to England (Johnson and Christou, p. 63; Baker Vol. 1, p. 89)

Conkey, Lunar, served as a Private in the 14th U.S. Infantry and was captured, probably at Beaver Dams, Upper Canada. Prisoner of War #4149 at Halifax, NS, interned 24 Jun 1813 and was discharged for exchange on 3 Feb 1814 (Johnson and Christou, p. 63; Baker Vol. 1, p. 90, spelled his first name Llunar)

Conkey, Piney, served as a Private in the 14th U.S. Infantry and was captured, probably at Beaver Dams, Upper Canada. Prisoner of War #4150 at Halifax, NS, interned 24 Jun 1813 and was discharged for exchange on 3 Feb 1814 (Johnson and Christou, p. 63; Baker Vol. 1, p. 90, spelled his first name Pliney)

Connelly, James, served as a Seaman and was born in Baltimore. Age: 20. Prison Depot: Dartmoor, Prisoner of War #2624. How Taken: Gave himself up off HM Ship-of-the-Line *Christian VII*. When Taken: 21 Dec 1812. Date Received: 21 Aug 1814. From what ship: HMT *Freya* from Chatham. Discharged on 26 Apr 1815. Prison Depot: Chatham, Prisoner of War #1586. Date Received: 18 Apr 1813. From what ship: HMS *Rosario*. Discharged on 11 Apr 1814 and sent to Dartmoor. (Johnson's Database, 2019)

Conner, Galen, served as a Mate and was born in Maryland. Age: 25. Prison Depot: Dartmoor, Prisoner of War #3605. Captured by HM Frigate *Barbadoes* on 31 Jan 1814 off St. Bartholomew, West Indies. Prize Name: *Gothland*. Ship Type: Merchant Vessel. Received: 30 Sep 1814. From what ship: HMT *Sybella*. Discharged on 4 Jun 1815. (Johnson's Database, 2019)

Conner, James (1790-1812), served as a Private in Capt. Reuben Gilder's Co., 14th U.S. Infantry, enlisted 27 Apr 1812 in Hagerstown, MD at age 22, born in York Co., PA, was wounded at Fort Erie, Upper Canada and died on 30 May 1812 at Four Mile Creek near Fort Niagara, NY (BLW# 5192-160-12; Johnson and Christou, p. 70)

Conner, Patrick (1766-1814), served as a Corporal in Capt. George Barker's Co., 22nd U.S. Infantry, enlisted 15 Jan 1813 in Cumberland, MD at the age of 47, 5' 9½"" tall, born in York, PA, was wounded at Chippewa, Upper Canada on 25 Jul 1814 and died at Buffalo, NY on 30 Jul 1814 (BLW# 26219-160-12; Johnson and Christou, p. 71)

Conner, William, served as a Private in Capt. John Lytle's Co., 4th U.S. Rifles, enlisted 21 May 1814, age 35, 5' 8" tall, born in Maryland or Virginia and was captured at Fort Erie on 17 Sep 1814. Prisoner of War #7872 at Halifax, NS, interned on 4 Dec 1814, discharged on 10 Apr 1815 and discharged from the service on 14 Jun 1815 at Conjocquita Creek, NY (Johnson and Christou, p. 71; Baker Vol. 1, p. 91, spelled his name Connor)

Conner, William, served as a Seaman and was born in Maryland. Age: 27. Prison Depot: Dartmoor, Prisoner of War #5731. How Taken: Gave himself up off MV

Warrior. When Taken: 12 Nov 1814. Date Received: 26 Dec 1814. From what ship: HMT *Argo*. Discharged on 11 Jul 1815. (Johnson's Database, 2019)

Conrad, John, served as a Lieutenant in Capt. Harry's Co., 24th Regiment, and died in 1814, but the date and cause of death were not stated (Marine p. 252)

Conway, Andrew, served as a Seaman and was born in Baltimore. Age: 20. Prison Depot: Portsmouth, Prisoner of War #670. How Taken: Gave himself up off HM Brig *Electra*. Date Received: 10 Feb 1813. From what ship: HMS *Electra*. Discharged on 6 Mar 1813 and sent to Chatham on HMS *Cornwall*. (Johnson's Database, 2019)

Conway (Cannoway), Charles, served as a Seaman and was born in Baltimore. Age: 43. Prison Depot: Plymouth 1, Prisoner of War #1174. Captured by HM Frigate *Stag*. When Taken: 18 Apr 1813. Where Taken: Bay of Biscayne. Prize Name: *Hebe*. Ship Type: Merchant Vessel. Received: 6 May 1813. From what ship: HMS *Stag*. Discharged and sent on 8 Sep 1813 to Dartmoor. Prison Depot: Dartmoor, Prisoner of War #47. Date Received: 8 Sep 1813 from Plymouth. Discharged and sent to Plymouth on 8 Jul 1814. (Johnson's Database, 2019)

Conway, John, served as a Marine, was taken from the barracks and admitted to the Naval Hospital in Washington, DC as Patient No. 3 on 13 Jun 1814 (illness or injury not stated) and was discharged 15 Jun 1814 and was admitted again as Patient No. 75 on 30 Nov 1814 with typhoid fever and was discharged on 4 Jan 1815 and sent to the barracks (Sharp's Database, 2018)

Conway, Michael, served as a Private in Capt. Clement Sullivan's Co., 14th U.S. Infantry, enlisted 2 Jun 1812 at the advanced age of 56, 5' 6" tall, born in County Galway, Ireland and was captured on 12 Jun 1813. Prisoner of War #5088 at Halifax, NS, interned 28 Dec 1813, discharged 3 Feb 1814, exchanged on 15 Apr 1814 and discharged from the service on 30 Apr 1815 at Greenbush, NY on a Surgeon's Certificate (Johnson and Christou, p. 72; Baker Vol. 1. p. 91)

Conwell, John, served as a Private in the 14th U.S. Infantry and was captured. Prisoner of War #3847 at Halifax, NS, interned 24 Jun 1813 and was discharged for exchange on 3 Feb 1814 (Johnson and Christou, p. 63; Baker Vol. 1, p. 91)

Cook, Benjamin, of Baltimore, served as a Seaman on the ship *Chesapeake* and was captured, but the date was not given. Prisoner of War #840 at Dartmoor and died on 6 Apr 1814 (Johnson's Database, 2019)

Cook, Benjamin (1787-1814) (African American), served as a Seaman and was born in Baltimore. Age: 26. Prison Depot: Plymouth 1, Prisoner of War #2119. Captured by HM Frigate *Hotspur* & HM Frigate *Pyramus*. When Taken: 26 Oct 1813. Where Taken: Bay of Biscayne. Prize Name: *Chesapeake*. Ship Type: Letter of Marque (Privateer). Date Received: 22 Nov 1813. From what ship: HMS

Pyramus. Discharged on 29 Nov 1813 and sent to Dartmoor. Prisoner of War #840 at Dartmoor. Died on 6 Apr 1814 from pneumonia. (Johnson's Database, 2019; Centennial Trails, United States Daughters of 1812, online at www.war1812trails.com/Dartmoor)

Cook, Edward, served as a Seaman and was born in Maryland. Age: 31. Prison Depot: Dartmoor, Prisoner of War #5854. Captured by HM Frigate *Grancius*. When Taken: 2 Dec 1814. Where Taken: off Lisbon, Portugal. Prize Name: *Leo*. Home Port: Baltimore. Ship Type: Privateer. Date Received: 26 Dec 1814. From what ship: HMT *Impregnable*. Discharged on 28 May 1815. (Johnson's Database, 2019)

Cook, Haz., served as a Private in the 14th U.S. Infantry (company not stated) and was captured on 24 Jun 1813, probably at Beaver Dams, Upper Canada. Prisoner of War #4629 at Halifax, NS, interned on 15 Nov 1813, discharged on 19 Nov 1813 and sent to England per order of Adm. Sir J. B. Warren (Johnson and Christou, p. 63; Baker Vol. 1, p. 91)

Cook, John, served as a Sergeant in 14th U.S. Infantry and was born in Maryland. Age: 20. Prison Depot: Chatham, Prisoner of War #3074. When Taken: 24 Jun 1813. Where Taken: Beaver Dams, Upper Canada. Date Received: 7 Jan 1814 from Halifax, NS. Discharged on 10 Oct 1814 and sent to U.S. on the Cartel *St. Philip*. (Johnson's Database, 2019)

Cook, John, served as a Private (company not stated) and was captured at the Battle of Bladensburg on 24 Aug 1814 (Marine, p. 174)

Cook, John, served as a Private in Capt. Samuel Dawson's Co., Frederick Co. Militia, from 26 Jul 1814, was engaged in the Battle of Bladensburg on 24 Aug 1814 and in the defense of Baltimore City on 12 Sep 1814 and was reported sick in Baltimore, but the exact date was not given (Mallick and Wright, p. 338)

Cook, William, served as a Private in Capt. Henry Grindage's Co., 14th U. S. Inf., enlisted 10 Sep 1812 and was captured. Prisoner of War 3836 at Halifax, NS, interned 24 Jun 1813, was discharged on 9 Nov 1813 and sent to England per order of Sir J. B. Warren (Johnson and Christou, pp. 72-73; Baker Vol. 1, p. 92)

Cooke, William, served as a Lieutenant in Capt. David Warfield's Co., 5th Regt., Baltimore United Volunteers, and was wounded in action at Bladensburg on 24 Aug 1814; he was in command of company at Bladensburg and at North Point on 12 Sep 1814 and was commissioned Captain on 8 Nov 1814 (Marine p. 253)

Cooksey, Richard K., served as a Private in Capt. George H. Steuart's Co. of Inf., 5th Regt., Baltimore Militia, from 19 Aug 1814, was mortally wounded at North Point on 12 Sep 1814 and died on 15 Sep 1814. His name is on the Baltimore Battle Monument. He may have been listed on the Prisoner of War list as Richard

K. Cook. (NARA; CMSR, Wright Vol. 2, p. 6; *Baltimore American*, 12 Jun 1819) Dr. James H. McCulloh, Jr. wrote this soon after the battle to the British commander: "In consequence of the humanity shown the following American prisoners of war, I do promise upon honor that they shall not directly or indirectly serve against the British until regularly exchanged." (Marine, p. 171)

Cooley, James, served as a Private in Capt. Barton Hackney's Co., Frederick Co. Militia, from 1 Sep 1814, participated in the Battle of North Point and was sick in hospital on 15 Sep 1814 in Baltimore (Mallick and Wright, p. 362)

Cooley, Joseph, served as a Private in Capt. John F. Huston's Co., Frederick Co. Militia, from 23 Jul 1814 and was reported as missing in action after the Battle of Bladensburg on 24 Aug 1814 (Mallick and Wright, pp. 82, 344)

Coon, John (1792-1813), served as a Corporal in Capt. John Burd's Co., 2nd Light Dragoons, U.S. Army, enlisted 2 Jun 1812 at the age of 20, 5' 5" tall, born in Washington Co., MD and died at Utica, NY on 6 Jun 1813; bounty land issued to Margaret Marshall, his mother (sic) and only heir at law (BLW# 27376-260-42; Johnson and Christou, p. 73)

Cooper, Daniel (Mulatto), served as a Seaman and was born in Baltimore. Age: 30. Prison Depot: Plymouth 1, Prisoner of War #583. Captured by HM Brig *Reindeer*. When Taken: 3 Feb 1813. Where Taken: Bay of Biscayne. Prize Name: *Cashiere*. Home Port: Baltimore. Ship Type: Letter of Marque. Date Received: 23 Feb 1813. From what ship: HMS *Surveillante*. Discharged and was sent to Dartmoor on 2 Apr 1813. Prison Depot: Dartmoor, Prisoner of War #90. Date Received: 2 Apr 1813 from Plymouth. Discharged and was sent to Dartmouth on 30 Jul 1813. (Johnson's Database, 2019)

Cooper, James (African American), served as a Seaman and was born in Tolbert, MD. Age: 22. Prison Depot: Portsmouth, Prisoner of War #148. Captured by HM Brig *Recruit*. When Taken: 29 Aug 1812. Where Taken: at sea. Prize Name: *William*. Home Port: Baltimore. Ship Type: Merchant Vessel. Date Received: 29 Oct 1812. From what ship: HM Ship-of-the-Line *Ardent*. Discharged on 19 Feb 1813 and sent to Chatham on HM Store Ship *Dromedary*. Prison Depot: Chatham, Prisoner of War #518. Date Received: 23 Feb 1813 from Portsmouth on HMS *Dromedary*. Discharged on 8 Jun 1813 and released to the Cartel *Rodrigo*. (Johnson's Database, 2019)

Cooper, James, served as a Boy onboard a ship and was born in Maryland. Age: 19. Prison Depot: Dartmoor, Prisoner of War #3797. Captured by HM Sloop *Martin*. When Taken: 30 Apr 1814. Where Taken: off Cape Lopez. Prize Name: *Hannah*, prize of the Privateer *Pike*. Ship Type: Privateer. Date Received: 5 Oct 1814. From what ship: HMT *President* from Halifax, NS. Discharged on 9 Jun 1815. (Johnson's Database, 2019)

Cooper, John (African American), served as a Seaman and was born in Baltimore. Age: 33. Prison Depot: Dartmoor, Prisoner of War #2571. Captured by HM Frigate *Hyperion*. When Taken: 25 Jun 1814. Where Taken: off Cape Finisterre, Spain. Prize Name: *Rattlesnake*. Home Port: Philadelphia. Ship Type: Privateer. Date Received: 21 Aug 1814. From what ship: HMS *Hyperion*. Discharged on 3 May 1815. (Johnson's Database, 2019)

Cooper, Peter (Mulatto), served as a Seaman and was born in Baltimore. Age: 23. Prison Depot: Plymouth 2, Prisoner of War #274. Captured by HM Brig *Onyx*. When Taken: 25 Dec 1814. Where Taken: at sea. Prize Name: *Netterville*. Ship Type: Merchant Vessel. Date Received: 2 Mar 1815. From what ship: HMS *Dannemark*. Discharged on 3 Mar 1815 and sent to Dartmoor. Prison Depot: Dartmoor, Prisoner of War #6398. Received: 3 Mar 1815. From what ship: HMT *Ganges* from Plymouth. Discharged on 11 Jul 1815. (Johnson's Database, 2019)

Cooper, Tannick, served as a Seaman and was born in Baltimore. Age: 34. Prison Depot: Plymouth 1, Prisoner of War #2487. How Taken: Gave himself up. Date Received: 15 Mar 1814. From what ship: HMS *Salvador del Mundo*. Discharged on 10 May 1814 and sent to Dartmoor. Prison Depot: Dartmoor, Prisoner of War #1083. Date Received: 10 May 1814 from Plymouth. Discharged on 27 Apr 1815. (Johnson's Database, 2019)

Cooper, Thomas (Mulatto), served as a Seaman and was born in Maryland. Age: 26. Prison Depot: Chatham, Prisoner of War #3812. How Taken: Gave himself up off HM Frigate *Phoenix*. When Taken: 17 Jul 1813. Received: 13 Jun 1814. From what ship: *Quebec* (sic). Discharged on 25 Sep 1814 and sent to Dartmoor on HMS *Leyden*. Prison Depot: Dartmoor, Prisoner of War #4744. Date Received: 9 Oct 1814 on: HMT *Freya* from Chatham. Discharged on 14 Jun 1815. (Johnson's Database, 2019)

Cooper, William (1794-1815), served as a Private in Capt. Horatio Stark's Co., 1st U.S. Infantry, enlisted on 2 Jul 1812 at the age of 18, 5' 6¼" tall, born in Montgomery Co., MD and died at Sackett's Harbor, NY on 2 Feb 1815 of a natural death (BLW# 18440-160-12; Johnson and Christou, p. 74)

Copasses, Matthew (alias Cabristal), served as a Seaman and was born in Maryland. Age: 18. Prison Depot: Chatham, Prisoner of War #1228. Captured by HM Frigate *Dryad*. When Taken: 7 Jan 1813. Where Taken: at sea. Prize Name: *Rossie*. Ship Type: Merchant Vessel. Date Received: 16 Mar 1813 from Portsmouth on HMS *Abundance*. Discharged on 24 Jul 1813 and released to the Cartel *Hoffning*. (Johnson's Database, 2019)

Cope, Henry, served as a Private in Capt. Thomas Montgomery's Co., 14th U.S. Infantry, enlisted on 12 Jul 1812 at the age of 20, 5' 5½" tall, born in Germany; wounded at Beaver Dams, Upper Canada, ten miles west of Niagara Falls, on 24

Jun 1813 and was discharged at Greenbush, NY on 6 May 1815 on a Surgeon's Certificate (BLW# 17396-160-1; Johnson and Christou, p. 74)

Copeland, Samuel, served as a Private in Capt. Samuel Lane's Co., 14ᵗʰ U.S. Inf., enlisted 24 Jun 1812 at Williamsport, MD at the age of 32, 5' 9¾" tall, born in Ireland and was discharged at Plattsburgh, NY on 11 Jul 1814 for infirmities (Johnson and Christou, p. 74)

Cordery, William (1781-1814), served as a Private in the 38ᵗʰ U.S. Infantry (company not stated), enlisted on 17 Apr 1814 at the age of 33, 5' tall, born in Worcester Co., MD and died on 20 Apr 1814; bounty land to daughter Martha Maddox and other heirs (BLW# 25041-160-12; Johnson and Christou, p. 75)

Cord, Jacob, served as a Private in Capt. David Cummings' Co., 14ᵗʰ U.S. Inf., enlisted 24 Oct 1812 and was captured. Prisoner of War #3914 at Halifax, NS, interned 24 Jun 1813, discharged 19 Nov 1814 sent to England, was later released and reportedly deserted on 10 Apr 1815 at Baltimore (Johnson and Christou, p. 75, spelled his name Cords; Baker Vol. 1, p. 93 spelled it Cord) Jacob Cord served as a Private in 14ᵗʰ U.S. Infantry and was born in Maryland. Age: 21. Prison Depot: Chatham, Prisoner of War #3057. When Taken: 24 Jun 1813. Where Taken: Beaver Dams, Upper Canada. Date Received: 7 Jan 1814 from Halifax, NS. Discharged on 10 Oct 1814 and sent to U.S. on the Cartel *St. Philip*. (Johnson's Database, 2019)

Coren, Hugh, served as a Seaman and was born in Maryland. Age: 24. Prison Depot: Plymouth 2, Prisoner of War #20. How Taken: Gave himself up off MV *Brothers*. When Taken: 14 Jan 1815. Where Taken: Liverpool, UK. Date Received: 3 Feb 1815. From what ship: HMS *Bittern*. Discharged on 4 Feb 1815 and sent to Dartmoor. Prison Depot: Dartmoor, Prisoner of War #6256. Date Received: 4 Feb 1815. From what ship: HMT *Ganges*. Discharged on 5 Jul 1815. (Johnson's Database, 2019)

Cornelius, John (1783-1814), served as a Private in the 38ᵗʰ U.S. Infantry, enlisted 15 Jan 1814 in Baltimore at the age of 31, 5' 8½" tall, born in Franklin Co., PA and died on 9 Jul 1814; heirs received half pay for five years in lieu of bounty land (Johnson and Christou, p. 75; Old War Pension File WF-13400)

Cornish, Charles (1773-1814) (African American), served as a Seaman and was born in Maryland. Age: 40. Prison Depot: Plymouth 1, Prisoner of War #2117. Captured by HM Frigate *Hotspur* & HM Frigate *Pyramus*. When Taken: 26 Oct 1813. Where Taken: Bay of Biscayne. Prize Name: *Chesapeake*. Ship Type: Letter of Marque (Privateer). Date Received: 22 Nov 1813. From what ship: HMS *Pyramus*. Discharged on 29 Nov 1813 and sent to Dartmoor. Prisoner of War #838 at Dartmoor. Died 10 Jan 1814, cause not stated. (Centennial Trails, United

States Daughters of 1812, online at www.war1812trails.com/Dartmoor; Johnson's Database, 2019)

Costin, Dennis, served as a Private in Capt. William Littlejohn's Co., 2nd U.S. Light Dragoons, also served in a Corps of Artillery, enlisted on 24 Dec 1813 in Baltimore at the age of 25, 5' 3½" tall, born in Amsterdam, Holland, and was discharged on 1 May 1818 as unfit for service (Johnson and Christou, p. 75)

Cotterell, Henry C., served as a Master and was born in Baltimore. Age: 28. Prison Depot: Plymouth 1, Prisoner of War #2530. Captured by HM Transport *Hydra*. When Taken: 3 Apr 1814. Where Taken: at sea. Prize Name: *Young Dixon*. Ship Type: Merchant Vessel. Date Received: 7 Apr 1814. From what ship: HMS *Fly*. Discharged on 10 May 1814 and sent to Dartmoor. Prison Depot: Dartmoor, Prisoner of War #1129. Date Received: 10 May 1814 from Plymouth. Escaped on 8 Aug 1814. (Johnson's Database, 2019)

Couet, John, served as a Seaman and was born in Charles Co., MD. Age: 32. Prison Depot: Plymouth 1, Prisoner of War #218. Captured by HM Frigate *Phoebe*. When Taken: 1 Jan 1813. Where Taken: Lat 44.4 Long 23. Prize Name: *Vengeance*. Ship Type: Letter of Marque. Date Received: 9 Jan 1813. From what ship: HMS *Phoebe*. Discharged and sent to Portsmouth on 8 Feb 1813 on HMS *Colossus*. Prison Depot: Chatham, Prisoner of War #482. Date Received: 19 Feb 1813. From what ship: HMS Modeste. Discharged on 24 Jul 1813 and released to the Cartel *Hoffning*. (Johnson's Database, 2019)

Courtney, George, served as a Private in Capt. Thomas Montgomery's Co., 14th U.S. Infantry, enlisted 2 Apr 1812 in Baltimore at the age of 41, 5' 4" tall, born in Ireland, occupation blacksmith, was captured at Beaver Dams, Upper Canada on 24 Jun 1813. Prisoner of War #4188 at Halifax, NS, discharged 27 Aug 1813, sent to England and was discharged on 20 Apr 1814 on a Surgeon's Certificate (Johnson and Christou, p. 76; Baker Vol. 1, p. 95)

Covington, Leonard, served as Brigadier General of the 1st Light Dragoons of the U.S. Army, born Maryland; commissioned as a Cornet, Light Dragoons, on 14 Mar 1792; promoted to Lieutenant on 25 Oct 1792; promoted to Captain on 11 Jul 1794; resigned on 22 Sep 1795; commissioned as a Lieutenant Colonel, Light Dragoons, on 9 Jan 1809; promoted to Colonel on 15 Feb 18-- and died from wounds received during the Battle of Chrystler's Field on 11 Nov 1813 (Johnson and Christou, p. 76; Marine, p. 255, stated he died on 14 Nov 1813)

Cowan, Mr., served as 2nd Mate on the privateer *Surprise* of Baltimore and drowned in a shipwreck on 5 Apr 1815 (Marine p. 255; *Niles Weekly Register*, 15 Apr 1815)

Cowman, Philip (1783-1851), served as a Private in Capt. Jacob Franklin's Co., Anne Arundel Co. Militia, having volunteered at the Cross Roads around 1 Aug 1812, served for 8 days between 14 Apr and 15 May 1813 and 19 days between 2 Aug and 29 Aug 1813; he allegedly served in 1814 and was discharged for sickness one day before the Battle of Bladensburg, but no roster has been found to confirm any service in 1814 and he was also alleged to have been discharged at Bladensburg on 1 Nov 1814; his bounty land application was rejected in 1851 and also his widow's in 1855. Elizabeth Dashields married Philip Cowman in Anne Arundel Co. at Herring Bay on 16 Oct 1805 and he died at West River on 7 Aug 1851. (Wright Vol. 4, pp. 17, 75; BLW# 55-rej-80524)

Cox, Abraham (African American), served as a Seaman and was born in Maryland. Age: 25. Prison Depot: Chatham, Prisoner of War #2590. How Taken: Gave himself up off HM Brig *Scorpion*. When Taken: 27 May 1813. Date Received: 5 Nov 1813. From what ship: HMS *Hindostan*. Discharged on 12 Aug 1814 and sent to Dartmoor on HMS *Alpheus*. (Johnson's Database, 2019)

Cox, Daniel (African American), served as a Seaman and was born in Frederick, MD. Age: 38. Prison Depot: Portsmouth, Prisoner of War #467. Captured by HM Ship-of-the-Line *Elephant*. When Taken: 28 Dec 1812. Where Taken: off Azores. Prize Name: *Sword Fish*. Home Port: Gloucester. Ship Type: Privateer. Date Received: 14 Jan 1813. From what ship: HMS *Elephant*. Discharged on 11 Mar 1813 and sent to Chatham on HM Store Ship *Abundance*. Prison Depot: Chatham, Prisoner of War #1147. Date Received: 16 Mar 1813 from Portsmouth Mundane. Discharged on 24 Jul 1813 and released to the Cartel *Hoffning*. (Johnson's Database, 2019)

Cox, Clement or Clemson, was allegedly killed on 12 Sep 1814 at North Point. His name is on the Baltimore Battle Monument in error as no contemporary records have been found for him; allegedly a private in Capt. Haubert's Co., 51st Regiment, he may actually be the John Kempson Cox who was also known as Kempson Cox. (*Baltimore American*, 12 Jun 1819, spelled his name Clemson Cox and stated he was killed in defending Baltimore from the British attack)

Cox, John (1769-1858), served as a Private in Capt. John Bond's Co., 41st Regt., Baltimore Co., joined 29 Aug 1814, was stationed at Kelley's Field in Baltimore and was discharged by a Surgeon on 8 Sep 1814; bounty land was issued to Thaddeus C. S. Duncan on 1 Dec 1859 (BLW# 55-80-224842; Wright Vol. 2, p. 67). He was born 11 Feb 1769, died 13 May 1858 and was buried next to his wife Susannah Cole (1785-1867) in Grace Falls Road United Methodist Church Cemetery in Baltimore County. (Smith's Database, 2019; www.findagrave.com)

Cox, John Kempson, served as a Private in Capt. Haubert's Co., 51st Regt., and was killed in action on 12 Sep 1814 at North Point. His name is on the Baltimore

Battle Monument. (NARA; CMSR listed him as Kempson Cox and Kimson Cox; Wright Vol. 2, pp. 30, 35; *Baltimore American*, 12 Jun 1819, reported his name as John K. Cox); see Clement or Clemson Cox, q.v.

Cox, Jonathan, served as a Private in Capt. George Steever's Co., 27th Regiment, Baltimore Militia, and was allegedlykilled on 12 Sep 1814 at North Point. His name is <u>not</u> on the Baltimore Battle Monument. (Huntsberry, p. 96; Wright Vol. 2, p. 15, and Marine p. 255, both did not mention his death)

Cozens, George, served as a Private in Capt. Reuben Gilder's Co., 14th U.S. Inf., enlisted 24 Mar 1814 and discharged on 12 Jul 1814 on Surgeon's Certificate because of wounds, date and place not stated; heirs received half pay for five years in lieu of bounty land (Johnson and Christou, p. 77)

Crabtree, John, served as a Private in the 14th U.S. Infantry and was captured. Prisoner of War #3964 at Halifax, NS, interned 24 Jun 1813 and was discharged for exchange on 3 Feb 1814 (Johnson and Christou, p. 77; Baker Vol. 1, p. 96)

Crafus, Richard (African-American) (1791-c1835), was a Seaman who may have been from Vienna on Maryland's Eastern Shore, or Salem, MA; he arrived at Dartmoor Prison on 9 Oct 1814, age 23, 6'4" tall, physically powerful and a masterful bare-knuckle boxer; known as "King Dick" he quickly asserted control of the African-American prisoners in Barracks No. 4 and ruled with an iron fist; "he swaggered through the prison with a large club in his hand, followed by two white, good-looking 'white lads' whom he dressed in fine clothing. King Dick might have been something of a dictator, but Number 4 barracks was, by all accounts, the safest, cleanest and best-run barracks at Dartmoor." (War of 1812 online at www.pbs.org/wned/war-of-1812/ essays/prisoners-war) Some historians believe he went to Boston after his release in 1815, taught boxing, was an auxiliary police officer and died c1835. (Information from list online at newenglandhistoricalsociety.com/richard-crafus-black-captor-King-War-1812)

Craig, James, served as a Private in Capt. John McKane's Co., 27th Regiment, Baltimore Militia, from 19 Aug 1814 and was killed at North Point on 12 Sep 1814. Name is on the Baltimore Battle Monument. (NARA; CMSR; *Baltimore American*, 12 Jun 1819)

Craig, William, served as a Seaman and was born in Dorset [Dorchester Co.], MD. Age: 29. Prison Depot: Plymouth 1, Prisoner of War #2612. How Taken: Gave himself up off HM Frigate *Alcmene*. When Taken: 25 Jan 1813. Date Received: 16 May 1814. From what ship: HMS *Repulse*. Discharged on 14 Jun 1814 and sent to Dartmoor. Prison Depot: Dartmoor, Prisoner of War #1239. Date Received: 14 Jun 1814 from Mill Prison. Discharged on 26 Apr 1815. (Johnson's Database, 2019)

Crane(?), James, served as a Marine and was taken from the barracks and admitted to the Naval Hospital in Washington, DC as Patient No. 72 on 14 Oct 1814 (injury or illness was not specified) and was discharged on 23 --- [illegible] 1814 and sent to the barracks (Sharp's Database, 2018)

Crane, Philip, served as a Corporal in Capt. Ezekiel F. Chambers' Co., 21st Regt., Kent County Militia, and was wounded at Caulk's Field on 31 Aug 1814. An entry on the muster roll dated 11 Sep – 23 Sep 1814 stated: "Sergeant John Magnor and Corporal Philip Crane who are both returned in this roll in pursuance to the directions of the commander of the Regiment were wounded in an action with the enemy in August last and have not been able to shoulder a musket since that period not being present in camp no rations were drawn for them of course." "Philip Crane, corporal, a ball between the tendons and the bone of the thigh near the knee" (Baltimore Patriot 9/22/1814, Wright Vol. 1, p. 24; Marine pp.120, 256)

Cranny, Edward, served as a Private in the 14th U.S. Infantry and was captured. Prisoner of War #168 at Halifax, NS, interned 24 Jun 1813 and discharged on 27 Aug 1814 and sent to England (Johnson and Christou, p. 78; Baker Vol. 1, p. 97)

Crasser, Jacob (1791-1813), served as a Private in Capt. Asabeal Nearing's Co., 19th U.S. Infantry, enlisted 7 Jul 1812 in Warren, Trumbull Co., OH, at the age of 21, 5' 8½' tall, was born in Maryland and died in October 1813; bounty land issued to Henry Crasser, his father and only heir at law (BLW# 25408-160-12; Johnson and Christou, p. 78)

Craventon, George, served as a Private in 14th U.S. Infantry and was captured. Prisoner of War #4010 at Halifax, NS, interned 24 Jun 1813 and was discharged for exchange on 3 Feb 1814 (Johnson and Christou, p. 78; Baker Vol. 1, p. 97)

Crea, Hugh, served as a Private in Capt. Peter Galt's Co., 6th Regt., Baltimore City Militia,from 19 Aug 1814 and died on 13 Sep 1814 (Wright Vol. 2, p. 11)

Crea, Hugh, served as a 2nd Gunner on board the privateer (armed brigantine) *Chausseur* of Baltimore commanded by Capt. Thomas Boyle and was reported killed in action on 26 Feb 1815 (*Niles Weekly Register*, 25 Mar 1815)

Creak, George, served as a Private in Capt. George Flautt's Rifle Co., Frederick Co., from 29 Apr 1813 and died on 30 May 1813 (Mallick and Wright, p. 87)

Creback, Joseph, served as a Private in Capt. James Haslett's Co., 38th U.S. Inf., enlisted 28 May 1813 and died on 9 Sep 1813 (Johnson and Christou, p. 79)

Cremer, David (1782-1812), served as a Private in Capt. Samuel Lane's Co., 14th U.S. Infantry, enlisted 27 May 1812 at the age of 30, 5' 9" tall, born in Baltimore and was killed by accident on 1 Dec 1812 at Conjocta Creek, NY; heirs received half pay for 5 years in lieu of bounty land (Johnson and Christou, p. 79)

Creswell, Hartford, served as a Private in Capt. John Rothrock's Co., 38th U.S. Inf., enlisted 28 May 1813 and died 22 Jan 1814 (Johnson and Christou, p. 79)

Cretzer, John, served as a Private in Capt. Berry's Artillery Co. and was slightly wounded on 13 Sep 1814 at Fort McHenry (Marine pp. 173, 257)

Crevisten, George (c1784-1855), served as a Private in the U.S. Light Dragoons under Lt. Col. Charles C. Boerstler and was wounded at Beaver Dams, Upper Canada, ten miles west of Niagara Falls, on 24 Jun 1813; born in Pennsylvania and later a resident of Harford County, he was also blacksmith for the troops, was taken prisoner and released after a short captivity. ("Harford County in the War of 1812," by Christopher T. George, *Harford Historical Bulletin* No. 76, Spring 1998, p. 19, citing *Encyclopedia of the War of 1812*, by Heidler and Heidler, pp. 45-46, 58-59). George Cravertson, Prisoner of War #792, taken on 26 Jun 1813 at Beaver Dams, received into custody on 7 Jul 1813 on the ship HM Steamboat *Malpomena* and discharged on 10 Aug 1813. (Johnson, p. 33) George Creviston or Crevenston married Martha Greenfield on 21 Apr 1818 and resided in Aberdeen, Harford Co., MD. (*Baltimore American*, 27 Apr 1818)

Crisher, Conrod, served as a Private in Capt. George Washington Magee's Co., Frederick Co. Militia, 1st Regiment, joined 22 Jul 1814, engaged in the Battle of Bladensburg and in the defense of Baltimore and on the muster roll dated 14 Oct 1814 – 10 Jan 1815 was reported "sick last muster, furloughed 15 days" (Mallick and Wright, p. 343)

Cromwell, Glacio (African American), served as a Seaman and was born in Baltimore. Age: 23. Prison Depot: Chatham, Prisoner of War #1584. How Taken: Gave himself up off HM Ship-of-the-Line *Christian VII*. When Taken: 21 Dec 1812. Date Received: 18 Apr 1813. From what ship: HMS *Rosario*. Discharged on 11 Apr 1814 and sent to Dartmoor. Prison Depot: Dartmoor, Prisoner of War #2622. Date Received: 21 Aug 1814. From what ship: HMT *Freya* from Chatham. Discharged on 26 Apr 1815. (Johnson's Database, 2019)

Cross, Jeremiah, served as a Private in Capt Henry Woodward's Co., Major Hammond's Battalion, for 7 days and was released by the physician on 15 Aug 1813; he was back in the service in 1st Lt. John Thomas 3rd Co., 32nd Regiment, Anne Arundel Co. Militia, from 24 Aug 1814 and was discharged by a Surgeon on 12 Sep 1814 as reported on the muster roll dated 24 Aug – 27 Sep 1814. (Wright Vol. 4, pp. 34, 43)

Cross, Middleton (1783-1815), served as a Sergeant in the 36th U.S. Infantry, enlisted 26 Jan 1815 at the age of 32, 6' 2¼" tall, born Maryland and died on 28

Feb 1815; bounty land issued to Mary Barkley, daughter, and other heirs of William Cross, his father (BLW# 1068-320-14; Johnson and Christou, p. 81)

Crow, James, served as a Sergeant in Capt. John Mowton's Co. of the 38th U.S. Infantry, enlisted 8 Jun 1813 for one year, re-enlisted 8 Mar 1814 and died on 5 Feb 1815 at Craney Island, VA; bounty land issued to Owen Crow, brother, and other heirs (BLW# 25521-160-12; Johnson and Christou, p. 82)

Crow, John, served as a Seaman and was born in Baltimore. Age: 27. Prison Depot: Portsmouth, Prisoner of War #1370. How Taken: Gave himself up off HM Transport *William Pitt No. 421*. Date Received: 4 Feb 1814. From what ship: HM Frigate *Bombay*. Discharged on 13 Feb 1814 and sent to Chatham on HMT *Malabar No. 352*. Age: 21 (sic). Prison Depot: Chatham, Prisoner of War #3524. Date Received: 23 Feb 1814 from Portsmouth on HMT *Malabar*. Discharged on 21 Jul 1814 and sent to Dartmoor on HMS *Portia*. Prison Depot: Dartmoor, Prisoner of War #1890. Date Received: 29 Jul 1814. Age 23 (sic). From what ship: HMS *Ville de Paris* from Chatham Depot. Discharged on 3 May 1815. (Johnson's Database, 2019)

Crowl, George, served as a Private in Capt. George Shryock's Co., Hagerstown, Washington Co. Militia, from 23 Jul 1814 and died on 31 Dec 1814 as reported on the muster roll dated 23 Jul 1814 – 10 Jan 1815 (Wright Vol. 9, p. 7)

Cullum, Jesse, served as a Private in the 40th Regiment, drafted on 10 Jul 1812 (company and dates of service were not stated) and was a Private in Capt. Henry P. Ruff's Co., 42nd Regiment, Harford Co. Militia, from 30 Apr 1813 and became an invalid, but the medical reason was not stated, and was discharged as unfit for duty on 4 Aug 1813. (Wright Vol. 3, p. 3 spelled his name Cullum, and p. 25 spelled his name Cullom) Jesse Cullum and Susanna Jones obtained a marriage license on 25 Jun 1801 (Harford Co. marriage record spelled his name Culham) Four children of Jesse and Susanna Colum (sic) were baptized on 14 Oct 1821, namely, Sarah age 9, Jesse age 7, Walter age 5 and Elizabeth age 4. (*St. Ignatius, Hickory, And Its Missions*, by Clarence V. Joerndt, 1972, p. 101)

Culpepper, Thomas C. (c1788-1826), served as a Private in Capt. Charles Gantt's Co., 31st Regt., Calvert Co. Militia, from 20 Aug to 24 Aug 1813 and was stationed at Drum Point and served between 18 Jul and 23 Jul 1814 in Capt. Joseph Griffiss' Co.; his widow Barbary J. Culpepper claimed he served in Capt. Stephen Johns' Co. and was engaged in the Battle of St. Leonard's Creek with Commodore Barney in the land service; he was taken prisoner by the English and kept in confinement for two weeks on board an English ship; her claim for bounty land was rejected (Wright Vol. 4, pp. 56, 77; BLW# 55-rej-113161)

Cumming, Robert, served as Major General, 1st Division of Militia, St. Mary's and Charles Cos., commissioned 9 Dec 1812 and later died, date and cause not stated (Wright Vol. 5, p. 10, but Vol. 7, p. 1, questionably listed service in 1813)

Cunning, John, served as a Private in Capt. Thomas Montgomery's Co., 14th U.S. Infantry, enlisted on 25 May 1812 for 5 years and died at Black Rock, NY on 28 Dec 1812; bounty land issued to is brother Barney Cunning and other heirs at law (BLW# 25482-160-12; Johnson and Christou, p. 83)

Cunningham, Kelly, served as a Private in 14th U.S. Infantry (company not stated) and was captured. Prisoner of War #3848 at Halifax, NS, interned 24 Jun 1813 and was discharged on 19 Nov 1813 and sent to England (Johnson and Christou, p. 83; Baker Vol. 1, p. 101, misspelled his first as Kellip)

Curtis, George, served as a Sergeant in Capt. Samuel Lane's Co., 14th U.S. Infantry, enlisted on 11 Jan 1812 for 18 months and died at Lewiston, NY from neck wounds received on 24 Jun 1813 at Beaver Dams, Upper Canada (Johnson and Christou, p. 84)

Curtis, Uria, served as a Private in the 14th U.S. Infantry and was later captured. Prisoner of War #4042 at Halifax, NS, interned 24 Jun 1813 and was discharged for exchange on 3 Feb 1814 (Johnson and Christou, p. 84; Baker Vol. 1, p. 102)

Curtis, William, served as a Boatswain and was born in Baltimore. Age: 38. Prison Depot: Dartmoor, Prisoner of War #4018. Captured by HM Ship-of-the-Line *Leander*. When Taken: 22 Jun 1814. Where Taken: off Cape Sable, NS. Prize Name: U.S. Brig *Rattlesnake*. Ship Type: Warship. Date Received: 6 Oct 1814. From what ship: HMT *Chesapeake* from Halifax, NS. Discharged on 9 Jun 1815. (Johnson's Database, 2019)

D

Dailey, Elijah, served as a Private in Capt. Joseph K. Stapleton's Co., 39th Regt. (Fowler's) Maryland Militia, Baltimore Militia, from 19 Aug 1814 and on 12 Sep 1814 he was wounded at the Battle of North Point by a musket ball in his right eye that remained in his head and which caused him the loss of his eye; a pension was granted on 17 May 1817, starting 20 Nov 1814, and he was living in Kent Co., MD in 1852. (BLW# 55-120-12614; Wright Vol. 2, p. 26) The will of Elijah Dailey, of Chestertown, was written on 20 May 1848 and proved on 26 Aug 1856. (*Abstracts of Kent County, Maryland Wills, Volume 2, 1816-1867*, by Christos Christou, Jr. and John Anthony Barnhouser, 1997, p.221)

Daily, William, served as a Private in Capt. Thomas Lawrence's Co., 22nd U.S. Infantry, enlisted 18 Feb 1813 for 5 years at the age of 36, 5' 9" tall, born in Maryland, and discharged at Pittsburgh on 10 Oct 1813 for a rupture (Johnson and Christou, p. 85)

Dairs, William, served as a Seaman and was born in Baltimore. Age: 26. Prison Depot: Portsmouth, Prisoner of War #638. How Taken: Gave himself up off HM Guard Ship *Royal William*. Date Received: 3 Feb 1813 on HMS *Royal William*. Discharged on 11 Mar 1813 and sent to Chatham on HM Store Ship *Abundance*. Prison Depot: Chatham, Prisoner of War #1304. Age 36 (sic). Date Received: 16 Mar 1813 from Portsmouth on HMS *Abundance*. Discharged on 23 Jul 1814 and sent to Dartmoor. (Johnson's Database, 2019)

Dalck, Andrew, served as 1st Corporal in Capt. John Hanna's Co., 5th Cavalry Regt., Baltimore City, and had one horse killedand a finger broken on 26 Aug 1814 (Wright, Vol. 2, p. 55; Marine, p. 260 listed him as a Corporal in Capt. Hanna's Co., Fells Point Light Dragoons, but did not mention his injury)

Dale, John, served as a Seaman and was born in Baltimore. Age: 25. Prison Depot: Dartmoor, Prisoner of War #4859. Captured by HM Brig *Sophie*. When Taken: 28 Mar 1814. Where Taken: West Indies. Prize Name: *Amelie*. Prize. Ship Type: Letter of Marque. Date Received: 9 Oct 1814. From what ship: HMT *Freya* from Halifax, NS. Discharged on 21 Jun 1815. (Johnson's Database, 2019)

Dallison, James (African American), served as a Seaman and was born in Baltimore. Age: 20. Prison Depot: Dartmoor, Prisoner of War #3906. Captured by HM Frigate *Loire*. When Taken: 10 Jul 1814. Where Taken: Chesapeake Bay. Prize Name: *Emeline*. Ship Type: Merchant Vessel. Date Received: 5 Oct 1814. From what ship: HMT *Orpheus* from Halifax, NS. Discharged on 9 Jun 1815. (Johnson's Database, 2019)

Dalmark, William, served as a Seaman and was born in Baltimore. Age: 32. Prison Depot: Dartmoor, Prisoner of War #2159. Captured by HM Frigate *Hyperion*. When Taken: 26 Jun 1814. Where Taken: off Cape Finisterre, Spain. Prize Name: *Rattlesnake*. Home Port: Philadelphia. Ship Type: Privateer. Date Received: 16 Aug 1814. From what ship: HMS *Dublin* from Halifax, NS. Discharged on 2 May 1815. (Johnson's Database, 2019)

Daniels, John (Mulatto), served as a Seaman and was born in Baltimore. Age: 45. Prison Depot: Plymouth 1, Prisoner of War #1924. Captured by HM Frigate *Leonidas*. When Taken: 12 Aug 1813. Where Taken: English Channel. Prize Name: sloop *Dianna & Betsey*, prize of the U.S. Brig *Argus*. Ship Type: Warship. Received: 23 Aug 1813 on HMS *Pelican*. Discharged on 8 Sep 1813 and sent to Dartmoor. Prison Depot: Dartmoor, Prisoner of War #646. Age 19(?). Received: 8 Sep 1813 from Plymouth. Discharged and sent to Mill Prison on 10 Jul (sic) 1813. (Johnson's Database, 2019)

Daniels, Peter, served as a Seaman on the privateer *Surprise* of Baltimore and drowned in a shipwreck on 5 Apr 1815 (Marine p. 261; *Niles Weekly Register*, 15 Apr 1815)

Dandsey, Hiram, from the *Ontario*, served as an Ordinary Seaman with the U.S. Chesapeake Flotilla, entered service on 15 Mar 1814 and was killed at the Battle of Bladensburg on 24 Aug 1814 (Shomette, p. 382; Sheads, p. 22)

Darby, Joseph (1779-1815), served as a Seaman and was born in Baltimore. Age: 35. Prison Depot: Bermuda, Prisoner of War #2033. Captured by HM Frigate *Severn*. When Taken: 22 Oct 1814. Where Taken: St. Georges. Prize Name: *Commodore Evans*. Ship Type: Merchant Vessel. Died on 29 Mar 1815 from consumption (tuberculosis). (Johnson's Database, 2019)

Dashiel, Richard, served as a Midshipman and was born in Queen Anne's Co., MD. Age: 24. Prison Depot: Dartmoor, Prisoner of War #4074. Captured by HM Frigate *Belvidera*. When Taken: 21 Apr 1813. Where Taken: off Delaware. Prize Name: *New Zealander* (whaler), prize of the U.S. Frigate *Essex*. Ship Type: Warship. Date Received: 6 Oct 1814. From what ship: HMT *Chesapeake* from Halifax, NS. Discharged and sent on 29 Nov 1814 to Ashburton on parole. (Johnson's Database, 2019)

Dashell, Levi (1788-1815), served as a Private in Capt. Charles Stansbury's Co., 38th U.S. Infantry, enlisted 24 May 1814 at the age of 26, 5' 8½" tall, born in Somerset Co., MD and died on 12 Feb 1815, but the place of death and medical reasons were not given; heirs received half pay for 5 years in lieu of bounty land (Johnson and Christou, p. 86)

Dashield, Peter, served as a Private in Capt. Kenneth McKenzie's Co., 14th U.S. Infantry, enlisted on 25 Oct 1812 and was later captured. Prisoner of War at Quebec and died there on 13 Oct 1813 (Johnson and Christou, p. 86; *American Prisoners of War Held in Quebec during the War of 1812*, by Eric Eugene Johnson, did not mention him, but cites Pvt. Peter Desheates, Prisoner of War #809, interned on 7 Jul 1813. Peter Desheates was probably Peter Dashield.)

David, Charles, served as a Seaman with the U.S. Chesapeake Flotilla under Comm. Barney, became sick with fever, was admitted to the Naval Hospital in Washington, DC as Patient No. 6 on 24 Aug 1814 and was discharged from the hospital on 4 Sep 1814 (Sharp's Database, 2018)

David, Elijah T. (1773-1812), served as a Private in Capt. John Stanard's Co., 20th U.S. Infantry, enlisted 21 Jul 1812 at the age of 39, 5' 7" tall, born in Prince George's Co., MD and died at Buffalo, NY on 3 Nov 1812, medical reasons not given (Johnson and Christou, p. 86)

David, John, served as a Private in the 14th U.S. Infantry (company not stated) and was later captured, probably at Beaver Dams, Upper Canada. Prisoner of War #4152 at Halifax, NS, interned 24 Jun 1813, discharged 24 Aug 1813 and sent to England (Johnson and Christou, p. 86; Baker Vol. 1, p. 105)

Davids, Thomas, served as a Mate and was born in Baltimore. Age: 29. Prison Depot: Plymouth 1, Prisoner of War #341. Captured by HM Sloop *Helena*. When Taken: 31 Dec 1813. Where Taken: off Western Islands, Scotland. Prize Name: *Postsea*, prize of the Privateer *Thrasher*. Ship Type: Privateer. Date Received: 22 Jan 1813. From what ship: HMS *Helena*. Discharged and sent to Chatham on 29 Mar 1813 on HMS *Braham*. (Johnson's Database, 2019)

Davidson, Henry, served as a Seaman and was born in Maryland. Age: 50. Prison Depot: Dartmoor, Prisoner of War #353. Captured by HM Frigate *Magiciene*. When Taken: 17 Jan 1813. Where Taken: off Western Islands, Scotland. Prize Name: *Thrasher*. Home Port: Gloucester. Ship Type: Privateer. Date Received: 1 Jul 1813 from Plymouth. Discharged and sent to Dartmouth on 30 Jul 1813. (Johnson's Database, 2019)

Davidson, James, served as a Private in Capt. John Montgomery's 1st Artillery Co., joined Aug 25 1814, wounded 12 Sep 1814 at North Point and was on the Prisoner of War list of those exchanged with the British. Dr. James H. McCulloh, Jr. wrote this soon after the battle to the British commander: "In consequence of the humanity shown the following American prisoners of war, I do promise upon honor that they shall not directly or indirectly serve against the British until regularly exchanged." (Wright Vol. 2, p. 46, Marine p. 171)

Davidson, John, served as a Private in Capt. Thomas Montgomery's Co., 14th U.S. Infantry, enlisted 24 Jul 1812 in Baltimore at the age of 29, 5' 4" tall, and was captured at Beaver Dams, Upper Canada on 24 Jun 1813. Prisoner of War #3776 at Halifax, NS, discharged for exchange on 3 Feb 1814, exchanged on 15 Apr 1814, returned to service and was discharged at Fort Hawkins, GA on 24 Jul 1817 (Johnson and Christou, p. 87; Baker Vol. 1, p. 105)

Davidson, Thomas, served as a Mate and was born in Baltimore. Age: 29. Prison Depot: Chatham, Prisoner of War #1418. Captured by HM Sloop *Helena*. When Taken: 31 Dec 1813. Where Taken: off Azores. Prize Name: *Postsea*, prize of the Privateer *Thrasher*. Ship Type: Privateer. Date Received: 5 Apr 1813 from Plymouth on HMS *Dwarf*. Discharged on 24 Jul 1813 and released to the Cartel *Hoffning*. (Johnson's Database, 2019)

Davis, Benjamin, served as a Private in the 14th U.S. Infantry and was captured. Prisoner of War #3865 at Halifax, NS, interned 6 Jun 1813 and was discharged for exchange on 3 Feb 1814 (Johnson and Christou, p. 86; Baker Vol. 1, p. 105)

Davis, Charles S., served as a Surgeon and was born in Baltimore. Age: 19. Prison Depot: Plymouth 1, Prisoner of War #2328. Captured by HM Brig *Pelican*. When Taken: 13 Jan 1814. Where Taken: at sea. Prize Name: *Siro*. Home Port: Baltimore. Ship Type: Letter of Marque. Date Received: 27 Jan 1814. From what ship: HMS *Pelican*. Discharged on 27 Jan 1814 and sent to Ashburton on parole. (Johnson's Database, 2019)

Davis, David (1788-1814), served as a Private in Capt. Christian Adreon's Co., 5th Regiment, Baltimore Militia, joined 27 Aug 1814 and died on 10 Oct 1814 from wounds received at Patapsco Neck. He is listed as a prisoner of war taken by the British. (Wright Vol. 2, p. 3; NARA; CMSR; Marine p. 171; Marine, p. 171; *Baltimore American*, 12 Jun 1819)Name is on the Baltimore Battle Monument. The David Davis history posted 4 Sep 2011 on Ancestry.com by Chuck Nelson cited *From Fletcher B. Speed Jr.'s Notes*: "Born in England. Came to Baltimore as a young man (through the port of New York). Was married to Esther Ellis, who was born in Wales. Was a barrister at the time he came here. Wounded at the Battle of North Point on Sept 12, 1814 and died of his wounds on Oct 10, 1814.

He left his wife and infant daughter, Mary Ellis Davis, who was born Aug. 27, 1814." Dr. James H. McCulloh, Jr. wrote this note soon after the battle to the British commander: "In consequence of the humanity shown the following American prisoners of war, I do promise upon honor that they shall not directly or indirectly serve against the British until regularly exchanged." (Marine p. 171). David Davies and Esther Evans were married in Baltimore on 29 Apr 1813. (*Methodist Records of Baltimore City, Maryland, Volume I, 1799-1829*, by Henry C. Peden, Jr., 1994, p. 33). Chuck Nelson posted David Davis' portrait online at Ancestry.com as shown above.

Davis, Ezra, served as a Private in the 14th U.S. Infantry and was later captured. Prisoner of War #4042 at Halifax, NS, interned 24 Jun 1813 and was discharged for exchange on 3 Feb 1814 (Johnson and Christou, p. 88; Baker Vol. 1, p. 105)

Davis, Hugh, served as a Private in Capt. Henry Grindage's Co., 14th U.S. Inf., enlisted at Nottingham, MD on 25 Aug 1812 for 5 years at the advanced age of 55, 5' 5¼" tall, born in Ireland or Wales. Prisoner of War #4024 at Halifax, NS, interned 24 Jun 1813, discharged for exchange on 3 Feb 1814, was returned to service and discharged on 10 Apr 1815 at Greenbush, NY for age and disability (Johnson and Christou, p. 88; Baker Vol. 1, p. 106)

Davis, Jacob (1789-1812), served as a Private in Capt. Samuel Lane's Co. of the 14th U.S. Infantry, enlisted on 13 Jun 1812 in Cumberland, MD, age 23, born in Jersey and died at Black Rock, NY on 5 Dec 1812; bounty land was issued to John Davis and other heirs (BLW# 23542-160-12; Johnson and Christou, p. 88)

Davis (Dawes?), James, served as a Private in the 36th U.S. Infantry, enlisted by Capt. Nelson on 23 Nov 1814 at Norfolk, VA, age 24, 6' 1" or 1½" tall, born at Middletown, Frederick Co., MD, "absent sick at Norfolk" and discharged on 13 Mar 1815 (Mallick and Wright, p. 95)

Davis, John (African American), served as a Seaman and was born in Baltimore. Age: 35. Prison Depot: Dartmoor, Prisoner of War#3483. How Taken: Gave himself up off HM Ship-of-the-Line *Prince*. When Taken: 14 Sep 1814. Date Received: 19 Sep 1814. From what ship: HMT *Salvador del Mundo*. Discharged on 4 Jun 1815. (Johnson's Database, 2019)

Davis, John, served as a Private in Capt. Joseph Marshall's Co., 14th U.S. Infantry, and was captured, but the date and place were not stated, probably Beaver Dams, Upper Canada. Prisoner of War #3903 at Halifax, NS, interned on 24 Jun 1813 and died of pneumonia on 25 Dec 1813 (Johnson and Christou, p. 88; Baker, Vol. 1, p. 107; BLW# 438-160-12)

Davis, John, served as a Private in the 14th U.S. Infantry and was captured on 24 Jun 1813, but the date and place were not stated, probably Beaver Dams, Upper Canada. Prisoner of War #3790 at Halifax, NS, interned 24 Jun 1813, discharged 19 Nov 1813 and sent to England, later released and discharged from service on 31 Mar 1815 (Johnson and Christou, p. 88; Baker Vol. 1, p. 106; Johnson's Database, 2019, did not list him)

Davis, John, served as a Private in Capt. Samuel Dawson's Co., Frederick Co. Militia, from 26 Jul 1814, engaged in the Battle of Bladensburg on 24 Aug 1814 and in the defense of Baltimore City on 12 Sep 1814 and was reported sick in Baltimore, but the date was not given (Mallick and Wright, pp. 93, 338)

Davis, John, served as a Private in Capt. Frederick Evans' Co., 2nd U.S. Artillery, enlisted 12 Feb 1814 at Columbia, PA, age 32, 5' 10½" tall, born in Maryland and discharged on 22 Apr 1815 because of pulmonary consumption (Johnson and Christou, p. 89)

Davis, John, served as a Seaman and was born in Maryland. Age: 29. Prison Depot: Chatham, Prisoner of War #2520. Captured by HM Frigate *Maidstone* & HM Brig *Nimrod*. When Taken: 17 Jul 1813. Where Taken: Grand Banks. Prize Name: *Yorktown*. Home Port: New York. Ship Type: Privateer. Date Received: 22 Oct 1813 from Portsmouth on HMT *Malabar*. Discharged on 8 Sep 1814 and sent to Dartmoor on HMS *Niobe*. Prison Depot: Dartmoor, Prisoner of War #3322. Date Received: 13 Sep 1814 on HMT *Niobe* from Chatham. Discharged on 28 May 1815. (Johnson's Database, 2019)

Davis, John, served as a Seaman and was born in Baltimore. Age: 32. Prison Depot: Dartmoor, Prisoner of War #4979. Captured by HM Frigate *Armide*. When Taken: 16 Aug 1814. Where Taken: off Nantucket, MA. Prize Name: *Invincible*. Home Port: Salem. Ship Type: Letter of Marque. Date Received: 28 Oct 1814. From what ship: HMT *Alkbar* from Halifax, NS. Discharged on 21 Jun 1815. (Johnson's Database, 2019)

Davis, John, served as a Boatswain and was born in Baltimore. Age: 48. Prison Depot: Dartmoor, Prisoner of War #3562. Captured by HM Frigate *Piqua*. When Taken: 26 Apr 1814. Where Taken: near Mona Passage, West Indies. Prize Name: *Hawk*. Home Port: Wilmington. Ship Type: Privateer. Date Received: 30 Sep 1814. From what ship: HMT *Sybella*. Discharged on 4 Jun 1815. (Johnson's Database, 2019)

Davis, John, served as a Seaman and was born in Baltimore. Age: 30. Prison Depot: Dartmoor, Prisoner of War #4890. How Taken: Gave himself up off HM Brig *Vestal*. When Taken: Jul 1814. Received: 24 Oct 1814. From what ship: HMT *Salvador del Mundo*. Discharged 21 Jun 1815. (Johnson's Database, 2019)

Davis, Joseph, served as a Seaman and was born in Baltimore. Age: 21. Prison Depot: Dartmoor, Prisoner of War #6252. How Taken: Gave himself up off MV *Kulabra*. When Taken: 25 Nov 1814. Received: 4 Feb 1815. From what ship: HMT *Ganges*. Discharged on 11 Jul 1815. (Johnson's Database, 2019)

Davis, Joseph, served as a Private in Capt. Denton Darby's Co., Frederick Co. Militia, joined 3 Aug 1814 and drowned on 16 Aug 1814, but the place was not stated (Mallick and Wright, pp. 94, 348)

Davis, Nathaniel, served as a Private in Capt. John Stanard's Co., 20th U.S. Infantry, also served in the U.S. Artificers, enlisted in Washington, DC on 5 Sep 1812, age 42, 5' 8" tall, born in Prince George's Co., and discharged on 14 Mar 1814 because of a rupture (Johnson and Christou, p. 89; BLW# 10877-160-12)

Davis, Peter L., served as a Private in Capt. Neale's Co., 36th U.S. Infantry, was wounded on 24 Aug 1814 on the field of battle at Bladensburg, was admitted to the Naval Hospital in Washington, DC as Patient No. 19, was discharged on 5 Sep 1814 and sent to the U.S. Hospital (Sharp's Database, 2018)

Davis, Robert (1775-1813), served as a Private in Capt. Kenneth McKenzie's Co., 14th U.S. Infantry, enlisted 17 Oct 1812 at the age of 37, 5' 4" tall, born in Baltimore and discharged at Greenbush, NY on 24 May 1815 on a Surgeon's Certificate, having been wounded in the arm at Beaver Dams, Upper Canada, ten miles west of Niagara Falls, on 24 Jun 1813 (BLW# 6849-160-12; Johnson and Christou, p. 89)

Davis, Shaddock, served as a Private in 14th U.S. Infantry (company not stated) and was later captured. Prisoner of War #3846 at Halifax, NS, interned 24 Jun 1813 and died there on 15 Sep 1813 of dysentery (Johnson and Christou, p. 90; Baker, Vol. 1, p. 108)

Davis, Thomas, served as a Seaman on the privateer *Chasseur* of Baltimore under Capt. Thomas Boyle and was severely wounded in action with HM Schooner *Lawrence* on 26 Feb or 27 Feb 1815 (Marine p. 263, stated it was 27 Feb 1815, but *Niles Weekly Register*, 25 Mar 1815, reported it was 26 Feb 1815)

Davis, Thomas, served as a Private in 14th U.S. Infantry (company not stated), enlisted on 13 Jul 1812 and was captured at Beaver Dams, Upper Canada on 24 Jun 1813. Prisoner of War #3771 at Halifax, NS, interned 24 Jun 1813, and discharged on 9 Nov 1813, sent to England, later released and discharged from the service on 31 Mar 1815 (Johnson and Christou, p. 90; Baker Vol. 1, p. 108)

Davis, William, served as a Private in Capt. John McChesney's Co., 6th U.S. Infantry, enlisted for 5 years at the age of 22, 5' 7½" tall, was born in Snow Hill, MD, was captured at Queenstown, Upper Canada. Prisoner of War, paroled on 25 Mar 1813 and discharged at Greenbush, NY on 19 Jul 1814 (Johnson and Christou, p. 90)

Davis, William, of Maryland, served as a Seaman on the ship *Desiree* and was reported by Capt. Jeduthan Upton, Jr. in 1814 as having been impressed into service and was a Prisoner of War on the prison ship *San Antonio* at Chatham, England (*Niles Weekly Register*, 26 Feb 1814), William Davis served as a Seaman and was born in Baltimore. Prison Depot: Dartmoor, Prisoner of War #1932. Age: 36. How Taken: Gave himself up off HM Frigate *Desiree*. When Taken: 8 Jan 1814. Date Received: 3 Aug 1814. From what ship: HMS *Alceste* from Chatham Depot. Discharged on 26 Apr 1815. (Johnson's Database, 2019)

Davison, Henry, served as a ship's Carpenter and was born in Maryland. Age: 50. Prison Depot: Plymouth 1, Prisoner of War #1013. Captured by HM Frigate *Magiciene* on 17 Jan 1813. Where Taken: off Western Islands, Scotland. Prize Name: *Thrasher*. Home Port: Gloucester. Ship Type: Privateer. Received: 20 Apr

1813. From what ship: HMS *Libria*. Discharged and sent to Dartmoor on 1 Jul 1813. (Johnson's Database, 2019)

Dawes (Davis?), James, served as a Private in the 36th U.S. Infantry, enlisted by Capt. Nelson on 23 Nov 1814 at Norfolk, VA, age 24, 6' 1" or 1½" tall, born at Middletown, Frederick Co., MD, "absent sick at Norfolk" and discharged on 13 Mar 1815 (Mallick and Wright, p. 95)

Daws, William H. (c1790-1812), served as a Private in Capt. Robert Kent's Co., 14th U.S. Infantry, enlisted 2 Jul 1812 and died on 25 Nov 1812 (BLW# 16685-160-12; Johnson and Christou, p. 91)

Dawson, Nicholas L., served as Paymaster in Cecil Co.'s 49th Militia Regiment, appointed on 4 Jul 1812 and listed as dead, but no date was given and cause was not stated, yet he was still serving as Paymaster under Major W. Boulden on 18 Apr 1813 (Wright Vol. 3, pp. 7, 12)

De Grot, John, served as a Private (company not stated) and was captured at the Battle of Bladensburg on 24 Aug 1814 (Marine, p. 174)

De Krafft, Edward, served as a Private (company not stated) and was captured at the Battle of Bladensburg on 24 Aug 1814 (Marine, p. 174)

De Noon, Charles, served as a Private in 14th U.S. Infantry (company not stated) and was captured, probably at Beaver Dams, Upper Canada. Prisoner of War #4806 at Halifax, NS, interned 24 Jun 1813, discharged on 27 Aug 1814 and sent to England (Johnson and Christou, p. 92; Baker Vol. 1, p. 110)

Deamer, John (1792-1814), served as a Private in Capt. Reuben Gilder's Co., 14th U.S. Infantry, enlisted 10 Mar 1814 at the age of 22, 5' 10" tall, born in Pennsylvania and died at Black Rock, NY on 13 Dec 1814 from sickness (Johnson and Christou, p. 92)

Deaver, Stephen, served as a Private in Capt. Frank Hampton's Co., 24th U.S. Infantry, enlisted 11 May 1813, age 24, 5' 9" tall, born in Baltimore, and was captured at Fort Niagara. Prisoner of War, later paroled and discharged from the service at Greenbush, NY on 8 May 1815 (Johnson and Christou, p. 92)

Deliney (Delignay), George, served as a Private in Capt. Samuel Lane's Co., 14th U.S. Infantry, enlisted 29 Sep 1812 for 5 years at Rising Sun, MD at the age of 24, 6' tall, born in Cecil Co. Prisoner of War #3931 at Halifax, NS, interned 24 Jun 1813, discharged on Feb 1814, exchanged on 15 Apr 1814 and deserted from Fort Severn on 12 Jul 1815 (Johnson and Christou, p. 93 spelled his name Deliney; Baker Vol. 1, p. 112 spelled it Delignay)

Dell, Peter, see Peter Dill, q.v.

Delsaver, Michael, served as a Private in Capt. William McIlvane's Co., 14th U.S. Infantry, enlisted 23 Jan 1813 [in Maryland?] at the age of 37, 5' 5" tall, born in Bridgetown, NJ, and was later captured. Prisoner of War #4061 at Halifax, NS, interned 24 Jun 1813, discharged for exchange on 3 Feb 1814 and discharged from the service on 5 Jan 1815 due to loss of an eye (Johnson and Christou, p. 93; Baker Vol. 1, p. 112)

Dempsey, George, served as a Private in Capt. Samuel Lane's Co., 14th U.S. Inf., enlisted 8 May 1812 at Williamsport, MD at age of 25, 5' 10½" tall, born in Pennsylvania. Prisoner of War #4093 at Halifax, NS, interned on 24 Jun 1813, discharged on 9 Nov 1813 and sent to England (Johnson and Christou, p. 93)

Denham, William, served as a Seaman and was born in Maryland. Age: 29. Prison Depot: Chatham, Prisoner of War #1298. How Taken: Gave himself up off HM Guard Ship *Royal William*. When Taken: 3 Feb 1813. Date Received: 16 Mar 1813 from Portsmouth on HMS *Abundance*. Discharged on 12 Oct 1813 and released to HMS *Ceres*. (Johnson's Database, 2019)

Denmade, Edward, served as a Private in 14th U.S. Infantry and was captured. Prisoner of War #4187 at Halifax, NS, interned 24 Jun 1813 and discharged 27 Aug 1813, sent to England (Johnson and Christou, p. 94; Baker Vol. 1, p. 113)

Dennight, Wilson, served as a Seaman and was wounded at the battle of Bladensburg, was admitted to the Naval Hospital in Washington, DC as Patient No. 34 on 3 Sep 1814 and was discharged on 10 Oct 1814 and sent to Baltimore (Sharp's Database, 2018)

Denningsburgh, William, served as a Private in Capt. Angus Langham's Co., 17th U.S. Inf., enlisted 1 Apr 1814 at Detroit, age 23, 5' 4½" tall, born in Baltimore Co., captured on Lake Huron on 3 Sep 1814, released on 30 Mar 1815 and discharged at Washington, DC on 27 Jun 1815 (Johnson and Christou, p. 94)

Dennis, Francis, served as a Seaman from Harford Co. and at age 22 he was a Prisoner of War at Dartmoor in Devon, England for 236 days from 28 Oct 1814 to 21 Jun 1815 ("Harford County in the War of 1812," by Christopher T. George, *Harford Historical Bulletin* No. 76, Spring 1998, p. 21 footnote). Francis Dennis served as a Seaman and was born in Havre de Grace, MD. Age: 22. Prison Depot: Dartmoor, Prisoner of War #4942. Captured by HM Frigate *Endymion* on 15 Aug 1814. Where Taken: off Nantucket, MA. Prize Name: *Herald*. Home Port: New York. Ship Type: Privateer. Date Received: 28 Oct 1814 from HMT *Alkbar* from Halifax, NS. Discharged on 21 Jun 1815. (Johnson's Database, 2019)

Dennis, Thomas, of Baltimore County, was captured in August 1812 and sent to England as a Prisoner of War; no military information was stated (*Niles Weekly Register*, 4 Sep 1813). Thomas Dennis served as a Seaman and was born in Kent

Co., MD. Age: 17. Prison Depot: Portsmouth, Prisoner of War #151. Captured by HM Brig *Recruit* on 29 Aug 1812 at sea. Prize Name: *William*. Home Port: Baltimore. Ship Type: Merchant Vessel. Date Received: 29 Oct 1812. From what ship: HM Ship-of-the-Line *Ardent*. Discharged on 19 Feb 1813, sent to Chatham on HM Store Ship *Dromedary*. Prison Depot: Chatham, Prisoner of War #521. Date Received: 23 Feb 1813 from Portsmouth on HMS *Dromedary*. Discharged on 8 Jun 1813 and released to the Cartel *Rodrigo*. (Johnson's Database, 2019)

Dennis, William, served as a Private in Capt. Richard Bennett's Co., 14th U.S. Infantry, enlisted 5 Apr 1813, was on board the fleet on Lake Ontario and died on 22 Aug 1813; bounty land issued to brother Thomas Dennis and other heirs at law (BLW# 18939-160-12; Johnson and Christou, p. 94)

Dennis, Wheatly, served as a Lieutenant in Capt. Dennis' Co., 37th Regiment, and diedin 1814. (Marine p. 266)

Denny, John, served as a Seaman in Joshua Barney's Flotilla and was wounded Bladensburg, was admitted to the Naval Hospital in Washington, DC as Patient No. 37 on 3 Sep 1914, was discharged on 4 Jan 1815 and sent to Baltimore (Sharp's Database, 2018; Marine p. 266, stated he was wounded and captured)

Denson, Charles, served as a Private in Capt. Isaac Barnard's Co., 14th U.S. Inf., enlisted 8 Feb 1813 and was captured (the date and place were not stated). Prisoner of War, sent to England, later released and discharged from service at Baltimore on 31 Mar 1815 due to abscess of lung (Johnson and Christou, p. 94)

Dent, Patrick, served as Surgeon's Mate, appointed 19 Aug 1809 and was listed as dead, no date and cause not stated, but apparently died in 1813 during the was since his replacement was appointed on 12 Apr 1813. (Wright Vol. 6, p. 1)

Deny, James (African American), served as a Seaman and was born in Maryland. Age: 28. Prison Depot: Chatham, Prisoner of War #317. Captured by HM Brig *Rifleman*. When Taken: 22 Aug 1812. Where Taken: off Scotland. Prize Name: *Joseph Ricketsen*. Ship Type: Merchant Vessel. Date Received: 23 Dec 1812 from Greenlaw Depot. Discharged on 10 May 1813 and released to the Cartel *Admittance*. (Johnson's Database, 2019)

Depass, George, served as a Private in 14th U.S. Infantry (company not stated), enlisted on 4 Mar 1813 and died on 15 Jun 1813; heirs received half pay for 5 years in lieu of bounty land (Johnson and Christou, p. 95)

Deroche, John Baptiste, served as a Private (command and captain were not stated) from Harford Co., MD, age 19, and was a Prisoner of War at Dartmoor in Devon, England for 196 days from 17 Dec 1814 to 1 Jul 1815 ("Harford County in the War of 1812," by Christopher T. George, *Harford Historical Bulletin* No. 76, Spring 1998, p. 21 footnote). John Baptiste Deroche served as a Seaman and was born in Havre de Grace, MD. Age: 19. Prison Depot: Dartmoor, Prisoner of War #5591. Captured by HM Brig *Jaseur*. When Taken: 21 Sep 1814. Where Taken: off Halifax. Prize Name: *Albion*, prize of the Privateer *Surprise*. Ship Type: Privateer. Date Received: 17 Dec 1814. From what ship: HMT *Loire* from Halifax, NS. Released on 1 Jul 1815. (Johnson's Database, 2019)

Desharn, George, served as a Seaman and was born in Baltimore. Age: 18. Prison Depot: Dartmoor, Prisoner of War #2304. Captured by HM Ship-of-the-Line *Saturn*. When Taken: 25 May 1814. Where Taken: off Sandy Hook, NJ. Prize Name: *Hussar*. Home Port: New York. Ship Type: Privateer. Date Received: 16 Aug 1814. From what ship: HMS *Dublin* from Halifax, NS. Discharged on 3 May 1815. (Johnson's Database, 2019)

Deshler, David, served as a Private in the U.S. Marine Corps, enlisted in Sep 1804 and was taken from the barracks and admitted to the Naval Hospital in Washington, DC as Patient No. 82 on 23 Dec 1814 with typhoid fever and died on 5 Jan 1815 (Sharp's Database, 2018); see David Dishler, q.v.

Desk, Michael (c1765-1814), served as a Private in Capt. Peter Pinney's Co., 27th Regiment, Baltimore Militia, joined on 24 Aug 1814 and was killed on 12 Sep 1814 at North Point. Name is on the Baltimore Battle Monument. (Wright Vol. 2, p. 20; NARA; CMSR; *Baltimore American*, 12 Jun 1819) Ann Desk, consort of Michael Desk who fell at the Battle of North Point, died on 26 Jun 1841. (*The [Baltimore] Sun*, 30 Jun 1841)

Devanghan, Jonathan, served as a Private in Capt. Thomas Sangster's Co., 12th U.S. Infantry, enlisted 25 May 1812 in Alexandria, DC, at the age of 40, 5' 9¼" tall, born in Maryland, discharged at Pittsburgh on 18 Aug 1815 on Surgeon's Certificate for old age (Johnson and Christou, p. 95)

Dew, Frederick, served as a Prize Master and was born in Baltimore. Age: 35. Prison Depot: Chatham, Prisoner of War #2752. Captured by HM Frigate *Spartan*. When Taken: 13 Jun 1813. Where Taken: off Delaware. Prize Name: *Globe*. Ship Type: Privateer. Date Received: 7 Jan 1814 from Halifax, NS. Discharged on 25 Sep 1814 and sent to Dartmoor on HMS *Leyden*. Prison Depot: Dartmoor, Prisoner of War #4383. Age 25 (sic). Date Received: 8 Oct 1814. From what ship: HMT *Leyden* from Chatham. Discharged on 14 Jun 1815. (Johnson's Database, 2019)

Dick, John, served as a Private in Capt. Nicholas Turbutt's Co., Frederick Co. Militia, Fredericktown area, from 1 Sep 1814, marched to Baltimore, stationed at Hampstead Hill and was discharged by surgeon, cause and date not given (Mallick and Wright, p. 357)

Dickerson, James, served as Seaman under Sailing Master Simmones Bunbury, U.S. Sea Fencibles, enlisted on 21 Feb 1814 at the advanced age of 50, 5' 5¼" tall, born in Philadelphia and was discharged on 7 Mar 1814 as unfit for service (Johnson and Christou, p. 96)

Didler, Henry, served as a Seaman and was born in Baltimore. Age: 20. Prison Depot: Chatham, Prisoner of War #3266. Captured by HM Ship-of-the-Line *Valiant* & HM Brig *Curlew*. When Taken: 26 Mar 1813. Where Taken: Georges Bank. Prize Name: *Volant*. Ship Type: Letter of Marque. Date Received: 23 Feb 1814 from Halifax, NS on HMT *Malabar*. Discharged on 22 Oct 1814 and sent to Dartmoor on HMS *Leyden*. Prison Depot: Dartmoor, Prisoner of War #5291. Date Received: 31 Oct 1814 on HMT *Leyden* from Chatham. Discharged on 29 Jun 1815. (Johnson's Database, 2019)

Diffenderffer, Richard, served as 4th Sergeant in Capt. Benjamin Edes' Co., 27th Regiment, Baltimore City Militia, from 19 Aug 1814 and on 12 Sep 1814 he was wounded by "a musket ball in his left knee which occasioned a long and painful confinement and has left an incurable lameness in his joint." This occurred while being engaged with the enemy at North Point in Capt. Poles' Co. in the 27th Regt. Statement dated 43 Jul 1816 by Surgeon T. Hamilton. (Pension #25023, p. 6; Wright Vol. 2, p. 17, did not mention injury). In Baltimore on 3 Oct 1842 Richard Deffenderffer, former Sergeant in the 27th Regiment, Maryland Militia, a resident of Baltimore for 47 years and previously of Anne Arundel Co., collected his own $24.00 pension due from 4 Mar to 4 Sep 1842. (Pierce, p. 49)

Dill (Dell), Peter, served as a Private in Capt. Reuben Gilder's Co., 14th U.S. Infantry, enlisted on 30 Aug 1812 in Maryland at the age of 33, 6' tall, born in Lancaster, PA and was captured on 24 Jun 1813 [at Beaver Dams] in Canada. Prisoner of War #5247 at Halifax, NS, interned on 28 Dec 1813 and discharged for exchange on 31 May 1814 (Johnson and Christou, p. 97 spelled his name Dill; Baker Vol. 1, p.112 spelled it Dell)

Dingall, George (African American), served as a Seaman and was born in Maryland. Age: 29. Prison Depot: Plymouth 1, Prisoner of War #673. How Taken: Gave himself up off Flag of Truce *Pennsylvania*. Date Received: 15 Mar 1813. From what ship: HMS *Bittern*. Discharged and was sent to Dartmoor on 1 Jul 1813. Prison Depot: Dartmoor, Prisoner of War #167. Date Received: 2 Apr 1813 from Plymouth. Discharged and was sent to Dartmouth on 30 Jul 1813. (Johnson's Database, 2019)

Discontine, Alex, served as a Marine with Commodore Porter, was wounded at "Battery Hazel White" (date not stated), was admitted to the Naval Hospital in Washington, DC as Patient No. 38 on 7 Sep 1814 and was discharged on 9 Dec 1814 and sent to barracks (Sharp's Database, 2018)

Diser, Samuel, served as a Private (company not stated) and was captured at the Battle of Bladensburg on 24 Aug 1814 (Marine, p. 174; Wright Vol. 2, p. 85, stated he was a Private in Capt. Robert C. Galloway's Co., 2nd Regiment, 11th Brigade, Baltimore, from 27 Jul 1814 and was "paroled," but no date was given)

Dishler, David, served as a Marine with Commodore Porter, was wounded at "Battery Hazel White" (date not stated), was admitted to the Naval Hospital in Washington, DC as Patient No. 38 on 7 Sep 1814 and was discharged on 21 Nov 1814 and sent to barracks (Sharp's Database, 2018); see David Deshler, q.v.

Disney, Joseph, served as a Private in Capt. Shepperd Leakin's Co., 38th U.S. Infantry, enlisted 12 Aug 1813 for 1 year and died at Fort McHenry on 15 or 18 Apr 1814 (Johnson and Christou, p. 97)

Disney, Samuel, served as a Private in Capt. Robert C. Galloway's Co., 2nd Regt., Baltimore, from 27 Jul 1814 and reported as "paroled," but the exact date was not given on the muster roll dated 27 Jul – 13 Oct 1814; he was discharged on 13 Oct 1814, probably in Baltimore, 18 miles from home (Wright Vol. 2, p. 85)

Disney, William, served as a Private in 1st Lt. Richard H. Battee's Co., Watkins' Regt., Anne Arundel Co. Militia, from 8 Jun 1813 and reported sick on furlough on 26 Aug 1813 on muster roll dated 16 Apr – 31 Jul 1813 (Wright Col. 4, p. 41)

Divers, John, served as 4th Sergeant in Capt. Benjamin Wilson's Co., 6th Cavalry District, Baltimore Co., from 1 Sep 1814 and a note attached to the pay roll stated, "I give it as my opinion that John Divers, attached to Capt. Wilson's Troop, is incompetent to perform duty at this time and probably may not be within two or three weeks. Shadrach Alfriend, Surgeon's mate of the Sixth Regt. of Cavalry." (Wright Vol. 2, p. 76)

Divinie, James, served as a Private in Capt. Samuel Sterett's Co., 5th Regiment, Baltimore Militia, from 19 Aug 1814 and reported as "sick unfit for duty," but no date was given (Wright Vol. 2, p. 6)

Dix, Timothy Jr., served as Lieutenant Colonel in the 14th U.S. Infantry, was born in New Hampshire and was commissioned a Major on 12 Mar 1812, promoted to Lieutenant Colonel on 20 Jun 1813 and died on 14 Nov 1813; bounty land issued to widow Lucy Hartwell Dix (BLW# 10501-160-50; Johnson and Christou, pp. 97-98)

Dixon, Benjamin, served as a Seaman and was born in Baltimore. Age: 30. Prison Depot: Plymouth 1, Prisoner of War #2231. How Taken: Gave himself up off an English MV. Date Received: 10 Jan 1814. From what ship: HMS *Scylla*. Discharged on 31 Jan 1814 and sent to Dartmoor. Prison Depot: Dartmoor, Prisoner of War #915. Date Received: 31 Jan 1814 from Plymouth. Discharged on 27 Apr 1815. (Johnson's Database, 2019)

Dixon, James, served as a Private in Capt. Samuel Lane's Co., 14th U.S. Infantry, enlisted 27 May 1812 for 5 years by Lt. Nelson in Cumberland, MD at the age of 19, 5' 7" tall, born in Frederick, MD, and was captured at Stoney Creek, Upper Canada on 12 Jun 1813. Prisoner of War #5094 at Halifax, NS, arrived at Salem from Halifax, interned 28 Dec 1813, discharged 31 May 1814, served at Fort Independence and deserted at Schenectady, NY on 19 Jan 1815 (Johnson and Christou, p. 98, Baker Vol. 1, p. 117, Mallick and Wright, p. 99)

Dobins, John, served as a Seaman and was born in Harford Co., MD. Age: 27. Prison Depot: Plymouth 1, Prisoner of War #628. How Taken: Gave himself up off HM Transport *William No. 69*. Date Received: 4 Mar 1813 from Plymouth. Sent to Dartmoor on 2 Apr 1813. (Johnson's Database, 2019)

Dominico, John (African American), served as a Cook and was born in Maryland. Age: 25. Prison Depot: Plymouth 2, Prisoner of War #196. Captured by HM Frigate *Statira*. When Taken: 1 Apr 1814. Where Taken: Lat 38N Long 24W. Prize Name: Chance. Home Port: Virginia. Ship Type: Privateer. Date Received: 2 Mar 1815. From what ship: HMS *Dannemark*. Discharged on 3 Mar 1815 and sent to Dartmoor. Prison Depot: Dartmoor, Prisoner of War #6440. Date Received: 3 Mar 1815 on HMT *Ganges* from Plymouth. Discharged on 11 Jul 1815. (Johnson's Database, 2019)

Donaldson, George, served as a Private in Capt. Reuben Gilder's Co., 14th U.S. Infantry, enlisted 11 Jan 1813 in Baltimore at the age of 28, 5' 6" tall, born in Baltimore Co., and discharged at Greenbush. NY on 25 Apr 1815 on Surgeon's Certificate (Johnson and Christou, p. 99)

Donaldson, James Lowry (1776-1814), served as a Lieutenant and Adjutant in the 27th Regt., Baltimore Militia, commanded by Lt. Col. Kennedy Long and was killed in action near North Point on 12 Sep 1814. His name is on the Baltimore Battle Monument. "James L. Donaldson, a lawyer of eminence, member of the legislature, and adjutant of the 27th regiment, killed." (CMSR; North Point dead and wounded Article in 4 Oct 1814 Columbian Register CT Vol. III 97, p. 4; Marine, p. 170; *Baltimore American*, 12 Jun 1819; *Baltimore Federal Gazette*, 24 Sep 1814) The death of "James Lowery Donaldson" was also reported in the *Niles Weekly Register* on 1 Oct 1814. From the Dielman-Hayward card file at the H. Furlong Baldwin Library at the Maryland Historical Society in Baltimore is the following: "James Lowry Donaldson died at North Point (battleground) on September 12, 1814, buried in St. Paul's Churchyard on September 15, 1814. An acre of square ground known as the James Lowry Donaldson Battle Acre dedicated by the veterans of the 27th and 5th Maryland, purchased and deeded to Baltimore County in memory of their fallen and dead comrades who died there on September 12, 1814. See 'The Defender,' September 12, 1834. James Lowry Donaldson was reburied at the sight of his death, so named for him, on

September 14, 1834." The *Baltimore Federal Gazette* on 24 Sep 1814 reported: "James Lowry Donaldson, Esq., who was killed in the late action near North Point, on the 12th instant, was a native of Ireland, but has resided in this country from the time he was eleven years old. He was the third son of Col. William Lowry, of this city, his name having been changed by an act of the assembly of this state, in compliance with the wishes of a relation ... For three successive years he received the highest proof of the confidence of his fellow-citizens, by being elected a delegate to represent them in the general assembly of this state ... he has left a widow and five small children ... The twenty-seventh regiment, in which he acted as adjutant, were warmly attached to him ... While in the active performance of his duty, he received a musket or rifle ball through his head, which put an immediate period to his life.") James Donaldson Lowry, of Baltimore City, on 7 Jan 1804, changed his name to James Lowry Donaldson in order to inherit from his uncle, James Lowry Donaldson, late of the City of London. (*Divorces and Names Changed in Maryland by Act of the Legislature, 1634-1867*, by Mary Keysor Meyer, 1991, p. 56) In 1963 Donald Franklin Stewart (born 1929), direct descendant of Lt. James Lowry Donaldson, stated James was the son of Col. William Lowry, was a native of Monaghan, Ireland and lived at 14 Connawaga Street in Baltimore. James' daughter Jane Donaldson married Capt. Richard Jackson of the Fairfax Dragoons in the War of 1812. (Society of the War of 1812 in the State of Maryland No. 561, National Application No. 3260, approved in 1964)

See James L. Donaldson's obituary on the next page.

Adjutant James L. Donaldson.

From the Baltimore Federal Gazette.

JAMES LOWRY DONALDSON, Esq. who was killed in the late action near North Point, on the 12th instant, was a native of Ireland, but has resided in this country from the time he was eleven years old. He was the third son of colonel William Lowry, of this city, his name having been changed by an act of the assembly of this state, in compliance with the wishes of a relation. Mr. Donaldson received a liberal education, and was bred to the profession of the law, which he was practising in this city with much reputation and success. For three successive years he received the highest proof of the confidence of his fellow-citizens, by being elected a delegate to represent them in the general assembly of this state, a station which, even his political opponents acknowledge, he filled with eminent ability.

Possessing a liberal and energetic mind and correct classical taste, he distinguished himself at the bar and in the senate as an orator, a civilian and a statesman; and his correct and gentlemanly conduct, ensured him the respect and esteem of his associates in both situations, even when differing from him in political sentiments. While his talents, integrity and activity raised him high in public estimation, his social virtues and friendly disposition endeared him to a large circle of acquaintances in private life, whose attachment to him increased with their intimacy, as it afforded them an opportunity of knowing his worth and merit.— Among those who long and intimately knew and sincerely esteemed him, was the writer of this article; who, although differing from him in political sentiments, never found that difference to affect in the slightest degree that friendship which he believes to have been mutual.

Mr. Donaldson was about thirty-three years of age; he has left a widow and five small children, to whom his loss will be irreparable; a numerous family of relatives, and his extensive circle of friends will also severely feel his loss.

The twenty-seventh regiment, in which he acted as adjutant, were warmly attached to him. A few minutes previous to the commencement of the action in which he was unhappily slain, he addressed them in a short but extremely appropriate and animating speech, which contributed not a little, as many of them have since stated, to induce that brave and steady resistance of the enemy, so highly honourable to the regiment. While in the active performance of his duty, he received a musket or rifle ball through his head, which put an immediate period to his life.

Dooley, James, served as a Commander and was born in Maryland. Age: 25. Prison Depot: Chatham, Prisoner of War #2785. Captured by HM Ship-of-the-Line *Victorious*. When Taken: 8 Jun 1813. Where Taken: Chesapeake Bay. Prize Name: *Rolla*. Type: Privateer. Received 7 Jan 1814 from Halifax, NS. Discharged on 4 Apr 1814 and sent to Ready on parole. (Johnson's Database, 2019)

Dorff, Patrick, served as a Private in Capt. John F. Huston's Co., Frederick Co. Militia, from 23 Jul 1814 and was taken prisoner in the Battle of Bladensburg on 24 Aug 1814 (Mallick and Wright, p. 99, spelled his name Dorff and p. 344 spelled it Dorf and p. 346 spelled it Dorff; Marine, p. 174, misspelled it Dorse)

Dorsey, Caleb, served as 2nd Sgt. in Capt. Roderick Burgess' Co., 32nd Regiment, Anne Arundel Co. Militia, from 22 Jul 1814 and was reported as "sick at home" on the muster roll dated 22 Jul – 19 Sep 1814. On 26 Jun 1857 Caleb Dorsey, age 68, a resident of Jefferson Co., KY, stated he was drafted in Anne Arundel Co.,

MD with his brothers Edward W. Dorsey and John T. W. Dorsey. (Wright Vol. 4, p. 42; BLW# 55-160-73584)

Dorsey, Charles, served as a Corporal in Capt. Aaron R. Levering's Co., 5th Regt., Baltimore Militia, Independent Blues, was wounded 12 Sep 1814 at North Point and reduced to a Private on 1 Oct 1814 (Wright Vol. 2, p. 5; Marine p. 270)

Dorsey, Daniel D. (1787-1814), served as a Private in Capt. James McDonald's Co., 14th U.S. Infantry, enlisted 17 Nov 1813 at the age of 26, 5' 10" tall, born in Maryland and died at Plattsburgh, NY on 28 Jun 1814; bounty land issued to his brother William Dorsey (BLW# 24256-160-12; Johnson and Christou, p. 100)

Dorsey, Edward H. (1789-1863), served as a Private in Capt. James Sterett's Co., 5th Cavalry Regiment, Baltimore City, joined on 23 Aug 1814 and while serving on picket guard duty on 12 Sep 1814 at North Point he, along with two others, became separated, with the British army in between them. They were ordered to surrender, but refused and leaped on their horses and escaped. They offered to pay for directions to Baltimore from a Negro man who said he would as he performed a service for some gentlemen and soon returned followed by British soldiers who forced them to surrender. The prisoners were taken to General Ross and gave an exaggerated account of the strength of the American forces. (Wright Vol. 2, p. 56; Marine, p. 150, citing *Oration by H. Clay Dallam, 1878*) Bounty land was issued to him in Mahaska, IA on 10 Feb 1852. (BLW# 50-40-123; Smith's Database, 2019) "Edward H. Dorsay, Sergeant, Baltimore Volunteers," captured on 13 Sep 1814, age 25, taken to Dartmouth, paroled on 8 Oct 1814 and discharged on 14 Mar 1815. (Johnson, p. 30)

Dorsey, Lloyd (1793-1860), served as a Private in Capt. John Heeter's Co., 44th Regiment, Montgomery Co. Militia, and reported "sick absent" on the muster roll dated 4 Aug – 27 Sep 1814. On 1 May 1855 Lloyd Dorsey, age 62, stated he volunteered on 4 Aug 1814 and on the way from Bladensburg to Baltimore [near Brookeville] he was detained by indisposition and got permission of his officers to be carried to his father's to be nursed until he recovered so as to join the company again in Baltimore, but the disease continued so as to prevent his attending payroll. (Wright Vol. 7, pp. 4, 23; BLW# 55-150-33996) After the war "Col. Dorsey" served in the State Legislature and died at home near Laytonsville on 26 Jun 1860 in his 68th year. (*Montgomery County Sentinel*, 6 Jul 1860)

Dorsey, Otho (1783-1857), served as a Private in Capt. John Fonsten's Co., Frederick Co. Militia, from 2 Sep 1814, marched to Baltimore, engaged in the defense of the city and reported "sick absent 26 Sep" 1814. Otho married Margaret Ann Lyon Brandenburg in 1846 in Carroll Co., MD and died in August 1857 without issue. (Mallick and Wright, p. 363; *Anne Arundel Gentry*, by Harry Wright Newman, 1971, Vol. 2, p. 140, citing Carroll Co. Will Book JB #2, p. 341)

Dorsey, Philip, served as a Private in Capt. Adam Barnes' Co., 32nd Regt., Anne Arundel Co. Militia, from 23 Aug 1814 and was sick on furlough (no date or cause given) as reported on the muster roll dated 23 Aug – 27 Sep 1814 (Wright Vol. 4, p. 42)

Dorsey, Richard B. (1790-1869), served as a Private in Capt. Samuel Sterett's Co., 5th Regt., Baltimore Volunteers, sometime between 19 Aug and 18 Nov 1814 on which muster roll he was reported "absent from the city" but no date or reasons were given (Wright Vol. 2, p. 56) On 12 Jan 1867 he was living at Dunnington Row, Capitol Hill, Washington, DC and wrote "Upon my return to Baltimore in 1814 I found my health did not improve and I there went to my father's family in Montgomery Co., Md. where I remained for some time." On 29 Nov 1867 he was living in Baltimore and stated he had served in "Capt. James Sterrett's Co., 5th Regt." In 1874 his widow Anna E. Dorsey (age 74) stated they married on 13 Dec 1818, her maiden name was Dorsey and he died in Washington, DC on 7 Jan 1869. (Wright Vol. 4, p. 81, BLW# 55-rej-331640)

Dougherty, Hamilton (1787-1814), served as a Private in Capt. Samuel Lane's Co. of the 14th U.S. Infantry, enlisted 21 May 1812 in Virginia at age 25, born Jefferson Co., VA. Prisoner of War (Chatham) and died at Chatham on 22 May 1814 (BLW# 21686-160-12; Johnson and Christou, p. 101)

Dougherty, John, served as a Private in Capt. Samuel Sterett's Co., 5th Regt., Baltimore Militia, from 19 Aug 1814 and was taken prisoner at North Point on 12 Sep 1814 (Wright Vol. 2, p. 6)

Dougherty, William, served as a Corporal in Capt. Samuel Lane's Co., 14th U.S. Infantry, enlisted 13 Jul 1812 for 5 years in Maryland at the age of 28, 5' 8½" tall, born in West Town, Chester Co., PA and captured on 12 Jun 1813. Prisoner of War #5017 at Halifax, NS, interned 28 Dec 1813, discharged 31 May 1814, returned to service and discharged on 13 Jul 1817 (Johnson and Christou, p. 101; Baker Vol. 1, p. 104, spelled his name Daugherty)

Douglas (Douglass), Mathew, served as a Seaman and was born in Maryland. Age: 24. Prison Depot: Plymouth 2, Prisoner of War #9. Captured by HM Schooner *Helicon*. When Taken: 17 Jan 1815. Where Taken: Lat 20N Long 52W. Prize Name: *Albion*. Prize. Ship Type: Privateer. Date Received: 3 Feb 1815. From what ship: HMS *Bittern*. Discharged on 4 Feb 1815 and sent to Dartmoor. Prison Depot: Dartmoor, Prisoner of War #6245. Received: 4 Feb 1815. From what ship: HMT *Ganges*. Discharged on 3 Jul 1815. (Johnson's Database, 2019)

Dowler, Thomas, served as a Private in Capt. Daniel Appling's Co., 1st U.S. Rifles, enlisted 25 May 1812 in Hiwassee Garrison, TN, age 25, 5' 9¾" tall, born in Washington Co., MD, was wounded at Lyon's Creek, Upper Canada on 18 Oct 1814 and discharged at Buffalo on 1 Aug 1815 (Johnson and Christou, p. 102)

Downes, Richard (1783-1873), served as a Private in Capt. John W. Lansdale's Co., Montgomery Co. and after the Battle of Bladensburg in Aug 1814 he was ordered to Baltimore, but was disabled and could not go. On 13 Sep 1871, age 88, he lived in Clarksville, Howard Co., MD and stated he married Tatitha --- on 7 Jan 1834 in Anne Arundel Co. On 12 Oct 1872 he stated he was born and raised near Colesville, Montgomery Co., MD, and he was around 27 when he enrolled and drilled under Capt. Lansdale. On 23 Apr 1878 Talitha Downes, age 63, stated Richard enlisted at age 28, was 5' 8" tall, black grey hair, and her maiden name was Wilson. She married "Richard M. Downs" on 7 Jan 1834 in Montgomery Co. Richard was married first to Sallie Bell who died in 1828 and he died on 21 Feb 1873. (Wright Vol. 7, p. 23; Pensions SO-24345, WO-18532)

Downs, William (1777-1815), served as a Private in Capt. Leroy Opie's Co. of the 5th U.S. Infantry, enlisted 5 Apr 1812 in Baltimore at the age of 35, 5' 8" tall, born in Baltimore, and discharged at Greenbush, NY on 1 Jun 1815 because of wounds (Johnson and Christou, p. 102)

Doyle, Patrick, served as an Ordinary Seaman of the U.S. Chesapeake Flotilla, entered service on 14 Jun 1814 and died on 28 Oct 1814 (Shomette, p. 394)

Drake, John, served as a Seaman and was born in Baltimore. Age: 35. Prison Depot: Chatham, Prisoner of War #1723. Captured by HMS *Horatio*. When Taken: 13 Dec 1812. Where Taken: Bay of Biscayne. Prize Name: *Powhattan*. Ship Type: Merchant Vessel. Date Received: 25 May 1813 from Portsmouth on HMS *Impetius*. Discharged on 24 Jul 1813 and released to the Cartel *Hoffning*. (Johnson's Database, 2019)

Drave, Nicholas, served as a Private in Capt. Robert C. Galloway's Co., 2nd Regiment, 11th Brigade, Baltimore, from 27 Jul 1814 and was reported dead on 28 Jul 1814 (Wright Vol. 2, p. 85)

Drayton, John (African American or Mulatto), served as a Seaman and was born in Baltimore. Age: 23. Prison Depot: Chatham, Prisoner of War #3930. How Taken: Gave himself up off HM Ship-of-the-Line *QueenCharlotte*. When Taken: 23 Sep 1814. Date Received: 24 Sep 1814. From what ship: HMS *Namur*. Discharged on 29 Sep 1814 and sent to Dartmoor on HMS *Freya*. Prison Depot: Dartmoor, Prisoner of War #4784. Date Received: 9 Oct 1814. From what ship: HMT *Freya* from Chatham. Discharged 11 Jul 1815. (Johnson's Database, 2019)

Drummond, John, served as a Private in 14th U.S. Infantry and was captured. Prisoner of War #4018 at Halifax, NS, interned 24 Jun 1813 and discharged 9 Nov 1813, sent to England (Johnson and Christou, p. 103; Baker Vol. 1, p. 124)

Dubois, David, served as a Private in the 14th U.S. Infantry and was captured. Prisoner of War #3921 at Halifax, NS, interned 24 Jun 1813, discharged 9 Nov 1813 and sent to England (Johnson and Christou, p. 103; Baker Vol. 1, p. 124)

Duckett, Richard (1775-1814), served as a Private in Capt. John Mowton's Co. of the 38th U.S. Infantry, enlisted on 14 Apr 1814 in Craney Island, VA at age 39, born in Baltimore and died on 8 Sep 1814 (Johnson and Christou, p. 103)

Duff, David (1777-1812), served as a Private in Capt. Samuel Lane's Co., 14th U.S. Infantry, enlisted on 26 May 1812 in Cumberland, MD at age 35, 5' 9" tall, born in Ireland and died at Black Rock, NY on 16 Dec 1812; bounty land was issued to Henry Duff (BLW# 23614-160-12; Johnson and Christou, pp. 103-104)

Duff, Henry, served as a Private in Capt. James Dillon 's Co., 27th Regiment, Baltimore Militia, and lost his right eye on 13 Sep 1814 at North Point (statement given under hand 15 Oct 1814 by Capt. James Dillin). He pensioned due to disability by March 1816 and transferred to PA on 3 Jan 1817. Formerly of Baltimore Union Greens attached to same regiment per Capt. Alexander Crooks. Certificate signed by Dr. T. Hamilton and Kennedy Long, Lt. Col., of 27th Regt., and S. Smith, late Major Genl. commanding. (Pension# 12815)

Duffy, John, served as a Private in Capt. Andrew C. Smith's Co., 49th Regiment, Cecil Co. Militia, for 30 days in April-May 1813 and was wounded during the attack on Frederick Town by the British and deemed "unfit for business and is still unsound." He was ordered into service at Elkton on 18 Apr 1813 and was discharged at Frederick Town in May 1813 in Cecil County. Capt. Smith wrote: "The tour of duty of each man was performed between the 17th of Apr 1813 and 22nd of May as stated but the particular days of the month when each commended and ended cannot possibly be ascertained and noted as my Roll was taken with my baggage by the enemy when they destroyed Frederick Town." (Wright Vol. 3, p. 12)

Dugan, James, served as a Private in Capt. Leroy Opie's Co., 14th U.S. Infantry, enlisted 27 May 1812 for 5 years at Frederick, MD at the age of 25, 5' 10" tall, born at Emmetsburg, MD, and was captured at Stoney Creek, Upper Canada on 8 Jun 1813. Prisoner of War at Halifax, later released and returned to service, but reported as deserted in Detroit on 26 Jun 1816 (Johnson and Christou, p. 104; Baker Vol. 1, pp. 124-125, did not mention him, but mentioned a James Duggin, Prisoner #255, Seaman, interned 26 Jul 1812, discharged 9 Oct 1812)

Duhard, Thomas, served as a 3rd Mate and was born in Baltimore. Age: 21. Prison Depot: Portsmouth, Prisoner of War #574. Captured by HM Frigate *Dryad*. When Taken: 7 Jan 1813. Where Taken: at sea. Prize Name: *Rossie*. Ship Type: Merchant Vessel. Date Received: 25 Jan 1813. From what ship: HM Ship-of-the-Line *Queen*. Discharged on 11 Mar 1813 and sent to Chatham on HM Store Ship *Abundance*.

Prison Depot: Chatham, Prisoner of War #1247. Date Received: 16 Mar 1813 from Portsmouth on HMS *Abundance*. Discharged on 24 Jul 1813 and released to the Cartel *Hoffning*. (Johnson's Database, 2019)

Dukehart, Thomas Frederick (1790-1848), served as Midshipman and Acting Master, U.S. Navy, under Commodore Joshua Barney and was captured at the Battle of Bladensburg on 24 Aug 1814, released on 7 Oct 1814 and discharged on 11 Dec 1814 (Marine, p. 174; Shomette, pp. 325, 361; NARA Naval Records, Muster Book, U.S. Flotilla, 3 Mar 1815) Capt. Thomas Dukehart died on 17 Jan 1848 in his 58th year and was long known as one of the most experienced ship masters out of the port of Baltimore. (*The [Baltimore] Sun*, 18 Jan 1848)

Dumour, Gideon (1790-1815), served as a Private in Capt. Samuel Raisin's Co., 36th U.S. Infantry, enlisted on 14 Jun 1814 at the age of 24, 5' 7" tall, born in Halifax, NC and died on 28 Jan 1815. (Johnson and Christou, p. 104)

Duncan, Abel, served as a Prize Master and was born in Baltimore. Age: 22. Prison Depot: Dartmoor, Prisoner of War #5650. Captured by HM Brig *Castilian*. When Taken: 30 Sep 1814. Where Taken: Long 14 Lat 52. Prize Name: Prize of the Privateer *Chasseur*. Home Port: Baltimore. Ship Type: Privateer. Date Received: 24 Dec 1814. From what ship: HMT *Impregnable*. Escaped on 1 Jun 1815. (Johnson's Database, 2019)

Duncan, George (African American), served as a Seaman and was born in Benedict, MD. Age: 28. Prison Depot: Chatham, Prisoner of War #3526. How Taken: Gave himself up. When Taken: 25 Feb 1814. Where Taken: London. Date Received: 26 Feb 1814. From what ship: HMS *Raisonable*. Discharged on 21 Jul 1814 and sent to Dartmoor on HMS *Portia*. Prison Depot: Dartmoor, Prisoner of War #1891. Received: 29 Jul 1814. From what ship: HMS *Ville de Paris* from Chatham Depot. Discharged on 2 May 1815. (Johnson's Database, 2019)

Dunn, Hezekiah, served as a Seaman and was born in Maryland. Age: 24. Prison Depot: Plymouth 1, Prisoner of War #100. Captured by HM Brig *Rover*. When Taken: 21 Oct 1812. Where Taken: off Bordeaux, France. Prize Name: *Experiment*. Ship Type: Merchant Vessel. Date Received: 25 Dec 1812. From what ship: HMS *Northumberland*. Discharged and sent to Portsmouth on 29 Dec 1812 on HMS *Northumberland*. Prison Depot: Portsmouth, Prisoner of War #354. Date Received: 31 Dec 1812. From what ship: HM Ship-of-the-Line *Northumberland*. Discharged on 4 Mar 1813 and sent to Chatham on HMS *Queen*. Prison Depot: Chatham, Prisoner of War #931. Date Received: 10 Mar 1813. From what ship: HMS *Tigress*. Discharged on 8 Jun 1813 and released to the Cartel *Rodrigo*. (Johnson's Database, 2019)

Duncan, James, served as a Private in Capt. Nathan Towson's Co., 2nd U.S. Artillery, enlisted on 24 Apr 1812 and was killed in action on 25 Jul 1814 (Johnson and Christou, pp. 104-105)

Dunn, James, served as a Private in Capt. John Kennedy's Co., 27th Regiment, Baltimore Militia, and was killed on 12 Sep 1814 at North Point, but his name is not on the Baltimore Battle Monument. (Huntsberry p. 93, stated he was killed, but Marine p. 273, did not mention his death)

Dunn, John, served as a Private in Capt. John Shrim's Co., 5th Regt., Baltimore Light Infantry, having volunteered when war was declared in 1812 and he continued in service and fought at Bladensburg on 23 Aug 1814 and at North Point on 12 Sep 1814 and was later discharged along with his company and regiment on 18 Nov 1814. (NARA; CMSR) His name is on the Baltimore Battle Monument. On September 2, 1814, ORDERED, That the commissioned and noncommissioned officers and privates, of the WASHINGTON BLUES, wear black crape on the left arm, for two weeks from this day, in respect for the memory of JOHN DUNN, late a member of this Co., who was killed in the Battle of Bladensburg on the 24th of August, 1814. Geo. H. Stewart, Captain. Mr. John Dunn, Respect to the memory of those who "die the willing martyrs for their country," is a debt which the generous heart delights to pay – We have to record the record the fall of a youthful soldier in the field of honor, in the death of Mr. John Dunn, who was killed in the battle of Bladensburg. The sympathy, which is justly excited at this early fate of a young champion of this country, is heightened by the amiable and respectable qualities, which endeared the departed to his brethren in arms, and to all his acquaintances. Let it be their consolation – "How sleep the brave who sink to rest. With all their country's wishes Blest." (*Baltimore American and Commercial Advertiser,* 12 Jun and 2 Jul 1819; *Baltimore Patriot*, 5 Sep 1813: Marine p. 273, did not mention his death; *Baltimore American*, 12 Jun 1819)

Dunn, John (1782-1814), served as a Private in Capt. Peter Schuyler's Co., 2nd U.S. Infantry, enlisted 7 Aug 1807 in Fredericktown, MD at the age of 25, 5' 9" tall, born in Morris, NJ and died at Fort Charlotte, AL on 24 Dec 1814 of fever (Johnson and Christou, p. 105)

Dunneal, Edward, served as a Private in Capt. David Cummings' Co., 14th U.S. Infantry, enlisted 3 Jul 1812 in Baltimore, age 43, 5' 3½" tall, born in Ireland and was later captured, date and place not stated. Prisoner of War, sent to England (prison not named), was later released (date not given) and was discharged from the service at Washington, DC on 20 Apr 1815 on a Surgeon's Certificate for a lost finger on his right hand (Johnson and Christou, p. 105)

Dunnevin, Walter, served as a Private in Capt. Isaac Barnard's Co., 14ᵗʰ U.S. Infantry, enlisted 7 Jan 1813 and died 12 May 1813; bounty land issued to niece Mary Buck and others (BLW# 25573-160-12; Johnson and Christou, p. 105)

Dunningberg, Henry, served as a Seaman and was born in Maryland. Age: 25. Prison Depot: Chatham, Prisoner of War #3007. Captured by HM Frigate *Shannon*. When Taken: 20 Aug 1813. Where Taken: at sea. Prize Name: *Yankee*. Ship Type: Privateer. Date Received: 7 Jan 1814 from Halifax, NS. Discharged on 25 Sep 1814 and sent to Dartmoor on HMS *Leyden*. Prison Depot: Dartmoor, Prisoner of War #4521. Received on 8 Oct 1814. From what ship: HMT *Leyden* from Chatham. Discharged on 15 Jun 1815. (Johnson's Database, 2019)

Dunnings, Charles, served as a Boy onboard a ship and was born in Baltimore. Age: 12. Prison Depot: Dartmoor, Prisoner of War #3855. Captured by HM Ship-of-the-Line *Majestic* & HM Brig *Dotterell*. When Taken: 22 May 1814. Where Taken: off Charleston, SC. Prize Name: *Dominica*. Ship Type: Merchant Vessel. Date Received: 5 Oct 1814 on HMT *Orpheus* from Halifax, NS. Discharged 9 Jun 1815. (Johnson's Database, 2019)

Dunnington, Dr. ----, was wounded by the accidental discharge of a gun in the hands of Pvt. Nehemiah Franklin in June 1814, per John McConchie's BLW# 55-160-49551 who had entered service in Charles Co., MD. (Wright Vol. 5, p. 76)

Dunnock, Joseph, served as a Private in Capt. James Almoney's Co., 41ˢᵗ Regt., Baltimore County, from 25 Aug 1814 and was reported "sick absent since 10 Oct" 1814 (Wright Vol. 2, p. 66)

Dunstan, John, served as a Seaman and was born in Baltimore. Age: 23. Prison Depot: Portsmouth, Prisoner of War #586. How Taken: Gave himself up off HM Transport *Diadem*. Date Received: 30 Jan 1813. From what ship: HMS *Diadem*. Discharged on 11 Mar 1813 and sent to Chatham on HM Store Ship *Abundance*. Prison Depot: Chatham, Prisoner of War #1255. Date Received: 16 Mar 1813 from Portsmouth on HMS *Abundance*. Discharged and released on 17 Jul 1814. (Johnson's Database, 2019)

Dunton, Robert, served as a Marine, was taken from the barracks and admitted to the Naval Hospital in Washington, DC as Patient No. 85 on 27 Dec 1814 with typhoid fever, was discharged on 20 Jan 1815 and sent to the barracks (Sharp's Database, 2018)

Dusheels (Dusheets), Arthur, served as a Seaman and was born in Maryland. Age: 20. Prison Depot: Plymouth 1, Prisoner of War #2113. Captured by HM Frigate *Hotspur* & HM Frigate *Pyramus*. When Taken: 26 Oct 1813. Where Taken: Bay of Biscayne. Prize Name: *Chesapeake*. Ship Type: Letter of Marque. Date Received: 22 Nov 1813. From what ship: HMS *Pyramus*. Discharged on 29 Nov

1813 and sent to Dartmoor. Prison Depot: Dartmoor, Prisoner of War #834. Date Received: 29 Nov 1813 from Plymouth. Discharged on 26 Apr 1815. (Johnson's Database, 2019)

Dustin, John, of Maryland, served as a Seaman on the ship *Dedham* and was reported by Capt. Jeduthan Upton, Jr. in 1814 as having been impressed into service and was being held as a Prisoner of War on the prison ship *San Antonio* at Chatham, England (*Niles Weekly Register*, 26 Feb 1814)

Duvall, Alvin, served as a Corporal in 14th U.S. Infantry (company not stated), enlisted on 21 Jul 1812 and was captured at Beaver Dams, Upper Canada on 24 Jun 1813. Prisoner of War at Halifax, NS and later paroled, but the date was not given (Johnson and Christou, p. 105, but Johnson, p. 60, did not list him)

Duvall, N. D. [possibly Nicholas D. Duvall], served as a Seaman and was born in Maryland. Age: 23. Prison Depot: Portsmouth, Prisoner of War #1091. Captured by HM Brig *Zenobia*. When Taken: 25 Jun 1813. Where Taken: off Lisbon, Portugal. Prize Name: *Hindostan*. Ship Type: Merchant Vessel. Date Received: 1 Oct 1813. From what ship: HM Ship-of-the-Line *Barham*. Discharged on 17 Oct 1813 and sent to Chatham on HM Store Ship *Weymouth*. Prison Depot: Chatham, Prisoner of War #2343. Date Received: 20 Oct 1813 from Portsmouth on an admiral's tender. Discharged on 4 Sep 1814 and sent to Dartmoor on HMS *Freya*. Prison Depot: Dartmoor, Prisoner of War #3170 (name listed as N. D. Durval). Date Received: 11 Sep 1814. From what ship: HMT *Freya* from Chatham. Discharged on 28 May 1815. Also listed as N. D. Dunvall, Seaman, age 23. Prison Depot: Portsmouth, Prisoner of War #1066. Captured by HM Brig *Zenobia*. When Taken: 25 Jun 1813. Where Taken: off Lisbon, Portugal. Prize Name: *Hindostan*. Ship Type: Merchant Vessel. Date Received: 19 Sep 1813. From what ship: HM Brig *Imogen*. Discharged on 29 Sep 1813 and sent to Chatham on HM Transport *Chatham*. (Johnson's Database, 2019)

Duvall, Trueman (c1788-1813), served as a Captain In the 34th Regiment, Prince George's Co. Militia, from 5 Aug to 2 Sep 1813 when stationed in Annapolis and died before 28 Dec 1813. (Wright Vol. 6, p. 17; Marine p. 275, mistakenly stated he died in 1814) The administrator of Duvall's estate on 28 Dec 1813 was Dennis Duvall. (Prince George's County Inventory Book TT, No. 1, p. 532)

Dye, William, served as a Master and was born in Charles Co., MD. Age: 37. Prison Depot: Plymouth 1, Prisoner of War #629. Captured by HM Ship-of-the-Line *Warspite*. When Taken: 26 Feb 1813. Where Taken: Bay of Biscayne. Prize Name: *Mars*. Ship Type: Merchant Vessel. Date Received: 4 Mar 1813. From what ship: MV *Mars*. Discharged and sent on 6 Mar 1813 to Ashburton on parole. (Johnson's Database, 2019)

Dyer, James, served as a Private in Capt. Fanning's Co., 2nd Regt., U.S. Infantry, when he was wounded (no details were given) and in Baltimore County on 13 Mar 1832 he had been a resident for about 13 years and previously lived in Pennsylvania, appointed William Lewis as his attorney to collect the pension due from 4 Sep 1831 to 4 Mar 1832. (Pierce, p. 57)

Dyer, John B., served as a Private in Capt. Clement Sullivan's Co., 14th U.S. Inf., enlisted 29 May 1812 and died 1 Oct 1812 at Fort Niagara, NY; heirs received half pay for 5 years in lieu of bounty land (Johnson and Christou, p. 106)

Dyer, Samuel, served as a Seaman and was born in Baltimore. Age: 15. Prison Depot: Dartmoor, Prisoner of War #2522. Captured by HM Sloop *Martin*. When Taken: 30 Jun 1814. Where Taken: off Halifax, NS. Prize Name: *Snap Dragon*. Ship Type: Privateer. Date Received: 16 Aug 1814. From what ship: HMT *Queen* from Halifax, NS. Discharged on 3 May 1815. (Johnson's Database, 2019)

E

Eades, John (1789-1815), served as a Private in Capt. John Duval's Co., 20th U.S. Infantry, enlisted 7 Sep 1813 at the age of 24, 5′ 7¾″ tall, born in Maryland and died on 30 Jan 1815, cause not stated (Johnson and Christou, p. 106)

Eaglehart, Nathan (1779-1813), served as a Private in Capt. Colin Buckner's Co., 5th U.S. Infantry, enlisted 4 Apr 1813 in Baltimore at age 34, 5′ 7″ tall, born in Accomack Co., VA and died on 28 Nov 1813 (Johnson and Christou, p. 106)

Early, Samuel (c1794-1814), served as a Private in Capt. John Brookes' Co., 38th U.S. Infantry, enlisted 23 Jul 1813 for 1 year, age not stated, 5′ 6″ tall, born in Prince George's Co., MD, re-enlisted for the war on 12 Aug 1814 and died on 27 Oct 1814; bounty land was issued to his brother Benoni Early and other heirs at law (BLW# 17678-160-12; Johnson and Christou, p. 107)

Earnest, Charles (c1788-1816), served as a Private in Capt. William B. Dyer's Co., 1st Rifle Bttn., from 19 Aug 1814, was wounded on 24 Aug 1814 at the Battle of Bladensburg and died on 31 Aug 1816; he was a ship carpenter, wife Sarah, son William born circa 1810 (at the Hartford Connecticut Asylum for Deaf and Dumb) and a daughter ---- born circa 1817 (sic); widow Sarah Earnest remarried on 20 Jan 1817 to Mr. Daggett who abandoned her. James Daggett married Sarah Arnest in Baltimore County on same date. Charles Earnest, the soldier, married Sarah Bradshaw on 9 Dec 1809 in Baltimore Co. (Marriage Records; Pension 27555; NARA; CMSR; Marine pp. 276, 280; Wright Vol. 2, p. 54). On 18 Mar 1825 Samuel B. Martin, late Surgeon in the 1st Bttn. of Maryland Riflemen, certified that Charles Earnest was wounded on 24 Aug 1814 at Bladensburg while a private in the 1st Rifle Bttn., commanded by Major W. Pinckney, and that he died of his chest wound after lingering a long time. Benjamin T. Boon made oath on

22 Apr 1825 that Charles Earnest died on 31 Aug 1816. In Baltimore on 13 Apr 1824 Edward J. Coale wad appointed on 10 Jul 1819 guardian of William Earnest, now a resident of the deaf and dumb asylum in Hartford, CT, who is pensioned as the surviving child of the soldier, collected $125.00 due him from 4 Sep 1823 to 4 Mar 1824. (Pierce, pp. 57-58)

Easterly, George, served as a Master and was born in Baltimore. Age: 36. Prison Depot: Plymouth 1, Prisoner of War #873. Captured by HM Frigate *Belle Poule*. When Taken: 19 Mar 1813. Where Taken: Bay of Biscayne. Prize Name: *John & Frances*. Ship Type: Merchant Vessel. Date Received: 30 Mar 1813. From what ship: HMS *Plymouth*. Discharged and was sent on 31 Mar 1813 to Ashburton on parole. (Johnson's Database, 2019)

Easton, John (1773-1815), served as a Private in Capt. Samuel Raisin's Co., 36th U.S. Infantry, enlisted 10 Jul 1813 in Waynesburg, PA, age 40, 5' 9" tall, born in District of Columbia, re-enlisted on 14 Dec 1814 and died at Georgetown, DC on 19 Jan 1815 (BLW# 11635-160-12; Johnson and Christou, pp. 107-108)

Eaton, John (1788-1815), served as a Private in the 14th U.S. Infantry, enlisted 14 Dec 1814 at the age of 26, 5' 10" tall, born in York, PA and died at Baltimore on 22 Feb 1815; bounty land was issued to his widow Justina Eaton and other heirs at law (BLW# 1050-320-12; Johnson and Christou, p. 108)

Eaton, John, served as a Seaman and was born in Baltimore. Age: 25. Prison Depot: Chatham, Prisoner of War #1224. Captured by HM Frigate *Dryad* on 7 Jan 1813 at sea. Prize Name: *Rossie*. Ship Type: Merchant Vessel. Date Received 16 Mar 1813 from Portsmouth on HMS *Abundance*. Discharged on 24 Jul 1813 and released to the Cartel *Hoffning*. (Johnson's Database, 2019)

Echard, Frederick, served as a Private in Capt. Ebenezer Childs' Co., 9th U.S. Infantry, enlisted 23 Dec 1813 in Boston at the age of 25, 5' 6" tall, born in Baltimore, was wounded in the thigh at Fort Erie, Upper Canada on 17 Sep 1814 and discharged at Pittsfield, NY on 13 Jun 1815 on Surgeon's Certificate (Johnson and Christou, p. 108)

Edgan, John, served as a Private in the 14th U.S. Infantry and was captured. Prisoner of War #4148 at Halifax, NS, interned 24 Jun 1813, discharged on 27 Aug 1813, sent to England (Johnson and Christou, p. 108; Baker Vol. 1, p. 130)

Edging, Martin, served as a Private in Capt. John Chunn's Co., 19th U.S. Infantry, enlisted 18 Jul 1812 at St. Clairsville, OH at the age of 32, 5' 11" tall, born in Easton, MD and captured at Fort Erie, Upper Canada by Commodore Yeo on 15 Aug 1814. Prisoner of War #7577 at Halifax, NS, interned on 27 Oct 1814 and discharged on 8 Apr 1815 (Johnson and Christou, p. 108; Baker Vol. 1, p. 130)

Edwards, Edward, served as a Private in Capt. Stephen Moore's Co. of the U.S. Volunteers, Baltimore, enlisted 8 Sep 1812 for 1 year and was killed at York, Upper Canada on 27 Apr 1813; bounty land issued to Aquila Edwards and other heirs (BLW# 26987-160-12; Johnson and Christou, p. 109; Wright Vol. 2, p. 57)

Edwards, Jesse, served as a Private (company not stated) and was captured at the Battle of Bladensburg on 24 Aug 1814 (Marine, p. 174)

Edwards, John (1784-1815), served as a Private in Capt. Hezekiah Johnson's Co., 1st U.S. Infantry, enlisted on 10 Jun 1814 in Frenchtown, NJ at the age of 30, 5' 6" tall, born in Maryland and died at Brownsville, NY on 8 or 9 Sep 1815 of fever (Johnson and Christou, p. 109)

Edwards, Thomas, served as a Private in Capt. Reuben Gilder's Co., 14th U.S. Infantry, enlisted 30 Mar 1814 at Towsontown, MD at the age of 38, 5' 8" tall, born in Baltimore City and was discharged at Greenbush, NY on 22 Apr 1815 for inability (Johnson and Christou, p. 109; BLW# 11785-160-12)

Eichelberger, Peter (1787-1875), served as a Private in Capt. Stephen H. Moore's Infantry Co., Baltimore Volunteers, from 8 Sep 1812 for 1 year and was sick in the hospital at Niagara, NY on 13 Apr 1813. (Wright Vol. 2, p. 57) Peter Eichelberger, Sr. was born on 3 Mar 1787 and died on 19 Apr 1875, burial place not stated (www.findagrave.com)

Eicholtz, John, served as a Private in the 5th U.S. Infantry, company and captain were not named, enlisted 29 Apr 1812 in Baltimore and was a prisoner of war, but date and place of capture were not stated (Johnson and Christou, p. 109)

Eli (Ely), George, of Harford Co., served as a Private in Capt. George Steever's Co., 27th Regiment, Baltimore Militia, from 19 Aug 1814 and was wounded on 12 Sep 1814 at North Point. (Wright Vol. 2, p. 15) He was born in 1777, married Ann Spencer, of Harford Co., died in Ohio, but date was not given. (Society of the War of 1812 in the State of Maryland No. 127, National No. 596, in 1896)

Elisha, Thomas, served as a Seaman and was born in Baltimore. Age: 27. Prison Depot: Chatham, Prisoner of War #1808. How Taken: Gave himself up. When Taken: 28 Jun 1813. Where Taken: London, UK. Date Received: 3 Jul 1813. From what ship: HMS *Raisonable*. Discharged on 25 Jul 1814 and sent to Dartmoor on HMS *Bittern*. Prison Depot: Dartmoor, Prisoner of War #2075. Date Received: 3 Aug 1814. From what ship: HMS *Bittern* from Chatham Depot. Discharged on 2 May 1815. (Johnson's Database, 2019)

Elliott, Joseph B., served as a Private in Capt. John Montgomery's 1st Artillery Co., Baltimore, from 19 Aug 1814 and was wounded on 12 Sep 1814 at North Point (Wright Vol. 2, p. 46; Marine p. 170 did not give his name)

Elliott, Thomas W., served as a Private in Capt. Nicholas Burke's Co., 6th Regt., Baltimore Militia, from 19 Aug 1814 and was discharged by the doctor, but the date and cause were not stated (Wright Vol. 2, p. 10)

Ellis, John, served as a Seaman and was born in Coopstown, MD [Harford Co.]. Age: 23. Prison Depot: Portsmouth, Prisoner of War #7. Captured by HM Frigate *Barbadoes*. When Taken: 22 Aug 1812. Where Taken: off Savannah, GA. Prize Name: U.S.R.M. Cutter *James Madison*. Ship Type: Warship. Date Received: 12 Oct 1812 San Antonio. From what ship: HM Ship-of-the-Line *Polyphemus*. Discharged on 19 Feb 1813 and sent to Chatham on HMS *Ulysses*. Prison Depot: Chatham, Prisoner of War #648. Age 33 (sic). Date Received: 24 Feb 1813 from Portsmouth on HMS *Ulysses*. Discharged on 10 May 1813 and released to the Cartel *Admittance*. (Johnson's Database, 2019)

Ellis, John, served as a Boatswain and was born in Maryland. Age: 23. Prison Depot: Chatham, Prisoner of War #20. Captured by HM Ship-of-the-Line *Cressy*. When Taken: 11 Aug 1812. Where Taken: Baltic Sea. Prize Name: *Navigator*. Ship Type: Merchant Vessel. Date Received: 29 Oct 1812. From what ship: HMS *Raisonable*. Discharged on 19 Mar 1813 and released to the *Navigator*. (Johnson's Database, 2019)

Ellis, William, served as a Seaman and was born in Baltimore. Age: 26. Prison Depot: Portsmouth, Prisoner of War #550. Captured by HM Frigate *Dryad*. When Taken: 7 Jan 1813. Where Taken: at sea. Prize Name: *Rossie*. Ship Type: Merchant Vessel. Date Received: 25 Jan 1813 on HM Ship-of-the-Line *Queen*. Discharged on 11 Mar 1813 and sent to Chatham on HM Store Ship *Abundance*. Prison Depot: Chatham, Prisoner of War #1223. Date Received: 16 Mar 1813 from Portsmouth on HMS *Abundance*. Discharged on 24 Jul 1813 and released to the Cartel *Hoffning*. (Johnson's Database, 2019)

Elvin, John, served as a Seaman and was born in Maryland. Age: 20. Prison Depot: Dartmoor, Prisoner of War #2458. Captured by HM Frigate *Orpheus*. When Taken: 20 Apr 1814. Where Taken: off Matanzas, Cuba. Prize Name: U.S. Sloop-of-War *Frolic*. Ship Type: Warship. Received: 16 Aug 1814 from HMT *Queen* from Halifax, NS. Discharged on 3 May 1815. (Johnson's Database, 2019)

Ely, Abraham, served as a Seaman and was born in Baltimore. Age: 29. Prison Depot: Chatham, Prisoner of War #2282. How Taken: Gave himself up. When Taken: 8 Sep 1813. Where Taken: London, UK. Date Received: 17 Sep 1813. From what ship: HMS *Raisonable*. Discharged on 4 Sep 1814 and sent to Dartmoor on HMS *Freya*. Prison Depot: Dartmoor, Prisoner of War #3131. Date Received: 11 Sep 1814. From what ship: HMT *Freya* from Chatham. Discharged on 27 Apr 1815. (Johnson's Database, 2019)

Elmore, Philip, served as a Private in the 14th U.S. Infantry and was captured. Prisoner of War #3963 at Halifax, NS, interned on 24 Jun 1813 and discharged for exchange on 3 Feb 1814 (Johnson and Christou, p. 110; Baker Vol. 1, p. 134)

Emmons, Henry, served as a Private in Capt. Samuel Lane's Co., 14th U.S. Inf., enlisted 28 Apr 1812 at Hagerstown, MD, age 26, 5' 11½" tall, born in Jersey. Prisoner of War #4066 at Halifax, NS, interned 24 Jun 1813, discharged 3 Feb 1814, was returned to service and deserted at Plattsburgh, NY on 20 Aug 1814 (Johnson and Christou, p. 110; Baker Vol. 1, p. 134 spelled his name Emmins)

Ennalls, Joseph, of Henry, served as a Captain In the 10th Cavalry District on 29 July 1812, was a Major on 6 Dec 1813 and died in July 1814 (Marine p. 279)

Ennels, Henry, served as a Private in Capt. James Barker's Co., 2nd U.S. Artillery, enlisted 27 Apr 1813 for 5 years in Philadelphia at the age of 37, 5' 9¾" tall, born in Maryland and was discharged on Surgeon's Certificate on 21 Jul 1815 (Johnson and Christou, p. 111)

Ent, John, served as 3rd Corporal in Capt. Thomas C. Worthington's Co., U.S. Army, enlisted at Annapolis on 4 Dec 1812 for 5 years at the age of 27, 5' 7½" tall, hazel eyes, brown hair, dark complexion, born in Germantown, PA, served in the 16th U.S. Infantry under Capt. J. Baldy, mustered at Philadelphia on 6 Jul 1814 and was discharged at Greenbush, NY on 22 or 25 Apr 1815, wounded (Mallick and Wright, pp. 108-109)

Ernest, Frederick, served as a Seaman and was wounded on 24 Aug 1814 at Bladensburg and his leg was amputated by a British surgeon; he was admitted to the Naval Hospital in Washington, DC as Patient No. 41 on 9 Sep 1814 and was discharged on 10 Oct 1814 and sent to Baltimore (Sharp's Database, 2018)

Etting, Samuel, served as a Private in Capt. Joseph H. Nicholson's Artillery Co. and was slightly wounded on 13 Sep 1814 at Fort McHenry (Marine p. 173)

Euler, Conrad, served as a Private in Capt. Dominic Bader's Co., 1st Rifle Bttn., Baltimore City, and was wounded, captured and taken as a prisoner of war on 12 Sep 1814 at North Point. Dr. James H. McCulloh, Jr. wrote this note soon after the battle to the British commander: "In consequence of the humanity shown the following American prisoners of war, I do promise upon honor that they shall not directly or indirectly serve against the British until regularly exchanged." (Wright Vol. 2, p. 53; Marine p. 171) In Baltimore on 5 Sep 1823 Conrad Euler, former private, Lt. Strischka's Co. of Yagers, 3rd Brigade, Maryland Militia [Joseph A. Strischka was the 2nd Lieutenant in Capt. Dominic Bader's Co.], in the late war and resident of this [Baltimore] city for about 10 years and previously of Philadelphia, collected his own $24.00 due from 4 Mar to 4 Sep 1823. Dr. John

Chapman and Dr. Horatio G. Jameson made oaths that Conrad Euler was still disabled from a wound in the right arm. (Pierce, p. 63)

Euler, Jacob, served as a 1st Sergeant in Capt. Dominic Bader's Rifle Co. and was wounded on 12 Sep 1814 at North Point. (Marine p. 280) Conrad Euler, administrator of Jacob Euler, late pensioner and former sergeant In Capt. Badon's (sic) Co. of Rifleman, Maryland Militia, who resided for 45 years in Baltimore and previously in Germany, collected $33.80 in arrears due from 4 Sep 1842 to 23 Feb 1843, the date of Jacob Euler's death. (Pierce, pp. 59-60)

Evans, Ebenezer, served in the Navy from 18 Feb 1814 and lost his sight at St. Leonards Creek, 2nd Battle, on 26 Jun 1814 (Shomette, p. 528; Sheads, p. 22)

Evans, Edward, served as a Private in the 14th U.S. Infantry and was captured. Prisoner of War #4184 at Halifax, NS, interned 24 Jun 1813, discharged on 27 Aug 1813, sent to England (Johnson and Christou, p. 110; Baker Vol. 1, p. 135)

Evans, George, served as 3rd Sergeant in Capt. Stephen H. Moore's Co. of U. S. Volunteers, Baltimore, from 8 Sep 1812 for 1 year and was "sick in hospital at Niagara," NY in 1813, but the exact date was not given (Wright Vol. 2, p. 57)

Evans, Jacob, served as a Prize Master and was born in Baltimore. Age: 22. Prison Depot: Plymouth 1, Prisoner of War #823. Captured by HM Brig *Piercer*. When Taken: 9 Mar 1813. Where Taken: off Isle Ross. Prize Name: *King George*, prize of the Privateer *Blockade*. Ship Type: Privateer. Received: 21 Mar 1813. From what ship: HMS *Piercer*. Discharged and sent to Dartmoor on 28 Jun 1813. Prison Depot: Dartmoor, Prisoner of War #308. Received: 28 Jun 1813 from Plymouth. Discharged on 15 Apr 1815. (Johnson's Database, 2019)

Evans, James, served as a Private in the 14th U.S. Infantry and was captured. Prisoner of War #4177 at Halifax, NS, interned 24 Jun 1813, discharged on 27 Aug 1813, sent to England (Johnson and Christou, p. 112; Baker Vol. 1, p. 135)

Evans, John, served as a Private in Capt. George Steever's Co., 27th Regiment, Baltimore Militia, from 9 Aug to 16 Aug 1813 and served as a Private in Capt. Peter Pinney's Co. from 19 Aug 1814 and was killed in Battle of North Point on 12 Sep 1814. His name is on the Baltimore Battle Monument (CMSR; Wright Vol. 2, p. 20; Marine p. 281; *Baltimore American*, 12 Jun 1819) July Court 1815: Elizabeth Evans, administratrix of John Evans, was ordered to sell a bake house and lot on Franklin Lane at Bowley's Wharf at public sale for not less than $4,000. (Baltimore Orphans Court Proceedings Book 9, p. 158)

Evans, John (1774-1815), served as a Private in Capt. Thomas Carbery's Co., 36th U.S. Infantry, enlisted 24 Feb 1814 in Leonardstown, MD at the age of 40, 5' 8" tall, born in Maryland and died in regimental hospital on 30 Jan 1815, place was not stated; bounty land issued to sister Susanna Drake (BLW# 11701-160-12; Johnson and Christou, p. 111)

Evans, John (1787-1814), served as a Seaman and was born in Baltimore. Age: 26. Prison Depot: Chatham, Prisoner of War #2846. Captured by HM Brig *Recruit* on 17 Aug 1813. Where Taken: coast of U.S. Prize Name: *Blockade*. Ship Type: Privateer. Died on 5 Mar 1814 from smallpox. (Johnson's Database, 2019)

Evans, John B. (c1785-1815), served as a Lieutenant in Capt. William Bean's Co., 12th Regiment, St. Mary's Co. Militia, volunteered at the beginning of the war being then in commission (muster roll date 15 Jul – 4 Aug 1813), also served in Capt. Cornelius Combs' Co. (muster roll dated 2 Feb – 11 Aug 1814) and then continued until summer of 1814 under Capt. Bean (muster rolls dated 4 Jun – 25 Jun 1814 and 12 Aug – 17 Aug 1814) when he became sick at Onion Field Camp and lingered until he died on 6 Mar 1815, never having recovered from the disease that he contracted from exposure in service. His widow Martha (Silence) Evans, whom he married on 4 Oct 1804, applied for bounty land in 1855, age 69. (BLW# 55-160-4201; Wright Vol. 5, pp. 16, 17, 23, 64)

Evans, Philip, served as a Private in Capt. Thomas Montgomery's Co., 14th U.S. Infantry, but enlistment date and place were not given, and was discharged at Burlington, VT on 21 Apr 1814 for inability (Johnson and Christou, p. 112)

Evans, William, served as a Private in Capt. Alexander Williams' Co., 2nd U.S. Artillery, enlisted 7 Sep 1813 in Philadelphia at the age of 39, 5' 11" tall, born in Maryland and was missing in action after the attack on Fort Erie, Upper Canada on 15 or 16 Aug 1814 (Johnson and Christou, p. 112)

Evans, William, served as a Seaman and was born in Baltimore. Age: 40. Prison Depot: Chatham, Prisoner of War #3861. Captured by HM Brig *Harpy*. When Taken: 18 Dec 1812. Where Taken: off Isle de France, Mauritius. Prize Name: *James*. Ship Type: Merchant Vessel. Date Received: 24 Aug 1814 from London. Discharged 22 Oct 1814 and sent to Dartmoor on HMS *Leyden*. Prison Depot: Dartmoor, Prisoner of War #5377. Received: 31 Oct 1814. From what ship: HMT *Leyden* from Chatham. Discharged on 27 Apr 1815. (Johnson's Database, 2019)

Everit, John, see William McCarty, q.v.

Everitt, Joseph, served as a Private in Capt. William Copper's Artillery Co., 21st Regiment, Kent Co. Militia, in 1813 and was reported as "excused on inability" on the muster roll dated 15 Apr – 12 May 1813 (Wright Vol. 1, p. 13)

Eversfield, John (1790-1857), served as a Private in Capt. Thomas Eversfield's Co., 17th Regiment, Prince George's Co. Militia, Nottingham Battalion, from 24 to 26 Jul 1813 and in Capt. Gavin Hamilton's Co. between 18 Aug and 17 Sep 1813 and was "sick and gone home," but no date was given; he was stationed at

Nottingham under Lt. Henry Swain from 17 to 24 Jun 1814 and served under Capt. Thomas Eversfield from 21 Aug 1814 until discharged on 3 Sep 1814. On 4 May 1858 Ann Perrie Eversfield, age 61, widow of John Eversfield, stated they were married on 6 Apr 1820 by Rev. Broadman, her former name was Wailes and John died at Oakland, near Bladensburg, on 18 Dec 1857. (Wright Vol. 6, pp. 4, 5, 7, 3, 35) John Eversfield was born on 13 Aug 1790, died on 18 Dec 1857 and was buried at St. John's Episcopal Church Cemetery in Beltsville, MD. (*Stones and Bones: Cemetery Records of Prince George's County, Maryland*, by Jean A. Sargent, ed., Prince George's County Genealogical Society, 1984, p. 148)

Everson, Richard, served as a Private in Capt. Robert T. Dade's Co.,` Cramer's Regiment, Montgomery Co. Militia, and was reported "sick in the City" on the muster roll dated 3 Aug – 10 Nov 1814 (Wright Vol. 7, p. 8)

F

Fable, Jesse, served as a Private under Joshua Barney in the U.S. Flotilla and was captured at Bladensburg on 24 Aug 1814 (Marine, p. 282)

Fable, John, served as a Private under Joshua Barney in the U.S. Flotilla and was captured at Bladensburg on 24 Aug 1814 (Marine, p. 281)

Fable, Joseph, served as a Private (company not stated) and was captured at the Battle of Bladensburg on 24 Aug 1814 (Marine, p. 174)

Fackney, John, served as a Seaman and was born in Maryland. Age: 25. Prison Depot: Dartmoor, Prisoner of War #2172. Captured by HM Frigate *Hyperion*. When Taken: 26 Jun 1814. Where Taken: off Cape Finisterre, Spain. Prize Name: *Rattlesnake*. Home Port: Philadelphia. Ship Type: Privateer. Received on 16 Aug 1814. From what ship: HMS *Dublin* from Halifax, NS. Discharged on 2 May 1815. (Johnson's Database, 2019)

Fagan, George, served as a Private in Capt. Joseph Green's Co., Frederick Co. Militia, from 14 Oct 1814 and was discharged by surgeon, but the date, place and cause were not stated (Mallick and Wright, p. 346)

Fagan, James, served as a Private in Capt. James McDonald's Co., 14th U.S. Infantry, enlisted 15 Feb 1814, age 35, 5' 7" tall, born in Ireland and discharged at Fort Moultrie, SC on 3 May 1816, wounded at Fort George, Upper Canada, but no date was given (BLW# 26303-160-12; Johnson and Christou, p. 113)

Fahnestock, Derrick, served as a Private in Capt. John Berry's Washington Artillery Co. and was slightly wounded on 13 Sep 1814 at Fort McHenry (Marine pp. 173, 282; Wright Vol. 2, p. 49) He was buried in Green Mount Cemetery.

Fairfield, Solomon, served as a Private in 14th U.S. Infantry and was captured. Prisoner of War #4046 at Halifax, NS, interned 24 Jun 1813 and died there on 24 Jun 1813 of small pox (Johnson and Christou, p. 114; Baker, Vol. 1, p. 136)

Fallier, George, served as a Private in Capt. William Roney's Co., 39th Regt., Baltimore Militia, from 20 Aug 1814, wounded on 13 Sep 1814 at Fort McHenry and died 19 Sep 1814. His name is on the Baltimore Battle Monument. (CMSR; Wright Vol. 2, p. 24; Marine p. 282; *Baltimore American*, 12 Jun 1819)

Fango, Matthew, served as a Quarter Gunner on the privateer *Surprise* of Baltimore and drowned in a shipwreck on 5 Apr 1815 (Marine p. 282; *Niles Weekly Register* 15 Apr 1815)

Farley (Ferley), John, served as a Seaman and was born in Baltimore. Age: 33. Prison Depot: Plymouth 1, Prisoner of War #1312. How Taken: Gave himself up off HM Ship-of-the-Line *Clarence*. Date Received: 10 May 1813. From what ship: HMS *Clarence*. Discharged on 8 Jul 1813 and sent to Chatham on HM Tender *Neptune*. Prison Depot: Chatham, Prisoner of War #1999. Date Received: 15 Jul 1813 from Plymouth.Discharged on 17 Jun 1814 and sent to Dartmoor on HMS *Pincher*. Prison Depot: Dartmoor, Prisoner of War #1840. Received on 21 Jul 1814. From what ship: HMT *Redbeard* & HMT *Pincher* from Chatham Depot. Discharged on 2 May 1815. (Johnson's Database, 2019)

Farman, Joseph, served as a Private in 14th U.S. Infantry and was born in Maryland. Age: 26. Prison Depot: Chatham, Prisoner of War #3065. When Taken: 24 Jun 1813. Where Taken: Beaver Dams, Upper Canada. Date Received: 7 Jan 1814 from Halifax, NS. Discharged on 10 Oct 1814 and sent to U.S. on the Cartel *St. Philip*. (Johnson's Database, 2019)

Farman, Joshua, served as a Private in the 14th U.S. Infantry and was captured. Prisoner of War #3968 at Halifax, NS, interned 24 Jun 1813, discharged 9 Nov 1813 and sent to England (Johnson and Christou, p. 114; Baker Vol. 1, p. 136)

Farquhar, John, served as a Seaman and was born in Baltimore. Age: 44. Prison Depot: Dartmoor, Prisoner of War #5936. Captured by HM Ship-of-the-Line *Bulwark*. When Taken: 23 Oct 1814. Where Taken: off Halifax, NS. Prize Name: *Harlequin*. Home Port: Portsmouth. Ship Type: Privateer. Date Received: 27 Dec 1814 from HMT *Penelope*. Discharged 3 Jul 1815. (Johnson's Database, 2019)

Farrell, Michael, served as a Private in Capt. Thomas Montgomery's Co., 14th U.S. Infantry, enlisted 12 May 1812 in Baltimore at age 48, 5' 6" tall, born in Galway, Ireland and captured on 12 Jun 1813. Prisoner of War #5110 at Halifax, NS, interned 8 Dec 1813, discharged 31 May 1814, returned to service and discharged from service at Greenbush, NY on 10 Apr 1815 for inability and old age (Johnson and Christou, p. 114; Baker Vol. 1, p. 137 spelled his name Farell)

Farrell, Richard, served as a Seaman and was born in Baltimore. Age: 23. Prison Depot: Dartmoor, Prisoner of War #5824. Captured by British gunboats. When Taken: 3 Sep 1814. Where Taken: Lake Huron. Prize Name: U.S. Schooner *Tigress*. Ship Type: Warship. Date Received: 26 Dec 1814. From what ship: HMT *Argo*. Discharged on 11 Jul 1815. (Johnson's Database, 2019)

Farry, Locklin, served as a Private in Capt. Reuben Gilder's Co., 14ᵗʰ U.S. Inf., enlisted 5 Apr 1813 at age 30, 5' 2" tall, born in Ireland and discharged at Burlington, VT on 9 Apr 1814 for inability due to an incurable bruise received at Chateaugay (Johnson and Christou, p. 115)

Fate, Thomas, served as a Seaman and was born in Maryland. Age: 34. Prison Depot: Plymouth 1, Prisoner of War #91. Captured by HM Brig *Rover*. When Taken: 21 Oct 1812. Where Taken: off Bordeaux, France. Prize Name: *Experiment*. Ship Type: Merchant Vessel. Date Received: 25 Dec 1812. From what ship: HMS *Northumberland*. Discharged and sent to Portsmouth on 29 Dec 1812 on HMS *Northumberland*. Prison Depot: Portsmouth, Prisoner of War #345. Date Received: 31 Dec 1812. From what ship: HM Ship-of-the-Line *Northumberland*. Discharged on 4 Mar 1813 and sent to Chatham on HMS *Queen*. Prison Depot: Chatham, Prisoner of War #922. Date Received: 10 Mar 1813. From what ship: HMS *Tigress*. Discharged on 8 Jun 1813 and released to the Cartel *Rodrigo*. (Johnson's Database, 2019)

Fauney, Jacob, served as Bugler in Capt. William Durbin's Co., Frederick Co. Militia, from 24 Aug 1814, marched off for Baltimore and was discharged for inability in 6 Sep 1814 (Mallick and Wright, p. 353)

Fazier, John, served as a Marine and was wounded on 24 Aug 1814 on the field of battle at Bladensburg, was admitted to the Naval Hospital in Washington, DC as Patient No. 14, was discharged on 14 Sep 1814 and sent to barracks (Sharp's Database, 2018)

Fenwick, Philip, served as a Private in Capt. Woodburn's Co., 45ᵗʰ Regiment, St. Mary's Co. Militia, from 29 Jul 1813 for 3 days and was "furlowed till he gets well." (Wright Vol. 5, p. 32)

Feres, John, served as a Private in the 14ᵗʰ U.S. Infantry and was captured at Beaver Dams, Upper Canada on 24 Jun 1813. Prisoner of War #3741 at Halifax, NS, interned on 24 Jun 1813, discharged on 9 Nov 1814 and sent to England per order of Adm. J. B. Warren (Johnson and Christou, p. 116; Baker Vol. 1, p. 137)

Ferguson, John, served as a Private under Lt. Col. George Armistead in the 1ˢᵗ U.S. Artillery, enlisted 17 Apr 1812 at Fort McHenry at the age of 38, 5' 9" tall, born in Pennsylvania and discharged at Fort Columbus, NY on 20 Sep 1813 for disability (Johnson and Christou, p. 116)

Ferguson, Thomas, served as a Seaman and was born in Baltimore. Age: 23. Prison Depot: Chatham, Prisoner of War #2509. Captured by HM Ship-of-the-Line *Victorious*. When Taken: 8 Jun 1813. Where Taken: Chesapeake Bay. Prize Name: *Globe*. Ship Type: Privateer. Date Received: 22 Oct 1813 from Portsmouth on HMT *Malabar*. Discharged on 8 Sep 1814 and sent to Dartmoor on HMS *Niobe*. Prison Depot: Dartmoor, Prisoner of War #3314. Age 25. Date Received: 13 Sep 1814. From what ship: HMT *Niobe* from Chatham. Discharged on 28 May 1815 (Johnson's Database, 2019)

Ferley, John, see John Farley, q.v.

Fernandes (Fernandez), Thomas, served as a Private in Capt. Samuel Dawson's Co., Frederick Co. Militia, from 26 Jul 1814, engaged in Battle of Bladensburg on 24 Aug 1814 and then in the defense of Baltimore City on 12 Sep 1814 and was reported "sick on furlough since Sep 26" 1814 (Mallick and Wright, p. 338)

Fetty, Jacob F., served as a Private in Capt. Isaac Barnard's Co., 14th U.S. Inf., enlisted 12 Nov 1812 and was killed at Beaver Dams, Upper Canada, ten miles west of Niagara Falls, on 24 Jun 1813 (Johnson and Christou, p. 116)

Fiddy, William (1796-1814), served as a Musician in Capt. Thomas Post's Co., 12th U.S. Infantry, enlisted 22 Aug 1813 for 5 years by Capt. Morgan in Virginia, age 17, 5' 1¼' tall, black eyes, black hair and dark complexton, born in Allegany Co., MD, mustered at Staunton VA, left sick in General Hospital at Sackett's Harbor, NY on 19 Sep 1814 and died there on 29 Oct or Nov 1814; bounty land was issued to his father Thompson Fiddy (BLW# 25469-160-12; Johnson and Christou, p. 116; Wright Vol. 10, p. 9)

Fielder, Robert (1782-1815), served as a Private in Capt. Hopley Yeaton's Co., 1st U.S Artillery, enlisted 19 Feb 1812 in Fort Nelson, VA, age 31, 5' 6½" tall, born St. Mary's Co., MD and died 18 May 1815 (Johnson and Christou, p. 117)

Fields, George (1793-1813), served as a Corporal in Capt. Daniel Appling's Co., 1st U.S. Rifles, enlisted 5 Apr 1813 at Fort Hampton, AL at age 20, 5' 10¾" tall, born in Maryland, and killed at Fort Erie, Upper Canada on 6 Aug 1814; bounty land was issued to his brother John Fields and other heirs at law (BLW# 21539-160-12; Johnson and Christou, p. 117)

Fields, Joseph, served as a Private in Capt. Edward W. Comegys' Co., 21st Regiment, Kent Co. Militia, in 1813 and was reported "sick" on the muster roll dated 5 Aug – 25 Aug 1813 (Wright Vol. 1, p. 15)

Fields, Thomas, served as a Private in Capt. William McIlvane's Co., 14th U.S. Infantry, enlisted 11 May 1812 for 5 years. Prisoner of War #4080 at Halifax, discharged on 3 Feb 1814, exchanged on 15 Apr 1814 and died on 30 Jun 1814, shot by a sentinel (Johnson and Christou, p. 117; Baker, Vol. 1, p. 140)

Fife, Andrew H., served as a Private in Capt. Stephen Moore's Co. in the U. S. Volunteers, Baltimore, enlisted 8 Sep 1812 for 1 year and then enlisted as a Gunner in Capt. John Gill's Co., U.S. Sea Fencibles on 20 Dec 1813 for 1 year. (Johnson and Christou, p. 117, did not mention his wound) Andrew H. Fife and Eliza Ann Roberts, both of Baltimore, were married 27 Sep 1817 by Rev. Healy. (*Baltimore Patriot*, 29 Sep 1817) In Baltimore on 6 Mar 1828 Andrew Fife, a former private in Capt. Stephen H. Moore's Co., U.S. Volunteers called the "Baltimore Blues" in the late war, and a resident of this city for 30 years and previously of Princess Anne Co., VA, who was wounded on 27 Apr 1815 at York, Upper Canada, appointed Thomas Dunlap as his attorney to collect his pension due from 4 Sep 1827 to 4 Mar 1828. (Pierce, p. 65)

Fish, Levin, served as a Private in the 12th U.S. Infantry, company and captain's name not stated, and died on 11 Feb 1814; heirs received half pay for 5 years in lieu of bounty land (Johnson and Christou, p. 118)

Fisher, Anthony, served as a Private in Capt. Nathan Towson's Co. and Capt. James Barker's Co., 2nd U.S. Artillery, enlisted 4 Aug 1812 for 5 years, age 22, 5' 2" tall, born in Baltimore and captured in the Battle of Stoney Creek on 6 Jun 1813. Prisoner of War #4446 at Halifax, NS, interned 9 Nov 1813, discharged for exchange on 31 May 1814 and discharged from the service at Fort Niagara, NY on 3 Aug 1817 (Johnson and Christou, p. 118; Baker Vol. 1, p. 141)

Fisher, Jacob, served as a Private in Capt. James Dorman's Co., 5th U.S. Infantry, enlisted 1 May 1812 for 5 years at Fredericktown, MD at the age of 35, 5' 6" tall, born in Pennsylvania and was discharged at Plattsburgh, NY on 4 Jul 1814 for old age and inability (Johnson and Christou, p. 118)

Fisher, James, served as a Seaman and was born in Maryland. Age: 29. Prison Depot: Dartmoor, Prisoner of War #2359. Captured by HM Sloop *Martin*. When Taken: 30 Jun 1814. Where Taken: off Halifax, NS. Prize Name: *Snap Dragon*. Ship Type: Privateer. Date Received: 16 Aug 1814. From what ship: HMT *Queen* from Halifax, NS. Discharged on 3 May 1815. (Johnson's Database, 2019)

Fisher, James, served as a Seaman and was born in Maryland. Age: 29. Prison Depot: Dartmoor, Prisoner of War #6546. How Taken: Gave himself up off HM Frigate *Quebec*. When Taken: 22 Feb 1813. Received: 7 Mar 1815 from HMT *Ganges* from Plymouth. Escaped on 1 Jun 1815. (Johnson's Database, 2019)

Fister, Jacob, served as a Private in Capt. Richard Arell's Co., 14th U.S. Infantry, enlisted 22 Jan 1813 for 5 years at Frederick, MD at the age of 23, 5' 7½' tall, born in Frederick, MD. Prisoner of War #3864 at Halifax, NS, interned 24 Jun 1813, discharged from prison on 3 Feb 1814 and discharged from the service on 22 Jan 1818 (Johnson and Christou, p. 119; Baker Vol. 1, p. 141)

Fishwick, John, served as a Private in Capt. Nicholas Burke's Co., 6th Regt., Baltimore Militia, from 19 Aug 1814 and was discharged by the doctor, but the date and cause were not stated (Wright Vol. 2, p. 10)

Fitzgerald, Samuel, served as a Private in Capt. William Jones' Co., 8th U.S. Infantry, enlisted 18 Jul 1812 in Georgia, age 26, 5' 9½" tall, born in Charles Co., MD and discharged on 21 Aug 1815 for debility (Johnson and Christou, p. 119)

Flaharty (Flaheety), Mathias, served as a Private in Capt. David Cummings' Co., 14th U.S. Infantry, enlisted on 28 Jul 1812 and was captured. Prisoner of War #4164 at Halifax, NS, interned 24 Jun 1813, was discharged on 27 Aug 1813 and sent to England on HMS *Regulus* (Johnson and Christou, p. 120 spelled his name Flaharty; Baker Vol. 1, p. 142, spelled it Flaheety)

Flanagan, Hugh, served as a Private in Capt. Samuel McDonald's Co., 6th Regt., Baltimore Militia, joined 25 Aug 1814 and was reported "absent in hospital," but the date and medical cause were not stated (Wright Vol. 2, p. 13)

Flaut (Flautt), Jacob, served as a Private in Capt. John Galt's Co., Frederick Co. Militia, from 31 Aug 1814 and reported as "sick absent 19 days" in Baltimore (Mallick and Wright, p. 361)

Fleagle, John, Jr. (1793-1879), served as a Private under Capt. Fonsten, 2 Sep – 27 Oct 1814. Statement in a letter by S. Franklin Fleagle in 1937 stated John Fleagle, Jr. fought in the War of 1812 and was shot in leg at Battle of North Point. The result of the wound was noticeable for the rest of his life, as he always walked lame and carried a cane. (Mallick and Wright, p. 116) John Fleagle died 24 Dec 1873, age 93 years, 2 months and 15 days and was buried in Grace Evangelical and Reformed Church Cemetery in Taneytown, MD. (*Names In Stone*, by Jacob M. Holdcraft, 1966, p. 409)

Fleetwood, Benjamin (c1779-1829), served as a Private in company of Capt. Daniel Schwartzauer, 27th Regiment, Baltimore Militia, was wounded at North Point on 12 Sep 1814 and listed as "in hospital" on the 19 Aug – 18 Nov 1814 muster roll. He was also shown on the list of Prisoners of War exchanged with the British. Dr. James H. McCulloh, Jr. wrote this note soon after the battle to the British commander: "In consequence of the humanity shown the following American prisoners of war, I do promise upon honor that they shall not directly or indirectly serve against the British until regularly exchanged." (Wright Vol. 2, p. 16, Marine p. 171) In Baltimore on 9 Mar 1830 Mayor Jacob Small made oath that Susan Fleetwood, here present, is the widow of Benjamin Fleetwood, a late invalid pensioner and former private in Capt. Schwarzauer's Co., 27th Regt., 2nd Bttn., Maryland Militia, and she collected $6.58 on 11 Mar 1830. James Phillips, Jr., owner of the brig *Sultana*, of the Port of Baltimore, made oath on 12 Mar

1830 that he was informed that Benjamin Fleetwood died aboard said brig on 24 Oct 1829 en route to New Orleans. (Pierce, p. 66)

Fleming, Michael, was a Seaman who was wounded on 24 Aug 1814 on the field of battle at Bladensburg, was admitted to Naval Hospital in Washington, DC as Patient No. 16, and deserted on 28 Sep 1814 (Sharp's Database, 2018)

Flenner, John (1784-1814), served as a Private in Capt. Edward Carrington's Co., 3rd U.S. Rifles, enlisted 7 Jun 1814 for 5 years in Beverly, VA at age 30, 5' 7" tall, born in Frederick, MD and died 24 Oct 1814 (Johnson and Christou, p. 120)

Fletcher, James, served as a Private in Capt. Joseph Marshall's Co., 14th U.S. Infantry, enlisted 9 Jul 1812 in Baltimore, age 16, 5' 8" tall, born in Alexandria, DC and discharged at Burlington, VT on 17 Mar 1814 for a contracted arm and indicating he was disabled when enlisted (Johnson and Christou, p. 121)

Fletcher, Levin, served as a Private in Capt. Thomas Kearney's Co., 14th U.S. Infantry, enlisted 29 May 1812 and died on 12 Jan 1813; bounty land issued to his brother James Fletcher (BLW# 26377-160-12; Johnson and Christou, p. 121)

Flitter, Ludwick, served as a Private in Capt. William Murray's Co., 36th Regt., Baltimore Co., from 25 Aug 1814 and reported as "sick absent since 10 Oct" (Wright Vol. 2, p. 62)

Flood, Francis, served as a Seaman and was born in Maryland. Age: 24. Prison Depot: Dartmoor, Prisoner of War #5132. How Taken: Gave himself up off HM Frigate *Crescent*. When Taken: 20 Oct 1814. Date Received: 31 Oct 1814. From what ship: HMT *Castilian*. Discharged 29 Jun 1815. (Johnson's Database, 2019)

Flowers, Andrew, served as a Private in Capt. Thomas Montgomery's Co., 14th U.S. Infantry, enlisted 8 Jun 1812 and died at Burlington, VT, of 25 Feb or 25 Apr 1814 from sickness; bounty land issued to brother Henry Flowers and other heirs at law (BLW# 25982-160-12; Johnson and Christou, p. 122)

Flowers, Benjamin, served as a Private in Capt. Philip B. Sadtler's Co., 5th Regiment, Baltimore Militia, and was wounded on 12 Sep 1814 at North Point (Wright Vol. 2, p. 7)

Flugle, John Jr., see John Fleagle, Jr.

Fogger (Foggart), Archibald, served as a Private in the 14th U.S. Infantry and was captured at Beaver Dams, Upper Canada on 24 Jun 1813. Prisoner of War #4096 at Halifax, NS and was discharged on 9 Nov 1813 and sent to England (Johnson and Christou, p. 122; Baker Vol. 1, p. 144 spelled his name Foggart)

Folger, Frederick, served as a Seaman and was born in Baltimore. Age: 27. Prison Depot: Portsmouth, Prisoner of War #1102. How Taken: Gave himself up off HM

Ship-of-the-Line *Swiftsure*. When Taken: 26 Dec 1812. Received: 5 Oct 1813 on HM Ship-of-the-Line *Achille*. Discharged 17 Oct 1813, sent to Chatham on HM Store Ship *Weymouth*. Prison Depot: Chatham, Prisoner of War #2368. Received: 20 Oct 1813 from Portsmouth on an admiral's tender. Discharged on 4 Sep 1814 and sent to Dartmoor on HMS *Freya*. Prison Depot: Dartmoor, Prisoner of War #3190. Received: 11 Sep 1814 on HMT *Freya* from Chatham. Discharged and sent to Dartmouth on 23 Sep 1814. (Johnson's Database, 2019)

Folks, James, served as a Private in Capt. John Heeter's Co., 44th Regiment, Montgomery Co. Militia, and was reported as taken prisoner on 24 Aug 1814 [at the Battle of Bladensburg] on the muster roll dated 4 Aug – 27 Sep 1814 (Wright Vol. 7, p. 4, spelled his name Fulks; Marine, p. 174, spelled it Folks)

Foot, Henry (1777-1814), served as a Private in the 44th U.S. Infantry, enlisted 3 May 1814 at Powder Magazine Barracks, LA at age 27, 5' 6" tall, born in Washington, MD (sic), and killed 23 Dec 1814 (Johnson and Christou, pp. 121)

Forbes, Sandy, served as a Seaman on the privateer *Globe* and was killed in action on 1 Nov 1813 (*Niles Weekly Register*, 19 Feb 1814)

Ford, Baptist, served as a Seaman and was born in Charles Co., MD. Age and Race not stated. Prison Depot: Jamaica, Prisoner of War #29. Captured by HM Frigate Gar*land*. When Taken: 3 Aug 1812. Where Taken: at sea. Prize Name: *Madisonia*. Ship Type: Merchant Vessel. Received: 22 Aug 1812 from HMS Gar*land*. Discharged 9 May 1813 and sent to U.S. (Johnson's Database, 2019)

Ford, John, served as a Seaman and was born in St. Mary's Co., MD. Age: 30. Prison Depot: Plymouth 2, Prisoner of War #518. Captured by HM Ship-of-the-Line *Elizabeth*. When Taken: 28 Feb 1815. Where Taken: West Indies. Prize Name: *MaryAnn*. Ship Type: Merchant Vessel. Date Received: 16 Apr 1815. From what ship: HMS *Swiftsure*. Discharged on 11 Jul 1815. and released to the Cartel *Wooddrop Sims*. (Johnson's Database, 2019)

Ford, John Francis (c1792-1822), served as 2nd Lieutenant in Capt. Gerrard N. Causin's Co., 4th Regimental Cavalry District, St. Mary's Co., in June 1814 and was in no engagement, but while acting under orders was wounded, remained so during the whole war and died in Dec 1822; widow Priscilla (Medley) Ford (who married John in 1818) married second to Capt. Charles G. Greenwell in 1826 and third to Henry W. Ford in 1835. (BLW# 55-120-24758; Wright Vol. 5, pp. 48, 64; *Marriages and Deaths, St. Mary's County, Maryland, 1634-1900*, by Margaret K. Fresco, 1982, pp. 106, 378)

Ford, Levi George (1779-1814), served as a Captain in the 8th Cavalry District on 12 Jun 1812 and died in 1814; he married Ann Bayard. (Marine p. 286; *1812 Ancestor Index Volume I, 1892-1970*, U.S. Daughters of 1812, 2005, p. 134)

Ford, Thomas, served as a Private in Capt. Stephen Gill's Co., 41st Regiment, Baltimore Co., from 25 Aug 1814 and was reported as "in hospital from Sep 27" 1814 (Wright Vol. 2, p. 68)

Ford, Timothy, served as a Private in Capt. Thomas Biddle's Co., 2nd U.S. Artillery, enlisted on 1 Aug 1812 for 5 years at the age of 48, 5' 6" tall, born in Baltimore Co., wounded at Fort George, Upper Canada on 27 Mar 1813 and was discharged at Boston, MA on 13 Jun 1815 on Surgeon's Certificate (BLW# 5677-160-12; Johnson and Christou, p. 123)

Ford, William, served as a Private in Capt. John Buck's Co., 38th U.S. Infantry, enlisted on 24 Nov 1813, age was not stated, 5' 9" tall, was born in Cecil Co., MD, re-enlisted on 7 Mar 1814 for the war and died at "Cantoment Baltimore" on 10 Dec 1814 (Johnson and Christou, p. 123)

Foreman, Elijah (c1785-1815), served as a Private in the 5th Calvary Regt. under Capt. James Horton and Col. Biays in the Maryland Chausseurs from 19 Aug 1814 to 23 Nov 1814 and was shot from his horse and badly wounded in the breast at the Battle of North Point on 12 Sep 1814 and died 19 Feb 1815 from his wound. Confirmed by Col. William Stansbury who was the Ensign of the company at that time; however, muster rolls did not state he was wounded; wife Elizabeth Foreman received his bounty land (BLW# 55-120-40258; Wright Vol. 2, p. 55; Marine p. 287)

Forman, Aaron (1788-1813), served as a Private in Capt. Mathew Arbuckle's Co., 2nd U.S. Infantry, enlisted 13 Jun 1808 in Fredericktown, MD at the age of 20, 5' 7" tall, born in Berkley, VA and died at Fort Charlotte, AL on 11 Dec 1813 (Johnson and Christou, p. 124)

Forrester, Charles, served as a Private in Capt. Peter Schuyler's Co., 2nd U.S. Infantry, enlisted in 1806, re-enlisted at Fort Stoddert on 20 Jul 1811 at the age of 39, 5' 6" tall, born in Queen Anne's Co., MD and discharged at Pass Christian on 31 Aug 1815 on a Surgeon's Certificate (Johnson and Christou, p. 124)

Forrester, Joseph (African American), served as a Seaman and was born in Baltimore. Age: 22. Prison Depot: Chatham, Prisoner of War #2462. Captured by *Shannon*, Nova Scotia Privateer. When Taken: 8 Nov 1813. Where Taken: off Newfoundland. Prize Name: *Thorn*. Ship Type: Privateer. Received: 21 Oct 1813 from Portsmouth on HMT *Malabar*. Discharged 4 Sep 1814. Sent to Dartmoor on HMS *Freya*. (Johnson's Database, 2019)

Forsyth, Robert, served as a Seaman and was born in Baltimore. Age: 23. Prison Depot: Chatham, Prisoner of War #2511. Captured by HM Ship-of-the-Line *Victorious*. When Taken: 8 Jun 1813. Where Taken: Chesapeake Bay. Prize Name: *Globe*. Ship Type: Privateer. Received: 22 Oct 1813 from Portsmouth on HMT

Malabar. Discharged on 8 Sep 1814 and sent to Dartmoor on HMS *Niobe.* Prison Depot: Dartmoor, Prisoner of War #3316. Date Received: 13 Sep 1814. From what ship: HMT *Niobe* from Chatham. Discharged on 28 May 1815. (Johnson's Database, 2019)

Foster, David (African American), served as a Seaman and was born in Maryland. Age: 38. Prison Depot: Plymouth 1, Prisoner of War #1105. Captured by HM Ship-of-the-Line *Superb.* When Taken: 15 Apr 1813. Where Taken: Bay of Biscayne. Prize Name: *Viper.* Home Port: New York. Ship Type: Privateer. Date Received: 22 Apr 1813. From what ship: HMS *Superb.* Discharged and sent to Dartmoor on 1 Jul 1813. Prison Depot: Dartmoor, Prisoner of War #410. Date Received: 1 Jul 1813 from Plymouth. Discharged on 20 Apr 1815. (Johnson's Database, 2019)

Foster, George, served as a Private in Capt. Nathan Towson's Co., 2nd U.S. Artillery, enlisted at age 39, date and place not stated, and was captured at the Battle of Stoney Creek on 12 Jun 1813. Prisoner of War #5072 at Halifax, NS, interned 28 Dec 1813 and discharged for exchange on 31 May 1814 (Johnson and Christou, p. 125, stated Quebec, but Baker Vol. 1, p. 146 stated Halifax)

Foster, Jacob, served as a Private in the 14th U.S. Infantry and was captured (no date). Prisoner of War, exchanged 15 Apr 1814 (Johnson and Christou, p. 126)

Foster, James, served as a Seaman and was born in Baltimore. Age: 36. Prison Depot: Dartmoor, Prisoner of War #3475. How Taken: Gave himself up off HM Ship-of-the-Line *Trident.* When Taken: 20 Jul 1814. Received: 19 Sep 1814 from HMT *Salvador del Mundo.* Discharged 11 Jul 1815. (Johnson's Database, 2019)

Foster, James B., served as a Private in Capt. John Brookes' Co., 38th U.S. Inf., enlisted 23 Jul 1813 and died 31 Jul 1813 (Johnson and Christou, p. 126)

Foster, John S., served as a Private in Capt. James Britton's Co., 14th U.S. Inf., enlisted 10 Apr 1813, age 27, 5' 5" tall, born in Marblehead, MA and discharged in Washington, DC on 25 Jul 1815 for "inability" (Johnson and Christos, p. 126)

Foster, Joseph, served as a Seaman and was born in Talbot Co., MD. Age: 18. Prison Depot: Plymouth 1, Prisoner of War #488. Captured by HM Brig *Reindeer.* When Taken: 3 Feb 1813. Where Taken: Bay of Biscayne. Prize Name: *Cashiere.* Home Port: Baltimore. Ship Type: Letter of Marque (Privateer). Date Received: 12 Feb 1813 from HMS *Reindeer.* Sent to Dartmoor on 28 Jun 1813. Prison Depot: Dartmoor, Prisoner of War #252. Date Received: 28 Jun 1813 from Plymouth. Sent to Dartmouth on 30 Jul 1813. (Johnson's Database, 2019)

Foster, Joseph (African American), served as a Seaman and was born in Baltimore. Age: 22. Prison Depot: Dartmoor, Prisoner of War #3267. Captured by HM Frigate *Shannon.* When Taken: 11 Oct 1812. Where Taken: off Halifax, NS. Prize Name: *Wiley Reynard.* Home Port: Boston. Ship Type: Privateer. Date

Received: 11 Sep 1814. From what ship: HMT *Freya* from Chatham. Discharged on 27 Apr 1815. (Johnson's Database, 2019)

Fowke, Gerard, served as a Private in Capt. John F. Gray's Co., 43rd Regiment, Charles Co. Militia, from 24 June 1814 and discharged on 3 Jul 1814 on account of sickness (Wright Vol. 5, pp. 39, 40)

Fowler, Isaac, served as a Seaman and was born in Baltimore. Age: 30. Prison Depot: Dartmoor, Prisoner of War #3042. How Taken: Gave himself up off HM Frigate *Galetea*. When Taken: 24 Aug 1814. Date Received: 2 Sep 1814. From what ship: HMT *Sultan*. Discharged on 28 Apr 1815. (Johnson's Database, 2019)

Fowler, Thomas (1790-1814), served as a Private in Capt. Thomas Montgomery's Co., 14th U.S. Infantry, enlisted 29 Apr 1812 at the age of 22, 5' 6" tall, born in Maryland and was killed in the Battle of Lyon's Creek on 19 Oct 1814 (BLW# 25705-160-12; Johnson and Christou, p. 127)

Fowler, William, served as 1st Sergeant in Capt. Henry Fowler's Co., Randall's Rifle Bttn., Baltimore Co., from 26 Aug 1813 an reported "sick absent from Sep 29" 1814 (Wright Vol. 2, p. 74)

Fowler, William, served as a Seaman and was born in St.Mary's Co., MD. Age: 35. Prison Depot: Dartmoor, Prisoner of War #3021. Captured by HM Frigate *Hyperion*. When Taken: 25 Jun 1814. Where Taken: off Cape Finisterre, Spain. Prize Name: *Rattlesnake*. Home Port: Philadelphia. Ship Type: Privateer. Date Received: 2 Sep 1814. From what ship: Naval Hospital, Plymouth. Discharged on 28 May 1815. (Johnson's Database, 2019)

Fowley, Henry, served as a Seaman and was born in Baltimore. Age and Race not stated. Prison Depot: Jamaica, Prisoner of War #48. How Taken: Gave himself up off HM Sloop *Atalante*. When Taken: 24 Aug 1812. Where Taken: Kingston, Jamaica. Date Received: 23 Aug 1812. From what ship: HMS Gar*land*. Discharged on 9 May 1813 and sent to U.S. (Johnson's Database, 2019)

Foxcroft, William (1792-1866), served as a Private in Capt. Adam Barnes' Co., Watkins' Regiment, Anne Arundel Co. Militia, from 16 Apr 1813 and was reported "sick in quarters" on muster roll dated 16 Apr – 31 Jul 1813. William Foxcroft, age 63, was living in Baltimore in 1855 and died on 7 Aug 1866, age 74. (Wright Col. 4, p. 41; BLW# 55-80-148; *The [Baltimore] Sun*, 8 Aug 1866)

Foxwell, George, served as a Seaman and was born in Maryland. Age: 28. Prison Depot: Chatham, Prisoner of War #304. Captured by HM Brig *Sarpedon*. When Taken: 12 Aug 1812. Prize Name: *Cygnet*. Ship Type: Merchant Vessel. Date Received: 23 Dec 1812 from Greenlaw Depot. Discharged on 10 May 1813 and released to the Cartel *Admittance*. (Johnson's Database, 2019)

Foy, Samuel, served as a Private in Capt. John Berry's Washington Artillery Co., Baltimore, from 19 Aug 1814, was severely wounded in action on 13 Sep 1814 at Fort McHenry and one of his legs was amputated. (Wright Vol. 2, p. 49, listed him as James/Samuel Foy; Marine pp. 173 and 289, listed him as Samuel Foy)

Fraher, Edward, served as a Private in Capt. Thomas Montgomery's Co., 14th U.S. Infantry, enlisted 28 May 1812, at the advanced age of 55, 5' 8" tall, born in Ireland and was captured, place not stated. Prisoner of War at Halifax, NS (Johnson and Christos, p. 127, but not listed in Baker Vol. 1, p. 148)

Frame, Edward, served as a Marine and was taken from the barracks and admitted to the Naval Hospital in Washington, DC as Patient No. 115 as of 1 Jun 1814, but his injury or illness was not stated (Sharp's Database, 2018)

Frame, Jacob, served as a Private under Capt. James F. Huston and Capt. Lewis Weaver in the Frederick Co. Militia from 23 Jul 1814, marched to Bladensburg and died on 23 Aug 1814 (Mallick and Wright, pp. 319, 344)

Franc, Christian, served as a Private in the 14th U.S. Infantry and was captured. Prisoner of War #3923 at Halifax, NS, interned 24 Jun 1813, discharged 9 Nov 1813 and sent to England (Johnson and Christou, p. 127; Baker Vol. 1, p. 148)

Francis, John (Mulatto), served as a Seaman and was born in Baltimore. Age: 38. Prison Depot: Portsmouth, Prisoner of War #816. How Taken: Gave himself up off HM Guard Ship *Royal William*. Date Received: 10 May 1813. From what ship: HMS *Puifrant*. Discharged on 17 May 1813 and sent to Chatham on HMS *Impeleux*. (Johnson's Database, 2019)

Francisco, John, served as a Private in the 14th U.S. Infantry and was captured. Prisoner of War #3928 at Halifax, NS, interned 24 Jun 1813 and discharged for exchange on 3 Feb 1814 (Johnson and Christou, p. 128; Baker Vol. 1, p. 149)

Franklin, S. W., served as a Lieutenant in Capt. Gray's Co., 43rd Regiment, and diedin 1814 (Marine p. 289; Wright Vol. 5, p. 39 did not list him in Capt. John F. Gray's Co., Charles Co. Militia, in June 1814 so he apparently had died by then)

Franklin, Zephaniah, served as a Private and was wounded by the accidental discharge of a gun in the hands of Pvt. Nehemiah Franklin in June 1814, per John McConchie's BLW# 55-160-49551 who had entered service in Charles Co. (Wright Vol. 5, p. 76)

Fray, James, served as a Seaman and was born in Baltimore. Age: 23. Prison Depot: Chatham, Prisoner of War #3374. Captured by HM Frigate *Maidstone* & HM Brig *Nimrod*. When Taken: 17 Jul 1813. Where Taken: Grand Banks. Prize Name: *Yorktown*. Home Port: New York. Ship Type: Privateer. Date Received: 23 Feb 1814 from Halifax, NS on HMT *Malabar*. Discharged on 10 Oct 1814 and sent to Dartmoor on HMS *Mermaid*. Prison Depot: Dartmoor, Prisoner of War #5227. Received: 31 Oct 1814 on HMT *Mermaid* from Chatham. Discharged on 29 Jun 1815. (Johnson's Database, 2019)

Frazer, Hulbert, served as a Private in 14th U.S. Infantry and was born in Maryland. Age: 29. Prison Depot: Chatham, Prisoner of War #3099. When Taken: 24 Jun 1813. Where Taken: Beaver Dams, Upper Canada. Date Received: 7 Jan 1814 from Halifax, NS. Discharged on 10 Oct 1814 and sent to U.S. on the Cartel *St. Philip*. (Johnson's Database, 2019)

Frazer, John, served as a Seaman and was born in Maryland. Age: 25. Prison Depot: Plymouth 1, Prisoner of War #1370. Captured by HM Frigate *Surveillante*. When Taken: 27 Apr 1813. Where Taken: Bay of Biscayne. Prize Name: *Tom*. Home Port: Baltimore. Ship Type: Letter of Marque (Privateer). Date Received: 15 May 1813. From what ship: HMS *Foxhound*. Discharged on 3 Jul 1813 and sent to Stapleton Prison. Prison Depot: Stapleton, Prisoner of War #366. Date Received: 11 Jul 1813 from Plymouth. Discharged on 16 Jun 1814 and sent to Dartmoor. (Johnson's Database, 2019)

Frazer, John, served as a Seaman on the privateer *Surprise* of Baltimore and drowned in a shipwreck on 5 Apr 1815 (Marine p. 289; *Niles Weekly Register*, 15 Apr 1815)

Frazier, Hubbard, served as a Private in the 14th U.S. Infantry (company not stated), enlisted 22 May 1812 for 5 years, age not stated, 5' 8" tall, born in Dorchester Co., MD and was captured at Beaver Dams, Upper Canada on 24 Jun 1813. Prisoner of War #3740 at Halifax, NS, discharged from prison on 9 Nov 1813 and discharged from military service on 22 May 1817 (Johnson and Christou, p. 128; Baker Vol. 1, p. 150 spelled his name Hulbard Fraser)

Frazier, John, served as a Master's Mate with the U.S. Chesapeake Flotilla, entered service on 17 Dec 1814, was reported sick (date and place were not stated) and died on 17 Jul 1814 (Shomette, p. 394)

Freeman, John, served as a Private in Capt. Joseph Hook's Co., 36th U.S. Inf., enlisted 18 Jun 1814 and died at Baltimore on 26 Dec 1814; bounty land to his sister Elizabeth Campbell (BLW# 11863-160-12; Johnson and Christou, p. 129)

Freeman, John, served as a Quarter Gunner and/or 2nd Gunner and was born in Maryland. Age: 35. Prison Depot: Plymouth 1, Prisoner of War #1812. Captured by HM Brig *Pelican*. When Taken: 14 Aug 1813. Where Taken: off St. David's Head, Wales. Prize Name: U.S. Brig *Argus*. Ship Type: Warship. Date Received: 17 Aug 1813. From what ship: USS *Argus*. Discharged on 27 Sep 1813 and sent to Dartmoor. Prison Depot: Dartmoor, Prisoner of War #687. Date Received: 27 Sep

1813 from Plymouth. Discharged and sent to Dartmouth on 2 Nov 1814. (Johnson's Database, 2019)

Freeman, Walter, served as a Private in Capt. Thomas T. Simmon's Co., 2nd Regiment, Anne Arundel Co. Militia, from 28 Sep 1814 and died on 28 Nov 1814, but the place and cause of death were not stated (Wright Vol. 4, p. 28)

Frenchaw, Joseph H., served as a Private in Capt. Joseph Marshall's Co., 14th U.S. Infantry, enlisted on 8 Feb 1814 and drowned in the Delaware River on 9 Oct 1814 (Johnson and Christou, p. 129)

Friday, Henry, served as a Private in Capt. Barton Hackney's Co., Frederick Co. Militia, from 1 Sep 1814, participated in the Battle of North Point and was sick and furloughed on 4 Oct 1814 in Baltimore (Mallick and Wright, p. 362)

Frizle, John, served as a Seaman and was born in Baltimore. Age: 27. Prison Depot: Dartmoor, Prisoner of War #3456. Captured by HM Sloop *Tartarus*. When Taken: 1 Sep 1814. Where Taken: off the Atlantic. Prize Name: Prize of the Privateer *Chasseur*. Home Port: Baltimore. Ship Type: Privateer. Date Received: 19 Sep 1814. From what ship: HMT *Salvador del Mundo*. Discharged on 4 Jun 1815. (Johnson's Database, 2019)

Frobus, Henry, served as a Seaman and was born in Baltimore. Age: 18. Prison Depot: Dartmoor, Prisoner of War #2347. Captured by HM Sloop *Martin*. When Taken: 30 Jun 1814. Where Taken: off Halifax, NS. Prize Name: *Snap Dragon*. Ship Type: Privateer. Date Received: 16 Aug 1814. From what ship: HMS *Dublin* from Halifax, NS. Discharged on 3 May 1815. (Johnson's Database, 2019)

Frog, Henry, served as a Private in Capt. John Bond's Co., 41st Regt., Baltimore Co., from 25 Aug 1814, was stationed at Kelley's Field in Baltimore and was discharged by a Surgeon on 6 Sep 1814 (Wright Vol. 2, p. 67)

Fry, Patrick (1788-1815), served as a Private in Capt. John Mowton's Co., 38th U.S. Infantry, enlisted 12 Jul 1814 in Norfolk, VA at age 26, 5' 4" tall, born in Baltimore and died at Craney Island, VA on 9 Mar 1815 [cause unknown, but probably service connected]; bounty land issued to Mary Cochran and other heirs at law (BLW# 10067-160-12; Johnson and Christou, p. 130)

Fuller, Darcus, served as 1st Corporal in Capt. John Stewart's Co., 51st Regiment, Baltimore Militia, from 23 Aug 1814 and was "sick absent from Aug 26" 1814 (Wright, Vol. 2, p. 310)

Fuller, Zachariah, from the *Ontario*, a Seaman of the U.S. Chesapeake Flotilla, entered service on 31 Dec 1813 and died on 22 May 1814 (Shomette, p. 403)

Fulton, Alexander (c1785-1860), served as a Private in Capt. John Sample's Co., 49th Regiment, Cecil Co. Militia, between 26 Aug and 27 Oct 1814. On 20 Jan 1853

Alexander Fulton, age 67, of Octoraro Hundred, stated he volunteered in the mass militia in Octoraro Hundred around 29 Aug 1814 and was discharged by Capt. Porter on account of sickness, date not given. In 1856 he stated he was age 72. On 24 Mar 1862 Rachel Fulton, age 70, stated they were married on 27 Nov 1817 by Rev. Clarkson and her former name was McKinley. Alexander died on 19 Nov 1860. (Wright Vol. 3, pp. 17, 50; BLW# 55-160-94966)

Fulton, James (1775-1824), served as a Private in Capt. Aaron R. Levering's Co., 5th Regiment, Baltimore Militia, Independent Blues, was wounded on 12 Sep 1814 at North Point and died on 8 Feb 1824 in his 49th year. He was buried in the cellar of Faith Presbyterian Church at Broadway and Gay Street. "This stone was erected by his affectionate relict Mary Neilson Fulton." (Wright Vol. 2, p. 5; Burials were copied by Edith Ensor Read, 1812 Society, and placed in File 52255 at the Maryland Historical Society) James Fulton was a native of Londonderry, Ireland and died 3 (sic) [possible transcription error] Feb 1814, age 48 years, at his residence near Baltimore. (*Baltimore Patriot*, 10 Feb 1824)

Fulton, John, served as a Private in Capt. Samuel Raisin's Co., 36th U.S. Infantry, and died in the hospital on 17 Feb 1815 (Johnson and Christou, p. 131)

Fulton, William, served as a Prize Master and was born in Baltimore. Age: 24. Prison Depot: Dartmoor, Prisoner of War #5017. Captured by HM Brig *Wasp* on 6 Sep 1814. Where Taken: off Cape Sable, NS. Prize Name: *Alexander*, prize of the Privateer *Monmouth*. Ship Type: Privateer. Date Received: 28 Oct 1814. From what ship: HMT *Alkbar* from Halifax, NS. Discharged on 21 Jun 1815. (Johnson's Database, 2019)

Furlong, William, served as a 2nd Mate and was born in Baltimore. Age: 19. Prison Depot: Plymouth 1, Prisoner of War #2319. Captured by HM Brig *Pelican*. When Taken: 13 Jan 1814. Where Taken: at sea. Prize Name: *Siro*. Home Port: Baltimore. Ship Type: Letter of Marque. Date Received: 25 Jan 1814. From what ship: HMS *Pelican*. Discharged on 31 Jan 1814 and sent to Dartmoor. Prison Depot: Dartmoor, Prisoner of War #979. Received: 31 Jan 1814 from Plymouth. Discharged 30 May 1814 and sent to London. (Johnson's Database, 2019)

G

Gage, Isaac, served as a Seaman and was born in Baltimore. Age: 27. Prison Depot: Stapleton, Prisoner of War #139. Captured by HM Brig *Royalist*. When Taken: 31 May 1813. Where Taken: Bay of Biscayne. Prize Name: *Governor Gerry*. Home Port: New Haven. Ship Type: Merchant Vessel. Date Received: 8 Jul 1813 from Plymouth. Age 28. Discharged on 13 Jun 1814 and sent to Dartmoor. Prison Depot: Dartmoor, Prisoner of War #1662. Date Received: 23 Jun 1814 from Stapleton. Discharged 1 May 1815. (Johnson's Database, 2019)

Gain, William, served as a Private in Capt. Eli Stocksdale Co., 36th Regiment, Baltimore Co., stationed at Hampstead Hlll in Baltimore City from 23 Aug 1814 and was reported "sick, absent since Oct 10" 1814 (Wright Vol. 2, p. 63)

Gaines, John, served as a Private in Capt. James Stuart's Co., 24th U.S. Infantry, enlisted 13 Jun 1813, age 44, 5′ 3″ tall, born in Baltimore, captured at Fort Niagara, NY on 19 Dec 1813. Prisoner of War at Quebec, exchanged on 11 May 1814 and discharged from the service at Fort Hawkins, GA on 31 Dec 1815 on a Surgeon's Certificate; wife named Dorcas Gaines (Old War Pension IF-14318 was rejected, but the reason was not stated; Johnson and Christou, p. 131; Johnson's Quebec book, p. 55, did not mention him)

Gale, William (African American), served as a Seaman and was born in Baltimore. Age: 20. Prison Depot: Chatham, Prisoner of War #3770. Captured by HM Ship-of-the-Line *San Domingo*. When Taken: 1 Mar 1814. Where Taken: off Savannah, GA. Prize Name: *Argus*. Ship Type: Privateer. Received: 26 May 1814. From what ship: HMS *Hindostan*. Discharged on 25 Sep 1814 and sent to Dartmoor on HMS *Niobe*. Prison Depot: Dartmoor, Prisoner of War #4156. Date Received: 6 Oct 1814. From what ship: HMT *Niobe* from Chatham. Discharged on 13 Jun 1815. (Johnson's Database, 2019)

Gallagher, George, served as a "Boy" in the Barney's Flotilla and was wounded at Montgomery Court House, had his leg amputated on the field, was admitted to the Naval Hospital in Washington, DC as Patient No. 43 on 17 Sep 1814 and was discharged on 18 Dec 1814 and sent to Baltimore (Sharp's Database, 2018; *en.wikipedia.org* article stated he served as a Seaman at battle of Bladensburg)

Gallagher, John (1789-1813), served as a Corporal in Capt. David Cummings' Co. of the 14th U.S. Infantry, enlisted 2 May 1812 in Williamsport, MD at the age of 23, born in Washington, MD and died at Lewiston, NY in July 1813; bounty land issued to his sister Elizabeth Gallagher and other heirs at law (BLW# 26227-160-12; Johnson and Christou, p. 131)

Galloway, Joseph, served as a Seaman and was born in Talbot Co., MD. Age: 21. Prison Depot: Plymouth 1, Prisoner of War #492. Captured by HM Brig *Reindeer*. When Taken: 3 Feb 1813. Where Taken: Bay of Biscayne. Prize Name: *Cashiere*. Home Port: Baltimore. Ship Type: Letter of Marque. Date Received: 12 Feb 1813. From what ship: HMS *Reindeer*. Discharged and sent to Dartmoor on 2 Apr 1813. Prison Depot: Dartmoor, Prisoner of War #9. Date Received: 2 Apr 1813 from Plymouth. Discharged and sent to Dartmouth on 30 Jul 1813. (Johnson's Database, 2019)

Galloway, Joseph (Mulatto), served as a Seaman and was born in Talbot Co., MD. Age: 21. Prison Depot: Dartmoor, Prisoner of War #648. Captured by HM Schooner *Telegraph*. When Taken: 13 Aug 1813. Where Taken: off St. Andrews,

142

Scotland. Prize Name: *Ellen & Emeline*. Ship Type: Merchant Vessel. Date Received: 8 Sep 1813 from Plymouth. Discharged and sent to Dartmouth on 30 Jul 1813 (Johnson's Database, 2019)

Galt, Robert, served as a Seaman and was born in Baltimore. Age: 19. Prison Depot: Chatham, Prisoner of War #342. Captured by HM Sloop *Helena*. When Taken: 31 Dec 1813. Where Taken: off Azores. Prize Name: *Postsea*, prize of the Privateer *Thrasher*. Ship Type: Privateer. Date Received: 19 Jan 1813. From what ship: HMS *Raisonable*. Discharged on 7 Apr 1813 and released to HMS *Raisonable*. (Johnson's Database, 2019)

Gamble, Stansbury, served as a Lieutenant in Capt. Lowman's Co., 35th Regt., and died in 1815, exact date and cause not stated (Marine p. 292; Wright Vol. 1, p. 36, stated Stansberry Gamble served as 1st Corporal in Capt. Nathan Baynard's Co., 35th Regt., Queen Anne's Co. Militia, from 7 to 14 May 1813)

Ganell, James, served as a Seaman and was born in Maryland. Age: 24. Prison Depot: Dartmoor, Prisoner of War #3764. Captured by HM Frigate *Lacedaemonian*. When Taken: 10 Jul 1814. Where Taken: off Charleston, SC. Prize Name: *Ann*. Ship Type: Privateer. Date Received: 30 Sep 1814 from HMT *President* from Halifax, NS. Discharged 9 Jun 1815. (Johnson's Database, 2019)

Gantt, Benjamin L., served as a Private in Capt. Jasper M. Jackson's Co., 34th Regt., Prince George's Co. Militia, from 21 Aug 1814 and was furloughed on 29 Aug 1814 for indisposition (Wright Vol. 6, p. 22)

Gardner, George (1784-1815), served as a Private in Capt. Charles Stansbury's Co., 38th U.S. Infantry, enlisted 23 Sep 1814 in Annapolis, age 30, 5' 6¾" tall, born in Anne Arundel Co. and died 2 Feb 1815 (Johnson and Christou, p. 132)

Gardner, Ignatius, served as a Private in Capt. John Heeter's Co., 44th Regt., Montgomery Co. Militia, from 4 Aug 1814 and reportedly deserted on 16 Aug, but he stated on 2 Jan 1851, age 65, in Knox Co., OH, that he volunteered at Rockville in June 1814 and was discharged at Hampstead Hill [in Baltimore] on 10 Sep 1814 because of inability to perform militia duty; however, his bounty land application was rejected. (Wright Vol. 7, pp. 4, 25; BLW# 50-rej-8813)

Gardner, Jacob, served as a Private in Capt. Stanton Sholes' Co., 2nd U.S. Artillery, enlisted 16 Mar 1814 at Greensburg, Beaver Co., PA at the age of 39, 5' 7" tall, was born in Maryland and discharged at Detroit, MI on 26 Oct 1815 on a Surgeon's Certificate (Johnson and Christou, p. 132)

Gardner, Mathew, served as a Private in Capt. Joseph Hook's Co. of the 36th U.S. Infantry, enlisted 7 Sep 1813 for 1 year, re-enlisted on 15 Aug 1814 for the war and died at Baltimore on 16 Nov 1814; bounty land was issued to widow Grace Gardner (BLW# 16617-160-12; Johnson and Christou, p. 133)

Garner, Charles, served as a Private (company not stated) and was wounded by the accidental discharge of a gun in the hands of Pvt. Nehemiah Franklin in June 1814, per John McConchie's BLW# 55-160-49551 who had entered service in Charles Co. (Wright Vol. 5, p. 76)

Garren, John, served as a Private in Capt. Thomas Lawrence's Co., 22nd U.S. Inf., enlisted 1 Jul 1813 at Uniontown, PA, age 21, 5' 9" tall, born in Baltimore, and discharged at Sackett's Harbor, NY on 11 Aug 1815 for chronic rheumatism and inability (Johnson and Christou, p. 133)

Garrett, Thomas, served as a Private in Capt. Jacob Deems' Co., 51st Regiment, from 23 Aug to 30 Aug 1813 and from 19 Aug 1814 until wounded on 12 Sep 1814 at North Point and died on 17 Sep 1814. Name is on the Baltimore Battle Monument. Payment was made by Adj. Acct, on 20 Dec 1816 to William Ray, atty. for the widow. (NARA; CMSR; Wright Vol. 2, pp. 29, 34; Marine p. 293)

Garrish, John, served as a Seaman of the U.S. Chesapeake Flotilla, entered service on 16 Dec 1813, was on board on 7 Apr 1814 and died on 13 Oct 1814 (Shomette p. 367)

Garrison, Bebel (African American), served as a Seaman and was born in Baltimore. Age: 26. Prison Depot: Dartmoor, Prisoner of War #5012. Captured by HM Schooner *Canso*. When Taken: 5 Aug 1814. Where Taken: off Azores. Prize Name: *Charlotte*, prize of the Privateer *Monmouth*. Home Port: Baltimore. Ship Type: Privateer. Date Received: 28 Oct 1814. From what ship: HMT *Alkbar* from Halifax, NS. Discharged on 21 Jun 1815. (Johnson's Database, 2019)

Garrison, C., of Baltimore, a Seaman on the *Invincible*, was captured (date and location were not stated) and imprisoned in Dartmoor, England prior to the massacre in the prison in 1815 at which time he was wounded in the right hand and arm (*Niles Weekly Register*, 17 Jun 1815)

Garrison, Cornelius, served as a Seaman and was born in Baltimore. Age: 24. Prison Depot: Dartmoor, Prisoner of War #5003. Captured by HM Frigate *Armide*. When Taken: 16 Aug 1814. Where Taken: off Nantucket, MA. Prize Name: *Helen*, prize of the Privateer *Invincible*. Home Port: Salem. Ship Type: Letter of Marque. Date Received: 28 Oct 1814. From what ship: HMT *Alkbar* from Halifax, NS. Discharged on 21 Jun 1815. (Johnson's Database, 2019)

Gary, John, served as a Private in Capt. Edward W. Comegys' Co., 21st Regt., Kent Co. Militia, in 1813 and was reported "absent sick" on the muster roll dated 5 Aug – 25 Aug 1813 (Wright Vol. 1, p. 15)

Gates, Jacob, served as a Private in the 14th U.S. Infantry and was captured. Prisoner of War #4011 at Halifax, NS, interned on 24 Jun 1813 and discharged for exchange on 3 Feb 1814 (Johnson and Christou, p. 134; Baker Vol. 1, p. 157)

Gates, James Jr., served as a Private in part of a detachment of Charles Co.'s 43rd Regiment stationed at Yateses circa 24 Jul 1814 and was reported as having been wounded with a bayonet that confined him for 15 days (Wright Vol. 5, p. 42)

Gates, Richard, served as a Private in the 36th U.S. Regiment and on 24 Aug 1814 was at the field of battle at Bladensburg, "diseased and destitute of shelter and food in with Lt. Harriden's order," was admitted to the Naval Hospital, Washington, DC, as Patient No. 27 on 27 Aug 1814, discharged on 5 Sep 1814 and sent to U.S. Hospital (Sharp's Database, 2018)

Gatton, Lewis, served as a Private in Capt. James Hazlett's Co., 38th Regt., and enlisted at Westernport, Allegany Co., MD; he served a few days when Capt. John Buck took command and he continued for 10 months and was discharged on account of sickness after having marched from Westport to Cumberland, form thence to Baltimore, and from Baltimore on board a sloop to Norfolk and from Norfolk to Crany Island and from there back to Baltimore where he was discharged in May 1813. He was living in Jackson Twp., Pike Co., OH in 1860, age 65. (BLW# 50-160-96732; Wright Vol. 5, p. 65)

Gault, Joseph, served as a Private in Capt. James F. Huston's Co., Frederick Co. Militia, from 23 Jul 1814 and died o n23 Aug 1814 (Mallick and Wright p. 123)

Gaylor, William, served as a Private (company not stated) and was captured at the Battle of Bladensburg on 24 Aug 1814 (Marine p. 174)

Gearhart, Jacob (1796-1814), served as a Private in Capt. James McDonald's Co. of the 14th U.S. Infantry, enlisted 11 Oct 1813 at the age of 17, born in Pennsylvania and died at Plattsburgh, NY on 9 Aug 1814 from sickness (BLW# 26303-160-12; Johnson and Christou, p. 135)

Gedson, John, served as a Seaman and was born in Fredericktown. Age: 39. Prison Depot: Plymouth 1, Prisoner of War #245. Captured by *Barton*, Liverpool letter of marque. When Taken: 29 Nov 1812. Where Taken: off Bermuda. Prize Name: *Junice & Lyda*, prize of the Privateer General Armstrong. Ship Type: Privateer. Date Received: 12 Jan 1813 from HMS *Bittern*. Discharged and sent to Portsmouth on 8 Feb 1813 on HMS *Colossus* (Johnson's Database, 2019)

Geers, John, served as a Private in Capt. Alexander Cummings' Co., 1st U.S. Light Dragoons, enlisted 4 Aug 1812 at Pittsburgh, PA at the age of 36, 6' tall, born in Kent Co., MD and discharged at Greenbush, NY on 10 Jun 1815 for rheumatism and debility (Johnson and Christou, p. 135)

Gennison, Michael (1779-1814), served as a Seaman and was born in Baltimore. Age: 25. Prison Depot: Dartmoor, Prisoner of War #5025. Captured by HM Brig *Wasp*. When Taken: 27 Jul 1814. Where Taken: Georges Bank. Prize Name: HM Schooner *Landrail*, prize of the Privateer *Syren*. Home Port: Baltimore. Ship Type:

Privateer. Date Received: 28 Oct 1814. From what ship: HMT *Alkbar* from Halifax, NS. Died on 12 Nov 1814. (Centennial Trails, U.S. Daughters of 1812, online at www.war1812trails.com/Dartmoor misspelled his name as Gennifon; Johnson's Database, 2019)

George, Ezekiel, served as a Private in Capt. Stephen H. Moore's Baltimore Volunteers Infantry Co., from 8 Sep 1812 for 1 year and "left sick in hospital at Sackett's Harbor Apr 13" 1813 [in New York State] (Wright Vol. 2, p. 57)

Gibbons, John, served as a Seaman of the U.S. Chesapeake Flotilla, entered service on 26 Mar 1814, was on board on 7 Apr 1814 and died on 7 Jan 1815 (Shomette p. 375)

Gibbs, Perry (African American), served as a Cook and was born in Georgetown, MD. Age: 26. Prison Depot: Chatham, Prisoner of War #156. How Taken: Gave himself up. When Taken: 28 Oct 1812. Where Taken: London, UK. Date Received: 5 Nov 1812. From what ship: HMS *Namur*. Discharged in Jul 1813 and released to the Cartel *Moses Brown*. (Johnson's Database, 2019)

Gibby, John, served as a Seaman and was born in Baltimore. Age: 21. Prison Depot: Plymouth 1, Prisoner of War #240. How Taken: Gave himself up. When Taken: 17 Nov 1812. Where Taken: Liverpool, UK. Received: 12 Jan 1813. From what ship: HMS *Bittern*. Discharged and sent to Portsmouth on 8 Feb 1813 on HMS *Colossus*. (Johnson's Database, 2019)

Gibey, John ("copper color"), served as a Seaman and was born in Baltimore. Age: 21, Prison Depot: Chatham, Prisoner of War #831. How Taken: Gave himself up off MV *John Barnes*. When Taken: 7 Nov 1813. Where Taken: Liverpool. Received: 1 Mar 1813 from Plymouth on HMS *Namur*. Discharged in July 1813 and released to the Cartel *Moses Brown*. (Johnson's Database, 2019)

Gibson, Edward, served as a Private in Capt. Thomas Montgomery's Co., 14th U.S. Infantry, enlisted 23 May 1812 and died in September 1813 (Johnson and Christou, p. 136)

Gibson, James, served as Colonel of the 4th Rifle Regiment; born in Maryland, graduated from the U.S. Military Academy on 12 Dec 1808 and commissioned a 1st Lieutenant in Light Artillery, promoted to Captain on 2 May 1810, promoted to Major and Assistant Inspector General on 2 Apr 1813, promoted to Colonel on 13 Jul 1813, transferred to the 4th U.S. Rifles on 21 Feb 1814 and was wounded in action at Ft. Erie, Upper Canada, on 17 Sep 1814 and died on 18 Sep 1814; bounty land issued to widow Matilda H. Evans (BLW# 5191-160-50; Johnson and Christou, p. 137; Marine, p. 295; *Niles Register*, 27 Oct 1814)

Gibson, James, served as a Private in Capt. David Warfield's Co., 5th Regiment, Baltimore Militia, and was wounded on 12 Sep 1814 at North Point. "Young

Gibson, (son of W. Gibson, Esq.), private, 5th Regiment, wounded. He was amongst the list of the Prisoners of War of the British." (North Point dead and wounded Article 4 Oct 1814 Columbian Register CT Vol. III 97, p. 4; Wright Vol. 2, p. 8) Dr. James H. McCulloh, Jr. wrote this soon after the battle to the British commander: "In consequence of the humanity shown the following American prisoners of war, I do promise upon honor that they shall not directly or indirectly serve against the British until regularly exchanged." (Marine, p. 171)

Gibson, John, served as a Marine and was wounded on the field of battle at Bladensburg on 24 Aug 1814, admitted to the Naval Hospital in Washington, DC as Patient No. 10, was discharged on 19 Oct 1814 and sent to barracks (Sharp's Database, 2018)

Gibson, Thomas, served as a Private in Richard Arell's Co., 14th U.S. Infantry, enlisted 18 May 1812 for 5 years in Baltimore at the age of 28, 5' 1½" tall, born in London, England, was captured, date and place not stated, but probably at Beaver Dams, Upper Canada. Prisoner of War #4091 at Halifax, NS, interned 24 Jun 1813, discharged for exchange on 3 Feb 1814 and exchanged on 5 Apr 1814 (Johnson and Christou, p. 137; Baker Vol. 1, p. 137)

Giddons, Andrew (African American), served as a Seaman and was born in Baltimore. Age: 39. Prison Depot: Dartmoor, Prisoner of War #3899. Captured by HM Frigate *Loire*. When Taken: 10 Jul 1814. Where Taken: Chesapeake Bay. Prize Name: *Robert*, prize of the Privateer *Mars*. Ship Type: Privateer. Date Received: 5 Oct 1814. From what ship: HMT *Orpheus* from Halifax, NS. Discharged on 9 Jun 1815. (Johnson's Database, 2019)

Gidelman, John, served as a Private in Capt. Richard Whartenby's Co., 5th U.S. Infantry, enlisted 8 Jan 1812 for 5 years at the age of 32, 5' 9" tall, born in Maryland and discharged at Washington, DC on 25 Jan 1816, lost his left eye while in the service; heirs received half pay for 5 years in lieu of bounty land (Johnson and Christou, p. 137)

Gilbert, Jurdonel, served as a Seaman and was born in Baltimore. Age: 26. Prison Depot: Plymouth 1, Prisoner of War #2427. Captured by HM Brig *Pelican*. When Taken: 14 Aug 1813. Where Taken: off St. David's Head, Wales. Prize Name: U.S. Brig *Argus*. Ship Type: Warship. Date Received: 12 Feb 1814. From what ship: HMS *Salvador del Mundo*. Discharged on 10 May 1814 and sent to Dartmoor. Prison Depot: Dartmoor, Prisoner of War #1036. Date Received: 10 May 1814 from Plymouth. Discharged and sent to Dartmouth on 19 Oct 1814. (Johnson's Database, 2019)

Gilbert, Thomas P., served as a Seaman of the U.S. Chesapeake Flotilla, entered service on 4 Nov 1813, was on board on 7 Apr 1814 and was killed at St. Leonards Creek, 1st Battle, on 10 Jun 1814 (Shomette, p. 68; Sheads, p. 22)

Gilchrist, John (1790-1815), served as a Private in 36th U.S. Infantry, enlisted on 20 Dec 1814 for the duration of the war at the age of 24, 5' 4" tall, born in Scotland and died on 16 Feb 1815 (Johnson and Christou, p. 138)

Gill, Cooper, served as a Private in 14th U.S. Infantry and died at Fort McHenry on 10 Sep 1814, two days prior to the battle (Johnson and Christou, p. 138)

Gill, John P., served as a Private in Capt. Stephen H. Moore's Co., Baltimore Volunteers Infantry Co., from 8 Sep 1812 for 1 year and was discharged as unfit for service, but no date was given (Wright Vol. 2, p. 57)

Gillen, James (c1790-1813) served as a Private in the 14th U.S. Infantry and died at Sackett's Harbor, NY on 3 Dec 1813 (Johnson and Christou, p. 138)

Gish, Thomas, served as a Private in Capt. Walter S. Hunt's, 41st Regiment, Baltimore Co., from 25 Aug 1814 and was reported as "sick-absent since Sep 2" 1814 (Wright Vol. 2, p. 68)

Gist, Jesse (1767-1815), served as a Private in Capt. William Allen's Co. of the 24th U.S. Infantry, enlisted 9 Sep 1812 at the age of 45, born in Baltimore Co. and died at Camp Russell, TN on 3 Jun 1815 (Johnson and Christou, p. 139)

Gittings, James C. (1796-1839), served as a Private in Capt. James Sterett's Co., 5th Cavalry Regiment, Baltimore City, joined on 21 Aug 1814 and while serving on picket guard duty on 12 Sep 1814 at North Point he, along with two others, became separated, with the British army in between them. They were ordered to surrender, but refused and leaped on their horses and escaped. They offered to pay for directions to Baltimore from a Negro man who said he would as he performed a service for some gentlemen and soon returned followed by British soldiers who forced them to surrender. The prisoners were taken to General Ross and gave an exaggerated account of the strength of the American forces. (Wright Vol. 2, p. 56; Marine, p. 150, citing *Oration by H. Clay Dallam, 1878*) He died on 12 Aug 1839 in his 42nd year and was buried next to his wife Rebecca Nicols Gittings (11 Feb 1804 – 13 May 1844) in the Gittings Family Cemetery at Long Green, Baltimore Co., MD. (Smith's Database, 2019; *Baltimore Cemeteries, Volume 1*, by Baltimore County Genealogical Society, 1985, p. 134)

Gittings, Michael D. (1796-1877), served as a Private in Capt. John Heeter's Co., 44th Regt., Montgomery Co. Militia, having volunteered at Rockville in Jun 1814 and was discharged in Baltimore following the battle of North Point, where he received a musket ball wound from the fire of the enemy in his right leg. He was also in the Battle of Bladensburg and his command had retreated to Capitol Hill near City of Washington and on 30 Aug 1814 his company marched to Baltimore and on 11 Sep 1814 they answered the call for volunteers and joined a reconnoitering party who marched to and engaged the enemy at North Point.

On 18 Mar 1878 Sophia C. Gittings, widow, stated Michael enlisted at age 18 years and 4 months, had light hair, light eyes and was sparsely built. Her maiden name was Jackson and they married in Clarksburg, Harrison Co., VA. [WV] on 2 Feb 1832. His first wife was Mary P. Williams who died in 1830. Sophia C. Gittings died in 1882. (Pensions SO-10913 and WO-12694; BLW# 50-40-91010 cancelled and BLW# 55-120-19635 granted; Wright Vol. 7, pp. 4, 26)

Gladden, William (1796-1815), served as a Private in Capt. Willis Foulk's Co., 22nd U.S. Inf., enlisted 29 Apr 1814 for the duration of the war in Washington, PA at the age of 18, 5' 7" tall, born in Maryland and died at Williamsville, NY on 20 Feb 1815 (Johnson and Christou, p. 139)

Gladding, George, served as a Private in the 14th U.S. Infantry, enlisted 19 Oct 1812 for 5 years and died at Sackett's Harbor, NY on 27 Dec 1813 (Johnson and Christou, p. 139)

Glanville, John, served as a Private under Capt. Thomas Page, 21st Regiment, Kent Co. Militia, from 20 Aug 1814, and was wounded in the arm at Caulk's Field on 31 Aug 1814 (Baltimore Patriot 9/22/1814, Marine pp. 120, 297; Wright Vol. 1, p. 20)

Glasgow, Theodore, served as a Private in Capt. John R. Dyer's Co., 17th Regiment, Prince George's Co. Militia, between 19 Aug and 13 Sep 1814 and was discharged by Major Manning for inability, but no date was given (Wright Vol. 6, p. 13)

Glisson, Charles, served as a Private in Capt. Lewis Willis' Co., 12th U.S. Infantry, enlisted 12 Feb 1815 at Washington, DC at the age of 42, 5' 8" tall, born in Anne Arundel Co., and discharged at Pittsburgh on 19 Aug 1815 on a Surgeon's Certificate due to old age (Johnson and Christou, p. 140)

Glynn, Hanson, served as a Officer and was born in Maryland. Age: 52. Prison Depot: Dartmoor, Prisoner of War #3826. Captured by HM Frigate *Niemen*. When Taken: 23 May 1814. Where Taken: off Egg Harbor, NJ. Prize Name: *Quiz*. Ship Type: Letter of Marque. Date Received: 5 Oct 1814. From what ship: HMT *Orpheus* from Halifax, NS. Discharged 9 Jun 1815. (Johnson's Database, 2019)

Goddard, Charles (1794-1872), served as a Private in Capt. James McConkey's Co., 27th Regt., Baltimore Militia, and was severely wounded at North Point on 12 Sep 1814 (Marine p. 297). Dr. James H. McCulloh, Jr. wrote this note soon after the battle to the British commander: "In consequence of the humanity shown the following American prisoners of war, I do promise upon honor that they shall not directly or indirectly serve against the British until regularly exchanged." (Marine, p. 171) In Baltimore on 10 Sep 1842 Charles Goddard, former private in 27th Regiment, Maryland Militia, and lifelong resident of this city, collected his own $36.00 due from 4 Mar to 4 Sep 1842 (Pierce, p. 74)

Godshall, George, served as a Private in Capt. William McIlvane's Co., 14th U.S. Infantry, enlisted 19 Dec 1812 for 5 years at the age of 26, 5' 7" tall, born in Pennsylvania and discharged at Greenbush, NY on 4 May 1815 for lameness (Johnson and Christou, p. 141)

Golder, George, served as a Private in Capt. David Warfield's Co., 5th Regiment, Baltimore United Volunteers, and was wounded at Bladensburg on 24 Aug 1814 (Wright Vol. 2, p. 8; Marine p. 297)

Goldsbury, William, served as a Seaman and was born in Maryland. Age: 32. Prison Depot: Plymouth 1, Prisoner of War #2111. Captured by HM Frigate *Hotspur* & HM Frigate *Pyramus*. When Taken: 26 Oct 1813. Where Taken: Bay of Biscayne. Prize Name: *Chesapeake*. Ship Type: Letter of Marque. Date Received: 22 Nov 1813. From what ship: HMS *Pyramus*. Discharged on 29 Nov 1813 and sent to Dartmoor. Prison Depot: Dartmoor, Prisoner of War #832. Date Received: 29 Nov 1813 from Plymouth. Discharged on 26 Apr 1815. (Johnson's Database, 2019)

Goodall, William, served as a Seaman and was born in Maryland. Age: 26. Prison Depot: Dartmoor, Prisoner of War #2272. Captured by HM Brig *Charybdis*. When Taken: 29 May 1814. Where Taken: off Cape Logan. Prize Name: *Success*, prize of the Privateer *Scourge*. Ship Type: Privateer. Date Received: 16 Aug 1814. From what ship: HMS *Dublin* from Halifax, NS. Discharged on 3 May 1815. (Johnson's Database, 2019)

Goodman, Cassius, served as a Seaman and was born in Baltimore. Age: 22. Prison Depot: Dartmoor, Prisoner of War #4019. Captured by HM Ship-of-the-Line *Leander*. When Taken: 22 Jun 1814. Where Taken: off Cape Sable, NS. Prize Name: U.S. Brig *Rattlesnake*. Ship Type: Warship. Date Received: 6 Oct 1814. From what ship: HMT *Chesapeake* from Halifax, NS. Discharged on 9 Jun 1815. (Johnson's Database, 2019)

Goodrich, A. C., served as a Private in the 14th U.S. Infantry and was captured. Prisoner of War #4027 at Halifax, NS, interned on 24 Jun 1813, was discharged on 9 Nov 1813 and sent to England per order of Sir J. B. Warren (Johnson and Christou, p. 142; Baker Vol. 1, p. 165)

Goodwin, Joseph, served as a Private in 14th U.S. Infantry and was captured at Beaver Dams, Upper Canada. Prisoner of War #3906 at Halifax, NS, interned on 24 Jun 1813, was discharged on 19 Nov 1813 and sent to England per order of Sir J. B. Warren (Johnson and Christou, p. 141; Baker Vol. 1, p. 165). Joseph Goodwin, Private, 14th U.S. Infantry, born in Maryland. Age: 25. Prison Depot:

Chatham, Prisoner of War #3055. When Taken: 9 Jun 1813. Where Taken: Beaver Dams, Upper Canada. Received: 7 Jan 1814 from Halifax, NS. Discharged on 17 Jun 1814. (Johnson's Database, 2019)

Goodwin, William (1785-1813), served as a Seaman and was born in Maryland. Age: 28. Prison Depot: Halifax, NS, Prisoner of War #3657. Captured by HM Brig *Manly*. When Taken: 2 Aug 1813. Where Taken: at sea. Prize Name: *Hope*, prize of the Privateer *Fox*. Ship Type: Privateer. Died on 11 Nov 1813 from fever. (Johnson's Database, 2019)

Goodwin, William, served as a Private in Capt. William Murray's Co., 36th Regt., Baltimore Co., from 25 Aug 1814 and died 23 Oct 1814 (Wright Vol. 2, p. 62)

Gordon, John, served as a Seaman and was born in Baltimore. Age: 27. Prison Depot: Chatham, Prisoner of War #2332. How Taken: Gave himself up off HM Frigate *Bucephalus*. When Taken: 20 Aug 1813. Date Received: 12 Oct 1813 from HMS *Raisonable*. Discharged on 25 Sep 1814 and sent to Dartmoor on HMS *Leyden*. Prison Depot: Dartmoor, Prisoner of War #4645. Date Received: 9 Oct 1814. From what ship: HMT *Leyden* from Chatham. Discharged on 15 Jun 1815. (Johnson's Database, 2019)

Gordon, Richard, served as a Private in Capt. William B. Dyer's Co., 1st Rifle Bttn., Baltimore City, from 19 Aug 1814 and was wounded, date not stated (Wright Vol. 2, p. 54, states he was wounded; Marine p. 299, states he was in Capt. Dyer's Co., Fells Point Rifleman, but does not mention being wounded)

Gordon, William, served as a Private in Capt. Robert Kent's Co., 14th U.S. Inf., enlisted 3 Aug 1812 and died 20 Nov 1812; heirs received half pay for 5 years in lieu of bounty land (Johnson and Christou, p. 142)

Gordon, William, served as a Seaman and was born in Maryland. Age: 33. Prison Depot: Dartmoor, Prisoner of War #3643. Captured by HM Frigate *Niemen*. When Taken: 28 Jan 1814. Where Taken: off Delaware. Prize Name: *Bordeaux Packet*. Home Port: Baltimore. Ship Type: Letter of Marque. Date Received: 30 Sep 1814. From what ship: HMT *Sybella*. Discharged and released on 30 Mar 1815. (Johnson's Database, 2019)

Gorsuch, Abram, served as a Private in Capt. James Almoney's Co., 41st Regt., Baltimore Co., from 25 Aug 1814 and was unable to muster on 1 Nov 1814 so his wife Anne Gorsuch attended in his place (Wright Vol. 2, p. 66) Abraham Gorsuch and Ann James were married on 21 Mar 1811 by Rev. Lewis Richards (*Maryland Marriages, 1801-1820*, by Robert Barnes, 1993, p. 71)

Gorsuch, Jared, see Gerrard Gossage, q.v.

Gorsuch, William, served as a Private (company not stated) and was captured at the Battle of Bladensburg on 24 Aug 1814 (Marine, p. 174). There was more than one man by this name in Baltimore Co. (Wright Vol. 2, pp. 39, 81, 83, 86)

Gosnell, Anthony, served as a Private in Capt. Jeremiah Ducker's Co., 2nd Regt., 11th Brigade, Baltimore Co., was stationed in Baltimore and reported "absent – sick on furlough since Sep 31" (sic) 1814 (Wright Vol. 2, p. 88)

Gossage, Gerrard (Jared), served as a Private in Capt. James Dorman's Co., 5th U.S. Infantry, enlisted 18 Mar 1813 in Baltimore at the age of 35, 5' 6" tall, born in Baltimore, was wounded at Lyon's Creek, Upper Canada on 19 Oct 1814 and discharged at Pittsburgh, PA on 16 Aug 1815 (Johnson and Christou, p. 143) [Gossage was most likely a misspoken and misspelled version of Gorsuch.]

Goswick, Thomas, served as a Private (company not stated) and was captured at the Battle of Bladensburg on 24 Aug 1814 (Marine, p. 174)

Gould, Thomas, served as a Boy onboard a ship and was born in Baltimore. Age: 14. Prison Depot: Plymouth 1, Prisoner of War #336. Captured by Rochefort, France. When Taken: 1 Jan 1813. Where Taken: Basque Roads, France. Prize Name: *Rossie*. Ship Type: Merchant Vessel. Date Received: 22 Jan 1813. From what ship: *Rossie*. Discharged and sent on 10 Apr 1813 to Ashburton on parole. (Johnson's Database, 2019)

Grace, Allen (African American), served as a Seaman and was born in Maryland. Age: 22. Prison Depot: Plymouth 1, Prisoner of War #1763. How Taken: Gave himself up on 6 Jul 1813. Where Taken: Liverpool, UK. Received: 23 Jun 1813. From what ship: HMS *PrinceFrederick*. Discharged on 8 Sep 1813 and sent to Dartmoor. Prison Depot: Dartmoor, Prisoner of War #529. Received: 8 Sep 1813 from Plymouth. Discharged on 26 Apr 1815. (Johnson's Database, 2019)

Grafton, William (1786-1879), served as a Private under Capt. Corbin Grafton and Capt. James Rampley, Harford Co. Militia, and on 6 Dec 1850, age 65, in Columbiana Co., OH, stated he was drafted at Cooptown on or about 28 Aug 1814; he served about 30 days when taken sick with measles, was removed to hospital in Baltimore near Hampstead Hill for about 10 days until the doctors declared him out of danger and released him and he rejoined his company and continued in service for about 2 weeks. On 13 Apr 1855, age 69, he stated his father was Daniel Grafton and the other William Grafton in his company was a cousin and son of Aquilla Grafton. Even though he emphasized that he was not the William Grafton who was marked on the rolls of said company as having deserted, such may not be the case because he deserted (actually absence without leave) and returned twice. The roll dated 28 Aug to 26 Sep 1814 stated "William Grafton, of Aquilla" was present and "William Grafton, of Daniel, deserted Sep 8" and the roll dated 21 Oct to 27 Oct 1814 stated "William Grafton, of D., deserted Oct 23, returned Oct 25." Be that as it may, his bounty land application was rejected. In 1865 William Grafton, of Daniel, age 79, was living in Wayne Twp., Columbiana Co., OH. (Wright Vol. 3, pp. 3, 20, 52, and p. 31 misspelled his name as Crafton; BLW# 55-rej-281186)

Graham, David, served as a Seaman and was born in Baltimore. Age: 21. Prison Depot: Plymouth 1, Prisoner of War #1838. Captured by HM Brig *Pelican* on 14 Aug 1813 off St. David's Head, Wales. Prize Name: U.S. Brig *Argus*. Ship Type: Warship. Date Received: 17 Aug 1813. From what ship: USS *Argus*. Discharged on 8 Sep 1813 and sent to Dartmoor. Prison Depot: Dartmoor, Prisoner of War #578. Age 25 (sic). Date Received: 8 Sep 1813 from Plymouth. Discharged and was sent to Dartmouth on 2 Nov 1814. (Johnson's Database, 2019)

Granger, James, served as a Private in Capt. Joseph H. Nicholson's Artillery Co., and was severely wounded on 13 Sep 1814 at Fort McHenry (Marine p. 173)

Grant, Peter, served as a Seaman and was born in Maryland. Age: 36. Prison Depot: Plymouth 1, Prisoner of War #785. Captured by HM Ship-of-the-Line *Warspite*. When Taken: 14 Mar 1813. Where Taken: Bay of Biscayne. Prize Name: *Cannoniere*. Home Port: New York. Ship Type: Privateer. Date Received: 19 Mar 1813. From what ship: HMS *Warspite*. Discharged and sent to Dartmoor on 28 Jun 1813. Prison Depot: Dartmoor, Prisoner of War #276. Received: 28 Jun 1813 from Plymouth. Discharged 20 Apr 1815. (Johnson's Database, 2019)

Graves, Jonathan, served as a Corporal in the U.S. Marine Corps, enlisted on 5 Aug 1800, was wounded on the field of battle at Bladensburg on 24 Aug 1814, was admitted to the Naval Hospital in Washington, DC as Patient No. 26 on 27 Aug 1814, and was discharged on 7 Oct 1814 and sent to barracks (Sharp's Database, 2018)

Graves, Peregrine, served as a Private in Capt. James Walker's Co., 45th Regt., St. Mary's Co. Militia, for 5 days between 14 Jul and 26 Jul 1813 and was furloughed sick (Wright Vol. 5, p. 29)

Gray, Capt. --, was wounded by accidental discharge of a gun in the hands of Pvt. Nehemiah Franklin in June 1814 and Lt. Roger Dunnington took command of the company, per John McConchie's BLW# 55-160-49551 who had entered service in Charles Co. (Wright Vol. 5, p. 76)

Gray, Charles (Mulatto), served as a Seaman and was born in Prince George's Co., MD. Age: 38. Prison Depot: Portsmouth, Prisoner of War #384. How Taken: Gave himself up off HM Ship-of-the-Line *Salvador del Mundo*. Date Received: 10 Jan 1813. From what ship: HM Guard Ship *Royal William*. Discharged on 4 Mar 1813 and sent to Chatham on HMS *Queen*. Prison Depot: Chatham, Prisoner of War #958. Age 33 (sic). Date Received: 10 Mar 1813. From what ship: HMS

Tigress. Discharged on 19 May 1813 and released to HMS *Ceres*. (Johnson's Database, 2019)

Gray, Francis, served as a Seaman and was born in Maryland. Age: 21. Prison Depot: Dartmoor, Prisoner of War #2981. Captured by HM Sloop *Heron*. When Taken: 25 Jan 1814. Where Taken: off St. Thomas, West Indies. Prize Name: *Frolic*. Ship Type: Privateer. Date Received: 29 Aug 1814. From what ship: HMT *Bittern*. Discharged on 19 May 1815. (Johnson's Database, 2019)

Gray, Henry W., served as a Private in Capt. R. B. Magruder's Co. of Artillery on 18 Feb 1814 and served in Capt. David Warfield's Co., Baltimore Militia, United Volunteers, from 19 Aug 1814, was captured at North Point on 12 Sep 1814 and "in captivity – exchanged 26 Nov" 1814 (Wright Vol. 2, pp. 2, 8; Marine, p. 172)

Gray, John D., served as a Sergeant in the 14th U.S. Infantry, enlisted 22 May 1812 for 18 months and was captured. Prisoner of War #4082 at Halifax, NS, interned on 24 Jun 1813, was discharged on 19 Nov 1813 and sent to England per order of Sir J. B. Warren (Johnson and Christou, p. 141, listed him as Sgt. John D. Gray; Baker Vol. 1, p. 170 listed him as Pvt. John Gray)

Gray, Joshua, served as a Private in Capt. Adam Barnes' Co., Watkins' Regt., Anne Arundel Co. Militia, from 16 Apr 1813 and was reported sick on furlough on the muster roll dated 16 Apr – 31 Jul 1813 (Wright Col. 4, p. 40)

Gray, Nathan (1786-1812), served as a Private in Capt. Samuel Lane's Co. of the 14th U.S. Infantry, enlisted 6 Jun 1812 at the age of 26, born in Jersey and died at Buffalo in Nov 1812 (Johnson and Christou, p. 145)

Gray, Samuel, served as a Private in Capt. John Berry's Artillery Co. and was slightly wounded on 13 Sep 1814 at Fort McHenry (Marine p. 173)

Gray, Thomas (Mulatto), served as a Seaman and was born in Baltimore. Age: 31. Prison Depot: Chatham, Prisoner of War #1793. How Taken: Gave himself up off HM Transport *Chatham*. When Taken: 10 Jun 1813. Date Received: 1 Jul 1813. From what ship: HMS *Raisonable*. Died on 4 Jan 1814 from pneumonia. (Johnson's Database, 2019)

Gray, William, served as a Private in Capt. John Berry's Co. and was wounded on 13 Sep 1814 at Fort McHenry (Huntsberry, p. 43, but Marine, p. 302, did not mention his wound)

Green, Benjamin, served as a Private in Capt. Michael Peters' Co., 39th Regt., Baltimore Militia, joined 19 Aug 1814 and was discharged by Dr. Hall that same day, but the medical reason was not stated (Wright Vol. 2, p. 30)

Green, George (1781-1815), served as a Private in Capt. Thomas Carbery's Co., 36th U.S. Infantry, enlisted 19 May 1814 in Cool Springs, St. Mary's Co., MD, at age 33, 5' 10" tall, born in Mathews Co., VA and died at regimental hospital on 18 Feb 1815 (BLW# 8986-160-12; Johnson and Christou, pp. 145-146)

Green, George (African American), served as a Seaman and was born in Baltimore. Age: 44. Prison Depot: Portsmouth, Prisoner of War #1118. How Taken: Gave himself up off HM Ship-of-the-Line *America*. Date Received: 5 Oct 1813. From what ship: HM Ship-of-the-Line *Achille*. Discharged on 17 Oct 1813 and sent to Chatham on HM Store Ship *Weymouth*. Prison Depot: Chatham, Prisoner of War #2382. Date Received: 20 Oct 1813 from Portsmouth on an admiral's tender. Discharged on 4 Sep 1814 and sent to Dartmoor on HMS *Freya*. Prison Depot: Dartmoor, Prisoner of War #3202. Date Received: 11 Sep 1814. From what ship: HMT *Freya* from Chatham. Discharged on 28 May 1815. (Johnson's Database, 2019)

Green, Henry (African American), served as a Seaman and was born in Baltimore. Age: 27. Prison Depot: Portsmouth, Prisoner of War #612. Captured by HM Ship-of-the-Line *Elephant*. When Taken: 28 Dec 1812. Where Taken: off Azores. Prize Name: *Sword Fish*. Home Port: Gloucester. Ship Type: Privateer. Received: 1 Feb 1813. From what ship: HM Frigate *Hermes*. Discharged on 11 Mar 1813 and sent to Chatham on HM Store Ship *Abundance*. Prison Depot: Chatham, Prisoner of War #1279. Received: 16 Mar 1813 from Portsmouth on HMS *Abundance*. Discharged 24 Jul 1813 and released to the Cartel *Hoffning*. (Johnson's Database, 2019)

Green, James (African American), served as a Seaman and was born in Dorset [Dorchester Co.], MD. Age: 36. Prison Depot: Chatham, Prisoner of War #135. How Taken: Gave himself up off HM Ship-of-the-Line *Lender*. When Taken: 26 Oct 1812. Where Taken: London, UK. Received: 5 Nov 1812 from HMS *Namur*. Discharged on 26 Jul 1814 and sent to Dartmoor on HMS *Raven*. (Johnson's Database, 2019)

Green, John (African American), served as a Seaman and was born in Baltimore. Age: 23. Prison Depot: Chatham, Prisoner of War #1342. How Taken: Gave himself up off HM Ship-of-the-Line *Cornwall*. When Taken: 21 Mar 1813. Date Received: 26 Mar 1813. From what ship: HMS *Raisonable*. Discharged on 23 Jul 1814 and sent to Dartmoor. Prison Depot: Dartmoor, Prisoner of War #1948. Age 24. Received: 3 Aug 1814. From what ship: HMS *Alceste* from Chatham Depot. Discharged on 2 May 1815. (Johnson's Database, 2019)

Green, John, served as a Seaman and was born in Baltimore. Age: 22. Prison Depot: Dartmoor, Prisoner of War #5521. Captured by HM Frigate *Galetea*. When Taken: 7 Sep 1814. Where Taken: English Channel. Prize Name: *James*. Ship Type: Privateer. Date Received: 17 Dec 1814. From what ship: HMT *Loire* from Halfiax. Discharged on 1 Jul 1815. (Johnson's Database, 2019)

Green, John (1775-1814), served as a Seaman under Sailing Master Simmones Bunbury, U.S. Sea Fencibles, enlisted on 16 Apr 1814 for 1 year at the age of 39, 5' 6" tall, born in Ireland and died at Fort McHenry on 23 Oct 1814 (Johnson and Christou, p. 146)

Green, Robert, served as a Seaman in a Sea Fencibles Co. under Sailing Master Simmones Bunbury and was slightly wounded on 13 Sep 1814 at Fort McHenry (Marine p. 173)

Green Robert, served as a Seaman of the U.S. Chesapeake Flotilla, entered service on 18 Sep 1813, was on board on 7 Apr 1814 and died in Baltimore on 16 Aug 1814 of disease (Shomette p. 362)

Green, Solomon (African American), served as a Seaman and was born in Baltimore. Age: 38. Prison Depot: Plymouth 1, Prisoner of War #2607. How Taken: Gave himself up off HM Frigate *Thames*. When Taken: 15 Nov 1812. Date Received: 16 May 1814. From what ship: HMS *Repulse*. Discharged on 14 Jun 1814 and sent to Dartmoor. Prison Depot: Dartmoor, Prisoner of War #1234. Date Received: 14 Jun 1814 from Mill Prison. Discharged on 26 Apr 1815. (Johnson's Database, 2019)

Green, Thomas, served as a Private in Capt. Reuben Gilder's Co., 14th U.S. Inf., enlisted 6 Aug 1812 at Cumberland, MD, age 27, 5' 9¼" tall, born in Virginia and was captured at Stoney Creek, Upper Canada on 12 Jun 1813. Prisoner of War #5135 at Halifax, NS, interned 28 Dec 1813 and was discharged for exchange on 31 May 1814 (Johnson and Christou, p. 146; Baker Vol. 1, p. 172)

Green, William (1777-1814), served as a Seaman and Quartermaster and was born in Baltimore. Age: 36. Prison Depot: Portsmouth, Prisoner of War #1363. Captured by HM Frigate *Crescent*. When Taken: 16 Sep 1813. Where Taken: at sea. Prize Name: *Elbridge Gerry*. Home Port: New York & Rhode Island. Ship Type: Privateer. Date Received: 1 Feb 1814. From what ship: HM Frigate *Sybille*. Discharged on 13 Feb 1814 and sent to Chatham on HMT *Malabar No. 352*. Prison Depot: Chatham, Prisoner of War #3507. Died on 19 Aug 1814 from fever. (Johnson's Database, 2019)

Greer, George (c1790-1826), served as a Private in Capt. Charles Pennington's Artillery Co., Baltimore, from 19 Aug 1814 and was severely wounded in his thigh on 13 Sep 1814 at Fort McHenry and determined to be unfit for duty (Wright Vol. 2, p. 47). "George Greer, merchant, wounded in Fort M'Henry." (North Point dead and wounded Article 4 Oct 1814 Columbian Register CT Vol. III 97, p. 4; Marine p. 173; Wright Vol. 2, p. 47; Society of the War of 1812 Application National No. 960 and No. 962 in 1907 stated he was born in Belfast, Ireland (date not given), married Mary Hall, of Baltimore, and died in 1826. St. Paul P. E. Church Records state George married Mary Hall on 11 May 1803)

Greer, Levin B., served as a Private in Capt. Gavin Hamilton's Co., 17th Regt., Prince George's Co. Militia, between 18 Aug and 17 Sep 1813 and reported as "sick and gone home," date not given (Wright Vol. 6, p. 5) Levin B. Grier served in Capt. Thomas Eversfield's Co. some time between 21 Aug and 6 Sep 1814 and was reported "sick and sent home" on 4 Sep 1814. (Wright Vol. 6, p. 13)

Gregg, James, served as a Private in Capt. William McIlvane's Co., 14th U.S. Inf., enlisted 24 Jan 1813 for 5 years and was captured. Prisoner of War #3925 at Halifax, NS, interned on 24 Jun 1813 and was discharged for exchange on 3 Feb 1814. He also served as a Private in Capt. Lawson's Co., Baltimore Patriots, and was buried in the Faith Presbyterian Church at Broadway and Gay St. (Johnson and Christou, p. 146; Baker Vol. 1, p. 173; Burials copied by Edith Ensor Read, 1812 Society, and placed in File 52255 at the Maryland Historical Society)

Gregg, John, supposedly served as a private in Capt. Cuddy Lawson's Co., 5th Regt., Baltimore Militia, but no such service record has been found; allegedly wounded or killed on 12 Sep 1814 at the Battle of North Point. Name is on the Baltimore Battle Monument (Marine, p. 304, did not mention his wound or death; *Baltimore American*, 12 Jun 1819, listed him without any proof). John Gregg married Harriet Hall in 1804. (*Baltimore Federal Gazette*, 2 Jun 1804)

Gregory, George, served as a Seaman and was born in Maryland. Age: 23. Prison Depot: Portsmouth, Prisoner of War #1413. Captured by HM Frigate *Belle Poule*. When Taken: 14 Dec 1813. Where Taken: Bay of Biscayne. Prize Name: *Squirrel*. Ship Type: Merchant Vessel. Date Received: 1 Mar 1814. From what ship: HMS *Helicon*. Discharged on 28 Apr 1814 and sent to Chatham on HMS *Favorite*. Prison Depot: Chatham, Prisoner of War #3551. Date Received: 7 May 1814 from Portsmouth on HMS *Favorite*. Discharged on 26 Sep 1814 and sent to Dartmoor on HMS *Leyden*. Prison Depot: Dartmoor, Prisoner of War #4298. Date Received: 7 Oct 1814 on HMT *Niobe* from Chatham. Discharged on 14 Jun 1815. There is another entry that appears to be for the same seaman, but the dates are slightly different: **George Gregory**, Seaman, born in Maryland. Age: 23. Prison Depot: Plymouth 1, Prisoner of War #2207. Captured by HM Frigate *Belle Poule*. When Taken: 14 Dec 1813. Where Taken: Bay of Biscayne. Prize Name: *Squirrel*. Ship Type: Merchant Vessel. Date Received: 27 Dec 1813 on HMS *Protector*. Discharged on 27 Feb 1814 and sent to Chatham on HMS *Haleyon*. (Johnson's Database, 2019)

Gregory, William, served as a Private in the U.S. Marine Corps, enlisted on 25 Sep 1812, was wounded at Bladensburg on 24 Aug 1814, was admitted to the Naval Hospital in Washington, DC as Patient No. 33 on 3 Sep 1814 and was discharged on 17 Oct 1814 and sent to barracks (Sharp's Database, 2018)

Grey, Samuel, served as a Private in Capt. Samuel Lane's Co., U.S. Infantry, enlisted 18 May 1812 for 5 years and was captured. Prisoner of War #3961 at Halifax, NS, interned on 24 Jun 1813, was discharged on 27 Aug 1813, sent to England on HMS *Regulus* and was later released., returned to service and was discharged on 18 May 1817 (Johnson and Christou, p. 148; Baker Vol. 1, p. 165)

Grey, Thomas (African American), served as a Cook and was born in Baltimore. Age: 28. Prison Depot: Plymouth 1, Prisoner of War #609. Captured by HM Frigate *Medusa*. When Taken: 4 Feb 1813. Where Taken: Bay of Biscayne. Prize Name: *Rolla*. Ship Type: Merchant Vessel. Date Received: 28 Feb 1813. From what ship: HMS *Surveillante*. Discharged and sent to Dartmoor on 2 Apr 1813. Prison Depot: Dartmoor, Prisoner of War #113. Date Received: 2 Apr 1813 from Plymouth. Discharged on 20 Apr 1815. (Johnson's Database, 2019)

Griffett, Joshua, served as a Private in Capt. John Bond's Co., 41st Regiment, Baltimore Co., joined 30 Aug 1814, stationed at Kelley's Field in Baltimore and was reported "absent sick" on that same day (Wright Vol. 2, p. 67)

Griffin, James, served as a Seaman and was born in Baltimore. Age: 27. Prison Depot: Chatham, Prisoner of War #146. How Taken: Gave himself up off MV *Country Square*. When Taken: 26 Oct 1812. Where Taken: London, UK. Date Received: 5 Nov 1812. From what ship: HMS *Namur*. Discharged on 19 Jan 1813 to the HMS *Scipion*. (Johnson's Database, 2019)

Griffin, James, served as a Seaman and was born in Maryland. Age: 20. Prison Depot: Portsmouth, Prisoner of War #473. Captured by HM Ship-of-the-Line *Elephant*. When Taken: 28 Dec 1812. Where Taken: off Azores. Prize Name: *Sword Fish*. Home Port: Gloucester. Ship Type: Privateer. Date Received: 14 Jan 1813. From what ship: HMS *Elephant*. Discharged on 11 Mar 1813 and sent to Chatham on HM Store Ship *Abundance*. (Johnson's Database, 2019)

Griffin, John, served as a Private in the 14th U.S. Infantry (company not stated) and was captured. Prisoner of War #3777 at Halifax, NS, interned 24 Jun 1813, discharged on 19 Nov 1813 and sent to England (Johnson and Christou, p. 148; Baker Vol. 1, p. 174)

Griffin, Samuel, served as a Seaman and was born in Maryland. Age: 20. Prison Depot: Chatham, Prisoner of War #1153. Captured by HM Ship-of-the-Line *Elephant*. When Taken: 28 Dec 1812. Where Taken: off Azores. Prize Name: *Sword Fish*. Home Port: Gloucester. Ship Type: Privateer. Date Received: 16 Mar 1813 from Portsmouth on HMS *Abundance*. Discharged on 24 Jul 1813 and released to the Cartel *Hoffning*. (Johnson's Database, 2019)

Griffith, Joshua, served as a Private in Capt. Adam Barnes' Co., Watkins' Regt., Anne Arundel Co. Militia, from 25 May 1813 and died later in 1813, but the date and cause of death were not stated (Wright Vol. 4, p. 40; Marine p. 305)

Griffith, Samuel, served as Surgeon's Mate in the 11th Regiment, Dorchester Co. Militia, commissioned 5 Jun 1812, later resigned and died in 1814, but the date and cause of death were not stated (Marine p. 305; Wright Vol. 1, p. iii)

Griffith, Sylvanus, served as a Lieutenant in Capt. Dedie's Co., 10th Regt., and died on 20 Sep 1813 (Marine p. 305)

Griffett, Joshua, served as a Private in Capt. John Bond's Co., 41st Regiment, Baltimore Co. Militia, from 25 Aug 1814 and was reported as "absent sick Aug 30" 1814 (Wright Vol. 2, p. 67)

Grimes, John, served as a Private in Capt. Isaac Barnard's Co., 14th U.S. Infantry, enlisted 28 Dec 1812 for 5 years in Baltimore at the age of 19, 5' 5½" tall, born in Baltimore, captured, date and place not stated. Prisoner of War exchanged on 15 Apr 1814 and discharged from the service at Raleigh, NC on 8 Jan 1818 (Johnson and Christou, p. 149, citing Pension Old War IF-25113)

Grimes, Nicholas, served as a Private in Capt. Samuel Lane's Co., 14th U.S. Inf., enlisted 25 May 1812 for 5 years at Cumberland, MD, age 21, 5' 11" tall, born in Frederick, MD, and captured on 24 Jun 1813, place not stated but probably Beaver Dams, Upper Canada. Prisoner of War #4807 at Halifax, NS, interned 27 Aug 1813, discharged from prison on 19 Nov 1813 and sent to England by order of Sir J. B. Warren. Prison Depot: Chatham, Prisoner of War #3130, age 23.Date Received: 7 Jan 1814 from Halifax, NS. Discharged on 10 Oct 1814, sent to U.S. on the Cartel *St. Philip*and was discharged from the service on 25 May 1817 (Johnson and Christou, p. 149; Baker Vol. 1, p. 175; Johnson's Database, 2019)

Grimes, Thomas (1774-1814), served as a Private in Capt. Miles Greenwood's Co., 16th U.S. Infantry, enlisted 22 Apr 1814 at Burlington, VT at the age of 40, 5' 6½" tall, born in Maryland and died at Plattsburgh, NY on 12 Oct 1814 (Johnson and Christou, p. 149)

Grimes, Thomas, served as a Private in 12th U.S. Infantry (company not stated), enlisted on 6 Jun 1812 for 5 years at the age of 44, 5' 9" tall, born in Prince George's Co., and was discharged on 23 Mar 1814 on a Surgeon's Certificate for rheumatism and lame back (Johnson and Christou, p. 149)

Grindle, Richard, served as a Private in Capt. Reuben Gilder's Co. of the 14th U.S. Infantry, enlisted 21 Feb 1813, discharged on 17 Jan 1814 for "inability" and died at Greenbush, NY on 15 Nov 1814 (Johnson and Christou, p. 150)

Griner, George, served as a Private in the 14th U.S. Infantry (company not stated) and was captured, probably at Beaver Dams, Upper Canada. Prisoner of War #4077 at Halifax, NS, interned on 24 Jun 1813 and was discharged for exchange on 3 Feb 1814 (Johnson and Christou, p. 150; Baker Vol. 1, p. 174)

Grizel, Joseph, served as a Private (company not stated) and was captured at the Battle of Bladensburg on 24 Aug 1814 (Marine, p. 174)

Groce, Jacob, served as a Private in Capt. Joseph Hook's Co., 36th U.S. Infantry, enlisted 2 Jun 1814 and was reportedly killed on 28 Sep 1814 while attempting to desert; yet, bounty land was granted to his sister Mary Hunter and other heirs at law (BLW# 25589-160-12; Johnson and Christou, p. 150)

Gromly, Constantine, served as a Private in Capt. Joseph Marshall's Co., 14th U.S. Infantry, enlisted 16 Sep 1812 and discharged at Greenbush, NY on 7 Jun 1815 for lameness (Johnson and Christou, p. 150; BLW# 12445-160-12)

Groves, George W., served as a Seaman and was born in Baltimore. Age: 28. Prison Depot: Dartmoor, Prisoner of War #3586. How Taken: Gave himself up off MV *Fortune*. When Taken: 16 Mar 1814. Received: 30 Sep 1814. From what ship: HMT *Sybella*. Discharged on 4 Jun 1815. (Johnson's Database, 2019)

Grubb, Andrew, served as a Seaman and was born in Baltimore. Age: 29. Prison Depot: Plymouth 1, Prisoner of War #2704. Captured by HM Brig *Foxhound*. When Taken: 27 May 1814. Where Taken: off Isles of Scilly, England. Prize Name: *Margaret*, prize of the Privateer *Surprise*. Home Port: Baltimore. Ship Type: Privateer. Date Received: 16 Jun 1814. From what ship: HMS *Foxhound*. Discharged on 20 Jun 1814 and sent to Dartmoor. Prison Depot: Dartmoor, Prisoner of War #1499. Received: 20 Jun 1814 from Mill Prison. Discharged on 1 May 1815. (Johnson's Database, 2019)

Gruet, James, served as a Private in the 14th U.S. Infantry and was captured. Prisoner of War #4070 at Halifax, NS, interned 6 Jun 1813 and discharged for exchange on 3 Feb 1814 (Johnson and Christou, p. 151; Baker Vol. 1, p. 176)

Gruet, William, served as a Private in the 14th U.S. Infantry and was captured. Prisoner of War #4075 at Halifax, NS, interned 24 Jun 1813 and discharged for exchange on 3 Feb 1814 (Johnson and Christou, p. 151; Baker Vol. 1, p. 176)

Guest, Basil, served as a Private in Capt. Peter Pinney's Co., 27th Regiment, Baltimore Militia, from 19 Aug 1814 and was discharged on 1 Sep 1814 by the Surgeon as an invalid (Wright Vol. 2, p. 20)

Gundy, James, served as a Boy onboard a ship and was born in Maryland. Age: 12. Prison Depot: Plymouth 1, Prisoner of War #2018. Captured by HM Brig *Royalist*. When Taken: 6 Sep 1812. Where Taken: coast of France. Prize Name:

Ned. Home Port: Baltimore. Ship Type: Letter of Marque (Privateer). Date Received: 30 Sep 1813. From what ship: HMS *Royalist*. Discharged on 3 Nov 1813 and sent to Dartmoor. Prison Depot: Dartmoor, Prisoner of War #742. Age 13. Date Received: 3 Nov 1813 from Plymouth. Discharged on 26 Apr 1815. (Johnson's Database, 2019)

H

Hackey, Edward, served as a Seaman and was born in Baltimore. Age: 20. Prison Depot: Dartmoor, Prisoner of War #4130. Captured by HM Frigate *Niemen*. When Taken: 28 Jun 1814. Where Taken: off Delaware. Prize Name: *Bordeaux Packet*. Home Port: Baltimore. Ship Type: Letter of Marque. Date Received: 6 Oct 1814 from HMT *Chesapeake* from Halifax, NS. Discharged on 13 Jun 1815. (Johnson's Database, 2019)

Haddaway, Edward, served as a Lieutenant in the U.S. Navy and died on 15 Jun 1817 at St. Michaels in Talbot Co. of a pulmonary complaint with which he had long been afflicted, possibly service connected (*Republican Star*, 17 Jun 1817)

Hagan, Isaac, served as a Private in Capt. Earle's Co., 14th U.S. Infantry and died at Cheektowaga Hospital, NY on 8 Feb 1815 from dysentery (Johnson and Christou, p. 152; https://wnyroots.tripod.com/Index-1812.html)

Hagan, John, served as a Private in Capt. Samuel Lane's Co., 14th U.S. Infantry, enlisted 17 Jun 1812 at Cumberland, MD, age 38, 5' 5" tall, born in New Jersey, and was captured, date and location not given, but probably at Beaver Dams, Upper Canada. Prisoner of War #3965 at Halifax, NS, interned 24 Jun 1813, discharged on 3 Feb 1814 by order of Rear Admiral Griffith and exchanged on 15 Apr 1814 (Johnson and Christou, p. 152; Baker Vol. 1, p. 178)

Hager, George, served as a Private in Capt. William McLaughlin's Co., 50th Regiment, Allegany County Militia, called into service to serve in the defense of Baltimore and was reported "sick absent" on muster roll dated 11 Aug – 13 Oct 1814 ("Allegany County Militia, Including Garrett County, 1794-1815," by F. Edward Wright and Marlene S. Bates, *Maryland Genealogical Society Bulletin*, Volume 32, No. 2, Spring 1991, p. 174; Wright Vol. 9, p. 6, stated Capt. Henry Lowrey's Co., but Wright Vol. 10, p. 2, stated Capt. William McLaughlin's Co.)

Haggerty, Levi (1790-1871), served as a Private in Capt. Kenneth McKenzie's Co., 14th U.S. Infantry, enlisted 24 Nov 1812 for 18 months, and was captured, date and place were not stated, but probably at Beaver Dams, Upper Canada. Prisoner of War at Halifax, NS, interned 24 Jun 1813, discharged on 3 Feb 1814, exchanged on 15 Apr 1814 and discharged from the service at Greenbush, NY on 23 Jun 1813. Levi married 1st to Rebecca Rockhole in 1820, married 2nd to Martha E. Herring in 1838, both times in Baltimore, and died on 11 Sep 1871 in Washington,

DC, although another record stated 29 Aug 1871. (Johnson and Christou, p. 153; Baker Vol. 1, p. 178 misspelled Levi as Sevii Haggerty; Pension SO-5254; WO-14641; BLW# 27369-160-42; *The (Baltimore) Sun*, 12 Sep 1871)

Haggerty, Mahlon (1789-1813), served as a Private in Capt. Colin Buckner's Co., 5th U.S. Infantry, enlisted 24 Mar 1813 in Baltimore at age 24, 5' 10½" tall, born in Maryland and died on 9 Dec 1813 (Johnson and Christou, p. 153)

Hahn, Joseph, served as a Private under Capt. William Knox and joined Capt. Gault's Co. at Taneytown in Jun or Aug 1814 and was discharged because of his disability (not specified) incurred by the service (Mallick and Wright, p. 136)

Haines, Benjamin, served as a Private in Capt. Richard Goodell's Co., 23rd U.S. Infantry, enlisted 15 Feb 1814 at the age of 38, 5' 5" tall, born in Maryland; appears to have died in service, date not stated (Johnson and Christou, p. 153)

Halbrook, Benjamin, served as a Seaman and was born in Baltimore. Age: 24. Prison Depot: Chatham, Prisoner of War #179. How Taken: Gave himself up off HM Transport *MaryAnn*. When Taken: 28 Oct 1812. Where Taken: London, UK. Received: 5 Nov 1812. From what ship: HMS *Namur*. Discharged on 19 Jan 1813 to the HMS *Scipion*. (Johnson's Database, 2019)

Hale, Shederick, served as a Seaman and was born in Baltimore. Age: 42. Prison Depot: Stapleton, Prisoner of War #293. Captured by HM Frigate *Iris*. When Taken: 10 Mar 1813. Where Taken: off Cape Ortegal, Spain. Prize Name: *Messenger*. Ship Type: Merchant Vessel. Date Received: 11 Jul 1813 from Plymouth. Discharged on 16 Jun 1814 and sent to Dartmoor. Prison Depot: Dartmoor, Prisoner of War #1573. Age 43. Date Received: 23 Jun 1814 from Stapleton. Discharged on 1 May 1815. (Johnson's Database, 2019)

Halfpenny, Robert, served as a Seaman and was born in Baltimore. Age: 19. Prison Depot: Plymouth 1, Prisoner of War #489. Captured by HM Brig *Reindeer*. When Taken: 3 Feb 1813. Where Taken: Bay of Biscayne. Prize Name: *Cashiere*. Home Port: Baltimore. Ship Type: Letter of Marque. Date Received: 12 Feb 1813. From what ship: HMS *Reindeer*. Discharged and sent to Dartmoor on 2 Apr 1813. Prison Depot: Dartmoor, Prisoner of War #6. Date Received: 2 Apr 1813 from Plymouth. Discharged and sent to Dartmouth on 30 Jul 1813. (Johnson's Database, 2019)

Halfpenny, William, served as a *Pilot* and was born in Baltimore. Age: 50. Prison Depot: Dartmoor, Prisoner of War #3823. Captured by HM Frigate *Niemen*. When Taken: 28 Jan 1814. Where Taken: off Delaware. Prize Name: *Bordeaux Packet*. Home Port: Baltimore. Ship Type: Letter of Marque. Date Received: 5 Oct 1814 on HMT *Orpheus* from Halifax, NS. Discharged on 9 Jun 1815. (Johnson's Database, 2019)

Hall, David, served as a 2nd Mate and was born in Maryland. Age: 22. Prison Depot: Plymouth 1, Prisoner of War #954. Captured by HM Frigate *Andromache*. When Taken: 14 Mar 1813. Where Taken: off Nantes, France. Prize Name: *Courier*. Home Port: Baltimore. Ship Type: Letter of Marque. Date Received: 7 Apr 1813 from HMS *Sea Lark*. Discharged and sent to Dartmoor on 28 Jun 1813. Prison Depot: Dartmoor, Prisoner of War #347. Received: 28 Jun 1813 from Plymouth. Discharged on 20 Apr 1815. (Johnson's Database, 2019)

Hall, Frederick (African-African), was a runaway slave who served under the name of William Williams in the 38th U.S. Regiment; see William Williams, q.v.

Hall, Henry (1785-1813), served as a Seaman and was born in Baltimore. Age: 27. Prison Depot: Chatham, Prisoner of War #1338. How Taken: Gave himself up off HM Brig *Echo*. When Taken: 1 Aug 1812. Date Received: 26 Mar 1813. From what ship: HMS *Raisonable*. Died on 18 Sep 1813 from phthisis pulmonalis (tuberculosis) and smallpox. (Johnson's Database, 2019)

Hall, John, served as a Seaman and was born in Maryland. Age: 22. Prison Depot: Chatham, Prisoner of War #3005. Captured by HM Frigate *Shannon*. When Taken: 20 Aug 1813. Where Taken: at sea. Prize Name: *Yankee*. Ship Type: Privateer. Date Received: 7 Jan 1814 from Halifax, NS. Discharged on 25 Sep 1814 and sent to Dartmoor on HMS *Leyden*. Prison Depot: Dartmoor, Prisoner of War #4685. Received: 9 Oct 1814. From what ship: HMT *Leyden* from Chatham. Discharged on 15 Jun 1815. (Johnson's Database, 2019)

Hall, John, served as a Seaman and was born in Maryland. Age: 28. Prison Depot: Plymouth 1, Prisoner of War #1771. Captured by HM Brig *Goldfinch*. When Taken: 27 Jun 1813. Where Taken: off Nantes, France. Prize Name: *Minerva*. Ship Type: Merchant Vessel. Date Received: 25 Jul 1813. From what ship: HMS *Pyramus*. Discharged on 10 Aug 1813 and released to HMS *Salvador del Mundo*. (Johnson's Database, 2019)

Hall, John, served as a Seaman and was born in Baltimore. Age: 31. Prison Depot: Chatham, Prisoner of War #2289. How Taken: Gave himself up off HM Ship-of-the-Line *Royal George*. When Taken: 29 Oct 1812. Date Received: 17 Sep 1813. From what ship: HMS *Raisonable*. Discharged on 11 Aug 1814 and sent to Dartmoor on HMS *Freya*. Prison Depot: Dartmoor, Prisoner of War #2686. Date Received: 21 Aug 1814. From what ship: HMT *Freya* from Chatham. Discharged on 26 Apr 1815. (Johnson's Database, 2019)

Hall, Nehemiah, served as a Private in Capt. Charles Timanus' Co., 36th Regt., Baltimore Co., and was discharged at Camp Deal 32 miles from his residence and died 7 Oct 1814, cause not stated, but it was probably service connected (Wright Vol. 2, p. 64)

Hall, Perry (African American), served as a Seaman and was born in Baltimore. Age: 25. Prison Depot: Chatham, Prisoner of War #2453. Captured by HM Frigate *Shannon*. When Taken: 11 Oct 1812. Where Taken: off Halifax, NS. Prize Name: *Wiley Reynard*. Home Port: Boston. Ship Type: Privateer. Date Received: 21 Oct 1813 from Portsmouth on HMT *Malabar*. Discharged on 4 Sep 1814 and sent to Dartmoor on HMS *Freya*. Prison Depot: Dartmoor, Prisoner of War #3252. Date Received: 11 Sep 1814 on HMT *Freya* from Chatham. Discharged on 27 Apr 1815. (Johnson's Database, 2019)

Hall, Robert (1794-1815), served as a Private in Capt. William Littlejohn's Co., 2nd U.S Light Dragoons, enlisted 19 Feb 1814 at the age of 20, 5' 6" tall, born in Baltimoreand died on 3 Jan or 10 Jan 1815 (Johnson and Christou, p. 155)

Hall, Thomas, served as a Prize Master and was born in Maryland. Age: 23. Prison Depot: Portsmouth, Prisoner of War #1490. Captured by HM Schooner *Canso*. When Taken: 11 May 1814. Where Taken: off Cape Clear, Ireland. Prize Name: *Traveler*, prize of the Privateer *Surprise*. Home Port: Baltimore. Ship Type: Privateer. Date Received: 1 Jun 1814. From what ship: HMS HMS *Canso*. Discharged on 30 Jun 1814 and sent to Plymouth on HM Brig *Steady*. (Johnson's Database, 2019)

Hall, Thomas (1777-1815), served as a Prize Master and was born in Maryland. Age: 36. Prison Depot: Dartmoor, Prisoner of War #1708. Captured by HM Schooner *Canso*. When Taken: 11 May 1814. Where Taken: off Cape Clear, Ireland. Prize Name: *Traveler*, prize of the Privateer *Surprise*. Home Port: Baltimore. Ship Type: Privateer. Date Received: 8 Jul 1814. From what ship: *Labrador*. Died on 18 Apr 1815 from phthisis pulmonalis (consumption or tuberculosis). (Johnson's Database, 2019; Centennial Trails, United States Daughters of 1812, online at www.war1812trails.com/Dartmoor)

Hallen, John, served as a Private in Capt. David Cummings' Co., 14th U.S. Inf., enlisted 1 Sep 1812 and was captured, date and place not stated. Prisoner of War, sent to England, later released, returned to service and deserted at Fort McHenry on 20 Apr 1815 (Johnson and Christou, p. 155)

Halson, James, served as a Private in the 14th U.S. Infantry and was captured. Prisoner of War #3855 at Halifax, NS, interned 24 Jun 1813 and was discharged for exchange on 3 Feb 1814 (Johnson and Christou, p. 155; Baker Vol. 1, p. 180)

Halton, William, served as a Farmer and was born in St. *Marys*. Age: 21. Prison Depot: Dartmoor, Prisoner of War #3897. Captured by HM Ship-of-the-Line *Albion*. When Taken: 31 May 1814. Where Taken: on shore at St. Mary's Co., MD. Date Received: 5 Oct 1814. From what ship: HMT *Orpheus* from Halifax, NS. Released on 23 Nov 1814. (Johnson's Database, 2019)

Hamill, Isaac, served as a Private in Capt. Andrew Porter's Co., 30th Regiment, Cecil Co. Militia, from 24 Apr 1813 and was "unwell at the time – excused" before 27 Apr 1813 (Wright Vol. 3, p. 10)

Hamilton, Joseph, served as a Private in Capt. Andrew Smith's Co., 51st Regt., Baltimore Militia, from 19 Aug 1814 and was discharged on 1 Sep 1814 by a Surgeon, but the cause was not reported (Wright Vol. 2, p. 38)

Hamilton, Robert M., served as a Master in the U.S. Navy and was captured at the Battle of Bladensburg on 24 Aug 1814 (Marine p. 174)

Hamilton, William, served as a Private in Capt. Henry Fleming's Co., 14th U.S. Infantry, enlisted 22 Nov 1812 at age 29, 5' 5½" tall, born in Prince George's Co., MD, discharged at Washington, DC on 7 Feb 1817 because of wounds received at Beaver Dams, Upper Canada, ten miles west of Niagara Falls, on 24 Jun 1813 (BLW# 8718-160-12; Johnson and Christou, p. 156)

Hammond, Hezekiah (1776-1815), served as a Private in Capt. Hopley Yeaton's Co., 1st U.S. Artillery, enlisted 31 Oct 1810 for 5 years in Washington, DC, age 34, 5' 9" tall, blue eyes, brown hair, fair complexion, born in Frederick Co., MD, sent to Fort Washington on 5 Nov 1810 and died at Fort Nelson, VA on 4 Mar 1815 (Johnson and Christou, p. 156; Mallick and Wright, p. 140)

Hammond, Simpson, served as a Sergeant in Capt. Duvall's Co. from 4 Aug 1814, as a substitute for Daniel Stoner, and "he said that after the Battle of Bladensburg they marched back to Bladensburg, thence to Washington City and encamped on Windmill Hill between the President's home and the Potomac River, where he was taken sick and unable to do his duty. After a short time in Georgetown he went home last part of Sep 1814. Confined under Doctor's care for more than 6 month; crippled with rheumatism, near death in 1858, but is better now (1859)" at which time he lived in Iowa and planned to move to Kansas Territory. (BLW# 55-160-88429; Mallick and Wright, p. 141)

Haney, Thomas, served as a Private in Capt. Henry P. Ruff's Co., 42nd Regiment, Harford Co. Militia, enlisted 30 Apr 1813 for 6 months, stationed at Annapolis and died on 16 Aug 1813, cause not stated (Wright Vol. 3, p. 25)

Hanks, Porter (c1780-1812), served as a 1st Lieutenant in the 1st U.S. Artillery, enlisted 17 Jan 1805 in Maryland, commissioned 2nd Lieutenant on 17 Jan 1805, promoted to 1st Lieutenant on 31 Dec 1806 and was killed at Detroit on 16 Aug 1812 (BLW# 4955-160-50; Johnson and Christou, p. 157)

Hanna, John, served as a Private in Capt. Stephen H. Moore's Co., Baltimore Volunteers Infantry Co., from 8 Sep 1812 for 1 year and died at Buffalo, NY on 13 Jan 1813 (Johnson and Christou, pp. 157-158; Wright Vol. 2, p. 57)

Hanna, Thomas, served as a Seaman and was born in Baltimore. Age: 32. Prison Depot: Dartmoor, Prisoner of War #5111. Captured by HM Sloop *Pylades*. When Taken: 13 Sep 1814. Where Taken: Long 65. Prize Name: *Nancy*, prize of the Privateer Portsmouth. Ship Type: Privateer. Received: 28 Oct 1814. From what ship: HMT *Alkbar* from Halifax, NS. Discharged on 29 Jun 1815. (Johnson's Database, 2019 , spelled his last name Hannah)

Hanna, William, served as a Private in Capt. Nathan Towson's Co. of 2nd U.S. Artillery, and died on 25 Mar 1813; wife Eleanor receved Old War Pension MC-4; heirs received half pay for 5 years in lieu of bounty land (Johnson and Christou, p. 158)

Hannum, Peter (1768-1813), served as a Private in Capt. David Cummings' Co., 14th U.S. Infantry, enlisted on 13 Aug 1812 at age 44, 5' 7½" tall, born in Pennsylvania and killed at Beaver Dams, Upper Canada, ten miles west of Niagara Falls, on 24 Jun 1813; bounty land issued to daughter Ann H, Hannum and other heirs at law (BLW# 17139-160-12; Johnson and Christou, p. 158)

Hansell, Philip, served as a Private in Capt. Samuel Lane's Co., 14th U.S. Inf., enlisted 20 Jun 1812 for 5 years at age 21, 5' 9¼" tall, born in Shepherdstown, VA and was captured, date and place not stated. Prisoner of War, exchanged on 15 Apr 1814 and was discharged at Montpelier, MS on 20 Jun 1817 (Johnson and Christou, p. 158)

Harbaugh, Charles (1790-1814), served as a Private in Capt. Colin Buckner's Co., 5th U.S. Infantry, enlisted 18 Feb 1813 for 5 years in Baltimore at the age of 23, 5' 5" tall, born in Baltimore and died 1 Jul 1814; bounty land issued to his father Leonard Harbaugh (BLW# 9764-160-12; Johnson and Christou, p. 158)

Harburn, Thomas, served as a Seaman and was born in Baltimore. Age: 30. Prison Depot: Dartmoor, Prisoner of War #1197. Captured by HM Frigate *Hotspur*. When Taken: 13 Jan 1813. Prize Name: *Imperatrice Reine*. Ship Type: Privateer. Date Received: 4 Jun 1814 from Dartmouth. Discharged on 28 Apr 1815. (Johnson's Database, 2019)

Harder, John, served as a Boy onboard a ship and was born in Maryland. Age: 17. Prison Depot: Portsmouth, Prisoner of War #1496. Captured by HM Schooner *Canso*. When Taken: 11 May 1814. Where Taken: off Cape Clear, Ireland. Prize Name: *Traveler*, prize of the Privateer *Surprise*. Home Port: Baltimore. Ship Type: Privateer. Date Received: 1 Jun 1814. From what ship: HMS HMS *Canso*. Discharged on 2 Jun 1814. Sent to Plymouth on HMS *Growler*. (Johnson's Database, 2019)

Hardesty, George (1778-1815), served as a Private in the 12th U.S. Infantry, enlisted 15 Nov 1814 at Winchester, VA at the age of 36, 6' 1" tall, born in Anne

Arundel Co. and died on 28 Mar or 6 Apr 1815; bounty land issued to his son James Hardesty and other heirs at law (Johnson and Christou, p. 159)

Hardie, Robert (1798-1881), served as a Seaman on the privateer *Nonsuch*, was captured and sent to Dartmoor prison, but no dates were given (Marine p. 312)

Harding, Charles (1787-1814), served as a Private in Capt. George Haig's Co., 2nd U.S. Light Dragoons, enlisted 16 Jul 1812 in Baltimore at the age of 25, 5' 6" tall, transferred to 1st U.S. Rifles on 4 Mar 1814 and was killed at Fort Erie, Upper Canada on 17 Sep 1814 (Johnson and Christou, p. 159)

Harding, Robert, served as a Private in Capt. Roderick Burgess' Co., 32nd Regt., Anne Arundel Co. Militia, from 22 Jul 1814 and was discharged by the Surgeon of the Regiment on 14 Sep 1814 as reported on the muster roll dated 22 Jul – 19 Sep 1814 (Wright Vol. 4, p. 42)

Hardwood, William, served as a Seaman and was born in Maryland. Age: 31. Prison Depot: Portsmouth, Prisoner of War #1147. Captured by HM Brig *Rebuff*. When Taken: 16 Jun 1813. Where Taken: off Cape St. Marys, Newfoundland. Prize Name: *Maydock*. Ship Type: Merchant Vessel. Date Received: 6 Oct 1813. From what ship: HM Sloop *Kingfisher*. Discharged on 17 Oct 1813 and sent to Chatham on HMT *Malabar No. 352*. (Johnson's Database, 2019)

Hardy, Amos, served as a Private in Capt. Thomas Montgomery's Co., 14th U.S. Infantry, enlisted 15 Jan 1813 at Alexandria, DC, age 24, 6' tall, born in Loudoun Co., VA and was captured. Prisoner of War #4051 at Halifax, NS, interned on 24 Jun 1813, discharged for exchange on 3 Feb 1814, exchanged on 15 Apr 1814, was returned to service and reported as deserted at Fort Severn, MD on 12 Jul 1815 (Johnson and Christou, p. 159; Baker Vol. 1, p. 185)

Hardy, George (1788-1814), served as a Private in Capt. James Paxton's Co., 5th U.S. Infantry, enlisted 31 Dec 1812 for 5 years in Lewisburg, VA, at the age of 24, 5' 2¼" tall, born in Frederick, MD and died at French Mills, NY on 3 Feb 1814 (Johnson and Christou, p. 159)

Hardy, John (1791-1813), served as a Corporal in Capt. Thomas Moore's Co., 12th U.S. Infantry, enlisted 22 Mar 1813 in Wheeling, VA at the age of 22, 5' 8" tall, born in Frederick Co., MD and was killed in action at Williamsburg, NY on 11 Nov 1813 (Johnson and Christou, pp. 159-160; Mallick and Wright, p. 145)

Hardy, Joseph, served as a Private in a Marine Battery under Sailing Master Rodman and was wounded on 13 Sep 1814 at Fort McHenry (Marine p. 173)

Hardy, Joseph (c1785-1814), served as a Private in Capt. James F. Huston's Co., Frederick Co., from 23 Jul 1814, on furlough after 4 Oct 1814 and died while on furlough on 19 Oct 1814 in Baltimore; he had married Catherine Ramsburger on 9 Jan 1807 in Frederick, MD. (Mallick and Wright, p. 145)

Hare, Henry, served as an Ensign in Capt. William Whiteford's Co., Harford Co. Militia, Extra Battalion, for "9 days plus 4 more days a prisoner" as noted on the muster roll dated 26 Apr – 3 May 1813 (Wright Vol. 3, p. 33) "The elder, Mr. Levy, was taken [by the British] about this time [3 May 1813], as was also Capt. Barnes, and one or two men. John O'Neill, Christopher Levy, James Sears, eldest son of Mrs. Sears, Capt. Whitefoot [Whiteford] and Ensign Hare were also made prisoners, as was one Whitloe, an aged citizen. Most of the Prisoners they released while on shore, but John O'Neill, Christopher Levy and James Sears they carried on board the fleet." (*Narrative Respecting the Conduct of the British From Their First Landing on Spesutia Island Till Their Progress to Havre de Grace*, by James Jones Wilmer, 1814, p. 13; *Concord Point Lighthouse Station at Havre de Grace*, by Jack L. Shagena, Jr. and Henry C. Peden, Jr., 2017, p. 35; "Harford County in the War of 1812," by Christopher T. George, *Harford Historical Bulletin* No. 76, Spring 1998, p. 33)

Harford, William, served as a Private in Capt. Conrad Hook's Co., Baltimore County, 2nd Regt. 11th Brigade, from 25 Jul 1814 and was killed in battle on 24 Aug 1814 at Bladensburg (Wright Vol. 2, p. 81)

Hargood, George, served as a Private in Capt. Isaac Barnard's Co., 14th U.S. Infantry, and was captured. Prisoner of War #3920 at Halifax, NS, interned 24 Jun 1813, discharged 19 Nov 1813 and sent to England (Pension Old War WF-13372 to widow Elizabeth Hargood; Pension Old War WF-14932 was Rejected; Johnson and Christou, p. 160; Baker Vol. 1, p. 185), George Hargood was born in Maryland. British Prison Depot: Chatham, Prisoner of War #3059. Age 29. When Taken: 24 Jun 1813. Where Taken: Beaver Dams, Upper Canada. Date Received: 7 Jan 1814 from Halifax. Discharged on 10 Oct 1814 and sent to U.S. on the Cartel *St. Philip.* (Johnson's Database, 2019)

Harker, John, served as a Boy onboard a ship and was born in Maryland. Age: 17. Prison Depot: Plymouth 1, Prisoner of War #2670. Captured by HM Schooner *Canso*. When Taken: 11 May 1814. Where Taken: off Cape Clear, Ireland. Prize Name: *Traveler*, prize of the Privateer *Surprise*. Home Port: Baltimore. Ship Type: Privateer. Date Received: 5 Jun 1814. From what ship: HMS *Gronville*. Discharged on 14 Jun 1814 and sent to Dartmoor. Prison Depot: Dartmoor, Prisoner of War #1294. Date Received: 14 Jun 1814 from Mill Prison. Discharged on 28 Apr 1815. (Johnson's Database, 2019)

Harman, John (1783-1815), served as a Private in Capt. Spotswood Henry's Co., 2nd U.S. Artillery, enlisted on 21 Jul 1812 for 5 years in Sullivan, NC at the age of 29, 5' 10½" tall, born in Maryland and died of wounds received in action in the

Mediterranean on 21 Jul 1815; bounty land issued to his son James Harman and other heirs at law (BLW# 15513-160-12; Johnson and Christou, p. 160)

Harman, William (1774-1813), served as a Private in Capt. Joseph Hook's Co., 36th U.S. Infantry, enlisted 6 May 1813 in Baltimore at the age of 39, born in Norfolk, VA and died on 20 Jun 1813 (Johnson and Christou, p. 160)

Harper, Henry, served as a Seaman of the U.S. Chesapeake Flotilla, entered service on 22 Feb 1814, was on board on 7 Apr 1814, reported sick (date not stated) and died on 12 Nov 1815 (Shomette p. 371)

Harrigan, Elisha, served as a Private in the 14th U.S. Infantry and was captured. Prisoner of War #4065 at Halifax, NS, interned 24 Jun 1813 and discharged for exchange on 3 Feb 1814 (Johnson and Christou, p. 160; Baker Vol. 1, p. 185)

Harrington, Thomas, served as a Private in Capt. Thomas Kearney's Co., 14th U.S. Infantry, enlisted 20 May 1812 for 5 years and died on 8 Feb 1813; bounty land issued to his sister Elizabeth Harrington and other heirs at law (BLW# 22181-160-12; Johnson and Christou, p. 161)

Harris, Andrew, served as a Private in the 14th U.S. Infantry, enlisted 18 May 1812, deserted, reassigned to Captain Leakin's Co., 38th Infantry, and died in hospital on 10 Apr 1814 (Johnson and Christou, p. 161)

Harris, George (1780-1813) (African American), served as a Seaman and was born in Baltimore. Age: 32. Prison Depot: Plymouth 1, Prisoner of War #67. Captured by HM Frigate *Medusa*. When Taken: 9 Nov 1812. Where Taken: off San Sebastian, Spain. Prize Name: *Independence*. Ship Type: Merchant Vessel. Date Received: 27 Nov 1812 from HMS *Wasp*. Sent to Portsmouth on 29 Dec 1812 on HM Ship-of-the-Line *Northumberland*. Prison Depot: Portsmouth, Prisoner of War #335. Died on 6 Mar 1813. (Johnson's Database, 2019)

Harris, James, served as a Seaman and was born in Maryland. Age 26. Prison Depot: Plymouth 1, Prisoner of War #99. Captured by HM Brig *Rover*. When Taken: 21 Oct 1812. Where Taken: off Bordeaux, France. Prize Name: *Experiment*. Ship Type: Merchant Vessel. Date Received: 25 Dec 1812. From what ship: HMS *Northumberland*. Discharged and sent to Portsmouth on 29 Dec 1812 on HMS *Northumberland*. Prison Depot: Portsmouth, Prisoner of War #353. Age 26, Received: 31 Dec 1812. From what ship: HM Ship-of-the-Line *Northumberland*. Discharged on 4 Mar 1813 and sent to Chatham on HMS *Queen*. Prison Depot: Chatham, Prisoner of War #930. Age 28. Received: 10 Mar 1813. From what ship: HMS *Tigress*. Discharged on 8 Jun 1813. Rreleased to the Cartel *Rodrigo*. (Johnson's Database, 2019)

Harris, John, served as a Seaman and was born in Maryland. Age: 25. Prison Depot: Plymouth 1, Prisoner of War #580. Captured by HM Brig *Reindeer*. When

Taken: 3 Feb 1813. Where Taken: Bay of Biscayne. Prize Name: *Cashiere*. Home Port: Baltimore. Ship Type: Letter of Marque. Date Received: 23 Feb 1813. From what ship: HMS *Surveillante*. Discharged and sent to Dartmoor on 2 Apr 1813. Prison Depot: Dartmoor, Prisoner of War #87. Date Received: 2 Apr 1813 from Plymouth. Discharged and sent to Dartmouth on 30 Jul 1813. (Johnson's Database, 2019)

Harris, Josiah, served as a Private in Capt. Thomas Montgomery's Co., 14th U.S. Infantry, enlisted 17 Feb 1813 and died at Burlington, VT, in Mar 1814 from sickness; bounty land was issued to his brothers William Harris and Zephaniah Harris, only heirs at law (BLW# 27428-160-42; Johnson and Christou, p. 161)

Harris, Samuel (1775-1858), served as 3rd Sergeant in Capt. Joseph H. Nicholson's Artillery Co., slightly wounded on 13 Sep 1814 at Fort McHenry; buried in Green Mount Cemetery (Marine p. 173; *The [Baltimore] Sun*, 7 Jun 1858)

Harrison, John, served as a Second Lieutenant and was born in Maryland. Age: 29. Prison Depot: Dartmoor, Prisoner of War #2515. Captured by HM Sloop *Martin*. When Taken: 30 Jun 1814. Where Taken: off Halifax, NS. Prize Name: *Snap Dragon*. Ship Type: Privateer. Date Received: 16 Aug 1814 from HMT *Queen* from Halifax, NS. Discharged on 3 May 1815. (Johnson's Database, 2019)

Harrison, Samuel (1791-1814), served as a Private in Capt. William Jett's Co., 20th U.S. Infantry, enlisted 26 Mar 1813 at the age of 22, 5' 10" tall, born in Calvert Co., MD and died in Jan 1814; bounty land issued to Isaac Harrison and other heirs at law (BLW# 12236-160-12; Johnson and Christou, p. 162)

Hart, Asa, served as a Seaman on the privateer *Globe* and was killed in action on 1 Nov 1813 (*Niles Weekly Register*, 19 Feb 1814)

Hart, Joshua (African American), served as a Seaman and was born in Baltimore. Age: 22. Prison Depot: Plymouth 1, Prisoner of War #1939. Captured by HM Frigate *President*. When Taken: 14 Aug 1813. Where Taken: off Nantes, France. Prize Name: *Marmion*. Ship Type: Merchant Vessel. Date Received: 27 Aug 1813. From what ship: HMS *Urgent*. Discharged on 8 Sep 1813 and sent to Dartmoor. Prison Depot: Dartmoor, Prisoner of War #655. Date Received: 8 Sep 1813 from Plymouth. Discharged on 26 Apr 1815. (Johnson's Database, 2019)

Hartley, David (1773-1812), served as a Private in Capt. Samuel Lane's Co., 14th U.S. Infantry, enlisted 22 Jun 1812 in O Bourg (sic), at the age of 39, 5' 6" tall, born in Ireland and died at Black Rock, New York on 5 Dec 1812 (Johnson and Christou, pp. 162-163)

Harvey, Anthony (African American), served as a Cook and was born in Baltimore. Age: 28. Prison Depot: Portsmouth, Prisoner of War #1321. Captured by HM Brig *Electra* on 7 Jul 1813 off St. Johns, Newfoundland. Prize Name:

Growler. Home Port: Salem. Ship Type: Privateer. Date Received: 24 Dec 1813. From what ship: HM Schooner Adonis. Discharged on 26 Dec 1813 and sent to Chatham on HMS *Nemesis*. Prison Depot: Chatham, Prisoner of War #3195. Date Received: 7 Jan 1813 from Portsmouth. Discharged on 25 Sep 1814 and sent to Dartmoor on HMS *Leyden*. (Johnson's Database, 2019)

Harwood, William, served as a Seaman and was born in Maryland. Age: 31. Prison Depot: Chatham, Prisoner of War #2429. Captured by HM Brig *Rebuff*. When Taken: 16 Jun 1813. Where Taken: off Cape St. Marys, Newfoundland. Prize Name: *Maydock*. Ship Type: Merchant Vessel. Date Received: 21 Oct 1813 from Portsmouth on HMT *Malabar*. Discharged on 4 Sep 1814 and sent to Dartmoor on HMS *Freya*. Prison Depot: Dartmoor, Prisoner of War #3238. Date Received: 11 Sep 1814. From what ship: HMT *Freya* from Chatham. Discharged on 28 May 1815. (Johnson's Database, 2019)

Haslett, Joseph (1772-1812), served as a Private in Capt. John Whistler's Co., 1st U.S. Infantry, enlisted 23 Sep 1806 in Lancaster, PA at age 34, 5' 10" tall, born in Maryland, re-enlisted 29 Sep 1811, was a prisoner of war (place and date not stated) and died at Boston, MA on 23 Dec 1812 (Johnson and Christou, p. 163)

Haslip, John, served as a Private in Capt. Clement Sullivan's Co., 14th U.S. Infantry, enlisted on 2 May 1812 and died on 4 Dec 1812; bounty land issued to his sister Nelly Haslip (BLW# 16485-160-12; Johnson and Christou, p. 164)

Haubert, Jacob (1796-1814), served as a Private in Capt. David Warfield's Co., 5th Regt., Baltimore Militia, from 19 Aug 1814 and was killed on 12 Sep 1814 at North Point. On 29 Dec 1814 in Baltimore County Frederick Haubert made oath that his son Jacob Haubert who was wounded in the late engagement with the enemy at North Point and who has since died was born in Feb 1796. Name is on the Baltimore Battle Monument. (CMSR; Wright Vol. 2, p. 80; Marine p. 172, states he died on 14 Sep 1814; *Baltimore American*, 12 Jun 1819)

Haubert, Michael, (1779-1814), served as a Captain of his own company in the 51st Regiment, Baltimore Militia, and died on 18 Oct 1814 (Wright Vol. 2, p. 35; however, Marine p. 316 states he resigned in Dec 1814; *Baltimore American*, 19 Oct 1814, reported, "Capt. Michael Haubert died yesterday, aged 35 years.")

Hauer, Henry, served as a Private in Capt. Thomas Contee Washington's Co., Frederick Co. Militia, and was reported "absent on duty, sick" at Fort Severn some time between 17 Aug and 31 Dec 1812 (Mallick and Wright, p. 331)

Haughn, Jonathan, served as a Private in Capt. George Washington Magee's Co., Frederick Co., joined on 22 Jul 1814 and was discharged on 1 Oct 1814 due to being "over age" (Mallick and Wright, p. 149)

Hawkenbrok, Henry, served as a Private in the 14th U.S. Infantry and was captured on 24 Jun 1813 [at Beaver Dams, Upper Canada]. Prisoner of War #3773 at Halifax, NS, interned 24 Jun 1813 and was discharged for exchange on 3 Feb 1814 (Johnson and Christou, p. 164; Baker Vol. 1, p. 189)

Hawkins, Isaac (Mulatto), served as a Seaman and was born in Maryland. Age: 31. Prison Depot: Chatham, Prisoner of War #2538. Captured by HM Frigate *Briton*. When Taken: 17 Jan 1813. Where Taken: off Bordeaux, France. Prize Name: *Columbia*. Ship Type: Merchant Vessel. Date Received: 22 Oct 1813 from Portsmouth on HMT *Malabar*. Discharged on 8 Sep 1814 and sent to Dartmoor on HMS *Niobe*. Prison Depot: Dartmoor, Prisoner of War #3334. Date Received: 13 Sep 1814. From what ship: HMT *Niobe* from Chatham. Discharged on 28 May 1815. (Johnson's Database, 2019)

Hawkins, James L., served as a Private in Capt. Joseph H, Nicholson's Artillery Co. and was slightly wounded on 13 Sep 1814 at Fort McHenry (Marine p. 173)

Hayes, Banjamin, served as a Seaman and was born in Maryland. Age: 24. Prison Depot: Plymouth 1, Prisoner of War #2267. Captured by HM Frigate *Euratos*. When Taken: 25 Dec 1813. Where Taken: at sea. Prize Name: *Fanny*. Prize. Ship Type: Privateer. Date Received: 20 Jan 1814. From what ship: HMS *Euratos*. Discharged on 31 Jan 1814 and sent to Dartmoor. Prison Depot: Dartmoor, Prisoner of War #931. Date Received: 31 Jan 1814 from Plymouth. Discharged on 27 Apr 1815. (Johnson's Database, 2019)

Hayes, John, served as a Gunner and was born in Baltimore. Age: 31. Prison Depot: Dartmoor, Prisoner of War #5435. Captured by HM Frigate *Armide*. When Taken: 16 Aug 1814. Where Taken: off Nantucket, MA. Prize Name: *Invincible*. Home Port: Salem. Ship Type: Letter of Marque. Date Received: 11 Nov 1814. From what ship: HMT *Impregnable*. Discharged and released on 1 Jul 1815. (Johnson's Database, 2019)

Hays, Bernard, served as a Private in Capt. Reuben Gilder's Co., 14th U.S. Inf., enlisted 11 Mar 1814 in Frederick, MD at age 22, 5' 9" tall, born in Hagerstown, was wounded at Lyon's Creek, Upper Canada and discharged at Greenbush, NY on 11 Apr 1815 because of wounds (Pension Old War IF-10228; BLW# 2712-160-12; Johnson and Christou, p. 165)

Hays, Reverdy, served as a Private in Capt. David Warfield's Co., 5th Regiment, Baltimore United Volunteers, and was wounded on 12 Sep 1814 at North Point (Marine pp. 172, 318)

Hays, Simeon, served as a Seaman on the privateer (letter-of-marque brig) *Matilda*, was captured (date not given) and sent to Dartmoor; exchanged and served on the privateer *Surprise*, was captured (date not given, but probably on 5 Apr 1815) and was again sent to Dartmoor (Marine, p. 318)

Hayward, George, served as a Private in Capt. Thomas Montgomery's Co., 14th U.S. Infantry, enlisted 19 May 1812 and died in 1814; his heirs received half pay for 5 years in lieu of bounty land (Johnson and Christou, p. 166)

Haywood, John (1787-1815) (African American), served as a Seaman and was born in Baltimore. Age: 25. Prison Depot: Chatham, Prisoner of War #2286. How Taken: Gave himself up off HM Ship-of-the-Line *Scipion*. When Taken: 20 Oct 1812. Date Received: 17 Sep 1813. From what ship: HMS *Raisonable*. Discharged on 4 Sep 1814 and sent to Dartmoor on HMS *Freya*. Prison Depot: Dartmoor, Prisoner of War #3134. Date Received: 11 Sep 1814. From what ship: HMT *Freya* from Chatham. Died on 6 Apr 1815 from gunshot wound [during the massacre] when shot in the prison yard. (Centennial Trails, United States Daughters of 1812, online at www.war1812trails.com/Dartmoor; Johnson's Database, 2019)

Hazletine, Thomas, served as a Private in Capt. Stephen Moore's Co. of the U.S. Volunteers, enlisted on 8 Sep 1812 for 1 year and was wounded at York, Upper Canada on 27 Apr 1813 (Johnson and Christou, p. 166; Wright Vol. 2, p. 57)

Head, Benjamin P. c1788-1814), served as a Private in Capt. Keller's Co., MD Militia, commissioned an Ensign in Capt. John Rothrock's Co., 38th U.S. Infantry, on 20 May 1813, dismissed on 19 Apr 1814 and died 22 Apr 1814 in Baltimore; he was married to Margaret Stembler on 2 Dec 1810 in Baltimore (Johnson and Christou, p. 166; Widow's Pension WO-762, WC-1316)

Hearsey, George T., served as a Private in Capt. David Warfield's Co., 5th Regt., Baltimore Militia, and was wounded on 12 Sep 1814 at North Point (Huntsberry p. 69, but Wright Vol. 2, p. 8, and Marine, p. 318, both did not mention wound; Marine, p. 172, stated he was a prisoner of war)

Heath, John, served as a Private in Capt. Josiah W. Heath's Co., 23rd Regiment, Somerset Co. Militia, for 1 day and was reported as "got crippled, taken sick, discharged" on the muster roll dated April 1814 (Wright Vol. 1, p. 55)

Heath, Richard K., served as 1st Major, 5th Regiment, Baltimore Militia, and was wounded on 12 Sep 1814 at North Point. "R. K. Heath, merchant, major, 5th regiment, had two horses shot under him and was slightly wounded." Another source stated, "Major Richard K. Heath, of the 5th, who led on the advance party to bring on the action, behaved as became an officer, the facts of his first horse being killed under him in the first skirmish, his second being badly wounded, and himself receiving a severe contusion on the head, by a musket ball, in the general action, are ample proofs of his bravery and exposure in discharge of his duty." (North Point dead and wounded Article 4 Oct 1814 Columbian Register CT Vol.

III 97, p. 4; Marine p. 165) "Died Wednesday morning last, Gen. Richard K. Heath, of the 14th Brigade, Maryland Militia – defended Baltimore in 1814 – interred with military and civic honors." (*Niles Weekly Register*, 15 Dec 1821)

Hedden, Amos, served as a Private in the 14th U.S. Infantry (company not stated), was captured and was a Prisoner of War at Halifax, NS. "Ames Hedden" of the 14th Regiment was Prisoner of War #3913, interned 24 Jun 1813 and sent to England on 9 Nov 1813; "Amos Hedden," whose regiment was not listed, was Prisoner of War #4640, interned 15 Nov 1813 and sent to England on 19 Nov 1813 (Johnson and Christou, p. 167; Baker Vol. 1, p. 192)

Hedrick, George, served as a Private in Capt. Nathan Towson's Co., 2nd U.S. Artillery, enlisted 12 Apr 1812 for 5 years in Baltimore at the age of 18, 5' 5¼" tall, born in Baltimore, and was captured at Stoney Creek, UC on 12 Jun 1813. "George Hedrick" was Prisoner of War #5034 at Halifax, NS, interned 28 Dec 1813, released and returned to service, date not given, and was discharged at Fort Niagara, NY on 30 Apr 1817; "George Hedricks" (also spelled Hedderick), same age, same rank, same company, captured at Stoney Creek, Henderson Harbor, and was Prisoner of War #287 at Quebec, interned 28 Jun 1813 and was discharged on 31 Oct 1813 (Johnson and Christou, p. 167, and Baker Vol. 1, p. 192, stated prison at Halifax, but Johnson, p. 68, stated prison at Quebec)

Heidelbaugh, George, served as a Private in Capt. Aaron R. Levering's Co., 5th Regiment, Baltimore Militia, joined 11 Sep 1814, was captured, taken prisoner, date and place not named, and exchanged on 26 Nov 1814 (Wright Vol. 2, p. 5)

Heinnan, Dennis (1787-1814), served as a Corporal in Capt. George Keyser's Co., 38th U.S. Infantry, enlisted 24 Sep 1814 in Baltimore at age 27, 5' 4½" tall, born in Ireland, drowned on 2 Dec 1814 in pursuit of a deserter; bounty land issued to his father William (BLW# 22952-160-12; Johnson and Christou, p. 168)

Heininger, Caleb, served as a Private in Capt. Henry Grindage's Co., 14th U.S. Infantry, enlisted 12 Sep 1812 at the age of 29, 5' 1" tall, born in Germany and discharged at Sackett's Harbor, NY on 11 Oct 1813 on a Surgeon's Certificate (Johnson and Christou, pp. 167-168)

Heisely (Heisley), Frederick Augustus (1792-1875), served as a Private in Capt. James F. Huston's Co., 1st Regiment of Maryland Militia, Frederick Co., from 23 Jul 1814, was wounded by a musket ball near the left hip joint on 24 Aug 1814 during the Battle of Bladensburg and was discharged from service on or about 3 Jan 1815. He left for Pennsylvania in 1818 and founded the F. A. Heisely Watch and Instrument Mfg. Co. in Pittsburgh. Surgeon's Affidavit prepared by Dr. Peter Fahnstock on 1 Feb 1844 in Pittsburgh stated that during the battle with the British troops at Bladensburg on 24 Aug 1814 Sgt. Heisley "received a musket ball in his left hip – a plain wound, the mark of which is apparent and the ball has never been abstracted, being lodged so deep in the part, as to render extraction, now impracticable, and he is thereby not only incapacitated for military duty, but, in the opinion of the undersigned, is totally disabled from obtaining his subsistance from manual labor." Thomas W. Morgan, Lieut., gave a similar statement on 7 Sep 1843 In Pittsburgh. On 20 Mar 1851 Frederick A. Heisely [his signature] wrote a letter to J. E. Heath, Esq., about the amount of his bounty land and included this statement about his service: "The company to which I was attached was organized on the 27th day of July 1814 at Frederick Barracks and marched on the 30th of same month and was attached to the First Regt. of Maryland Drafts and on the 21st of August same year marched for Bladensburg were (sic) I was wounded on the 24th of same month in the hip and on the 28th was placed under the care of Dr. Wm. Taylor, then Hospital Surgeon at Frederick Town under whose hands I remained until about the 4th of September following when I arrived at camp near Baltimore and was there a few days when I was advised by Dr. Nelson, one of the Surgeons of the Regt., to return home which advice I took and on my arrival home my brother took my place and went on and served the balance of my time which ended in January 1815 which my Certificate of Discharge will show." F. A. Heisely was born in Frederick, MD on 3 Jul 1792, died in Pittsburgh, PA on 21 May 1875 and was buried in Allegheny Cemetery, Section 22, Lot 77, Grave 1. (Mallick & Wright, p. 152; Bounty Land Warrant Application Records online at Fold3, pp. 9, 22, 26; also, online at www.findagrave.com/memorial/80258852/frederick-augustus-heisely, some information and instrument pictures posted by Thomas G. Raub)

Helms, Abraham (1782-1814), served as a Private in Capt. James Paxton's Co., 12th U.S. Infantry, enlisted 8 Jul 1812 in Botetourt Co., VA at the age of 30, 5' 7½" tall, born in Maryland, severely wounded during the Battle of La Cole, Upper Canada on 30 Mar 1814 and died from wounds at Burlington, VT on 14 May or 18 May 1814; bounty land was issued to his father John D. Helms (BLW# 16498-160-12; Johnson and Christou, p. 168)

Helvenstine, George W. (1778-1813), served as a Sergeant in Capt. George Seviers' Co., 1st U.S. Rifles, enlisted 1 Jan 1808 for 5 years at age 30, 5' 10" tall, was born in Washington, MD and died at Sackett's Harbor, NY on 14 Dec 1813 (Johnson and Christou, p. 168)

Hemmingway, John, served as a Private in Capt. Frederick Evans' Co., 2nd U.S. Artillery, enlisted 18 Jul 1814 at Fort McHenry at the age of 39, 5' 6" tall, born in Boston and discharged on 10 Aug 1815 at Elkton, MD for inability (Johnson and Christou, p. 168; BLW# 440-160-12)

Henderson, David (1776-1813), served as a Private in Capt. Joseph Hook's Co., 36th U.S. Infantry, enlisted 20 May 1813 for 1 year in Annapolis at the age of 37,

5' 9¾" tall, born in Scotland and died on 25 or 26 – [Aug?] 1813 (Johnson and Christou, p. 168)

Henderson, George W., served as a Private and was born in Maryland. Age: 46. Prison Depot: Dartmoor, Prisoner of War #5838. When Taken: 17 Sep 1814. Where Taken: Fort Erie, Upper Canada. Prize Name: 4th U.S. Rifles. Land Forces. Date Received: 26 Dec 1814. From what ship: HMT *Argo*. Discharged on 29 Jun 1815. (Johnson's Database, 2019)

Hendrickson, John, served as a Seaman and was born in Maryland. Age: 30. Prison Depot: Dartmoor, Prisoner of War #4122. Captured by HM Frigate *Niemen*. When Taken: 28 Jun 1814. Where Taken: off Delaware. Prize Name: *Bordeaux Packet*. Home Port: Baltimore. Ship Type: Letter of Marque. Date Received: 6 Oct 1814 on HMT *Chesapeake* from Halifax, NS. Discharged on 13 Jun 1815. (Johnson's Database, 2019)

Henricks, Jeremiah, served as a Seaman and was born in Baltimore. Age: 16. Prison Depot: Portsmouth, Prisoner of War #31. Captured by HM Frigate *Barbadoes*. When Taken: 22 Aug 1812. Where Taken: off Savannah, GA. Prize Name: U.S.R.M. Cutter *James Madison*. Ship Type: Warship. Date Received: 12 Oct 1812 San Antonio. From what ship: HM Ship-of-the-Line *Polyphemus*. Discharged on 19 Feb 1813 and sent to Chatham on HMS *Ulysses*. Prison Depot: Chatham, Prisoner of War #670. Date Received: 24 Feb 1813 from Portsmouth on HMS *Ulysses*. Discharged 10 May 1813 and released to Cartel *Admittance*. (Johnson's Database, 2019)

Henry, George, served as a Private in the 14th U.S. Infantry and was captured, probably at Beaver Dams, Upper Canada. Prisoner of War #4017 at Halifax, NS, interned 24 Jun 1813, discharged on 9 Nov 1813 and sent to England (Johnson and Christou, p. 169; Baker Vol. 1, p. 193)

Henry, James, served as a Private in Capt. David Cummings' Co., 14th U.S. Inf., enlisted 1 Jun 1812 and was captured. Prisoner of War #4155 at Halifax NS, interned 24 Jun 1813, discharged on 27 Aug 1813, was sent to England, later released, returned to service and deserted at Fort McHenry on 20 Apr 1815 (Johnson and Christou, p. 169; Baker Vol. 1, p. 194)

Henry, Samuel, served as a Private in Capt. James Dorman's Co., 5th U.S. Inf., enlisted 27 Feb 1812 for 5 years in Baltimore, age 21, 5' 9" tall, born in Adams Co., PA, was captured on 10 Jun 1813 at Stoney Creek, Upper Canada. Prisoner of War #3910 at Halifax, NS, interned 24 Jun 1813, discharged for exhange on 3 Feb 1814, exchanged on 15 Apr 1815 (sic), returned to service and deserted at Detroit, MI on 15 Feb 1816 (Johnson and Christou, p. 169; Baker Vol. 1, p. 194, stated he served in the 6th U.S. Regiment)

Hensow, John, served as a Seaman and was born in Baltimore. Age: 27. Prison Depot: Dartmoor, Prisoner of War #3783. Captured by *Rebecca*, British Privateer. When Taken: 13 Apr 1814. Where Taken: off Delaware. Prize Name: *James*. Ship Type: Privateer. Date Received: 5 Oct 1814. From what ship: HMT *President* from Halifax, NS. Discharged 9 Jun 1815. (Johnson's Database, 2019)

Henwood, Eliza, served as a Cook and was born in Maryland. Age: 26. Prison Depot: Chatham, Prisoner of War #214. How Taken: Gave himself up off MV *Perverance*. When Taken: 2 Nov 1812. Date Received: 15 Nov 1812. From what ship: HMS *Raisonable*. Discharged in Jul 1813 and released to the Cartel *Moses Brown*. (Johnson's Database, 2019)

Herbert, Thomas, served as a Private in Capt. Richard Clarke's Co., 12th Regt., St. Mary's Co. Militia, from 23 Aug to 31 Aug 1813 and "still on duty on board a N. Caroline Schooner captured on the 29th inst. on suspicion of having been trading with the British." (Wright Vol. 5, p. 13)

Herkwright, John, served as a Seaman and was born in Maryland. Age: 24. Prison Depot: Plymouth 2, Prisoner of War #463. Captured by HM Brig *Barbadoes*. When Taken: 11 Jan 1815. Where Taken: off St. Bartholomew, West Indies. Prize Name: *Fox*. Home Port: Baltimore. Ship Type: Privateer. Date Received: 16 Apr 1815. From what ship: HMS *Swiftsure*. Discharged on 2 Jun 1815 and released to the Cartel *Soverign*. (Johnson's Database, 2019)

Herrick, Thomas, served as a Private in Capt. Nathan Towson's Co., 2nd U.S. Artillery, enlisted 13 Apr 1812 for 5 years and died at Black Rock, NY on 11 Jan 1815 (Johnson and Christou, pp. 169-170)

Herring, Gardner, served as a Private in Capt. Clement Sullivan's Co., 14th U.S. Infantry, enlisted 3 Jun 1812 in Cambridge, MD, age 28, 5' 6¼" tall, born in Kent Co., MD, and was discharged at Greenbush, NY on 2 Dec 1813 on a Surgeon's Certificate (Johnson and Christou, p. 170)

Herring, Henry, served as a Private in Capt. John Bond's Co., 41st Regiment, Baltimore Co., from 25 Aug 1814 and reported as "absent-sick Sep 1" 1814 (Wright Vol. 2, p. 67)

Herring, John (1787-1814), served as a Private in Capt. Clement Sullivan's Co., 14th U.S. Infantry, and was captured at Beaver Dams, Upper Canada, ten miles west of Niagara Falls, on 24 Jun 1813. Age 26, born in Maryland. Prison Depot: Halifax, NS. Prisoner of War #3785 and died at Halifax on 11 Jan 1814 of dysentery; bounty land issued to Gardner Herring and other heirs at law (BLW# 26805-160-12; Johnson and Christou, p. 170; Baker, Vol. 1, p. 194; Johnson's Database, 2019)

Herrings, Joshua, served as a Private in Capt. David Millikin's Co., 22nd U.S. Inf., enlisted 27 Jul 1813 at Waynesboro, PA, age 25, 5' 11" tall, born in Baltimore, and discharged at Sackett's Harbor, NY on 11 Aug 1815 for partial blindness (Johnson and Christou, p. 170)

Herron, James, served as a Private in Capt. Henry Grindage's Co., 14th U.S. Infantry, enlisted on 18 Sep 1812 at the age of 32, 5' 7" tall. Prisoner of War (Halifax), captured at Beaver Dams, Upper Canada, ten miles west of Niagara Falls, on 24 Jun 1813 and discharged at Boston, MA on 7 Aug 1814 because of wounds (BLW# 6691-160-12; Johnson and Christou, p. 170, but Baker, Vol. 1, p. 194, did not mention him)

Herry, Tobias, served as a Private in Capt. Daniel McFarland's Co., 22nd U.S. Infantry, enlisted 21 May 1812 in Washington, PA at the age of 38, 5' 7" tall, born in Maryland, wounded at Chippewa, Upper Canada on 25 Jul 1814 and discharged at Buffalo, NY on 1 Aug 1815 (Johnson and Christou, p. 170)

Hetzer, George, served as a Sergeant in Capt. Samuel Lane's Co., 14th U.S. Inf., enlisted 2 May 1812 in Maryland, age 21, 5' 6" tall, born in Washington, MD and was slightly wounded at Black Rock, NY on 28 or 29 Nov 1812. Prisoner of War at Halifax, NS, having been captured at Beaver Dams, Upper Canada, ten miles west of Niagara Falls, on 24 Jun 1813 (Johnson and Christou, p. 171, but Baker, Vol. 1, p. 194, did not mention him)

Hewey, John, served as a Private in the 14th U.S. Infantry and was captured, probably at Beaver Dams, Upper Canada. Prisoner of War #4050 at Halifax, NS, interned 24 Jun 1813 and discharged for exchange on 3 Feb 1814 (Johnson and Christou, p. 171; Baker Vol. 1, p. 195)

Heyden, Daniel, served as a Private in the 14th U.S. Infantry and was captured, probably at Beaver Dams, Upper Canada. Prisoner of War #4012 at Halifax, NS, interned 24 Jun 1813 and discharged for exchange on 3 Feb 1814 (Johnson and Christou, p. 171; Baker Vol. 1, p. 195)

Heywood, John (Mulatto), served as a Seaman and was born in Baltimore. Age: 25. Prison Depot: Portsmouth, Prisoner of War #800. How Taken: Gave himself up off HM Ship-of-the-Line *Scepter*. When Taken: Where Taken: Mahon (Island of Minorca). Date Received: 21 Apr 1813. From what ship: HM Guard Ship *Royal William*. Discharged on 27 Apr 1813 and sent to Chatham on HMS *Citoyenne*. Prison Depot: Chatham, Prisoner of War #1659. Date Received: 9 May 1813. From what ship: HMS *Raisonable*. Discharged on 13 Aug 1814 and sent to Dartmoor. Prison Depot: Dartmoor, Prisoner of War #2719. Date Received: 21 Aug 1814. From what ship: HMT *Freya* from Chatham. Discharged on 26 Apr 1815. (Johnson's Database, 2019)

Hichew, David, see David Hiteshew, q.v.

Hicks, Isaac, served as a Private in Capt. William McIlvane's Co., 14th U.S. Infantry, enlisted on 13 Jun 1812 at age 32, 5' 10½" tall, born in Frederick Co., VA and was captured on 12 Jun 1813. Prisoner of War #5165 at Halifax, NS, interned 28 Dec 1813 and discharged for exchange on 3 Feb 1814 (Johnson and Christou, p. 171; Baker Vol. 1, p. 195)

Higginbotham, William, served as a Seaman and was born in Baltimore. Age: 36. Prison Depot: Dartmoor, Prisoner of War #3824. Captured by HM Frigate *Niemen*. When Taken: 28 Jan 1814. Where Taken: off Delaware. Prize Name: *Bordeaux Packet*. Home Port: Baltimore. Ship Type: Letter of Marque. Date Received: 5 Oct 1814 on HMT *Orpheus* from Halifax, NS. Discharged on 9 Jun 1815. (Johnson's Database, 2019)

Higgins, David, served as a Marine, was taken from the barracks and admitted to the Naval Hospital in Washington, DC as Patient No. 67 on 1 Aug 1814 (injury or illness was not specified) and was discharged on 8 Aug 1814 and sent to the barracks (Sharp's Database, 2018)

Higgins, Joshua C., served as a Major in the 2nd Regiment, Anne Arundel Co. Militia, commissioned on 2 Jul 1807, battalion commander in 1814 (muster roll dated 19-21 July 1814) and died in 1815, but the date and cause of death were not stated (Wright Vol. 4, pp. 11, 19; Marine p. 322)

High, Jacob, served as a Private in Capt. Robert C. Galloway's Co., 2nd Regiment, 11th Brigade, Baltimore Militia, from 27 Jul 1814 and was wounded on 24 Aug 1814 at Bladensburg (Wright Vol. 2, p. 86)

Hilderbrand, George (1792-1814), served as a Private in Capt. James F. Huston's Co., from 23 Jul 1814 and died on 16 Aug 1814 (Mallick and Wright, p. 155, stating he was born on 19 Aug 1792, son of Joseph and Magdalene)

Hill, Jeremiah, served as a Seaman and was born in Baltimore. Age: 27. Prison Depot: Portsmouth, Prisoner of War #1344. Captured by *Chance*, Jersey Privateer. When Taken: 15 Dec 1813. Where Taken: coast of France. Prize Name: *Watson*, prize of the Privateer *True Blooded Yankee*. Ship Type: Privateer. Date Received: 4 Jan 1814. From what ship: Earl S. Vincent Packet. Discharged on 5 Jan 1814 and sent to Chatham on HMS *Poictiers*. Prison Depot: Chatham, Prisoner of War #3226. Captured by *Chance*, Jersey Privateer. When Taken: 13 Dec 1813. Where Taken: coast of France. Prize Name: *Watson*, prize of the Privateer *True Blooded Yankee*. Ship Type: Privateer. Date Received: 13 Jan 1814 from Portsmouth on HMS *Poictiers*. Discharged on 25 Sep 1814 and sent to Dartmoor on HMS *Leyden*. Prison Depot: Dartmoor, Prisoner of War #4708. Date

Received: 9 Oct 1814 on HMT *Leyden* from Chatham. Discharged on 15 Jun 1815. (Johnson's Database, 2019)

Hill, John (1774-c1814), served as a Private in Capt. Reuben Chamberlain's Co., 2nd U.S. Infantry, enlisted 19 Jul 1808 in Columbia Springs at the age of 34, 5' 10" tall, born Cecil Co., MD, re-enlisted at Fort Bowyer on 24 Jul 1813 for five years and died at Mobile, AL, but the date and cause of death were not stated (Johnson and Christou, p. 172)

Hill, Pompey (African American), served as a Seaman and was born in Maryland. Age: 34. Prison Depot: Portsmouth, Prisoner of War #558. Captured by HM Frigate *Dryad* on 7 Jan 1813 at sea. Prize Name: *Rossie*. Ship Type: Merchant Vessel. Date Received: 25 Jan 1813. From what ship: HM Ship-of-the-Line *Queen*. Discharged on 11 Mar 1813 and sent to Chatham on HM Store Ship *Abundance*. Prison Depot: Chatham, Prisoner of War #1231. Date Received: 16 Mar 1813 from Portsmouth on HM Store Ship *Abundance*. Discharged on 24 Jul 1813 and released to the Cartel *Hoffning*. (Johnson's Database, 2019)

Hill, Richard, was a Seaman who was wounded on 24 Aug 1814 on the field of battle at Bladensburg, was admitted to the Naval Hospital in Washington, DC as Patient No. 15, was discharged on 30 Oct 1814 and sent to Baltimore (Sharp's Database, 2018)

Hill (Hile), Shadrick (African American), served as a Seaman and was born in Baltimore. Age: 40. Prison Depot: Plymouth 1, Prisoner of War #1277. Captured by HM Frigate *Medusa*. When Taken: 12 Apr 1813. Where Taken: Bay of Biscayne. Prize Name: *Caroline*. Ship Type: Merchant Vessel. Date Received: 10 May 1813. From what ship: HMS *Medusa*. Discharged on 2 Sep 1813 and sent to Dartmoor. (Johnson's Database, 2019)

Hill, Stephen, served as a Private in the 14th U.S. Infantry (company not stated) and was born in Maryland; enlisted 12 Nov 1812 for 18 months and was later captured. Prisoner of War #3919 at Halifax, NS, interned 24 Jun 1813, was discharged on 9 Nov 1813 and sent to England. Prison Depot: Chatham, Prisoner of War #3058. Age 23. When Taken: 24 Jun 1813. Where Taken: Beaver Dams, Upper Canada. Date Received: 7 Jan 1814 from Halifax, NS. Discharged on 10 Oct 1814 and sent to U.S. on the Cartel *St. Philip*. (Johnson and Christou, p. 172; Baker Vol. 1, p. 197; Johnson's Database, 2019)

Hill, Thomas (1784-1822), served as a Private in Capt. Alexander Williams' Co., 2nd U.S. Artillery, enlisted on 2 May 1813, age 29, 5' 7½" tall, born in Baltimore, wounded at Chippewa, Upper Canada on 5 Jul 1814 in left leg, discharged at Greenbush, NY on 24 Apr 1815 due to wounds and diedin 1822; heirs received half pay for 5 years in lieu of bounty land (Johnson and Christou, p. 172)

Hilliard, Robert B., served as a Master and was born in Maryland. Age: 32. Prison Depot: Plymouth 1, Prisoner of War #101. Captured by HM Cutter *Fancy*. When Taken: 19 Dec 1812. Where Taken: Bay of Biscayne. Prize Name: *Argus*. Ship Type: Merchant Vessel. Date Received: 27 Dec 1812. From what ship: *Fancy*, Cutter. Discharged and sent on 8 Dec 1812 to Ashburton on parole. (Johnson's Database, 2019)

Hindman, John (African American), served as a Seaman and was born in Annapolis. Age: 41. Prison Depot: Plymouth 2, Prisoner of War #269. Captured by HM Brig *Onyx*. When Taken: 25 Dec 1814. Where Taken: at sea off San Domingo (Haiti). Prize Name: *Netterville*. Ship Type: Merchant Vessel. Date Received: 2 Mar 1815. From what ship: HMS Dannemark. Discharged on 3 Mar 1815 and sent to Dartmoor. Prison Depot: Dartmoor, Prisoner of War #6393. Date Received: 3 Mar 1815 on HMT *Ganges* from Plymouth. Discharged on 11 Jul 1815. (Johnson's Database, 2019)

Hinds, John, served as a Private in Capt. Robert C. Galloway's Co., 2nd Regiment, 11th Brigade, Baltimore Militia, from 27 Jul 1814 and was reported "missing since the action at Bladensburgh" on 24 Aug 1814 (Wright Vol. 2, p. 86)

Hinhart, Ab. [Abraham], served as a Seaman on the privateer *Globe* and was killed in action 1 Nov 1813 (*Niles Weekly Register*, 19 Feb 1814)

Hinton, Reason (1782-1814), served as a Private in Capt. Shepperd Leakin's Co., 38th U.S. Infantry, enlisted 25 Jan 1814 in Baltimore at the age of 32, 5' 10" tall, born in Upper Marlboro, MD and died at Baltimore on 22 Aug 1814 (Johnson and Christou, p. 174)

Hiteshew, Abraham (1789-1873), served as a Private in Capt. William Knox's Co., Frederick Co. Militia, joined 26 Aug 1814 and discharged at Baltimore on 21 Oct 1814 due to sickness. He was born 28 Mar 1789, died 1 Aug 1873 and was buried at Grace Evangelical & Reformed Church, Taneytown, MD. (Mallick and Wright, p. 157; *Names In Stone*, by Jacob M. Holdcraft, 1966, p. 575)

Hiteshew David (c1794-1814), served as a Private in Capt. John Fonsten's Co., Frederick Co. Militia, joined 2 Sep 1814, marched to Baltimore and engaged in the defense of the city on 12 Sep 1814, was "sick absent on Oct 11" 1814 and died on 23 Oct 1814 (Mallick and Wright, p. 154, spelled his name Hichew)

Hobbs, Brice (1775-1812), served as a Private in Capt. Simon Owens' Co., 1st U.S. Infantry, enlisted 5 Apr 1810 in Chambersburg, PA at the age of 35, 5' 10½" tall, born in Frederick, MD and died at Belle Fontaine, MO, on 1 Nov 1812 (Johnson and Christou, p. 174)

Hobbs, William C. (c1773-1815), served as Captain of his own company in the 36th U.S. Infantry, born in Maryland, commissioned a 1st Lieutenant on 30 Apr

1813, promoted to Captain on 30 Sep 1814 and died on 8 Feb 1815, cause not stated; bounty land issued to his widow Christina Hobbs (BLW# 11342-160-12; Johnson and Christou, p. 174) William C. Hobbs married Christina Schnertzell on 30 May 1794 in Frederick Co., MD. (*Maryland Marriages, 1778-1800*, by Robert Barnes, 1979, p. 105)

Hobert, James, served as a Seaman and was born in Maryland. Age: 49. Prison Depot: Dartmoor, Prisoner of War #4961. Captured by HM Frigate *Endymion*. When Taken: 15 Aug 1814. Where Taken: off Nantucket, MA. Prize Name: *Herald*. Home Port: New York. Ship Type: Privateer. Date Received: 28 Oct 1814. From what ship: HMT *Alkbar* from Halifax, NS. Discharged on 21 Jun 1815. (Johnson's Database, 2019)

Hockenbrough, Henry, served as a Private in Capt. Richard Arell's Co., 14th U.S. Infantry, enlisted 15 Aug 1812 in Baltimore at the age of 38, 5' 5¾" tall, born in Germany, and was captured, date and place were not stated. Prisoner of War, exchanged on 15 Apr 1814 and discharged at Annapolis on 18 Oct 1815 as unfit for service (Johnson and Christou, p. 175)

Hoff, Michael, served as a Corporal in 14th U.S. Infantry, enlisted 24 Nov 1813 for 18 months and was captured. Prisoner of War, sent to England, returned to service and was discharged on 31 Mar 1815 (Johnson and Christou, p. 175)

Hoffman, George W., served as a Private in Capt. Peter Pinney's Co., 27th Regt., Baltimore Militia, from 25 Aug 1814 and was discharged in Sep 1814 by the Surgeon, but the exact date and cause were not stated (Wright Vol. 2, p. 20)

Hoffman, Henry (1773-1814), served as a Private in Capt. James McDonald's Co., 14th U.S. Infantry, enlisted 7 Feb 1814 at the age of 41, 5' 6" tall, born in Virginia and was killed in the Battle of Lyon's Creek on 19 Oct 1814; bounty land issued to son Jacob Hoffman and other heirs at law (BLW# 25344-160-12; Johnson and Christou, p. 175)

Hoffman, Philip, served as a Private in the 14th U.S. Infantry and was captured. Prisoner of War #4125 at Halifax, NS, interned 24 Jun 1813 and discharged for exchange on 3 Feb 1814 (Johnson and Christou, p. 175; Baker Vol. 1, p. 198)

Hoffman, William Davis (1795-1866), served as a Private in the companies of Capt. Joseph Green and then Capt. James F. Huston between 23 Jul 1814 and 10 Jan 1815 and was "injured at Bladensburg" on 24 Aug 1814. (Mallick and Wright, p. 159, did not mention service at Bladensburg nor his injury; Pension WO-24544, WC-17219, BLW# 50-80-27262) He was born on 11 Oct 1795, died on 20 Mar 1866. and was buried beside his wife Susanna Densifor Hoffman (1806-1881) in Middletown Cemetery at Freeland, Baltimore Co., MD. (Smith's Database, 2019;

pictures of his gravestone engraved "Veteran War 1812" are shown on line at www.findagrave.com courtesy of Beckey Russell and family)

Hogan, William, of Maryland, served as a Seaman on the ship *Desiree* and was reported by Capt. Jeduthan Upton, Jr. in 1814 as having been impressed into service and was being held as a Prisoner of War on the prison ship *San Antonio* at Chatham, England (*Niles Weekly Register*, 26 Feb 1814)

Hogart, William, served as a Private in Capt. James Gibson's Co. of U.S. Light Artillery, enlisted 26 Jan 1812 for 5 years at the age of 33, 5' 10" tall, born in Baltimore, and was captured at Queenston Heights, Upper Canada on 3 Oct 1812, later released, returned to service and discharged at Fort Independence, MA on 26 Jan 1817 (Johnson and Christou, pp. 175-176)

Holbrook, Thomas, served as a Private in Capt. George Washington Magee's Co., New Windsor, Frederick Co. Militia, 1st Regiment, joined 23 Jul 1814 in Baltimore Town, engaged in the Battle of Bladensburg and was captured and taken prisoner on 24 Aug 1814, paroled on 26 Aug 1814, re-joined his regiment on 6 Dec 1814 and discharged at Annapolis on or by 15 Jan 1815 (Mallick and Wright, pp. 159, 343; Marine, p. 174; Wright Vol. 2, p. 77)

Holiday, Thomas, served as a Private (company not stated) and was captured at the Battle of Bladensburg on 24 Aug 1814 (Marine, p. 174)

Holland, George, served as a Private in the 14th U.S. Infantry and was captured later. Prisoner of War at Quebec and died there on 17 Jul 1813 (Johnson and Christou, p. 176; Johnson's Quebec book, p. 72, did not mention him)

Holland, Henry, served as a Private in Capt. Adam Barnes' Co., Watkins' Regt., Anne Arundel Co. Militia, from 16 Apr 1813 and was reported "sick in hospital" on the muster roll dated 16 Apr – 31 Jul 1813 (Wright Col. 4, p. 40)

Holland, John (1771-1813), served as a Private in the 14th U.S. Infantry at the age of 42 and was captured later. Prisoner of War at Quebec and died there on 17 Jul 1813. (Johnson and Christou, p. 176)

Holland, Joseph, served as a Private in Capt. Roderick Burgess' Co., 32nd Regt., Anne Arundel Co. Militia, from 22 Jul 1814 and was reported "sick from 23 Aug 1814" on the muster roll dated 22 Jul – 19 Sep 1814 (Wright Vol. 4, p. 42)

Holland, Richard, served as a Seaman and was born in Maryland. Age: 25. Prison Depot: Plymouth 1, Prisoner of War #1616. Captured by HM Frigate *Belle Poule*. When Taken: 11 May 1813. Where Taken: Bay of Biscayne. Prize Name: *Revenge*. Home Port: Charleston. Ship Type: Letter of Marque (Privateer). Date Received: 14 Jun 1813. From what ship: HMS *Royalist*. Discharged on 30 Jun 1813 and sent to Stapleton. Prison Depot: Stapleton, Prisoner of War #153. Received: 8 Jul 1813 from Plymouth. Discharged on 13 Jun 1814 and sent to Dartmoor. Prison Depot: Dartmoor, Prisoner of War #1432. Date Received: 19 Jun 1814 from Stapleton. Discharged 28 May 1815. (Johnson's Database, 2019)

Hollings, Thomas (c1790-1813) served as a Private in Capt. Isaac Barnard's Co., 14th U.S. Infantry, enlisted on 15 Jan 1813 for 5 years and died on 7 Aug 1813; bounty land was issued to his father Jesse Hollings who was his only heir (BLW# 22920-160-12; Johnson and Christou, p. 176)

Hollingsworth, Horatio, served as a Private in Capt. David Warfield's Co., 5th Regiment, Baltimore Militia, United Volunteers, joined 31 Aug 1814 and was wounded on 12 Sep 1814 at North Point (Wright Vol. 2, p. 8; Marine p. 326)

Hollingsworth, Jacob, served as a Private in the 38th U.S. Infantry, enlisted on 26 Oct 1813 for 1 year and was either discharged or died at Baltimore on 31 Oct 1813 (Johnson and Christou, p. 176)

Hollingsworth, Levi (1765-1822), served as a Private in Capt. Samuel Sterett's Co., 5th Regt., Baltimore Militia, was wounded at North Point on 12 Sep 1814 and died in 1822 (North Point dead and wounded Article 4 Oct 1814 Columbian Register CT Vol. III 97, p. 4; Wright Vol. 2, p. 6; Baltimore Will Book 11, p. 451)

Holmes, John, served as a Seaman and was taken from the barracks and admitted to the Naval Hospital in Washington, DC as Patient No. 2 as of 1 Jun 1814, but his injury or illness was not stated (Sharp's Database, 2018)

Holmes, Joseph, served as a Private in Capt. John H. Rogers' Co., 51st Regiment, Baltimore Militia, from 19 Aug 1814 and was discharged some time in Nov 1814 by a Surgeon, but the medical reason was not reported (Wright Vol. 2, p. 37)

Holmes, Thomas, served as a Private in Capt. Gerrard Wilson's Co., 6th Regt., Baltimore Militia, from 19 Aug 1814 and was discharged by the doctor on 19 Oct 1814 as unfit for service (Wright Vol. 2, p. 11)

Holmes, Vincent, served as a Private in Capt. Gerrard Wilson's Co., 6th Regt., Baltimore Militia, from 19 Aug 1814 and was discharged by the doctor on 19 Oct 1814 as unfit for service (Wright Vol. 2, p. 11)

Holmes, Walter (1785-1814), served as a Private in Capt. Shepperd Leakin's Co., 38th U.S. Infantry, enlisted 30 Aug 1814 in Baltimore at the age of 29, 5' 9½" tall, born in Philadelphia and died at Camp Snowden on 19 Oct or 19 Nov 1814 (Johnson and Christou, p. 177)

Holston, Hamilton, served as Ship Steward on the privateer (armed brigantine) *Chausseur* of Baltimore commanded by Capt. Thomas Boyle and was slightly wounded in action on 26 Feb 1815 (*Niles Weekly Register*, 25 Mar 1815)

Holston, James, served as a Private in Capt. Kenneth McKenzie's Co., 14th U.S. Infantry, enlisted 28 Dec 1812 for 18 months and was later captured. Prisoner of War, exchanged on 15 Apr 1814 and discharged at Greenbush, NY on2 3 Jun 1814 (Johnson and Christou, p. 177)

Holton, Robert (c1795-1832), served as a Private in Capt. Combs' Co., 12th Regt., St. Mary's Co., and was stationed at Cedar Point and Point Lookout for 3 days between 16 Apr and 11 May 1813. (Wright Vol. 5, pp. 22, 72) On 15 Oct 1852 Eliza Guyther, age 49, widow of Robert Holton, stated they were married on 2 Aug 1827 by Rev. Whitfield, her former name was Eliza A. Waughop and Robert died in 1832; she later married W. W. Guyther in 1838 and he died in 1846; her bounty land claim was rejected (BLW# 55-rej-329150). Robert Holton also apparently served as a Seaman on the merchant vessel *Mary* and was captured on 9 Jul 1814 "at sea by HMS *Loire*, received from *Dragon*. Fame (sic) per order Capt. Skipney senior officer," interned at Halifax, NS on 1 Aug 1814 as Prisoner of War #6807 and discharged on 30 Aug 1814. (Baker Vol. II, p. 201)

Holton, William (c1795-1825), served as a Private in Capt. Forrest's Co., was taken prisoner in St. Mary's Co. in the summer of 1813 and carried to England where he remained for 9 months, per Capt. William B. Scott who added in 1851 that he saw Holton on board the enemy's vessels and supplied him with money and other necessaries (BLW# 50-160-10057; Wright Vol. 5, p. 72). The records show that he served under Capt. James Forrest for 16 days between 10 Feb and 24 Jun 1814 (Wright Vol. 5, p. 47). William Holton also apparently served as a Seaman on the merchant vessel *Mary* and was captured on 9 Jul 1814 "at sea by HMS *Loire*, received from *Dragon*. HMS *Chesapeake* for England," interned at Halifax, NS on 1 Aug 1814 as Prisoner of War #6806 and discharged on 18 Aug 1814 (Baker, Vol. 1, p. 201). On 2 Jan 1851 Elizabeth Bowling, age 53, widow of William Holton, stated they were married on 20 Jan 1818 by Rev. Anger, in Charles Co., her former name was Thompson and William died on 3 Jan 1825 in St. Mary's Co. (BLW# 50-160-10057)

Holtzman, Jacob, served as a Private in the U.S. Marine Corps, enlisted 4 Jun 1807 and was taken from the barracks and admitted to the Naval Hospital in Washington, DC as Patient No. 83 on 23 Dec Jul 1814 with typhoid fever and died on 26 Dec 1814 (Sharp's Database, 2018)

Hood, Frederick, served as a Private in Capt. George Steele's Co., 14th U.S. Infantry, enlisted 7 Sep 1812 in Baltimore at the age of 30, 5' 8½" tall, born in Philadelphia, and was captured at Stoney Creek, Upper Canada on 12 Jun 1813. Prisoner of War #5127 at Halifax, NS, interned on 28 Dec 1813 and discharged for exchange on 31 May 1814, was returned to service and deserted on 16 Jul 1815 (Johnson and Christou, p. 178; Baker Vol. 1, p. 202)

Hook, Aaron, served as a Seaman and was born in Maryland. Age: 20. Prison Depot: Plymouth 1, Prisoner of War #114. Captured by HM Ship-Sloop *Jalouse*. When Taken: 1 Dec 1812. Where Taken: off Cape St. Vincent, Portugal. Prize Name: *Otter*. Ship Type: Merchant Vessel. Date Received: 30 Dec 1812. From what ship: HMS *Leonidas*. Discharged and sent to Portsmouth on 4 Jan 1813 on HMS *Revolutionnaire*. (Johnson's Database, 2019)

Hook, Benjamin, see Benjamin Horn, q.v.

Hook, Greenbury (1787-1814), served as a Sergeant in Capt. Willis Foulk's Co., 22nd U.S. Infantry, enlisted 26 May 1812 in Washington, DC, age 25, 5' 7" tall, born in Maryland and died at Williamsville, NY on 14 Oct 1814 from fever; his bounty land was issued to his brother James Hook and other heirs at law (BLW# 22096-160-12; Johnson and Christou, p. 178)

Hooker, Jonsey, served as a Private in Capt. George Washington Magee's Co., Frederick Co. Militia, 1st Regt., New Windsor area, from 22 Jul 1814, engaged in the Battle of Bladensburg and in the defense of Baltimore and was reported "sick on furlough" on 1 Oct 1814 (Mallick and Wright, p. 342)

Hooper, Barton, served as a Private in the 12th U.S. Infantry and enlisted on 11 Aug 1812 at Charles Town for 5 years, age 25, 5' 11" tall, light eyes, dark hair, dark complexion, born in Frederick Co., MD, "absent sick" at Williamsville, NY since 9 Jun 1814, sent to the general hospital in Burlington, VT on 5 May 1814, discharged on 25 or 26 Nov 1814 and discharged from service at Pittsburgh, PA on 17 Aug 1815 due to an ulcerated leg (Mallick and Wright, p. 161)

Hooper, James, served as a Seaman in the U.S. Chesapeake Flotilla under Commodore Joshua Barney and was wounded and captured at the Battle of Bladensburg on 24 Aug 1814 (Marine p. 327)

Hooper, John, served as a Seaman on the schooner *Lawrence* of Baltimore and was stabbed through the hand during an encounter with the British brig *Eagle* in early 1815. (*Niles Weekly Register*, 25 Mar 1815)

Hoover, George (1790-1813?) served as a Private in the 14th U.S. Infantry (company not stated) at the age of 23 and was captured at Beaver Dams, Upper Canada on 26 Jun 1813. Prisoner of War #900 at Quebec, interned 21 Jul 1813 and either died on 9 Aug 1813 or was released (Johnson and Christou, p. 178, stated George Hoover died, but Johnson's Quebec book, p. 73, stated George Hover (sic) was discharged on 10 Aug 1813 and sent to HMS *Malpomena*)

Hopkins, -----, served as a Private in the 14th U.S. Infantry (compan not stated) and died at Sackett's Harbor, NY on 4 Nov 1813 (Johnson and Christou, p. 178)

Hopkins, Daniel, served as a Seaman and was captured at sea. Prison Depot: Plymouth 1, Prisoner of War #1537. Age 28. Born in Maryland. Captured by HM Frigate *Andromache*. When Taken: 14 Mar 1813. Where Taken: off Nantes, France. Prize Name: *Courier*. Home Port: Baltimore. Ship Type: Letter of Marque (Privateer). Date Received: 29 May 1813. From what ship: HMS *Hannibal*. Discharged on 30 Jun 1813 and sent to Stapleton. Prison Depot: Stapleton, Prisoner of War #101. Date Received: 8 Jul 1813 from Plymouth. Discharged on 13 Jun 1814 and sent to Dartmoor. Prison Depot: Dartmoor, Prisoner of War #1391. Date Received: 19 Jun 1814 from Stapleton. Discharged on 28 Apr 1815. (Johnson's Database, 2019)

Hopkins, Edward, served as an Ensign in Capt. Joseph Merrick's Co., 36th U.S. Infantry, born in Maryland, commissioned on 30 Apr 1813 and was killed in a duel on 26 May 1814 (Johnson and Christou, p. 178)

Hopkins, John, served as a Private in Capt. Thomas Montgomery's Co., 14th U.S. Infantry (company noy stated), enlisted on 5 Aug 1812 for 5 years and died at Lewiston, NY on 15 Aug 1813 (Johnson and Christou, p. 179)

Hopkins, Joseph, served as a Private in Capt. Thomas Gittings' Co. in the Extra Battalion, Montgomery Co. Militia, and was reported as discharged by surgeon (no date) on the muster roll dated 26 Jul – 2 Sep 1813 (Wright Vol. 7, p. 6)

Hopkins, Philip, served as a Private in Capt. Thomas Montgomery's Co., 14th U.S. Infantry, enlisted 11 Jan 1813 and died in August 1813; heirs received half pay for 5 years in lieu of bounty land (Johnson and Christou, p. 179)

Hopkins, Samuel (African American), served as a Seaman and was born in Baltimore. Age: 36. Prison Depot: Chatham, Prisoner of War #96. How Taken: Gave himself up off MV *Fleetwood*. When Taken: 26 Oct 1812. Where Taken: London, UK. Received: 4 Nov 1812. From what ship: HMS *Namur*. Discharged on 24 Feb 1813 and released to HMS *Ceres*. (Johnson's Database, 2019)

Hopper, Benjamin, served as a Private in Capt. Philip Smith's Co., Frederick Co. Militia, and deserted on 18 Jul 1813, but returned on 19 Jul 1813 and was on "sick leave in Aug/Sep" 1813 (Mallick and Wright, pp. 162, 336)

Horn, Benjamin, served as a Private in Capt. John Fonsten's Co., Frederick Co. Militia, from 2 Sep 1814, marched to Baltimore and engaged in the defense of the city and was "sick absent" on 9 Oct 1814 (Mallick and Wright, p. 363, stated his name was shown as Benjamin Hook on the sick/dead list)

Hornblower, William, see William Stevens, q.v.

Horney, David, served as a Private in Capt. Richard Whartenby's Co., 5th U.S. Infantry, enlisted 6 Jan 1812 in Baltimore, age 30, 5' 8½" tall, born in Kent Co., MD, and captured at Stoney Creek, Upper Canada on 12 Jun 1813. Prisoner of War #5081 at Halifax, NS, interned 28 Dec 1813, was discharged for exchange on 31 May 1814, returned to service and was discharged at Fort McHenry on 30 Jun 1817 (Johnson and Christou, p. 179; Baker Vol. 1, p. 203, stated he was also listed as "Prisoner #5080 in roster")

Horsman, John, of Maryland, served as a Seaman on the ship *LaHogue* and was reported by Capt. Jeduthan Upton, Jr. in 1814 as having been impressed into service and was being held as a Prisoner of War on the prison ship *San Antonio* at Chatham, England (*Niles Weekly Register*, 26 Feb 1814)

Horsydise, William, served as a Chief Mate and was born in Maryland. Age: 31. Prison Depot: Plymouth 1, Prisoner of War #1408. Captured by HM Brig *Orestes*. When Taken: 15 Apr 1813. Where Taken: Bay of Biscayne. Prize Name: *Henry Clements*. Ship Type: Merchant Vessel. Date Received: 20 May 1813. From what ship: HMS *Orestes*. Discharged on 23 May 1813 and sent to Ashburton on parole. (Johnson's Database, 2019)

Hose, Frederick, served as a Private in Capt. Thomas Montgomery's Co., 14th U.S. Infantry, enlisted 4 Oct 1812 at Hagerstown, MD, age 45, 5' 7" tall, born in Hagerstown and was discharged at Washington, DC on 8 Nov 1815 for disability (Johnson and Christou, p. 149; BLW# 883-160-12)

Hoskins, John, served as a Private in Capt. Thomas Montgomery's Co., 14th U.S. Infantry, enlisted 19 May 1813 in Sharpsburg, MD at the age of 24, born in Sharpsburg, MD and discharged at Fort Niagara, NY on 31 Aug 1813 due to a head wound (BLW# 8844-160-12; Johnson and Christou, p. 180)

Hoss, John, served as a Private in Capt. James McElroy's Co., 16th U.S. Infantry, enlisted 21 Sep 1812 at Harrisburg, PA at the age of 43, 5' 11" tall, born in Maryland and discharged at Sackett's Harbor, NY on 15 Aug 1815 for old age and rheumatism (Johnson and Christou, p. 180)

Hough, Thomas (1775-1815), served as a Private in Capt. Joseph Nelson's Co., 36th U.S. Infantry, enlisted 28 Jun 1814 at the age of 39 and died on or about 31 Jan 1815; bounty land issued to his son Joseph Hough and other heirs at law (BLW# 26182-160-12; Johnson and Christou, p. 180)

Houghton, Timothy, served as a Seaman and was born in Baltimore. Age: 41. Prison Depot: Dartmoor, Prisoner of War #3859. Captured by HM Ship-of-the-Line *Bulwark*. When Taken: 11 Jul 1814. Where Taken: off Nantucket, MA. Prize Name: *Thorn*. Ship Type: Merchant Vessel. Date Received: 5 Oct 1814. From what ship: HMT *Orpheus* from Halifax, NS. Discharged on 9 Jun 1815. (Johnson's Database, 2019)

Houseman (Hooseman), John, served as a Seaman and was born in Maryland. Age: 22. Prison Depot: Portsmouth, Prisoner of War #624. How Taken: Gave himself up off HM Guard Ship *Royal William*. Date Received: 3 Feb 1813. From what ship: HMS *Royal William*. Discharged on 11 Mar 1813 and sent to Chatham on HM Store Ship *Abundance*. Prison Depot: Chatham, Prisoner of War #1290. Date Received: 16 Mar 1813 from Portsmouth on HMS *Abundance*. Discharged on 23 Jul 1814 and sent to Dartmoor. Prison Depot: Dartmoor, Prisoner of War #1924. Age 23. Received: 3 Aug 1814. From what ship: HMS *Alceste* from Chatham. Discharged on 2 May 1815. (Johnson's Database, 2019)

Hovey, Samuel, served as a Private in Capt. Henry Fleming's Co., 14th U.S. Infantry, and was captured, date and place not stated, but probably at Beaver Dams, Upper Canada. Prisoner of War #3971 (Halifax), interned 24 Jun 1813, discharged on 3 Feb 1814 for exchange per order of Rear Adm. Griffith and died some time in Feb 1814 (Johnson and Christou, p. 180; Baker, Vol. 1, p. 204)

Howard, Benjamin, served as a Private in Capt. Richard Whartenby's Co., 5th U.S. Infantry, enlisted 6 Mar 1812 for years at the age of 41, 5' 7" tall, born in Maryland and discharged at Plattsburgh, NY on 24 Mar 1814 for wounds he had received in service (Johnson and Christou, pp. 180-181)

Howard, David, served as a Private in Capt. John Montgomery's Co., 1st Regt. Artillery, Baltimore, from 25 Aug 1814, was wounded at North Point on 12 Sep 1814 and died on 13 Sep 1814. His name is on the Baltimore Battle Monument (CMSR; Wright Vol. 2, p. 46; *Baltimore American*, 12 Jun 1819; Marine p. 170 did not list his name)

Howard, George W., served as 1st Sergeant in Capt. Edward Aisquith's Co., 1st Rifle Bttn., Baltimore City, from 19 Aug 1814 and was wounded on 12 Sep 1814 at North Point (Wright Vol. 2, p. 53)

Howard, John, served as a Private in Capt. Edward Aisquith's Co., 1st Rifle Bttn., Baltimore City, from 19 Aug 1814 and was taken prisoner at North Point on 12 Sep 1814 (Wright Vol. 2, p. 53)

Howard, Joseph, served as a Private and substitute for Jacob Hoover in Capt. Thomas Contee Worthington's Co. from 17 Aug 1812, was stationed at Fort Severn and died 26 Dec 1812 (Wright Vol. 8, p. 332; Mallick and Wright, p. 163)

Howard, Levite, served as a Private in the U.S. Marine Corps, was taken from the barracks and admitted to the Naval Hospital in Washington, DC as Patient No. 138 as of 1 Jun 1814 (discharge date not stated), was admitted again as Patient No. 70 on 3 Aug 1814 and discharged on 24 Aug 1814, and was again admitted as Patient No. 50 on 7 Oct 1814 with a fever and died on 4 Jan 1815 as a result of typhus (Sharp's Database, 2018)

Howard, Samuel, served as a Private in Capt. John Hatherly's Co., 22nd Regt., Anne Arundel Co. Militia, joined on 13 Dec 1814 and died on 18 Dec 1814 as shown on the muster roll dated 13 Dec 1814 – 1 Mar 1815 (Wright Vol. 4, p. 37)

Howard, William, served as a Boatswain and was born in Baltimore. Age: 24. Prison Depot: Plymouth 1, Prisoner of War #1330. Captured by HM Sloop *Pheasant*. When Taken: 23 Apr 1813. Where Taken: Bay of Biscayne. Prize Name: *Fox*. Ship Type: Letter of Marque. Date Received: 14 May 1813. From what ship: HMS Pleasant. Discharged on 3 Jul 1813 and sent to Stapleton Prison. Prison Depot: Stapleton, Prisoner of War #330. Age 26. Date Received: 11 Jul 1813 from Plymouth. Discharged: Enlisted on 25 Mar 1814 in British naval service. (Johnson's Database, 2019)

Howdy, Joseph, served as a Seaman and was born in Maryland. Age: 24. Prison Depot: Dartmoor, Prisoner of War #6526. How Taken: Gave himself up off MV *Triton*. When Taken: Nov 1814. Received: 3 Mar 1815. From what ship: HMT *Ganges* from Plymouth. Discharged on 11 Jul 1815. (Johnson's Database, 2019)

Howell, John, served as a Seaman and was born in Baltimore. Age: 46. Prison Depot: Chatham, Prisoner of War #2290. How Taken: Gave himself up off HM Brig *Paulina*. When Taken: 30 May 1813. Date Received: 17 Sep 1813. From what ship: HMS *Raisonable*. Discharged on 4 Sep 1814 and sent to Dartmoor on HMS *Freya*. Prison Depot: Dartmoor, Prisoner of War #3135. How Taken: Gave himself up off HM Brig *Paulina*. When Taken: 29 May 1813. Date Received: 11 Sep 1814. From what ship: HMT *Freya* from Chatham. Discharged on 28 May 1815. (Johnson's Database, 2019)

Howland, John M., served as 4th Sergeant in Capt. Steuart's Co., Washington Blues, and was captured at Bladensburg on 24 Aug 1814 (Marine, pp. 174, 329)

Hoy, Barney, served as a Private in the 14th U.S. Infantry and was captured. Prisoner of War #4178 at Halifax, NS, interned 24 Jun 1813, discharged on 27 Aug 1813 and sent to England on HMS *Regulus* (Johnson and Christou, p. 182; Baker Vol. 1, p. 206)

Hoy, Philip (African American), served as a Seaman and was born in Baltimore. Age: 35. Prison Depot: Chatham, Prisoner of War #104. How Taken: Gave himself up off MV *Dominich*. When Taken: 26 Oct 1812. Where Taken: London, UK. Date

Received: 4 Nov 1812. From what ship: HMS *Namur*. Discharged in Jul 1813 and released to the Cartel *Moses Brown*. (Johnson's Database, 2019)

Hubbard, Hugh, served as a Private in Capt. Thomas Montgomery's Co., 14th U.S. Infantry, enlisted 11 Jul 1812 at Cambridge, MD at the age of 18, 5' 6½" tall, was born at Newmarket, MD and discharged at Greenbush, NY on 20 Mar 1815 for a rupture on his right side (Johnson and Christou, p. 182)

Hubbard, Jacob, served as a Private and was captured at North Point on 12 Sep 1814. Dr. James H. McCulloh, Jr. wrote this soon after the battle to the British commander: "In consequence of the humanity shown the following American prisoners of war, I do promise upon honor that they shall not directly or indirectly serve against the British until regularly exchanged." (Marine, p. 171)

Hubbard, Thomas, served as a Landsman of the U.S. Chesapeake Flotilla, entered service on 28 Mar 1814 and was killed at St. Leonards Creek, 2nd Battle, on 26 Jun 1814 (Shomette, p. 379; Sheads, p. 22)

Huberre, Joseph, served as a Marine and was wounded on 24 Aug 1814 on the field of battle at Bladensburg, admitted to the Naval Hospital in Washington, DC as Patient No. 29, was discharged on 14 Oct 1814 and sent to barracks (Sharp's Database, 2018)

Hudson, James, served as a Seaman and was born in Baltimore. Age: 24. Prison Depot: Plymouth 1, Prisoner of War #2441. How Taken: Gave himself up by the crew of the *Mary*. When Taken: Prize Name: *Mary*, prize of the Privateer *Prince de Neufchatel*. Ship Type: Privateer. Date Received: 14 Feb 1814. From what ship: HMS *Halcyon*. Discharged on 10 May 1814 and sent to Dartmoor. Prison Depot: Dartmoor, Prisoner of War #1049. Date Received: 10 May 1814 from Plymouth. Discharged on 27 Apr 1815. (Johnson's Database, 2019)

Huff, Michael, served as a Private in the 14th U.S. Infantry and was captured. Prisoner of War #4059 at Halifax, NS, interned 24 Jun 1813, discharged on 19 Nov 1813 and sent to England on HMS *Regulus* (Johnson and Christou, p. 183; Baker Vol. 1, p. 207)

Huffington, Jesse, served as a Sailing Master on a barge under Commodore Joshua Barney and was captured at the Battle of Bladensburg on 24 Aug 1814 (Shomette, p. 325; Marine, p. 174)

Hugg, Richard, served as a Private in Capt. Peter Pinney's Co., 27th Regiment, Baltimore Militia, from 19 Aug 1814 and was wounded in battle on 12 Sep 1814 at North Point (Wright Vol. 2, p. 20)

Huggins, James, served as a Private in Capt. Clement Guiton's Co., 2nd Regt., 11th Brigade, Baltimore Militia, from 27 Jul 1814 and was reported as "sick-absent since Sep 12" 1814 (Wright Vol. 2, p. 86)

Hughes, John, served as a Seaman and was born in Baltimore. Age: 24. Prison Depot: Portsmouth, Prisoner of War #834. How Taken: Gave himself up off HM Ship-of-the-Line *Boyne*. Date Received: 5 Jun 1813. From what ship: HM Guard Ship *Royal William*. Discharged on 10 Jun 1813 and sent to Chatham on HMS *Arethusa*. Prison Depot: Chatham, Prisoner of War #1775. Date Received: 14 Jun 1813. From what ship: HMS *Arathursa*. Discharged on 24 Jul 1814 and sent to Dartmoor on HMS *Lyffey*. Prison Depot: Dartmoor, Prisoner of War #2051. Date Received: 3 Aug 1814. From what ship: HMS *Lyffey* from Chatham Depot. Discharged on 26 Apr 1815. (Johnson's Database, 2019)

Hughes, William, served as a Seaman and was born in Baltimore. Age: 34. Prison Depot: Dartmoor, Prisoner of War #3633. Captured by HM Brig *Doterel*. When Taken: 14 Dec 1813. Where Taken: off Charleston, SC. Prize Name: *Monarch*. Ship Type: Merchant Vessel. Date Received: 30 Sep 1814. From what ship: HMT *Sybella*. Discharged on 4 Jun 1815. (Johnson's Database, 2019)

Hughes, William (1771-1812), served as a Private in Capt. Peter Schuyler's Co. of the 2nd U.S. Infantry, enlisted 18 Oct 1807 for 5 years at Columbia Springs at the age of 36, 5' 7" tall, born in Maryland and died at Mount Vernon on 3 Jul 1812 (Johnson and Christou, p. 184)

Hukill, Levi, served as Cornet, Lieutenant and Captain in 1st U.S. Light Dragoons, born in Maryland, commissioned a Cornet on 3 May 1808, promoted to 1st Lieutenant on 18 Jan 1810, promoted to Captain on 7 Jun 1813, served as a Major, Assistant Inspector General, from 6 Aug 1813 to 5 Dec 1813 and died on 5 Dec 1813 (Johnson and Christou, p. 184)

See image of Levi Hukill on the next page.

Portrait is in private hands. Photo provided by the William J. Hull family.

Hull, Edward, served as a Private in Capt. Benjamin C. Howard's Co., 5th Regiment, Baltimore Militia, from 19 Aug 1814 and was killed on 24 Aug 1814 [at Bladensburg]. William Buchanan, Register of Wills for Baltimore County, certified that Letters of Administration had been granted unto Ann Hull in the personal estate of Edward Hull, deceased, according to law, on 16 Nov 1814. Receipt signed by Polly Hull. His brother George Hull served with him and wrote in 1842 to Congress stating: We [were] called by Gen C. Winder, by express, to assist him at Bladensburg, where all history says they disgrace there part. An we would have done more if we had catridges, for we only had eight rounds, for only two were given to us at Elk Ridge. () We had discharged our pieces in the morning for two days. The first five rounds: we drove above there right wing back about 200 yards. When they got reinforced we fell back to our firmer ground, then gave them three rounds and (broke). Col T. Sterrett was near one at the time- being personally aquainted for 2 some years- He swung his sword at me, looked at me and said "Rally your men, they are giving way again". I looked up at him and said Colonol, there is not a man in the regiment [that] has a cartridge, where they were giving way, or not. I don't know, I saw we was outflanked, but could not see them in front for the smoke, but with the rest, I started in a fairly smart trot I tell you.From there the Fifth was again sent forward at North Point, being whipped at Bladensburg 20 days before. The Mechanics, under Howard, and the Blues under Heath, lead the advance - by request-, I was along side of B. Howard, and at the hills, by Heath, which his first (history says he had two horses shot under him, but the first one was a mare) For when he fell, he was astraddled of her until he unbuckled his holsters, [he] came near me and exclaimed " By God boys, "they have got my mare, but they shant have any pistols!" (Having them in his hand) "Give it to them!" "My brother Edward fell at Bladensburg, in my platoon. It cost me something to get him from Bladensburg to Baltimore where he was buried in the Christ Church burying ground with honors of war. He had been married only about six months. His wife dead, and no children, should your honorable body think his body and uniform was worth as much as an enlisted soldier, it might refund me the expense of taking him home."George Hull of Cincinnati OH (NARA; Wright Vol. 2, p. 4)

Hunderville, John, served as a Private in 14th U.S. Infantry and was born in Maryland. Age: 26. Prison Depot: Chatham, Prisoner of War #3061. When Taken: 24 Jun 1813. Where Taken: Beaver Dams, Upper Canada. Date Received: 7 Jan 1814 from Halifax, NS. Discharged on 10 Oct 1814 and sent to U.S. on the Cartel *St. Philip*. (Johnson's Database, 2019)

Hunt, James, served as a Seaman and was born in Baltimore. Age: 24. Prison Depot: Plymouth 2, Prisoner of War #176. Captured by HM Ship-of-the-Line *Leviathan*. When Taken: 20 Mar 1814. Where Taken: at sea. Prize Name: *Farmer's Daughter*. Ship Type: Merchant Vessel. Date Received: 2 Mar 1815. From what ship: HMS *Dannemark*. Discharged on 3 Mar 1815 and sent to Dartmoor. Prison Depot: Dartmoor, Prisoner of War #6419. Date Received: 3 Mar 1815. From what ship: HMT *Ganges* from Plymouth. Discharged on 3 Jul 1815. (Johnson's Database, 2019)

Hunt, John H., served as a Private in Capt. Walter S. Hunt's, 41st Regiment, Baltimore Co. Militia, from 25 Aug 1814 and was "discharged by Surgeon Sep –" 1814 (Wright Vol. 2, p. 68)

Hunter, Alexander, served as a Seaman and was born in Baltimore. Age: 25. Prison Depot: Dartmoor, Prisoner of War #2953. Captured by *Rose & Thistle*. When Taken: 24 Feb 1814. Where Taken: off St. Bartholomew, West Indies. Prize Name: *Ellen & Elizabeth*. Ship Type: Merchant Vessel. Date Received: 24 Aug 1814. From what ship: HMT *Hannibal*. Discharged on 19 May 1815. (Johnson's Database, 2019)

Hunter, George, served as a Seaman and was born in Fredericktown. Age: 27. Prison Depot: Plymouth 1, Prisoner of War #1120. Captured by HM Ship-of-the-Line *Superb*. When Taken: 15 Apr 1813. Where Taken: Bay of Biscayne. Prize Name: *Viper*. Home Port: New York. Ship Type: Privateer. Date Received: 22 Apr 1813. From what ship: HMS *Superb*. Discharged and sent to Dartmoor on 1 Jul 1813. Prison Depot: Dartmoor, Prisoner of War #424. Date Received: 1 Jul 1813 from Plymouth. Discharged on 20 Apr 1815. (Johnson's Database, 2019)

Hunter, James, served as a Seaman and was born in Maryland. Age: 28. Prison Depot: Chatham, Prisoner of War #2510. Captured by HM Ship-of-the-Line *Victorious*. When Taken: 8 Jun 1813. Where Taken: Chesapeake Bay. Prize Name:

Globe. Ship Type: Privateer. Received: 22 Oct 1813 from Portsmouth on HMT *Malabar*. Discharged on 8 Sep 1814 and sent to Dartmoor on HMS *Niobe*. Prison Depot: Dartmoor, Prisoner of War #3315. Date Received: 13 Sep 1814. From what ship: HMT *Niobe* from Chatham. Discharged on 28 May 1815. (Johnson's Database, 2019)

Hunter, James, served as a Private in the 14th U.S. Infantry, enlisted 30 Nov 1812 and was captured at Beaver Dams, Upper Canada on 24 Jun 1813. Prisoner of War #4143 at Halifax, NS, interned 24 Jun 1813, discharged on 27 Aug 1813 and sent to England on HMS *Regulus*. Prison Depot: Chatham, Prisoner of War #3141. Received on 7 Jan 1814 from Halifax. Age 27. Born in Maryland. Discharged on 10 Oct 1814 and sent to U.S. on the Cartel *St. Philip*. (Johnson's Database, 2019; Johnson and Christou, p. 185; Baker Vol. 1, p. 209)

Hunter, James, served as a Private in Capt. Michael Haubert's Co., 51st Regt., Baltimore City Militia, from 23 Aug 1813 and was discharged by a Surgeon on 29 Aug 1813 (Wright Vol. 2, p. 30)

Hunter, Joseph, served as a Private in Capt. David Cummings' Co., 14th U.S. Infantry, enlisted 25 Jul 1812 and was captured at Beaver Dams, Upper Canada, ten miles west of Niagara Falls, on 24 Jun 1813. Prisoner of War #3733 at Halifax and died there on 30 Aug 1813; bounty land issued to Robert Hunter, his brother and only heir (BLW# 25878-160-12; Johnson and Christou, p. 185; Baker, Vol. 1, p. 209)

Huntsberry, Henry, served as a Private in Capt. George Shryock's Company, Hagerstown, Washington Co. Militia, from 23 Jul 1814 and was discharged on 5 Dec 1814 by a Surgeon at Annapolis (Wright Vol. 9, p. 8)

Hurd, John, served as a Private in the 14th U.S. Infantry and was later captured. Prisoner of War #3821 at Halifax, NS, interned 6 Jun 1813, discharged on 19 Nov 1813 and sent to England on HMS *Success* (Johnson and Christou, p. 182; Baker Vol. 1, p. 206)

Hurst, Jacob, served as a Private in Capt. Lawson Cuddy's Co., 41st Regiment, Baltimore Co., from 25 Aug 1814 and was reported "sick-absent since Oct 11" 1814 (Wright Vol. 2, p. 67)

Hurstley, Charles, served as a Seaman and was born in Harford. Age: 26. Prison Depot: Chatham, Prisoner of War #2047. How Taken: Gave himself up off HM Brig *Philomel*. When Taken: 28 Dec 1812. Date Received: 4 Aug 1813. From what ship: HMS *Christian VII*. Discharged on 25 Jul 1814 and sent to Dartmoor on HMS *Bittern*. (Johnson's Database, 2019)

Hurtt, Samuel, served as a Seaman and was born in Harford Co., MD. Age: 24. Prison Depot: Portsmouth, Prisoner of War #564. Captured by HM Frigate *Dryad*.

When Taken: 7 Jan 1813. Where Taken: at sea. Prize Name: *Rossie*. Ship Type: Merchant Vessel. Date Received: 25 Jan 1813. From what ship: HM Ship-of-the-Line *Queen*. Discharged on 11 Mar 1813 and sent to Chatham on HM Store Ship *Abundance*. (Johnson's Database, 2019)

Hush, Samuel (1787-1814), served as a Private in Capt. George Washington Magee's Co., New Windsor, Frederick Co. Militia, on 22 Jul 1814, age 27, 5' 10" tall, auburn hair, blue eyes, light complexion, and a shoemaker in Baltimore City when he joined the company; was wounded in the leg at Bladensburg on 24 Aug 1814 and being exposed to inclement weather in the entrenchments, was given a furlough of five days to be removed from camp to his home in Baltimore for typhus fever, but died before furlough expired. Muster roll states he died 24 Dec 1814, but widow's bounty land application stated 23Dec 1814. (BLW# 50-40-40923, 55-120-2737, Pension WO-25385; Society of the War of 1812 Application National No. 178 in 1894 stated he died 25 Dec 1814) Samuel Hush married Mary Ann Leary (1791-1879) on 27 Mar 1807 and Mary Ann Hush married second to Joseph Carr on 2 Oct 1818 and he died on 14 Nov 1818 or 19 Apr 1820 (Wright Vol. 2, p. 77; Mallick and Wright, pp. 166, 343; Marine p. 332, states he died from the effects of fatigue and exposure on 25 Dec 1814)

Huston, James F., served as Captain of his own company in the Frederick Co. Militia from 23 Jul 1814, was taken sick in Annapolis, returned to Fredericktown and never rejoined his company (Mallick and Wright, p. 344)

Hutchins, Edward (African American), served as a Seaman and was born in Maryland. Age: 22. Prison Depot: Plymouth 1, Prisoner of War #1525. Captured by HM Frigate *Andromache*. When Taken: 14 Mar 1813. Where Taken: off Nantes, France. Prize Name: *Courier*. Home Port: Baltimore. Ship Type: Letter of Marque. Date Received: 29 May 1813. From what ship: HMS *Hannibal*. Sent to Stapleton. Prison Depot: Stapleton, Prisoner of War #87. Date Received: 8 Jul 1813 from Plymouth. Discharged on 13 Jun 1814 and sent to Dartmoor. Prison Depot: Dartmoor, Prisoner of War #1380. Date Received: 19 Jun 1814 from Stapleton. Discharged on 28 Apr 1815. (Johnson's Database, 2019)

Hutchins, Perry, served as a Private in Capt. Andrew Slicer's Co., 32nd Militia Regiment, Anne Arundel Co., and was listed as "dead" on the muster roll dated 21 Aug – 17 Oct 1814, but the exact date was not given (Wright Vol. 4, p. 44)

Hutchinson, Lamore (African American), served as a Seaman and was born in Maryland. Age: 19. Prison Depot: Dartmoor, Prisoner of War #3881. Captured by HM Frigate *Niemen*. When Taken: 21 May 1814. Where Taken: off Cape Hatteras, NC. Prize Name: *Patriot*. Ship Type: Merchant Vessel. Date Received: 5 Oct 1814. From what ship: HMT *Orpheus* from Halifax, NS. Discharged on 9 Jun 1815. (Johnson's Database, 2019)

Huzza, John, served as a Private in Capt. Edward Aisquith's Co., 1st Rifle Bttn., Baltimore City, from 19 Aug 1814 and was taken prisoner on 12 Sep 1814 at North Point (Wright Vol. 2, p. 53)

Hyatt, Joseph, served as a Private in Capt. Reuben Gilder's Co., 14th U.S. Inf., enlisted 1 Oct or 31 Dec 1812 at age 42, born in Frederick, MD, 5' 7½" tall, dark eyes, dark hair, fair complexion. Prisoner of War in Halifax, NS, arrived at Salem from Halifax, entered hospital 26 Mar 1814, joined regiment at Plattsburgh, NY on 14 May 1814, was wounded in right breast at Cook's Mills on 19 Oct 1814 and discharged at Greenbush, NY on 28 Mar 1815 (Johnson and Christou, p. 187; Mallick and Wright, p. 167; Baker, Vol. 1, p. 211, did not mention him. Johnson's Quebec book, p. 77, stated Joseph Hyett was Prisoner of War #972, taken at Fort Schisher on 5 Jul 1813, interned at Quebec and discharged for exchange on 31 Oct 1813). A newspaper notice in 1819 stated, "Jos. Hyatt cautions persons from receiving a land warrant granted to him for militia services, the warrant having been lost." (*Political Examiner & Public Advertiser*, Frederick, MD, 6 Jan 1819) On 12 Apr 1831 "Jose" Hyatt, former private in Capt. Reuben Gilder's Co., 14th Regt., U.S. Infantry, in the late war and resident of this county for at least 59 years, appointed John Duer as his attorney to collect his pension of $16.00 due from 4 Sep 1830 to 4 Mar 1831 (Pierce, p. 94)

Hyde, Nathan, an American seaman who was impressed into British service in 1806, "made his escape last February [1816] and arrived in Baltimore ten days since – other Americans remain on board the *Northumberland 74*". (*Niles Weekly Register*, 12 Aug 1816)

I

Iler, Jacob, served as a Private (company not stated) and was captured at the Battle of Bladensburg on 24 Aug 1814 (Marine, p. 174); see Jacob Euler, q.v.

Ingle, John, served as a Seaman and was born in Baltimore. Age: 26. Prison Depot: Plymouth 1, Prisoner of War #1271. Captured by HM Frigate *Medusa*. When Taken: 12 Apr 1813. Where Taken: Bay of Biscayne. Prize Name: *Caroline*. Ship Type: Merchant Vessel. Date Received: 10 May 1813. From what ship: HMS *Medusa*. Discharged on 3 Jul 1813 and sent to Stapleton Prison. Prison Depot: Stapleton, Prisoner of War #288. Date Received: 11 Jul 1813 from Plymouth. Discharged on 16 Jun 1814 and sent to Dartmoor. Prison Depot: Dartmoor, Prisoner of War #1569. Age 27. Date Received: 23 Jun 1814 from Stapleton. Discharged on 1 May 1815. (Johnson's Database, 2019)

Ireland, Jonathan served as a Private in the 14th U.S. Infantry (company not stated) and was later captured. Prisoner of War #3828 at Halifax, NS, interned 6 Jun 1813, discharged on 9 Nov 1813 and sent to England on HMS *Success* (Johnson and Christou, p. 188; Baker Vol. 1, p. 212)

Irvine, Baptist, served as 2nd Lieutenant and Acting Adjutant in the Baltimore Volunteers Infantry Co. under Capt. Stephen H. Moore and commanded by Lt. Col. Francis McClure; enlisted on 8 Sep 1812 and was wounded at York, Upper Canada on 27 Apr 1813 (Johnson and Christou, p. 188; Wright Vol. 2, p. 57)

Isaac, Joseph (1782-1866), served as Captain of his own company and was stationed at Annapolis from 21 Jul to 2 Sep 1813 during which part of the time in August he was sick and his lieutenant was placed in charge temporarily; he was stationed at Nottingham from 24 to 27 Jun 1814 and at Milltown from 19 Jul to 30 Jul 1814 (Wright Vol. 6, pp. 15, 19, 21, 58; Pension SO-18958 of Pvt. George Gray; BLW# 55-120-80143 of Capt. Joseph Isaac in Jan 1851 states he was age 66, thus born in 1784, but his Holy Trinity Episcopal Church tombstone states Col. Joseph Isaac died on 14 Jan 1866, age 83, thus born in 1782)

Isnogle (Icenogal), David, served as a Private in Capt. Benjamin Watson's Co., 25th U. S. Infantry, enlisted in Ohio by Ensign Riley on 3 Apr 1813 for duration of the war, born in Frederick Co., MD, age 22, 5' 7" tall, hazel eyes, light hair, fair complexion, was wounded on 6 Jul 1814, was in general hospital as of 30 Sep 1814, was at Sackett's Harbor, NY on 2 Apr and 7 May 1815 and was discharged on 17 May 1815 (Mallick and Wright, p. 168)

Ivory, William, served as a Marine and was taken from the barracks to the Naval Hospital in Washington, DC and admitted as Patient No. 51 on 7 Oct 1814 with fever and died on 30 Nov 1814 (Sharp's Database, 2018)

J

Jack, John (1779-1815) (African American), served as a Seaman and was born in Baltimore. Age: 36. Prison Depot: Dartmoor, Prisoner of War #6514. How Taken: Gave himself up off HM Frigate *Orontes*. When Taken: Feb 1815. Date Received: 3 Mar 1815 from Plymouth on HMT *Ganges*. Died on 14 Mar 1815 from pneumonia. (Johnson's Database, 2019; Centennial Trails, United States Daughters of 1812, online at www.war1812trails.com/Dartmoor)

Jackson, Allison (African American), served as a Seaman and was born in Charles City. Age: 26. Prison Depot: Portsmouth, Prisoner of War #807. How Taken: Gave himself up off HM Frigate *Hotspur*. Date Received: 21 Apr 1813. From what ship: HM Guard Ship *Royal William*. Discharged on 27 Apr 1813 and sent to Chatham on HMS *Citoyenne*. (Johnson's Database, 2019)

Jackson, Frederick (African American), served as a Seaman and was born in Maryland. Age: 22. Prison Depot: Portsmouth, Prisoner of War #1393. Captured by *Vittoria*, Guernsey Privateer. When Taken: 28 Jan 1814. Where Taken: off Bordeaux, France. Prize Name: *Pilot*. Home Port: Baltimore. Ship Type: Letter of Marque. Date Received: 7 Feb 1814. From what ship: *Mary* from Guernsey.

Discharged on 13 Feb 1814 and sent to Chatham on HMT *Malabar No. 352*. Prison Depot: Chatham, Prisoner of War #3521. Date Received: 23 Feb 1814 from Portsmouth on HMT *Malabar*. Discharged on 26 Sep 1814 and sent to Dartmoor on HMS *Leyden*. Prison Depot: Dartmoor, Prisoner of War #4289. Received: 7 Oct 1814. From what ship: HMT *Niobe* from Chatham. Discharged on 14 Jun 1815. (Johnson's Database, 2019)

Jackson, Henry, served as a 3rd Lieutenant and was born in Maryland. Age: 25. Prison Depot: Plymouth 1, Prisoner of War #1414. Captured by HM Frigate *Leonidas*. When Taken: 23 May 1813. Where Taken: off Cape Clear, Ireland. Prize Name: *Paul Jones*. Home Port: New York. Ship Type: Privateer. Date Received: 26 May 1813. From what ship: HMS *Leonidas*. Discharged on 30 Jun 1813 and sent to Stapleton. Prison Depot: Stapleton, Prisoner of War #93. Date Received: 8 Jul 1813 from Plymouth. Escaped on 2 Sep 1813 from the black hole. (Johnson's Database, 2019)

Jackson, J. K. (African American), served as a Seaman and was born in Kent Co., MD. Age: 30. Prison Depot: Chatham, Prisoner of War #1700. Captured by *Thetis*, British Privateer. When Taken: 2 May 1813. Where Taken: Bay of Biscayne. Prize Name: *Governor Middleton*. Ship Type: Merchant Vessel. Date Received: 15 May 1813. From what ship: HMS *Viper*. Discharged on 2 Nov 1813 and released to HMS *Ceres*. (Johnson's Database, 2019).

Jacobs, Ignatius (1794-1883), served as a Private under Capt. James F. Huston and Capt. Lewis Weaver, Frederick Co. Militia, and was sick in Fredericktown since 26 Aug 1814; Thomas Moore served as substitute (Mallick and Wright, pp. 345, 346). He died on 3 Oct 1883, age 89 years, 6 months and 3 days and was buried next to his wife Martha Jacobs (1800-1857) in Jerusalem Cemetery near Myersville, MD. (*Names In Stone*, by Jacob M. Holdcraft, 1966, p. 618)

Jackson, John, served as a Seaman on the privateer *Surprise* of Baltimore and drowned in a shipwreck on 5 Apr 1815 (Marine p. 334; *Niles Weekly Register*, 15 Apr 1815)

Jacobs, John W., served as a Private in Capt. Thomas Kearney's Co., 14th U.S. Infantry, enlisted 11 Jul 1812 and was later captured. Prisoner of War #3857 at Halifax, NS, interned 24 Jun 1813, discharged 9 Nov 1813 and sent to England, later released and discharged from the service on 31 Mar 1815 (Johnson and Christou, p. 190; Baker Vol. 1, p. 212, listed him as John Jacobs)

James, Benjamin (Mulatto), served as a Seaman and was born in Maryland. Age: 31. Prison Depot: Dartmoor, Prisoner of War #2554. Captured by HM Frigate *Eridanus*. When Taken: 13 Aug 1814. Where Taken: Lat 40, Long 16. Prize Name: *Coromandel*, prize of the Privateer *York*. Home Port: Baltimore. Ship Type:

Privateer. Received: 16 Aug 1814. From what ship: HMT *Salvador del Mundo*. Discharged on 5 Jul 1815. (Johnson's Database, 2019)

James, John, served as a Seaman and was born in Baltimore. Age: 27. Prison Depot: Dartmoor, Prisoner of War #3616. Captured by HM Brig *Doterel*. When Taken: 14 Dec 1813. Where Taken: off Charleston, SC. Prize Name: *Monarch*. Ship Type: Merchant Vessel. Date Received: 30 Sep 1814. From what ship: HMT *Sybella*. Discharged on 4 Jun 1815. (Johnson's Database, 2019)

James, William (African American), served as a Seaman and was born in Maryland. Age: 37. Prison Depot: Sierra Leone Roster, Prisoner of War #41. Captured by HM Frigate *Thais*. When Taken: 31 Mar 1813. Where Taken: off Liberia, Africa. Prize Name: *Rambler*. Home Port: Bristol. Ship Type: Privateer. Discharged: Gone on Cartel, ship not named. (Johnson's Database, 2019)

Jameson, Daniel, served as a Seaman and was born in Baltimore. Age: 28. Prison Depot: Dartmoor, Prisoner of War #2384. Captured by HM Frigate *Orpheus*. When Taken: 20 Apr 1814. Where Taken: off Matanzas, Cuba. Prize Name: U.S. Sloop-of-War *Frolic*. Ship Type: Warship. Date Received: 16 Aug 1814. From what ship: HMT *Queen* from Halifax, NS. Discharged and sent to Dartmouth on 19 Oct 1814. (Johnson's Database, 2019)

Jamison, John (1792-1875), served as a Private in Capt. Henry Steiner's Co., Frederick Co. Militia, from 25 Aug 1814 and was "sick on furlough," but no date was given (Mallick and Wright, pp. 169, 353; *Frederick Examiner*, 22 Sep 1875)

Jarboe, James, served as a Captain in the 12th Regiment, St. Mary's Co., was commissioned on 12 Jun 1812, stationed at Clifton Factory on 29 Apr 1813 and stationed for 18 days between 16 Jul and 4 Aug 1813 from Herring Creek to Saint Indigoes. (Wright Vol. 5, p. 21; Marine p. 335) Sgt. Cornelius Kirby stated in 1851 he volunteered at Clifton Factory in 1812 and served in said company until Capt. James Jarboe was captured by the enemy. (Wright Vol. 5, p. 78)

Jarman, Walter, served as a Private in Capt. Robert C. Gallaway's Co., 46th Regiment, Baltimore Co. Militia, stationed at Carroll's Island on the lower end of Middle River Neck at the mouth of Gunpowder River and was reported "dead, no wife or near relation," but date of death was not given on the muster roll dated 19 Apr – 22 Apr 1813 (Wright Vol. 2, p. 71)

Jarrett, Abraham, served as a Seaman and was born in Maryland. Age: 50. Prison Depot: Plymouth 2, Prisoner of War #483. Captured by HM Brig *Barbadoes*. When Taken: 11 Jan 1815. Where Taken: off St. Bartholomew, West Indies. Prize Name: *Fox*. Home Port: Baltimore. Ship Type: Privateer. Date Received: 16 Apr 1815. From what ship: HMS *Swiftsure*. Discharged on 2 Jun 1815 and released to the Cartel *Soverign*. (Johnson's Database, 2019)

Jefferson, James, served as a Private in Capt. Aaron R. Levering's Co., 5th Regiment, Baltimore Militia, from 19 Aug 1814 and was discharged on 31 Aug 1814 due to inability (Wright Vol. 2, p. 5)

Jeffry, Isaac, served as a Seaman on the privateer *Surprise* of Baltimore and drowned in a shipwreck on 5 Apr 1815 (Marine p. 336; *Niles Weekly Register*, 15 Apr 1815)

Jellers, John G. (1787-1814), served as a Private in Capt. William Adams' Co., 13th U.S. Infantry, enlisted on 8 Mar 1814 at the age of 27, 5' 2" tall, born in Baltimore and died at Sackett's Harbor, NY on 19 Sep 1814 from fever (Johnson and Christou, p. 191)

Jenkins, George (1789-1814) served as a Private in Capt. George H. Steuart's Co., 5th Regiment, Baltimore Militia, from 19 Aug 1814 and was killed at North Point on 12 Sep 1814. His name is on the Baltimore Battle Monument. (CMSR; Wright Vol. 2, p. 6; *Baltimore American*, 12 Jun 1819)

Jenkins, Nathaniel (1794-1815) (African American), served as a Seaman and was born in Baltimore. Age: 19. Prison Depot: Stapleton, Prisoner of War #388. Captured by HM Frigate *Surveillante*. When Taken: 27 Apr 1813. Where Taken: Bay of Biscayne. Prize Name: *Tom*. Home Port: Baltimore. Ship Type: Letter of Marque. Date Received: 11 Jul 1813 from Plymouth. Discharged on 16 Jun 1814 and sent to Dartmoor. Prison Depot: Dartmoor, Prisoner of War #1636. Age 20. Date Received: 23 Jun 1814 from Stapleton. Died on 21 Feb 1815 from variola (smallpox). (Johnson's Database, 2019; Centennial Trails, U.S. Daughters of 1812, online at www.war1812trails.com/Dartmoor)

Jenkins, Solomon, served as a Seaman on the privateer *Surprise* of Baltimore and drowned in a shipwreck on 5 Apr 1815 (Marine p. 336; *Niles Weekly Register*, 15 Apr 1815)

Jenkins, William, served as a Private and Gunner in Sailing Master Rodman's Marine Battery and was wounded on 12 Sep 1814 at Fort McHenry (Marine pp. 173, 336)

Jennings, John, served as a Seaman and was born in Annapolis. Age: 29 or 39. Prison Depot: Chatham, Prisoner of War #905. How Taken: Gave himself up off HM Ship-of-the-Line *San Juan*. When Taken: 9 Aug 1812. Date Received: 1 Mar 1813 from Plymouth on HMS *Namur*. Discharged on 25 Sep 1814 and sent to Dartmoor on HMS *Leyden*. Prison Depot: Dartmoor, Prisoner of War #4630. Date Received: 9 Oct 1814 on HMT *Leyden* from Chatham. Discharged on 27 Apr 1815. (Johnson's Database, 2019)

Jennings, Samuel (African American), served as a Seaman and was born in Baltimore. Age: 41. Prison Depot: Dartmoor, Prisoner of War #5951. Captured by

HM Ship-of-the-Line *Bulwark*. When Taken: 23 Oct 1814. Where Taken: off Halifax, NS. Prize Name: *Harlequin*. Home Port: Portsmouth. Ship Type: Privateer. Received: 27 Dec 1814. From what ship: HMT *Penelope*. Discharged on 3 Jul 1815. (Johnson's Database, 2019)

Jennings (Jennins), Samuel (African American), served as a Seaman and was born in Baltimore. Age: 40. Prison Depot: Plymouth 1, Prisoner of War #358. Captured by HM Frigate *Andromache*. When Taken: 11 Jan 1813. Where Taken: off Bordeaux, France. Prize Name: *Louisa*, prize of the Privateer *Decatur*. Ship Type: Privateer. Date Received: 4 Feb 1813. From what ship: HMS *Cornwall*. Discharged and sent to Chatham on 29 Mar 1813 on HMS *Braham*. Prison Depot: Chatham, Prisoner of War #1433. Date Received: 6 Apr 1813 from Plymouth on HMS *Decoy*. Discharged on 24 Jul 1813 and released to the Cartel *Hoffning*. (Johnson's Database, 2019)

Jenny, John, served as a Private in Capt. David Cummings' Co., 14th U.S. Inf., enlisted 20 May 1812 and was captured at Beaver Dams, Upper Canada. On 24 Jun 1813. Prisoner of War #3759 at Halifax, NS, interned 24 Jun 1813, discharged on 9 Nov 1813 and sent to England on HMS *Success*. Prison Depot: Chatham, Prisoner of War #3107. Received: 7 Jan 1814 from Halifax. Age 21. Born in Maryland, Discharged 10 Oct 1814 and sent to U.S. on Cartel *St. Philip*. (Johnson and Christou, p. 192; Baker Vol. 1, p. 212; Johnson's Database, 2019)

Jephson, John (1767-1814), served as a Private in Capt. James Dillon's Co., 27th Regiment, Baltimore Militia, from 19 Aug 1814, was wounded on 12 Sep 1814 at North Point and died on 7 Oct 1814. His name is on the Baltimore Battle Monument. (CMSR; Marine, p. 336; *Baltimore American*, 12 Jun 1819; Wright Vol. 2, p. 17, mistakenly stated he was discharged on 7 Oct 1814) Dr. James H. McCulloh, Jr. wrote this note soon after the battle to the British commander: "In consequence of the humanity shown the following American prisoners of war, I do promise upon honor that they shall not directly or indirectly serve against the British until regularly exchanged." (Marine, p. 171) John Jephson died 7 Oct 1814, age 47, of a wound he received at North Point; his funeral from his late residence in Franklin Street, near Gray's Gardens. (*Baltimore American*, 8 Oct 1814) He wrote his will that was proved on 12 Oct 1814, mentioned his wife Catherine and stated he was sound of mind, but sick of body due to his afflicting illness. (Baltimore County Wills Book No. 9, p. 486)

Jeremy, Stephen (Mulatto), served as a Seaman and was born in Baltimore. Age: 27. Prison Depot: Portsmouth, Prisoner of War #472. Captured by HM Ship-of-the-Line *Elephant*. When Taken: 28 Dec 1812. Where Taken: off Azores. Prize Name: *Sword Fish*. Home Port: Gloucester. Ship Type: Privateer. Date Received: 14 Jan 1813. From what ship: HMS *Elephant*. Discharged on 11 Mar 1813 and sent to Chatham on HM Store Ship *Abundance*. Prison Depot: Chatham, Prisoner of War #1152. Received: 16 Mar 1813 from Portsmouth Mundane (sic). Discharged on 24 Jul 1813 and released to the Cartel *Hoffning*. (Johnson's Database, 2019)

Jewell, Samuel, served as a Seaman and was born in Maryland. Age: 20. Prison Depot: Portsmouth, Prisoner of War #352. Captured by HM Brig *Rover*. When Taken: 21 Oct 1812. Where Taken: off Bordeaux, France. Prize Name: *Experiment*. Ship Type: Merchant Vessel. Date Received: 31 Dec 1812. From what ship: HM Ship-of-the-Line *Northumberland*. Discharged on 4 Mar 1813 and sent to Chatham on HMS *Queen*. (Johnson's Database, 2019)

Jewell, Samuel, served as a Seaman and was born in Maryland. Age: 20. Prison Depot: Chatham, Prisoner of War #929. Captured by HM Brig *Rover*. When Taken: 21 Oct 1812. Where: off Bordeaux, France. Prize Name: *Experiment*. Ship Type: Merchant Vessel. Date Received: 10 Mar 1813. From what ship: HMS *Tigress*. Discharged on 8 Jun 1813 and was released to the Cartel *Rodrigo*. (Johnson's Database, 2019)

Jifford, T., served as a Seaman on the privateer *Globe* and was wounded in action on 1 Nov 1813 (Marine p. 336)

Johnson, Abraham (1776-1831), served as Lieutenant in Capt. Lawson Cuddy's Co., 41st Regiment, Baltimore Co. Militia, from 25 Aug 1814 and was reported as "sick-absent since Sep 22" 1814. He died on 20 Feb 1831, age 55, Baltimore Co., and bounty land was issued to his widow Jemima Johnson in 1855. (BLW# 55-160-29377; *Baltimore American*, 23 Feb 1831; Wright Vol. 2, p. 67; Widow's Pension WO-11560; Smith's Database, 2019)

Johnson, Benjamin, served as a Private in Capt. Edward Orrick's Co., 41st Regt., Baltimore Co. Militia from 25 Aug 1814 and was discharged by a Surgeon on 26 Aug 1814 (Wright Vol. 2, p. 70)

Johnson, Charles, served as a Private in Capt. Henry Myers' Co., 39th Regiment, Baltimore City, from 19 Aug 1814 and was "sick in quarters with syphilis" as reported on the muster roll of 19 Aug – 18 Nov 1814 (Wright Vol. 2, p. 25)

Johnson, Christopher, served as a Private in Capt. Isaac Raven's Co., Baltimore Co., 2nd Regiment, 11th Brigade, from 27 Jul 1814, was captured at Bladensburg on 24 Aug 1814 and reported as "a prisoner of war on parole" on the muster roll dated 27 Jul – 1 Dec 1814 (Wright Vol. 2, p. 83; Marine, p. 174)

Johnson, Francis (Mulatto), served as a Seaman and was born in Maryland. Age: 28. Prison Depot: Chatham, Prisoner of War #2830. Captured by HM Brig *Fantome*. When Taken: 5 Oct 1813. Where Taken: off Portland, ME. Prize Name: *Portsmouth Packet*. Home Port: Portsmouth. Ship Type: Privateer. Date

Received: 7 Jan 1814 from Halifax, NS. Discharged on 27 Mar 1814 and released to HMS *Ceres*. (Johnson's Database, 2019)

Johnson, Henry (African American), served as a Boy onboard a ship and was born in Baltimore. Age: 15. Prison Depot: Plymouth 1, Prisoner of War #2677. Captured by HM Ship-of-the-Line *Sterling Castle*. When Taken: 10 May 1814. Where Taken: Lat 36 Long 37. Prize Name: *John*, prize of the Privateer *Amelia*. Ship Type: Privateer. Date Received: 5 Jun 1814. From what ship: HMS *Gronville*. Discharged on 14 Jun 1814 and sent to Dartmoor. Prison Depot: Dartmoor, Prisoner of War #1301. Date Received: 14 Jun 1814 from Mill Prison. Discharged on 28 Apr 1815. (Johnson's Database, 2019)

Johnson, Hezekiah, served as a Private in Capt. John Chunn's Co., 17th U.S. Inf., enlisted 27 Feb 1813 for 5 years at Newark, OH at the age of 33, 5′ 6″ tall, born in Cecil Co., MD and was discharged on 2 Feb 1816 on a Surgeon's Certificate (Johnson and Christou, p. 194)

Johnson, Isaac, served as a Private in the 14th U.S. Inf. (company not stated) and was captured, probably at Beaver Dams, Upper Canada in 24 Jun 1813. Prisoner of War #3863 at Halifax, NS, interned 24 Jun 1813 and discharged for exchange on 3 Feb 1813 (Johnson and Christou, p. 194; Baker Vol. 1, p. 217)

Johnson, Isaac, served as a Private (company not stated) and was captured at the Battle of Bladensburg on 24 Aug 1814 (Marine, p. 174)

Johnson, James, served as a Seaman and was born in Talbot Co., MD. Age: 19. Prison Depot: Plymouth 1, Prisoner of War #1267. Captured by HM Frigate *Medusa*. When Taken: 12 Apr 1813. Where Taken: Bay of Biscayne. Prize Name: *Caroline*. Ship Type: Merchant Vessel. Date Received: 10 May 1813. From what ship: HMS *Medusa*. Discharged on 3 Jul 1813 and sent to Stapleton Prison. Prison Depot: Stapleton, Prisoner of War #284. Captured by HM Frigate *Iris*. When Taken: 10 Mar 1813. Where Taken: off Cape Ortegal, Spain. Prize Name: *Messenger*. Ship Type: Merchant Vessel. Received: 11 Jul 1813 from Plymouth. Discharged on 16 Jun 1814 and sent to Dartmoor. (Johnson's Database, 2019)

Johnson, James, served as a Seaman of the U.S. Chesapeake Flotilla, entered service on 23 Oct 1813 and died on 5 Dec 1813 (Shomette p. 363)

Johnson, John (African American), served as a Seaman and was born in Baltimore. Age: 29. Prison Depot: Dartmoor, Prisoner of War #3051. How Taken: Gave himself up off HM Ship-of-the-Line *Sultan*. When Taken: 2 Sep 1814. Date Received: 2 Sep 1814. From what ship: HMT *Sultan*. Discharged on 28 Apr 1815. (Johnson's Database, 2019)

Johnson, John, served as a Seaman and was born in Maryland. Age: 17. Prison Depot: Dartmoor, Prisoner of War #2357. Captured by HM Sloop *Martin*. When

Taken: 30 Jun 1814. Where Taken: off Halifax, NS. Prize Name: *Snap Dragon*. Ship Type: Privateer. Date Received: 16 Aug 1814. From what ship: HMT *Queen* from Halifax, NS. Discharged on 3 May 1815. (Johnson's Database, 2019)

Johnson, John, served as a Private in Capt. Samuel Raisin's Co., 36th U.S. Infantry, enlisted 1 Nov 1814 for 5 years and "died in barracks" on 22 Jan 1815 (Johnson and Christou, p. 195)

Johnson, John, served as a Seaman on the privateer *Surprise* of Baltimore and drowned in a shipwreck on 5 Apr 1815 (Marine p. 337; *Niles Weekly Register*, 15 Apr 1815)

Johnson, Joseph, served as a Seaman and was born in Maryland. Age: 20. Prison Depot: Dartmoor, Prisoner of War #1565. Captured by HM Frigate *Iris*. When Taken: 10 Mar 1813. Where Taken: off Cape Ortegal, Spain. Prize Name: *Messenger*. Ship Type: Merchant Vessel. Date Received: 23 Jun 1814 from Stapleton. Discharged on 1 May 1815. (Johnson's Database, 2019)

Johnson, Noble, served as a Private in Capt. Clement Sullivan's Co., 14th U.S. Infantry, enlisted 9 May 1812 in Cambridge, MD, age 20, 5' 8½" tall, born in Dorchester Co., MD and was captured at Beaver Dams, Upper Canada on 24 Jun 1813. Prisoner of War # 5248 at Halifax, NS, interned on 28 Dec 1813 and discharged for exchange on 31 May 1814; Matilda Johnson, widow, received a pension (File WO-42378; Johnson and Christou, p. 195; Baker Vol. 1, p. 219)

Johnson, Peter W., served as a Private in Capt. Shepperd Leakin's Co., 38th U.S. Infantry, enlisted 25 Mar 1814 at the age of 28, 5'10" tall, born in Baltimore and was discharged on 23 Nov 1814 on a Surgeon's Certificate for a rupture (Pension Old War File IF-25187; Johnson and Christou, p. 195)

Johnson, Robert, served as a Seaman and was born in Baltimore. Age: 24. Prison Depot: Portsmouth, Prisoner of War #1244. Captured by HM Ship-of-the-Line *Illustrious*. When Taken: 22 Oct 1813. Where Taken: at sea off a British south sea whaler (prize). Ship Type: Merchant Vessel. Date Received: 26 Nov 1813. From what ship: HMS *Illustrious*. Discharged on 26 Dec 1813 and sent to Chatham on HMS *Diomede*. Prison Depot: Chatham, Prisoner of War #2887. Name spelled Johnstone. Date Received: 7 Jan 1814. Discharged on 25 Sep 1814 and sent to Dartmoor on HMS *Leyden*. Prison Depot: Dartmoor, Prisoner of War #4433. Date Received: 8 Oct 1814. From what ship: HMT *Leyden* from Chatham. Discharged on 14 Jun 1815. (Johnson's Database, 2019)

Johnson, Thomas, served as a Seaman and was born in Baltimore. Age: 27. Prison Depot: Portsmouth, Prisoner of War #848. How Taken: Gave himself up off HM Ship-of-the-Line *Malta*. Received: 15 Jun 1813 from HM Sloop *Helena*. Discharged on 2 Jul 1813 and sent to Chatham on HMS *Tribune*. Prison Depot:

Chatham, Prisoner of War #1856. Date Received: 7 Jul 1813 from Portsmouth on HMS *Tribune*. Discharged on 25 Jul 1814 and sent to Dartmoor on HMS *Bittern*. Prison Depot: Dartmoor, Prisoner of War #2097. Date Received: 3 Aug 1814. From what ship: HMS *Bittern* from Chatham Depot. Discharged on 2 May 1815. (Johnson's Database, 2019)

Johnson, Truman, served as a Private in Capt. Nathan Towson's Co., 2nd U.S. Artillery, age 29, and was captured at Battle of Stoney Creek, Upper Canada on 6 June 1813. Prisoner of War #284 at Quebec, interned on 28 Jun 1813 and was released on 31 Oct 1813 to HMT *Malabar* (Johnson and Christou, p. 195; Johnson's Quebec book, p. 80)

Johnson, William, served as a Corporal in Capt. William McDonald's Co., 5th U.S. Infantry, enlisted on 8 Mar 1811 in Baltimore for 5 years and was later captured, date and place not stated. Prisoner of War on parole, discharged from the service on 3 Mar 1816 (Johnson and Christou, pp. 195-196)

Johnson, William, served as a Private in the 14th U.S. Infantry and was captured on 24 Jun 1813 at Beaver Dams, Canada. Prisoner of War #3816 at Halifax, NS, interned 27 Aug 1813 and discharged for exchange on 3 Feb 1814 (Johnson and Christou, p. 196; Baker Vol. 1, p. 220)

Johnston (Johnson), Jeremiah, served as a Private in Capt. George Kesling's Co., 19th U.S. Infantry, enlisted 10 Apr 1814 by Lt. Cisnea in Chillicothe, OH at the age of 23, 5' 9" tall, black hair, black eyes, dark complexion, born in Allegany Co., MD and was accidently wounded a short time after his enlistment and remained lame, never joined his regiment and was discharged on 16 Feb 1815 (BLW# 8813-160-12; Johnson and Christou, p. 194, Wright Vol. 10, p. 9)

Johnston, John, served as a Private in Capt. Thomas Quantrill's Co., 39th Regt., Baltimore Militia, from 25 Aug 1814 and died on 22 Sep 1814, cause of death was not stated (Wright Vol. 2, p. 28)

Johnston, John W., served as a Private in Capt. William Littlejohn's Co., 2nd U.S. Light Dragoons, enlisted 7 Sep 1813 at the advanced age of 48, 5' 9½" tall, born in Queen Anne's Co., and was discharged on 24 Jun 1815 as an invalid, but the medical reason was not stated (Johnson and Christou, p. 196)

Johnston, Joshua (1788-1814), served as a Private in Capt. James McDonald's Co., 14th U.S. Infantry, enlisted Aug 1813 at the age of 25, 5' 10" tall, born in Maryland and drowned in May 1814 (Johnson and Christou, p. 196)

Johnston, Perry (African American), served as a Seaman and was born in Maryland. Age: 26. Prison Depot: Plymouth 2, Prisoner of War #4. Captured by HM Schooner *Helicon*. When Taken: 17 Jan 1815. Where Taken: Lat 20N Long 52W. Prize Name: *Albion*. Prize. Ship Type: Privateer. Date Received: 3 Feb 1815.

From what ship: HMS *Bittern*. Discharged on 4 Feb 1815 and sent to Dartmoor. Prison Depot: Dartmoor, Prisoner of War #6240. Date Received: 4 Feb 1815. From what ship: HMT *Ganges*. Discharged on 5 Jul 1815. (Johnson's Database, 2019)

Johnston, Samuel (African American), served as a Seaman and was born in Baltimore. Age: 25. Prison Depot: Plymouth 2, Prisoner of War #529. Captured by HM Frigate *Barbadoes*. When Taken: 6 Dec 1815. Where Taken: off St. Bartholomew, West Indies. Prize Name: *Gallant*. Ship Type: Merchant Vessel. Date Received: 16 Apr 1815. From what ship: HMS *Swiftsure*. Discharged on 2 Jun 1815 and released to the Cartel *Soverign*. (Johnson's Database, 2019)

Jolly, Benjamin, served as a Private in Capt. Henry Lowrey's Co., Allegany Co. Miltiia, joined after 14 Oct 1814 and died on 26 Dec 1814 (Wright Vol. 9, p. 6)

Jonathan, Jonathan (sic), served as a Seaman and was born in Baltimore. Age: 26. Prison Depot: Dartmoor, Prisoner of War #4749. How Taken: Gave himself up off HM Ship-of-the-Line *Minden*. When Taken: 4 Oct 1813. Date Received: 9 Oct 1814. From what ship: HMT *Freya* from Chatham. Discharged on 15 Jun 1815. (Johnson's Database, 2019)

Jones, Benjamin, see Peter Jones, q.v.

Jones, Cabal, served as a 2nd Mate and was born in Kent Co., MD. Age: 29. Prison Depot: Portsmouth, Prisoner of War #543. Captured by HM Frigate *Briton*. When Taken: 17 Dec 1812. Where Taken: off Bordeaux, France. Prize Name: *Leader*. Ship Type: Merchant Vessel. Date Received: 25 Jan 1813. From what ship: HM Ship-of-the-Line *Queen*. Discharged on 11 Mar 1813 and sent to Chatham on HM Store Ship *Abundance*. (Johnson's Database, 2019)

Jones, David, served as a Seaman and was born in Baltimore. Age: 19. Prison Depot: Chatham, Prisoner of War #175. How Taken: Gave himself up. When Taken: 27 Oct 1812. Where Taken: London, UK. Date Received: 5 Nov 1812. From what ship: HMS *Namur*. Discharged in Jul 1813 and released to the Cartel *Moses Brown*. (Johnson's Database, 2019)

Jones, Enoch, served as a Private in Capt. Nathan Towson's Co., 2nd U.S. Artillery, enlisted 4 May 1812 for 5 years in Baltimore at the age of 29, 5' 6½" tall, born in Baltimore, captured during the Battle of Stoney Creek, Upper Canada in June 1813. Prisoner of War at Quebec, released on 31 Oct 1813 and discharged from the service on 30 Jun 1817 (Johnson and Christou, p. 197; Johnson's Quebec book, p. 81, did not mention him)

Jones, Harry (African American), served as a "Boy" in the Chesapeake Flotilla, was wounded on 24 Aug 1814 at Bladensburg, admitted to the Naval Hospital in Washington, DC as Patient No. 35 on 3 Sep 1814, was discharged on 30 Oct 1814 and sent to Baltimore (Sharp's Database, 2018;.*www.en.wikipedia.org* article stated he was a free black and served as a Seaman)

Jones, Henry, served as a Mate and was born in Baltimore. Age: 27. Prison Depot: Chatham, Prisoner of War #172. How Taken: Gave himself up. When Taken: 27 Oct 1812. Where Taken: London, UK. Date Received: 5 Nov 1812. From what ship: HMS *Namur*. Discharged in Jul 1813 and released to the Cartel *Moses Brown*. (Johnson's Database, 2019)

Jones, Henry (African American), served as a Seaman and born in Maryland. Age: 25. Prison Depot: Dartmoor, Prisoner of War #5590. Captured by HM Sloop *Plover* on 8 Sep 1814 off St. Johns, Newfoundland. Prize Name: *Young William*, prize of the Privateer *Surprise*. Home Port: Baltimore. Ship Type: Privateer. Date Received: 17 Dec 1814. From what ship: HMT *Loire* from Halfiax, NS. Discharged and released on 1 Jul 1815. (Johnson's Database, 2019)

Jones, James, served as a Seaman and was born in Baltimore. Age: 28. Prison Depot: Plymouth 2, Prisoner of War #276. Captured by HM Brig *Onyx*. When Taken: 25 Dec 1814. Where Taken: at sea. Prize Name: *Netterville*. Ship Type: Merchant Vessel. Received: 2 Mar 1815. From what ship: HMS *Dannemark*. Discharged on 3 Mar 1815 and sent to Dartmoor. Prison Depot: Dartmoor, Prisoner of War #6400. Date Received: 3 Mar 1815. From what ship: HMT *Ganges* from Plymouth. Discharged on 11 Jul 1815. (Johnson's Database, 2019)

Jones, James (1788-1815), served as a Private in Capt. Heman Fay's Co., 1st U.S. Artillery, enlisted 21 Apr 1814 for 5 years in Annapolis at the age of 26, 5' 6" tall, born in New Jersey and died on 8 Mar 1815; bounty land issued to William Jones, his father and heir (BLW# 14338-160-12; Johnson and Christou, p. 198)

Jones, James, served as a Private in Capt. William Gates' Co., 32nd U.S. Infantry, enlisted 21 Nov 1813 for 5 years at Wilkesboro, PA at the age of 40, 5' 4" tall, born in Prince George's Co., MD and was discharged on 29 Aug 1817 for inability (Johnson and Christou, pp. 197-198)

Jones, Joshua (1773-1813), served as a Private in Capt. Andrew Madison's Co., 12th U.S. Infantry, enlisted 16 Nov 1812 for 5 years in Morgantown, VA at the age of 39, 5' 8" tall, born in Baltimore Co. and died at Sackett's Harbor, NY on 17 Nov 1813 (Johnson and Christou, p. 198)

Jones, Lewis, served as a Seaman and was born in Maryland. Age: 25. Prison Depot: Chatham, Prisoner of War #3657. Captured by HM Brig *Moselle & Brilliant*, Privateer. When Taken: 12 Aug 1813. Where Taken: near Charleston, SC. Prize Name: *Caroline*. Ship Type: Merchant Vessel. Date Received: 23 Apr 1814. From what ship: HMS *Raisonable*. Discharged on 25 Sep 1814 and sent to Dartmoor on HMS *Niobe*. Prison Depot: Dartmoor, Prisoner of War #4595. Date

Received: 9 Oct 1814. From what ship: HMT *Leyden* from Chatham. Discharged on 15 Jun 1815. (Johnson's Database, 2019)

Jones, Major, regiment not stated, "of Broad Creek, Kent Island, was captured on the way home; accompanied by Messrs. Barrow, Teat, Legg and Capt. Benjamin Waters; they were going to attend sale of Lloyd Bewley's property distrained on by Major Jones." (*Republican Star*, Talbot Co., MD, 10 Aug 1813)

Jones, Peter (alias Benjamin Jones) (African American), served as a Seaman and was born in Maryland. Age: 24. Prison Depot: Plymouth 1, Prisoner of War #1178. How Taken: Gave himself up off HM Ship-of-the-Line *Magnificent*. When Taken: 2 May 1813. Date Received: 6 May 1813. From what ship: HMS *Stag*. Discharged and sent to Chatham on 8 Jul 1813 on HM *Hired Dart*, tender *Neptune*. Prison Depot: Chatham, Prisoner of War #1990. Date Received: 15 Jul 1813 from Plymouth. Discharged on 17 Jun 1814 and sent to Dartmoor on HMS *Pincher*. Prison Depot: Dartmoor, Prisoner of War #1801. Date Received: 20 Jul 1814. From what ship: HMS *Milford* from Plymouth. Discharged on 1 May 1815. (Johnson's Database, 2019)

Jones, Richard, served as a Seaman and was born in Baltimore. Age: 25. Prison Depot: Plymouth 1, Prisoner of War #991. Captured by HM Frigate *Medusa*. When Taken: 2 Apr 1813. Where Taken: Bay of Biscayne. Prize Name: *Lightning*. Ship Type: Merchant Vessel. Date Received: 16 Apr 1813. From what ship: HMS *Fairy*. Discharged and sent to Dartmoor Prison on 27 Jul 1813. Prison Depot: Dartmoor, Prisoner of War #680. Date Received: 27 Sep 1813 from Plymouth. Discharged on 26 Apr 1815. (Johnson's Database, 2019)

Jones, Samuel, served as a Private in Capt. John Fonsten's Co., Frederick Co. Militia, from 2 Sep 1814, marched to Baltimore, engaged in the defense of the city on 12 Sep 1814 and was discharged by [surgeon's] certificate on 11 Oct 1814, but the medical reason was not stated (Mallick and Wright, p. 363)

Jones, Sandy, served as a Drummer, was taken from the barracks and admitted to the Naval Hospital in Washington, DC as Patient No. 89 on 30 Dec 1814 with typhoid fever, was discharged on 5 Jan 1815 and sent to the barracks (Sharp's Database, 2018)

Jones, Talbot (1771-1834), served as a Private in Capt. Samuel Sterett's Co., 5th Regiment, Baltimore Militia, from 19 Aug 1814, was taken prisoner on 13 Sep at North Point, was later paroled and discharged on 3 Oct 1814; a native of Armagh, Ireland, he died at home on Lexington St. in Baltimore on 28 Mar 1834 and was buried in St. Peter's Episcopal Cemetery. (Wright Vol. 2, p. 6; *Baltimore American*, 31 Mar 1834; *Baltimore City Deaths and Burials, 1834-1840*, by Henry C. Peden, Jr., 1998, p. 191)

Jones, Theodore, served as a Seaman and was born in Maryland. Age: 26. Prison Depot: Portsmouth, Prisoner of War #1355. How Taken: Gave himself up off HM Ship-of-the-Line *Bulwark*. Date Received: 28 Jan 1814. From what ship: HMS Bulmark. Discharged on 13 Feb 1814 and sent to Chatham on HMT *Malabar No. 352*. Prison Depot: Chatham, Prisoner of War #3489. Received: 23 Feb 1814 on HMT *Malabar*. Discharged on 26 Sep 1814 and sent to Dartmoor on HMS *Leyden*. Prison Depot: Dartmoor, Prisoner of War #4158. Date Received: 6 Oct 1814. From what ship: HMT *Niobe* from Chatham. Discharged on 13 Jun 1815. (Johnson's Database, 2019)

Jones, Thomas, served as a Private in Capt. Barton Hackney's Co., Frederick Co. Militia, from 1 Sep 1814, participated in the Battle of North Point on 12 Sep 1814 and was discharged by a Surgeon on 4 Oct 1814, but the medical reason was not stated (Mallick and Wright, pp. 174, 362)

Jones, Thomas (1776-1815), served as a Private in Capt. Joseph Kean's Co., 4th U.S. Rifles, enlisted 8 Aug 1814 for 5 years in McConnelstown, PA at the age of 39, 6' tall, born in Maryland and died on 8 Aug 1815, but the medical reason was not stated (Johnson and Christou, p. 199)

Jones, Thomas, served as a Seaman and was born in Baltimore. Age: 22. Prison Depot: Plymouth 1, Prisoner of War #1670. How Taken: Gave himself up off MV *Good Intent*. When Taken: 4 May 1813. Where Taken: Liverpool, UK. Date Received: 17 Jun 1813. From what ship: HMS *Bittern*. Discharged on 30 Jun 1813 and sent to Stapleton. Prison Depot: Stapleton, Prisoner of War #407. Date Received: 20 Jul 1813. From what ship: *Bridgewater*. Discharged on 16 Jun 1814 and sent to Dartmoor. Prison Depot: Dartmoor, Prisoner of War #1494. Date Received: 19 Jun 1814 from Stapleton. Discharged on 1 May 1815. (Johnson's Database, 2019)

Jones, Thomas (1775-1815) (African American), served as a Cook and was born in Baltimore. Age: 38. Prison Depot: Portsmouth, Prisoner of War #1281. Captured by HM Brig *Electra*. When Taken: 7 Jul 1813. Where Taken: off St. Johns, Newfoundland. Prize Name: *Growler*. Home Port: Salem. Ship Type: Privateer. Date Received: 22 Dec 1813. From what ship: HM Ship of-the-Line *Bellerophon*. Discharged on 26 Dec 1813 and sent to Chatham on HMS *Nemesis*. Prison Depot: Chatham, Prisoner of War #2688. Discharged on 8 Sep 1814 and sent to Dartmoor on HMS *Niobe*. Prison Depot: Dartmoor, Prisoner of War #3434. Date Received: 13 Sep 1814. Died on 23 Feb 1815 from phthisis pulmonalis (tuberculosis). (Centennial Trails, United States Daughters of 1812, online at www.war1812trails.com/Dartmoor; Johnson's Database, 2019)

Jones, Thomas (African American), served as a Seaman and was born in Baltimore. Age: 25. Prison Depot: Portsmouth, Prisoner of War #1335. How

Taken: Gave himself up off HM Ship-of-the-Line *Invincible*. Date Received: 27 Dec 1813. From what ship: HMS *Nemesis*. Discharged on 27 Dec 1813 and sent to Chatham on HMS *Nemesis*. Prison Depot: Chatham, Prisoner of War #3022. Date Received: 7 Jan 1814. Discharged on 26 Sep 1814 and sent to Dartmoor on HMS *Leyden*. Prison Depot: Dartmoor, Prisoner of War #4688. Date Received: 9 Oct 1814. From what ship: HMT *Leyden* from Chatham. Discharged on 15 Jun 1815. (Johnson's Database, 2019)

Jones, Thomas, served as a Chief Mate and was born in Maryland. Age: 27. Prison Depot: Plymouth 1, Prisoner of War #1251. Captured by HM Frigate *Medusa*. When Taken: 12 Apr 1813. Where Taken: Bay of Biscayne. Prize Name: *Caroline*. Ship Type: Merchant Vessel. Date Received: 10 May 1813. From what ship: HMS *Medusa*. Discharged on 9 Jul 1813 and sent to Ashburton on parole. (Johnson's Database, 2019)

Jones, William (Mulatto), served as a Seaman and was born in Baltimore. Age: 25. Prison Depot: Chatham, Prisoner of War #3224. Captured by *Vittoria*, Guernsey Privateer. When Taken: 26 Dec 1813. Where Taken: Bay of Biscayne. Prize Name: *Volunteer*. Ship Type: Merchant Vessel. Date Received: 13 Jan 1814 on HMS *Poictiers*. Discharged on 25 Sep 1814 and sent to Dartmoor on HMS *Leyden*. (Johnson's Database, 2019)

Jones, William (African American), served as a Seaman and was born in Baltimore. Age: 28. Prison Depot: Plymouth 1, Prisoner of War #1182. How Taken: Gave himself up off HM Ship-of-the-Line *Clarence*. Date Received: 6 May 1813. From what ship: HMS *Stag*. Discharged and sent to Chatham on 8 Jul 1813 on HM *Hired Dart*, tender *Neptune*. Prison Depot: Chatham, Prisoner of War #1994. Date Received: 15 Jul 1813 from Plymouth. Discharged on 18 Oct 1813 and released to HMS *Ceres*. (Johnson's Database, 2019)

Jones, William, served as a Seaman and was born in Baltimore. Age: 25. Prison Depot: Plymouth 1, Prisoner of War #968. Captured by HM Frigate *Medusa* & HM Brig *Lyra*. When Taken: 28 Mar 1813. Where Taken: off Cape Ortegal, Spain. Prize Name: *Ferox*. Ship Type: Merchant Vessel. Date Received: 9 Apr 1813. From what ship: HMS *Lyra*. Discharged and sent on 21 Jun 1813 to the U.S. ship *Hope*. (Johnson's Database, 2019)

Jones, William, served as a Boy onboard a ship and was born in Baltimore. Age: 15. Prison Depot: Dartmoor, Prisoner of War #5135. Captured by HM Brig *Castilian*. When Taken: 29 Sep 1814. Where Taken: off Ireland. Prize Name: *Calabria*. Ship Type: Merchant Vessel. Date Received: 31 Oct 1814 from HMT *Castilian*. Discharged on 29 Jun 1815. (Johnson's Database, 2019)

Jones, William, served as a Private (company not stated), born in Baltimore, age 20, and was captured in the Battle of Stoney Creek, Upper Canada on 6 Jun 1813.

Prisoner of War #286 at Quebec, interned 28 Jun 1813 and released for exchange on 31 Oct 1813 on HMT *Malabar* (Johnson and Christou, p. 199; Johnson's Quebec book, p. 82)

Jones, William, served as a Private in 8th U.S. Infantry (company not stated), enlisted 1 Dec 1812 for 5 years at the age of 19, 5' 4" tall, born in Maryland and discharged on 21 Feb 1817 for wounds received in action against the Indians near Rock Island, IL (Johnson and Christou, p. 200)

Jones, William, served as a Private in Capt. Samuel Lane's Co., 14th U.S. Inf., enlisted 15 May 1812 for 5 years in Shephardstown, VA at the age of 31, 5' 10" tall, and was killed in camp near Buffalo, NY on 11 Oct 1812; bounty land issued to Martha H. Richards and Letitia Harvey, his only heirs (BLW# 27268-160-12; Johnson and Christou, p. 199)

Jones, William, served as a Sergeant in Capt. David Cummings' Co., 14th U.S. Infantry, enlisted 24 Jun 1812 at Fort Cumberland, MD, age 25, 5' 11" tall, born in Caswell, NC and was later captured. Prisoner of War #3826 at Halifax, NS, interned 6 Jun 1813, escaped ("run") on 27 Sep 1813, returned to service and was discharged in March 1815 (Johnson and Christou, p. 199; Johnson's Quebec book, p. 223)

Jones, William, served as a Private in Capt. James Dorman's Co., 5th U.S. Inf., enlisted 4 Aug 1812 in Baltimore at the age of 21, 5' 6½" tall, born in Maryland and was captured on Lake Ontario (no date given). Prisoner of War (date and location not stated), released, returned to service and deserted at Pittsburgh, PA on 18 Aug 1815 (Johnson and Christou, p. 200)

Jones, William L., served as a Sergeant in the 14th U.S. Infantry, enlisted 5 Jan 1813 and was later captured. Prisoner of War, sent to England, later released and discharged from the service on 31 Mar 1815 (Johnson and Christou, p. 200)

Jones, Zachariah (1786-1815), served as a Private in Capt. Bernard Peyton's Co., 20th U.S. Infantry, enlisted 4 Jul 1813 at the age of 27, 5' 7" tall, light eyers, light hair, fair complexion, born in Frederick, MD and mustered at Norfolk, VA on 15 Mar 1815, transferred to 35th U.S. Infantry on 20 Mar 1815, was sick in Regimental Hospital and died in General Hospital on 14 May or 30 Jun 1815 of indisposition; bounty land issued to his brother Thomas Jones and other heirs at law (BLW# 21729-160-12; Mallick and Wright, p. 174, stated he died on 14 May 1815, but Johnson and Christou, p. 200, stated he died on 30 Jun 1815)

Jordan, John (1789-1814), served as a Private in Capt. James McDonald's Co., 14th U.S. Infantry, enlisted 21 Feb 1814 for the war at the age of 25, 5' 6" tall, born in Ireland, and killed in the Battle of Lyon's Creek on 19 Oct 1814 (Johnson and Christou, p. 201)

Jordan, Joseph (1783-1813), served as a Seaman and was born in Maryland. Age: 30. Prison Depot: Plymouth 1, Prisoner of War #1813. Captured by HM Brig *Pelican*. When Taken: 14 Aug 1813. Where Taken: off St. David's Head, Wales. Prize Name: U.S. Brig *Argus*. Ship Type: Warship. Date Received: 17 Aug 1813. Received dead. Died on 17 Aug 1813 and received for interment at Mill Prison Hospital. (Johnson's Database, 2019)

Jordan, William, served as a Private in Capt. Samuel Raisin's Co., 36th U.S. Inf., enlisted 30 May 1814 in Richmond, VA, age not given, 5' 9" tall, born in Henrico Co., VA and died in barracks on 14 Jan 1815 (Johnson and Christou, p. 201)

Jordan, William, served as a Captain in the 26th Regiment, Talbot Co. Militia, in 1813 and it was reported on 10 May 1813 that Capt. Jordan was very ill at the time the company was mustered out, in consequence of which the command devolved on Lt. William Austin (Wright Vol. 1, p. 96)

Jordon, Robert, served as a Private in the 38th U.S. Infantry (compnay not stated) and died on 22 Feb 1815 (Johnson and Christou, p. 201)

Joseph, John, served as a Private in Capt. James Charles' Co., 12th U.S. Inf., enlisted 30 Jun 1812 at Baltimore, age 35, 5' 8" tall, born in Bordeaux, France and was captured at Stoney Creek, Upper Canada on 12 Jun 1813. Prisoner of War #5151 at Halifax, NS, interned 28 Dec 1813, discharged 31 May 1814, returned to service and was discharged at Buffalo, NY on 10 Jun 1815 due to loss of right eye (Johnson and Christou, p. 201, Baker Vol. 1, p. 224)

Joshihorn, Joseph, served as a Private in the 5th U.S. Infantry, enlisted 6 Feb 1813 for 5 years in Baltimore at the age of 33, 5' 9" tall, born in Virginia and discharged at Greenbush, NY on 9 Dec 1813 on a Surgeon's Certificate (Johnson and Christou, p. 201)

Joy, Edward (1776-1864), served as a Private in Capt. Peter Pinney's Co., 27th Regiment, Baltimore Militia, from 19 Aug 1814 and was severely wounded on 12 Sep 1814 at North Point (Wright Vol. 2, p. 20) He married Elizabeth Wheeler. (*1812 Ancestor Index Volume I, 1892-1970*, National Society United States Daughters of 1812, 2005, p. 283)

Joyce, Abel (1782-1815), served as a Private in Capt. Thomas Carbery's Co., 36th U.S. Infantry, enlisted 2 Mar 1814 in Leonardstown, MD at the age of 32, 5' 9" tall, born in Maryland and died in regimental hospital on 5 Feb 1815 (Johnson and Christou, p. 201)

Justice, William, served as a Private in the U.S. Marine Corps, enlisted in Nov 1799 and was taken from the barracks and admitted to the Naval Hospital in Washington, DC as Patient No. 73 on 4 Nov 1814 (injury or illness was not specified) and was discharged on 29 Dec 1814 and sent to the barracks (Sharp's Database, 2018)

K

Kanady (Kanada), James, served as a Able Seaman and was born in Baltimore. Age: 20. Prison Depot: Portsmouth, Prisoner of War #715. How Taken: Gave himself up off HM Frigate *Dryad*. Date Received: 27 Feb 1813. From what ship: HM Frigate *Dryad*. Discharged on 6 Mar 1813 and sent to Chatham on HMS *Cornwall*. Prison Depot: Chatham, Prisoner of War #1117. Date Received: 14 Mar 1813 from Portsmouth on HMS *Beagle*. Discharged on 11 Aug 1814 and sent to Dartmoor on HMS *Freya*. Prison Depot: Dartmoor, Prisoner of War #2602. Date Received: 21 Aug 1814 on HMT *Freya* from Chatham. Discharged on 26 Apr 1815. (Johnson's Database, 2019)

Kane, Dennis, served as a Private in Capt. William Littlejohn's Co., 2nd U.S. Light Dragoons, enlisted 13 Jan 1814 in Baltimore at the age of 23, 5' 11½" tall, born in Donegal, Ireland, and discharged on 24 Jun 1815 as an invalid (Johnson and Christou, p. 201)

Kearns, John (1775-1821), served as a Private in Capt. Nathan Towson's Co., 2nd U.S. Artillery, enlisted 22 May 1812 in Baltimore at age 37, 5' 11" tall, born in Ireland, wounded during the Battle of Chippewa, Upper Canada on 25 Jul 1814 and discharged at Baltimore on 1 May 1815 (BLW# 13753-160-12; Johnson and Christou, p. 203) In Baltimore Co. on 6 Apr 1821 Ann Roberts made oath that John Kearns was an invalid pensioner and former private in Capt. N. Towson's Co., U.S. Corps of Artillery, and he died 11 Mar 1821. On 24 Mar 1821 John Kipp was appointed administrator of John Kearns' estate and collected $49.80 in arrears due from 4 Sep 1820 to 11 Mar 1821. (Pierce, pp. 99-100)

Keane (Keen), William Jr., served as a Private in Capt. John Montgomery's 1st Artillery Co., joined Aug 25 1814, age 18, dark hair, dark blue eyes, 5' 5" tall; received a left hip wound (by ball ammo) at North Point on 12 Sep 1814. (Wright Vol. 2, p. 46; Pension File #25193; Johnson and Christou, p. 204) Dr. James H. McCulloh, Jr. wrote this note soon after the battle to the British commander: "In consequence of the humanity shown the following American prisoners of war, I do promise upon honor that they shall not directly or indirectly serve against the British until regularly exchanged." (Marine, p. 171)

Keene, Jesse, served as a Private in Capt. Walter S. Hunt's, 41st Regiment, Baltimore Co., from 25 Aug 1814 and reported as "sick-absent since Sep 20" 1814 (Wright Vol. 2, p. 69)

Keho, Patrick, served as a Private in Capt. David Cummings' Co., 14th U.S. Infantry, enlisted 9 May 1812 in Baltimore, age 34, 5' 4" tall, and was captured, date and place not stated. Prisoner of War, sent to England, later released and discharged from the service on20 Apr 1815 on a Surgeon's Certificate for an ulcerated leg (Johnson and Christou, p. 204)

Keith, James, served as a Private in Capt. Charles Timanus' Co., 36th Regt., Baltimore Co., joined 7 Sep 1814 at Turnpike Gate on Frederick Road, 2 miles from residence, discharged at Camp Deal, 6 miles from residence, and died on 9 Oct 1814, cause not stated, probably service connected (Wright Vol. 2, p. 64)

Kell, Francis, served as a Seaman and was born in Baltimore. Age: 22. Prison Depot: Plymouth 2, Prisoner of War #271. Captured by HM Brig *Onyx*. When Taken: 25 Dec 1814. Where Taken: at sea off San Domingo (Haiti). Prize Name: *Netterville*. Ship Type: Merchant Vessel. Date Received: 2 Mar 1815. From what ship: HMS Dannemark. Discharged on 3 Mar 1815 and sent to Dartmoor. Prison Depot: Dartmoor, Prisoner of War #6395. Date Received: 3 Mar 1815. From what ship: HMT *Ganges* from Plymouth. Discharged on 11 Jul 1815. (Johnson's Database, 2019)

Keller, John (1784-1869), served as a Private under Capt. James F. Huston and Capt. Lewis Weaver in the militia in upper Frederick Co., was called into service on 23 Jul 1814, was sick in Baltimore on 30 Aug 1814 and reportedly deserted on 27 Oct 1814 (Mallick and Wright, pp. 176, 345). He was born 22 Sep 1784, died 25 Sep 1869 and was buried in Monrovia at Bush Creek German Brethren Church Cemetery. (*Names In Stone*, by Jacob M. Holdcraft, 1966, p. 645)

Keller, Philip, served as a Private in Capt. Eli Stocksdale Co., 36th Regiment, Baltimore Co., stationed at Hampstead Hill in Baltimore City from 23 Aug 1814 and was reported "sick, absent since Sep 26" 1814 (Wright Vol. 2, p. 63)

Kellinger (Killinger), John, served as a Seaman and was born in Maryland. Age: 32. Prison Depot: Stapleton, Prisoner of War #186. Captured by HM Frigate *Belle Poule*. When Taken: 11 May 1813. Where Taken: Bay of Biscayne. Prize Name: *Revenge*. Home Port: Charleston. Ship Type: Letter of Marque. Date Received: 8 Jul 1813 from Plymouth. Discharged on 13 Jun 1814 and sent to Dartmoor. Prison Depot: Dartmoor, Prisoner of War #1458. Date Received: 19 Jun 1814 from Stapleton. Discharged 28 Apr 1815. (Johnson's Database, 2019)

Kelly, Charles, served as a Private in Capt. Robert Kent's Co., 14th U.S. Infantry, enlisted on 22 Jul 1812 at age 28, 5' 7" tall, born Ireland; Prisoner of War #3960 (Halifax), sent to England, interned at Halifax on 24 Jun 1813, discharged from Halifax on 27 Aug 1813 and discharged from servce at Washington, DC, on 26 Jun 1815 because of wounds received in action (BLW# 7039-160-12; Pension Old War IF-1970; Johnson and Christou, p. 205; Baker, Vol. 1, p. 227)

Kelly, Edward, served as a Private in Capt. Nicholas Turbutt's Co., Frederick Co. Militia, Fredericktown area, from 1 Sep 1814, marched to Baltimore, stationed at Hampstead Hill and died in hospital, cause and date not given (Mallick and Wright, p. 357)

Kelly, John, served as a Private in U. S. Rifles in 1814, enlisted at Shepherds-town, VA by Capt. H. V. Swearingen for five years, age 24, 5' 7" or 8" tall, grey or light eyes, light hair, brown complexion, born in Fredericktown, MD, "absent sick" at Sackett's Harbor, NY since 16 Jul 1814; served at Lake Erie on 30 Sep 1814, late Capt. Armistead's Co., served in Lt. L. Laval's Co. and was discharged at Carlisle Barracks, PA for disability on 13 Jul 1814 (Mallick and Wright, p. 177)

Kelly, Michael (c1790-1813), served as a Private in Capt. Nathan Towson's Co., 2nd U.S. Artillery, and was killed in Battle of Stoney Creek on 6 Jun 1813; heirs received his half pay for 5 years in lieu of bounty land (Johnson and Christou, p. 205, also spelled his name Kelley)

Kelly, Michael (1765-1815), served as a Private in Capt. Reuben Gilder's Co., 14th U.S. Infantry, enlisted 24 Mar 1814 in Baltimore at the age of 49, 5' 10" tall, born in Ireland and died at Greenbush, NY on 24 Mar 1815 from sickness; bounty land issued to son Edward Kelly and other heirs at law (BLW# 11933-160-12; Johnson and Christou, p. 205)

Kelly, Patrick, served as a Private in Capt. John Fonsten's Co., Frederick Co. Militia, from 2 Sep 1814, marched to Baltimore, engaged in the defense of the city and reported "sick absent 24 Sep" 1814 (Mallick and Wright, p. 363)

Kelly, Solomon (1789-1814), served as a Private in Capt. William Adair's Co., 17th U.S. Infantry, enlisted 27 May 1814 by Capt. James Hunter for the duration of the war at the age of 25, 5' 7" tall, born in Frederick Co., MD and died at Fort Erie, Upper Canada on 24 Oct 1814 (Johnson and Christou, p. 205)

Kelly, William, served as a Corporal in Capt. David Cummings' Co., 14th U.S. Infantry, enlisted 2 Aug 1812 at the age of 40, 5' 7" tall, was wounded in the mouth during the Battle of Beaver Dams, Upper Canada, ten miles west of Niagara Falls, on 24 Jun 1813, was captured and sent to England (Halifax) as Prisoner of War #4146 and discharged on 27 Aug 1813; he was discharged from the service at Baltimore on 30 Apr 1815 on a Surgeon's Certificate (BLW# 3228-160-12; Johnson and Christou, p. 206; Baker, Vol. 1, p. 227). In Lancaster, PA on 26 Mar 1824 William Kelley (sic), former sergeant in Capt. Cummings' Co. 14th U.S. Infantry when disabled in the late war, and a resident of this city for four years, previously of Lancaster County, appointed Charles Moss as his attorney to collect the pension due him from 4 Sep 1823 to 4 Mar 1824 and he (Kelly) was paid $48.00 on 27 Mar 1824. (Pierce, p. 101)

Kelly, William, served as a Private in Capt. Conrad Hook's Co., Baltimore Co., 2nd Regt., 11th Brigade, stationed at Camp Hampstead in Baltimore from 25 Jul 1814 and was listed as "absent sick Nov 28" 1814 (Wright Vol. 2, p. 81)

Kelly, William, "of Maryland, revolutionary veteran," was "impressed from a prison ship at Quebec" In 1813 (*Niles Weekly Register*, 20 Nov 1813)

Kendrick, Noah (1787-1814), served as a Private in Capt. Andrew Madison's Co., 12th U.S. Infantry, enlisted 27 Sep 1813 at the age of 26, 5' 8½" tall, born in Talbot Co., MD and died at Buffalo, NY on 7 Dec 1814 from sickness (Johnson and Christou, p. 206)

Kendrick, William, was a Seaman who was wounded on 24 Aug 1814 on the field of battle at Bladensburg, was admitted to Naval Hospital in Washington, DC as Patient No. 13, was discharged on 28 Sep 1814 and sent to the Navy Yard (Sharp's Database, 2018)

Kennard, Joseph (1793-1813) (African American), served as a Seaman and was born in Maryland. Age: 22. Prison Depot: Chatham, Prisoner of War #800. Captured by HM Ship-of-the-Line *Colossus*. When Taken: 5 Jan 1813. Where Taken: off Western Islands, Scotland. Prize Name: *Dolphin*. Home Port: Philadelphia. Ship Type: Merchant Vessel. Date Received: 27 Feb 1813 from Plymouth on HMS *Namur*. Died on 1 Aug 1813 from phthisis (tuberculosis). (Johnson's Database, 2019)

Kennedy, John, served as a Private in Capt. James Dorman's Co., 5th U.S. Infantry, enlisted 19 Jun 1811 for 5 years in Baltimore at the age of 25, 5' 6¾" tall, born in Trenton, NJ and discharged at Pittsburgh, PA on 17 Aug 1815 for "incapacity" (Johnson and Christou, p. 206)

Kennedy, John, served as a Private in the 7th U.S. Infantry (company not stated), enlisted 13 Aug 1814 by Lt. Riley at Hopkinsville, KY for 5 years, age 40, hazel eyes, fair hair and fair complexion, born in Cumberland, MD. Transferred to Capt. Vail's Co. at New Orleans on 22 Dec 1814 and discharged on 21 Apr 1815 for inability (Wright Vol. 10, p. 9)

Kennedy, Lawrence (1786-1815), served as a Private in Capt. Charles Stansbury's Co., 38th U.S. Infantry, enlisted 9 Nov 1814 for 5 years in Cumberland at age 28, 6' 4½" tall, born in Ireland and died on 10 Feb 1815, cause was not stated, but probably service connected (Johnson and Christou, p. 206)

Kennedy, Thomas, served as a Private in Capt. David Cummings' Co., 14th U.S. Infantry, enlisted 9 May 1812 for 5 years and died on 5 Apr 1813, but the cause was not stated, probably service connected (BLW# 3229-160-12; Johnson and Christou, p. 206)

Kennedy, William, served as a Private in Capt. Thomas Montgomery's Co., 14th U.S. Infantry, enlisted 14 Jul 1812 in Baltimore at the age of 38, 5' 10" tall, and was discharged at Greenbush, NY on 16 Apr 1815 for consumption and inability (Johnson and Christou, p. 206)

Kent, Emanuel Jr., served as a Private in Capt. Charles Pennington's Artillery Co., Baltimore, from 19 Aug 1814 and was severely wounded on 13 Sep 1814 at Fort McHenry, lost his right arm, survived the war and died in 1818. (Wright Vol. 2, p. 47; Marine, p. 173; Baltimore County Will Book 10, p. 470)

Kent, Robert, served as 4th Sergeant in Capt. Stephen H. Moore's Co., U.S. Volunteers, Baltimore City, from 8 Sep 1812 for 1 year and was wounded at Newark on 27 May 1813 (Wright Vol. 2, p. 57, inexplicably stated "Robert Kent, 4th Sgt, reduced from 4th Sgt Jan 1 1813;" Johnson and Christou, p. 207)

Kepler, Abijah (1788-1812), served as a Private in Capt. Samuel Lane's Co., 14th U.S. Infantry, enlisted 25 May 1812 for 5 years in Cumberland at the age of 24, 6' tall, born in York, PA and was killed at Carlisle Barracks, PA on 20 Jul 1812 (Johnson and Christou, p. 207)

Keplinger, John, served as a Private in Capt. Thomas Montgomery's Co., 14th U.S. Infantry, enlisted on 24 Dec 1812 and died on 27 Dec 1813; bounty land issued to Catehrine Hauer, Margaret Currell and Elizabeth Mount, his sisters and ony heirs at law (BLW# 27181-160-42; Johnson and Christou, p. 207)

Kerby, Thomas, served as a Private in Capt. William Brown, Jr.'s Co., 6th Regt., Baltimore Militia, from 19 Aug 1814 and was discharged on 19 Oct 1814 by the Surgeon, but the medical reason was not stated (Wright Vol. 2, p. 9)

Kesler, John, served as a Private in Capt. John H. Rogers' Co., 51st Regiment, Baltimore Militia, from 19 Aug 1814 and was taken prisoner on 12 Sep 1814 at the Battle of North Point (Wright Vol. 2, p. 37)

Kesselring, Lewis, served as a Private in Capt. John Galt's Co., 31 Oct – 27 Oct 1814, lost his leg owing to exposure to the cold; born circa 1786 and resided in Huntington Co., PA in 1855 (Mallick and Wright, p. 178; BLW# 55-120-24941)

Kettle, William, served as a Private in the U.S. Inf., born in Frederick Co., MD, enlisted 17 Jan 1813 by Lt. Larkins at Carlisle, PA for 5 years, age 21, 5' 5" tall, blue eyes, brown hair, light complexion, born in Frederick Co., MD, left sick at Williamsville, NY on 20 Oct 1814 and 26 Oct 1814, wounded, and joined from Williamsville on 27 Apr 1815, was confined in Watertown jail by civil authority on 31 Dec 1817, sent to state's prison on 31 Jan 1818 for 5 years and on 30 Jun 1818 was dropped. (Johnson and Christou, p. 207; Mallick and Wright, p. 178)

Key, Francis Scott (1779-1843), a distinguished lawyer from Georgetown, and later of Frederick, was held as a prisoner in the British fleet during the attack on Fort McHenry on 12 Sep 1814. "Having gone on board in the cartel ship *Minden*, in the company of Col. John R. Skinner, under the protection of a flag of truce, to effect the release of some captive friends (Dr. Beanes, a highly esteemed physician of Upper Marlborough in Maryland), he was himself detained during the expedition. They were placed on board the *Surprise*, where they were courteously treated. Finally they were transferred to their own vessel, the *Minden*, which was anchored in sight of the Fort. Of vivid and poetic temperance, he felt deeply the danger which their preparations foreboded, and the long and terrible hours which passed in sight of that conflict whose issue he could not know. It was under those circumstances that he composed 'The Star Spangled Banner,' descriptive of the scenes of that doubtful night and of his own excited feelings" and it ultimately became our National Anthem. (J. Thomas Scharf's *The Chronicles of Baltimore*, Vol. 1, pp. 351-352) He was born on 1 Aug 1779, died on 11 Jan 1843 and was buried in Mt. Olivet Cemetery in Frederick Co., MD. (*Names in Stone*, by Jacob M. Holdcraft, 1966, p. 656)

Keyser, Peter, served as a Lieutenant in the 38th U.S. Infantry, commissioned as a 3rd Lieutenant on 20 May 1813, promoted to 2nd Lieutenant on 22 Apr 1814 and died on 1 Oct 1814 (Johnson and Christou, p. 208)

Keysler, George, served as a Private in Capt. John Stanard's Co., 20th U.S. Infantry, enlisted 23 Jan 1813 at Dumfries, MD, age 14 (sic), 5' tall, born in Baltimore, transferred to 12th U.S. Inf., and was discharged at Pittsburgh on 17 Aug 1815 on a Surgeon's Certificate for epilepsy (Johnson and Christou, p. 206)

Kholehaus, Frederick, served as a Private in Capt. Luke Kiersted's Co., 6th Regt., Baltimore Militia, from 20 Aug 1814 and discharged on 22 Sep 1814 because of fits (Wright Vol. 2, p. 12)

Kidwell, William, served as a Private in Capt. Thomas Eversfield's Co., 17th Regiment, Prince George's Co. Militia, Nottingham Battalion, from 24 to 26 Jul 1813, was stationed at Nottingham Courthouse from 17 to 23 Jun 1814 under Capt. James Baden, and from 21 Aug 1814 under Capt. Eversfield until "sick and sent home" on 6 Sep 1814. On 13 Nov 1850 William Kidwell, age 65, stated he was drafted and enrolled at Nottingham around 1 Sep 1812 (sic) and served about 12 months in total. (Wright Vol. 6, pp. 4, 7, 13, 41; BLW# 55-rej-18991)

Kierle, John W., served as a Private in Capt. William Brown, Jr.'s Co., 6th Regt., Baltimore Militia, from 19 Aug 1814 and was discharged on 11 Nov 1814 by the Surgeon, but the medical reason was not stated (Wright Vol. 2, p. 9)

Killman, Henry, served as a Private in Capt. George C. Collins' Co., Voluntary Artillery, Lt. Col. Jacob Small's Regiment, was stationed at Annapolis from 8 Aug

1812 and was reported "sick and on furlough to Baltimore," but no date was given on the muster roll dated 8 Aug – 14 Oct 1812 (Wright Vol. 2, p. 58)

Kilpatrick, John, served as a Private in Capt. Edward Orrick's Co., 41st Regiment, Baltimore Co. Militia, from 25 Aug 1814 and was discharged by a Surgeon on 30 Aug 1814 (Wright Vol. 2, p. 70)

Kindle (Kindale), Samuel, served as a Corporal in Capt. William McIlvane's Co., 14th U.S. Infantry, enlisted 29 Jan 1813 at the age of 24, 5' 8¾" tall, born in New Jersey and was later captured. Prisoner of War #4049 at Halifax, discharged for exchange on 3 Feb 1814, exchanged on 15 Apr 1814, returned to service and was discharged at Plattsburgh, NY on 28 Jul 1814 (Johnson and Christou, p. 209 spelled his name Kindle and Kindale; Baker Vol. 1, p. 229, spelled it Kindle)

King, Edward (1787-1813), served as a Private in Capt. Francis Johnston's Co., 2nd U.S. Infantry, enlisted 22 Oct 1807 in Fredericktown, MD at the age of 20, 5' 8" tall, born Prince George's Co., MD, re-enlisted at Fort Stoddert on 12 Oct 1812 and died at Dauphin Island on 18 Jul 1813 (Johnson and Christou, p. 209)

King, John, served as a Marine and was taken from the barracks and admitted to the Naval Hospital in Washington, DC as Patient No. 78 on 6 Dec 1814 with an ulcer and was discharged on 28 Dec 1814 and sent to the barracks (Sharp's Database, 2018)

King, John B. (c1789-1815), served as a Private in Capt. John H. Chew's Co., 31st Regiment, Calvert Co. Militia, was stationed at St. Leonards's Creek on 9 and 10 Jun 1814, at Hunting Creek from 10 to 12 Jul 1814, in service again from 18 to 21 Jul 1814, in Capt. John Ireland's Co. from 22 to 26 Jul 1814, in Capt. Chew's Co. for 8 days between 2 Aug and 17 Aug 1814 and died 6 Feb 1815 in Calvert Co., cause not stated. In 1858 Ann (Errix) King, age 68, residing in Baltimore, stated she married John B. King alias John King on 22 Feb 1810 in Calvert Co. by Rev. Gant. (Wright Vol. 4, pp. 51, 52. 54, 55, 101; BLW# 55-160-83230)

King, William, served as a Private in Capt. David Cummings' Co., 14th U.S. Inf., enlisted 1 Jun 1812 and was captured at Beaver Dams, Upper Canada on 24 Jun 1813. Prisoner of War #3751 at Halifax, NS, interned 24 Jun 1813, discharged on 19 Nov 1813 and sent to England per order of Sir J. B. Warren. Born in Maryland. Age: 27. Prison Depot: Chatham, Prisoner of War #3104. Date Received: 7 Jan 1814 from Halifax, NS. Discharged on 10 Oct 1814 and sent to U.S. on the Cartel *St. Philip*. ((Johnson and Christou, p. 210; Baker Vol. 1, p. 230; Johnson's Database, 2019)

Kingdom, John, served as a Seaman and was born in Maryland. Age: 18. Prison Depot: Plymouth 2, Prisoner of War #180. Captured by HM Ship-of-the-Line *Leviathan*. When Taken: 20 Mar 1814 or 29 May 1814. Where Taken: at sea. Prize

Name: *Farmer's Daughter*. Ship Type: Merchant Vessel. Received: 2 Mar 1815. From what ship: HMS *Dannemark*. Discharged on 3 Mar 1815 and sent to Dartmoor. Prison Depot: Dartmoor, Prisoner of War #6423. Received: 3 Mar 1815. From what ship: HMT *Ganges* from Plymouth. Age 38 (sic). Discharged on 11 Jul 1815. (Johnson's Database, 2019)

Kingsbury, Thomas (1792-1815), served as a Private in Capt. Thomas Sangster's Co., 12th U.S. Infantry, enlisted 3 May 1814 for 5 years at the age of 22, 5' 10" tall, born in Hagerstown, MD and died at Washington, DC on 9 Jan 1815, cause was not stated, but probably service connected; bounty land was issued to his father Domilian Kingsbury (BLW# 3952-160-12; Johnson and Christou, p. 210)

Kirby, Anthony, served as a Seaman and was born in Baltimore. Age: 20. Prison Depot: Dartmoor, Prisoner of War #3828. Captured by HM Frigate *Niemen*. When Taken: 22 May 1814. Where Taken: off Egg Harbor, NJ. Prize Name: *Modelle*. Ship Type: Merchant Vessel. Date Received: 5 Oct 1814. From what ship: HMT *Orpheus* from Halifax, NS. Discharged on 9 Jun 1815. (Johnson's Database, 2019)

Kirby, George, served as a Private in Capt. John R. Dyer's Co., 17th Regiment, Prince George's Co. Militia, between 19 Aug and 13 Sep 1814 and was "sent home sick on furlough," but no date was given (Wright Vol. 6, p. 13)

Kirby, John, served as an Ensign in Capt. William Chalmers' Co., 51st Regiment, from 23 Aug to 30 Aug 1813, was on the rolls again on 19 Aug 1814 and was wounded on 12 Sep 1814 at North Point (Marine pp. 170, 348; Wright Vol. 2, pp. 29, 33, did not mention his wound)

Kirk, John (1785-1815), served as a Private in Capt. Francis Johnston's Co., 2nd U.S. Infantry, enlisted 28 Jan 1808 in Columbia Springs at the age of 23, 5' 6¼" tall, was born in Baltimore and died at Fort Charlotte, AL on 1 Feb 1815, cause not stated, but was probaby service connected (Johnson and Christou, p. 210)

Kiser, John (1787-1813), served as a Private in Capt. Samuel Lane's Co., 14th U.S. Infantry, enlisted 11 Jun 1812 in Shippensburg, PA, at the age of 25, by Lt. Stergis to serve until 11 Dec 1813, 5' 8" tall, blue eyes, fair hair and complexion, was born in Cumberland, MD and was killed at Beaver Dams, Upper Canada, ten miles west of Niagara Falls, on 24 Jun 1813 (Johnson and Christou, pp. 210-211; Wright Vol. 10, p. 9)

Kithcart, Robert, see Robert Cathcart, q.v.

Kitton, Abraham, served as a Boy onboard a ship and was born in Baltimore. Age: 14. Prison Depot: Plymouth 2, Prisoner of War #272. Captured by HM Brig *Onyx*. When Taken: 25 Dec 1814. Where Taken: at sea. Prize Name: *Netterville*. Ship Type: Merchant Vessel. Date Received: 2 Mar 1815. From what ship: HMS

Dannemark. Discharged on 3 Mar 1815 and sent to Dartmoor. Prison Depot: Dartmoor, Prisoner of War #6396. Date Received: 3 Mar 1815. From what ship: HMT *Ganges* from Plymouth. Discharged and released on 11 May 1815. (Johnson's Database, 2019)

Klay, John, served as a Private under Capt. Denton Darby, joined 3 Aug 1814 and drowned, but no date and location were given (Mallick and Wright, p. 180)

Klee, John, served as a Sergeant in Capt. Philip B. Sadtler's Co., 5th Regiment, Baltimore Militia, from 16 Aug to 13 Aug 1813 and served as 4th Sergeant from 19 Aug 1814 to 18 Nov 1814 (Wright, Vol. 2, pp. 7, 24, made no mention of an injury). In Baltimore on 18 Feb 1830 John Milchsack made oath that Mrs. Catherine Klee, also present, was the widow of John Klee who was an invalid pensioner and former sergeant in Capt. Sadler's (sic) Co., 5th Regt., Maryland Militia, and he had died on 27 Jan 1830. (Pierce, p. 103)

Kline, Peter (alias Peter Little), served as a Private in Capt. Samuel Lane's Co., 14th U.S. Infantry, date not stated. Prisoner of War, exchanged on 15 Apr 1814, and was discharged on 25 Apr 1815 due to rupture (Mallick and Wright, p. 192)

Knabbs, James (1794-1815), served as a Seaman and was born in Baltimore. Age: 22. Prison Depot: Dartmoor, Prisoner of War #4798. Captured by HM Frigate *Pique*. When Taken: 7 May 1814. Where Taken: off Porto Rico, West Indies. Prize Name: *President*. Ship Type: Privateer. Date Received: 9 Oct 1814. From what ship: HMT *Freya* from Halifax, NS. Died on 26 Feb 1815 from perissneuoniria (pneumonia). (Johnson's Database, 2019)

Knabbs, William, of Baltimore, served as a Seaman on the ship *Dominique* and was captured, but date was not given. Prisoner of War #4798 at Dartmoor and died on 3 Feb 1815 (Centennial Trails, United States Daughters of 1812, online at www.war1812trails.com/Dartmoor)

Knight, Absalom Jr. (1789-1814), served as a Private in Capt. Reuben Gilder's Co., 14th U.S. Infantry, enlisted on 7 May 1813 for 5 years at the age of 24, 5' 5" tall, born in Maryland and died at Plattsburgh, NY on 18 Nov 1814 (BLW# 15385-160-12; Johnson and Christou, p. 211)

Knight, Joshua, served as a Private in Capt. Henry Fleming's Co., 14th U.S. Inf., enlisted 11 Feb 1813 and died on 12 Jun 1813, place and cause not stated; widow Mary Knight and heirs received half pay for 5 years in lieu of bounty land (Pension Old War File IF-10818; Johnson and Christou, p. 211)

Knight, William, served as a Private in Capt. Richard Whartenby's Co., 5th U.S. Infantry, enlisted 18 May 1813 at Georgetown, DC, at the very young age of 12 (sic), 4' 5" tall, born in Annapolis and was captured at Stoney Creek, Upper Canada on 12 Jun 1813. Prisoner of War #5298 at Halifax, NS, interned on 5 Jan

1814, discharged for exchange on 16 May 1814 and was discharged from the service on 18 May 1817 (Johnson and Christou, p. 212; Baker Vol. 1, p. 232)

Knower, John (1776-1813), served as a Seaman under Sailing Master Simmones Bunbury, U.S. Sea Fencibles, enlisted 9 Dec 1813 at age 40 (sic), 5' 8¼" tall, born in Middletown, MD (sic) and died at Baltimore on 26 Dec 1813 (Johnson and Christou, p. 212) Obituary stated he was formerly of Worcester, MA and died at age 37 (sic), leaving a widow and three children (*Baltimore Whig*, 6 Jan 1814)

Knowlton, Silas, served as a Private in Capt. Henry Myers' Co., 39th Regiment, Baltimore Militia, from 19 Aug 1814 and was discharged as being insane on 14 Sep 1814 [possibly from post traumatic stress disorder] (Wright Vol. 2, p. 25)

Kolb, Jacob (1784-1812), served as a Private in Capt. John Brahan's Co., 2nd U.S. Infantry, enlisted 8 Apr 1808 in Staunton, VA at the age of 24, 5' 6" tall, born in Frederick Co., MD and died at Mount Vernon on 29 Aug 1812 (Johnson and Christou, p. 212, spelled his name Kolp, but it was in all likelihood Kolb)

Kolb, John (1792-1815), served as a Private in Capt. Reuben Gilder's Co. 14th U.S. Infantry, enlisted 3 Mar 1814 in Fredericktown, MD at the age of 22, 5' 8" tall, born in Baltimore and died at Greenbush, NY on 9 Apr 1815; bounty land issued to his brother Daniel Kolb and other heirs (BLW# 25287-160-12; Johnson and Christou, p. 212)

Koontz (Kuntz), Abraham, served as a Private in Capt. John Kerlinger's Co., 36th Regiment, Baltimore Co., joined 7 Sep 1814 and died on 3 Oct 1814. Ordered in December 1814 that David Keefer sell by public sale all the personal estate of Abraham Koontz except the house and lot where a credit of three months and return an account sales thereof to the court. (Wright Vol. 2, p. 62; Baltimore County Orphans Court Proceeding 1814-1817, Vol. 9, p. 73)

Koontz (Koontze), Jacob, served as a Private in the 12th U.S. Infantry (company not stated), enlisted 8 Jun 1813 at New Market by Lt. Towls for 18 months, age 34, 5' 7½" tall, dark eyes, dark hair, fair complexion, born in Frederick Co., MD and was missing in action on 11 Nov 1813; he was present on the roll of Capt. Moore's Co. at Plattsburgh, NY on 15 Apr 1814. Prisoner of War (date and place not stated), was exchanged and received at Chazy on 11 May 1814, arrived at Plattsburgh in 1814 (date not stated) and was discharged at Buffalo, NY on 8 Dec 1814 (Mallick and Wright, p. 184)

Kountz (Kuntz), David, served as a Private in Capt. Samuel Lane's Co., 14th U.S. Infantry, enlisted 9 Jun 1812 at Shepherdstown, VA, age 24, 5' 8½" tall, born in Lancaster, PA and was captured. Prisoner of War #3993 at Halifax, NS, interned 24 Jun 1813, discharged 9 Nov 1813 and sent to England (Pension WO-17639 to his widow Elizabeth Kuntz; Johnson and Christou, p. 212 spelled his name both Kountz and Kuntz; Baker Vol. 1, p. 233 spelled it Kountz)

Kow, Frederick, served as a Private in Capt. Samuel Lane's Co., 14th U.S. Inf., enlisted 25 Jun 1812 at Hagerstown, MD at the age of 35, 5' 8" tall, born in Hagerstown and was discharged at Greenbush, NY on 4 May 1815 for inability (Johnson and Christou, p. 212)

Kromhout (Krompout), Barney, served as a Seaman and Steward and was born in Baltimore. Age: 23. Prison Depot: Plymouth 1, Prisoner of War #532. Captured by HM Brig *Foxhound*. When Taken: 8 Feb 1813. Where Taken: English Channel. Prize Name: *Terrible*. Ship Type: Merchant Vessel. Date Received: 15 Feb 1813. From what ship: HMS *Foxhound*. Discharged and sent to Dartmoor on 2 Apr 1813. Prison Depot: Dartmoor, Prisoner of War #44. Date Received: 2 Apr 1813 from Plymouth. Discharged and sent to Dartmouth on 30 Jul 1813. (Johnson's Database, 2019)

L

Labec, Constant, served as a Seaman of the U.S. Chesapeake Flotilla, entered service on 16 Mar 1814 and was killedat the Battle of Baldensburg on 24 Aug 1814 (Shomette, p. 388)

Lacy, John, served as a Private In Capt. John B. Snowden's Co., Baltimore Co., 2nd Regiment, 11th Brigade, from 25 Jul 1814 and was reported as "prisoner on parole beginning Aug 22, later deserted," but no date was given on the muster roll dated 25 Jul – 1 Dec 1814 (Wright Vol. 2, p. 82)

Lain, Benjamin, see Benjamin Lake, q.v.

Lake, Benjamin (1788-1813), served as a Private in the 14th U.S. Infantry, age 25, born in Plattsburgh, NY, was captured later. Prisoner of War at Quebec and died there on 22 Jul 1813 (Johnson and Christou, p. 214)

Lake, James, served as a Private in Capt. Henry Neale's Co., 36th U.S. Infantry, enlisted 23 Jul 1813 for 1 year and died 26 Jul 1813, place and cause of death were not stated (Johnson and Christou, p. 214)

Lamb, John (1774-1844), served as a Private in Capt. John Montgomery's 1st Artillery Co., Baltimore, on 15 Aug 1812, was a private in the same company from 19 Aug 1814 and was wounded by a "canister shot in the hip above left knee" and captured on 12 Sep 1814 at North Point; age 40, light brown hair, dark blue eyes, 6' tall (Wright Vol. 2, p. 46; Marine, p. 351; Pension File #25211; BLW# 55-120-40542). Dr. James H. McCulloh, Jr. wrote this note soon after the battle to the British commander: "In consequence of the humanity shown the following American prisoners of war, I do promise upon honor that they shall not directly or indirectly serve against the British until regularly exchanged." (Marine, p. 171). In Baltimore on 3 May 1845 George Gelbach, administrator of John Lamb, deceased, late invalid pensioner who resided in this city for 20 years and previously in Pennsylvania, collected $57.60 arrears due from 4 Sep 1843 to 10 Apr 1844, the date of Lamb's death, for his three surviving children, names not given (Pierce, p. 104)

Lambert, Lewis, served as a Private (company not stated) and was captured at the Battle of Bladensburg on 24 Aug 1814 (Marine, p. 174)

Lambeth, John, served as a Private in Capt. Thomas T. Simmons' Co., 2nd Regt., Anne Arundel Co. Militia, from 28 Sep 1814 and was reported "sick, absent with leave" on the muster roster dated 18 Oct – 1 Dec 1814 (Wright Vol. 4, p. 28)

Lambie, James, served as a Private in Capt. Charles Pennington's Artillery Co., Baltimore Independent Artillerists, and was slightly wounded on 13 Sep 1814 at Fort McHenry (Marine, pp. 173, 351)

Landsbury, John, served as a Master and was born in Annapolis. Age: 33. Prison Depot: Dartmoor, Prisoner of War #5576. How Taken: Gave himself up off a fishing boat on the Baltimore River. Date Received: 17 Dec 1814. From what ship: HMT *Loire* from Halfiax, NS. Discharged and released on 1 Jul 1815. (Johnson's Database, 2019)

Lane, Benjamin (1785-1813), served as a Private in Capt. Samuel Lane's Co., 14th U.S. Infantry, enlisted on 6 Jan 1813 at the age of 28, 5' 8" tall, and was captured at Beaver Dams, Upper Canada, on 24 Jun 1813. Prisoner of War #515 at Quebec, interned 7 Jul 1813 and died on 23 Jul 1813 of dysentery; bounty land issued to Daniel Lane and other heirs (BLW# 15331-160-12; Johnson and Christou, p. 214; Johnson's Quebec book, p. 86, spelled his name Lain)

Lane, James (Mulatto), served as a Chief Mate and was born in Maryland. Age: 22. Prison Depot: Plymouth 1, Prisoner of War #2096. Captured by HM Ship-of-the-Line *Magnificant*. When Taken: 30 Oct 1813. Where Taken: off Lorient, France. Prize Name: *Amiable*. Ship Type: Letter of Marque (Privateer). Date Received: 9 Nov 1813. From what ship: *Amiable*, Privateer. Discharged on 11 Nov 1813 and sent to Ashburton on parole. (Johnson's Database, 2019)

Larew, Abraham, see Abraham Lerew (Larew), q.v.

Larkins, Thomas, served as a Seaman and was born in Baltimore. Age: 20. Prison Depot: Chatham, Prisoner of War #275. How Taken: Gave himself up. When Taken: 10 Dec 1812. Where Taken: London, UK. Date Received: 23 Dec 1812. From what ship: HMS *Raisonable*. Discharged on 24 Jul 1813 and released to the Cartel *Hoffning*. (Johnson's Database, 2019)

Larwood, William, served as a Private in Capt. William McIlvane's Co., 14th U.S. Infantry, enlisted 20 May 1813 and was captured, date and place not stated. Prisoner of War, exchanged on 15 Apr 1813 and discharged at Greenbush, NY on 1 Jun 1815 on disability (Johnson and Christou, p. 216)

Latham, Edward (1778-1814), served as a Private in 14th U.S. Infantry (company not stated) and was captured at Beaver Dams, Upper Canada in 24 Jun 1813. Born in Baltimore. Age: 35. Prisoner of War #3768 at Halifax, NS, interned 24 Jun 1813, discharged 9 Nov 1813 and sent to England on HMS *Success*. Prison Depot: Chatham. Prisoner of War #3111. Died on 1 May 1814 from fever. (Johnson and Christou, p. 216; Baker Vol. 1, p. 237; Johnson's Database, 2019)

Latimore, Thomas, served as a Seaman of the U.S. Chesapeake Flotilla, entered service on 31 Mar 1814 and died on 31 May 1814 (Shomette p. 377)

Lauter, Thomas, served as a Seaman on board the privateer (armed brigantine) *Chausseur* of Baltimore commanded by Capt. Thomas Boyle and was severely wounded in action on 26 Feb 1815 (*Niles Weekly Register*, 25 Mar 1815)

Law, James, served as a Private in Capt. John Stewart's Co., 51st Regiment, Baltimore Militia, from 23 Aug 1814 and was discharged by the Surgeon, but the date and medical reason were not given (Wright Vol. 2, p. 31)

Lawder, George, served as a Seaman in Joshua Barney's Flotilla and sustained a "wound and fracture" on 24 Aug 1814 on the field of battle at Bladensburg, yet was not admitted to the Naval Hospital in Washington, DC as Patient No. 49 until 7 Oct 1814 and was discharged on 1 Apr 1815 (Sharp's Database, 2018)

Lawless, John, served as a Private in Capt. Joseph Marshall's Co., 14th U.S. Infantry, enlisted 4 Oct 1812 at the age of 34, 5' 6½" tall, born in Baltimore, wounded at Beaver Dams, Upper Canada, ten miles west of Niagara Falls, on 24 Jun 1813 and was discharged at Greenbush, NY on 24 May 1815 on Surgeon's Certificate (Johnson and Christou, p. 217; Pension Old War IF-20227)

Lawless, John, served as a Private in Capt. George Steever's Co., 6th Regiment, Baltimore Militia, from 19 Aug 1814, was captured at North Point and reported as "in captivity 12 Sep" on the 19 Aug – 18 Nov 1814 rolls (Wright Vol. 2, p. 15)

Lawless, Philip, served as a Private in Capt. Reuben Gilder's Co., 14th U.S. Infantry, enlisted 7 Mar 1814 in Maryland at age of 37, born in Frederick, MD, 5' 10½" tall, grey eyes, dark hair and light complexion, was wounded in the left thigh by accident, was left at Pittsfield and was discharged at Greenbush, NY on 8 Jun 1815 (BLW# 6389-160-12; Johnson and Christou, p. 217; Mallick and Wright, p. 193) In Frederick Co. on 4 Mar 1829 Philip Lawless, a disabled soldier in Capt. Reuben Guilder's (sic) Co., 14th U.S. Regt. in the late war, and a resident of this county for at least 51 years, appointed John Duer as his attorney to collect his $32.00 pension due from 4 Sep 1828 to 4 Mar 1829 (Pierce, p. 106)

Lawson, James (1787-1813) (African American), served as a Seaman and Steward and was born in Baltimore. Age: 25 or 27. Prison Depot: Dartmoor, Prisoner of War #210. Captured by HM Ship-of-the-Line *Warspite*. When Taken: 26 Feb 1813. Where Taken: off Basque Roads, France. Prize Name: *Mars*. Ship Type: Merchant Vessel. Received: 2 Apr 1813 from Plymouth. Died on 5 Jan 1814 from smallpox. (Johnson's Database, 2019)

Lawson, Mathew, served as a Seaman and was born in Baltimore. Age: 31. Prison Depot: Portsmouth, Prisoner of War #224. Captured by HM Brig *Zephyr*. When Taken: 10 Dec 1812. Where Taken: at sea. Prize Name: *Antelope*. Home Port: New York. Ship Type: Privateer. Received: 27 Dec 1812 on HMS *Zephyr*. Discharged on 19 Feb 1813 and sent to Chatham on HM Store Ship *Dromedary*. Prison Depot: Chatham, Prisoner of War #588. Date Received: 23 Feb 1813 on HMS *Dromedary*. Discharged on 2 Jul 1813 and released to the Cartel *Moses Brown*. (Johnson's Database, 2019)

Lawson, Richard, served as a Private in Capt. Aaron R. Levering's Co., 5th Regiment, Baltimore Militia, from 19 Aug 1814, was captured, taken prisoner and exchanged on 26 Nov 1814 (Wright Vol. 2, p. 5)

Layfield, Littleton, served as a Seaman and was born in Maryland. Age: 20. Prison Depot: Plymouth 1, Prisoner of War #1373. Captured by HM Frigate *Surveillante*. When Taken: 27 Apr 1813. Where Taken: Bay of Biscayne. Prize Name: *Tom*. Home Port: Baltimore. Ship Type: Letter of Marque. Date Received: 15 May 1813. From what ship: HMS *Foxhound*. Discharged on 3 Jul 1813 and sent to Stapleton Prison. Prison Depot: Stapleton, Prisoner of War #368. Date Received: 11 Jul 1813 from Plymouth. Discharged on 16 Jun 1814 and sent to Dartmoor. Prison Depot: Dartmoor, Prisoner of War #1622. Age 21. Date Received: 23 Jun 1814 from Stapleton. Discharged on 1 May 1815. (Johnson's Database, 2019)

Layton, William, served as a Boy onboard a ship and was born in East Town. Age: 18. Prison Depot: Plymouth 1, Prisoner of War #942. Captured by *Brothers*, Guernsey Privateer, on 26 Mar 1813. Where Taken: Bay of Biscayne. Prize Name: *Gleamer*. Ship Type: Merchant Vessel. Date Received: 8 Apr 1813. From what ship: *Wasp*, sloop from Guernsey. Discharged and sent to Chatham on 8 Jul 1813 on HM *Hired Dart*, tender *Neptune*. (Johnson's Database, 2019)

Lazelear, Benjamin, served as a Private in the 14th U.S. Infantry and was later captured. Prisoner of War #3984 at Halifax, NS, interned on 24 Jun 1813 and died there on 22 Sep 1813 (Johnson and Christou, p. 218; Baker, Vol. 1, p. 239)

Lazure, Jacob W. (1792-1814), served as a Private in Capt. Reuben Gilder's Co., 14th U.S. Infantry, enlisted 9 Jun 1813 for 5 years at the age of 21, 6' 4" tall, was born in Maryland and died at Brownsville, NY on 29 Dec 1814 (Johnson and Christou, p. 218)

Leach, Benjamin (1778-1815), served as a Private in Capt. Simon Owens' Co., 1st U.S. Infantry, enlisted 14 Apr 1809 in Winchester at the age of 31, 5' 8" tall, born in Frederick, MD, re-enlisted at Winchester of 8 Jun 1814 for the war and died on 27 Jan 1815, place and cause not stated (Johnson and Christou, p. 218)

Leach, George, served as a Private in Capt. Robert C. Galloway's Co., 2nd Regt., 11th Brigade, Baltimore, from 27 Jul 1814 and was reported as "sick – absent without leave Oct 5" 1814 (Wright Vol. 2, p. 86)

Leach, Ralph (1790-1834), served as a Private in Capt. Thomas Owings' Co., 32nd Regt., Anne Arundel Co. Militia, from 13 May to 26 May 1813 in Annapolis, and as a Private in Capt. Adam Barnes' Co. from 23 Aug 1814 and was "sick on furlough Sep 20" as reported on the muster roll dated 23 Aug – 27 Sep 1814. On 24 Nov 1854 Rachael Leach, age 64, of Howard Co., widow of Ralph Leach, stated he was drafted in Anne Arundel Co. in July 1814 and was discharged at Baltimore. They were married on 25 Apr 1815 by Rev, Hood and her maiden name was Hobbs. On 26 Jun 1855 Rachel Leach stated she was age 66 and resided in Howard Co. On 26 Jun 1855 Warfield Hobbs, Walter Sellman and Samuel Grimes stated Ralph Leach served under Capt. Adam Barnes from 23 Aug to about 13 Sep 1814, was taken sick and furloughed by Dr. Stockett around 17 Sep 1814. (Wright Vol. 4, pp. 41, 43, 102-103; BLW# 55-120-70653)

League, Abraham, served as a Private in Capt. Thomas L. Lawrence's Co., 6th Regiment, Baltimore Militia, from 19 Aug 1814 and was discharged because of sickness, but the date was not stated (Wright Vol. 2, p. 12)

Leahy, John, served as a Sergeant in Capt. Joseph Barton's Co., 15th U.S. Infantry, enlisted 19 Dec 1812 in Baltimore, age 29, 6' tall, born in Hunterdon Co., NJ and was discharged at Fort Erie, Upper Canada on 16 Jun 1815 on a Surgeon's Certificate (Johnson and Christou, p. 219)

Leazer, Elisha, served as a Private in Capt. Samuel Lane's Co., 14th U.S. Infantry, enlisted 6 Jun 1812 in Allegany Co., MD at the age of 27, 5' 7¾" tall, born in Bedford, PA and was captured on 24 Jun 1813 at Beaver Dams, Upper Canada. Prisoner of War #3810 at Halifax, NS, interned 27 Aug 1813, was discharged for exchange on 3 Feb 1814, exchanged 15 Apr 1814 and deserted at Fort Severn, MD on 15 Jul 1815 (Johnson and Christou, p. 219 spelled his name Leazer and on p. 229 spelled it Lozier; Baker Vol. 1, p. 241 spelled his name Leazer)

Lecompte, William, served as a Private in Capt. Richard Arell's Co., 14th U.S. Infantry, enlisted 19 May 1812 and later captured, date and place not stated. Prisoner of War, exchanged on 15 Apr 1814, returned to service and died at Williamsville, NY on 10 Jan 1815; bounty land issued to Joseph Lecompte, his uncle, and other heirs (BLW# 26733-160-12; Johnson and Christou, p. 219)

Ledman, Francis (1785-1814), served as a Corporal, 11th U.S. Infantry, enlisted 6 Jul 1814 in Burlington, VT at the age of 29, 6' tall, born in Maryland and died on 25 Dec 1814 from sickness (Johnson and Christou, p. 219)

Lee, David, served as a Private in Capt. Henry Craig's Co., 1st U.S. Artillery, enlisted 2 Jun 1814 in Youngstown, PA at the age of 20, 5' 8¾" tall, born in Cecil Co., was wounded at Fort Erie, Upper Canada on 18 Oct 1814 and discharged at Buffalo, NY on 2 Aug 1815 (Johnson and Christou, p. 219)

Lee, Edward (Mulatto), served as a Seaman and was born in Dorset [Dorchester Co.], MD. Age: 25. Prison Depot: Portsmouth, Prisoner of War #799. How Taken: Gave himself up off HM Ship-of-the-Line *Scepter*. Date Received: 21 Apr 1813. From what ship: HM Guard Ship *Royal William*. Discharged on 27 Apr 1813 and sent to Chatham on HMS *Citoyenne*. Prison Depot: Chatham, Prisoner of War #1658. Date Received: 9 May 1813. From what ship: HMS *Raisonable*. Discharged on 13 Aug 1814 and sent to Dartmoor. Prison Depot: Dartmoor, Prisoner of War #2718. Date Received: 21 Aug 1814. From what ship: HMT *Freya* from Chatham. Discharged on 26 Apr 1815. (Johnson's Database, 2019)

Lee, Henry III ("Light-Horse Harry") (1756-1818), was a retired cavalry officer who served in the Revolutionary War, was Governor of Virginia and left public life in 1801; however, during the civil unrest in Baltimore on 27 Jul 1812, Lee received grave injuries while helping to resist an attack on his friend Alexander Contee Hanson, editor of the *Baltimore Federal Republican* who was attacked by a Democratic-Republican mob because his paper opposed the War of 1812. Lee, Hanson and two dozen other Federalists had taken refuge in the offices of the paper. The group surrendered to Baltimore City officials the next day and they were jailed. Laborer George Woolslager led a mob that forced its way into the jail and removed the Federalists, beating and torturing them over the next three hours. All were severely injured and one Federalist, James Lingan, died. Lee suffered extensive internal injuries as well as head and face wounds, and even his speech was affected. His symptoms were consistent with what is now called post-traumatic stress disorder. After unsuccessful convalescence at his home, he sailed to the West Indies in an effort to recuperate from his injuries. On his way back to Virginia, Lee died on 25 Mar 1818, at Dungeness, GA on Cumberland Island, cared for by Nathaniel Greene's daughter Louisa. "Light-Horse Harry" was buried with full military honors, provided by an American fleet stationed near St. Mary's, GA, in a small cemetery at Dungeness. In 1913 his remains were moved to the Lee family crypt at Lee Chapel on the campus of Washington & Lee University in Lexington, Virginia. (For more details about the civil unrest in Baltimore in 1812, see *Chronicles of Baltimore*, pp. 313-339)

Lee, Jacob, served as a Private in Capt. William McLaughlin's Co., 50th Regt., Allegany Co. Militia, called into service in the defense of Baltimore, reported as "sick in hospital" on the muster roll dated 11 Aug – 13 Oct 1814 and discharged by surgeon on 27 Oct 1814 ("Allegany County Militia (Including Garrett Co.), 1794-1815," by F. Edward Wright and Marlene S. Bates, *Maryland Genealogical Society Bulletin,* Vol. 32, No. 2, Spring 1991, p. 174; Wright Vol. 9, p. 6 states Capt. Henry Lowery's Co.; Wright Vol. 10, p. 2 states Capt. William McLaughlin)

Lee, John, served as a Private in Capt. John Owings' Co., 36th Regt., Baltimore Co., from 25 Aug 1814, stationed at Stinchomb's Old Field and was "discharged sick Sep 27" 1814 at Camp Deal (Wright Vol. 2, p. 63)

Lee, John, served as a Private in Capt. Colin Buckner's Co., 5th U.S. Infantry, enlisted 17 Feb 1813 in Baltimore at the age of 38, 5' 10" tall, born in Bucks Co., PA and was discharged at Buffalo, NY on 21 Jun 1815 on a Surgeon's Certificate (Johnson and Christou, p. 220)

Lee, Samuel (African American), served as a Seaman and was born in Maryland. Age: 25. Prison Depot: Portsmouth, Prisoner of War #559. Captured by HM Frigate *Dryad*. When Taken: 7 Jan 1813. Where Taken: at sea. Prize Name: *Rossie*. Ship Type: Merchant Vessel. Date Received: 25 Jan 1813. From what ship: HM Ship-of-the-Line *Queen*. Discharged on 11 Mar 1813 and sent to Chatham on HM Store Ship *Abundance*. Prison Depot: Chatham, Prisoner of War #1232. Date Received: 16 Mar 1813 on HMS *Abundance*. Discharged on 24 Jul 1813 and released to the Cartel *Hoffning*. (Johnson's Database, 2019)

Lee, Washington, served as a Steward of the U.S. Chesapeake Flotilla, entered service on 23 Apr 1814, reported sick (date not stated) and died on 9 Nov 1814 (Shomette, p. 379; Sheads, p. 22)

Lee, William, served as a Seaman and was born in Baltimore, MD. Age: 31. Prison Depot: Chatham, Prisoner of War #78. Captured by HM Brig *Sarpedon*. When Taken: 12 Aug 1812. Where Taken: Great Belt, Denmark. Prize Name: Cuba. Ship Type: Merchant Vessel. Received: 4 Nov 1812. From what ship: HMS *Namur*. Discharged on 10 May 1813 and released to the Cartel *Admittance*. (Johnson's Database, 2019)

Leith, John, served as a Private (company not stated) and was captured at the Battle of Bladensburg on 24 Aug 1814 (Marine, p. 174)

Leizer, Peter, see Peter Lizer, q.v.

Lemand, James (1772-1814), served as a Private in Capt. T. Montgomery's Co., 14th U.S. Infantry, enlisted 21 Apr 1812 at the age of 40, 5' 5" tall, born in Baltimore and was killed at Chippewa, Upper Canada on 15 Oct 1814; bounty land was issued to Mary Lemand, guardian of the children of James Lemand (BLW# 2865-160-12; Johnson and Christou, p. 220)

Lemars, John, served as a Seaman on privateer *High Flyer* and was wounded in action in December 1812 (Marine p. 355)

Lemmon, Nicholas, served as a Private In Capt. John B. Snowden's Co., 2nd Regiment, 11th Brigade, Baltimore Co., and listed as "dead"on the muster roll dated 25 Jul – 1 Dec 1814, but exact date was not given (Wright Vol. 2, p. 82)

Leone, G. C., served as a Private in Capt. Thomas L. Lawrence's Co., 6th Regt., Baltimore City, from 19 Aug 1814 and was discharged by the doctor because of sickness, but no date was given (Wright Vol. 2, p. 12)

Lerew (Larew), Abraham, served as an Ensign in Capt. James Haslett's Co., 2nd Regiment, 11th Brigade, Baltimore City, from 22 May 1813 and resigned on 30 May 1813. He then appeared as an Ensign in Capt. John Matthews' Co. on the muster roll dated 12 May – 2 Jul 1813 and served as a Private in a Company pf Volunteer Artillerists under Capt. Joseph H. Nicholson, Baltimore, commanded by Lieut. Col. George Armistead from 19 Aug 1814 and was severely wounded on 13 Sep 1814 at Fort McHenry. (Marine p. 173; Wright, pp. 51, 78, 79)

Letters, Daniel, served as a Private in Capt. William McLaughlin's Co., 50th Regt., Allegany Co. Militia, was called into service in the defense of Baltimore and was reported as "sick in hospital" in September on the muster roll dated 11 Aug – 13 Oct 1814 ("Allegany County Militia (Including Garrett Co.), 1794-1815," by F. Edward Wright and Marlene S. Bates, *Maryland Genealogical Society Bulletin,* Volume 32, No. 2, Spring 1991, p. 174; Wright Vol. 10, p. 2)

Levely, William, served as a Private in Capt. Aaron R. Levering's Co., 5th Regt., Baltimore City Militia, from 19 Aug 1814, was captured, place not stated, taken prisoner and exchanged on 26 Nov 1814 (Wright Vol. 2, p. 5)

Levering, Jesse, served as a Private in Capt. Samuel Sterett's Co., 5th Regt., Baltimore Militia, and was listed as wounded at North Point on muster roll dated 19 Aug – 18 Nov 1814 (Wright Vol. 2, p. 6)

Levering, John, served as a Private in Capt. Samuel Sterett's Co., 5th Regiment, Baltimore City Militia, was promoted to 2nd Corporal on 12 Sep 1814 and wounded same day (Wright Vol. 2, p. 6) In Baltimore Co. on 18 May 1820 John Levering, former private in acting Capt. Reese's Co. of Volunteers, 5th Regiment, Maryland Militia, and a resident of Baltimore for about 30 years and previously of Pennsylvania, collected his own $32 pension due from 4 Mar 1819 to 4 Mar

1820. Earlier, on 18 Dec 1819, Dr. Joseph Birkhead and Dr. Thomas E. Bond made oaths that John Levering was still disabled from a gunshot wound to the mouth. (Pierce, pp. 109-110)

Leverton, John, served as a Private in Capt. Clement Sullivan's Co., 14th U.S. Infantry, enlisted 20 May 1812 for 5 years and was captured at Beaver Dams, Upper Canada on 24 Jun 1813. Prisoner of War #4785 at Halifax, NS, interned 24 Jun 1813, discharged on 9 Nov 1813, sent to England on HMS *Success*, was later released, returned to service and was discharged on 19 May 1817 (Johnson and Christou, p. 221); Baker Vol. 1, p. 244)

Levi, Henry (1787-1813), served as a Corporal in 23rd U.S. Infantry and was born in Maryland. Age: 26. Prison Depot: Halifax, NS, Prisoner of War #3936. When Taken: 26 Jun 1813. Where Taken: Beaver Dams, Upper Canada. Died on 27 Oct 1813 from inflammation of lungs. (Johnson's Database, 2019)

Levy, Christopher, served as a Private in the 42nd Regiment, Harford Co. Militia, was captured when the British attacked and burned Havre de Grace on 3 May 1813, was taken onboard the ship *Maidstone* and released two days later by the valiant efforts of a town delegation led by Matilda O'Neill, teenage daughter of Lt. John O'Neill who was also captured. "The elder, Mr. Levy, was taken [by the British] about this time, as was also Capt. Barnes, and one or two men. John O'Neill, Christopher Levy, James Sears, eldest son of Mrs. Sears, Capt. Whitefoot [Whiteford] and Ensign Hare were also made prisoners, as was one Whitloe, an aged citizen. Most of the Prisoners they released while on shore, but John O'Neill, Christopher Levy and James Sears they carried on board the fleet ... The Levy's are hatters in this town, hard working, honest, industrious men." (*Narrative Respecting the Conduct of the British From Their First Landing on Spesutia Island Till Their Progress to Havre de Grace*, by James Jones Wilmer, 1814, pp. 19-20; *Concord Point Lighthouse Station at Havre de Grace*, by Jack L. Shagena, Jr. and Henry C. Peden, Jr., 2017, p. 35; "Harford County in the War of 1812," by Christopher T. George, *Harford Historical Bulletin* No. 76, Spring 1998, p. 33)

Levy, Mr., see Christopher Levy, q.v.

Lewis, David R., served as a Private in Capt. James Many's Co., 1st U.S. Artillery, enlisted 10 Aug 1806 in Baltimore for 5 years at the age of 30, 5' 11" tall, born in Maryland, re-enlisted on 31 Dec 1812 and was discharged at New York on 17 Nov 1814 on a Surgeon's Certificate for deafness (Johnson and Christou, p. 221)

Lewis, Dudley, served as a Private in the 14th U.S. Infantry and was captured. Prisoner of War #3833 at Halifax, NS, interned 6 Jun 1813 and was discharged for exchange on 3 Feb 1814 (Johnson and Christou, p. 221; Baker Vol. 1, p. 245)

Lewis, Isaac (1787-1815), served as a Private in Capt. Hopley Yeaton's Co., 1st U.S. Artillery, enlisted 21 Feb 1814 in Fort Nelson, VA at the age of 27, 5' 7" tall, born in Prince George's Co., MD and died at Fort Nelson, VA on 25 Feb 1815 (BLW# 27427-160-12; Johnson and Christou, p. 221)

Lewis, John, served as a Seaman, born in Annapolis, and was captured at sea. How Taken: Gave himself up off HM Frigate *Theban* and sent to England. When Taken: 24 Jun 1813. Age 28. Received: 24 Aug 1814 from London. Prison Depot: Chatham, Prisoner of War #3857.Discharged on 26 Sep 1814 and sent to Dartmoor on HMS *Leyden*. Prison Depot: Dartmoor, Prisoner of War #4756. Received: 9 Oct 1814. From what ship: HMT *Freya* from Chatham. Discharged on 15 Jun 1815. (Johnson's Database, 2019)

Lewis, John (African American), served as a Seaman, born in Maryland, and was captured. Captured by HM Frigate *Medusa* and sent to England. When Taken: 9 Nov 1812. Age 25. Where Taken: off San Sebastian, Spain. Prize Name: *Independence*. Ship Type: Merchant Vessel. Prison Depot: Plymouth 1, Prisoner of War #61. Received: 27 Nov 1812. From what ship: HMS *Wasp*. Discharged and sent to Portsmouth on 29 Dec 1812 on HMS *Northumberland*. Prison Depot: Portsmouth, Prisoner of War #329. Date Received: 31 Dec 1812. From what ship: HM Ship-of-the-Line *Northumberland*. Discharged on 4 Mar 1813 and sent to Chatham on HMS *Queen*. Prison Depot: Chatham, Prisoner of War #1058. Received: 11 Mar 1813 from Yarmouth on HMS *Tenders*. Discharged on 8 Jun 1813 and released to the Cartel *Rodrigo*. (Johnson's Database, 2019)

Lewis, Samuel, served as a Seaman and was taken from the barracks and admitted to the Naval Hospital in Washington, DC as Patient No. 9 as of 1 Jun 1814, but his injury or illness was not stated (Sharp's Database, 2018)

Liddle, Morris, served as a Seaman, born in Maryland, and was captured at sea. How Taken: Gave himself up off HM Frigate *Ulysses* and sent to England. Prison Depot: Portsmouth, Prisoner of War #666. Date Received: 7 Feb 1813. Age 26. From what ship: HMS *Ulysses*. Discharged on 6 Mar 1813 and sent to Chatham on HMS *Cornwall*. (Johnson's Database, 2019)

Linard, Alfred, served as a Private in the 14th U.S. Infantry and was captured. Prisoner of War #3850 at Halifax, NS, interned 24 Jun 1813, discharged 9 Nov 1813 and sent to England (Johnson and Christou, p. 223; Baker Vol. 1, p. 248)

Lingan, James McCubbin (1751-1812), was a retired Brigadier General who served in the Revolutionary War and was subsequently a senior officer in the Maryland State Militia. He was taken prisoner at Fort Washington early in the war and spent several years aboard a prison hulk. After independence, Lingan served as a government official in Georgetown. At the outbreak of the War of 1812, Lingan was an outspoken advocate of freedom of the press and was murdered by a mob while defending the offices of an anti-war newspaper in Baltimore. When the offices of the *Baltimore Federal Republican* were besieged and burnt by a mob angry at anti-war editorials run by the newspaper, Lingan protested at the act and sheltered newspaper editor Alexander Contee Hanson in Georgetown. On 17 Jul 1812 Hanson resumed printing the newspaper at new offices in Baltimore and another mob formed within hours, again storming the building and destroying the presses. Hanson, with Lingan, Henry Lee III and others who had hastened from Washington to try to calm the crowd, were arrested by local militia and taken to Baltimore City Jail in an attempt to calm the situation. The crowd, led by an athletic butcher named John Mumma, followed them to the prison and stormed the building. Lingan attempted to stop the mob by displaying a bayonet wound he had received in the Revolutionary War, but this only inflamed the crowd and Hanson, Lingan and Lee were severely beaten and left for dead. Hanson and Lee survived, although the latter was left partially blinded after hot wax was poured into his eyes. Lingan, however, died from his serious injuries and was buried at St. John's Church in Georgetown at a funeral attended by thousands of mourners. George Washington Custis read the eulogy, praising Lingan's defence of free press and crying "Oh Maryland! Would that the waters of the Chesapeake could wash this foul stain from thy character!" 96 years later, Lingan's remains were removed from the burial ground in Georgetown and transferred to Arlington National Cemetery. This cemetery was established in 1864 on the grounds of *Arlington*, the Lee farm and home of George Washington Parke Custis. (For more details about the civil unrest in Baltimore, see *Chronicles of Baltimore*, pp. 313-339) James McCubbin Lingan was born 13 May 1751 and died 28 Jul 1812. His wife Janet Henderson was born 2 Sep 1765 and died 5 Jul 1832. (tombstone)

Lingo, William, served as a Private in Capt. Thomas Ramsey's Co., 1st U.S. Rifles, enlisted 19 May 1813 at the age of 18, 5' 6" tall, born in Maryland, wounded at Fort Erie, Upper Canada on 12 Aug 1814 and was discharged at Buffalo, NY on 1 Aug 1815 (Johnson and Christou, p. 223, inadvertently listed him twice)

Linsey, Alexander, served as a Seaman and was born in Baltimore. Age: 16. Prison Depot: Plymouth 1, Prisoner of War #1695. Captured by HM Brig *Royalist*. When Taken: 31 May 1813. Where Taken: Bay of Biscayne. Prize Name: *Governor Gerry*. Home Port: New Haven. Ship Type: Merchant Vessel. Date Received: 26 Jun 1813. From what ship: HMS *Duncan*. Discharged on 30 Jun 1813 and sent to Stapleton. Prison Depot: Stapleton, Prisoner of War #201. Date Received: 8 Jul 1813 from Plymouth. Discharged on 13 Jun 1814 and sent to Dartmoor. Prison Depot: Dartmoor, Prisoner of War #1471. Captured by HM Brig *Lyra*. When Taken: 29 May 1813. Where Taken: Bay of Biscayne. Prize Name: *Governor Gerry*.

Home Port: New Haven. Ship Type: Merchant Vessel. Date Received: 19 Jun 1814 from Stapleton. Discharged on 28 Apr 1815. (Johnson's Database, 2019)

Linthicum, Abner Jr. (1795-1845), served as Drilling Officer under Capt. Ball and was Captain of his own company in the 22nd Regiment, Anne Arundel Co. Militia, stationed at Fort Madison from 11 Apr to 1 May 1813; his first wife Rachel Stewart died in 1838 or 1839 and his second wife Mary Bryan, whom he married in 1842 in Govanstown, Baltimore Co., was aged 82 in 1891 when she stated, "During my husband's lifetime I was accustomed to hearing him called Captain Linthicum and hearing him speak of the time he was Captain of a company of militia stationed at Fort Madison opposite Annapolis. Then a youth of 18 or 19 years whilst there he contracted a fever the effects of which he never entirely recovered, and from which he died in September 1845." Abner died on 29 Sep 1845 and was buried on the home place in Anne Arundel Co. (Wright Vol. 4, pp. 37, 103; Pension WO-45048; Anne Arundel Co. Will, 1845)

Linthicum, Wesley, served as a Private in 1st Lt. John Thomas 3rd's Co., 32nd Regt., Anne Arundel Co. Militia, from 24 Aug 1814 and "furloughed – sick at home " on the muster roll dated 24 Aug – 27 Sep 1814. On 23 Sep 1852 Wesley Linthicum, age 61, of Howard Co., stated he volunteered in Anne Arundel Co. on 24 Aug 1814 and was discharged at Baltimore in 1814. He was still living on 17 Aug 1855, age 63. (Wright Vol. 4, pp. 43, 104, spelled his name Westley)

Liser, Jacob, served as a Private in Capt. George Shryock's Co., Hagerstown, Washington Co. Militia, from 23 Jul 1814 and reported as sick in the hospital in Baltimore, but no date was given, probably on 6 Oct 1814 (Wright Vol. 9, p. 8)

Liser, Jonas, served as a Private in Capt. George Shryock's Co., Hagerstown, Washington Co. Militia, from 23 Jul 1814 and reported as sick in the hospital in Baltimore on 6 Oct 1814 (Wright Vol. 9, p. 8)

Liser, William, served as a Private in Capt. George Shryock's Co., Hagerstown, Washington Co. Militia, from 23 Jul 1814 and was reported as sick in hospital in Baltimore on 6 Oct 1814 (Wright Vol. 9, p. 8)

Lissel, Joseph, served as a Seaman, born in St. Mary's Co., MD, and was captured at sea. How Taken: Gave himself up. When Taken: 28 Nov 1812. Age 32. Where Taken: London. Prison Depot: Chatham, Prisoner of War #260. Date Received: 7 Dec 1812. From what ship: HMS *Raisonable*. Discharged on 24 Jul 1813 and released to the Cartel *Hoffning*. (Johnson's Database, 2019)

Little, Ezekiel (1778-1813), served as a Private in Capt. Colin Buckner's Co., 5th U.S. Infantry, enlisted 18 Feb 1813 at age 35, 6' tall, born in Anne Arundel Co., MD and died on 18 Aug 1813 (Johnson and Christou, p. 224)

Little, Peter (alias Peter Kline), served as a Private in Capt. Samuel Lane's Co., 14th U.S. Infantry, date not stated. Prisoner of War, exchanged on 15 Apr 1814, and discharged on 25 Apr 1815, ruptured (Mallick and Wright, p. 192)

Little, Morris, of Maryland, served as a Seaman on the ship *Ulysses* and was reported by Capt. Jeduthan Upton, Jr. in 1814 as having been impressed into service and was being held as a Prisoner of War on the prison ship *San Antonio* at Chatham, England (*Niles Weekly Register*, 26 Feb 1814)

Livers, John (1775-1815), served as a Private in Capt. Joseph Marshall's Co., 14th U.S. Infantry, enlisted 30 Oct 1813 at age 38, 5' 6" tall, born in Maryland and died at Greenbush, NY on 9 Feb 1815 (Johnson and Christou, pp. 224-225)

Lives, William G. (1794-1814), served as a Seaman under Sailing Master Simmones Bunbury, U.S. Sea Fencibles, enlisted on 3 Jan 1814 at the age of 20, 5' 9" tall, born in New York and died 16 Jul 1814 (Johnson and Christou, p. 225)

Livingston, Thomas, served as a Private in Capt. William Jett's Co., 20th U.S Infantry, enlisted 1 May 1813 in Baltimore, age 28, 6' 1" tall, born in Baltimore and discharged at Greenbush, NY on 4 May 1815 on a Surgeon's Certificate (Johnson and Christou, p. 223)

Lizer (Leizer, Lizar), Peter (1791-1814), served as a Private in Capt. Joseph Henderson's Co., 22nd U.S. Infantry, enlisted 23 Mar 1814 by Lt. Culbertson at the age of 23, 6' 1" tall, grey eyes, dark hair, dark complexion, born in Frederick Co., MD, mustered at Pittsburgh, PA on 30 Apr 1814 and in June 1814 and was killed on 25 Jul 1814 (Johnson and Christou, p. 220; Mallick and Wright, p. 188)

Lloyd, John, served as a Private in Capt. Edward Orrick's Co., 41st Regiment, Baltimore Co., from 25 Aug 1814 and reported as "sick-absent since Aug 30" 1814 (Wright Vol. 2, p. 70 spelled his name Loyd)

Loar, George, served as a Private in Capt. Henry Lowery's Co., Allegany Co. Militia, and was discharged by a Surgeon on 5 Dec 1814 (Wright Vol. 9, p. 6)

Locher (Lochner, Loerher), Adam, served as a Private in Capt. George W. Magee's Co., Frederick Co. Militia, 1st Regiment, New Windsor area, from 22 Jul 1814, engaged in the Battle of Bladensburg and was reported missing in action on 24 Aug 1814 (Mallick and Wright, p. 342)

Locker, Michael, served as a Seaman, born in St. Mary's Co., MD, and was captured at sea. How Taken: Gave himself up off HM Brig *Hecate* and sent to England. Prison Depot: Chatham, Prisoner of War #3875. Age 21. When Taken: 26 Aug 1814. Date Received: 28 Aug 1814 from London. Discharged on 26 Sep 1814 and sent to Dartmoor on HMS *Leyde*. Prison Depot: Dartmoor, Prisoner of

War #4717. Date Received: 9 Oct 1814. From what ship: HMT *Freya* from Chatham. Discharged on 15 Jun 1815. (Johnson's Database, 2019)

Lockridge, Robert, served as a Private in Capt. Carney's Co., 13th U.S. Infantry, and was wounded, date and location not stated. In Baltimore on 5 Mar 1827 he stated he was disabled in the late war and had been a resident of this city for about nine years and previously of Philadelphia. He collected his own $24 due from 4 Sep 1826 to 4 Mar 1827. An earlier voucher from 4 Mar to 4 Sep 1826 gave his residence as Washington Co. for eight years and previously in Albany, NY. (Pierce, p. 111; Johnson and Christou, p. 225, did not mention him)

Lockwood, Benjamin, served as a Seaman and was born in Baltimore. Age: 39. Prison Depot: Chatham, Prisoner of War #3724. Captured by HM Ship-of-the-Line *Minden*. When Taken: 17 Nov 1812. Where Taken: off Cape of Good Hope, South Africa. Prize Name: Valentine. Ship Type: Merchant Vessel. Date Received: 23 May 1814 from London. Discharged on 22 Oct 1814 and released to HMS *Argonant*. (Johnson's Database, 2019)

Logan, William, served as a Seaman and was born in Baltimore. Age: 23. Prison Depot: Dartmoor, Prisoner of War #5956. Captured by HM Ship-of-the-Line *Bulwark*. When Taken: 23 Oct 1814. Where Taken: off Halifax, NS. Prize Name: *Harlequin*. Home Port: Portsmouth. Ship Type: Privateer. Date Received: 27 Dec 1814. From what ship: HMT *Penelope*. Discharged on 3 Jul 1815. (Johnson's Database, 2019)

Logan, William, served as a Seaman and was born in Baltimore. Age: 23. Prison Depot: Plymouth 1, Prisoner of War #1533. Captured by HM Frigate *Andromache*. When Taken: 14 Mar 1813. Where Taken: off Nantes, France. Prize Name: *Courier*. Home Port: Baltimore. Ship Type: Letter of Marque. Date Received: 29 May 1813. From what ship: HMS *Hannibal*. Discharged on 30 Jun 1813 and sent to Stapleton. Prison Depot: Stapleton, Prisoner of War #97. Date Received: 8 Jul 1813 from Plymouth. Discharged on 13 Jun 1814 and sent to Dartmoor. Prison Depot: Dartmoor, Prisoner of War #1387. Date Received: 19 Jun 1814 from Stapleton. Discharged 28 Apr 1815. (Johnson's Database, 2019)

Logere, Henry C., served as a USMC Sergeant and was born in Baltimore. Age: 25. Prison Depot: Dartmoor, Prisoner of War #4014. Captured by HM Ship-of-the-Line *Leander*. When Taken: 22 Jun 1814. Where Taken: off Cape Sable, NS. Prize Name: U.S. Brig *Rattlesnake*. Ship Type: Warship. Date Received: 6 Oct 1814. From what ship: HMT *Chesapeake* from Halifax, NS. Discharged on 9 Jun 1815. (Johnson's Database, 2019)

Logue, Joshua, served as a Private In Capt. John B. Snowden's Co., Baltimore Co., 2nd Regiment, 11th Brigade, from 25 Jul 1814 and was reported as "sick on furlough," but no date was given on the muster roll (Wright Vol. 2, p. 82)

Lollis, Phillip, see Phillip Lawless, q.v.

Lomax, Lawson, served as a Private in Capt. Thomas Sangster's Co., 12th U.S. Infantry, enlisted 15 May 1812 at Alexandria, VA for 18 months at the age of 23 or 25 (sic), 5' 7" or 8½" (sic) tall, born in Frederick Co., MD and mustered in Burlington, VT on 28 Feb 1814 and was sick at Sackett's Harbor, NY on 30 Apr 1814; appears to have enlisted again at Alexandria, VA by Lt. Randolph on 28 Jan 1815 for the duration of the war and was discharged at Fredericksburg on 15 Mar 1815 (Mallick and Wright, pp. 193-194)

Long, Daniel (1785-1812), served as a Private in Capt. Samuel Lane's Co., 14th U.S. Infantry, enlisted on 15 May 1812 in Shephardstown, MD at the age of 27, 5' 8" tall, and died at Black Rock, NY on 16 Dec 1812 from wounds received in action on 28 Nov 1812 (BLW# 7241-160-12; Johnson and Christou, p. 226)

Long, George, served as a Private in Capt. Thomas Blair's Co., Allegany Co. Militia, and was reported "sick in the hospital" on the muster roll dated 2 Sep – 28 Oct 1814 ("Allegany County Militia (Including Garrett Co.), 1794-1815," by F. Edward Wright and Marlene S. Bates, *Maryland Genealogical Society Bulletin,* Volume 32, No. 2, Spring 1991, p. 177; Wright Vol. 10, p. 6)

Long, Henry (1782-1887), an "Old Defender," died at Jarrettsville on 4 Sep 1887, age 95; he was wounded at Bladensburg in 1812 (sic) and had been on a government pension for over 50 years. (*The Aegis*, 9 Sep 1887, mistakenly reported his name as Henry Levy and other newspapers repeated the error) Henry Long, of Black Horse, Harford Co., applied for a pension on 8 Apr 1873 and stated he was wounded in the hip at Bladensburg on 24 Aug 1814 and the disability still continued. (Fold3, p. 11; Bethel Presbyterian Church Cemetery) He stated he served under a Capt. Leach, but records indicate Capt. George Steever's Co., 6th Regt., Baltimore City, from 19 Aug 1814. (Wright Vol. 2, p. 15)

Long, James, served as a Seaman and was born in Baltimore. Age: 36. Prison Depot: Portsmouth, Prisoner of War #1497. Captured by HM Schooner *Canso.* When Taken: 11 May 1814. Where Taken: off Cape Clear, Ireland. Prize Name: *Traveler,* prize of the Privateer *Surprise.* Home Port: Baltimore. Ship Type: Privateer. Date Received: 1 Jun 1814. From what ship: HMS HMS *Canso.* Discharged on 2 Jun 1814 and sent to Plymouth on HMS *Growler.* (Johnson's Database, 2019)

Long, Joseph, served as a Seaman and was born in Baltimore. Age: 36. Prison Depot: Plymouth 1, Prisoner of War #2669. Captured by HM Schooner *Canso.* When Taken: 11 May 1814. Where Taken: off Cape Clear, Ireland. Prize Name: *Traveler,* prize of the Privateer *Surprise.* Home Port: Baltimore. Ship Type: Privateer. Received: 5 Jun 1814. From what ship: HMS *Gronville.* Discharged on 14 Jun 1814 and sent to Dartmoor. Prison Depot: Dartmoor, Prisoner of War

#1293. Date Received: 14 Jun 1814 from Mill Prison. Discharged on 28 Apr 1815. (Johnson's Database, 2019)

Long, Mr., served as 1st Lieutenant under Commodore Joshua Barney and was wounded on 16 Sep 1814, along with six of his crew members (who were not identified) during an engagement "with his Britannic Majesty's packet ship *Princess Amelia*." (J. Thomas Scharf's *The Chronicles of Baltimore*, Vol. 1, p. 359)

Long, Robert W., served as an Ensign in the 14th U.S. Infantry (company not stated), commissioned on 27 May 1812, resigned on 15 Feb 1813 and died on 9 Mar 1813 (Johnson and Christou, p. 227; *Baltimore American*, 11 Mar 1813)

Long, Sylvanus, served as Lieutenant on the privateer *Rossie* and was mortally wounded in action with the *Princess Amelia*, date not stated (Marine p. 359)

Longford, Samuel, served as a Seaman and was born in Maryland. Age: 23. Prison Depot: Plymouth 1, Prisoner of War #1307. Captured by HM Frigate *Surveillante*. When Taken: 22 Apr 1813. Where Taken: at sea. Prize Name: *Eliza*. Ship Type: Merchant Vessel. Date Received: 10 May 1813. From what ship: HMS *Medusa*. Discharged on 3 Jul 1813 and sent to Stapleton Prison. Prison Depot: Stapleton, Prisoner of War #317. Received: 11 Jul 1813 from Plymouth. Discharged on 16 Jun 1814 and sent to Dartmoor. Prison Depot: Dartmoor, Prisoner of War #1592. Age 24. Date Received: 23 Jun 1814 from Stapleton. Discharged and sent to Mill Prison on 30 Jun 1814. (Johnson's Database, 2019)

Longwell (Longwhell), Amos, served as a Seaman and was born in Maryland. Age: 24. Prison Depot: Portsmouth, Prisoner of War #554. Captured by HM Frigate *Dryad*. When Taken: 7 Jan 1813. Where Taken: at sea. Prize Name: *Rossie*. Ship Type: Merchant Vessel. Date Received: 25 Jan 1813. From what ship: HM Ship-of-the-Line *Queen*. Discharged on 11 Mar 1813 and sent to Chatham on HM Store Ship *Abundance*. Prison Depot: Chatham, Prisoner of War #1227. Date Received: 16 Mar 1813 om HMS *Abundance*. Discharged on 24 Jul 1813 and released to the Cartel *Hoffning*. (Johnson's Database, 2019)

Loughborough, Foster, was a Seaman who sustained a hemorrhage on 24 Aug 1814 on the field of battle at Bladensburg, was admitted to the Naval Hospital in Washington, DC as Patient No. 17 and discharged on 28 Aug 1814 (Sharp's Database, 2018)

Loughguski, Matthias, served as a Private under Brevet Major Gray in the 2nd Regiment, U.S. Infantry, and was "wounded in the late war," but the date and location were not stated. On 20 Mar 1828 in Baltimore he stated he had been a resident of Baltimore County for six or seven years and previously in Adams Co., PA. He collected his own pension of $24.00 due from 4 Mar 1827 to 4 Mar 1828. Also, on 20 Mar 1828, Dr. Henry W. Webster and Dr. F. E. B. Hintze made oaths that his disability continued from a musket ball passing through his left ankle producing anchylosis varicose veins. (Pierce, p. 115)

Louis, Joseph, served as a Seaman and was born in Baltimore. Age: 21. Prison Depot: Plymouth 2, Prisoner of War #15. How Taken: Gave himself up off MV *Philbes*. When Taken: 26 Dec 1814. Where Taken: Greenock, Scotland. Date Received: 3 Feb 1815. From what ship: HMS *Bittern*. Discharged on 4 Feb 1815 and sent to Dartmoor. (Johnson's Database, 2019)

Loura, John, see John Lowrye (Loura), q.v.

Love, David (1781-1814), served as a Private in Capt. Thomas Moore's Co., 12th U.S. Infantry, enlisted 22 May 1813 by Lt. A. McDonald for 5 years in Wheeling, VA, at the age of 32, 5' 10" tall, born in Frederick Co., MD and died at French Mills, NY on 2 Jan 1814 from sickness (Johnson and Christou, p. 227; Mallick and Wright, p. 195)

Loveitson, John, served as a Private in 14th U.S. Infantry and was born in Maryland. Age: 29. Prison Depot: Chatham, Prisoner of War #3102. When Taken: 24 Jun 1813. Where Taken: Beaver Dams, Upper Canada. Date Received: 7 Jan 1814 from Halifax, NS. Discharged on 10 Oct 1814 and sent to U.S. on the Cartel *St. Philip*. (Johnson's Database, 2019)

Lovely, Henry, served as a Master and was born in Baltimore. Age: 29. Prison Depot: Plymouth 1, Prisoner of War #2327. Captured by HM Brig *Pelican*. When Taken: 13 Jan 1814. Where Taken: at sea. Prize Name: *Siro*. Home Port: Baltimore. Ship Type: Letter of Marque. Date Received: 27 Jan 1814. From what ship: HMS *Pelican*. Discharged on 27 Jan 1814 and sent to Ashburton on parole. (Johnson's Database, 2019)

Lovett, Joseph, served as a Sergeant in Capt. Sullivan Burbank's Co., 21st U.S. Infantry, enlisted 12 May 1814 in Batavia, NY, age 36, 6' tall, born in Baltimore City and was furloughed at Williamsville, NY on account of a severe wound, date not stated (Johnson and Christou, p. 228)

Lowe, Isaac (African American), served as a Seaman and was born in Maryland. Age: 34. Prison Depot: Plymouth 2, Prisoner of War #3. Captured by HM Schooner *Helicon*. When Taken: 17 Jan 1815. Where Taken: Lat 20N Long 52W. Prize Name: *Albion*. Prize. Ship Type: Privateer. Date Received: 3 Feb 1815. From what ship: HMS *Bittern*. Discharged on 4 Feb 1815 and sent to Dartmoor. Prison Depot: Dartmoor, Prisoner of War #6239. Received: 4 Feb 1815. From what ship: HMT *Ganges*. Discharged on 5 Jul 1815. (Johnson's Database, 2019)

Lowe, John, served as a Seaman and was born in Baltimore. Age: 18. Prison Depot: Plymouth 1, Prisoner of War #1245. Captured by HM Frigate *Andromache*. When Taken: 14 Mar 1813. Where Taken: off Nantes, France. Prize

Name: *Courier*. Home Port: Baltimore. Ship Type: Letter of Marque. Date Received: 9 May 1813. From what ship: HMS *Andromache*. Discharged on 3 Jul 1813 and sent to Stapleton Prison. Prison Depot: Stapleton, Prisoner of War #247. Received: 11 Jul 1813 from Plymouth. Discharged 16 Jun 1814 and sent to Dartmoor. Prison Depot: Dartmoor, Prisoner of War #1533. Received: 23 Jun 1814 from Stapleton. Discharged 1 May 1815. (Johnson's Database, 2019)

Lowe, Samuel, served as a Private in Capt. Isaac Barnard's Co., 14th U.S. Inf., enlisted 1 Feb 1813 at the age of 22, 5' 5¼" tall and captured at Beaver Dams, Upper Canada on 24 Jun 1813. Prisoner of War #5102 at Halifax, NS, interned 28 Dec 1813, discharged for exchange on 31 May 1814 and discharged from the service on 7 Aug 1814 (Johnson and Christou, p. 228; Baker Vol. 1, p. 253)

Lowman, Emory (c1790-1837), served as a Private in Capt. John Berry's Artillery Co., Baltimore, from 19 Aug 1814, was severely wounded in action on 13 Sep 1814 at Fort McHenry and an arm was amputated (Wright Vol. 2, p. 49; Marine, p. 173; Baltimore County Will Book No. 16, p. 288)

Lowrey, James, served as a Private in the 14th U.S. Infantry and was captured, probably at Beaver Dams, Upper Canada. Prisoner of War #4173 at Halifax, NS, interned 24 Jun 1813, discharged 27 Aug 1813 and sent to England (Johnson and Christou, p. 229; Baker Vol. 1, p. 253)

Lowry, Moses, served as a Private in Capt. Isaac Raven's Co., Baltimore Co., 2nd Regiment, 11th Brigade, from 27 Jul 1814 and was "discharged Aug 3 – sick" (Wright Vol. 2, p. 83)

Lowry, Obadiah (1779-1815), served as a Private in Capt. Samuel Raisin's Co., 36th U.S. Infantry, enlisted 10 Jul 1814 in Norfolk, VA, age 35, 5' 7" tall, born in Halifax, VA and died in hospital on 6 Mar 1815 (Johnson and Christou, p. 229)

Lowrye (Loura), John, served as a Private in Capt. George Shryock's Co., Hagerstown, Washington Co. Militia, from 23 Jul 1814 and was reported "sick on furlough," but no date was given (Wright Vol. 9, p. 8)

Lozier, Elisha, see Elisha Leazer, q.v.

Lucas, Benjamin, served as a Private in Capt. Joseph Marshall's Co., 14th U.S. Infantry, enlisted 2 Sep 1814, age 32, 5' 10½" tall, born in Cecil Co., discharged at Greenbush, NY on 25 May 1815 as a cripple (Johnson and Christou, p. 229; BLW# 462-160-12)

Lucas, Benjamin, served as a Seaman and was born in Baltimore. Age: 21. Prison Depot: Portsmouth, Prisoner of War #179. Captured by HM Transport *Diadem*. When Taken: 7 Oct 1812. Where Taken: S. Andera (St. Andrews, Scotland). Prize Name: Baltimore. Home Port: Baltimore. Ship Type: Privateer. Date Received: 3

Nov 1812 San Antonio. From what ship: HMS *Diadem*. Discharged on 19 Feb 1813 and sent to Chatham on HM Store Ship *Dromedary*. Prison Depot: Chatham, Prisoner of War #548. Date Received: 23 Feb 1813 on HMS *Dromedary*. Discharged on 8 Jun 1813 and released to the Cartel *Rodrigo*. (Johnson's Database, 2019)

Lucas, Daniel, served as a Private in Capt. Lawson Cuddy's Co., 41st Regiment, Baltimore Co., from 25 Aug 1814 and was reported "sick-absent since Oct 19" 1814 (Wright Vol. 2, p. 67, spelled his name Lucus)

Lucas, David, served as a Private in Capt. George Birch's Co., 1st U.S. Artillery, enlisted 7 Jun 1813 in Centreville, MD, age 26, 5' 4" tall, born in Centreville, discharged 4 Sep 1815 on Surgeon's Certificate (Johnson and Christou, p. 229)

Lucas, Mr., served as a Private (company not stated) and a discharged soldier from the U.S. Army who had been wounded at New Orleans, died on 10 Dec 1815 at Fort McHenry (*Baltimore American*, 15 Dec 1815)

Luckenbeel, John (1892-1874), served as a Private in Capt. Peter Snyder's Co., 2nd PA Regt., from 5 Sep 1814, rendezvous at York, PA, born in Frederick Co., MD, served in Baltimore in 1814, sick in hospital and was on furlough since 21 Nov 1814; moved to Ohio in 1833 and was mayor of the town of Western Star in Medina County when he died on 28 Dec 1874 (Mallick and Wright, p. 196)

Luckett, Alexander, served as a Private in Capt. James Rhea's Co., 1st U.S. Inf., enlisted in March 1809 for 5 years at Detroit, MI, age 31, 5' 6½" tall, born in Maryland and was a Prisoner of War on parole, but the date and place were not stated (Johnson and Christou, p. 230)

Luckett, Alexander, served as a Corporal in Capt. Israel Turner's Co., 13th U.S. Infantry, enlisted 26 Jan 1814 at Greenbush, NY, age 29, 5' 7" tall, born in Port Tobacco, MD. Prisoner of War on parole, but the date and place not stated; discharged at Plattsburgh, NY on 20 Aug 1815 (Johnson and Christou, p. 230)

Luckett, John Roger Nelson, served as Captain of his own company, 2nd U.S. Infantry; born in Maryland, he was commissioned an Ensign on 26 Mar 1804, promoted to 2nd Lieutenant on 30 Nov 1805, promoted to 1st Lieutenant on 17 Aug 1807, promoted to Captain on 6 Jul 1812 and died on 5 May 1813 (Johnson and Christou, p. 230)

Luckey, Samuel, served as a Private in the 14th U.S. Infantry and was captured. Prisoner of War #3985 at Halifax, NS, interned 24 Jun 1813 and died there on 13 Sep 1813 of dysentery (Johnson and Christou, p. 230; Baker, Vol. 1, p. 254)

Lusk, John B. (1783-1812), served as a Private in Capt. Samuel Lane's Co., 14th U.S. Infantry, enlisted 14 Jun 1812 for 5 years in Hagerstown, MD at the age of

29, 6' 1" tall, born in Pennsylvania and was killed in camp on 27 Nov 1812 (Johnson and Christou, pp. 230-231)

Lutz, Joseph, served as a Corporal in Capt. Nathan Towson's Co., 2nd U.S. Artillery, enlisted 31 May 1812 in Baltimore at the age of 20, 5' 7¼" tall, born in Baltimore; wounded in the elbow at Chippewa, Upper Canada on 5 Jul 1814 and discharged at Baltimore on 1 May 1815 (Johnson and Christou, p. 231)

Lynch, Elijah, served as a Private in Capt. Robert Kent's Co., 14th U.S. Infantry, enlisted 12 Aug 1812, was wounded in the hand in action on 11 Nov 1813 and discharged at Burlington, VT on 6 Apr 1814 (Johnson and Christou, p. 231)

Lynch, John, served as a Captain in the 11th Regiment, Dorchester Co. Militia, in 1814 and was reported as unable to serve on 16 Apr 1813 "in consequence of his indisposition," but returned to service on 17 Apr 1813 (Wright Vol. 1, p. 66)

Lynch, John, served as a 2nd Lieutenant in the 14th U.S. Infantry and was born in Maryland, commissioned an Ensign on 9 Oct 1812, promoted to 3rd Lieutenant on 13 Mar 1813, promoted to 2nd Lieutenant on 15 Aug 1813 and was killed in the Battle of Chrystler's Field, Upper Canada on 11 Nov 1813 (Johnson and Christou, p. 231; Marine p. 361)

Lynch, John, served as a Private in the 14th U.S. Infantry and was captured. Prisoner of War #3833 at Halifax, NS, interned 6 Jun 1813 and was discharged for exchange on 3 Feb 1814 (Johnson and Christou, p. 231; Baker Vol. 1, p. 245)

Lynch, Thomas, served as a Seaman, born in Maryland, and was captured at sea. How Taken: Gave himself up off HM Frigate *Orpheus* and sent to England. Prison Depot: Portsmouth, Prisoner of War #1153. Date Received: 7 Oct 1813. Age 38. From what ship: HM Frigate *Spartan*. Discharged on 17 Oct 1813 and sent to Chatham on HMT *Malabar No. 352*. Prison Depot: Chatham, Prisoner of War #2400. Date Received: 21 Oct 1813 on HMT *Malabar*. Escaped on 10 Jun 1814 from HM Prison Ship *CrownPrince*. (Johnson's Database, 2019)

Lynch, William, served as a Seaman and was born in Maryland. Age: 21. Prison Depot: Plymouth 1, Prisoner of War #97. Captured by HM Brig *Rover*. When Taken: 21 Oct 1812. Where Taken: off Bordeaux, France. Prize Name: *Experiment*. Ship Type: Merchant Vessel. Date Received: 25 Dec 1812. From what ship: HMS *Northumberland*. Discharged and sent to Portsmouth on 29 Dec 1812 on HMS *Northumberland*. Prison Depot: Portsmouth, Prisoner of War #351. Date Received: 31 Dec 1812. From what ship: HM Ship-of-the-Line *Northumberland*. Discharged on 4 Mar 1813 and sent to Chatham on HMS *Queen*. Prison Depot: Chatham, Prisoner of War #928. Date Received: 10 Mar 1813. From what ship: HMS *Tigress*. Discharged on 8 Jun 1813 and released to the Cartel *Rodrigo*. (Johnson's Database, 2019)

Lynch, William, served as a Seaman and was born in Maryland. Age: 23. Prison Depot: Dartmoor, Prisoner of War #4857. Captured by HM Brig *Hardy*. When Taken: 28 Mar 1814. Where Taken: West Indies. Prize Name: *Fairy*. Ship Type: Privateer. Date Received: 9 Oct 1814. From what ship: HMT *Freya* from Halifax, NS. Discharged on 21 Jun 1815. (Johnson's Database, 2019)

Lynch, William, served as a Private in Capt. Richard Bell's Co., 5th U.S. Infantry, enlisted 26 Feb 1813 for 5 years in Baltimore at the age of 40, 5' 10" tall, born in Ireland, discharged at Plattsburgh, NY on 5 Jul 1815 on Surgeon's Certificate and placed on pension rolls on 4 Jan 1816 (Johnson and Christou, p. 232)

Lyons, Jonathan (1771-1815), served as a Private in 39th U.S. Infantry (company not stated), enlisted 15 Feb 1815 at the age of 44, 5' 7" tall, born in Queen Anne's Co., and died on 17 Apr 1815; bounty land issued to his son Richard Lyons and other heirs at law (BLW# 850-320-14; Johnson and Christou, p. 232)

Lyons, Peter, served as a Seaman and was born in Baltimore. Age: 37. Prison Depot: Plymouth 1, Prisoner of War #320. Captured by HM Frigate *Dryad*. When Taken: 8 Jan 1813. Where Taken: off Bordeaux, France. Prize Name: *Porcupine*. Ship Type: Merchant Vessel. Date Received: 21 Jan 1813. From what ship: HMS *Abercrombie*. Discharged and sent to Chatham on 29 Mar 1813 on HMS *Braham*. Prison Depot: Chatham, Prisoner of War #1402. Received: 5 Apr 1813 from Plymouth on HMS *Dwarf*. Discharged on 24 Jul 1813 and released to the Cartel *Hoffning*. (Johnson's Database, 2019)

M

Ma----n(?), William, served as a Private in Capt. Bedington Hands' Co., 21st Regiment, Kent Co. Militia, in 1813 and it was reported he "has certificate of inability" on the muster roll dated 13 Apr – 13 May 1813 (Wright Vol. 1, p. 12)

Maas, Andrew, served as a Private in Capt. William Roney's Co., 39th Regiment, Baltimore Militia, from 19 Aug 1814 and was reported "missing since 12 Sep" 1814, allegedly killed at North Point, but not reported as such on the rolls; yet, his name is on the Baltimore Battle Monument. (Wright Vol. 2, p. 24, spelled his name Mass; NARA; CMSR; *Baltimore American*, 12 Jun 1819, stated he was killed in defending Baltimore from the British attack)

Mack, David (1787-1814), served as a Private in Capt. Joseph Marshall's Co., 14th U.S. Infantry, enlisted 21 Sep 1814, age 27, 5' 2" tall, born in Pennsylvania and died at Batavia, NY on 29 Nov 1814 (Johnson and Christou, p. 232)

Mackay, Joseph or James (African American), served as a Seaman and was born in Baltimore. Age: 21. Prison Depot: Dartmoor, Prisoner of War #5027. Captured by HM Brig *Wasp*. When Taken: 27 Jul 1814. Where Taken: Georges Bank. Prize Name: HM Schooner *Landrail*, prize of the Privateer *Syren*. Home Port:

Baltimore. Ship Type: Privateer. Date Received: 28 Oct 1814. From what ship: HMT *Alkbar* from Halifax, NS. Discharged on 21 Jun 1815. (Johnson's Database, 2019)

Mackey, Benjamin, served as a Private in Capt. John Foster's Co., 22nd U.S. Infantry, enlisted 8 Jul 1813 for 5 years in Uniontown, PA at the age of 28, 5' 8" tall, born in Baltimore and discharged at Sackett's Harbor, NY on 8 Jul 1815, reported wounded (Johnson and Christou, p. 233)

Maccubbin, Nicholas Zachariah (c1785-1813), served as a Private in Capt. Jonathan Pinkney's Artillery Co. attached to the 8th Brigade, for 45 days between 9 Apr and 29 May 1813, was a Private in Capt. Joseph Sands' Co., 22nd Regiment, Anne Arundel Co. Militia, for 5 days between 11 May and 29 May 1813 and was stationed at Annapolis for 26 days between 2 Aug and 31 Aug 1813. He died **on** 25 Dec 1813 in Annapolis, cause was not stated. His widow Catherine "Kitty" Maccubbin, age 70, in 1855, stated her maiden name was Welch and she married Nicholas in Annapolis in 1806 by Rev. Wyatt. (Wright Vol. 4, pp. 13, 31, 32, 105; BLW# 55-160-12; Anne Arundel Co. records indicate Nicholas Z. Maccubbin and Kitty Welch obtained a license on 8 Apr 1806)

Mackubin, Richard Creagh (1795-1814), served as a Private in Capt. Jonathan Pinkney's Artillery Co., 2nd Regiment, attached to the 8th Brigade, in 1813 and served as a Private in Ensign Brewer's Detachment in the 36th Regiment at Bladensburg in 1814; he was wounded and with a comrade in arms crossed the Potomac River and they made their way to the Lee farm *Arlington* where he died on 25 Aug 1814 and was buried there. The bodies of other soldiers from Maryland who were killed in 1814 were brought to Arlington Cemetery decades later and reburied there, so it appears that they took Mackubin's casket and reburied it along with those Marylanders in rows together in Section 13. His original flat gravestone is inscribed: To the Memory / of / Richard C. Mackubin / A Volunteer from Annapolis / (His Native City) / in Maryland / In the defense / of his Country's Capitol / He fell at the Battle / of Bladensburgh / on the 24th Aug. 1814 / in the twentieth year of his age. An upright military marker is inscribed: "8213. R. C. Mackubin. U. S. Soldier. War of 1812." (Wright Vol. 4, pp. 13, 40; Marine p. 368; www.findagrave.com/photos/2015)

Madden, John (African American), served as a Seaman and was born in Talbot Co., MD. Age: 26. Prison Depot: Plymouth 2, Prisoner of War #275. Captured by HM Brig *Onyx* on 25 Dec 1814. Where Taken: at sea. Prize Name: *Netterville*. Ship Type: Merchant Vessel. Received: 2 Mar 1815. From what ship: HMS Dannemark. Discharged on 3 Mar 1815 and sent to Dartmoor. Prison Depot: Dartmoor, Prisoner of War #6399. Received: 3 Mar 1815. From what ship: HMT *Ganges* from Plymouth. Discharged on 11 Jul 1815. (Johnson's Database, 2019)

Maddox, Gilbert, served as a Private in Capt. Thomas Burgess' Co., 43rd Regiment, Charles Co. Militia, from 1 Aug to 5 Aug 1813 at Port Tobacco and for 11 days between 4 Jul and 15 Jul 1814 in Capt. Gustavus Brown's Co. On 18 Feb 1851 Violetta Shannon, age 60, widow of Gilbert Maddox, stated she married Gilbert Maddox on 22 Mar 1814 and he died about 1815; she married James Shannon on 16 Jul 1816. (Wright Vol. 5, pp. 38, 40, 77; BLW# 55-160-93077)

Magaurin, Henry, served as a Private in Capt. George Steever's Co., 27th Regt., Baltimore Militia, from 19 Aug and was wounded on 12 Sep 1814 at North Point (Wright Vol. 2, p. 15) In Baltimore on 6 Mar 1829 Henry Magauran (sic), former private in Capt. Steeve's (sic) Co., 27th Regt., MD Militia, in the late war when disabled, and a resident of Baltimore for 20 years and previously of Pennsylvania, collected his own $24.00 pension due from 4 Sep 1828 to 4 Mar 1829 (Pierce, p. 124)

Magee, Robert, served as a Private in Capt. David Cummings' Co., 14th U.S. Infantry, enlisted 3 Jun 1812 and was captured at Beaver Dams, Upper Canada on 24 Jun 1813. Prisoner of War #4081 at Halifax, NS, interned 24 Jun 1813 and discharged on 9 Nov 1813 and sent to England per order of Sir. J. B. Warren (Johnson and Christou, p. 234; Baker Vol. 1, p. 257)

Magness, William, served as a Private in Capt. Henry Grindage's Co., 14th U.S. Infantry, enlisted 1 Jul 1813 and died on 23 Feb 1814; bounty land issued to his sister Mary Ann Clark (BLW# 17407-160-12; Johnson and Christou, p. 234)

Magnor, John, served as a Sergeant in Capt. Ezekiel F. Chambers Co., 21st Regt., Kent County Militia, from 19 Aug 1814 and was wounded at Caulk's Field on 31 Aug 1814. "Sergeant John Magnor and Corporal Philip Crane who are both returned in this roll in pursuance to the directions of the commander of the regiment were wounded in an action with the enemy in August last and have not been able to shoulder a musket since that period not being present in camp no rations were drawn for them of course." John Magnor, sergt. Slightly in the thigh. (Baltimpre Patriot 9/22/1814, Wright Vol. 1, pp. 1, 12, 15, 17, 19, 21, 24; Marine pp. 120, 122, 370)

Magruder, B. H., served as a Private in Capt. James K. Stapleton's Co., 39th Regiment, Baltimore Militia, and reported as "sick in quarters with syphilis" on the muster roll dated 19 Aug – 18 Nov 1814 (Wright Vol. 2, p. 26)

Magruder, Carlton, served as a Private in Capt. Robert T. Dade's Co., Cramer's Regt., Montgomery Co., and reported as "sick absent 30 days" on the muster roll dated 3 Aug – 10 Nov 1814 (Wright Vol. 7, p. 8, spelled his name McGruder)

Magruder, Dennis F., served as a Private in Capt. David Warfield's Co., 5th Regiment, Baltimore United Volunteers, and was wounded at Bladensburg on 24 Aug 1814 (Marine p. 370)

Mahu, Pedro Alexander, served as a Private from Harford Co. (company and enlistment date were not stated), age 36, was a Prisoner of War at Dartmoor in Devon, England for 241 days from 31 Oct 1814 to 29 Jun 1815 ("Harford County in the War of 1812," by Christopher T. George, *Harford Historical Bulletin* No. 76, Spring 1998, p. 21 footnote); see Pedro Alexander, q.v.

Major (Mager), Lawrence, served as a Private in Capt. William Durbin's Co., Frederick Co. Militia, from 24 Aug 1814, marched off for Baltimore and was discharged for inability, but date was not stated (Mallick and Wright, p. 353)

Malone, Caleb, served as a Private in the 14th U.S. Infantry, enlisted 17 Aug 1813 for 5 years and died in Brownsville, NY on 2 Feb 1815; bounty land issued to widow Susanna Malone (BLW# 17845-160-50; Johnson and Christou, p. 235)

Malone, John, served as a Private in Capt. Frank Hampton's Co., 24th U.S. Inf., enlisted 29 Jun 1813 for 5 years, age 35, 5' 10" tall, born in Baltimore, and was captured at Fort Niagara, NY on 19 Dec 1813. Prisoner of War at Quebec, was exchanged on 11 May 1814 and discharged from the service on 28 Jun 1818 (Johnson and Christou, p. 235; Johnson's Quebec book, p. 95, did not list him)

Man, George, served as a Private in the U.S. Army (company and enlistment date not stated) and died on 9 Jul 1813 (*Baltimore American*, 23 Jul 1813)

Manahan, David, served as a Private in Capt. Samuel Lane's Co., 14th U.S. Inf. enlisted 21 May 1812 at Westminster, MD at the age of 25, 5' 4½" tall, born in Maryland and was captured at Beaver Dams, Upper Canada on 24 Jun 1813. Prisoner of War #4094 at Halifax, NS, interned 24 Jun 1813, discharged 9 Nov 1813 and sent to England. Prison Depot: Chatham, Prisoner of War #3079. Date Received: 7 Jan 1814 from Halifax. Age 28 (sic). Born in Maryland. Discharged on 10 Oct 1814 and sent to U.S. on the Cartel *St. Philip*. Discharged from the service on 30 Apr 1815 (Johnson and Christou, p. 235; Baker Vol. 1, p. 258; Johnson's Database, 2019, misspelled his name as Manaham)

Manifold William, served as a Private in Capt. John Smithson's Co., 42nd Regt., Harford Co. Militia, from 12 Oct 1814 and was discharged "for conscience sake" on 21 Oct 1814 (Wright Vol. 2, p. 19)

Manley, Randolph (1787-1814), served as a Seaman and was born in Maryland. Age: 26. Prison Depot: Portsmouth, Prisoner of War #1123. Captured by HM Brig *Rebuff*. When Taken: 12 May 1813. Where Taken: off Cape St. Vincent, Portugal. Prize Name: *Sampson*. Ship Type: Merchant Vessel. Date Received: 5 Oct 1813 from HM Ship-of-the-Line *Achille*. Discharged on 17 Oct 1813 and sent to

Chatham on HMT *Malabar No. 352*. Prison Depot: Chatham, Prisoner of War #2420. Died on 25 May 1814 from fever. (Johnson's Database, 2019)

Manning, Ignatius, served as a Private in Capt. James Walker's Co., 45th Regt., St. Mary's Co. Militia, for 4 days between 14 Jul and 26 Jul 1813 and was furloughed sick (Wright Vol. 5, p. 29)

Manning, Jesse, served as a Private in Capt. William Murray's Co., 36th Regt., Baltimore Co., from 25 Aug 1814, served at Hampstead Hill in Baltimore and was reported "sick-absent since Sep 15" 1814 (Wright, Vol. 2, p. 63)

Manning, Samuel (1783-1814), served as a Private in Capt. Reuben Gilder's Co., 14th U.S. Infantry, enlisted 9 Aug 1813 at age 25, 5'7" tall, born in Baltimore, wounded at Lyon's Creek, Upper Canada on 19 Oct 1814 and died at Buffalo, NY on 9 Nov 1814 (BLW# 15618-160-12; Johnson and Christou, pp. 235-236)

Mansfield, John, served as a Private in Capt. John Stanard's Co., 20th U.S. Inf., enlisted 12 Aug 1812 by Capt. John Macrae for 5 years at the age of 19, 5' 4½" tall, born in Frederick Co., "absent sick at Williamsville," NY in May 1813, and was discharged at Greenbush, NY on 14 Oct 1813 on a Surgeon's Certificate as unfit for duty (Mallick and Wright, p. 198; Johnson and Christou, p. 236)

Manson, Henry (1786-1832), served as a Seaman under Sailing Master Simmones Bunbury, U.S. Sea Fencibles, enlisted 28 Dec 1813 at age 27, 5' 6½" tall, born in Denmark and discharged on 22 Dec 1814; he was placed on the pension rolls on 1 Dec 1820 and died on 27 Nov 1832 (Johnson and Christou, p. 236). In Baltimore on 19 May 1821 Henry Manson, former private in Capt. Bunbury's Co., Corps of Sea Fencibles, in the late war, and a life-long resident of Baltimore except when following his occupation of seaman, collected his own $26.83 pension due from 14 Aug 1820 to 4 Mar 1821. (Pierce, p. 126)

Manville, Joshua (1786-1814), served as a Private in Capt. Reuben Gilder's Co. of the 14th U.S. Infantry, enlisted 21 Dec 1812 at the age of 26, born in South America, re-enlisted on 27 Feb 1814 for the war and died at Plattsburgh, NY on 28 May 1814 (Johnson and Christou, p. 236)

March, William (1794-1814), served as a Private in 14th U.S. Infantry (company not stated) and was captured at Beaver Dams, Upper Canada on 26 Jun 1813. Born in Maryland. Age: 19. Prison Depot: Halifax, NS, Prisoner of War #3924. Died 7 Jan 1814 from consumption (tuberculosis). (Johnson's Database, 2019; Baker, Vol. 1, p. 259)

Maria, John, from the *Scorpion*, served as an Ordinary Seaman with the U.S. Chesapeake Flotilla, entered service on 11 Jan 1813 and was killed on2 4 Aug 1814 at the Battle of Bladensburg (Shomette, p. 397)

Marion, John (African American), served as a Seaman and was born in Baltimore. Age: 25. Prison Depot: Dartmoor, Prisoner of War #6067. Captured by HM Brig *Recruit*. When Taken: 6 Apr 1814. Where Taken: Lat. 29N Long. 76W. Prize Name: *Chasseur*. Ship Type: Privateer. Received: 28 Dec 1814. From what ship: HMT *Penelope*. Discharged 3 Jul 1815. (Johnson's Database, 2019)

Marlow, Thomas (1792-181), served as a Sergeant in Capt. Joseph Marshall's Co., 14th U.S. Infantry, enlisted 23 Mar 1814 at Upper Marlboro, MD at the age of 22, 5' 9" tall, born in Prince George's Co., MD and died at Canandaigua, NY on 15 Jan 1815 from diarrhea; bounty land issued to his sister Martha Ann Early and other heirs at law (BLW# 24113-160-12; Johnson and Christou, p. 237)

Marriott, Elisha (c1787-1814), served as 3rd Sergeant, Capt. Christian Adreon's Co., 5th Regiment, Baltimore Militia, from 19 Aug 1814 and died 24 Aug 1814 at Bladensburg [not in Baltimore]. His name is on the Baltimore Battle Monument. Warrant No. 17614 sent 21 May 1852. On 8 Nov 1851 Ann Jones, aged 56 years, a resident of Baltimore City, declares she is the widow of Elisha Marriott, deceased, who was a 3rd Sergeant of Capt. Christopher Adreon's Co. in 5th Regt. commanded by Lt. Col. Joseph Sterett, being Maryland Militia infantry, and her husband volunteered on the 19th of August 1814 for the term of said war and continued in actual service until 24th day of August 1814 and was engaged in the battle with said British forces at Bladensburg and during said action was shot and killed as will appear by the muster rolls of said Co. She has no certificate of said facts they being filed in the pension office. She further states that she was married to Elisha Marriott on 23rd day of Jan 1814 by Rev. Dr. G. Roberts, a clergyman, her name before said marriage was Ann Tool and her said husband died as above stated at Bladensburg on the sd. 24th of August 1814. She has no cert of marriage nor can she obtain any record evidence from court nor is there any private family record to establish said marriage. She has to refer to the evidence herewith submitted. She also states that she was again married to Malon Jones in the City of Baltimore on the 4th day of Nov 1817 by Stephen Russell, a clergyman, that said Malon Jones was a private in a Co. commanded by Capt. George Steevers attached to the 27th Regiment M.M. Commanded by Lt. Col. Kennedy Long and volunteered at Baltimore City on the 19th August 1814 for the term of said war and continued in actual service until 18th day of Nov 1814 and was honorably discharged at Baltimore City. Her last husband Malon Jones became very dissipated and left her and the City of Baltimore on or about 6th day of February 1842 and she has not heard from him directly or indirectly but one since he left her by an 27 Dec 1842 at which time she was informed that the said Malon Jones was dead and that she has been left by said Jones without any means of support and has been compelled to support herself and in all maters and things to as a widow and that she knows no better or does consider herself a widow and that she does believe that he is dead as above reported and she is informed by the laws of Maryland he being absent over 7 years she having heard nothing from him in said time. She makes this declaration to obtain bounty land she is entitled to. Signed Ann Jones formerly Ann Marriott. On Nov 8 1851 Araminta Euvalt and Rebecca Hess respectable inhabitants of said City declare that they knew the said Elisha Marriott and Ann Marriott or Ann Jones and they lived as husband and wife and that the said Malon Jones left her and died, they having known her for 40 years past and for more than 8 years past. (NARA; CMSR; Wright Vol. 2, p. 3; Marine, p. 372, did not state he was wounded or killed; BLW# 115755)

Marriott, James H., served as a Private in Capt. Christian Adreon's Co., 5th Regiment, Baltimore Militia, from 19 Aug 1814 and died from wounds received at Patapsco Neck. Name is on the Baltimore Battle Monument. (NARA; CMSR; Wright Vol. 2, p. 3; Marine, p. 372; *Baltimore American*, 12 Jun 1819) Dr. James H. McCulloh, Jr. wrote this note soon after the battle to the British commander: "In consequence of the humanity shown the following American prisoners of war, I do promise upon honor that they shall not directly or indirectly serve against the British until regularly exchanged." (Marine, p. 171)

Marriott, William (1781-1843), served as a Captain of a company under Gen. Winder, volunteered in Annapolis in 1813, was wounded in service and drew a pension for years before his death in Knox Co., OH on 18 Jul 1843. He was referred to as Capt. William Marriott, of Thomas, and married Edith Waters on 29 Apr 1804 in Prince George's Co., MD by Rev. Scott. In 1851 Edith Marriott, age 66, widow, was living in Claibourn Twp., Union Co., OH and she was still living there in 1855, age 70. (Wright Vol. 4, pp. 15, 106; BLW# 55-rej-84059)

Marsh, Dennis, served as a Private in Capt. David Warfield's Co., 5th Regiment, Baltimore United Volunteers, from 19 Aug 1814, was wounded on 12 Sep 1814 at the Battle of North Point and was discharged on 22 Oct 1814 (Marine pp. 172, 372; Wright Vol. 2, p. 8, did not mention that he had been wounded)

Marsh, Henry, served as a Private in Capt. James Dorman's Co., 5th U.S. Inf., enlisted 18 May 1812 at Alexandria, DC at the age of 21, 5' 10¾" tall, born in Baltimore and discharged at Greenbush, NY on 30 May 1812 on a Surgeon's Certificate for frost bite on his right leg (Johnson and Christou, p. 236)

Marshall, Joseph, served as Captain of his own company in 14th U. S. Infantry; commissioned 1st Lieutenant on 12 Mar 1812, promoted to Captain on 15 Aug 1813 and was captured. Prisoner of War #4200 at Dartmouth, England, age 38, paroled 1 Sep 1813, discharged on 31 May 1814 and discharged from service on 15 Jun 1815; placed on pension roll on 11 May 1830 (Johnson and Christou, p.

237; *American Prisoners of War Paroled at Dartmouth, Halifax, Jamaica and Odiham during the War of 1812*, by Eric Eugene Johnson, p. 37)

Marshall, Leonard, served as a Private in Capt. Andrew Slicer's Co., 32nd Regt., Anne Arundel Co. Militia, joined 22 Aug 1814 and listed as dead (no date or cause given) on muster roll dated 21 Aug – 17 Oct 1814 (Wright Vol. 4, p. 44)

Marshall, Levi, served as a Seaman and was born in Maryland. Age: 39. Prison Depot: Chatham, Prisoner of War #1783. How Taken: Gave himself up off St. Vincent, Portugal. When Taken: May 1813. Date Received: 1 Jul 1813. From what ship: HMS *Raisonable*. Discharged on 22 Oct 1814 and released to HMS *Argonaut*. (Johnson's Database, 2019)

Marshall, Levy, served as a Seaman and was born in Baltimore. Age: 29. Prison Depot: Dartmoor, Prisoner of War #3546. Captured by HM Frigate *Piqua*. When Taken: 26 Apr 1814. Where Taken: near Mona Passage, West Indies. Prize Name: *Hawk*. Home Port: Wilmington. Ship Type: Privateer. Date Received: 30 Sep 1814. From what ship: HMT *Sybella*. Discharged on 4 Jun 1815. (Johnson's Database, 2019)

Martin, ----, served as a "Sea Captain" with Comm. Barney and was wounded on 24 Aug 1814 "from the seat of war" on the field of battle at Bladensburg, was admitted to the Naval Hospital in Washington, DC as Patient No. 32 and was discharged on 26 Sep 1814 and sent to Baltimore (Sharp's Database, 2018)

Martin, Anthony (c1790-1814), served as a Private in Capt. John Fonsten's Co., Frederick Co. Militia, from 2 Sep 1814, marched to Baltimore, engaged in the defense of the city on 12 Sep 1814, was "sick absent" on 29 Sep 1814 and died in Baltimore. Anthony Martin married Robina Addlesperger or Ensperger on 4 or 24 Feb 1810 in Westminster, MD. (Wright Vol. 8, p. 364; Mallick and Wright, p. 200; BLW# 55-120-37692)

Martin, Isaac, served as a Boy onboard a ship and was born in Baltimore. Age: 16. Prison Depot: Plymouth 1, Prisoner of War #1483. Captured by HM Frigate *Leonidas*. When Taken: 23 May 1813. Where Taken: off Cape Clear, Ireland. Prize Name: *Paul Jones*. Home Port: New York. Ship Type: Privateer. Received: 26 May 1813. From what ship: HMS *Leonidas*. Discharged on 30 Jun 1813 and sent to Stapleton. Prison Depot: Stapleton, Prisoner of War #60. Received: 8 Jul 1813 from Plymouth. Discharged on 13 Jun 1814 and sent to Dartmoor. Age: 16. Prison Depot: Dartmoor, Prisoner of War #1361. Received on 19 Jun 1814 from Stapleton. Discharged on 28 Apr 1815. (Johnson's Database, 2019)

Martin, J. B., served as a Surgeon (company not stated) and was captured at the Battle of Bladensburg on 24 Aug 1814 (Marine, p. 174)

Martin, James H., served as a Sailing Master on a barge under the command of Commodore Joshua Barney and was severely wounded during the Battle of Bladensburg on 24 Aug 1814 (Shomette, p. 325). James H. Martin, Acting Sailing Master, USN, entered the Chesapeake Bay Flotilla on 5 Jul 1814. Commodore Joshua Barney stated in a letter to William Jones, Secretary of the Navy, on 29 Aug 1814 that Sailing Master Martin was wounded in action on 24 Aug 1814 at Bladensburg, MD. He was admitted to the Naval Hospital in Washington, DC as Patient No. 25 on 26 Aug 1814, was discharged on 4 Jan 1815 and sent to Baltimore; he resigned on 15 Apr 1815. (Sharp's Database, 2018)

Martin, John, served as a Private in Capt. Samuel Sterett's Co., 5th Regiment, Baltimore Militia, from 19 Aug 1814 and was wounded at North Point on 12 Sep 1814 (Wright Vol. 2, p. 6)

Martin, Jonathan, served as a Seaman and was born in Baltimore. Age: 37. Prison Depot: Portsmouth, Prisoner of War #28. Captured by HM Frigate *Barbadoes*. When Taken: 22 Aug 1812. Where Taken: off Savannah, GA. Prize Name: U.S.R.M. Cutter *James Madison*. Ship Type: Warship. Date Received: 12 Oct 1812 San Antonio. From what ship: HM Ship-of-the-Line *Polyphemus*. Discharged on 19 Feb 1813 and sent to Chatham on HMS *Ulysses*. Prison Depot: Chatham, Prisoner of War #667. Date Received: 24 Feb 1813 on HMS *Ulysses*. Discharged on 10 May 1813 and released to the Cartel *Admittance*. (Johnson's Database, 2019)

Martin, Philip, served as a Seaman and was born in Baltimore. Age: 25. Prison Depot: Dartmoor, Prisoner of War #3523. Captured by HM Ship-of-the-Line *Conquestador*. When Taken: 3 Aug 1814. Where Taken: off Grand Banks. Prize Name: *Sabine*. Prize. Ship Type: Privateer. Date Received: 28 Sep 1814. From what ship: HMT *Salvador del Mundo*. Discharged on 4 Jun 1815. (Johnson's Database, 2019)

Martin, William (1777-1813), served as a Private in Capt. Samuel Raisin's Co., 36th U.S. Infantry, enlisted on 17 May 1813 in Cambridge, MD at the age of 36, 5' 6½" tall, born in Dorchester Co., MD and died at Camp Cold Spring on 15 Oct 1813 (Johnson and Christou, p. 239)

Martin, William, served as a Private in Capt. David Cummings' Co., 14th U.S. Infantry, enlisted for 5 years (date was not given), age 25, 5' 8" tall, born in Baltimore and was captured at Beaver Dams, Upper Canada on 24 Jun 1813. Prisoner of War #4636 at Halifax, NS, interned 15 Nov 1813, discharged 19 Nov 1813 and sent to England. Prison Depot: Chatham, Prisoner of War #3164. Date Received: 7 Jan 1814 from Halifax. Age 21 (sic), Born in Baltimore. Discharged on 10 Oct 1814 and sent to U.S. on the Cartel *St. Philip*. Discharged from the service at Fort Hawkins, GA on 9 Apr 1817. (Johnson and Christou, p. 239; Baker Vol. 1, p. 262; BLW# 12890-160-12; Johnson's Database, 2019)

Martin, William, served as a Private in Capt. John Kerlinger's Co. in Lt. Col. William Nace's Regiment, Baltimore County Militia, from 19 Aug 1813 and was reported "sick absent," but the date was not stated (Information from original 1813 roster; Wright Vol. 2, p. 41, did not mention being "sick absent")

Mason, Ira, served as a Private in the 14th U.S. Infantry and was captured. Prisoner of War #4038 at Halifax, interned 24 Jun 1813 and died there on 24 Oct 1813 of smallpox (Johnson and Christou, p. 239; Baker, Vol. 1, p. 263)

Mason, Richard (1777-1815), served as a Private in Capt. William Littlejohn's Co., 2nd U.S. Light Dragoons, U.S. Army, enlisted 9 Sep 1813 at Head of Elk, MD [Cecil County] at the age of 36, 5' 6½" tall, born in Maryland and died on 3 Apr 1815 (Johnson and Christou, p. 239)

Mason, William, served as a Prize Master and was born in Baltimore. Age: 25. Prison Depot: Dartmoor, Prisoner of War #2523. Captured by HM Frigate *Cyane*. When Taken: 22 May 1814. Where Taken: off Newfoundland. Prize Name: *Aeolus*, prize of the Privateer *Pike*. Ship Type: Privateer. Date Received: 16 Aug 1814. From what ship: HMT *Queen* from Halifax, NS. Discharged on 3 May 1815. (Johnson's Database, 2019)

Mass, Andrew, see Andrew Maas, q.v.

Massington, Charles, served as a Private in a Marine Battery under Sailing Master Rodman from 10 Oct 1813, was on board on 7 Apr 1814 and was killed at Fort McHenry on 13 Sep 1814 (Shomette, p. 365; Marine pp. 173, 379, spelled his name Messenger)

Matire(?), John, served as a Private in Capt. George Shryock's Co., Hagerstown, Washington Co. Militia, from 23 Jul 1814, sick on furlough on 1 Oct and was discharged by a Surgeon on 8 Dec 1814 at Annapolis (Wright Vol. 9, p. 8)

Matney, George, served as a Private in Capt. Andrew Madison's Co., 12th U.S. Infantry, enlisted 11 Sep 1812 by Lt. Harrison for 5 years, age 20, 5' 5½" tall, dark eyes, dark hair, dark complexion, born in Allegany Co., MD and left sick at Plattsburgh, NY on 29 Aug 1814. Discharged at Fort Erie, Upper Canada on 17 Jun 1815 on a Surgeon's Certificate for epilepsy (Johnson and Christou, p. 240; Wright Vol. 10, p. 10, stated he was discharged at Buffalo, NY on 9 Jun 1815)

Matthews, Cornelius, served as a Seaman and was born in Baltimore. Age: 25. Prison Depot: Chatham, Prisoner of War #3866. Captured by HM Brig *Thistle*. When Taken: 24 Feb 1813. Where Taken: off St. Bartholomew, West Indies. Prize Name: *Harriett*. Prize. Ship Type: Privateer. Date Received: 25 Aug 1814 from

London. Discharged on 22 Oct 1814 and sent to Dartmoor on HMS *Leyden*. Prison Depot: Dartmoor, Prisoner of War #5381. Date Received: 31 Oct 1814. From what ship: HMT *Leyden* from Chatham. Discharged and released on 1 Jul 1815. (Johnson's Database, 2019)

Matthews, Leonard, served as a }Supercargo" and was born in Maryland. Age: 28. Prison Depot: Plymouth 1, Prisoner of War #2316. Captured by HM Brig *Pelican*. When Taken: 13 Jan 1814. Where Taken: at sea. Prize Name: *Siro*. Home Port: Baltimore. Ship Type: Letter of Marque. Date Received: 25 Jan 1814. From what ship: HMS *Pelican*. Discharged on 25 Jan 1814 and sent to Ashburton on parole. (Johnson's Database, 2019)

Mattock, Joseph, served as a Private in Capt. David Cummings' Co., 14th U.S. Infantry, enlisted on 12 Jul 1812 when still a minor, without the consent of his parents or guardians, and was captured at Beaver Dams, Upper Canada on 24 Jun 1813. Prisoner of War #3793 at Halifax, NS, interned on 27 Aug 1813 and was discharged on 9 Nov 1813 and sent to England on HMS *Success* (Johnson and Christou, p. 240; Baker Vol. 1, p. 265, spelled his name Mattack)

Mawe, Michael, served as a Private (company not stated) and was captured at the Battle of Bladensburg on 24 Aug 1814 (Marine, p. 174)

Maxwell, John G. (1788-1815), served as a Private in Capt. Matthew Magee's Co., 4th U.S. Rifles, enlisted 5 May 1814 at age 26, 5' 10" tall, born in Baltimore and died 29 Mar 1815; bounty land issued to his sister Eliza Hustead and other heirs at law (BLW# 24858-160-12; Johnson and Christou, p. 241)

Maxwell, Robert, served as a Private in Capt. David Cummings' Co., 14th U.S. Infantry, enlisted on 11 Feb 1813 for 5 years at the age of 29, 5' tall, born in Ireland and was later captured. Prisoner of War #4163 at Halifax, interned 24 Jun 1813, discharged on 27 Aug 1813 and sent to England, later released and was discharged from the service at Montgomery, AL on 13 Feb 1818 (Johnson and Christou, p. 241; Baker Vol. 1, p.265)

Maxwell, William F. (1784-1813), served as a Private under Lt. Col. George Armistead in the 1st U.S. Artillery, enlisted 27 Apr 1812 at Fort McHenry at the age of 28, 5'10" tall, born in Ireland and died at Fort Columbus, NY on 1 Apr 1813 (Johnson and Christou, p. 241)

Maybe, Jacob, served as a Private in the 14th U.S. Infantry (company not stated) and was captured, probably at Beaver Dams, Upper Canada. Prisoner of War #4036 at Halifax, NS, interned 24 Jun 1813 and was discharged for exchange on 3 Feb 1814 (Johnson and Christou, p. 241; Baker Vol. 1, p. 265)

McAllen, Dennis, from the *Ontario*, served as a Seaman of the U.S. Chesapeake Flotilla, entered service on 15 Mar 1814, was on board on 7 Apr 1814 and died on 11 Oct 1814 (Shomette, p. 400)

McBride, James, served as a Seaman and was born in Baltimore. Age: 27. Prison Depot: Plymouth 1, Prisoner of War #1313. How Taken: Gave himself up off HM Ship-of-the-Line *Clarence*. Date Received: 11 May 1813. From what ship: HMS *Clarence*. Discharged on 8 Jul 1813 and sent to Chatham on HM Tender *Neptune*. Prison Depot: Chatham, Prisoner of War #2000. Date Received: 15 Jul 1813 from Plymouth. Discharged on 17 Jun 1814 and sent to Dartmoor on HMS *Pincher*. Prison Depot: Dartmoor, Prisoner of War #1841. Date Received: 21 Jul 1814. From what ship: HMT *Redbeard* & HMT *Pincher* from Chatham. Discharged on 2 May 1815. (Johnson's Database, 2019)

McCallom, ----, served as a Marine and was taken from the barracks to the Naval Hospital in Washington, DC and admitted as Patient No. 55 on 4 Jul 1814 and discharged on 31 Dec 1814 unfit for military duty (Sharp's Database, 2018)

McCarrier, Stephen, served as a Private in Capt. Richard Arell's Co., 14th U.S. Infantry, enlisted 13 Sep 1812 at Baltimore, age 28, 5' 10" tall, born in Chester Co., PA. Prisoner of War, date and place of capture not stated, was exchanged on 15 Apr 1814 and discharged at Greenbush, NY on 20 Mar 1815 with loss of two fingers on right hand (Johnson and Christou, p. 243)

McCarthy, David, served as a Seaman on the privateer *Nonsuch* of Baltimore under Capt. Lively and was killed in action on 28 Sep 1812 during a battle with a British schooner off Martinique (*Niles Weekly Register*, 14 Nov 1812; J. Thomas Scharf's *The Chronicles of Baltimore*, Vol. 1, p. 359)

McCarthy, Samuel, served as a Seaman and was born in Baltimore. Age: 18. Prison Depot: Dartmoor, Prisoner of War #6490. Captured by HM Sloop *Dasher*. When Taken: 12 Feb 1814. Where Taken: off coast of U.S. Prize Name: *Louisa*, prize of the Privateer *Expedition*. Ship Type: Privateer. Date Received: 3 Mar 1815. From what ship: HMT *Ganges* from Plymouth. Discharged on 11 Jul 1815. (Johnson's Database, 2019)

McCarty, Charles, served as a Private in Capt. William McIlvane's Co., 14th U.S. Infantry, enlisted 22 May 1812 at Denton, MD at age 24, 5' 10½" tall, born in Caroline Co., MD and was captured on 12 Jun 1813 in Canada. Prisoner of War #5311 at Halifax, NS, Interned 3 Feb 1814 (sic), was discharged for exchange on 3 Feb 1814, exchanged on 15 Apr 1814 and discharged from service on 22 May 1817 (Johnson and Christou, p. 243; Baker Vol. 1, p. 266)

McCarty, J., served as a Marine and was taken from the barracks and admitted to the Naval Hospital in Washington, DC as Patient No. 59 on 8 Jul 1814 (injury or illness was not specified) and was discharged on 11 Jul 1814 and sent to the barracks (Sharp's Database, 2018)

McCarty, William (1789-1813), served as a Private in Capt. Colin Buckner's Co., 5th U.S. Infantry, enlisted 12 May 1813 in Baltimore at the age of 24, 5' 10" tall, born in Harford Co., MD and died on 13 Jul 1813; bounty land issued to his heirs that included James Everit, father of William McCarty, alias John Everit (BLW# 12825-160-12; Johnson and Christou, p. 243)

McCausland, Hugh, served as a Private in Capt. James Dorman's Co., 5th U.S. Infantry, enlisted 5 May 1812 for 5 years in Baltimore, age 34, 5' 6" tall, born in Ireland and was captured at Fort Erie in Nov 1812. Prisoner of War, paroled, and discharged from the service on 4 May 1817 (Johnson and Christou, p. 243)

McClellan, Robert, served as a Seaman with Commodore Barney and was wounded at Upper Marlboro, admitted to the Naval Hospital in Washington, DC as Patient No. 42 on 12 Sep 1814 and was discharged on 14 Oct 1814 and sent to Baltimore (Sharp's Database, 2018)

McClellan (McClelland), William (1771-1814), served as a Private in Capt. David Warfield's Co., 5th Regiment, Baltimore Militia, from 19 Aug 1814 and was killed on 12 Sep 1814 at North Point. His name is on the Baltimore Battle Monument. (NARA; CMSR; Wright Vol. 2, p. 8, spelled his name McClelland; Marine, p. 172) Letters of administration on the estate of William McClelland on 28 Sep 1814 were granted to Elijah P. Barrows. (*Baltimore American*, 12 Jun 1819) William McClellan, merchant, was slain in the Battle of North Point and was buried in Westminster Cemetery. (*Baltimore's Westminster Cemetery & Westminster Presbyterian Church: A Guide to the Markers and Burials, 1775-1943*, by Mary Ellen Hayward and R. Kent Lancaster, 1984, p. 26)

McCloud, Thomas, served as a Private in Capt. Joseph Wood's Co., Frederick Co. Militia, from 14 Oct 1814 and was reported sick in hospital, but no date or place were given (Mallick and Wright, p. 359)

McClure, Edward, served as a Private in Capt. Peter Pinney's Co., 27th Regt., Baltimore Militia, from 19 Aug 1814, was exempted from duty on 1 Sep 1814 by the Surgeon, reason was not stated, but he served as a volunteer in battle on 12 Sep 1814 at North Point (Wright Vol. 2, p. 20)

McClure, John, served as a Private in Capt. Samuel Lane's C., 14th U.S. Infantry, enlisted 26 Jun 1812 and was later captured. Prisoner of War #4095 at Halifax, interned 24 Jun 1813 and discharged for exchange on 3 Feb 1814 (Johnson and Christou, p. 244; Baker Vol. 1, p. 267, misspelled his name McClerce)

McClure, William, served as a Private in Capt. Thomas Montgomery's Co., 14th U.S. Infantry, enlisted 5 Jun 1812 for 5 years at the advanced age of 54, 5' 10" tall, born in Ireland and was discharged at Plattsburgh, NY on 18 Mar 1814 due to old age and inability (Johnson and Christou, p. 245)

McCoates, Samuel, served as a Seaman from Harford County on the privateer (letter-of-marque ship) *Baltimore,* commanded by Capt. Edward Veasey, was captured, taken into custody and imprisoned at Chatham on 23 Feb 1813 and was released for home aboard the Cartel *Rodrigo* four months later on 8 Jun 1813. ("Harford County in the War of 1812," by Christopher T. George, *Harford Historical Bulletin* No. 76, Spring 1998, pp. 17, 18, 20, citing *The Fatal Cruise of the Argus*, by Ira Dye, pp. 294-296, and *Records Relating to American Prisoners of War, 1812-1815, in the Public Record Office, London*, Admiralty Papers) Samuel McCoates served as a Seaman and was born in Harford Co., MD. Age: 30. Prison Depot: Chatham, Prisoner of War #551. Captured by HM Transport *Diadem*. When Taken: 7 Oct 1812. Where Taken: S. Andera (St. Andrews, Scotland). Prize Name: *Baltimore*. Home Port: Baltimore. Ship Type: Privateer. Received: 23 Feb 1813 on HMS *Dromedary*. Discharged 8 Jun 1813 and released to the Cartel *Rodrigo*. (Johnson's Database, 2019)

McColister, Nicholas, served as a Private in Capt. Joshua M. Amos' Co., 42nd Regt., Harford Co. Militia, from 27 Aug 1814 until 12 Oct 1814 when discharged by Dr. Miller, cause not stated (Wright Vol. 3, p. 29)

McComas, Henry Gough (1795-1814), served as a Private in Capt. Edward Aisquith's Rifle Co., Sharp Shooters, and was killed on 12 Sep 1814 at North Point. His name is on the Baltimore Battle Monument as well as the Wells and McComas Monument. (Wright Vol. 2, p. 53; *Baltimore American*, 12 Jun 1819) "Daniel Wells and Henry G. McComas are alleged to have killed General Robert Ross, leader of the British forces, before they themselves fell in battle. They were originally buried in Second Baptist (New Jerusalem) Cemetery near Broadway before entombment in a vault in Green Mount Cemetery. It appears that they were as venerated as medieval saints' relics for they were brought from the vault to lie in state in the hall of the old Maryland Institute in September 1858. Thousands of people visited (one assumes did not view) the bodies before they were placed in a funeral car and hence paraded down Baltimore Street to 'Ashland Square, the place of interment.' On the 44th Anniversary of the battle and after Mayor Thomas Swann gave an address before 'an immense audience', they were finally put to rest. It wasn't until thirteen years later, however, that the monument's base was erected after being funded through public subscription." (*The Very Quiet Baltimoreans*, by Jane B Wilson, 1991, pp. 97-98) "Baltimore, 13 Dec 1814: Sir, the bearer of this is the father of Henry McComas who was killed in the advance on the 12th Sept [and] he wishes to obtain the pay due him. Signed: Edward Aisquith." (NARA; CMSR) Henry Gough McComas served with his older brother Zacheous Onion McComas (1792-1867) and they were sons of Frederick Christian McComas and Susannah Onion. (Marine p. 363; Genealogical research by the authors, 2019)

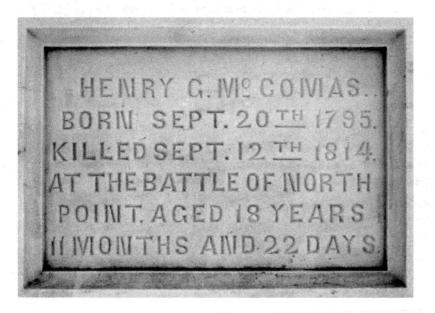

HENRY G. MᶜCOMAS.
BORN SEPT. 20 ᵀᴴ 1795.
KILLED SEPT. 12 ᵀᴴ 1814.
AT THE BATTLE OF NORTH
POINT. AGED 18 YEARS
11 MONTHS AND 22 DAYS.

McCombs, Frederick, served as a Private in Capt. Stephen H. Moore's Co., Baltimore Volunteers, from 8 Sep 1812, was promoted to 4th Corporal on 1 Jan 1813, wounded at Newark and in hospital on 13 Apr 1813 (Wright Vol. 2, p. 57)

McConchie, John T. S., served as a Private under Captain Dunnington and Captain Burgess, Charles and St. Mary's Cos., initially serving in 1813 and was discharged. and was drafted on 15 Jun 1814 under Capt. John F. Gray, served until 14 Jun 1814 and was discharged; soon after returning home he was called out again under Capt. Thomas Burgess for 28 days and engaged the enemy at Benedict, killing one British soldier and taking five prisoners. In his second service he was engaged at Cedar Point when the warehouse burned and was granted a furlough to go home, being unfit because of a sore leg. In 1855, age 63, he was living in Washington, DC. (BLW# 55-160-49551; Wright Vol. 5, p. 76)

McConnell, Samuel, served as a Seaman on board the privateer (armed brigantine) *Chasseur* of Baltimore commanded by Capt. Thomas Boyle and was killed in action on 26 Feb 1815 (*Niles Weekly Register*, 25 Mar 1815)

McConity, Hugh (1780-1814), served as a Private in Capt. Reuben Gilder's Co., 14th U.S. Infantry, enlisted 26 Jun 1813 at the age of 33, 5' 6" tall, born in Ireland

and died at Buffalo, NY on 4 Nov 1814 from wounds received during the Battle of Lyons Creek on 19 Oct 1814 (Johnson and Christou, p. 245)

McCorkill, James, served as a Private in Capt. Richard Arell's Co., 14th U.S. Inf., enlisted 19 Jul 1812 at Westchester, PA, age 23, 5' 9" tall, born in Chester, PA and was captured at Beaver Dams, PA on 24 Jun 1813. Prisoner of War #3803 at Halifax, NS, interned 27 Aug 1813, discharged for exchange on 3 Feb 1814, exchanged on 15 Apr 1814, returned to service and deserted at Fort Severn, MD on 13 Jul 1815 (Johnson and Christou, pp. 245-246; Baker Vol. 1, p. 267 misspelled his name as James McCorchill)

McCoul, Robert, served as a Private in Capt. Robert Lawson's Co., 5th Regt., Baltimore Militia, was captured at the Battle of Bladensburg on 24 Aug 1814 and exchanged on 6 Oct 1814 (Marine, p. 174 spelled his name McCall and p. 417 spelled his name McCoul; Wright Vol. 2, p. 4 spelled his name McCoul)

McCowan, Michael, served as a Private in Capt. Thomas Montgomery's Co. of the 14th U.S. Infantry, enlisted 13 Apr 1813 and died in Feb 1814 (BLW# 13120-160-12; Johnson and Christou, p. 246)

McCoy, James, served as a Private in Capt. Richard Whartenby's Co., 5th U.S. Infantry, enlisted 29 May 1811 at Baltimore at the age of 25, 5' 6½" tall, born in Ireland and discharged at Greenbush, NY on 4 May 1815 for general debility (Johnson and Christou, p. 246)

McCray, Philip (1780-1814), served as a Private in Capt. Reuben Gilder's Co. of the 14th U.S. Infantry, enlisted 5 Apr 1813 at age 33, born in Ireland and died on 20 Nov 1814 of sickness (BLW# 25907-160-12; Johnson and Christou, p. 247)

McCree, James, served as Surgeon, 25th Regiment, Somerset Co. Militia, under Lt. Col. Thomas Humphreys, appointed on 7 Dec 1813 and reported dead, but the date and cause of death were not stated; his replacement was appointed on 15 Jul 1814 (Wright Vol. 1, p. 11; Marine, p. 364 listed him as James McCrie and McCrea, surgeon in 25th Regt., and indicated he died in 1814)

McCrory, James, served as a Private in the 14th U.S. Infantry and was captured at Beaver Dams, Upper Canada on 24 Jun 1813. Prisoner of War #3800 at Halifax, NS, interned 27 Aug 1813, was discharged on 19 Nov 1813 and sent to England (Johnson and Christou, p. 246; Baker Vol. 1, p. 267)

McCulloch, James W., served as 4th Corporal in Capt. David Warfield's Co., 5th Regt., Baltimore United Volunteers, promoted to 6th Sergeant and wounded on 24 Aug 1814 at Bladensburg (Marine, p. 365; Wright Vol. 2, p. 7) Dr. James H. McCulloh, Jr. wrote this note soon after the battle to the British commander: "In consequence of the humanity shown the following American prisoners of war, I do promise upon honor that they shall not directly or indirectly serve against the

British until regularly exchanged." (Marine, p. 171 stated he was wounded at Bladensburg)

McCurd, James, served as a Private in Capt. William Adams' Co., 13th U.S. Inf., enlisted 2 Feb 1814 in New York at the age of 27, 5' 8½" tall, born in Baltimore and discharged on 9 Sep 1815 for debility (Johnson and Christou, p. 247)

McDaniel, Alexander, served as a Private in Capt. Peter Pinney's Co., 27th Regt., Baltimore Militia, from 19 Aug 1814 and was reported "missing since 27 Aug" 1814 (Wright Vol. 2, p. 16)

McDaniels, John, served as a Mate and was born in Baltimore. Age: 22. Prison Depot: Dartmoor, Prisoner of War #3530. Captured by HM Ship-of-the-Line *Conquestador*. When Taken: 22 Aug 1814. Where Taken: Long 19 Lat 107. Prize Name: *Rover*, prize of the Privateer York. Home Port: Baltimore. Ship Type: Privateer. Date Received: 28 Sep 1814. From what ship: HMT *Salvador del Mundo*. Discharged and released on 12 Jun 1815. (Johnson's Database, 2019)

McDennis, Patrick, served as a Private in the 14th U.S. Infantry, enlisted 25 Jan 1813 for 18 months and was later captured. Prisoner of War #4157 at Halifax, NS, interned 24 Jun 1813, discharged on 27 Aug 1813 and sent to England, later released and discharged from service on 31 Mar 1815 (Johnson and Christou, p. 248; Baker Vol. 1, p. 267)

McDonald, Henry, served as a Private in Capt. E. G. Williams' Co., 1st Cavalry, Washington Co. Militia, from 11 Aug 1814 and was discharged on 2 Sep 1814 by a certificate from the doctor (Wright Vol. 9, p. 2)

McDonald, James, served as a Lieutenant in Capt. James McDonald's Co., 14th U.S. Infantry, born in Maryland, commissioned a 1st Lieutenant on 12 Mar 1812, promoted to Captain on 1 Oct 1813 and died at Buffalo, NY on 11 Nov 1814 (Johnson and Christou, p. 248)

McDonald, John, served as a Seaman and was born in Baltimore. Age: 25. Prison Depot: Dartmoor, Prisoner of War #622. Captured by HM Brig *Pelican*. When Taken: 14 Aug 1813. Where Taken: off St. David's Head, Wales. Prize Name: U.S. Brig *Argus*. Ship Type: Warship. Date Received: 8 Sep 1813 from Plymouth. Discharged and sent to Dartmouth on 2 Nov 1814.

McElroy, Eleazer, served as a Private in the U.S. Marine Corps, enlisted 16 Sep 1807 and was taken from the barracks and admitted to the Naval Hospital in Washington, DC as Patient No. 81 on 21 Dec 1814 with typhoid fever and died on 26 Dec 1814 (Sharp's Database, 2018)

McElroy, Robert, served as a Private in the U.S. Marine Corps and was taken from the barracks and admitted to the Naval Hospital in Washington, DC as

Patient No. 76 on 30 Nov 1814 with "affec" (name of illness illegible) and was discharged on 7 Jan 1815 and sent to the barracks (Sharp's Database, 2018)

McFadden, John, served as a Seaman and was born in Baltimore. Age: 23. Prison Depot: Dartmoor, Prisoner of War #4118. Captured by HM Frigate *Niemen*. When Taken: 28 Jun 1814. Where Taken: off Delaware. Prize Name: *Bordeaux Packet*. Home Port: Baltimore. Ship Type: Letter of Marque. Date Received: 6 Oct 1814 from HMT *Chesapeake* from Halifax, NS. Discharged on 13 Jun 1815. (Johnson's Database, 2019)

McFadon (McFaden), James, served as a 2nd Prize Master and was born in Baltimore. Age: 26. Prison Depot: Plymouth 1, Prisoner of War #2265. Captured by HM Frigate *Euratos*. When Taken: 25 Dec 1813. Where Taken: at sea. Prize Name: *Fanny*. Prize. Ship Type: Privateer. Date Received: 20 Jan 1814 on HMS *Euratos*. Discharged on 31 Jan 1814 and sent to Dartmoor. Prison Depot: Dartmoor, Prisoner of War #929. Received: 31 Jan 1814 from Plymouth. Escaped 3 Jun 1814. (Johnson's Database, 2019)

McFadon, John Jr., served as a Private in Capt. Samuel Sterett's Co., 5th Regt., Baltimore Militia, from 19 Aug 1814 and was wounded at North Point on 12 Sep 1814 (Wright Vol. 2, p. 6)

McFalland, William, served as a Private in Capt. Henry Lowery's Co., Allegany Co. Militia, and was sick in hospital after 14 Oct 1814 (Wright Vol. 9, p. 5)

McFarland (McFarlan), Peter, served as a Private in Capt. Joseph Wood's Co., Frederick Co. Militia, from 3 Aug 1814, was in the entrenchments during the Battle of North Point on 12 Sep 1814 and was "sick absent with leave 12 Oct" 1814 (Mallick and Wright, p. 358)

McFarren, John (1793-1868), served as 4th Sergeant in Capt. Edward Aisquith's Rifle Co., Sharp Shooters, Baltimore City, from 19 Aug 1814 and was wounded on 12 Sep 1814 at North Point (Wright Vol. 2, p. 53, Marine p. 365)

McGaby, Edward, served as a Private in Capt. James Dorman's Co., 5th U.S. Infantry, enlisted 8 Jul 1812 in Baltimore at the age of 32, 5' 5½" tall, born in Scotland and was discharged at Pittsburgh, PA on 16 Aug 1815 on a Surgeon's Certificate (Johnson and Christou, p. 236)

McGee, James, served as a Private in Capt. John Fonsten's Co., Frederick Co. Militia, from 2 Sep 1814, marched to Baltimore, engaged in the defense of the city, and was reported "sick absent" on 24 Sep 1814 (Wright Vol. 8, p. 364; Mallick and Wright, p. 205)

McGee, James (1786-1815), served as a Private in Capt. David Cummings' Co., 14th U.S. Infantry, enlisted 29 Oct 1814 in Williamsport, MD at age of 28, 5' 6" tall, born in Ireland and died 14 Aug 1815 (Johnson and Christou, pp. 249-250)

McGee, John, served as a Seaman and was born in Baltimore. Age: 32. Prison Depot: Dartmoor, Prisoner of War #3958. Captured by HM Frigate *Loire*. When Taken: 10 Dec 1813. Where Taken: off Block Island, RI. Prize Name: *Rolla*. Home Port: Baltimore. Ship Type: Privateer. Date Received: 5 Oct 1814. From what ship: HMT *President* from Halifax, NS. Discharged on 9 Jun 1815. (Johnson's Database, 2019)

McGinley, Andrew, served as a Private in Capt. Kenneth McKenzie's Co., 14th U.S. Infantry, and was wounded at Fort George, Upper Canada on 27 May 1813 (Johnson and Christou, p. 250)

McGlindey, Michael, served as a Private in Capt. Joseph Hook's Co., 36th U.S. Infantry, enlisted 14 Jun 1814 and died 20 Aug 1814; bounty land issued to George McGlindey (BLW# 27096-160-12; Johnson and Christou, p. 250)

McGowan, Ennis, served as a Marine and was taken from the barracks and admitted to the Naval Hospital in Washington, DC as Patient No. 57 on 6 Jul 1814 (injury or illness was not specified) and was discharged on 8 Jul 1814 and sent to the barracks (Sharp's Database, 2018)

McGriffin, John, served as a Private in Capt. Alexander Brookes' Co., 3rd U.S. Artillery, enlisted 29 Jan 1813 for 5 years at Caningsburgh (sic), age 32, 5' 7" tall, born in Cecil Co., and later captured. Prisoner of War, exchanged on 28 Apr 1814 and discharged from service on 2 Jan 1818 (Johnson and Christou, p. 251)

McGuire, ----, served as a Marine, was taken from the barracks and admitted to the Naval Hospital in Washington, DC as Patient No. 88 on 28 Dec 1814 with typhoid fever, was discharged on 20 Jan 1815 and sent to the barracks (Sharp's Database, 2018)

McGuire, Hugh, served as a Private in the 14th U.S. Infantry and was captured. Prisoner of War #4167 at Halifax, NS, interned 24 Jun 1813, was discharged on 27 Aug 1813 and sent to England on HMS *Regulus* (Johnson and Christou, p. 251; Baker Vol. 1, p. 269, spelled his name Hugh McGwire)

McGuire, John, served as a Seaman and was born in Baltimore. Age: 24. Prison Depot: Dartmoor, Prisoner of War #5506. Captured by HM Frigate *Maidstone*. When Taken: 30 Oct 1814. Where Taken: off Cape Sable, NS. Prize Name: Ann Dorothy. Prize. Ship Type: Privateer. Received: 17 Dec 1814. From what ship: HMT *Loire* from Halfiax. Discharged on 29 Jun 1815. (Johnson's Database, 2019)

McIver, William, served as a Private in the 14th U.S. Infantry and was captured. Prisoner of War #3956 at Halifax, NS, interned 24 Jun 1813, was discharged on 27 Aug 1813 and sent to England on HMS *Regulus* (Johnson and Christou, p. 252; Baker Vol. 1, p. 269)

McKeever, Charles, served as a Private in the 14th U.S. Infantry and was later captured. Prisoner of War #4185 at Halifax, NS, interned on 24 Jun 1813, was discharged on 27 Aug 1813 and sent to England on HMS *Regulus* (Johnson and Christou, p. 252; Baker Vol. 1, p. 269)

McKeige, Denis, served as a Seaman and was born in Maryland. Age: 34. Prison Depot: Dartmoor, Prisoner of War #3015. How Taken: Gave himself up off HM Ship-of-the-Line *Zealous*. When Taken: 27 Aug 1814. Date Received: 2 Sep 1814. From what ship: HMT *Centaur*. Discharged on 28 May 1815. (Johnson's Database, 2019)

McKelip, Joseph, served as a Private in Capt. Samuel Lane's Co., 14th U.S. Infantry, enlisted on 15 Jun 1812 for 1 year and died at Black Rock, NY on 16 Dec 1812 (Johnson and Christou, p. 252)

McKeller, Benjamin, served as a Private in Capt. William McIlvane's Co., 14th U.S. Infantry, enlisted on 30 Nov 1812 for 18 months and was later captured. Prisoner of War, exchanged on 15 Apr 1815 and discharged at Plattsburgh, NY on 5 Jul 1814 (Johnson and Christou, p. 252)

McKenny, John, served as a Private in Capt. Thomas Sangster's Co., 14th U.S. Infantry, enlisted 8 Jul 1812 at Baltimore, age 20, born in Ireland and reported to be a "Prisoner of War since 1 Jan 1814" (Johnson and Christou, p. 252)

McKenny, John, served as a Private in Capt. John R. Dyer's Co., 17th Regiment, Prince George's Co. Militia, between 19 Aug and 13 Sep 1814 and was taken prisoner, detained for 2 days and discharged at Fort Washington, but no dates were given (Wright Vol. 6, p. 13)

McKenzie, Alexander, served as 3rd Sergeant in Capt. Edward Aisquith's Rifle Co., Sharp Shooters, Baltimore City, from 19 Aug 1814 and was wounded on 12 Sep 1814 at North Point (Marine p. 367)

McKenzie, John (African American), served as a Seaman and was born in Baltimore. Age: 36. Prison Depot: Chatham, Prisoner of War #2100. How Taken: Gave himself up off HM Ship-of-the-Line *Barfleur*. When Taken: 27 May 1813. Received: 9 Aug 1813. From what ship: HMS *Thames*. Discharged on 12 Aug 1814 and sent to Dartmoor on HMS *Alpheus*. Prison Depot: Dartmoor, Prisoner of War #2879. Date Received: 24 Aug 1814. From what ship: HMT *Alpheus* from Chatham. Discharged on 19 May 1815. (Johnson's Database, 2019)

McKenzie, Kenneth, (1776-1817), served as a Captain of his own company in the 14th U.S. Infantry at age 36; born in Maryland, commissioned on 6 Jul 1812. Prisoner of War at Dartmouth with two prisoner numbers, #4914 and #4776, paroled on 1 Sep 1813 from the HMS *Regulus*, discharged 10 Nov 1813, paroled on 15 Nov 1813, sent to Prison Ship *Success*, discharged 19 Nov 1813, sent to Ashburton, England on 23 Jun 1814, discharged on 15 Jun 1815 and died on 29 Sep 1817 (Johnson and Christou, p. 253; Johnson, pp. 37-38)

McKerbie, Alexander, served as a Prize Master and was born in Baltimore. Age: 28. Prison Depot: Plymouth 1, Prisoner of War #2671. Captured by HM Ship-of-the-Line *Sterling Castle*. When Taken: 10 May 1814. Where Taken: Lat 36 Long 37. Prize Name: *John*, prize of the Privateer *Amelia*. Ship Type: Privateer. Date Received: 5 Jun 1814. From what ship: HMS *Gronville*. Discharged on 14 Jun 1814 and sent to Dartmoor. (Johnson's Database, 2019)

McKertre, Abraham, served as a Prize Master and was born in Baltimore. Age: 28. Prison Depot: Dartmoor, Prisoner of War #1295. Captured by HM Ship-of-the-Line *Sterling Castle*. When Taken: 10 May 1814. Where Taken: off Cape Clear, Ireland. Prize Name: *John & Frances*, prize of the Privateer *Amelia*. Ship Type: Privateer. Date Received: 14 Jun 1814 from Mill Prison. Discharged on 28 Apr 1815. (Johnson's Database, 2019)

McKinney, Philip, served as a Private in 1st Lt. John Weer's Co., 36th Regiment, Baltimore Co., from 26 Aug 1814 and died on 1 Oct 1814 (Wright Vol. 2, p. 60)

McKinnon, Nathaniel (African American), served as a Seaman and was born in Baltimore. Age: 22. Prison Depot: Stapleton, Prisoner of War #171. Captured by HM Frigate *Magiciene*. When Taken: 5 Jun 1813. Where Taken: Bay of Biscayne. Prize Name: *Tickler*. Ship Type: Letter of Marque. Date Received: 8 Jul 1813 from Plymouth. Discharged on 13 Jun 1814 and sent to Dartmoor. Prison Depot: Dartmoor, Prisoner of War #1445. Date Received: 19 Jun 1814 from Stapleton. Discharged on 28 Apr 1815. (Johnson's Database, 2019)

McKissick (McKissic), James, served as a Private in Capt. John Galt's Co., Frederick Co. Militia, from 31 Aug 1814 and was reported "sick absent 14 Oct" in Baltimore (Mallick and Wright, pp. 205, 361)

McLane, James (1789-1815), served as a Private in Capt. Samuel Raisin's Co. , 36th U.S. Infantry, enlisted 21 Sep 1814 in the District of Columbia at the age of 25, 5' 8¼" tall, born in Fairfax, VA and died in hospital on 3 Jan 1815 (Johnson and Christou, p. 253)

McLaughlin, James, served as a Private in Capt. George Stockton's Co., 28th U.S. Infantry, enlisted 1 Jun 1812 in Elizabethtown, KY at the age of 29, 5' 10" tall, born in St. Mary's Co., MD, wounded at Fort Meigs, OH and was discharged at

Detroit on 11 Nov 1815 (BLW# 5730-160-12; Johnson and Christou, p. 254) In Frederick Co. on 18 Mar 1822 James McLaughlin, a former private in Capt. Brooke's Co., 5th Regt., U.S. Inf., in the late war, stated he had been a resident of this county for eight years and previously of Baltimore Co. He appointed John Duer as his attorney to collect his $72 pension due from 4 Mar 1821 to 4 Mar 1822; also, on 18 Mar 1822, Dr. W. Bradley Tyler and Dr. John H. McElfresh made oaths that he continues to be disabled through loss of right eye, partial loss of sight in left eye, and wounds of right arm and leg. (Pierce, p. 122)

McLaughlin, William, served as a Private in Capt. George Stockton's Co., 28th U.S. Infantry, enlisted 1 Jun 1813 at Elizabethtown, KY at the age of 29, 5' 10" tall, born in St. Mary's Co., MD, lost an arm during the siege of Fort Meigs and was discharged on 10 Nov 1815 (Johnson and Christou, p. 254)

McLean, Thomas, served as a Boy onboard a ship and was born in Maryland. Age: 18. Prison Depot: Dartmoor, Prisoner of War #2257. Captured by HM Brig *Curlew*. When Taken: 25 May 1814. Where Taken: off Halifax, NS. Prize Name: *Ontario*, prize of Privateer *Lawrence*. Home Port: Baltimore. Ship Type: Privateer. Date Received: 16 Aug 1814. From what ship: HMS *Dublin* from Halifax, NS. Discharged 3 May 1815. (Johnson's Database, 2019)

McMinn, Joseph, served as a Private inCapt. Jacob Wolf's and William Curtis' Comp, Md Mil from 26 Jul to 13 Oct 1814 in Wolf's Comp and from 14 Oct 1814 to 10 Jan 1815 in Curtis' Comp. He was injured in the eye at Fort McHenry and lost his eye. He applied from Hope, Clarke Co, Missouri Separate Pension applications and Bounty Land files including widow Sarah's pension. He served in First Regt under Col. John Ragan. He married Mrs. Sarah S. Morrison on Oct 1, 1876 in Clark Co MO. He died Apr 17, 1886. She died Sep 4, 1888. He had an invalid pension for life in 1854 for the loss of one eye and then later a service pension in 1871 and then switched back to higher invalid pension. His first wife was Elizabeth Livick whom he married at Augusta Co VA in 1820. He signed up in Washington Co MD in fall of 1813 and then discharged in spring of 1815 in Annapolis MD. (NARA SO 11,165, SC 14907, WO 44167 WC 34574; Wt 31350-80-50. 33-465-80-55, Wright Vol 2 p 27)

McNab, John, served as a Private in Capt. Reuben Gilder's Co., 14th U.S. Inf., enlisted 3 May 1813 for 5 years and died at Sackett's Harbor, NY on 3 Nov 1813; bounty land issued to his brother Isaac McNab and other heirs at law (BLW# 25422-160-12; Johnson and Christou, p. 254)

McNeil, James Jr. (1785-1831) served as a Private in the 1st Artillery Regiment, Capt. Charles Pennington's Co., Baltimore Independent Artillerists, and was severely wounded on 13 Sep 1814 at Fort McHenry, lost his right leg, survived the war and died on 22 Dec 1831 in his 45th year. He was a native of Ireland and was buried in the Faith Presbyterian Church, Broadway and Gay Street. (Wright Vol. 2, p. 47, spelled his name McNeal; Marine, p. 173, spelled it McNeil; Burials copied by Edith Ensor Read, 1812 Society, placed in File 52255 at the Maryland Historical Society, spelled his name McNeil; and, also on microfilm, p. 6, and his name was spelled McNeal; Baltimore County Will Book No. 14, p. 107)

McNelly, Thomas, served as a ship's Carpenter and was born in Maryland. Age: 57. Prison Depot: Plymouth 1, Prisoner of War #1116. Captured by HM Ship-of-the-Line *Superb*. When Taken: 15 Apr 1813. Where Taken: Bay of Biscayne. Prize Name: *Viper*. Home Port: New York. Ship Type: Privateer. Date Received: 22 Apr 1813. From what ship: HMS *Superb*. Discharged and sent to Dartmoor on 1 Jul 1813. Prison Depot: Dartmoor, Prisoner of War #420. Received: 1 Jul 1813 from Plymouth. Discharged on 20 Apr 1815. (Johnson's Database, 2019)

McQuinn, Donald, served as a Corporal in Capt. Isaac Barnard's Co., 14th U.S. Infantry, enlisted 30 Nov 1812 for 5 years, wounded on 24 Jun 1813. Prisoner of War, exchanged on 15 Apr 1814, and discharged at Washington, DC on 5 Oct 1814 (BLW# 10687-160-12; Johnson and Christou, p. 256) In Baltimore on 4 Mar 1826 Donald McQuin (sic), former corporal in Capt. Barnard's Co. of Infantry in the late war, and a resident of this city nearly all his life, appointed Robert Bradley as his attorney to collect his $36 pension due from 4 Sep 1825 to 4 Mar 1826 (Pierce, p. 124)

McRay, William, served as a Private in the 14th U.S. Infantry and was later captured. Prisoner of War #4183 at Halifax, NS, interned on 24 Jun 1813, was discharged on 27 Aug 1813 and sent to England on HMS *Regulus* (Johnson and Christou, p. 256; Baker Vol. 1, p. 271)

McRhea, Edward, served as a Private in the 14th U.S. Infantry and was later captured. Prisoner of War #4058 at Halifax, NS, interned on 24 Jun 1813 and was discharged for exchange on 3 Feb 1814 (Johnson and Christou, p. 256; Baker Vol. 1, p. 271)

Mead, Benjamin, served as a Private in Capt. William Smith's Co., 16th U.S. Infantry, enlisted 9 Apr 1813 for 5 years in Wilmington, DE, age 40, 5' 6" tall, born in Charles Co., MD, and discharged at Buffalo, NY on 19 Jun 1815 due to a scrotal hernia (Johnson and Christou, p. 256)

Meath, Solomon (African American), served as a Seaman and was born in Maryland. Age: 24. Prison Depot: Portsmouth, Prisoner of War #1228. How Taken: Gave himself up off HM Ship-of-the-Line *Invincible*. When Taken: 14 Jan 1813. Date Received: 24 Nov 1813. From what ship: HM Transport *Leopard*. Discharged on 26 Dec 1813 and sent to Chatham on HMS *Diomede*. Prison Depot: Chatham, Prisoner of War #3023. Age 25. Date Received: 7 Jan 1814. Discharged on 26 Sep 1814 and sent to Dartmoor on HMS *Leyden*. Prison Depot: Dartmoor,

Prisoner of War #4689. Date Received: 9 Oct 1814. From what ship: HMT *Leyden* from Chatham. Discharged on 11 Jul 1815. (Johnson's Database, 2019)

Mechane, Almond, served as a Private in the 14th U.S. Infantry and was later captured, probably at Beaver Dams, Upper Canada. Prisoner of War #3990 at Halifax, NS, interned on 24 Jun 1813 and was discharged for exchange on 3 Feb 1814 (Johnson and Christou, p. 256; Baker Vol. 1, p. 272)

Medcalf, John (1774-1815), served as a Private in Capt. Edmund Duvall's Co., 42nd U.S. Infantry, enlisted 25 Dec 1813 at Bladensburg, MD, age 39, 5' 2" tall, born in Annapolis and died in New York on 18 Jun 1815; heirs received half pay for 5 years in lieu of bounty land (Johnson and Christou, p. 256)

Medler, John, served as a Seaman and was born in Maryland. Age: 40. Prison Depot: Plymouth 2, Prisoner of War #547. How Taken: Gave himself up off HMS *Harmony*. When Taken: 4 Sep 1814. Where Taken: Barbados, West Indies. Date Received: 16 Apr 1815. From what ship: HMS *Swiftsure*. Discharged on 2 Jun 1815 and released to the Cartel *Soverign*. (Johnson's Database, 2019)

Meiniffe, Charles, served as a Seaman and was born in Baltimore. Age: 21. Prison Depot: Plymouth 1, Prisoner of War #2002. Captured by HM Brig *Royalist*. When Taken: 6 Sep 1812. Where Taken: coast of France. Prize Name: *Ned*. Home Port: Baltimore. Ship Type: Letter of Marque. Date Received: 22 Sep 1813. From what ship: HMS *Royalist*. Discharged on 27 Sep 1813 and sent to Dartmoor. Prison Depot: Dartmoor, Prisoner of War #721. Date Received: 27 Sep 1813 from Plymouth. Discharged and sent to Plymouth on 7 Dec 1813. (Johnson's Database, 2019)

Melville, John, served as a Seaman and was born in Baltimore. Age: 19. Prison Depot: Plymouth 1, Prisoner of War #326. Captured by HM Frigate *Dryad*. When Taken: 8 Jan 1813. Where Taken: off Bordeaux, France. Prize Name: *Porcupine*. Ship Type: Merchant Vessel. Date Received: 21 Jan 1813. From what ship: HMS *Abercrombie*. Discharged and sent to Chatham on 29 Mar 1813 on HMS *Braham*. Prison Depot: Chatham, Prisoner of War #1408. Date Received: 5 Apr 1813 from Plymouth on HMS *Dwarf*. Discharged 24 Jul 1813 and released to the Cartel *Hoffning*. (Johnson's Database, 2019)

Melvin, William, served as a Private in the 14th U.S. Infantry and was later captured. Prisoner of War #4182 at Halifax, NS, interned on 24 Jun 1813, was discharged on 27 Aug 1813 and sent to England on HMS *Regulus* (Johnson and Christou, p. 257; Baker Vol. 1, p. 273)

Menillo, John, of Baltimore, served as a Seaman on the ship *Rattlesnake* and was captured, but date was not given. Prisoner of War #4917 at Dartmoor and died on 18 Nov 1814 (Centennial Trails, United States Daughters of 1812, online at www.war1812trails.com/Dartmoor)

Mercer, Chamont (Mulatto or Yellow), served as a Steward and was born in Prince George's Co., MD. Age: 25. Prison Depot: Plymouth 1, Prisoner of War #400. Captured by HM Frigate *Iris*. When Taken: 17 Jan 1813. Where Taken: at sea. Prize Name: *Union*. Home Port: Philadelphia. Ship Type: Merchant Vessel. Date Received: 5 Feb 1813 on HMS San Josef. Discharged and sent to Chatham on 29 Mar 1813 on HMS *Braham*. Prison Depot: Chatham, Prisoner of War #146. Received: 6 Apr 1813 on Tender *Eliza*. Discharged 24 Jul 1813. Released to the Cartel *Hoffning*. (Johnson's Database, 2019)

Mercer, John, served as a Private in Capt. Thomas Montgomery's Co., 14th U.S. Infantry, enlisted 14 Jun 1812 in Wilmington, DE, age 35, 5' 8" tall, born in Cecil Co., MD and discharged at Greenbush, BY on 18 Mar 1815 due to a rupture (Johnson and Christou, pp. 257-258)

Merchant, Richard, served as a Private in Capt. Stephen H. Moore's Co., Baltimore Volunteers Infantry Co., from 8 Sep 1812 for 1 year and sick in hospital in Niagara, NY, but no date was given, probably 13 Apr 1813 (Wright Vol. 2, p. 57)

Meredith, Benjamin, served as a Private in Capt. Robert Lawson's Co., 5th Regt., Baltimore Militia, from 19 Aug 1814, was captured and taken prisoner at North Point on 12 Sep 1814, exchanged on 6 Nov (sic) and discharged 2 Sep (sic) 1814 (Wright Vol. 2, pp. 4-5)

Merpaux, Brian, served as a Seaman and was born in Baltimore. Age: 23. Prison Depot: Portsmouth, Prisoner of War #187. Captured by HM Transport *Diadem*. When Taken: 7 Oct 1812. Where Taken: S. Andera (St. Andrews, Scotland). Prize Name: *Baltimore*. Home Port: Baltimore. Ship Type: Privateer. Received: 10 Nov 1812. From what ship: HMS *Diadem*. Discharged on 19 Feb 1813 and sent to Chatham on HM Store Ship *Dromedary*. (Johnson's Database, 2019)

Merriken, Jacob (1791-1814), served as a Private in Capt. Christian Adreon's Co., 5th Regt., Baltimore Union Volunteers, participated in the battle at North Point on12 Sep 1814 and was reported sick, not killed, on the muster roll dated 18 Oct – 18 Nov 1814 (NARA; CMSR; Marine, p. 378); therefore, Jacob is not the J. Merriken inscribed on the Baltimore Battle Monument, but it was Joseph.

Merriken, Joseph (1777-1815), served as a Private in Capt. Thomas Watkins' Co., 39th Regt., under Col. Benjamin Fowler, and was mortally wounded at the Battle of North Point on 12 Sep 1814 (according to *Citizen Soldiers*, by Hickman, 1848, that cites a statement made by David M. Merriken, grandson of Joseph; Wright Vol. 2, p. 27, states Joseph Merriken served as a Private under Lt. William Wooddy in the 39th Regiment as listed on the muster roll dated 19 Aug to 18 Nov

1814; however, his wound was not mentioned). The Merriken on the Baltimore Battle Monument is Joseph Merriken, not Jacob Merriken as some have claimed. It is based on the following: In 1853 Ann Merriken, age 75, of Annapolis, but visiting the City of Baltimore, his widow, applied and was granted a pension of half pay. She stated Joseph died "from disease contracted and injury received while in the line of duty Sept 1 (sic) 1814 and is proved by several credible witnesses who certify to the facts of their own person knowledge. The deceased soldier ruptured a blood vessel and fell in the streets of Baltimore and was taken to his residence and lingered till March 20, 1815 when he died. His name is among those whose names are inscribed on the battle monument in Balto." Statements also made by Ann Hyde, John Henry Smith, Joseph Richardson and Joseph S. Merriken, age 51 in 1853, son of the soldier. Dr. Howard was the surgeon of the regiment who took care of Joseph Merriken during and after the war in which he served as a sergeant. Ann Merriken stated she married Joseph on 6 Feb 1798 [actually, the Anne Arundel County marriage license of Joseph Merriken and Anne Gray was dated 1 Feb 1799], that he served from 18 Aug 1814 to 19 Nov 1814, and he fell from excessive fatigue and in his fall ruptured a blood vessel on 1 (sic) Sep 1814 from which he later died on 20 Mar 1815. (Fold3 Pension and BLW File) Prior to the War of 1812 Joseph Merriken, age 22, served as a Corporal in Capt. John Merriken's Co., Anne Arundel Co. Militia, on 22 Mar 1799. (Wright Vol. 4, p. 2) Joseph Merrican also served as a Private in Capt. William Roney's Co., 39th Regiment, Baltimore Militia, from 16 Aug to 23 Aug 1813 (Wright, Vol. 2, p. 23) In Baltimore on 8 Aug 1863 the Court was satisfied that Ann Merriken, late pensioner and widow of Joseph Merriken, died in Annapolis on 9 Feb 1863 and left two children, Ann Hyde and Joseph S. Merriken. On the same date Emma Weedon and Sarah A. Marr made oaths that Ann resided in Annapolis for 46 years and previously in Baltimore. The said two children of Ann and Joseph then collected $18.07 due from 4 Sep 1862 to 9 Feb 1863. (Pierce, pp. 129-130)

Messenger, Charles, served as a Private in a Marine Battery under Sailing Master Rodman from 10 Oct 1813, was on board on 7 Apr 1814 and was killed at Fort McHenry on 13 Sep 1814 (Marine pp. 173, 379, spelled his name Messenger; Shomette, p. 365, spelled his name Massington)

Metakern, Seth, served as a Private in the 14th U.S. Infantry and was later captured. Prisoner of War #3988 at Halifax, NS, interned on 24 Jun 1813 and was discharged for exchange on 3 Feb 1814 (Johnson and Christou, p. 259; Baker Vol. 1, p. 274)

Metcalf, Mordecai, served as a Corporal in the 22nd U.S. Infantry, enlisted 7 or 17 June 1814 by Lt. Morrow for 5 years, age 22, 5' 11" tall, black eyes, black hair, dark complexion, born in Fredericksburg, MD (sic) and mustered in Lt. J. R. Guy's

Detachment, Fort Fayette, on 16 Jun 1814; ordered to Buffalo on 16 Jun 1814, joined at Buffalo from Lt. Guy's Detachment on 30 Sep 1814 and absent at Buffalo since 2 Oct 1814 by reason of sickness; was at Shomac Bay on 31 Dec 1816 and 28 Feb 1817; confined to Watertown jail by civil authority and sent to state prison for 5 years on 31 Jan 1818, reason not stated, and he was dropped from the rolls (Mallick and Wright, p. 208)

Metty, Martin, served as a Private in Capt. Gerrard Wilson's Co., 6th Regt., Baltimore Militia, from 19 Aug 1814 and was discharged by the doctor on 19 Oct 1814 as unfit for service (Wright Vol. 2, p. 11)

Mezich, Elisha (Mulatto), served as a Seaman and was born in Maryland. Age: 38. Prison Depot: Plymouth 1, Prisoner of War #1681. Captured by HM Frigate *Belle Poule*. When Taken: 11 May 1813. Where Taken: Bay of Biscayne. Prize Name: *Revenge*. Home Port: Charleston. Ship Type: Letter of Marque. Date Received: 26 Jun 1813. From what ship: HMS *Duncan*. Discharged on 30 Jun 1813 and sent to Stapleton. Prison Depot: Stapleton, Prisoner of War #187. Date Received: 8 Jul 1813 from Plymouth. Discharged on 13 Jun 1814 and sent to Dartmoor. (Johnson's Database, 2019)

Middleton, John (Mulatto), served as a Seaman and was born in Maryland. Age: 24. Prison Depot: Portsmouth, Prisoner of War #1353. How Taken: Gave himself up off HM Frigate *Rosamond*. When Taken: 28 Dec 1813. Date Received: 28 Jan 1814. From what ship: HM Ship-of-the-Line *Prince*. Discharged on 13 Feb 1814 and sent to Chatham on HMT *Malabar No. 352*. Prison Depot: Chatham, Prisoner of War #348. Date Received: 23 Feb 1814 from Portsmouth on HMT *Malabar*. Discharged on 26 Sep 1814 and sent to Dartmoor on HMS *Leyden*. Prison Depot: Dartmoor, Prisoner of War #4732. Date Received: 9 Oct 1814. From what ship: HMT *Freya* from Chatham. Discharged on 15 Jun 1815. (Johnson's Database, 2019)

Mids, Michael, served as a Seaman and was born in Baltimore. Age: 21. Prison Depot: Portsmouth, Prisoner of War #1390. Captured by *Vittoria*, Guernsey Privateer. When Taken: 28 Jan 1814. Where Taken: off Bordeaux, France. Prize Name: *Pilot*. Home Port: Baltimore. Ship Type: Letter of Marque (Privateer). Date Received: 7 Feb 1814. From what ship: *Mary* from Guernsey. Discharged on 13 Feb 1814 and sent to Chatham on HMT *Malabar No. 352*. Prison Depot: Chatham, Prisoner of War #3518. Age 21. Date Received: 23 Feb 1814 from Portsmouth on HMT *Malabar*. Discharged on 26 Sep 1814 and sent to Dartmoor on HMS *Leyden*. Prison Depot: Dartmoor, Prisoner of War #4286. Age 26 (sic). Date Received: 7 Oct 1814 on HMT *Niobe* from Chatham. Discharged on 14 Jun 1815. (Johnson's Database, 2019)

Mietellan, John, served as a Private in the 14th U.S. Infantry (company not stated) and was later captured, probably at Beaver Dams, Upper Canada. Prisoner of War #4020 at Halifax, NS, interned 24 Jun 1813 and was discharged for exchange on 3 Feb 1814 (Johnson and Christou, p. 259; Baker Vol. 1, p. 275)

Miflin, Richard (African American), served as a Seaman and was born in Baltimore. Age: 26. Prison Depot: Dartmoor, Prisoner of War #5635. Captured by HM Brig *Racehorse*. When Taken: Dec 1812. Where Taken: off Table Bay, South Africa. Prize Name: *Monticello*. Ship Type: Merchant Vessel. Date Received: 24 Dec 1814. From what ship: HMT *Tay*. Discharged on 27 Apr 1815. (Johnson's Database, 2019)

Mildews, Calop, served as a Private in Capt. Robert C. Galloway's Co., 2nd Regt., 11th Brigade, Baltimore, for "1 month, discharged Sep 28 by doctor" in 1814 (Wright Vol. 2, p. 86)

Miles, Morris, served as a Private in Capt. Reuben Gilder's Co., 14th U.S. Inf., enlisted 11 Feb 1813 for 5 years at the age of 25, born in Prince George's Co., MD, was wounded at LaCole Mill, Lower Canada on 30 Mar 1814 and was discharged at Fort Hawkins, GA on 11 Feb 1818 (BLW# 19452-160-12; Johnson and Christou, p. 260)

Miller, Adam, served as a Private in Capt. Andrew Smith's Co., 51st Regiment, Baltimore Militia, joined 12 Sep 1814, was reported "in captivity" and no date was given, but it was most probably at North Point (Wright Vol. 2, p. 38)

Miller, Andrew, served as a Private in Capt. Jacob Deems' Co., 51st Regiment, Baltimore Militia, from 19 Aug 1814 and reported "in captivity, taken at North Point on 12 Sep 1814" (Wright Vol. 2, p. 34; Marine, p. 379, stated he was captured at North Point and taken to Barbados) Andrew Miller, of Baltimore, married Caroline Dawes, of Dumfries, VA, date not given (Society of the War of 1812 Application National No. 10 in 1889)

Miller, Enoch, served as a Marine, was taken from the barracks and admitted to the Naval Hospital in Washington, DC as Patient No. 66 on 31 Jul 1814 (injury or illness was not specified) and was discharged on 3 Aug 1814 and sent to the barracks (Sharp's Database, 2018)

Miller, Francis, served as a Musician in Capt. Richard Bell's Co. of the 5th U.S. Infantry, enlisted 29 Jul 1812 in Baltimore and died at Plattsburgh, NY on 10 Jul 1814 (BLW# 25806-160-12; Johnson and Christou, p. 260)

Miller, Frederick (1786-1814), served as a Private in Capt. James McDonald's Co., 14th U.S. Infantry, enlisted 27 Jan 1814 in Baltimore at the age of 17, 5' 2" all, born in Baltimore and died on 2 Jun 1814; bounty land issued to his mother Martha Miller (BLW# 9687-160-12; Johnson and Christou, p. 260)

Miller, Gattel (Gastel), served as a Private in the 14th U.S. Infantry (company not stated) and was captured at Beaver Dams, Upper Canada on 24 Jun 1813. Prisoner of War #3769 at Halifax, interned on 24 Jun 1813 and died on 18 Oct 1813 of dysentery (Johnson and Christou, p. 260; Baker, Vol. 1, p. 275)

Miller, George, served as a Private and was killed at Bladensburg on 24 Aug 1814 while serving in an Anne Arundel Co. Detachment of Volunteers under the command of Ensign William Brewer and attached to the 36th Regiment of Infantry commanded by Lt. Col. Scott (Wright Vol. 4, p. 40; Marine p. 380)

Miller, George (1767-1814), served as a Private in Capt. Samuel Lane's Co. of the 14th U.S. Infantry, enlisted 27 Jun 1812 for 18 months at age 45, 5' 10" tall, born in Pennsylvania and died at Sackett's Harbor, NY on 14 Jan 1814 (Johnson and Christou, p. 261)

Miller, George, served as a Private in Capt. Daniel Shawen's Co., Frederick Co. Militia, from 5 Sep 1814 and was reported "sick absent" on 6 Oct 1814 (Mallick and Wright, pp. 210, 365)

Miller, George, served as a Private in Capt. Thomas Contee Washington's Co., Frederick Co. Militia, from 17 Aug 1812 and was "discharged for inability" at Fort Severn before 31 Dec 1812 and was sick on leave when the company was discharged (Mallick and Wright, pp. 210, 332; BLW# 55-80-6944)

Miller, James, served as a Private in Capt. David Cummings' Co., 14th U.S. Infantry, enlisted 18 Aug 1813 and was later captured. Prisoner of War #4165 at Halifax, NS, interned 24 Jun 1813, sent to England on 27 Aug 1813, later released and was discharged at Fort McHenry on 30 Apr 1815 due to old age and rheumatism (Johnson and Christou, p. 261; Baker Vol. 1, p. 276)

Miller, James, served as a Private in Capt. Stephen Lee's Co., 19th U.S. Infantry, enlisted 27 Aug 1813, age 29, 5' 7½" tall, born in Baltimore City and captured at Fort Niagara, NY on 19 Dec 1813. Prisoner of War #1332 at Quebec, interned 29 Jan 1814 when received from Montreal by land carriage, exchanged on 4 May or 11 May 1814 and discharged from service at Greenbush, NY on 8 May 1815 (Johnson and Christou, p. 261; Johnson's Quebec book, p. 105)

Miller, John, served as a Private in Capt. Daniel Shawen's Co., Frederick Co. Militia, from 5 Sep 1814 and died 9 Oct 1814 (Mallick and Wright, pp. 211, 365)

Miller, John, served as a Seaman of the U.S. Chesapeake Flotilla, entered service on 6 Dec 1813, was on board on 7 Apr 1814 and was "shot and killed by ensign" on 3 Sep 1814 (Shomette p. 367)

Miller, John, served as a Seaman and was born in Baltimore. Age: 39. Prison Depot: Plymouth 2, Prisoner of War #122. Captured by HM Ship-of-the-Line

Leander, HM Ship-of-the-Line *Newcastle* & HM Frigate *Acasta*. When Taken: 28 Dec 1814. Where Taken: Lat 35N Long 52W. Prize Name: *Prince de Neufchatel*. Home Port: New York. Ship Type: Privateer. Date Received: 18 Feb 1815. From what ship: HMS *Sybille*. Discharged on 19 Feb 1815 and sent to Dartmoor. Prison Depot: Dartmoor, Prisoner of War #6356. Date Received: 19 Feb 1815. From what ship: HMT *Ganges* from Plymouth. Discharged and released on 6 Jul 1815. (Johnson's Database, 2019)

Miller, John, served as a Seaman and was born in Baltimore. Age: 30. Prison Depot: Dartmoor, Prisoner of War #3646. How Taken: Gave himself up off HM Ship-of-the-Line *Barfleur*. Date Received: 30 Sep 1814. From what ship: HMT *Sybella*. Discharged on 4 Jun 1815. (Johnson's Database, 2019)

Miller, John (African American), served as a Cook and was born in Queen Anne's Co., MD. Age: 25. Prison Depot: Plymouth 1, Prisoner of War #633. Captured by HM Frigate *Belle Poule*. When Taken: 14 Feb 1813. Where Taken: Bay of Biscayne. Prize Name: *Criterion*. Ship Type: Merchant Vessel. Received: 4 Mar 1813. From what ship: HMS *Strenuous*. Discharged and sent to Dartmoor on 2 Apr 1813. Prison Depot: Dartmoor, Prisoner of War #134. Received: 12 Apr 1813 from Plymouth. Discharged on 20 Apr 1815. (Johnson's Database, 2019)

Miller, Samuel, served as a Private in Capt. Samuel Lane's Co., 14th U.S. Inf., enlisted on 18 Aug 1812, age 35, 5' 4" tall, born in Cecil Co., MD and discharged at Plattsburgh, NY on 11 Jul 1814 for infirmities (Johnson and Christou, p. 262)

Miller, Samuel, served as a Private (company not stated) and was captured at the Battle of Bladensburg on 24 Aug 1814 (Marine, p. 174)

Miller, Samuel (1775-1855), served in the U.S. Marine Corps, was promoted to 1st Lieutenant on 7 Mar 1809 and promoted to Captain on 18 Jun 1814; he was wounded "from the seat of war" at the battle of Bladensburg on 24 Aug 1814 and admitted to the Naval Hospital in Washington, DC on 28 Aug 1814; he was subsequently discharged (date was not given) and was brevetted a Major for his service at Bladensburg. (Sharp's Database, 2018)

Miller, Valentine, served as a Private in Capt. William Durbin's Co., Frederick County Militia, joined 24 Aug 1814 and discharged on 9 Sep 1814 for inability (Mallick and Wright, p. 211)

Miller, William, served as a Private in Capt. Jacob Michael's Co., 42nd Regiment, Harford Co. Militia, from 28 Aug 1814 until discharged on 9 Sep 1814 by the Surgeon, medical reason not stated (Wright Vol. 3, p. 31)

Miller, William, served as a Seaman and was born in Baltimore. Age: 20. Prison Depot: Dartmoor, Prisoner of War #5434. How Taken: Gave himself up off HM Ship-of-the-Line *Ruby*. When Taken: 5 Nov 1814. Date Received: 11 Nov 1814.

From what ship: HMT *Impregnable*. Discharged and released on 1 Jul 1815. (Johnson's Database, 2019)

Millican, William, served as a Seaman and was born in East Town, MD. Age: 24. Prison Depot: Chatham, Prisoner of War #114. How Taken: Gave himself up off MV *Urbana*. When Taken: 26 Oct 1812. Where Taken: London. Received: 4 Nov 1812. From what ship: HMS *Namur*. Discharged on 11 Jan 1813 and released to the *Rebecca*. (Johnson's Database, 2019)

Mills, Stephen, served as a Private in Capt. David Cummings' Co., 14th U.S. Infantry, enlisted 13 Mar 1812 and was captured. Prisoner of War #4809, interned 15 Nov 1813, discharged on 19 Nov 1813 and sent to England (Johnson and Christou, p. 263; Baker Vol. 1, p. 278)

Mills, William, served as a Seaman and was born in Maryland. Age: 30. Prison Depot: Plymouth 1, Prisoner of War #1536. Captured by HM Frigate *Andromache*. When Taken: 14 Mar 1813. Where Taken: off Nantes, France. Prize Name: *Courier*. Home Port: Baltimore. Ship Type: Letter of Marque. Date Received: 29 May 1813. From what ship: HMS *Hannibal*. Discharged on 30 Jun 1813 and sent to Stapleton. Prison Depot: Stapleton, Prisoner of War #100. Date Received: 8 Jul 1813 from Plymouth. Discharged on 13 Jun 1814 and sent to Dartmoor. Prison Depot: Dartmoor, Prisoner of War #1390. Received: 19 Jun 1814 from Stapleton. Discharged on 28 Apr 1815. (Johnson's Database, 2019)

Mines, Artemas (African American), served as a Steward and was born in Maryland. Age: 22. Prison Depot: Plymouth 1, Prisoner of War #2000. Captured by HM Brig *Royalist*. When Taken: 6 Sep 1812. Where Taken: coast of France. Prize Name: *Ned*. Home Port: Baltimore. Ship Type: Letter of Marque. Date Received: 22 Sep 1813 from HMS *Royalist*. Discharged on 27 Sep 1813 and sent to Dartmoor. Prison Depot: Dartmoor, Prisoner of War #719. Date Received: 27 Sep 1813 from Plymouth. Discharged 26 Apr 1815. (Johnson's Database, 2019)

Mitchell, Carr, served as a Seaman and was born in Maryland. Age: 17. Prison Depot: Plymouth 1, Prisoner of War #1713. Captured by HM Frigate *Iris*. When Taken: 8 Jun 1813. Where Taken: Bay of Biscayne. Prize Name: *Joseph*. Ship Type: Merchant Vessel. Date Received: 4 Jul 1813. From what ship: HMS *Iris*. Discharged 22 Aug 1813. Released to HMS *Redpole*. (Johnson's Database, 2019)

Mitchell, Charles, served as a Private in Capt. David Cummings' Co., 14th U.S. Infantry, enlisted 6 Mar 1813 and was captured on 24 Jun 1813. Prisoner of War #3894, interned 24 Jun 1813, discharged on 19 Nov 1813 and sent to England, later released and deserted at Baltimore on 20 Apr 1815 (Johnson and Christou, p. 264; Baker Vol. 1, p. 278, stated he was in the 23rd U.S. Infantry)

Mitchell, Henry, of Maryland, served as a Seaman on the ship *LaHogue* and was reported by Capt. Jeduthan Upton, Jr. in 1814 as having been impressed into service and was being held as a Prisoner of War on the prison ship *San Antonio* at Chatham, England (*Niles Weekly Register*, 26 Feb 1814)

Mitchell, Jacob (1794-1814) (African American), served as a Seaman and was born in Baltimore. Age: 24. Prison Depot: Plymouth 1, Prisoner of War #1265. Captured by HM Frigate *Medusa*. When Taken: 12 Apr 1813. Where Taken: Bay of Biscayne. Prize Name: *Caroline*. Ship Type: Merchant Vessel. Date Received: 10 May 1813. From what ship: HMS *Medusa*. Discharged on 3 Jul 1813 and sent to Stapleton Prison. Prison Depot: Stapleton, Prisoner of War #282. Date Received: 11 Jul 1813 from Plymouth. Died on 25 May 1814 in hospital. (Johnson's Database, 2019)

Mitchell, John (African American), served as a Seaman and was born in Maryland. Age: 22. Prison Depot: Plymouth 1, Prisoner of War #2523. Captured by HM Frigate *Seahorse*. When Taken: 22 Mar 1814. Where Taken: at sea. Prize Name: *Hope*, prize of the Privateer *True Blooded Yankee*. Ship Type: Privateer. Date Received: 6 Apr 1814. From what ship: HMS *Queen Charlotte*. Discharged on 10 May 1814 and sent to Dartmoor. Prison Depot: Dartmoor, Prisoner of War #1123. Date Received: 10 May 1814 from Plymouth. Discharged on 28 Apr 1815. (Johnson's Database, 2019)

Mitchell, John, served as a Seaman and was born in Baltimore. Age: 23. Prison Depot: Portsmouth, Prisoner of War #162. Captured by HM Transport *Diadem*. When Taken: 7 Oct 1812. Where Taken: S. Andera (St. Andrews, Scotland). Prize Name: Baltimore. Home Port: Baltimore. Ship Type: Privateer. Date Received: 3 Nov 1812 San Antonio. From what ship: HMS *Diadem*. Discharged on 19 Feb 1813 and sent to Chatham on HM Store Ship *Dromedary*. Prison Depot: Chatham, Prisoner of War #531. Date Received: 23 Feb 1813 from Portsmouth on HMS *Dromedary*. Discharged on 8 Jun 1813 and released to the Cartel *Rodrigo*. (Johnson's Database, 2019)

Mitchell, John, served as a Seaman and was born in Baltimore. Age: 18. Prison Depot: Plymouth 1, Prisoner of War #192. Captured by HM Frigate *Phoebe*. When Taken: 23 Dec 1812. Where Taken: off Azores. Prize Name: *Hunter*. Home Port: Salem. Ship Type: Privateer. Date Received: 9 Jan 1813. From what ship: HMS *Phoebe*. Discharged and sent to Portsmouth (sic) on 8 Feb 1813 on HMS *Colossus*. Prison Depot: Chatham, Prisoner of War #460. Date Received: 19 Feb 1813. From what ship: HMS *Modeste*. Discharged on 24 Jul 1813 and released to the Cartel *Hoffning*. (Johnson's Database, 2019)

Mitchell, John, served as a Private in Capt. Thomas T. Simmons' Co., 2nd Regt., Anne Arundel Co. Militia, from 28 Sep 1814, was furloughed on 12 Oct 1814 and reported as "very sick at home" on 17 Oct 1814 (Wright Vol. 4, pp. 28, 43)

Mitchell, Joseph, served as a Private in Capt. Benjamin Thomas' Co., 49th Regt., Cecil Co. Militia, for 14 days between 18 Apr 1813 and 16 May 1813 and was "discharged on account of sickness" (Wright Vol. 3, p. 13)

Mitchell, Reuben (1795-1815), served as a Gunner and was born in Maryland. Age: 29. Prison Depot: Dartmoor, Prisoner of War #5500. When Taken: 22 Aug 1814. Where Taken: Chesapeake Bay. Prize Name: U.S. *Gunboat No. 2* (under Commodore Barney). Ship Type: Warship. Date Received: 17 Dec 1814. From what ship: HMT *Loire* from Halifax, NS. Died on 11 May 1815 from variola (smallpox). (1815 Centennial Trails, United States Daughters of 1812, online at www.war1812trails.com/Dartmoor; Johnson's Database, 2019)

Mitchell, William (1767-1813), served as a Private in 14th U.S. Infantry at the age of 46 and was captured. Prisoner of War #95 at Quebec, interned 8 Jun 1813 and died on 4 Aug 1813 (Johnson and Christou, p. 264; Johnson's Quebec book, p. 106)

Mix, Lewis, served as a Private in Capt. John Stewart's Co., 51st Regt., Baltimore Militia, joined 21 Aug 1814 and was wounded, but the place and date were not stated (Wright Vol. 2, p. 32, spelled his name Mis/Mia/Mix, and Marine p. 382, spelled it Mix, but did not mention his wound)

Money, Thomas M. (1776-1814), served as a Private in the 20th U.S. Infantry, enlisted 28 Apr 1812 at the age of 36, 5' 8" tall, born in Charles Co., MD and died on 4 Feb 1814, place and cause were not stated; pension issued to widow Margaret Money (Johnson and Christou, p. 265; Old War File IF-10530)

Monk, Philip (African American), served as a Seaman and was born in Baltimore. Age: 22. Prison Depot: Dartmoor, Prisoner of War #6300. Captured by HM Ship-of-the-Line *Leander*. When Taken: 4 Jan 1815. Prize Name: *John*, prize of the Privateer *Perry*. Home Port: Baltimore. Ship Type: Privateer. Date Received: 19 Feb 1815 from HMT *Ganges* from Plymouth. Discharged on 5 Jul 1815. (Johnson's Database, 2019)

Montgomery, John, served as a Private (company not stated) and was captured at the Battle of Bladensburg on 24 Aug 1814 (Marine, p. 174)

Moon, Joseph, served as a Private in the 14th U.S. Infantry and was captured [at Beaver Dams, Upper Canada] on 24 Jun 1813. Prisoner of War #4660 at Halifax, NS, interned 15 Nov 1813, discharged 9 Nov 1813 and sent to England (Johnson and Christou, p. 265; Baker Vol. 1, p. 281)

Mooney, George, served in the Navy from 10 Sep 1813 and drowned in a submarine at St. Leonards Creek, 2nd Battle, on 26 Jun 1814 (Shomette, p. 851; Sheads, p. 22)

Moore, Andrew (1777-1812), served as a Seaman on the privateer *Matilda*, age 35, born in Maryland, and died at the poor house and hospital in Savannah on 16 Oct 1812 (*Baltimore Federal Gazette*, 14 Nov 1812)

Moore (More), G., served as a Private in Capt. William Ray's Miles River Co., 26th Regiment, Talbot Co. Militia, in 1813 and was reported as "sick and not attending," but the specific dates were not indicated on the muster rolls dated 10 May – 11 May 1813 and 4 Aug – 30 Aug 1813 (Wright Vol. 1, p. 97)

Moore, Henry, served as a Seaman and was born in Baltimore. Age: 29. Prison Depot: Chatham, Prisoner of War #277. How Taken: Gave himself up. When Taken: 14 Dec 1812. Where Taken: London, UK. Date Received: 23 Dec 1812. From what ship: HMS *Raisonable*. Discharged on 24 Jul 1813 and released to the Cartel *Hoffning*. (Johnson's Database, 2019)

Moore, James, served as a Private in Capt. Joseph Marshall's Co., 14th U.S. Infantry, enlisted 13 Aug 1814 at Elkton, MD at the age of 22, 5' 5" tall, born in Delaware and discharged at Greenbush, NY on 4 May 1815 on a Surgeon's Certificate for a rupture (Johnson and Christou, p. 262, BLW# 19995-160-12)

Moore, James, served as a Private in Capt. Byrd Willis' Co., 20th U.S. Infantry, enlisted 9 Jun 1813 at Stevensburg, VA at the age of 25, 5' 6" tall, born in St. Mary's Co., MD and discharged at Burlington, VT on 24 Mar 1814 on Surgeon's Certificate due to a fractured arm (Johnson and Christou, pp. 265-266)

Moore, John, served as a Seaman and was born in Baltimore. Age: 30. Prison Depot: Chatham, Prisoner of War #2035. How Taken: Gave himself up. When Taken: 26 Jul 1813. Where Taken: London, UK. Date Received: 1 Aug 1813. From what ship: HMS *Raisonable*. Discharged on 4 Aug 1814 and sent to Dartmoor on HMS *Liverpool*. Prison Depot: Dartmoor, Prisoner of War #2814. Date Received: 24 Aug 1814. From what ship: HMT *Liverpool* from Chatham. Discharged on 19 May 1815. (Johnson's Database, 2019)

Moore, John (African American), served as a Seaman and was born in Maryland. Age: 29. Prison Depot: Plymouth 1, Prisoner of War #2116. Captured by HM Frigate *Hotspur* & HM Frigate *Pyramus*. When Taken: 26 Oct 1813. Where Taken: Bay of Biscayne. Prize Name: *Chesapeake*. Ship Type: Letter of Marque. Date Received: 22 Nov 1813. From what ship: HMS *Pyramus*. Discharged on 29 Nov 1813 and sent to Dartmoor. Prison Depot: Dartmoor, Prisoner of War #837. Date Received: 29 Nov 1813 from Plymouth. Discharged on 26 Apr 1815. (Johnson's Database, 2019)

Moore, Robert Scott (1792-1817), served as 3rd Lieutenant in Capt. Charles Pennington's Co., 1st Artillery Regt., Baltimore Independent Artillerists, from 19 Aug 1814 and was "stationed at Fort McHenry during the bombardment of 13 September 1814. The fatigue and exposure he went under on that mermonable [memorable] occasion brought on a desease [disease] of the Breast and of which he labored until 2nd Jan 1817 when he departed this life in a hope of a Blessed Immortality. Age 21 years, 6 mo." Robert Scott Moore, youngest son of Robert Moore, late merchant of Baltimore, formerly of Londonderry, Ireland, was buried in the Faith Presbyterian Church cellar at Broadway and Gay Street. (Wright Vol. 2, p. 47; Burials copied by Edith Ensor Read, 1812 Society, and placed in File 52255 at the Maryland Historical Society; she wrote, "In the cellar of the Chapel had to dig down twenty inches to get this information.") Robert Scott Moore, younger brother of Col. Samuel Moore of South Charles Street, died on 2 Jan 1817, age 25 (*Baltimore Patriot*, 6 Jan 1817)

Moore, Samuel, served as 1st Major in Long's 27th Regiment, Baltimore Militia, and was wounded on 12 Sep 1814 at the Battle of North Point (North Point dead and wounded Article 4 Oct 1814 Columbian Register CT Vol. III 97, p. 4; Marine p. 170) "Major Moore, of the 27th, was severely but not dangerously wounded." (J. Thomas Scharf's *The Chronicles of Baltimore*, Vol. 1, p. 351)

Moore, Samuel C. (1790-1815), served as a Private in Capt. John Rothrock's Co., 38th U.S. Infantry, enlisted 9 Sep 1813 at the age of 23, 5' 10" tall, born in Somerset Co., MD and diedin 1815; bounty land issued to John B. Moore and other heirs at law (BLW# 15909-160-12; Johnson and Christou, p. 266)

Moore, Stephen H., served as Captain of Baltimore Volunteers Infantry Co. (Independent Blues) from 8 Sep 1812 for 1 year and was wounded at York, Upper Canada on 27 Apr 1813; bounty land issued to his widow Jane Moore (BLW# 9756-160-50; Wright Vol. 2, p. 57; Johnson and Christou, p. 266)

Moore, Symond, served as a Private in Capt. Reuben Gilder's Co., 14th U.S. Inf., enlisted 12 May 1812 in Baltimore at age 26, 5' 5¾" tall, born in Minnack, Duchess Co., NY and later captured. Prisoner of War at Halifax, later released and discharged from the service at Greenbush, NY on 1 Jun 1815 for debility (Johnson and Christou, p. 26; Baker Vol. 1, p. 282, did not mention him)

Moore, William, served as a Private in Capt. James Dorman's Co., 5th U.S. Infantry, enlisted 27 Apr 1812 in Alexandria, DC, age 29, 5' 10½" tall, born in Harford Co., MD, wounded at Black Rock, NY and discharged at Pittsfield, NY on 13 Jun 1815 on a Surgeon's Certificate (Johnson and Christou, p. 266) William Moore was deposed on 31 Jul 1826 and stated he was upwards of 52 years of age. (*Harford County, Maryland Deponents, 1775-1835*, by Henry C. Peden, Jr., 2017, p. 142)

Moran, William (1783-1815), served as a Private in Capt. Hezekiah Bradley's Co., 2nd U.S. Infantry, enlisted 1 Mar 1814 in Washington, MD, at the age of 31, 5' 9" tall, born in Montgomery Co., MD and died at New Orleans on 25 Dec 1815 (Johnson and Christou, pp. 266-267)

Moran, William, served as a Sergeant in Capt. Lizur Canfield's Co., 23rd U.S. Infantry, enlisted 28 Aug 1812 at age 34, 5' 7¾" tall, was born in Baltimore and discharged at Sackett's Harbor, NY for disability, but the extent of his medical problem was not indicated (Johnson and Christou, p. 267)

Moreland, Theodore (1793-1815), served as a Private in Capt. Samuel Raisin's Co., 36th U.S. Infantry, enlisted on 21 Aug 1814 at the age of 21, 5' 5" tall, was born in Charles Co. and died on 27 Jan 1815. Barren Roby and Josias Marshall, acquaintances of Theodore Moreland, dec., late a private soldier in the U.S. Army, stated on 19 Feb 1821 that Matthew Moreland is the brother of said soldier, both of whom are the sons of Stephen Moreland who is also dead. They further stated that Matthew Moreland and his two sisters Anne Moreland and Rebecca Moreland are the legal heirs of the estate of the said Theodore Moreland. On 29 Mar 1822 acquaintances Leonard R. Richards and John B. Turner confirmed the information regarding Theodore Moreland's heirs. (BLW# 12-160-25774; Johnson and Christou, p. 267; Wright Vo. 5, p. 80)

Morgan, Jeremiah, served as a Private (company not stated) and was captured at the Battle of Bladensburg on 24 Aug 1814 (Marine, p. 174)

Morgan, Jesse, served as a Private in Capt. Peter Pinney's Co., 27th Regiment, Baltimore Militia, on 19 Aug 1814, became sick and never mustered since 20 Aug 1814 (Wright Vol. 2, p. 20)

Morgan, James (African American), served as a Seaman and was born in Baltimore. Age: 35. Prison Depot: Chatham, Prisoner of War #155. How Taken: Gave himself up. When Taken: 27 Oct 1812. Where Taken: London, UK. Date Received: 5 Nov 1812. From what ship: HMS *Namur*. Discharged in Jul 1813 and released to the Cartel *Moses Brown*. (Johnson's Database, 2019)

Morgan, Lodowick, served as 2nd Lieutenant in Capt. Lodowick Morgan's Co., 1st U.S. Rifles, from 3 May 1808, was promoted to 1st Lieutenant on 21 May 1809, promoted to Captain on 1 Jul 1811, promoted to Major on 24 Jan 1814 and was killed in action at Fort Erie, Upper Canada on 12 Aug 1814 (Johnson and Christou, p. 268)

Three new plaques were placed at the Centreville War Memorial in 2014 that included Major Lodowick Morgan (above center) who died on August 12, 1814.

Morgan, Thomas, served as a Private in Capt. Thomas F. W. Vinson's Co., 32nd Regt., Montgomery Co. Militia, Extra Battalion, from 1 Aug 1814 was reported missing in action on 24 Aug 1814 at Bladensburg (Wright Vol. 7, p. 5)

Morganthall, George, served as a Private in Capt. George Shryock's Co., Hagerstown, Washington Co. Militia, from 23 Jul 1814 and was reported as "sick on furlough," but no date was given (Wright Vol. 9, p. 8)

Morris, Andrew (African American), served as a Seaman and was born in Maryland. Age: 18. Prison Depot: Chatham, Prisoner of War #3775. Captured by HM Ship-of-the-Line *San Domingo*. When Taken: 1 Mar 1814. Where Taken: off Savannah, GA. Prize Name: *Argus*. Ship Type: Privateer. Date Received: 26 May 1814. From what ship: HMS *Hindostan*. Discharged on 25 Sep 1814 and sent to Dartmoor on HMS *Niobe*. Prison Depot: Dartmoor, Prisoner of War #4624. Date Received: 9 Oct 1814. From what ship: HMT *Leyden* from Chatham. Discharged on 15 Jun 1815. (Johnson's Database, 2019)

Morris, Morris (Maurice), served as a Private in Capt. Richard Arell's Co., 14th U.S. Infantry, enlisted 13 Aug 1812 in Baltimore at age 40, 5' 8" tall, born in Montgomery Co., PA and was captured on 12 Jun 1813. Prisoner of War #5087at Halifax, NS, interned 28 Dec 1813, discharged from prison on 31 May 1814 and discharged from the service at Greenbush, NY on 19 Jun 1815 for old age and infirmity (Johnson and Christou, p. 269; Baker Vol. 1, p. 284)

Morris, Thomas, served as a Seaman and was born in Maryland. Age: 22. Prison Depot: Plymouth 1, Prisoner of War #422. Captured by HM Frigate *Iris*. When Taken: 17 Jan 1813. Where Taken: at sea. Prize Name: *Union*. Home Port: Philadelphia. Ship Type: Merchant Vessel. Date Received: 5 Feb 1813. From what ship: HMS *San Josef*. Discharged and sent to Chatham on 29 Mar 1813 on HMS *Braham*. Prison Depot: Chatham, Prisoner of War #1492. Received: 6 Apr 1813 from Plymouth on an admiral's tender. Discharged 26 Jul 1813. Released to the Cartel *Hoffning*. (Johnson's Database, 2019)

Morrison, Arthur, served as a Private in Capt. Thomas Blair's Co., Allegany Co. Militia, and was reported as "sick in camp" on the muster roll dated 2 Sep – 28 Oct 1814 ("Allegany County Militia (Including Garrett Co.), 1794-1815," by F. Edward Wright and Marlene S. Bates, *Maryland Genealogical Society Bulletin*, Volume 32, No. 2, Spring 1991, p. 177; Wright Vol. 10, p. 6)

Mowbray, Aaron, served as a Private in Capt. Clement Sullivan's Co., 14th U.S. Infantry, enlisted 25 Apr 1812 for 5 year and died on or about 19 Sep 1812, but cause and place not stated; bounty land issued to his brother William Mowbray and other heirs at law (BLW# 23329-160-12; Johnson and Christou, p. 270)

Moxly, William, served as a Private in Capt. Thomas F. W. Vinson's Co., 32nd Regt., Montgomery Co., Extra Battalion, from 1 Aug 1814 was reported missing in action on 24 Aug 1814 at Bladensburg. (Wright Vol. 7, p. 5) He may be the William Moxley who died in 1845. (Montgomery Co. Will Book No. 4, p. 392)

Mozer, John D., served as a Private in Capt. Philip B. Sadtler's Co., 4th Regiment, Baltimore City, from 19 Aug 1814 and was wounded at Bladensburg on 24 Aug 1814 (Wright Vol. 2, p. 7)

Mullen, James, served as a Seaman in Commodore Barney's Flotilla and was wounded at Montgomery Court House, was admitted to the Naval Hospital in Washington, DC as Patient No. 44 on 17 Sep 1814 with fever, was discharged on 8 Dec 1814 and sent to Baltimore; he was again admitted to the hospital as Patient No. 86 on 27 Dec 1814 with typhoid fever and was discharged on 4 Jan 1815 at which time he was reported to be a Marine. (Sharp's Database, 2018)

Muller, Francis Xavier, of Baltimore, served as a Seaman on the privateer *Paul Jones* in 1812 and while attempting to swim ashore in the Savannah River was taken down by an alligator (*Niles Weekly Register*, 24 Oct 1812)

Mullin, Charles, served as a Private in Capt. Caleb Holder's Co., 17th U.S. Infantry, enlisted on 16 Dec 1812 for 5 years at the age of 40, 5' 5" tall, was born in Cecil Co., MD and discharged on 8 Jun 1816 on a Surgeon's Certificate (Johnson and Christou, p. 262)

Mullins, Owen, served as a Private in the 14th U.S. Infantry and was captured. Prisoner of War #3858 at Halifax, interned on 24 Jun 1813 and discharged for exchange on 3 Feb 1914 (Johnson and Christou, p. 271; Baker Vol. 1, p. 287)

Mulvy, Michael (1793-1814), served as a Private in Capt. Daniel McFarland's Co., 22nd U.S. Infantry, enlisted on 22 Jul 1812 in Washington, PA at the age of 19, was born in Marylandand died at Franklin, NY on 1 Jan 1814 (Johnson and Christou, p. 271)

Murdock, John B., served as a Private in Capt. John Galt's Co., Frederick County Militia, joined 31 Aug 1814 and reported "dead"on 18 Oct 1814. (Mallick and Wright, pp. 217, 361)

Murphy, James (1788-1818), served as a Private in Capt. Reuben Gilder's Co., 14th U.S. Infantry, enlisted 2 Mar 1813 at the age of 25, 5' 5" tall, born in Clonmel, Ireland, was discharged at Greenbush, NY on 4 May 1815 on a Surgeon's Certificate because of wounds received in leg and wrist, placed on the pension roll on 9 Aug 1815 and died on 24 Jun 1818 (BLW# 14283-160-12; Johnson and Christou, p. 272)

Murphy, James, served as a Private in Capt. Thomas Blair's Co., Allegany Co. Militia, and was reported as "sick in camp" on the muster roll dated 2 Sep – 28 Oct 1814 ("Allegany County Militia (Including Garrett Co.), 1794-1815," by F. Edward Wright and Marlene S. Bates, *Maryland Genealogical Society Bulletin,* Volume 32, No. 2, Spring 1991, p. 177; Wright Vol. 10, p. 6)

Murphy, John, served as Captain of the privateer *Globe* in 1812 and served as Captain of the privateer *Grampus* in 1814 and was killed in action 4 Sep 1814 (Marine p. 388)

Murphy, John, served as a Private in the 14th U.S. Infantry, enlisted by Lt. Nelson at Fort Cumberland, Allegany Co., MD on 2 Jun 1812 for 5 years; served as a Corporal in Capt. Samuel Lane's Co. at the age of 21, 5' 8¼" tall, born at Fort Cumberland, MD and was captured. Prisoner of War #4124 at Halifax, NS, interned 24 Jun 1813, discharged for exchange on 3 Feb 1814, exchanged on 15 Apr 1814, returned to service, deserted on 27 Nov 1814, reduced to Private, rejoined on 30 Nov 1815, appointed Corporal on 13 Mar 1816, reduced to Private on 25 Apr 1815 and was discharged from the service at Raleigh, NC on 3 or 4 Jun 1817. (*Maryland Genealogical Society Bulletin,* Volume 32, No. 2, Spring 1991, p. 180, citing *Registers of Enlistment in the U. S. Army, 1798-1914,* M233; Johnson and Christou, p. 272; Baker Vol. 1, p. 288; Wright Vol. 10, p. 10)

Murphy (Murphey), Samuel, served as a Private in Capt. Perrin Willis' Co., 2nd U.S. Infantry, enlisted 21 Nov 1814 at Washington, DC for 5 years at the age of 21, 6' tall, born in Montgomery Co., MD and discharged at Carlisle Barracks, PA on 7 Jul 1815 because of a rupture (Johnson and Christou, p. 271)

Murray, Amon, served as a Private in Capt. Clement Sullivan's Co., 14th U.S. Infantry, enlisted 20 May 1812 and died on 3 Dec 1812; bounty land issued to Ann Lanham and other heirs (BLW# 7090-160-12; Johnson and Christou, p. 271)

Murray, Edward, served as a Private in Capt. James Dorman's Co., 5th U.S. Infantry, enlisted 10 Aug 1812 in Baltimore at the age of 28, 5' 9" tall, born in Ireland and was discharged at Greenbush, NY for incapacity, but the date was not given (Johnson and Christou, p. 273)

Murray, Edward, served as a Private in Capt. Samuel Sterett's Co., 5th Regt., Baltimore Militia, and was taken prisoner on 12 Sep 1814 at North Point (Wright Vol. 2, p. 6)

Murray, James, of Maryland, served as a Seaman on the ship *Messenger* and was captured, but date was not given. Prisoner of War #4100676 at Dartmoor and died on 17 Oct 1813 (Centennial Trails, United States Daughters of 1812, online at www.war1812trails.com/Dartmoor)

Murray, James (1794-1813), served as a Seaman and was born in Baltimore. Age: 24. Prison Depot: Dartmoor, Prisoner of War #676. Captured by HM Frigate *Iris*. When Taken: 10 Mar 1813. Where Taken: off Cape Ortegal, Spain. Prize Name: *Messenger*. Ship Type: Merchant Vessel. Died on 17 Oct 1813 from pneumonia. (Johnson's Database, 2019)

Murray, John or Richard (sic) (1774-1814) (Mulatto), served as a Seaman and Cook and was born in Maryland. Age: 40. Prison Depot: Chatham, Prisoner of War #3572. How Taken: Gave himself up off a cutter. When Taken: 25 Feb 1814. Where Taken: off Bordeaux, France. Prize Name: *Commodore Perry*. Ship Type: Merchant Vessel. Date Received: 7 May 1814. From what ship: HM Sloop (not readable). Discharged on 25 Sep 1814 and sent to Dartmoor on HMS *Niobe*. Prison Depot: Dartmoor, Prisoner of War #4209. Received: 7 Oct 1814. From what ship: HMT *Niobe* from Chatham. Discharged on 13 Jun 1815. (Johnson's Database, 2019)

Murray, William H., served as 4th Sergeant in Capt. David Warfield's Co., 5th Regt., Baltimore Militia, and was reported "wounded," but no date and place were given on the muster roll dated 19 Aug – 18 Nov 1814 (Wright Vol. 2, p. 7)

Muschett (Muskett), Walter, served as a Private in Capt. David Warfield's Co., 5th Regt., Baltimore United Volunteers, and was wounded on 12 Sep 1814 at North Point (Wright Vol. 2, p. 8) Dr. James H. McCulloh, Jr. wrote this note soon after the battle to the British commander: "In consequence of the humanity shown the following American prisoners of war, I do promise upon honor that they shall not directly or indirectly serve against the British until regularly exchanged." (Marine, p. 171)

Myerheifer, John, served as a Corporal in the 38th U.S. Infantry, enlisted 1 Mar 1814 by Capt. Rothrock at Craney Island, age 30, 5' 9" tall, brown/black eyes, black hair, brown complexion, born in Fredericktown, MD, absent in General

Hospital at Norfolk on 15 Mar 1815 and discharged at Craney Island on 15 Mar 1815 (sic). (Mallick and Wright, p. 319)

Myers, Edward, served as a Seaman and was born in Maryland. Age: 22. Prison Depot: Dartmoor, Prisoner of War #2292. Captured by HM Ship-of-the-Line *Saturn*. When Taken: 25 May 1814. Where Taken: off Sandy Hook, NJ. Prize Name: *Hussar*. Home Port: New York. Ship Type: Privateer. Date Received: 16 Aug 1814. From what ship: HMS *Dublin* from Halifax, NS. Discharged on 3 May 1815. (Johnson's Database, 2019)

Myers, Frederick, served as a Seaman and was born in Baltimore. Age: 37. Prison Depot: Plymouth 1, Prisoner of War #324. Captured by HM Frigate *Dryad*. When Taken: 8 Jan 1813. Where Taken: off Bordeaux, France. Prize Name: *Porcupine*. Ship Type: Merchant Vessel. Date Received: 21 Jan 1813 on HMS *Abercrombie*. Discharged and sent to Chatham on 29 Mar 1813 on HMS *Braham*. Prison Depot: Chatham, Prisoner of War #1406. Date Received: 5 Apr 1813 from Plymouth on HMS *Dwarf*. Discharged on 24 Jul 1813 and released to the Cartel *Hoffning*. (Johnson's Database, 2019)

Myers, John, served as a Private in the 14th U.S. Infantry, enlisted 26 Feb 1813 for 18 months and was captured later. Prisoner of War #3949, interned 24 Jun 1813, was discharged on 19 Nov 1813 and sent to England, later released and was discharged from the service at Baltimore on 31 Mar 1815 (Johnson and Christou, p. 274; Baker Vol. 1, p. 289, stated he was in the 15th U.S. Infantry)

Myers, Michael, served as a Private in Capt. Samuel Lane's Co., 14th U.S. Inf., enlisted 13 Jun 1812 in Lewistown at the age of 18, 5' 7" tall, was wounded at Black Rock, NY on 28 Nov 1813 and deserted at Fort McHenry on 20 Apr 1815 (Johnson and Christou, p. 274)

Myers, Michael, served as a Private in the 14th U.S. Infantry and was captured. Prisoner of War #4037 at Halifax, NS, interned 24 Jun 1813, discharged 9 Nov 1813 and sent to England (Johnson and Christou, p. 275; Baker Vol. 1, p. 289)

N

Nabbs, William, served as a Landsman of the U.S. Chesapeake Flotilla, entered service on 22 Mar 1814, was on board on 7 Apr 1814 and was killed at St. Leonards Creek, 2nd Battle, on 26 Jun 1814 (Shomette, p. 375; Sheads, p. 22)

Nagel, George, served as a Seaman and was born in Maryland. Age: 32. Prison Depot: Plymouth 1, Prisoner of War #1836. Captured by HM Brig *Pelican*. When Taken: 14 Aug 1813. Where Taken: off St. David's Head, Wales. Prize Name: U.S. Brig *Argus*. Ship Type: Warship. Date Received: 17 Aug 1813. From what ship: USS *Argus*. Discharged on 8 Sep 1813 and sent to Dartmoor. Prison Depot:

Dartmoor, Prisoner of War #576. Date Received: 8 Sep 1813 from Plymouth. Discharged and sent to Dartmouth on 2 Nov 1814. (Johnson's Database, 2019)

Naperny, John, served as a Private in the 14th U.S. Infantry and was captured. Prisoner of War #4181 at Halifax, NS, interned 24 Jun 1813, discharged 27 Aug 1813 and sent to England (Johnson and Christou, p. 274; Baker Vol. 2, p. 290)

Nash, Archibald (1788-1813), served as a Private in Capt. Samuel Lane's Co., 14th U.S. Infantry, enlisted 21 May 1812 in Westminster, MD, age 24, 5' 2" tall, born in Maryland and killed at Beaver Dams, Upper Canada, ten miles west of Niagara Falls, on 24 Jun 1813 (Johnson and Christou, p. 275)

Nash, Daniel (1783-1815), served as a Seaman and was born in Dorset [Dorcehster Co.], MD. Age: 31. Prison Depot: Dartmoor, Prisoner of War #3485. How Taken: Gave himself up off HM Ship-of-the-Line *Prince*. When Taken: 14 Sep 1814. Date Received: 19 Sep 1814. From what ship: HMT *Salvador del Mundo*. Died 14 Feb 1815 from variola (smallpox). (Johnson's Database, 2019)

Nash, Ephraim, served as a Private in Capt. Daniel Schwartzauer's Co., 27th Regiment, Baltimore Militia, from 19 Aug 1814 and reported as "in captivity 12 Sep" at North Point (Wright Vol. 2, p. 16)

Nash, William, served as a Seaman and was born in Baltimore. Age: 40. Prison Depot: Chatham, Prisoner of War #1691. Captured by *Thetis*, British Privateer. When Taken: 2 May 1813. Where Taken: Bay of Biscayne. Prize Name: *Governor Middleton*. Ship Type: Merchant Vessel. Date Received: 15 May 1813. From what ship: HMS *Viper*. Died on 30 Sep 1813 from phthisis (tuberculosis). (Johnson's Database, 2019)

Neal, Dennis, served as a Seaman and was born in Maryland. Age: 25. Prison Depot: Plymouth 1, Prisoner of War #1562. Captured by HM Frigate *Andromache*. When Taken: 14 Mar 1813. Where Taken: off Nantes, France. Prize Name: *Courier*. Home Port: Baltimore. Ship Type: Letter of Marque. Date Received: 29 May 1813. From what ship: HMS *Hannibal*. Discharged on 30 Jun 1813 and sent to Stapleton. Prison Depot: Stapleton, Prisoner of War #124. Date Received: 8 Jul 1813 from Plymouth. Discharged on 13 Jun 1814 and sent to Dartmoor. Prison Depot: Dartmoor, Prisoner of War #1407. Received: 19 Jun 1814 from Stapleton. Discharged on 28 Apr 1815. (Johnson's Database, 2019)

Neal, John, served as a Gunner and was born in Baltimore. Age: 36. Prison Depot: Plymouth 1, Prisoner of War #2275. Captured by HM Brig *Pelican*. When Taken: 13 Jan 1814. Where Taken: at sea. Prize Name: *Siro*. Home Port: Baltimore. Ship Type: Letter of Marque. Date Received: 23 Jan 1814. From what ship: HMS *Pelican*. Discharged on 31 Jan 1814 and sent to Dartmoor. Prison Depot:

Dartmoor, Prisoner of War #939. Date Received: 31 Jan 1814 from Plymouth. Discharged on 27 Apr 1815. (Johnson's Database, 2019)

Neale, Benjamin, served as a Private in Capt. George Steever's Co., 27th Regiment, Baltimore Militia, from 9 Aug to 16 Aug 1813 and served in Capt. John McKane's Co., 27th Regiment, from 19 Aug 1814 and was killed on 12 Sep 1814 at North Point. His name is on the Baltimore Battle Monument. (NARA; CMSR; *Baltimore American*, 12 Jun 1819; Wright Vol. 2, p. 18, listed him, but did not mention that he was killed)

Neel, William, served as a Seaman and was born in Fredericktown, MD. Age: 23. Prison Depot: Plymouth 1, Prisoner of War #2545. Captured by HM Post Ship *Crocodile*. When Taken: 6 Aug 1813. Where Taken: off Corsuma. Prize Name: *Mary*, prize of the Privateer *Blockade*. Ship Type: Privateer. Date Received: 16 Apr 1814. From what ship: Transport *Fanny*. Discharged on 10 May 1814 and sent to Dartmoor. Prison Depot: Dartmoor, Prisoner of War #1138. Date Received: 10 May 1814 from Plymouth. Discharged on 28 Apr 1815. (Johnson's Database, 2019)

Negro Peter, served on board the privateer (armed brigantine) *Chausseur* of Baltimore commanded by Capt. Thomas Boyle and was severely wounded in action on 26 Feb 1815 and later died (*Niles Weekly Register*, 25 Mar 1815)

Neil, Jeremiah (1786-1815), served as a Private in Capt. Joseph Marshall's Co., 14th U.S. Infantry, enlisted 18 Jun 1814 in Baltimore, age 28, 5' 10½" tall, born in Baltimore, died at Utica, NY on 12 Jan 1815, cause not stated; heirs received half pay for 5 years in lieu of bounty land (Johnson and Christou, p. 276)

Nesbitt, Shadrack, served as a Private in Capt. Reuben Gilder's Co., 14th U.S. Infantry, enlisted 19 May 1812 for 5 years in Maryland at the age of 21, 5' 6" tall, born in Dorchester Co., MD and captured at Stoney Creek, Upper Canada on 12 Jun 1813. Prisoner of War #5091 at Halifax, interned 28 Dec 1813, was discharged for exchange on 31 May 1814, returned to the service and was discharged at Montpelier, MS (sic) on 18 May 1817 (Johnson and Christou, p. 276; Baker Vol. 1, p. 290 spelled his name Shedrick Nesbett)

Neveling, John, served as a Private in Capt. Jacob Deems' Co., 51st Regiment, Baltimore Militia, joined 20 Aug 1814 and was discharged on 7 Sep 1814 by a Surgeon, but the cause was not reported (Wright Vol. 2, p. 34)

Newcomb, Tilton, served as a Lieutenant and was born in Maryland. Age: 31. Prison Depot: Dartmoor, Prisoner of War #4877. Captured by HM Brig *Barracouta*. When Taken: 9 Oct 1814. Where Taken: off Western Islands, Scotland. Prize Name: *Saratoga*. Ship Type: Privateer. Date Received: 24 Oct

1814. From what ship: HMT *Salvador del Mundo*. Discharged on 21 Jun 1815. (Johnson's Database, 2019)

Newland, Thomas, served as a Private in the 14th U.S. Infantry and was later captured. Prisoner of War #4171 at Halifax, NS, interned on 24 Jun 1813, was discharged on 27 Aug 1813 and sent to England on the HSM *Regulus* (Johnson and Christou, p. 277; Baker Vol. 2, p. 292)

Newman, Stokely, served as a Private in Capt. Reuben Gilder's Co., 14th U.S. Infantry, enlisted 12 Aug 1812 in Chester at the age of 26, 5' 11½" tall, born in Lewistown, DE. Prisoner of War #5251 at Halifax, captured on 13 Sep 1813, discharged from prison and exchanged 31 May 1814; wounded at Cook's Mills, Upper Canada on 19 Oct 1814 and discharged at Greenbush, NY on 28 Mar 1815 (BLW# 3990-160-12; Johnson and Christou, pp. 277-278, but p. 360 listed him as Newman Stokeley; Baker, Vol. 2, p. 292) In Baltimore on 22 Jun 1825 Stokely Newman, former private in Capt. Gilder's Co., 14th Regiment, disabled in the late war and a resident of Queen Anne's Co. before and since the war, collected his own $12 .00 due from 4 Sep 1824 to 4 Mar 1825 (Pierce, p. 125)

Newnam, James, of Baltimore, was captured (company or vessel and date and location were not stated) and imprisoned in Dartmoor, England prior to the massacre in the prison in 1815 during which time he was dangerously wounded (*Niles Weekly Register*, 17 Jun 1815)

Nicholas, George (c1787-1813), served as Surgeon's Mate in 14th U.S. Infantry, commissioned on 14 Oct 1812. A doctor late of Centreville, Queen Anne's Co., MD, he died in Baltimore on 17 Mar 1813, age about 26, leaving a sister on the Eastern Shore, aged 14, as his only relation. (Johnson and Christou, p. 278; *Baltimore Federal Gazette*, 18 Mar 1813 and 19 Mar 1813)

Nicholls, William, served as a Private in Capt. William McIlvane's Co., 14th U.S. Infantry, enlisted 13 Apr 1813, age 40, 5' 6¾" tall, born in Delaware, also served onboard the fleet with Commodore Chauncey, and was discharged on 4 May 1815 at Greenbush, NY for infirmities (Johnson and Christou, p. 278)

Nichols, Adam, served as a Private in Capt. Henry Steiner's Co., Frederick Co. Militia, from 25 Aug 1814 and was reported "sick on furlough," but no date was given (Mallick and Wright, p. 354) He may be the J. Adam Nickel (1785-1864) who was buried in Mt. Olivet Cemetery in Frederick, MD. (*Names In Stone*, by Jacob M. Holdcraft, 1966, p. 846)

Nichols, John, served as a Private in Capt. Joseph Isaac's Co., 34th Regiment, Prince George's Co. Militia, between 21 Jul 1813 and 2 Sep 1813, was stationed at Annapolis for six days and was then reported sick (Wright Vol. 6, p. 15)

Nichols, John, served as a Private in Capt. Josiah Woods' Co., 10th U.S. Inf., enlisted 1 Jun 1813 at age 43, 5' ½" tall, born in Maryland and was discharged on 28 Feb 1814 on a Surgeon's Certificate (Johnson and Christou, p. 279)

Nicholson, Benjamin, served as 1st Lieutenant in the 14th U.S. Infantry; born in Maryland, commissioned on 12 Mar 1812, promoted to Captain on 3 Mar 1813 and died on 13 May 1813 from wounds received at the capture of York, Upper Canada on 27 Apr 1813 (Johnson and Christou, p. 279, Marine, p. 392). Capt. Nicholson, the "aide-de-camp to Brig. Gen. Pike, died on board Commodore Chauncy's fleet on the Lakes." (*Baltimore Federal Gazette*, 27 May 1813)

Nicholson, Charles (African American), served as a Seaman and was born in Baltimore. Age: 25. Prison Depot: Portsmouth, Prisoner of War #955. How Taken: Gave himself up off HM Ship-of-the-Line *Swiftsure*. When Taken: 26 Dec 1812. Date Received: 28 Jul 1813. From what ship: HM Sloop *Volentaire*. Discharged on 7 Aug 1813 and sent to Chatham on HMS *Rinaldo*. Prison Depot: Chatham, Prisoner of War #2170. Received: 16 Aug 1813 from Portsmouth on an admiral's tender. Discharged on 15 Oct 1813 and released to HMS *Ceres*. (Johnson's Database, 2019)

Nicholson, James, served as a Seaman and was born in Maryland. Age: 21. Prison Depot: Dartmoor, Prisoner of War #4443. Captured by HM Brig *Electra*. When Taken: 7 Jul 1814. Where Taken: off St. Johns, Newfoundland. Prize Name: *Growler*. Home Port: Salem. Ship Type: Privateer. Date Received: 8 Oct 1814. From what ship: HMT *Leyden* from Chatham. Discharged on 14 Jun 1815. (Johnson's Database, 2019)

Nicholson, William, served as a Ship's Carpenter and on 24 Aug 1814 was on the field of battle at Bladensburg, and later "died at his house from a wound," but the date and place of residence were not stated (Sharp's Database, 2018)

Nicum, John (1774-1814), served as a Private in Capt. Harris Hickman's Co., 17th U.S. Infantry, enlisted 23 Apr 1814 in Franklin Co., OH at age of 40, 5' 10" tall, born in Maryland and died on 2 Nov 1814; bounty land issued to John Nicum and other heirs at law (BLW# 23025-160-12; Johnson and Christou, p. 279)

Norman, Michael, served as a Seaman and was born in Baltimore. Age: 25. Prison Depot: Plymouth 1, Prisoner of War #2686. How Taken: Gave himself up off HM Ship-of-the-Line *Cornwallis*. Date Received: 7 Jun 1814. From what ship: *Inap*. Discharged on 14 Jun 1814 and sent to Dartmoor. Prison Depot: Dartmoor, Prisoner of War #1310. Date Received: 14 Jun 1814 from Mill Prison. Discharged on 28 Apr 1815. (Johnson's Database, 2019)

Norris, Luther A., served as a Private in Capt. Aaron R. Levering's Co., 5th Regiment, Baltimore Militia, and was wounded on 12 Sep 1814 at North Point

(Wright Vol. 2, p. 5) Dr. James H. McCulloh, Jr. wrote this note soon after the battle to the British commander: "In consequence of the humanity shown the following American prisoners of war, I do promise upon honor that they shall not directly or indirectly serve against the British until regularly exchanged." (Marine, p. 171)

Norris, Patrick, served as a Private in Capt. Joseph Marshall's Co., 14th U.S. Infantry, enlisted 5 Aug 1814 in Boonesboro, MD at age 33, 5' 9" tall, born in Boonsbury (sic), was wounded in left shoulder, place and date not stated, and was discharged at Greenbush, NY on 4 Apr 1815; placed on pension roll on 25 Dec 1819 (BLW# 23543-160-12; Johnson and Christou, p. 280) In Washington Co., MD on 5 Sep 1842 Patrick Norris, former private in Capt. J. Marshall's Co., 14th Regiment, U.S. Infantry, and lifelong resident of the county, appointed C. C. Jameson as his attorney to collect his $24.00 pension due from 4 Mar to 4 Sep 1842 (Pierce, p. 137)

Norris, Thomas, served as a Private in Capt. Samuel Sterett's Co., 5th Regt., Baltimore Militia, joined on 1 Sep 1814 and was taken prisoner at North Point on 12 Sep 1814 (Wright Vol. 2, p. 6)

Norris, William (1776-1815), served as a Private in Capt. Joseph Marshall's Co., 14th U.S. Infantry, enlisted 15 Aug 1814 at age 38, 5' 10" tall, born in Maryland and died at Greenbush, NY on 22 Jan 1815 from diarrhea; bounty land issued to his son George Norris (BLW# 26899-160-12; Johnson and Christou, p. 280)

North, Henry (1785-1815), served as a Private in Capt. George Keyser's Co., 38th U.S. Infantry, enlisted 18 Nov 1814 in Baltimore at the age of 19, 5' 4½" tall, born in Dorchester Co., MD and died on 24 Jan 1815; bounty land issued to his sister Mary North (BLW# 27004-160-12; Johnson and Christou, p. 280)

North, James (c1790-1812), served as a Private in Capt. Thomas Kearney's Co., 14th U.S. Infantry, enlisted 15 May 1812 and died 27 Dec 1812; bounty land issued to son James North (BLW# 26979-160-12; Johnson and Christou, p. 280)

North, Thomas, served as a Seaman and was born in Maryland. Age: 39. Prison Depot: Stapleton, Prisoner of War #416. How Taken: Gave himself up off Portuguese MV *Senora del Manda*. When Taken: 9 Nov 1813. Date Received: 9 Nov 1813. From what ship: Naval *Rendezvous Bristol*. Discharged on 16 Jun 1814 and sent to Dartmoor. Prison Depot: Dartmoor, Prisoner of War #1653. How Taken: Gave himself up. When Taken: 9 Nov 1813. Where Taken: Bristol, UK. Date Received: 23 Jun 1814 from Stapleton. Discharged on 1 May 1815. (Johnson's Database, 2019)

Norton, Theophilus J., served as a Private in Capt. Kenneth McKenzie's Co., 14th U.S. Infantry, enlisted 16 Jan 1813 in Baltimore for 18 months at the age of 23,

5′ 6″ tall, born in Philadelphia, lost a leg at Fort George, Upper Canada on 27 May 1813 and was discharged at Baltimore on 28 Nov 1814 on a Surgeon's Certificate (Johnson and Christou, p. 281) In Baltimore Co. on 12 Mar 1821 Theophilus J. Norris, former sergeant in Capt. Kenneth's Co. (sic), 14th Regt., U.S. Infantry, in the late war when disabled, and a resident of Baltimore for about 4 or 5 years and previously of different places, and he collected his own $48.00 pension due from 4 Sep 1820 to 4 Mar 1821. (Pierce, p. 137)

Notter, Benjamin, served as a Private in Capt. Reuben Gilder's Co., 14th U.S. Infantry, enlisted 5 Sep 1812 in Baltimore at the advanced age of 48, 5′ 8″ tall, born in Ireland and was discharged at Greenbush, NY on 1 Jun 1815 because of age and infirmities (Johnson and Christou, p. 281)

Nowlton, Ebenezer, served as a Private in the 14th U.S. Infantry and was later captured. Prisoner of War #3929 at Halifax, NS, interned on 24 Jun 1813 and discharged for exchange on 3 Feb 1814 (Johnson and Christou, p. 281; Baker Vol. 2, p. 297)

Noyle, Jacob, served as a Private and was captured at North Point on 12 Sep 1814. Dr. James H. McCulloh, Jr. wrote this soon after the battle to the British commander: "In consequence of the humanity shown the following American prisoners of war, I do promise upon honor that they shall not directly or indirectly serve against the British until regularly exchanged." (Marine, p. 171)

Nunamacker, Michael (1780-1814), served as a Private in Capt. Alexander McIlhenney's Co., 5th U.S. Infantry, enlisted 10 Apr 1813 in Lancaster, PA at the age of 33, 5′ 6″ tall, born in Maryland and died on 12 Jan 1814 (Johnson and Christou, p. 281)

Nusser (Nussear), John, served as a Private in Capt. Joseph Hook's Co., 36th U.S. Infantry, enlisted 23 or 24 Jul 1814 at Baltimore at the age of 33 or 38 (sic), 5′ 7″ or 7½″ tall, gray eyes, dark hair, dark complexion, born in Frederick Co., MD, absent sick since July 1814, mustered at Ft. Covington on 31 Dec 1814, was reported "deserted" on 21 Mar 1815, yet discharged at Ft. Covington on 30 Mar 1815 (Mallick and Wright, p. 224)

Nutter, Charles, served as a Surgeon, 25th Regiment, Somerset County Militia, under Lt. Col. Thomas Humphreys, appointed 28 Nov 1808, reported dead in 1813 (date and cause not stated) and his replacement was appointed on 7 Dec 1813. (Wright Vol. 1, p. iii; Marine p. 394, listed him as "---- Nutton, surgeon")

Nybro, Godfred, served as a Private in the 14th U.S. Infantry and was captured at Beaver Dams, Upper Canada on 24 Jun 1813. Prisoner of War #3841 at Halifax, NS, interned 15 Nov 1813, discharged 19 Nov 1813 and sent to England (Johnson and Christou, p. 282; Baker Vol. 2, p. 292)

Nye, John, served as a Private in Capt. Thomas Montgomery's Co., 14th U.S. Infantry (company not stated), enlisted 10 Feb 1813 at the age of 27, 5' 6" tall, born in Somerset Co., PA, was wounded in battle in June 1813 and discharged at Washington, DC on 31 May 1815 due to loss of right arm (BLW# 2645-160-12; Old War Pension IF-26748; Johnson and Christou, p. 282)

O

Oakam, Archibald (African American), served as a Seaman and was born in Baltimore. Age: 21. Prison Depot: Dartmoor, Prisoner of War #3590. Captured by HM Brig *Hardy*. When Taken: 26 Mar 1814. Where Taken: West Indies. Prize Name: *Fairy*. Ship Type: Privateer. Date Received: 30 Sep 1814. From what ship: HMT *Sybella*. Discharged on 4 Jun 1815. (Johnson's Database, 2019)

O'Conner, Jeremiah (1779-1815), served as a Private in Capt. Charles Stansbury's Co., 38th U.S. Infantry, enlisted 9 Dec 1814 in Cumberland at the age of 35, born in Ireland and died 6 Feb 1815; bounty land to his brother and only heir Thomas O'Connor (BLW# 18443-160-12; Johnson and Christou, p. 283)

O'Conner, John, served as a Private in Capt. Humphrey's Co., 6th Regt., U.S. Infantry, and in Baltimore on 31 May 1828 he stated he had been disabled in the late war and was a resident of this city; he collected his own $36 pension due from 4 Sep 1827 to 4 Mar 1828. His statement was sworn before W. L. Gill, Justice of the Peace, stating no further detail was possible "from the deafness of the pensioner no communication can be held with him." (Pierce, p. 138)

Odenbaugh, Charles, (1771-1813), served as a Private in Capt. Daniel McFarland's Co., 22nd U.S. Infantry, enlisted 29 May 1812 in Washington, DC at the age of 41, 5' 7¾" tall, born in Baltimore and died at Fort Niagara, NY on 22 Apr 1813 from dropsy (Johnson and Christou, p. 283)

Offutt, Colmore (1785-1855), served as a Private in Capt. John Heeter's Co., 44th Regiment, Montgomery Co. Militia, having volunteered at Rockville around 3 Aug 1814 and he did not obtain a regular discharge because he was sick with dysentery; however, muster roll dated 4 Aug – 27 Sep 1814 reported Colmore was absent without leave since 28 Aug 1814; immediately after the Battle of Bladensburg John Offutt was sent by his father to bring Colmore home from "Tennally town, D. C." where he was sick. He married Elizabeth Ann Poole on 7 Feb 1847 in Montgomery Co., was age 65 in 1850 and died on 5 Feb 1855. (Wright Vol. 7, pp. 4, 35; BLW# 55-160-36814)

Ogden, Amos, served as a Private in Capt. Clement Guiton's Co., 2nd Regt., 11th Brigade, Baltimore, from 27 Jul 1814 and was reported "sick on furlough since Sep 1" 1814 (Wright Vol. 2, p. 86)

Ogle, James, served as a Private in Capt. George Haig's Co., 2nd U.S. Light Dragoons, enlisted 11 Jul 1812 at Leesburg, VA at the age of 23, 5' 8½" tall, born in Baltimore, and was discharged on 21 Jul 1815 on a Surgeon's Certificate (Johnson and Christou, p. 284)

Oiler (Ohler), George (c1783-1813), served as a Private in Capt. Samuel Lane's Co., 14th U.S. Infantry, enlisted 16 May 1812 for 5 years, age 30, 5' 7" tall, sandy eyes, brown hair, brown complexion, born in Frederick, MD and captured at Beaver Dams, Upper Canada, ten miles west of Niagara Falls, in June of 1813. Prisoner of War #3820 at Halifax, NS, age 29, interned 13 Jun 1813 and died there on 19 Sep 1813 from paralytic (Johnson and Christou, p. 284; Baker, Vol. 2, p. 298; Mallick and Wright, p. 225; Johnson's Database, 2019)

Oliver, Anthony (African American), served as a Seaman and was born in Baltimore. Age: 47. Prison Depot: Dartmoor, Prisoner of War #5430. Captured by HM Frigate *Maidstone* & HM Brig *Nimrod*. When Taken: 17 Jul 1813. Where Taken: Grand Banks. Prize Name: *Yorktown*. Home Port: New York. Ship Type: Privateer. Date Received: 31 Oct 1814. From what ship: HMT *Leyden* from Chatham. Released on 1 Jul 1815. (Johnson's Database, 2019)

Oliver, William, served as a Private in Capt. Reuben Gilder's Co., 14th U.S. Infantry, enlisted 1 May 1813 and died on 14 Oct 1813; bounty land issued to his brother Joshua Oliver (BLW# 19853-160-12; Johnson and Christou, p. 284)

O'Neal, Con., served as a Private in the 14th U.S. Infantry, enlisted 30 Oct 1812 and was later captured. Prisoner of War #3954 at Halifax, NS, interned on 24 Jun 1813, discharged on 27 Aug 1813 and sent to England, later released and discharged from service on 31 Mar 1815 (Johnson and Christou, p. 284; Baker Vol. 2, p. 299, spelled his name Con. O'Neill)

O'Neal, William, Jr. (1795-1865), served as a Private in Capt. John Heeter's Co., 44th Regt., Montgomery Co., and was wounded in action 24 Aug 1814 from a gunshot which he received at Bladensburg and the ball passed through his leg about 1 inch above the ankle joint. It entered in front and passed through the bone and large tendon attached to the heel that rendered the wound very painful and dangerous, a great number of the bone were discharged from it. The wound was not closed until sometime April last. "I examined and seen the blood on his ancle (sic) while retreating with the help of his gun" per 15 Feb 1816 statement of Richard West who was 8 to 11 feet from William O'Neale (sic) when he was wounded. After the war he became Sheriff of Montgomery County and died 29 Dec 1865 in his 71st year. (BLW# 50-40-12451 and BLW# 55-120-7194; Wright Vol. 7, pp. 4, 35; *Montgomery County Sentinel*, 19 Jan 1866) In Montgomery Co. on 13 Sep 1842 William O'Neale (sic), former private in Capt. Heeter's Co., MD Volunteer Militia, and resident of this county for at least six years, appointed Lancaster Ould as his attorney to collect his $24.00 pension due from 4 Mar to 4 Sep 1842 (Pierce, p. 141)

O'Neill, John (1768-1838), served in the militia under Gen. "Light Horse Harry" Lee in the Whiskey Rebellion of 1794 and was an Ensign in 1797 during the naval war with France. He was appointed Ensign in Capt. Charles Foreman's Co., 42nd Regt., Harford Co. Militia, on 16 Dec 1809 and promoted to Lieutenant in Capt. Thomas Courtney's Co. on 6 Nov 1811. He had resigned his commission on 27 Apr 1813, yet a week later he was hailed as the brave Lt. John O'Neill, the defender of Havre de Grace, when the British attached and burned the town on 3 May 1813. In an act of defiance O'Neill went to the Potato Battery near his home and single-handedly fired a cannon that recoiled and severely injured his thigh; he was captured and taken onboard the ship *Maidstone*, but through the valiant efforts of his teenage daughter Matilda and a delegation from the town he was released two days later. He was listed as "the brave John O'Neal" in the 1814 tax records and his braveness most likely led to his appointment as the first keeper of the Concord Point Lighthouse on 3 Nov 1827 by President John Quincy Adams. He held that position until his death and was buried in nearby Angel Hill Cemetery. (Adjutant General Militia Appointments, 1794-1817, p. 51; *Narrative Respecting the Conduct of the British From Their First Landing on Spesutia Island Till Their Progress to Havre de Grace*, by James Jones Wilmer, 1814, pp. 19-20; "Harford County in the War of 1812," by Christopher T. George, *Harford Historical Bulletin* No. 76, Spring 1998, p. 33; *Havre de Grace Record*, 2 May 1963; *Concord Point Lighthouse Station at Havre de Grace*, by Jack L. Shagena, Jr. and Henry C. Peden, Jr., 2017, pp. 35-37, 119-124) "The brave O'Neil, hero of Havre de Grace, has been released by the enemy and has returned to that place." (*Republican Star*, Talbot Co., MD, 18 May 1813)

Orn, Benjamin (1784-1814), served as a Private in Capt. Reuben Gilder's Co., 14th U.S. Infantry, enlisted 11 Oct 1813, age 19, 5' 7" tall, born in Pennsylvania and died at Black Rock, NY on 29 Dec 1814 from sickness; bount land issued to his brother Joseph Orr (BLW# 26305-160-12; Johnson and Christou, p. 285)

O'Rourke, Charles, served as a Private in Capt. David Warfield's Co., 5th Regt., Baltimore United Volunteers, and was wounded on 12 Sep 1814 at North Point (Marine p. 396)

Orr, William, served as a Private in Capt. John Stanard's Co., 20th U.S. Infantry, enlisted 11 Aug 1812 at Leesburg, VA at the age of 26, 6' tall, born in Maryland, and discharged at Pittsburgh on 17 Aug 1815 because of an ulcerated leg (Johnson and Christou, p. 285)

Osborn, Elisha, served as a Marine and was wounded on 24 Aug 1814 on the field of battle at Bladensburg, was admitted to the Naval Hospital, Washington,

DC, as Patient No. 36 on 3 Sep 1814, was discharged on 31 Dec 1814 and sent to barracks (Sharp's Database, 2018, also noted this was possibly Aisha Osborn, Drum Major, USMC, who enlisted in August 1804)

Osborne, Thomas, served as a Sergeant in Capt. Kenneth McKenzie's Co., 14th U.S. Infantry, enlisted on 30 Nov 1812 for 18 months and was later captured [at Beaver Dams, Upper Canada]. Prisoner of War #3989 at Halifax, NS, interned 24 Jun 1813, was discharged for exchange on 3 Feb 1814, exchanged on 15 Apr 1814, and discharged at Greenbush, NY on 23 Jun 1814 (Johnson and Christou, p. 287, mistakenly stated he enlisted on 30 Nov 1814; Baker Vol. 2, p. 299)

Osburn, Moses, served as a Private in Capt. Samuel Lane's Co., 14th U.S. Inf., enlisted 10 Jun 1812 and was killed at Carlisle Barracks, PA on 20 Aug 1812; bounty land issued to his daughter Jane Skeen and other heirs at law (BLW# 26468-160-12; Johnson and Christou, p. 286)

Osgood, David, served as a Seaman and was born in Baltimore. Age: 24. Prison Depot: Portsmouth, Prisoner of War #661. How Taken: Gave himself up at the Cowes Rendezvous. Date Received: 6 Feb 1813. Discharged on 6 Mar 1813 and sent to Chatham on HMS *Cornwall*. Prison Depot: Chatham, Prisoner of War #1065. Received: 14 Mar 1813 from Portsmouth on HMS *Cornwell*. Discharged on 11 Aug 1814 and sent to Dartmoor. Prison Depot: Dartmoor, Prisoner of War #2584. Received on 21 Aug 1814 on HMT *Freya* from Chatham. Discharged on 3 May 1815. (Johnson's Database, 2019)

Ostender, Gabriel, served as a Private in the 14th U.S. Infantry and was later captured. Prisoner of War #3974 at Halifax, NS, interned on 24 Jun 1813 and was discharged for exchange on 3 Feb 1814 and exchanged on 15 Apr 1814 (Johnson and Christou, p. 286; Baker Vol. 2, p. 300, spelled his name Ostener)

Ott, Frederick, served as a Private under Capt. James F. Huston and Capt. Lewis Weaver in Frederick County Militia and was sick in Fredericktown on 25 Aug 1814 (Mallick and Wright, p. 345, and p. 346 stated he deserted on 8 Dec 1814)

Ouselburgh, Philip, served as a Private in the 14th U.S. Infantry and was later captured, probably at Beaver Dams, Upper Canada. Prisoner of War #4065 at Halifax, NS, interned 24 Jun 1813 and discharged for exchange on 3 Feb 1814 (Johnson and Christou, p. 286; Baker Vol. 2, p. 300)

Owen, Richard H. (c1776-1858), served as a Private in Capt. David Warfield's Co., 5th Regiment, Baltimore City Militia, from 19 Aug 1814 and was wounded on 12 Sep 1814 at North Point (Huntsberry, p. 69, mentioned his wound and Wright Vol. 2, p. 8, and Marine p. 397, did not, but they all listed him as R. H. Owen). R. H. Owen died in Baltimore at the home of his nephew R. F. Maynard on 18 Sep 1858, age about 82, and was buried at St. Thomas Episcopal Church, Owings

Mills, Baltimore County. (*St. Thomas Parish Deaths and Burials, Owings Mills, Maryland, 1728-1995*, by Family Line Publications (no author cited, but published by F. Edward Wright), 1995, p.80; *The [Baltimore] Sun*, 20 Sep 1858; Baltimore City Will Book No. 28, p. 296, gave his name as Richard H. Owen)

Owens, Joseph, served as 4th Sergeant in Capt. Samuel Sterett's Co., 5th Regt., Baltimore Militia, having been promoted from private to 4th Sergeant on 12 Sep 1814 and was wounded the same day at North Point (Wright Vol. 2, p. 6)

P

Pack, Abraham (African American), served as a Seaman and was born in Harford Co., MD. Age: 26. Prison Depot: Plymouth 1, Prisoner of War #584. Captured by HM Brig *Reindeer*. When Taken: 3 Feb 1813. Where Taken: Bay of Biscayne. Prize Name: *Cashiere*. Home Port: Baltimore. Ship Type: Letter of Marque. Received: 23 Feb 1813. From what ship: HMS *Surveillante*. Discharged and sent to Dartmoor Prison on 2 Apr 1813. Prison Depot: Dartmoor in Devon, England for 119 days from 2 Apr to 30 Jul 1813. Prisoner of War #91. Received: 2 Apr 1813 from Plymouth. Discharged and sent to Dartmouth on 30 Jul 1813. (Johnson's Database, 2019; "Harford County in War of 1812," by Christopher T. George, *Harford Historical Bulletin* No. 76, Spring 1998, p. 21 footnote)

Packman, George, served as a Seaman and was born in Baltimore. Age: 32. Prison Depot: Chatham, Prisoner of War #1054. Captured by HM Frigate *Medusa*. When Taken: 9 Nov 1812. Where Taken: off San Sebastian, Spain. Prize Name: *Independence*. Ship Type: Merchant Vessel. Received: 11 Mar 1813 from Yarmouth on HMS *Tenders*. Discharged on 8 Jun 1813 and released to the Cartel *Rodrigo*. (Johnson's Database, 2019)

Padgett, John (1792-1814), served as a Corporal in Capt. Joseph Hook's Co. of the 36th U.S. Infantry, enlisted 27 Jun 1813 in Baltimore at the age of 21, born in Charles Co., MD and died on 7 Feb 1814 (Johnson and Christou, p. 287)

Paine, William G. (1787-1814), served as a Musician in the company of Capt. Thomas Montgomery, 14th U.S. Infantry, enlisted 12 Jun 1812 at the age of 25, born in Connecticut; wounded at Williamsburg, NY and died at Burlington, VT on 23 Feb 1814 (Johnson and Christou, pp. 287-288)

Page, Cato (African American), served as a Seaman and was born in Baltimore. Age: 23. Prison Depot: Dartmoor, Prisoner of War #2958. Captured by: picked up in a boat from HM Frigate *Fox*. Date Received: 24 Aug 1814. From what ship: HMT *Hannibal*. Discharged on 19 May 1815. (Johnson's Database, 2019)

Page, Moses, served as a Seaman, was taken from the barracks and admitted to the Naval Hospital in Washington, DC as Patient No. 10 as of 1 Jun 1814, but the nature of his injury or illness was not stated (Sharp's Database, 2018)

Palmer, John, served as a Seaman and was born in Maryland. Age: 27. Prison Depot: Plymouth 1, Prisoner of War #2115. Captured by HM Frigate *Hotspur* & HM Frigate *Pyramus*. When Taken: 26 Oct 1813. Where Taken: Bay of Biscayne. Prize Name: *Chesapeake*. Ship Type: Letter of Marque. Received: 22 Nov 1813. From what ship: HMS *Pyramus*. Discharged 29 Nov 1813 and sent to Dartmoor. Prison Depot: Dartmoor, Prisoner of War #836. Age 37 (sic). Received: 29 Nov 1813 from Plymouth. Discharged on 26 Apr 1815. (Johnson's Database, 2019)

Pannell, Hugh, served as a Seaman and was born in Baltimore. Age: 28. Prison Depot: Plymouth 1, Prisoner of War #455. Captured by HM Ship-of-the-Line *Colossus*. When Taken: 5 Jan 1813. Where Taken: off Western Islands, Scotland. Prize Name: *Dolphin*. Home Port: Philadelphia. Ship Type: Letter of Marque. Date Received: 6 Feb 1813. From what ship: HMS *Rhin*. Discharged and sent to Chatham on 29 Mar 1813 on HMS *Braham*. Prison Depot: Chatham, Prisoner of War #1557. Received: 8 Apr 1813 from Plymouth on HMS Olympia. Discharged on 27 Jul 1813 and released to the Cartel *Hoffning*. (Johnson's Database, 2019)

Pannison, Henry (African American), served as a Cook and was born in Maryland. Age: 34. Prison Depot: Dartmoor, Prisoner of War #3569. Captured by HM Frigate *Piqua*. When Taken: 26 Apr 1814. Where Taken: near Mona Passage, West Indies. Prize Name: *Hawk*. Home Port: Wilmington. Ship Type: Privateer. Received: 30 Sep 1814. From what ship: HMT *Sybella*. Discharged on 4 Jun 1815. (Johnson's Database, 2019)

Paradise, John, served as a Private in Capt. Richard Arell's Co., 14th U.S. Inf., enlisted 3 Sep 1812 for 5 years at Snow Hill, MD, age 22, 5' 6½" tall, born in Worcester Co., MD, and was captured [Beaver Dams, Upper Canada). Prisoner of War #3979 at Halifax, NS, interned 24 Jun 1813, discharged for exchange on 3 Feb 1814, exchanged on 15 Apr 1814, discharged from service on 2 Sep 1817 (Johnson and Christou, p. 288; Baker Vol. 12, p. 302)

Parker, Henry, served as a 3rd Lieutenant in 14th U.S. Infantry, commissioned an Ensign on 12 May 1813, promoted to 3rd Lieutenant on 14 Nov 1813 and died from wounds received at LaCole Mill, Lower Canada, on 30 Mar 1814 (Johnson and Christou, p. 288)

Parker, John, served as a Private in Capt. Lawson Cuddy's Co., 41st Regiment, Baltimore Co., from 30 Aug 1814 and was reported "missing since Oct 13" 1814 (Wright Vol. 2, p. 67)

Parker, Zebadiah, served as a Private in Capt. Jeremiah Ducker's Co., 2nd Regt., 11th Brigade, Baltimore Co., stationed in Baltimore from 14 Oct 1814 and reported "absent-sick on furlough since Sep 30" 1814 (Wright Vol. 2, p. 88)

Parkinson, William, served as a Private in Capt. Leroy Opie's Co., 5th U.S. Infantry, enlisted 31 May 1813 for 5 years in Baltimore, by Lt. Bird, at the age of 28, 5' 10½" tall, gray eyes, light hair, dark complexion, born in Cumberland, mustered 28 Feb and 30 Apr 1815 at Buffalo, NY and discharged at Fort Erie, Upper Canada on 21 Jun 1815 on a Surgeon's Certificate for inability (Johnson and Christou, p. 289; Wright Vol. 10, p. 10)

Parks, Richard, served as a Seaman and was born in Baltimore. Age: 44. Prison Depot: Chatham, Prisoner of War #779. Captured by HM Sloop *Hyacinth* and HM Frigate *Argo*. When Taken: 27 Aug 1812. Where Taken: Straits of Gibraltar. Prize Name: *Eliza*. Home Port: New York. Ship Type: Merchant Vessel. Date Received: 27 Feb 1813 from Plymouth on HMS *Namur*. Discharged on 10 May 1813 and released to the Cartel *Admittance*. (Johnson's Database, 2019)

Parks, Selby, served as a Private in Capt. Richard Arell's Co., 14th U.S. Infantry, enlisted 13 Apr 1812 at Baltimore at age 20, 5' 9¾" tall, born in Somerset Co., MD, and captured at Beaver Dams, Upper Canada, on 24 Jun 1813. Prisoner of War #3778 at Halifax, NS, interned 24 Jun 1813, discharged for exchange on 3 Feb 1814, exchanged on 15 Apr 1814, returned to service and deserted at Fort Severn, MD on 19 Jul 1815 (Johnson and Christou, p. 289; Baker Vol. 2, p. 304)

Parnell, Hugh, served as a Seaman and was born in Baltimore. Age: 28. Prison Depot: Dartmoor, Prisoner of War #4121. Captured by HM Frigate *Niemen*. When Taken: 28 Jun 1814. Where Taken: off Delaware. Prize Name: *Bordeaux Packet*. Home Port: Baltimore. Ship Type: Letter of Marque. Date Received: 6 Oct 1814. From what ship: HMT *Chesapeake* from Halifax, NS. Discharged on 13 Jun 1815. (Johnson's Database, 2019)

Parsons, Thomas, served as a Private in Capt. John T. Randall's Rifle Co., Baltimore Co., from 26 Jul 1814 and was wounded in action on 24 Aug 1814 at Bladensburg; shown on muster roll of 14 Oct – 1 Dec 1814 of Capt. Benjamin Gorsuch's Co., 2nd Regt., 11th Brigade, as wounded in action and was discharged on 1 Dec 1814 at Camp Hampstead in Baltimore City (Wright Vol. 2, pp. 74, 88)

Pasley, David (c1790-1812) served as a Private in Capt. Thomas Montgomery's Co., 14th U.S. Infantry, enlisted on 13 Apr 1812 for 5 years and died on 21 Dec 1812 (Johnson and Christou, p. 290)

Pastorias, Samuel, served as a Private in Capt. John Stewart's Co., 51st Regt., Baltimore Militia, joined 21 Aug 1814 and was wounded, but the place and date were not given (Wright Vol. 2, p. 32)

Patterson, Joseph (Mulatto), served as a Seaman and was born in Baltimore. Age: 17. Prison Depot: Dartmoor, Prisoner of War #6080. Captured by HM Frigate *Niemen*. When Taken: 18 Sep 1814. Where Taken: off Delaware. Prize

Name: *Daedalus*. Home Port: Baltimore. Ship Type: Letter of Marque. Date Received: 28 Dec 1814. From what ship: HMT *Penelope*. Discharged on 3 Jul 1815. (Johnson's Database, 2019)

Paxton, Joseph, served as a Private in Capt. Henry Lowery's Co., Allegany Co. Militia, and was discharged by a Surgeon on 20 Nov 1814 (Wright Vol. 9, p. 6)

Pater, Stephen, served as a Private in Capt. John D. Miller' Co., 39th Regiment, joined 1 Sep 1814 and died 2 Nov 1814 (Wright 2, p. 25)

Patterson, Archibald, served as a Private in Capt. David Cummings' Co., 14th U.S. Infantry, enlisted 16 Apr 1812 and later captured. Prisoner of War #4190 at Halifax, NS, interned 24 Jun 1813, discharged 27 Aug 1813 and sent to England on HMS *Regulus* (Johnson and Christou, p. 290; Baker Vol. 2, p. 305)

Patterson, Thomas, served as a Private in Capt. Richard Arell's Co., 14th U.S. Infantry, enlisted 3 Jul 1812 at Baltimore, age 25, 5' 7½" tall, born in Stafford, VA and later captured. Prisoner of War #4073 at Halifax, NS, interned 24 Jun 1813, discharged for exchange on 3 Feb 1814, exchanged on 15 Apr 1814, returned to service and deserted at Fort Severn, MD on 15 Jul 1815 (Johnson and Christou, p. 289; Baker Vol. 2, p. 306)

Patton, David, served as a Corporal in the 14th U.S. Infantry, enlisted 11 Nov 1812 for 18 months and was captured on 2 4 Jun 1813 [Beaver Dams, Upper Canada]. Prisoner of War #4819 at Halifax, NS, interned 15 Nov 1813 and discharged 19 Nov 1813, sent to England, later released and discharged from the service on 21 Mar 1815 (Johnson and Christou, p. 291; Baker Vol. 2, p. 306)

Paul, John, served as a Private in Capt. John O'Fallon's Co., 2nd U.S. Rifles, enlisted 18 Aug 1814 in Ohio or Newport, KY at the age of 35, 5' 8" tall, born in Maryland, and discharged at Detroit on 23 Sep 1818 on a Surgeon's Certificate, but the nature of his disability was not stated (Johnson and Christou, p. 291)

Payne, Richard, served as a Private in the 14th U.S. Infantry and was captured. Prisoner of War #3986 at Halifax, NS, interned 24 Jun 1813 and discharged for exchange on 3 Feb 1814 (Johnson and Christou, p. 291; Baker Vol. 2, p. 307)

Peach, Isaac (1775-1815), served as a Private in Capt. Reuben Gilder's Co., 14th U.S. Infantry, enlisted 8 Oct 1813 for 5 years at the age of 38, 5' 6" tall, born in Maryland and died at Cheektowaga Hospital, NY on 8 Feb 1815 (Johnson and Christou, p. 292; https://wnyroots.tripod.com/Index-1812.html)

Peach, Joseph, served as a Private in Capt. Joseph Isaac's Co., 34th Regiment, Prince George's Co. Militia, between 21 Jul and 2 Sep 1813, was stationed at Annapolis for 11 days and was reported "absent sick sent home by order of surgeon," but the nature of his illness was not stated (Wright Vol. 6, p. 15)

Peach, William, from the *Ontario*, served as an Ordinary Seaman with the U.S. Chesapeake Flotilla, entered service on 21 Dec 1812 and died on 29 Sep 1814 (Shomette, p. 383; Sheads, p. 22)

Peak, John, served as a Pilot in the U.S. Flotilla and was wounded on 24 Aug 1814 on the field of battle at Bladensburg, was admitted to the Naval Hospital in Washington, DC as Patient No. 20, and was discharged on 28 Aug 1814 (Sharp's Database, 2018)

Pearce, Charles, served as a Seaman and was born in Baltimore. Age: 35. Prison Depot: Dartmoor, Prisoner of War #5957. Captured by HM Ship-of-the-Line *Bulwark*. When Taken: 23 Oct 1814. Where Taken: off Halifax, NS. Prize Name: *Harlequin*. Home Port: Portsmouth. Ship Type: Privateer. Date Received: 27 Dec 1814 from HMT *Penelope*. Discharged 3 Jul 1815. (Johnson's Database, 2019)

Pearce (Peirce, Pierce), Edward, served as a Seaman and was born in Baltimore. Age: 26. Prison Depot: Plymouth 1, Prisoner of War #46. How Taken: Gave himself up off HM Frigate *Circe*. Date Received: 25 Nov 1813. From what ship: HMS *Stork*. Discharged and sent to Portsmouth on 29 Dec 1812 on HMS *Northumberland*. Prison Depot: Portsmouth, Prisoner of War #317. Date Received: 31 Dec 1812. From what ship: HM Ship-of-the-Line *Northumberland*. Discharged on 4 Mar 1813 and sent to Chatham on HMS *Queen*. Prison Depot: Chatham, Prisoner of War #1048. Date Received: 11 Mar 1813 from Yarmouth on HMS *Tenders*. Discharged on 4 Aug 1814 and sent to Dartmoor on HMS *Liverpool*. Prison Depot: Dartmoor, Prisoner of War #2747. Date Received: 24 Aug 1814. From what ship: HMT *Liverpool* from Chatham. Discharged on 26 Apr 1815. (Johnson's Database, 2019)

Pearson, Benjamin, served as a Seaman and was born in Baltimore. Age: 35. Prison Depot: Dartmoor, Prisoner of War #2125. How Taken: Gave himself up off HM Ship-of-the-Line *Mulgrave*. When Taken: 17 Nov 1812. Received: 8 Aug 1814. From what ship: HMT *Raven* from Chatham. Discharged on 26 Apr 1815. Prison Depot: Chatham, Prisoner of War #244. Received: 1 Dec 1812. From what ship: HMS *Raisonable*. Discharged on 25 Jul 1814 and sent to Dartmoor on HMS *Bittern*. (Johnson's Database, 2019)

Pearson, Charles, served as a Seaman and was born in Baltimore. Age: 35. Prison Depot: Dartmoor, Prisoner of War #3452. How Taken: Gave himself up off HM Sloop *Lender*. When Taken: 14 Sep 1814. Date Received: 19 Sep 1814. From what ship: HMT *Salvador del Mundo*. Discharged and released on 11 Jun 1815. (Johnson's Database, 2019)

Peasely, David (c1790-1814) served as a Private in the 14th U.S. Infantry and died on 21 Nov 1814; heirs received half pay for 5 years in lieu of bounty land (Johnson and Christou, p. 292)

Pebase, John, served as a Private in Capt. Henry Fleming's Co., 14th U.S. Infantry and was captured, but the date and place was not stated. "Prisoner of War, received from Chazy on 11 May 1814" (Johnson and Christou, p. 292)

Pedersen, John, see John Peterson, q.v.

Pembroke, James, served as a Cook of the U.S. Chesapeake Flotilla, entered service on 23 May 1814, reported sick (date and illness not stated) and died on 29 May 1814 (Shomette, p. 391)

Pembroke, Thomas C. (1786-1815), served as a Sergeant in Capt. Richard Clarke's Co., 12th Regiment, St. Mary's Co. Militia, from 10 Jul to 4 Aug 1813, from 23 Aug to 31 Aug 1813, from 24 Sep to 5 Oct 1813, from 2 Jun to 11 Jun 1814, from 18 Jul to 8 Aug 1814 and died on 30 Nov 1815, age 29. He married first to Winefred Dunbar on 12 Oct 1806 and second to Mary McKay on 7 Nov 1809. Mary Pembrook (sic), widow, applied for and was granted bounty land in 1855. Thomas C. Pembroke was buried in a "Private Cemetery located in the woods near Seaside View Road at Ridge, 1st District. Has 3 Dunbar gravestones, 1 Pembroke and Dr. Sydney Evans, 1810-1886." (Wright Vol. 5, pp. 12, 13, 14, 22, 27, and p. 81 stated he died 15 Nov 1815 and spelled his name Pembroke, Pembrook and Pembrooke; BLW# 55-160-55093 spelled his name Pembrook; *Marriages and Deaths, St. Mary's County, Maryland, 1634-1900*, by Margaret K. Fresco, 1982, pp. 236, 440, spelled his name Pembroke)

Pendel, Thomas, served as a Sergeant in Capt. Nathan Towson's Co., 2nd U.S. Artillery, enlisted 27 Jun 1812 at the age of 25, 5' 11" tall, wounded at Black Rock, NY and was dischaged at Boston on 12 Jun 1815 on Surgeon's Certificate, but the nature of his wound was not stated (Johnson and Christou, p. 293)

Pennywell, Patty, served as a Private in Capt. John Baldy's Co., 16th U.S. Inf., enlisted 9 Mar 1814 in Philadelphia at age 20, 5' 1" tall, born in Worcester Co., MD and was discharged at Buffalo, NY on 17 Jun 1815 for "mental incapacity" (Johnson and Christou, p. 295)

Penfield, John, served as a Seaman and was born in Baltimore. Age: 26. Prison Depot: Portsmouth, Prisoner of War #1365. How Taken: Gave himself up off HM Brig *Swinger*. Date Received: 2 Feb 1814. From what ship: HMS *Swinger*. Discharged on 13 Feb 1814 and sent to Chatham on HMT *Malabar No. 352*. Prison Depot: Chatham, Prisoner of War #3494. Date Received: 23 Feb 1814 from Portsmouth on HMT *Malabar*. Discharged on 26 Sep 1814 and sent to Dartmoor on HMS *Leyden*. John Penfold (sic) served as a Seaman and was born in Baltimore. Age: 26. Prison Depot: Dartmoor, Prisoner of War #4163. How Taken: Gave himself up off HMS *Minos*. When Taken: 2 Feb 1814. Received: 6 Oct 1814. From what ship: HMT *Niobe* from Chatham. Discharged on 13 Jun 1815. (Johnson's Database, 2019)

Perce, Elem, see Clem Pierce, q.v.

Perdum, Mordecai, served as a Private in Capt. Basil Dorsey's Co., Frederick County Militia, from 30 Jul 1814 and was furloughed on 9 Sep 1814 until well (Mallick and Wright, pp. 228, 348)

Peregrine, Taggert, served as a Seaman and was born in Maryland. Age: 28. Prison Depot: Plymouth 1, Prisoner of War #1266. Captured by HM Frigate *Medusa*. When Taken: 12 Apr 1813. Where Taken: Bay of Biscayne. Prize Name: *Caroline*. Ship Type: Merchant Vessel. Date Received: 10 May 1813. From what ship: HMS *Medusa*. Discharged on 3 Jul 1813 and sent to Stapleton Prison. Prison Depot: Stapleton, Prisoner of War #283. Date Received: 11 Jul 1813 from Plymouth. Discharged on 16 Jun 1814 and sent to Dartmoor. Prison Depot: Dartmoor, Prisoner of War #1564. Age 29. Date Received: 23 Jun 1814 from Stapleton. Discharged on 1 May 1815. (Johnson's Database, 2019)

Perrie, Charles S., served as a Private in Capt. Gavin Hamilton's Co., 17th Regt., Prince George's Co. Militia, between 18 Aug and 17 Sep 1813 and reported as "sick and gone home," but no date was given; he served under Capt. Thomas Eversfield from 21 Aug 1814 until "sick and sent home Sep 6" 1814. (Wright Vol. 6, p. 5 spelled his name Perry, and p. 13 spelled his name Perrie)

Perrigue (Perrague), James, served as a Corporal in Capt. William McIlvane's Co., 14th U.S. Infantry, enlisted 29 Jan 1813 and was later captured. Prisoner of War #3926 at Halifax, NS, interned 24 Jun 1813 and discharged for exchange on 3 Feb 1814 (Johnson and Christou, p. 294; Baker Vol. 2, p. 311)

Perry, James, served as a Private in Capt. James Dorman's Co., 5th U.S. Infantry, enlisted 4 May 1812 in Alexandria, DC, age 24, 5' 8" tall, born in Baltimore, wounded in the Battle of Lyon's Creek, discharged at Pittsburgh on 16 Aug 1815 and placed on the pension roll on 11 Dec 1815 (Johnson and Christou, p. 294)

Perry, Richard, served as a Private in Capt. Kenneth McKenzie's Co., 14th U.S. Infantry, enlisted 24 Nov 1812 and was later captured. Prisoner of War #4029 at Halifax, NS, interned 24 Jun 1813 and discharged for exchange on 3 Feb 1814 (Johnson and Christou, p. 295; Baker Vol. 2, p. 311, stated 6th U.S. Infantry)

Perry, William, served as a Private in Capt. William McIlvane's Co., 14th U.S. Infantry, enlisted 31 Dec 1812 at age 28, 5' 6" tall, born in Harford Co., MD, wounded at Plattsburgh, NY by a bayonet and was discharged at Greenbush, NY on 1 May 1815 by a Surgeon's Certificate (BLW# 6977-160-12; Johnson and Christou, p. 295; Pension File Old War IF-3671)

Persons, James (c1790-1813), served as a Private in the 14th U.S. Infantry and died at Sackett's Harbor, NY on 29 Oct 1813 (Johnson and Christou, p. 295)

Peters, Henry, served as a Private in Capt. Andrew Smith's Co., 51st Regt., Baltimore City Militia, from 23 Aug 1814 and was "discharged for inability" on 26 Aug 1814 (Wright Vol. 2, p. 31)

Peters, John, served as a Private in Capt. Samuel Dawson's Co., Frederick Co., Militia, from 26 Jul 1814, later promoted to Corporal, and was wounded at the Battle of North Point on 12 Sep 1814 with a ball cutting the flesh above the left knee; moved to Ohio before 1850, his wife died in 1869 and he lived in Belmont Co., OH in Dec 1871 (BLW# 50-40-7913 and 55-160-16743; Pension SO-16515, SC-10431; Mallick and Wright, p. 229)

Peter, Thomas (African American), served as a Seaman and was born in Baltimore. Age: 39. Prison Depot: Portsmouth, Prisoner of War #1097. When Taken: 25 Nov 1813. Where Taken: Mahon (Island of Minorca). How Taken: Gave himself up off HM Ship-of-the-Line *Berwick*. Date Received: 5 Oct 1813. From what ship: HM Ship-of-the-Line *Achille*. Discharged on 17 Oct 1813 and sent to Chatham on HM Store Ship *Weymouth*. Prison Depot: Chatham, Prisoner of War #2363. Date Received: 20 Oct 1813 from Portsmouth on an admiral's tender. Discharged on 25 Sep 1814 and sent to Dartmoor on HMS *Leyden*. Prison Depot: Dartmoor, Prisoner of War #4646. Date Received: 9 Oct 1814. From what ship: HMT *Leyden* from Chatham. Discharged on 15 Jun 1815. (Johnson's Database, 2019)

Peters, William (1783-1813), served as a Private in Capt. Nathan Towson's Co., 2nd U.S. Artillery, enlistment date not given, age 30, and died from wounds received in Battle of Stoney Creek [in June 1813] (Johnson and Christou, p. 295)

Peters, William (1788-1863), served as a Private in Capt. Stephen H. Moore's Co., Baltimore Volunteers Infantry Co., from 8 Sep 1812 for 1 year and was sick in hospital at Niagara, NY on 13 Apr 1813 (Wright Vol. 2, p. 57) He died 21 Nov 1863 and buried in Green Mount Cemetery. (*The [Baltimore] Sun*, 23 Nov 1863)

Peters, William (1786-1812), served as a Lieutenant in the U.S. Navy and died at St. Mary's, MD on 3 Nov 1812 in his 27th year (*Baltimore Whig*, 29 Nov 1812; *Marriages and Deaths, St. Mary's County, Maryland, 1634-1900*, by Margaret K. Fresco, 1982, p. 441, citing *National Intelligencer*, 3 Dec 1812)

Peterson, Alexander (African American), served as a Seaman and was born in Maryland. Age: 25. Prison Depot: Plymouth 2, Prisoner of War #32. How Taken: Gave himself up. When Taken: Where Taken: Greenock, Scotland. Date Received: 8 Feb 1815. From what ship: HMS *Impregnable*. Discharged on 10 Feb 1815 and sent to Dartmoor. Prison Depot: Dartmoor, Prisoner of War #6270. Date Received: 10 Feb 1815. From what ship: HMT *Ganges* from Plymouth. Discharged on 5 Jul 1815. (Johnson's Database, 2019)

Peterson, James, served as a Seaman and was born in Maryland. Age: 46. Prison Depot: Dartmoor, Prisoner of War #3625. Captured by HM Brig *Doterel*. When Taken: 14 Dec 1813. Where Taken: off Charleston, SC. Prize Name: *Monarch*. Ship Type: Merchant Vessel. Date Received: 30 Sep 1814. From what ship: HMT *Sybella*. Discharged on 4 Jun 1815. (Johnson's Database, 2019)

Peterson (Pederson), John, served as a Seaman and was born in Baltimore. Age: 33. Prison Depot: Chatham, Prisoner of War #1802. How Taken: Gave himself up off HM Ship-of-the-Line *Spencer*. When Taken: 28 or 29 May 1813. Where Taken: London. Received: 3 Jul 1813. From what ship: HMS *Raisonable*. Discharged on 25 Jul 1814 and sent to Dartmoor on HMS *Bittern*. Prison Depot: Dartmoor, Prisoner of War #2965. Age 34. Received: 24 Aug 1814. From what ship: HMT *Hannibal*. Discharged on 19 May 1815. (Johnson's Database, 2019)

Petry, John, served as a Private in Capt. Henry Fleming's Co., 14th U.S. Inf., enlisted 6 Mar 1813 at the advanced age of 49, 5' 9½" tall, born in Philadelphia, PA and was discharged at Plattsburgh, NY on 17 May 1814 on a Surgeon's Certificate for a hernia (Johnson and Christou, p. 295)

Phillips, Archibald, served as a Private in Capt. Conrad Hook's Co., Baltimore County, 2nd Regt., 11th Brigade, stationed at Camp Hampstead Hill in Baltimore from 25 Jul 1814 and was reported "absent sick," but no date was given on the muster roll dated 25 Jul – 1 Dec 1814 (Wright Vol. 2, p. 81)

Phillips, William (African American), served as a Seaman and was born in Baltimore. Age: 29. Prison Depot: Chatham, Prisoner of War #2285. How Taken: Gave himself up off HM Ship-of-the-Line *Scipion*. When Taken: 20 Oct 1812. Date Received: 17 Sep 1813. From what ship: HMS *Raisonable*. Discharged on 4 Sep 1814 and sent to Dartmoor on HMS *Freya*. Prison Depot: Dartmoor, Prisoner of War #3133. Date Received: 11 Sep 1814. From what ship: HMT *Freya* from Chatham. Discharged on 27 Apr 1815. (Johnson's Database, 2019)

Pidgeon, John, served as a Private in Capt. Christian Adreon's Co., 5th Regt., Baltimore Militia, and was wounded on 12 Sep 1814 at North Point (Wright Vol. 2, p. 3) Dr. James H. McCulloh, Jr. wrote this soon after the battle to the British commander: "In consequence of the humanity shown the following American prisoners of war, I do promise upon honor that they shall not directly or indirectly serve against the British until regularly exchanged." (Marine, p. 171) In Baltimore Co. on 4 Sep 1839 John Pidgeon, former private in 5th Regt., MD Militia, and a resident of Baltimore for 4½ years, previously of New York City, collected his own $48.00 pension due from 4 Mar to 4 Sep 1839 (Pierce, p. 148)

Piercal, Henry, served as a Private in Capt. Stephen H. Moore's Co., Baltimore Volunteers Infantry Co., from 8 Sep 1812 for 1 year and was "sick at Buffalo," NY on 28 Feb 1813 (Wright Vol. 2, p. 57)

Pierce, Clem, served as a Private in Capt. Jeremiah Ducker's Co., Randall's Rifle Bttn., Baltimore Co., from 25 Jul 1814 to 1 Dec 1814 (Wright Vol. 2, pp. 72, 87), but Marine, p. 402, stated one "Elem Perce" was a Private in Capt. Ducker's Co., 7th Regt., and was wounded at Bladensburg; Wright did not mention a wound)

Piercy, Jacob, served as a Private in Capt. Colin Buckner's Co., 5th U.S. Infantry, enlisted 26 Feb 1813 at Baltimore, age 44, 5' 8" tall, born in Philadelphia and was discharged at Greenbush, NY on 12 Jun 1814 because of a rupture (BLW# 5206-160-12; Johnson and Christou, p. 297)

Pike, David, served as a Private in Capt. Nathan Towson's Co., 2nd U.S. Artillery, enlisted 22 May 1812 and died in the hospital some time during 1813 (Johnson and Christou, p. 297)

Pilch, James, served as a Private in Capt. John Hanna's Co., 5th Cavalry Regt., Baltimore City, from 19 Aug 1814 and was "dismissed on 12 Sep for shyness in battle at North Point" (Wright Vol. 2, p. 55)

Pindergast, Robert, served as an Ordinary Seaman with the U.S. Chesapeake Flotilla, entered service on 1 Feb 1814, was on board on 7 Apr 1814 and died on 3 Sep 1814 (Shomette p. 370)

Pinkney, William (1764-1822), served as Major in command of the 1st Rifle Bttn., commissioned on 8 Jan 1813, was stationed at Baltimore from 19 Aug to 14 Nov 1814 and was reportedly wounded, but date and place were not given (Wright Vol. 2, p. 53; Marine p. 405 stated William Pinkney, Jr. was wounded) William Pinkney, U.S. Senator from Maryland, died 25 Feb 1822, about age 60 years, in Washington, DC (*Baltimore Patriot*, 26 Feb 1822)

Pinkney, William Jr. (1789-1853), served as Adjutant in the 1st Rifle Co. under Major William Pinkney, was commissioned on 24 Jan 1813 and wounded at Bladensburg in 1814 (Wright Vol. 2, p. 53, stated Major William Pinkney was stationed at Baltimore from 19 Aug to 18 Nov 1814 and was wounded; William Pinkney, Jr. was his Adjutant; Marine, p. 405, stated Adjutant William Pinkney, Jr. was born in 1789, was wounded in 1814 and died in 1853; however, the obituary of Col. William Pinkney stated he died on 18 Oct 1853 in his 84th year, thus born in 1770. This is mistake in the newspaper since he was actually in his 64th year and not his 84th year. "The deceased was the oldest son of the late William Pinkney and by his abilities, scrupulous honor and integrity shewed himself worthy of his illustrious father. During the War of 1812, Col. Pinkney was present at the battles of Bladensburg and North Point as Adjutant of Rifle Battlion, and on both [of] those occasions distinguished himself by his intelligence and bravery. He discharged several important offices under the general government with the highest credit to himself; was amiable and exemplary in all the relations of private life; and both deserved and earned the esteem and friendship of all who knew him." (*The [Baltimore] Sun*, 22 Oct 1853)

Pirkins, Hector (1791-1859), a native of Connecticut, but for 40 years a citizen of Baltimore, lost a leg in the Battle of Chippewa [in Upper Canada on 25 Jul 1814] and died on 29 Mar 1859, age 68, at his home at 172 N. Eden Street. (*The [Baltimore] Sun*, 30 Mar 1859)

Pitcher, Jacob, served as a Private in the 14th U.S. Infantry (company was not stated) and captured, probably at Beaver Dams, Upper Canada on 24 Jun 1813. Prisoner of War #4100 at Halifax, NS, interned 24 Jun 1813 and discharged for exchange on 3 Feb 1814 (Johnson and Christou, p. 298; Baker Vol. 2, p. 319)

Pittman, Henry, served as a Seaman and was born in Baltimore. Age: 23. Prison Depot: Chatham, Prisoner of War #2503. Captured by HM Frigate *Nymphe*. When Taken: 30 Jun 1813. Where Taken: off Halifax, NS. Prize Name: *Thomas*. Home Port: Portsmouth. Ship Type: Privateer. Date Received: 22 Oct 1813 from Portsmouth on HMT *Malabar*. Discharged on 8 Sep 1814 and sent to Dartmoor on HMS *Niobe*. (Johnson's Database, 2019)

Place, George, served as a Marine, was taken from the barracks and admitted to the Naval Hospital in Washington, DC as Patient No. 73 on 9 Aug 1814 (injury or illness was not specified) and was discharged on 19 Aug 1814 and sent to the barracks (Sharp's Database, 2018)

Plante (Plants), Edward T., served as a Private in Capt. Nathan Towson's Co., 2nd U.S. Artillery, enlistment date not given, age 19, and was captured during the Battle of Stoney Creek [in June 1813]. Prisoner of War #302 at Quebec, interned 28 Jun 1813 and released on 31 Oct 1813 (Johnson and Christou, p. 298; Johnson's Quebec book, p. 122)

Plester, Stephen, served as a Seaman and was born in Baltimore. Age: 25. Prison Depot: Plymouth 2, Prisoner of War #528. Captured by HM Frigate *Barbadoes*. When Taken: 6 Dec 1815. Where Taken: off St. Bartholomew, West Indies. Prize Name: *Gallant*. Ship Type: Merchant Vessel. Date Received: 16 Apr 1815. From what ship: HMS *Swiftsure*. Discharged on 2 Jun 1815 and released to the Cartel *Soverign*. (Johnson's Database, 2019)

Pluck, Michael, served as a Crewman on the privateer *Sarah Ann* of Baltimore, age 26, was captured and sent to Jamaica in 1812; born in Baltimore, parents dead, has a sister in Pennsylvania named Ann Welsh (*Niles Weekly Register*, 14 Nov 1812, but the same paper on 2 Oct 1813 stated he was sent to Bermuda)

Poe, Jacob (1775-1860), served as a Private in Capt. John Bond's Co., 41st Regt., Baltimore Co. Militia, joined 30 Aug 1814 and was reported "absent sick Sep 1 – Oct 20" 1814 (Wright Vol. 2, p. 67). Jacob Poe, son of Capt. George Poe and

Catharine Dawson, married Bridget Amelia Fitzgerald Kennedy (1775-1844) in 1803 and died on 25 Jul 1860, age 84, in Baltimore at the home of his son Neilson Poe (1809-1884) at 25 Lexington St. (*The [Baltimore] Sun*, 26 Jul 1860; Poe Chart, by Francis Barnum Culver, renowned genealogist in the early 1900s)

Pogue, James Jr., served as a Private in Capt. David Warfield's Co., 5th Regt., Baltimore Militia, and was wounded on 12 Sep 1814 at North Point (Huntsberry p. 69; Marine, p. 406 and Wright Vol. 2, p. 8, did not mention being wounded; Wright misspelled his name Pague)

Pogue, John G., served as a Private in Capt. David Warfield's Co., 5th Regiment, Baltimore Militia, from 19 Aug 1814, captured at North Point on 12 Sep 1814 and reported on roll as "in captivity" (Wright Vol. 2, p. 8; Marine, p. 172)

Polkinghorn, Richard, served as a Private in Capt. Christian Adreon's Co., 5th Regiment, Baltimore Militia, and was reported "in captivity as of Nov 18" 1814 (Wright Vol. 2, p. 3)

Pollett, Edward, served as a Seaman and was born in Baltimore. Age: 22. Prison Depot: Portsmouth, Prisoner of War #1262. Captured by HM Frigate *Niger*. When Taken: 13 Nov 1813. Where Taken: off Cape Finisterre, Spain. Prize Name: *Dart*. Ship Type: Privateer. Date Received: 19 Dec 1813. From what ship: HMS Fortunee. Discharged on 26 Dec 1813 and sent to Chatham on HMS *Diomede*. Prison Depot: Chatham, Prisoner of War #2904. Received: 7 Jan 1814 from Portsmouth. Died on 21 Apr 1814 from fever. (Johnson's Database, 2019)

Pool, Basil, served as a Private in Capt. John Fonsten's Co., Frederick Co. Militia, from 2 Sep 1814, marched to Baltimore, engaged in the defense of the city, and was reported "sick absent" on 3 Oct 1814 (Mallick and Wright pp. 230, 364)

Pool, John (c1780-1815), served as a Private in Capt. Benjamin McCeney's Co., 2nd Regiment, Anne Arundel Co. Militia, for 14 days between 10 Aug and 29 Aug 1813, stationed for 6 days near Pig Point from 17 to 22 Jun 1814, for 3 days in August 1814 and joined Capt. Thomas T. Simmons' Co., 32nd Regiment, on 8 Sep 1814 and possibly served to 17 Oct 1814 (muster roll dated 22 Aug – 17 Oct 1814). On 26 Nov 1850 Verlinda Pool, age 70, of Anne Arundel Co., widow of John Pool, stated he volunteered at Pig Point in Anne Arundel Co. on 1 Jul 1813 and was drafted on 1 Jul 1814 and went to Baltimore City with Capt. Thomas Simmons and was at the Battle of Baltimore. They were married on 2 Nov 1804 in Anne Arundel Co. by Rev. Compton and her maiden name was Beder. John Pool died at home on 11 Mar 1815. In 1855 Verlinda Pool, age 69 (sic), lived in Calvert Co. (BLW# 55-120-18372; Wright Vol. 4, pp. 20, 21, 44, 114)

Pool, John, of Maryland, served as a Seaman on the ship *Java* and was reported by Capt. Jeduthan Upton, Jr. in 1814 as having been impressed into service and was being held as a Prisoner of War on the prison ship *San Antonio* at Chatham, England (*Niles Weekly Register*, 26 Feb 1814)

Pool, John, served as a Seaman and was born in Maryland. Age: 22. Prison Depot: Chatham, Prisoner of War #2080. How Taken: Gave himself up off HM Ship-of-the-Line *Armada*. When Taken: 8 Jun 1813. Date Received: 9 Aug 1813. From what ship: HMS *Thames*. Discharged on 4 Aug 1814 and sent to Dartmoor on HMS *Liverpool*. Prison Depot: Dartmoor, Prisoner of War #2842. How Taken: Gave himself up off HM Frigate *Armide* on 8 Jun 1813. Date Received: 24 Aug 1814. From what ship: HMT *Liverpool* from Chatham. Discharged on 19 May 1815. (Johnson's Database, 2019)

Poole, John (African American), served as a Seaman and was born in Baltimore. Age: 27. Prison Depot: Portsmouth, Prisoner of War #615. How Taken: Gave himself up off HM Guard Ship *Royal William*. When Taken: 3 Feb 1813. Date Received: 3 Feb 1813. From what ship: HMS *Royal William*. Discharged on 11 Mar 1813 and sent to Chatham on HM Store Ship *Abundance*. Prison Depot: Chatham, Prisoner of War #1282. Received: 16 Mar 1813 from Portsmouth on HMS *Abundance*. Discharge date was not listed, but he was sent to Dartmoor. Prison Depot: Dartmoor, Prisoner of War #1917. Age 28. Date Received: 3 Aug 1814. From what ship: HMS *Alceste* from Chatham Depot. Discharged on 2 May 1815. (Johnson's Database, 2019)

Pope, Moses (1791-1814), served as a Private in Capt. James Dorman's Co., 5th U.S. Infantry, enlisted 30 May 1812 in Baltimore for 5 years at age 21, 5' 8" tall, born in Baltimore and was killed in the Battle of Lyon's Creek on 19 Oct 1814 (Johnson and Christou, p. 300)

Porter, Henry, served as a Private in Capt. William McLaughlin's Co., 50th Regt., Allegany Co. Militia, was called into service in the defense of Baltimore and reported "sick in hospital" in Sep 1814 as noted on muster roll dated 11 Aug – 13 Oct 1814 ("Allegany County Militia (Including Garrett Co.), 1794-1815," by F. Edward Wright and Marlene S. Bates, *Maryland Genealogical Society Bulletin*, Vol. 32, No. 2, Spring 1991, p. 174; Wright Vol. 9, p. 6, states he was in Capt. Henry Lowery's Co.; Wright Vol. 10, p. 2, states Capt. William McLaughlin's Co.)

Porter, Nathan, served as a Private in Capt. Conrad Hook's Co., Baltimore Co., 2nd Regt., 11th Brigade, stationed at Camp Hampstead in Baltimore from 25 Jul 1814 and was listed as "sick absent since Sep 25" 1814 (Wright Vol. 2, p. 81)

Porter, Rezin, served as a Private in Capt. Roderick Burgess' Co., 32nd Regt., Anne Arundel Co. Militia, from 22 Jul 1814 and was discharged by the Surgeon (no date or cause was given) and then returned to service on 18 Sep 1814 as reported on the muster roll dated 22 Jul – 19 Sep 1814. In 1850 Reason Porter, age 63, and Sarah Porter, age 61, both born in Maryland, lived in Rome Twp., Athens Co., OH and in 1860 Reason Porter, age 81, lived at that same location. (Wright Vol. 4, pp. 42, 114; 1850, 1860 OH Censuses; Smith's Database, 2019)

Porter, William, served as a Private in Capt. Stephen Moore's Co., Baltimore Volunteers Infantry Co., enlisted 8 Sep 1812 for 1 year and was wounded at York, Upper Canada on 27 Apr 1813 (Johnson and Christou, p. 301; Wright Vol. 2, p. 57, states he was wounded at Newark and in the hospital, no date given)

Posey, Valentine, served as a Passenger and Acting Mate and was born in Baltimore or Charles Co., MD. Age: 24. Prison Depot: Portsmouth, Prisoner of War #824. Captured by HM Frigate *Iris*. When Taken: 10 Mar 1813. Where Taken: off Cape Ortegal, Spain. Prize Name: *Messenger*. Ship Type: Merchant Vessel. Date Received: 13 May 1813. From what ship: HM Frigate *Medusa*. Discharged on 17 May 1813 and sent to Chatham on HMS *Impeleux*. Prison Depot: Chatham, Prisoner of War #1733. Date Received: 25 May 1813 from Portsmouth on HMS *Impetius*. Discharged on 24 Jul 1814 and sent to Dartmoor on HMS *Lyffey*. (Johnson's Database, 2019)

Potter, John, served as a Private in Capt. Joseph Hook's Co., 36th U.S. Infantry, enlisted 24 May 1813 in Baltimore, age 39, 5' 11" tall, born in Anne Arundel Co., MD and was captured near Washington, DC on 24 Aug 1814. Prisoner of War #7313 at Halifax, NS, interned 30 Sep 1813 and discharged on 5 Mar 1815 (Johnson and Christou, p. 301; Baker Vol. 2, p. 323)

Pottinger, William, served as a Midshipman and was born in Maryland. Age: 20. Prison Depot: Plymouth 1, Prisoner of War #1928. Captured by HM Brig *Pelican*. When Taken: 14 Aug 1813. Where Taken: off St. David's Head, Wales. Prize Name: U.S. Brig *Argus*. Ship Type: Warship. Date Received: 23 Aug 1813. From what ship: HMS *Pelican*. Discharged on 26 Aug 1813 and sent to Ashburton on parole. (Johnson's Database, 2019)

Potts, Lyman, served as a Marine and was taken from the barracks and admitted to the Naval Hospital in Washington, DC as Patient No. 61 on 22 Jul 1814 (injury or illness was not specified) and was discharged on 29 Jul 1814 and sent to the barracks (Sharp's Database, 2018)

Powell, Elijah, served as a Seaman and was born in Harford Co., MD. Age: 34. Prison Depot: Portsmouth, Prisoner of War #572. Captured by HM Frigate *Dryad*. When Taken: 7 Jan 1813. Where Taken: at sea. Prize Name: *Rossie*. Ship Type: Merchant Vessel. Date Received: 25 Jan 1813. From what ship: HM Ship-of-the-Line *Queen*. Discharged on 11 Mar 1813 and sent to Chatham on HM Store Ship *Abundance*. Prison Depot: Chatham, Prisoner of War #1245. Date Received: 16 Mar 1813 from Portsmouth on HMS *Abundance*. Discharged on 24 Jul 1813 and released to the Cartel *Hoffning*. (Johnson's Database, 2019)

Powell, Joseph (African American), served as a Seaman and was born in Baltimore. Age: 32. Prison Depot: Portsmouth, Prisoner of War #1226. Captured by Spanish Army. When Taken: 2 Jul 1813. Where Taken: off Passage Harbor. Prize Name: *Falcon* (schooner), prize of the U.S. Frigate *President*. Ship Type: Warship. Received: 21 Nov 1813. From what ship: *Fortan*. Discharged 26 Dec 1813 and sent to Chatham on HMS *Diomede*. (Johnson's Database, 2019)

Powers, John, served as a Private in the 14th U.S. Infantry and was born in Baltimore. Age: 22. Prison Depot: Chatham, Prisoner of War #3112. When Taken: 24 Jun 1813. Where Taken: Beaver Dams, Upper Canada. Date Received: 7 Jan 1814 from Halifax, NS. Discharged on 10 Oct 1814 and sent to U.S. on the Cartel *St. Philip*. (Johnson's Database, 2019)

Powers, Joseph, served as a Private in Capt. David Cummings's Co., 14th U.S. Infantry, enlisted 18 May 1812 and captured ay Beaver Dams, Upper Canada on 24 Jun 1813. Prisoner of War #3770 at Halifax, NS, interned 24 Jun 1813 and discharged on 9 Nov 1813 and sent to England (Johnson and Christou, p. 302; Baker Vol. 2, p. 324)

Powers, William, served as a Seaman and was born in Georgetown, MD. Age: 18. Prison Depot: Portsmouth, Prisoner of War #149. Captured by HM Brig *Recruit*. When Taken: 29 Aug 1812. Where Taken: at sea. Prize Name: *William*. Home Port: Baltimore. Ship Type: Merchant Vessel. Received: 29 Oct 1812. From what ship: HM Ship-of-the-Line *Ardent*. Discharged on 19 Feb 1813 and sent to Chatham on HM Store Ship *Dromedary*. (Johnson's Database, 2019; *Niles Weekly Register*, 4 Sep 1813, reported that William Power, of Baltimore County, was captured in August 1812 and sent to England as a Prisoner of War)

Prendewell, James, served as a Seaman and was born in Baltimore. Age: 20. Prison Depot: Portsmouth, Prisoner of War #168. Captured by HM Transport *Diadem*. When Taken: 7 Oct 1812. Where Taken: S. Andera (St. Andrews, Scotland). Prize Name: *Baltimore*. Home Port: Baltimore. Ship Type: Privateer. Date Received: 3 Nov 1812 San Antonio. From what ship: HMS *Diadem*. Discharged on 19 Feb 1813 and sent to Chatham on HM Store Ship *Dromedary*. Prison Depot: Chatham, Prisoner of War #537. Date Received: 23 Feb 1813 from Portsmouth on HMS *Dromedary*. Discharged on 8 Jun 1813 and released to the Cartel *Rodrigo*. (Johnson's Database, 2019)

Preston, Armond (Ormand), served as a Private in Capt. Richard Arell's Co., 14th U.S. Infantry, enlisted 21 May 1812 in Baltimore at age of 26, 5' 9½" tall, born in Poultary, Rutland Co., VT and was later captured. Prisoner of War #4084 at Halifax, interned on 24 Jun 1813, discharged for exchange on 3 Feb 1814, exchanged on 15 Apr 1814 and deserted at Fort Severn, MD on 14 Jul 1815 (Johnson and Christou, p. 302; Baker Vol. 2, p. 325)

Preston, Benjamin, served as a Private in Capt. William Bird's Co., 5th U.S. Inf., enlisted 19 May 1814 for 5 years in Baltimore at the age of 39, 5' 5" tall, born in Harford Co., MD, and was discharged at Buffalo, NY on 21 Jun 1814 because of hard drinking (Johnson and Christou, p. 302)

Pretzman, George (1791-1814), served as a Private in Capt. John Buck's Co., 38th U.S. Infantry, enlisted 9 Jun 1814 by Ensign Martin for the duration of the war at the age of 23, 5' 10½" tall, gray eyes, brown hair, dark complexion, born in Frederick, MD and died in General Hospital at Baltimore on 2 or 12 Dec 1814 (BLW# 27403-160-42; Johnson and Christou, pp. 302-303, stated he died on 12 Dec 1814; Mallick and Wright, p. 233, stated he died on 2 Dec 1814)

Price, Edward, of Maryland, served as a Seaman on the ship *Circe* and was reported by Capt. Jeduthan Upton, Jr. in 1814 as having been impressed into service and was being held as a Prisoner of War on the prison ship *San Antonio* at Chatham, England (*Niles Weekly Register*, 26 Feb 1814)

Price, Edward V., served as Paymaster of the 45th Regiment, St. Mary's Co., and died in office on 24 Jul 1813 (Wright Vol. 5, p. 10)

Price, Elias (1789-1868), served as a Private in Capt. John Heeter's Co., 44th Regiment, Montogmery Co. Militia, and stated in Oct 1850, age 61, that he had volunteered around 1 Aug 1814 and became very sick and being in his own county obtained leave from his captain to remain a few days until he was able to march; he was absent only 2 or 3 days; however, the company muster roll dated 4 Aug – 27 Sep 1814 reported he was absent without leave since 28 Aug 1814; Elias stated he rejoined his company at Baltimore on 30 or 31 Aug 1814 and continued in service until his company was discharged. On 26 Oct 1878 Deborah Price, age 73, widow of Elias, stated they were married in 1825 by cohabitation and public acknowledgement of each other as man and wife, and he died near Brookeville on 11 Jun 1868. Deborah Price, of Olney, Montgomery Co., died on 28 Apr 1882. (Wright Vol. 7, pp. 4, 38; Pension WO-34432)

Price, Job, served as a Private in 14th U.S. Infantry and was born in Maryland. Age: 24. Prison Depot: Chatham, Prisoner of War #3158. When Taken: 24 Jun 1813. Where Taken: Beaver Dams, Upper Canada. Date Received: 7 Jan 1814 from Halifax, NS. Discharged on 10 Oct 1814 and sent to U.S. on the Cartel *St. Philip*. (Johnson's Database, 2019)

Price, Johnson, served as a Private in Capt. Thomas Montgomery's Co., 14th U.S. Infantry, enlisted 7 May 1812 for 5 years at Cambridge, MD, age 18, 5' 6" tall, born in Dorchester Co., MD and later captured, date and place not stated. Prisoner of War at Montreal, later released, date not given, returned to service and was discharged on 7 May 1817 (Johnson and Christou, p. 303)

Price, Merritt, served as a Private in Capt. Clement Sullivan's Co., 14th U.S. Infantry, enlisted 8 Jun 1812 for 5 years at Leonardtown, MD, age 18, 5' 8" tall, born in St. Mary's Co., MD and was captured at Beaver Dams, Upper Canada on 24 Jun 1813. Prisoner of War #3795 at Halifax, interned on 27 Aug 1813, discharged for exchange on 3 Feb 1813, exchanged on 15 Apr 1814 and was discharged from the service at Montpelier, VT on 8 Jun 1817 (Johnson and Christou, p. 303; Baker Vol. 2, p. 325)

Price, Nehemiah, served as a Private in Capt. Thomas T. Simmons' Co., 2nd Regt., Anne Arundel Co. Militia, from 28 Sep 1814 and was reported "absent sick" on the muster roster dated 18 Oct – 1 Dec 1814 (Wright Vol. 4, p. 28)

Pringle, William, served as a Private in Capt. Colin Buckner's Co., 5th U.S. Infantry, enlisted 5 Feb 1813 for 5 years in Baltimore at the age of 25, 5' 6¼" tall, born in Philadelphia, and discharged on 31 May 1814 for injuries received in service, but the date and nature of his injuries were not stated (Johnson and Christou, p. 304)

Pritchard, Carvel (1774-1814), served as a Private in Capt. Thomas Ramsey's Co. of the 1st U.S. Rifles, enlisted 29 Jan 1814 for 5 years in Cincinnati at the age of 40, 5' 9" tall, born in Cecil Co., MD and died on 12 Jul 1814, probably at Newport, KY (Johnson and Christou, p. 304)

Pritchard, John Jr., served as a Private in Capt. James Newnam's Co., 4th Regt., Talbot Co., from 14 Apr to 21 Apr 1813 at Chloras Point and on 9 May and 10 May 1813 at Easton and died some time before 19 Apr 1814 at which time militia pay was due to the members of Capt. Thomas Henrix's Co. and John Pritchard [without the Jr.] was reported dead at that time; however, John Pritchard's name does not appear on any extant muster roll of Capt. Thomas Henrix's Co., 4th Regiment, Talbot Co. (Wright Vol. 1, p. 85; *Republican Star*, Talbot Co., MD, 19 Apr 1814)

Pritchard, Parvall (1772-1814), served as a Private in Capt. Robert Desha's Co. of the 24th U.S. Infantry, enlisted 28 Jul 1812 for 18 months at age 40, 5' 9" tall, born in Cecil Co., MD, re-enlisted on 29 Jul 1813 for five years in Capt. Thomas Ramsey's Rifle Co. and died on 12 Jul 1814. (Johnson and Christou, p. 304)

Probus, Henry, served as a Private in Capt. John Symmes' Co., 1st U.S. Infantry, enlisted 4 Apr 1814 in Cincinnati at the age 21, 5' 11" tall, born in Maryland, and was wounded at Chippewa, Upper Canada on 25 Jul 1814 (Johnson and Christou, p. 304)

Prosser, Uriah (1743-1814), served as a Private in Capt. Benjamin Edes' Co., 27th Regt., Baltimore Militia, from 10 Sep 1814 and was killed in action on 12 Sep 1814 at North Point. Name is on the Baltimore Battle Monument. (CMSR; *Baltimore American*, 12 Jun 1819, spelled his name incorrectly as Prosper) "Uriah

Prosser, formerly of Philadelphia, shoemaker, a soldier of the Revolution who volunteered [in the War of 1812] although above military duty age [age 69] was killed alongside his son, fighting nobly" at North Point. (*New York Commercial Advertiser*, c.16 Sep 1814)

Pryor, John, served as a Private in Capt. Reuben Gilder's Co., 14th U.S. Infantry, and died at the hospital in Cheektowaga, NY on 22 Nov 1814 from dysentery (Johnson and Christou, p. 305; https://wnyroots.tripod.com/Index-1812.html)

Pumphrey, Aquila, served as a Private in Capt. Thomas T. Simmons' Co., 2nd Regiment, Anne Arundel Co. Militia, from 28 Sep 1814 and was reported "sick, Nov 29" on the muster roster dated 18 Oct – 1 Dec 1814 (Wright Vol. 4, p. 28)

Pumphrey, Cockey (c1775-1814), served as a Private in Capt. Charles Pumphrey's Co., 22nd Regiment, Anne Arundel Co. Militia, for 7 days between 13 Apr and 5 May 1813 and was stationed at Fort Madison and Bodkin Point. On 21 Jan 1851 Margarett Pumphrey, age 73, of Baltimore City, widow of Cockey Pumphrey, stated he volunteered at Magity [Magothy River] in April 1813 and was "discharged by death" on 7 Feb 1814. They were married on 8 Oct 1796 in Anne Arundel Co. by Rev. Hagerty; her maiden name was Margaret Cromwell. (BLW# 50-rej-70186; Wright Vol. 4, pp. 37, 115)

Purnal, Elisha, served as a Seaman and was born in Maryland. Age: 24. Prison Depot: Chatham, Prisoner of War #2522. Captured by HM Frigate *Maidstone* & HM Brig *Nimrod*. When Taken: 17 Jul 1813. Where Taken: Grand Banks. Prize Name: *Yorktown*. Home Port: New York. Ship Type: Privateer. Date Received: 22 Oct 1813 from Portsmouth on HMT *Malabar*. Discharged and released in Oct 1814. (Johnson's Database, 2019)

Purnell, John, served as a Private in Capt. Reuben Gilder's Co., 14th U.S. Inf., enlisted 12 Aug 1812 for 5 years and discharged at Burlington, VT on 30 Mar 1814 due to an emaciation of his right thigh and leg (Johnson and Christou, p. 305; BLW# 24222-160-12, Pension Old War IF-3748)

Q

Quantrill, Thomas, served as a Captain from Hagerstown in the 24th Regiment on 16 Jun 1812 and was attached to Lt. Col. Fowler's 39th Regiment in Baltimore when wounded on 12 Sep 1814 at the Battle of North Point (Wright Vol. 2, p. 28, Marine pp. 165, 170)

Queen, Daniel (African American), served as a Seaman and was born in Prince George's Co., MD. Age: 31. Prison Depot: Chatham, Prisoner of War #3951. How Taken: Gave himself up off HM Ship-of-the-Line *Blenheim*. When Taken: 27 Aug 1814. Received: 21 Oct 1813. From what ship: *Quebec* (sic). Discharged 22 Oct 1814 and sent to Dartmoor on HMS *Leyden*. (Johnson's Database, 2019)

Quinn, David, served as a Private (company not stated) and was wounded on 24 Aug 1814 on the field of battle at Bladensburg, was admitted to the Naval Hospital, Washington, DC, on 25 Aug 1814 as Patient No. 22 and discharged on 9 Sep 1814 by order of Gen. Mason (Sharp's Database, 2018)

R

Radley, Robert (1771-1813), served as a Private in the 36th U.S. Infantry, enlisted 3 May 1813 in Baltimore at age 42, 5' 5¼" tall, born in Charleston (sic), MD and died on 15 Aug 1813 (Johnson and Christou, p. 305)

Ragan, John, of Washington Co., served as Lieutenant Colonel of the 24th Regiment and specially formed the 1st Regiment in service of the U.S, consisting of companies from Western Maryland; this regiment served from 21 Jul 1814 to 10 Jan 1815 and he was in command at the Battle of Bladensburg on 24 Aug 1814 where he was injured and captured; he was later released and was in command of a company at the Battle of New Orleans in January 1815 (Marine pp. 174, 411; Mallick and Wright, p. 234) Amelia Ragan, relict of the late Col. John Ragan, died on 25 Aug 1822 in her 34th year, leaving three children. (*The Maryland Herald and Hagers-Town Weekly Advertiser*, 27 Aug 1822)

Rage, James, served as a Private in Capt. Samuel Lane's Co., 14th U.S. Infantry, enlisted 19 Jun 1812 for 5 years and was killed at Carlisle Barracks, PA on 25 Jul 1812 (Johnson and Christou, p. 306)

Rainey, Joseph, served as a Private in Capt. Samuel Raisin's Co., 36th U.S. Infantry, enlisted on 21 Jun 1814 for the duration of the war and died in hospital on 21 Jan 1815, place and cause of death were not stated (Johnson and Christou, p. 306)

Ramsden, William, served as a Seaman and was born in Baltimore. Age: 21. Prison Depot: Dartmoor, Prisoner of War #5600. Captured by HM Brig *Wasp*. When Taken: 14 Sep 1814. Where Taken: off Cape Sable, NS. Prize Name: *Alexander*, prize of the Privateer *Monmouth*. Ship Type: Privateer. Date Received: 17 Dec 1814. From what ship: HMT *Loire* from Halfiax. Discharged on 5 Jul 1815. (Johnson's Database, 2019)

Ramsour (Ramsower), Henry, served as a Private in Capt. James Dorman's Co., 5th U.S. Infantry, enlisted 26 May 1812 for 5 years at Frederick Town at the age of 22, 5' 6½" tall, hazel eyes, light hair, fair complexion, born in Frederick Co.; was a hospital guard on 28 Apr 1814, joined his regiment on 4 May 1814, sent to hospital at Plattsburgh, NY on 1 Aug 1814, "absent sick since" at Buffalo, NY on 1 Mar and 30 Apr 1815, discharged at Greenbush, NY on 1 May or 10 May 1815 due to an ulcerated leg (Mallick and Wright, p. 236)

Randale, Frederick, served as a Seaman and was born in Maryland. Age: 30. Prison Depot: Plymouth 1, Prisoner of War #419. Captured by HM Frigate *Iris*. When Taken: 17 Jan 1813. Where Taken: at sea. Prize Name: *Union*. Home Port: Philadelphia. Ship Type: Merchant Vessel. Received: 5 Feb 1813 from HMS San Josef. Discharged and sent to Chatham on 29 Mar 1813 on HMS *Braham*. Prison Depot: Chatham, Prisoner of War #1489. Received: 6 Apr 1813 from Plymouth on an admiral's tender. Discharged on 26 Jul 1813 and released to the Cartel *Hoffning*. (Johnson's Database, 2019)

Randall, Aquila (1780-1814), served as a Private in Capt. Benjamin C. Howard's Co., 5th Regiment, Baltimore Mechanical Volunteers, from 19 Aug 1814 and was killed on 12 Sep 1814 at North Point. Name is on Baltimore Battle Monument on the Aquila Randall Monument. His estate was administered upon by John C. Randall on 16 Nov 1814. (NARA; CMSR; Wright Vol. 2, p. 4; *Baltimore American*, 12 Jun 1819; Marine, p. 411, listed him as Aquila A. Randall). In 1817 "A monument was erected in Baltimore to the memory of Acquilla Randall, member of 'First Mechanical Volunteers' who died 12 Sept. 1814 – in defense of Baltimore – aged 24 years." (*Niles Weekly Register*, 2 Aug 1817). Aquila Randall was buried in Green Mount Cemetery. In 2017 the Society of the War of 1812 in the State of Maryland rededicated the Aquila Randall Monument.

Randall, Enoch, served as a Private in Capt. Larkin Hammond's Co., Calvert Co., under Lt. Col. Frisby Tilghman's Cavalry Troops, joined 27 Aug 1814 and absent sick (no date or cause given) as reported on the muster roll dated 22 Aug – 22 Sep 1814 (Wright Vol. 4, p. 48)

Randolph, Henry, served as a Seaman and was born in Baltimore. Age: 24. Prison Depot: Plymouth 2, Prisoner of War #564. Captured by HMS *Muros*. When Taken: 8 Dec 1814. Where Taken: West Indies. Prize Name: *Mary*. Ship Type: Merchant Vessel. Date Received: 16 Apr 1815. From what ship: HMS *Swiftsure*. Discharged on 2 Jun 1815 and released to the Cartel *Soverign*. (Johnson's Database, 2019)

Ranter, Thomas, served as a Mate and was born in Maryland. Age: 23. Prison Depot: Plymouth 1, Prisoner of War #248. Captured by HM Ship-Sloop *Jalouse*. When Taken: 12 Dec 1812. Where Taken: Lat 43 Long 20. Prize Name: Rising Sun. Ship Type: Merchant Vessel. Date Received: 16 Jan 1813. From what ship: HMS *Stork*. Discharged and sent on 18 Jan 1813 to Ashburton on parole. (Johnson's Database, 2019)

Ratcliff, William, from the *Shark*, served as a "Boy" (a minor in training to become an officer) of the U.S. Chesapeake Flotilla, entered service on 1 Jan 1813, reported sick (date not stated) and died 12 Nov 1814 (Shomette, p. 386)

Raven, James, served as a Cooper and was born in Baltimore. Age: 25. Prison Depot: Dartmoor, Prisoner of War #2219. Captured by HM Ship-of-the-Line *Saturn*. When Taken: 25 May 1814. Where Taken: off Sandy Hook, NJ. Prize Name: *Hussar*. Home Port: New York. Ship Type: Privateer. Date Received: 16 Aug 1814. From what ship: HMS *Dublin* from Halifax, NS. Discharged on 2 May 1815. (Johnson's Database, 2019)

Ray, John, served as a Private in Capt. George Washington Magee's Co., 1st Regiment, Frederick Co. Militia, New Windsor area, from 22 Jul 1814, engaged in the Battle of Bladensburg on 24 Aug 1814 and was reported "sick absent 27 Aug" 1814 (Mallick and Wright, p. 342)

Ray, John, served as a Private in Capt. David Cummings's Co., 14th U.S. Infantry, enlisted 1 Jun 1812 for 5 years and was later captured. Prisoner of War, sent to England, later released, date was not given, returned to service and deserted at Fort McHenry on 28 Apr 1815 (Johnson and Christou, p. 308)

Read, Benjamin, served as a Private in Capt. William Henshaw's Co., 5th U.S. Infantry, enlisted 19 Mar 1813 in Baltimore at the age of 27, 6' 1" tall, born in Baltimore and died at Buffalo on 18 Dec 1814 (Johnson and Christou, p. 308)

Ray, William, served as a Seaman and was born in Baltimore. Age: 20. Prison Depot: Chatham, Prisoner of War #3790. Captured by HM Sloop *Atalante*. When Taken: 16 Nov 1812. Where Taken: off Cape of Good Hope, South Africa. Prize Name: *Ocean*, south seaman. Ship Type: Merchant Vessel. Date Received: 26 May 1814. From what ship: HMS *Hindostan*. Discharged on 22 Oct 1814 and sent to Dartmoor on HMS *Leyden*. Prison Depot: Dartmoor, Prisoner of War #4317. Age 21. Date Received: 7 Oct 1814. From what ship: HMT *Niobe* from Chatham. Discharged on 27 Apr 1815. (Johnson's Database, 2019)

Reans, John, served as a Seaman and was born in Baltimore. Age: 19. Prison Depot: Chatham, Prisoner of War #1588. How Taken: Gave himself up off HM Ship-of-the-Line *Christian VII*. When Taken: 21 Dec 1812. Date Received: 18 Apr

1813. From what ship: HMS *Rosario*. Discharged on 31 Aug 1813 and released to HMS *Ceres*. (Johnson's Database, 2019)

Reardon, John W., served as a Corporal in Capt. Thomas Read's Co. in the 19th U.S. Infantry, enlisted 28 Aug 1812 in Ohio for 18 months at the age of 21, 5' 8" tall, born in Maryland, and was discharged on 25 Oct 1814 because of wounds (Johnson and Christou, p. 308)

Reardon, Samuel, served as a Private in Capt. William Taylor's Co., 18th U.S. Infantry, later served in the 4th U.S. Infantry, enlisted 15 Sep 1814 for 5 years in Chester, SC, age 40, 5' 9½" tall, born in Harford Co., MD and was discharged at Sullivan Island on 5 Apr 1816 on a Surgeon's Certificate (Johnson and Christou, p. 292, misspelled his name as Peardon)

Recruit, Richard, served as a Private in Capt. Barton Hackney's Co., Frederick County Militia, from 1 Sep 1814, participated in the Battle of North Point on 12 Sep 1814 and was "sick in hospital" on 22 Sep 1814 in Baltimore (Mallick and Wright, pp. 237, 362)

Redman, David, served as a Seaman and was born in Maryland. Age: 21. Prison Depot: Portsmouth, Prisoner of War #1152. How Taken: Gave himself up off HM Ship-of-the-Line *Scepter*. Date Received: 7 Oct 1813. From what ship: HM Frigate *Spartan*. Discharged on 17 Oct 1813 and sent to Chatham on HMT *Malabar No. 352*. Prison Depot: Chatham, Prisoner of War #2399. Date Received: 21 Oct 1813 from Portsmouth on HMT *Malabar*. Discharged on 4 Sep 1814 and sent to Dartmoor on HMS *Freya*. Prison Depot: Dartmoor, Prisoner of War #3218. Date Received: 11 Sep 1814. From what ship: HMT *Freya* from Chatham. Discharged on 28 May 1815. (Johnson's Database, 2019)

Redmond (Redman), Martin, served as a Private in Capt. Richard Arell's Co., 14th U.S. Infantry (company and enlistment date not given) and was captured at Beaver Dams, Upper Canada on 24 Jun 1813. Prisoner of War #3763 at Halifax, NS, interned 24 Jun 1813 and discharged for exchange on 3 Feb 1814 (Johnson and Christou, p. 309; Baker Vol. 2, p. 333)

Reed (Reid), John, served as Quartermaster in the Extra Battalion, Dorchester Co. Militia, for 10 days between 10 Apr and 25 May 1813 at or near Cambridge and died, "payroll signed by Henry Keene, administrator of John Reed" (Wright Vol. 1, p. 73, spelled his name Reed; Marine p. 415, spelled his name Reid)

Reed (Reid), Thomas (African American), served as a Seaman and was born in Maryland. Age: 36. Prison Depot: Dartmoor, Prisoner of War #3583. How Taken: Gave himself up. When Taken: Jun 1814. Where Taken: Mahon (Island of Minorca). Received: 30 Sep 1814. From what ship: HMT *Sybella*. Discharged on 4 Jun 1815. (Johnson's Database, 2019)

Reeder, James, served as a Private in Capt. Barton Hackney's Co., Frederick County Militia, from 1 Sep 1814, participated in the Battle of North Point and was "sick in hospital" on 17 Sep 1814 in Baltimore (Mallick and Wright, p. 362)

Reeder, Robert Dougan (1784-1814), served as a Sergeant in Capt. Enoch J. Millard's Co., 12th Regiment, St. Mary's Co. Militia, in Nov 1813, served as a Private for 2 days in Aug 1814, and joined the regular army as a Private in Capt. Henry G. Neale's Co., 36th U.S. Infantry enlisted 4 Aug 1814 at the age of 30, 5' 6" tall, light complexion, blue eyes, light hair, was born in St. Mary's Co., and discharged on 24 Nov 1814, "incapable of performing the duty of a soldier in consequence of dysentery under which he had labored for some weeks past in the hospital at Grulesf(?) Town and imperfect(?) sight which daily increases ... on his legs and gene...s (sic) bad habit of body ... Certificate of disc (dead)." The bounty land application dated 20 May 1818 and filed by Joseph Harris, guardian to Helen Ann Reeder, the only child and heir of Robert D. Reeder, requested patent for the land sent to him at Leonardtown in St. Mary's Co. (Wright Vol. 5, pp. 20, 23, 24, 25, 83; BLW# 12-160-18136; Johnson and Christou, p. 310). Robert Dougan Reeder married Helen Hebb in 1805. (*Marriages and Deaths, St. Mary's County, Maryland, 1634-1900*, by Margaret K. Fresco, 1982, p. 250)

Rees, William, served as a Steward and was born in Baltimore. Age: 26. Prison Depot: Chatham, Prisoner of War #182. How Taken: Gave himself up off MV *Echo*. When Taken: 29 Oct 1812. Where Taken: London, UK. Received: 5 Nov 1812. From what ship: HMS *Namur*. Discharged on 7 Jun 1813 and released to HMS *Ceres*. (Johnson's Database, 2019)

Reese, John, served as an Ensign in Capt. Samuel Sterett's Co., 5th Regiment, Baltimore Militia, and was commanding as Lieutenant in place of Capt. Sterett when wounded at North Point on 12 Sep 1814, the same day he was promoted (North Point dead and wounded Article 4 Oct 1814 Columbian Register CT Vol. III 97, p. 4; Wright Vol. 2, p. 6; Marine pp. 170, 414)

Reese, John S., served as a Private in Capt. Edward Orrick's Co., 41st Regiment, Baltimore Co. Militia, from 25 Aug 1814 and reported as "sick-absent since Sep 14" 1814 (Wright Vol. 2, p. 70)

Reeves, Asa, served as a Private in Capt. Horatio Stark's Co., 7th U.S. Infantry, enlisted 22 Apr 1812 for 5 years at the age of 21, 6' tall, born in Maryland and died at Sackett's Harbor, NY on 27 Dec 1814 (Johnson and Christou, p. 310)

Reigle, John Adam (c1792-1848), served as a Private in Capt. Thomas T. Simmons' Co., 2nd Regt., Anne Arundel Co. Militia, from 28 Sep 1814 and was reported as "furloughed Oct 23, sick at home" on the muster roster dated 18 Oct – 1 Dec 1814, noting his home was 36 miles from Baltimore. On 14 Dec 1850 Eliza Ann Reigle, age 54, widow of John A. Reigle, stated they married in mid-January

1813 by Rev. Weems and her maiden name was Eliza Ann Lusby. John Reigle was drafted at Annapolis and died in Anne Arundel Co. on 27 Feb 1848. (Wright Vol. 4, pp. 28, 116; Anne Arundel County records indicate John Adam Reigle and Eliza Ann Lusby obtained a marriage license on 8 Feb 1813)

Reintzell, George, served as a Private and was captured at North Point on 12 Sep 1814. Dr. James H. McCulloh, Jr. wrote soon after the battle to the British commander: "In consequence of the humanity shown the following American prisoners of war, I do promise upon honor that they shall not directly or indirectly serve against the British until regularly exchanged." (Marine, p., 171)

Renark, Thomas, served as a Private in Capt. Nathan Towson's Co., 2nd U.S. Artillery, enlistment date not given, and was captured at the Battle of Stoney Creek, Upper Canada in June 1813 (Johnson and Christou, p. 310)

Reppert (Reppart), George (1777-1851), served as a Private in Capt. Daniel Schwartzauer's Co., 27th Regiment, Baltimore Militia, and was wounded on 12 Sep 1814 at North Point (Wright Vol. 2, p. 16) Dr. James H. McCulloh, Jr. wrote this note after the battle to the British commander: "In consequence of the humanity shown the following American prisoners of war, I do promise upon honor that they shall not directly or indirectly serve against the British until regularly exchanged." (Marine, p. 171) In Baltimore on 6 Sep 1842 George Reppart (a German), former private in Capt. Schwarzauer's (sic) Co., 27th Regt., MD Militia, and a resident of this city for 41 years and previously of Albany, NY, collected his own $48.00 pension due from 4 Mar to 4 Sep 1842. (Pierce, p. 154; *1812 Ancestor Index Volume III, 1992-2002*, National Society United States Daughters of 1812, 2003, p. 134, gave his name as George Lewis Reppert)

Resser, Jacob, served as a Private in Capt. John Berry's Washington Artillery Co. and was slightly wounded 13 Sep 1814 at Fort McHenry (Marine pp. 173, 415)

Reynolds, Bryan, allegedly served as a Private in Capt. John Montgomery's Artillery Co., Baltimore City, and was allegedly wounded on 12 Sep 1814 at North Point. Name is on the Baltimore Battle Monument, but documentation for his service has not yet been found and not listed in Wright's or Marine's books (*Baltimore American*, 12 Jun 1819, spelled his name Brian Reynolds)

Reynolds, Daniel, served as a Private in Capt. Reuben Gilder's Co. of the 14th U.S. Infantry, enlisted 10 Nov 1812 and died at Sackett's Harbor, NY on 23 Jan 1814; bounty land issued to daughter Agnes Reynolds and other heirs at law (BLW# 21599-160-12; Johnson and Christou, p. 311)

Reynolds, Gilbert, served as a Private in Capt. Richard Bell's Co., 5th U.S. Inf., enlisted 14 Jan 1812 for 5 years at Baltimore at the age of 21, 5' 7½" tall, born in Gloucester, NJ and was captured at Stoney Creek, Upper Canada on 12 Jun 1813.

Prisoner of War #5173 at Halifax, NS, interned 28 Dec 1813, discharged for exchange on 31 May 1814, returned to service, transferred to the Corps of Artillery and was discharged on 14 Jan 1815 (Johnson and Christou, p. 311; Baker Vol. 2, p. 335)

Reynolds, James, served as a Private in Capt. Andrew Smith's Co., 51ˢᵗ Regt., Baltimore Militia, joined 15 Sep 1814 and died 9 Nov 1814 (Wright Vol. 2, p. 38)

Reynolds, Richard, served as a Private in Capt. Cuddy Lawson's Co. Baltimore Patriots, 5ᵗʰ Regiment, and was allegedly killed on 12 Sep 1814 at North Point, but the muster roll stated he was discharged on 3 Oct 1814. His name is not on the Baltimore Battle Monument. (Huntsberry, p. 71; Wright Vol. 2, p. 5, and Marine p. 416, both did not mention his death)

Rhea, John, served as a Private in the 14ᵗʰ U.S. Infantry and was captured at Beaver Dams, Upper Canada, on 24 Jun 1813. Prisoner of War #3792 at Halifax, NS, interned 24 Jun 1813 and was discharged 9 Nov 1813 and sent to England on HMS *Success* (Johnson and Christou, p. 311; Baker Vol. 2, p. 336)

Rhodes, John, served as a Private in George Armistead's Co., 1ˢᵗ U.S. Artillery, enlisted 29 Aug 1811 at Fort McHenry, age 38, 5' 9" tall, born in Germany and was discharged on 6 Oct 1815 for disability (Johnson and Christou, p. 311)

Rhodrick, Joseph, served as a Seaman and was born in St. Mary"s Co., MD. Age: 39. Prison Depot: Plymouth 1, Prisoner of War #681. Captured by *Chance*, Jersey Privateer. When Taken: 15 Feb 1813. Where Taken: off Bordeaux, France. Prize Name: *Hope*. Ship Type: Merchant Vessel. Date Received: 15 Mar 1813. From what ship: *Growler*. Discharged and was sent to Dartmoor on 2 Apr 1813. Prison Depot: Dartmoor, Prisoner of War #174. Received: 2 Apr 1813 from Plymouth. Discharged on 20 Apr 1815. (Johnson's Database, 2019)

Rice, James, served as a Seaman and was born in St. Mary's Coi., MD. Age: 20. Prison Depot: Dartmoor, Prisoner of War #3507. Captured by HM Schooner *Whiting*. When Taken: Aug 1814. Where Taken: off Western Islands, Scotland. Prize Name: *Chasseur*. Ship Type: Privateer. Date Received: 24 Sep 1814. From what ship: HMT *Salvador del Mundo*. Discharged on 4 Jun 1815. (Johnson's Database, 2019)

Rice, John, served as a Private in Capt. Thomas Montgomery's Co., 14ᵗʰ U.S. Infantry, enlisted 22 Jun 1812 and was later captured, but date and place were not stated. Prisoner of War, exchanged on 11 May 1814 and reported deserted at Plattsburgh, NY in June 1814 (Johnson and Christou, p. 312)

Rice, John, of Maryland, served as a Seaman on the ship *LaHogue* and was reported by Capt. Jeduthan Upton, Jr. in 1814 as having been impressed into service and was being held as a Prisoner of War on the prison ship *San Antonio* at Chatham, England (*Niles Weekly Register*, 26 Feb 1814)

Rice, John, served as a Private in Capt. T. P. Moore's Co., 12th U.S. Infantry, enlisted 13 Jul 1813 by Lt. Morgan in Virginia, age 18, 5′ 4½″ tall, gray eyes, dark hair, dark complexion, born in Allegany Co., MD, left sick at Winchester, VA since 13 Sep 1813 (as of 31 Dec 1813), mustered at Staunton, VA on 10 May 1814, at Buffalo, NY on 28 Feb and 30 Apr 1815 and was discharged at Buffalo on 31 May or 1 Jun 1815 (Wright Vol. 10, p. 11)

Rice, William, see William Rise, q.v.

Rich, Elisha, served as a Seaman and was born in Baltimore. Age: 29. Prison Depot: Chatham, Prisoner of War #2021. How Taken: Gave himself up off HM Sloop-Brig *Rosario*. Received: 15 Jul 1813 from Plymouth. Discharged on 17 Jun 1814 and sent to Dartmoor on HMS *Pincher*. (Johnson's Database, 2019)

Rich, William (African American), served as a Seaman and was born in Maryland. Age: 23. Prison Depot: Plymouth 1, Prisoner of War #1017. How Taken: Gave himself up off HM Ship-of-the-Line *Malta*. Where Taken: Gibraltar. Date Received: 20 Apr 1813. From what ship: HMS *Libria*. Discharged and sent to Dartmoor (sic) on 1 Jul 1813. Prison Depot: Chatham, Prisoner of War #1980. Date Received: 15 Jul 1813 from Plymouth. Discharged on 23 Feb 1814 and released to HMS *Ceres*. (Johnson's Database, 2019)

Richards, David, served as a Private in Capt. James McConkey's Co., 27th Regt., Baltimore Militia, from 19 Aug 1814 until discharged on 29 Oct 1814 (Wright Vol. 2, p. 19, does not mention being wounded) In Baltimore on 27 Mar 1821 David Richards, former private in Capt. McKonkey's (sic) Co., Maryland Militia, in the late war when disabled, and resident of Philadelphia for about 5 months and previously of Maryland, collected his own $24.00 pension due from 4 Sep 1820 to 4 Mar 1821. (Pierce, p. 155)

Richards, John (1784-1815), served as a Private in Capt. Charles Stansbury's Co., 38th U.S. Infantry, enlisted 5 Nov 1814 in Baltimore at age 30, 5′4 ½″ tall, born in Maryland, died 14 Mar 1815, place and cause not stated; heirs received half pay for 5 years in lieu of bounty land (Johnson and Christou, p. 312)

Richards, John, served as a Seaman and was born in Charles City. Age: 28. Prison Depot: Portsmouth, Prisoner of War #933. Captured by HM Ship-of-the-Line *Fame*. When Taken: 24 Jun 1813. Taken at sea. Prize Name: --?--, prize of the Privateer *True Blooded Yankee*. Ship Type: Privateer. Date Received: 1 Jul 1813. From what ship: HM Brig *Hope*. Discharged on 2 Jul 1813 and sent to Chatham on HMS *Scorpion*. (Johnson's Database, 2019)

Richards, Sandy (African American), served as a Seaman and was born in Baltimore. Age: 44. Prison Depot: Chatham, Prisoner of War #3408. Captured by HM Frigate *Crescent*. When Taken: 16 Sep 1813. Where Taken: off Cape Cod, MA. Prize Name: *Elbridge Gerry*. Home Port: New York & Rhode Island. Ship Type: Privateer. Date Received: 23 Feb 1814 from Halifax, NS on HMT *Malabar*. Discharged on 22 Oct 1814 and sent to Dartmoor on HMS *Leyden*. Prison Depot: Dartmoor, Prisoner of War #5308. Age 45. Date Received: 31 Oct 1814. From what ship: HMT *Leyden* from Chatham. Discharged on 29 Jun 1815. (Johnson's Database, 2019)

Richardson, Allison, served as a Drummer (company not stated) and was taken from the barracks with a fracture (body part was not specified) and admitted to the Naval Hospital in Washington, DC as Patient No. 56 on 5 Jul 1814 and was discharged on 17 Aug 1814 and sent to barracks (Sharp's Database, 2018)

Richardson, Amos (1781-1815), served as a Private in Capt. Charles Stansbury's Co., 38th U.S. Infantry, enlisted 24 Aug 1814 in Annapolis at age 33, 5' 9" tall, born in Dorchester Co., MD and died on 12 Jan 1815, place and cause were not stated; widow Eleanor Richardson and heirs received half pay for five years in lieu of bounty land (Johnson and Christou, p. 312; Pension Old War Minor 480)

Richardson, Daniel, served as a Seaman and was born in Maryland. Age: 25. Prison Depot: Chatham, Prisoner of War #808. Captured by HM Frigate *Andromache*. When Taken: 10 Dec 1812. Where Taken: off Bordeaux, France. Prize Name: *Leader*. Ship Type: Merchant Vessel. Date Received: 27 Feb 1813 from Plymouth on HMS *Namur*. Discharged in July 1813 and released to the Cartel *Moses Brown*. (Johnson's Database, 2019)

Richardson, Daniel, served as a Seaman and was born in Maryland. Age: 24. Prison Depot: Plymouth 1, Prisoner of War #280. Captured by HM Frigate *Briton*. When Taken: 10 Dec 1812. Where Taken: off Bordeaux, France. Prize Name: *Leader*. Ship Type: Merchant Vessel. Received: 21 Jan 1813. From what ship: HMS *Abercrombie*. Discharged and sent to Portsmouth on 8 Feb 1813 on HMS *Colossus*. (Johnson's Database, 2019)

Richardson, David K., served as a Corporal in Capt. Robert Lawson's Co., 5th Regt., Baltimore Militia, was captured at the Battle of Bladensburg on 24 Aug 1814 and exchanged on 6 Oct 1814 (Marine, pp. 174, 417; Wright Vol. 2, p. 4)

Richardson, James, served as a Private in Capt. John Kennedy's Co., 27th Regt., Baltimore Militia, from 19 Aug 1814 and was killed on 12 Sep 1814 at North Point. His name is on the Baltimore Battle Monument. (CMSR; *Baltimore American*, 12 Jun 1819; Wright Vol. 2, p. 18, mentioned his service but not his death; Marine p. 417, also mentioned his service but not his death)

Richardson, Perry (African American), served as a Seaman and was born in Maryland. Age: 21. Prison Depot: Portsmouth, Prisoner of War #610. Captured by HM Ship-of-the-Line *Elephant*. When Taken: 28 Dec 1812. Where Taken: off Azores. Prize Name: *Sword Fish*. Home Port: Gloucester. Ship Type: Privateer. Date Received: 1 Feb 1813. From what ship: HM Frigate *Hermes*. Discharged on 11 Mar 1813 and sent to Chatham on HM Store Ship *Abundance*. Prison Depot: Chatham, Prisoner of War #1277. Received: 16 Mar 1813 from Portsmouth on HMS *Abundance*. Discharged on 24 Jul 1813 and released to Cartel *Hoffning*. Subsequently, Perry Richardson (African American), Seaman, born in Maryland, age 25, was again captured and imprisoned. Prison Depot: Dartmoor, Prisoner of War #3940. Captured by HM Frigate *Loire*. When Taken: 10 Dec 1813. Where Taken: off Block Island, RI. Prize Name: *Rolla*. Home Port: Baltimore. Ship Type: Privateer. Received: 5 Oct 1814. From what ship: HMT *President* from Halifax, NS. Wounded [during the prison massacre] on 6 Apr 1815, shot in prison yard. Discharged 9 Jun 1815. (Johnson's Database, 2019)

Richie, Allen, served as a Private in Capt. Samuel Lane's Co., 14th U.S. Infantry, enlisted 4 Sep 1812, age 21, 5' 11½" tall, born in Ireland and later captured, probably at Beaver Dams, Upper Canada. Prisoner of War #3882, interned 24 Jun 1813, discharged 19 Nov 1813 and sent to England (Johnson and Christou, p. 313; Baker Vol. 2, p. 339)

Richman, Joshua, served as a Seaman and was born in Maryland. Age: 21. Prison Depot: Plymouth 1, Prisoner of War #699. Captured by HM Ship-of-the-Line *Superb*. When Taken: 9 Feb 1813. Where Taken: Bay of Biscayne. Prize Name: *Star*. Ship Type: Merchant Vessel. Date Received: 19 Mar 1813. From what ship: HMS *Warspite*. Discharged and sent to Dartmoor on 2 Apr 1813. Prison Depot: Dartmoor, Prisoner of War #189. Date Received: 2 Apr 1813 from Plymouth. Discharged on 20 Apr 1815. (Johnson's Database, 2019)

Ricker, James, served as a Seaman and was born in Baltimore. Age: 22. Prison Depot: Dartmoor, Prisoner of War #1672. Captured by HM Frigate *Ceres*. When Taken: 5 Jun 1814. Where Taken: English Channel. Prize Name: *Vivid*, prize of the Privateer *Surprise*. Home Port: Baltimore. Ship Type: Privateer. Received: 2 Jul 1814 from Plymouth. Discharged 1 May 1815. (Johnson's Database, 2019)

Ricker, John, served as a Private in Capt. Isaac Barnard's Co., 14th U.S. Infantry, enlisted 13 Aug 1814 at the age of 26, 5' 3" tall, born in Baltimore and was discharged on 5 Dec 1814 on a Surgeon's Certificate for epileptic fits; bounty land was issued to his son John Ricker, Jr. and other heirs at law (Johnson and Christou, p. 313; BLW# 25321-169-12)

Ricketts, Benjamin, served as a 3rd Lieutenant in 14th U.S. Infantry (company not stated), was commissioned on 12 May 1813 and died in November 1813 (Johnson and Christou, p. 313)

Rictor, Christian (1787-1814), served as a Private in Capt. Reuben Gilder's Co., 14th U.S. Infantry, enlisted 21 Jan 1814 at the age of 27, born in Pennsylvania, was wounded at Lyon's Creek, Upper Canada on 19 Oct 1814 and died at Williamsville, NY on 18 Nov 1814 (Johnson and Christou, p. 314)

Riddle, Lawson, served as a Private in Capt. Henry Woodward's Co., 22nd Regiment, Anne Arundel Co. Militia, for 20 days between 28 Jul and 1 Sep 1813, in Capt. Adam Barnes' Co., 32nd Regiment, between 23 Aug and 27 Sep 1814, in Capt. Andrew Slicer's Co., 32nd Regiment, from 27 Sep to 17 Oct 1814 and in Capt. Thomas T. Simmons' Co., 2nd Regt., Anne Arundel Co. Militia, from 18 Oct 1814 and was reported "absent sick" on the muster roster dated 18 Oct – 1 Dec 1814. On 13 Nov 1850 Lawson Riddle, age 60, of Laurel, Prince George's Co., stated he was drafted in Anne Arundel Co. on 8 Aug 1814 and was discharged at Baltimore on 8 Feb 1815. In 1855, age 63, Lawson was living in Baltimore City. On 16 Mar 1871 Lawson Riddle, age 84, of Clarksville, Howard Co., MD, applied for a pension, stating he was drafted at Chestnut Spring in July or August 1813 and was discharged at Annapolis. His wife was Marry (sic) Riddle and they were married on 15 Aug 1820 at Union Factory. (Wright Vol. 4, pp. 28, 34, 44, 116, 138; BLW# 55-120-83693; Pension SO-15538, SC-17005)

Riddle, Robert, served as a Private in the 14th U.S. Infantry and was captured. Prisoner of War #4039 at Halifax, NS, interned 24 Jun 1813 and discharged for exchange on 3 Feb 1814 (Johnson and Christou, p. 314; Baker Vol. 2, p. 339)

Ridenour, Conrad, served as a Private in Capt. Henry Fleming's Co., 14th U.S. Infantry, enlisted 1 Feb 1813 for 18 months, age 30, 5' 9" tall, born in Maryland and was captured at Beaver Dams, Upper Canada on 24 Jun 1813. Prisoner of at Halifax, NS, later released, date not given, and discharged on 20 Jun 1815 (Johnson and Christou, p. 314, but Baker Vol. 2, p. 339, did not mention him)

Rideout, John J., served as a Seaman and was born in Baltimore. Age: 28. Prison Depot: Portsmouth, Prisoner of War #948. How Taken: Gave himself up off HM Frigate *Unicorn*. When Taken: 17 Jun 1813. Date Received: 8 Jun 1813. From what ship: HMS *Eldegon*. Discharged on 7 Aug 1813 and sent to Chatham on HMS *Rinaldo*. Prison Depot: Chatham, Prisoner of War #2163. Date Received: 16 Aug 1813 from Portsmouth on an admiral's tender. Discharged on 17 Jun 1814 and was sent to Dartmoor on the *Penebar*. [Rideout's name was mistakenly copied as Rectout by the compiler.] The record showed J. J. Rideout was at Prison Depot: Dartmoor, Prisoner of War #1815. Date Received: 20 Jul 1814. From what ship:

HMS *Milford* from Plymouth. Discharged on 26 Apr 1815. (Johnson's Database, 2019)

Rideout, James (African American), served as a Seaman and was born in Annapolis. Age: 37. Prison Depot: Plymouth 1, Prisoner of War #2549. How Taken: Gave himself up. When Taken: 25 Jan 1814. Where Taken: Scotland. Date Received: 16 Apr 1814. From what ship: HMS *PrinceFrederick*. Discharged on 10 May 1814 and sent to Dartmoor. Prison Depot: Dartmoor, Prisoner of War #1142. Date Received: 10 May 1814 from Plymouth. Discharged on 28 Apr 1815. (Johnson's Database, 2019)

Ridgely, Daniel Bowley (c1789-1814), served as a Private in Capt. Larkin Hammond's Co., Light Dragoons, 32nd Regiment, Ann Arundel Co., on 3 Sep 1808, was commissioned a 2nd Lieutenant on 23 Apr 1812 and served in Capt. Larkin Hammond's Co., 3rd Cavalry District, from 16 Apr to 24 Apr 1813. He married Mary Hammond circa 28 Jan 1811, lived at Elk Ridge and died intestate before 4 Feb 1814 (date of estate inventory). Mrs. Mary Ridgely died on 26 Jun 1840 at her residence in Baltimore Co. (Marine p. 418; Wright Vol. 4, pp. 6, 46; *Anne Arundel Gentry*, by Harry Wright Newman, 1979, Vol. 3, pp. 149-150)

Ridgeway, Jonathan, served as a Private in Capt. Gavin Hamilton's Co., 17th Regiment, Prince George's Co. Militia, from 18 to 28 Jul 1813 at Accokeek Church, was stationed at Nottingham in Capt. David Crawford's Co. for 3 or 4 days about 17 Jun 1814, was stationed at Nottingham and Port Tobacco for six days between 18 Jul and 2 Aug 1814 and was reported "sick and sent home," but the exact date was not given; he returned to service in Capt. John Carter's Co., 17th Regiment, from 19 Aug to 2 Sep 1814 at Tanyard Spring. On 20 Dec 1850 Jonathan Ridgeway, age 64, and again on 7 May 1855, age 69, resided in Tuscarawas Co., OH and stated he enrolled in Prince George's Co., MD about June 1813 and was discharged on 30 or 31 Aug 1814 at Bladensburg. (Wright Vol. 6, pp. 4, 6, 11, 12, 13, 46; BLW# 55-160-2433)

Riggin (Riggins), Leban (Laban), served as a Corporal in Capt. David Cummings' Co., 14th U.S. Infantry, enlisted 10 Jun 1812 for 5 years at age 39, 5' 9" tall, born in Wester, NC and was captured at Beaver Dams, Upper Canada on 24 Jun 1813. Prisoner of War #3976 at Halifax, NS, interned 24 Jun 1813, discharged 9 Nov 1813, sent to England, later released and was discharged from the service on 10 Jun 1817 (Johnson and Christou, pp. 314-315; Baker Vol. 2, p. 339, spelled his name Leban Riggins and listed him twice as Prisoner of War #3976 and Prisoner of War #4650). Leban Riggins served as a Private in the 14th U.S. Infantry and was born in Maryland. Age: 26. Prison Depot: Chatham, Prisoner of War #3066. When Taken: 24 Jun 1813. Where Taken: Beaver Dams, Upper Canada. Date Received: 7 Jan 1814 from Halifax, NS. Discharged on 10 Oct 1814 and sent to U.S. on the Cartel *St. Philip*. (Johnson's Database, 2019)

Riggs, James, served as a Private in Capt. Larkin Hammond's Co., Anne Arundel Co., Tilghman's Cavalry Troops, having volunteered at Annapolis around 1 Apr 1814 and continued in service about six months when he was taken sick at Baltimore about the last of Sep 1814; he was permitted to go home on furlough and before he got well the company was discharged; muster rolls, however, indicate Riggs served under Capt. Hammond between 16 Apr and 24 Apr 1813 at Annapolis, from 22 Aug 1814 until reported "absent without leave" on 6 Sep 1814 (yet he received bounty land in 1855). In 1852 James Riggs, age 77, lived in Guernsey Co., OH and in 1855, age 80, he lived in Belmont Co., OH. (Wright Vol. 4, pp. 46, 48, 117; BLW# 55-120-71534; Smith's Database, 2019)

Righter, Frederick, served as a Private in Capt. Andrew Smith's Co., 51st Regt., Baltimore Militia, from 19 Aug 1814 and was discharged on 2 Sep 1814 by a Surgeon, but the cause was not reported (Wright Vol. 2, p. 38)

Riley, John, served as a Private in Capt. Lawson Cuddy's Co., 41st Regiment, Baltimore Co. Militia, from 25 Aug 1814 and was reported "sick-absent since Oct 11" 1814 (Wright Vol. 2, p. 68)

Riley, Lewis, served as a Seaman on the privateer *Nonsuch* of Baltimore under Capt. Levely and was killed in action on 28 Sep 1812 during a battle with a British schooner off Martinique (*Niles Weekly Register*, 14 Nov 1812; J. Thomas Scharf's *The Chronicles of Baltimore*, Vol. 1, p. 359)

Riley, Pheril, served as a Private in Capt. John R. Dyer's Co., 17th Regiment, Prince George's Co. Militia, between 19 Aug 1814 and 13 Sep 1814, was taken prisoner, detained 2 days and was discharged at Fort Washington, but no dates were given (Wright Vol. 6, p. 13)

Rimmer, John (c1790-1812) served as a Private in 14th U.S. Infantry, enlisted 17 Apr 1812 and died on 22 May 1812; bounty land issued to his sister Mary Ann Parker and other heirs (BLW# 13137-160-12; Johnson and Christou, p. 315)

Rinehart, Daniel (1786-1818), served as a Private in Capt. George Washington Magee's Co., Frederick Co. Militia, 1st Regiment, joined 22 Jul 1814, engaged in the Battle of Bladensburg and in the defense of Baltimore; on the muster roll dated 14 Oct 1814 – 10 Jan 1815 he was reported "sick last muster, furloughed 15 days" and joined the regiment on 10 Nov 1814 (Mallick and Wright, pp. 243, 343, spelled his name Rineheart and stated he was enlisted in the regular army on 19 or 21 Apr 1814 by Capt. Smith in Baltimore; Marine, p. 175, spelled his name Rynehart). At enlistment in Baltimore, as a Private in the 38th Regiment, Daniel "Rineheart" was 5"9" tall, blue eyes, brown hair, light complexion, age 28 [transcribed as 38 or 28] and was born in Baltimore. The Recruiting Return shows him at Fort McHenry on 16 Feb and 28 Feb 1815, serving in Capt. Thomas Sangston's Detachment at Fort Covington on 30 Apr 1815. (Johnson and

Christou, p. 243) Daniel Rinehart died 9 Aug 1818, age 32 years, 5 months and 12 days, and was buried in Wolf Cemetery at Union Bridge in Carroll Co., MD. (*Names In Stone*, by Jacob M. Holdcraft, 1966, p. 947) There were two men named Daniel Rinehart during this time period so additional research will be necessary before drawing any conclusions regarding their identity.

Ringgold, Thomas (African American), served as a Seaman and was born in Baltimore. Age: 32. Prison Depot: Chatham, Prisoner of War #3743. Captured by HM Ship-of-the-Line *San Domingo*. When Taken: 1 Mar 1814. Where Taken: off Savannah, GA. Prize Name: *Argus*. Ship Type: Privateer. Date Received: 26 May 1814. From what ship: HMS *Hindostan*. Discharged on 25 Sep 1814 and sent to Dartmoor on HMS *Niobe*. Prison Depot: Dartmoor, Prisoner of War #4607. Date Received: 9 Oct 1814. From what ship: HMT *Leyden* from Chatham. Discharged on 15 Jun 1815. (Johnson's Database, 2019)

Ringold, Peregrin, served as a Seaman and was born in Baltimore. Age: 36. Prison Depot: Plymouth 1, Prisoner of War #2308. Captured by HM Brig *Pelican*. When Taken: 13 Jan 1814. Where Taken: at sea. Prize Name: *Siro*. Home Port: Baltimore. Ship Type: Letter of Marque. Date Received: 23 Jan 1814. From what ship: HMS *Pelican*. Discharged on 31 Jan 1814 and sent to Dartmoor. Prison Depot: Dartmoor, Prisoner of War #971. Date Received: 31 Jan 1814 from Plymouth. Discharged on 27 Apr 1815. (Johnson's Database, 2019)

Ringold, Thomas B., served as a Seaman and was born in Prince George's Co., MD. Age: 34. Prison Depot: Chatham, Prisoner of War #358. Captured by HM Sloop *Helena*. When Taken: 31 Dec 1813. Where Taken: off Azores. Prize Name: *Postsea*, prize of the Privateer *Thrasher*. Ship Type: Privateer. Date Received: 19 Jan 1813. From what ship: HMS *Raisonable*. Discharged on 24 Jul 1813 and released to the Cartel *Hoffning*. (Johnson's Database, 2019)

Ringrove, William, served as a Boy onboard a ship and was born in Maryland. Age: 12. Prison Depot: Dartmoor, Prisoner of War #3555. Captured by HM Frigate *Piqua*. When Taken: 26 Apr 1814. Where Taken: near Mona Passage, West Indies. Prize Name: *Hawk*. Home Port: Wilmington. Ship Type: Privateer. Date Received: 30 Sep 1814. From what ship: HMT *Sybella*. Discharged on 4 Jun 1815. (Johnson's Database, 2019)

Rinnear, William, served as a Private in Capt. Joseph Marshall's Co., 14th U.S. Infantry and was discharged on 3 Dec 1814 due to a rupture, after serving for four months (Johnson and Christou, p. 316)

Rise (Rice), William (1786-1864), served as a Private in Capt. Daniel Shawen's Co., Frederick County Militia, from 5 Sep 1814 and was reported "sick absent" on 6 Oct 1814 (Mallick and Wright, pp. 244, 365, spelled his name Rise). William

Rice died on 4 Sep 1864, age 78, and was buried in St. John's Catholic Cemetery in Frederick. (*Names In Stone*, by Jacob M. Holdcraft, 1966, p. 939)

Ritchie, James, served as a Seaman and was born in Baltimore. Age: 23. Prison Depot: Dartmoor, Prisoner of War #3986. Captured by HM Ship-of-the-Line *Leander*. When Taken: 22 Jun 1814. Where Taken: off Cape Sable, NS. Prize Name: U.S. Brig *Rattlesnake*. Ship Type: Warship. Date Received: 6 Oct 1814. From what ship: HMT *Chesapeake* from Halifax, NS. Discharged on 9 Jun 1815. (Johnson's Database, 2019)

Roach, Reuben (African American), served as a Seaman and was born in Maryland. Age: 29. Prison Depot: Plymouth 1, Prisoner of War #1183. How Taken: Gave himself up off HM Ship-of-the-Line *Dublin*. Date Received: 8 May 1813. From what ship: HMS *Dublin*. Discharged and sent to Chatham on 8 Jul 1813 on HM *Hired Dart*, tender *Neptune*. Prison Depot: Chatham, Prisoner of War #1995. Date Received: 15 Jul 1813 from Plymouth. Discharged on 17 Jun 1814 and sent to Dartmoor on HMS *Pincher*. (Johnson's Database, 2019)

Roach, Stephen, served as a Private in Capt. Thomas Montgomery's Co., 14th U.S. Infantry, enlisted 26 May 1812 and was killed during the Battle of LaCole Mill, Lower Canada on 30 Mar 1814; bounty land issued to James Roach and other heirs at law (BLW# 17625-160-12; Johnson and Christou, p. 316)

Robbins, William, served as a Seaman on the privateer *Surprise* of Baltimore and drowned in a shipwreck on 5 Apr 1815 (Marine p. 420; *Niles Weekly Register*, 15 Apr 1815)

Robert, George (African American), "a native born coloured man" and Seaman on the privateer *Sarah Ann* of Baltimore, was captured and sent to Jamaica late in 1812 (*Niles Weekly Register*, 14 Nov 1812, but the same paper on 2 Oct 1813 stated he was sent to Bermuda and spelled his last name Roberts)

Roberts, George, served as a Seaman and was born in Baltimore. Age: 30. Prison Depot: Dartmoor, Prisoner of War #1192. Captured by *Rolla*. When Taken: 25 Sep 1813. Prize Name: *La Miquelonnaise*, French Privateer. Date Received: 4 Jun 1814 from Dartmouth. Discharged on 6 Apr 1815. (Johnson's Database, 2019)

Roberts, James, served as a Private in 1st Lt. Richard H. Battee's Co., Watkins' Regiment, Anne Arundel Co. Militia, from 8 Jun 1813 and died on 26 Aug 1813, but the place and cause of death were not stated (Wright Vol. 4, p. 41)

Roberts, John (1790-1815), served as a Seaman and was born in Baltimore. Age: 23. Prison Depot: Plymouth 1, Prisoner of War #1411. How Taken: Gave himself up. When Taken: 10 May 1813. Where Taken: Cove of Cork, Ireland. Date Received: 22 May 1813. From what ship: HMS *Talbot*. Discharged on 8 Sep 1813 and sent to Dartmoor. Prison Depot: Dartmoor, Prisoner of War #486. Date

Received: 8 Sep 1813 from Plymouth. Died on 12 May 1815 from gunshot wound [during the massacre] on 6 Apr 1815, shot in prison yard. (Johnson's Database, 2019; Centennial Trails, United States Daughters of 1812, online at www.war1812trails.com/Dartmoor)

Roberts, William, served as a Seaman and was born in Maryland. Age: 31. Prison Depot: Chatham, Prisoner of War #326. How Taken: Gave himself up off MV *Eliza*. When Taken: 3 Jan 1813. Where Taken: London, UK. Date Received: 11 Jan 1813. From what ship: HMS *Raisonable*. Discharged on 28 Apr 1813 and released to the *David Scott*. (Johnson's Database, 2019)

Roberts, William (African American), served as a Seaman and was born in Baltimore. Age: 36. Prison Depot: Chatham, Prisoner of War #2038. How Taken: Gave himself up. When Taken: 24 Jul 1813. Where Taken: London, UK. Date Received: 1 Aug 1813. From what ship: HMS *Raisonable*. Discharged on 4 Dec 1813 and released to HMS *Ceres*. (Johnson's Database, 2019)

Roberts, William, served as a Private in the 14th U.S. Infantry and was later captured, probably at Beaver Dams, Upper Canada. Prisoner of War #3938 at Halifax, NS, interned 24 Jun 1813 and died there on 28 Sep 1813 of affliction of the chest (Johnson and Christou, p. 317; Baker, Vol. 2, p. 341)

Roberts, Zachariah (1777-1846), served as a Private in Capt. Nathan Towson's Co., 2nd U.S. Artillery, enlisted 25 Jan 1812 for 5 years in Baltimore at age of 34, 5' 7½" tall, born in Baltimore, was wounded at Chippewa, Upper Canada on 5 Jul 1814 and discharged at Baltimore on 1 May 1815; placed on pension roll on 2 May 1815 (Johnson and Christou, p. 317; *The [Baltimore] Sun*, 31 Oct 1846)

Robey (Roby), Peter H., served as a Private in Capt. Edward Tatnall's Co., 4th U.S. Infantry, enlisted 28 May 1814 at Washington, GA, age 27, 5' 6" tall, born in Charles Co., MD and was discharged at Fort Moultrie, SC on 16 Sep 1815 due to a rupture (Johnson and Christou, p. 320; BLW# 9320-160-12)

Robinson, ----, served as a Sergeant in the Marines and was taken from the barracks and admitted to the Naval Hospital in Washington, DC as Patient No. 2 on 4 Jun 1814 (injury or illness not stated) and was discharged on 15 Jun 1814 and sent to the barracks (Sharp's Database, 2018)

Robinson, Benjamin, served as a Private in Capt. James Britton's Co., 14th U.S. Infantry, enlisted on 19 Apr 1813 and died later in the war, but date and cause of death were not stated (BLW# 26603-160-12; Johnson and Christou, p. 318)

Robinson, Caleb R., served as a 2nd Lieutenant in Capt. William Addison's Co., U.S. Sea Fencibles, commissioned on 17 Mar 1814 and died on 28 Jan 1815, but place and cause of death were not stated (Johnson and Christou, p. 318)

Robinson, Daniel, served as a Private in the 14th U.S. Infantry and was later captured, probably at Beaver Dams, Upper Canada. Prisoner of War #3907 at Halifax, NS, interned in 24 Jun 1813 and was discharged for exchange on 3 Feb 1814 (Johnson and Christou, p. 318; Baker Vol. 2, p. 341)

Robinson, David, served as Acting Midshipman on a barge under Commodore Joshua Barney in the U.S. Flotilla and was captured at the Battle of Bladensburg on 24 Aug 1814 (Marine, p. 174)

Robinson, Dorsey, served as a Seaman of the U.S. Chesapeake Flotilla, entered service on 27 Nov 1813 and died on 2 Oct 1814 (Shomette p. 367)

Robinson, Edward, served as a Seaman and was born in Talbot Co., MD. Age: 24. Prison Depot: Portsmouth, Prisoner of War #195. How Taken: Gave himself up. Date Received: 22 Nov 1812. From what ship: HM Guard Ship *Royal William*. Discharged on 19 Feb 1813 and sent to Chatham on HM Store Ship *Dromedary*. (Johnson's Database, 2019)

Robinson, George (African American), served as a Seaman and was born in Talbot Co., MD. Age: 25. Prison Depot: Dartmoor, Prisoner of War #5782. How Taken: Gave himself up off HM Sloop *Ariel*. When Taken: 8 Dec 1812. Date Received: 26 Dec 1814. From what ship: HMT *Argo*. Discharged on 3 Jul 1815. (Johnson's Database, 2019)

Robinson, James, served as Acting 1st Sergeant in Capt. Luke Kiersted's Co., 6th Regiment, Baltimore Militia, from 19 Aug 1814 until 11 Sep 1814 when he was "reverted to private because of sickness" (Wright Vol. 2, p. 11)

Robinson, John, served as a Private in Capt. Montgomery's Baltimore Union Artillery, wounded and captured 12 Sep 1814 at North Point (Marine, p. 422) Dr. James H. McCulloh, Jr. wrote this note soon after the battle to the British commander: "In consequence of the humanity shown the following American prisoners of war, I do promise upon honor that they shall not directly or indirectly serve against the British until regularly exchanged." (Marine, p. 171)

Robinson (Robertson), John (1794-1855), served as a Private in Capt. William Durbin's Co., Frederick Co. Militia, joined 24 Aug 1814, absent without leave on 29 Sep 1814, returned to service and was furloughed in Baltimore, being sick and unfit for service in Oct 1814; he lived in Frederick Co. and Baltimore City and died in Carroll County on 15 Jul 1855. (Mallick and Wright, p. 245)

Robinson, Joseph (1779-1814), served as a Private in Capt. Thomas Carbery's Co., 36th U.S. Infantry, enlisted 27 Apr 1814 at Georgetown, DC at the age of 35, 5' 10" tall, born in Cork, Ireland and died at Georgetown, DC on 4 Oct 1814 (Johnson and Christou, p. 319)

Robinson, Joseph, served as 1st Sergeant in Capt. Luke Kiersted's Co., 6th Regt., Baltimore Militia, from 19 Aug 1814 and then as "acting 1st Sergeant until 11 Sep when he reverted to private because of sickness" (Wright Vol. 2, p. 11)

Robinson, T. G., served as a physician aboard the privateer *Prince of Neufchatel* and was wounded in action on 11 Sep 1814 (Marine p. 422)

Robinson, Thomas, served as a Private in Capt. Abraham Pyke's Co., 1st Artillery Co., Baltimore, from 19 Aug 1814 and died 17 Sep 1814. (Wright Vol. 2, p. 49)

Robinson, William (Mulatto), served as a Seaman and was born in Baltimore. Age: 21. Prison Depot: Chatham, Prisoner of War #3924. How Taken: Gave himself up off HM Ship-of-the-Line *Revenge*. When Taken: 23 Sep 1814. Date Received: 24 Sep 1814. From what ship: HMS *Namur*. Discharged on 29 Sep 1814 and sent to Dartmoor on HMS *Freya*. Prison Depot: Dartmoor, Prisoner of War #4778. Date Received: 9 Oct 1814. From what ship: HMT *Freya* from Chatham. Discharged on 15 Jun 1815. (Johnson's Database, 2019)

Roddy, W. B., served as a Marine Fifer and was born in Maryland. Age: 22. Prison Depot: Dartmoor, Prisoner of War #3272. Captured by HM Frigate *Orpheus*. When Taken: 20 Apr 1814. Where Taken: off Matanzas, Cuba. Prize Name: U.S. Sloop-of-War *Frolic*. Ship Type: Warship. Date Received: 13 Sep 1814 from Naval Hospital, Plymouth. Discharged on 28 May 1815. (Johnson's Database, 2019)

Rodgers, George, served as a Private in Capt. Richard Arell's Co., 14th U.S. Inf., enlisted 2 Jun 1812 in Baltimore, age 23, 5' 5" tall, born in Baltimore and was later captured. Prisoner of War, exchanged on 15 Apr 1814, returned to service and deserted at Fort Severn, MD on 16 Jul 1815 (Johnson and Christou, p. 320)

Roe (Rowe), Michael, served as a Private in Capt. Nathan Towson's Co., 2nd U.S. Artillery, enlistment date not given, age 30, and was captured at the Battle of Stoney Creek, Upper Canada on 12 Jun 1813. Prisoner of War #5075, interned 28 Dec 1813 and was discharged for exchange on 31 May 1814 (Johnson and Christou, p. 320; Baker Vol. 2 p. 349)

Roesener, John, served as a Private in Capt. Philip B. Sadtler's Co., 5th Regt., Baltimore Militia, from 19 Aug 1814 and died 19 Sep 1814 (Wright Vol. 2, p. 7)

Rogers, Thomas, a crewman on the privateer *Sarah Ann* of Baltimore, was captured and sent to Jamaica late in 1812; born in Waterford, Ireland, resident of U.S. many years, naturalized at Baltimore Custom House, has a wife and there children there (*Niles Weekly Register*, 14 Nov 1812, but the same paper on 2 Oct 1813 stated he was sent to Bermuda)

Rohr, Peter, served as a Private under Capt. James F. Huston and Capt. Joseph Green in the Frederick County Militia, joined 23 Jul 1814, furloughed 23 Sep 1814 and discharged in Baltimore on 6 Dec 1814 by a Surgeon's Certificate, but the medical reason was not specified (Mallick and Wright, pp. 246, 346)

Roles, John, served as a Seaman and was born in Maryland. Age: 22. Prison Depot: Plymouth 1, Prisoner of War #1532. Captured by HM Frigate *Andromache*. When Taken: 14 Mar 1813. Where Taken: off Nantes, France. Prize Name: *Courier*. Home Port: Baltimore. Ship Type: Letter of Marque (Privateer). Date Received: 29 May 1813. From what ship: HMS *Hannibal*. Discharged on 30 Jun 1813 and sent to Stapleton. Prison Depot: Stapleton, Prisoner of War #96. Age 23. Date Received: 8 Jul 1813 from Plymouth. Discharged on 13 Jun 1814 and sent to Dartmoor. Prison Depot: Dartmoor, Prisoner of War #1386. Date Received: 19 Jun 1814 from Stapleton. Discharged on 28 Apr 1815. (Johnson's Database, 2019)

Roles Reason, served as a Private in Capt. Henry Grindage's Co., 14th U.S. Inf., enlisted 9 Aug 1812 for 1 year at the age of 31, 5' 5 ½" tall, and was captured at Stoney Creek, Upper Canada on 12 Jun 1813. Prisoner of War #5096 at Halifax, interned on 28 Dec 1813, discharged for exchange on 31 May 1814 and was discharged from the service on 7 Aug 1814, re-enlisted on 9 Aug 1814 for the duration of the war and served in Capt. Porter's Co., 27th U.S. Regiment, until discharged at New York on 17 Jun 1815 (Johnson and Christou, pp. 320-321; Baker Vol. 2, p. 346)

Root, John (1785-1813), served as a Private in the 14th U.S. Infantry in 1813, age 28, born in New York. Prisoner of War #429 at Quebec, interned on 7 Jul 1813 and died there on 22 Aug or 23 Aug 1813 (Johnson and Christou, p. 321, stated he died 22 Aug 1813; Johnson, pp. 132-133, stated he died 23 Aug 1813)

Root, John, served as a Private in Capt. William Curtis' Co., Washington Co. Militia, from 14 Oct 1814 and died on 1 Dec 1814 (Wright Vol. 9, p. 4)

Rooter, John (1787-1814), served as a Seaman and was born in Maryland. Age: 26. Prison Depot: Portsmouth, Prisoner of War #1336. Captured by *Friends*, Antigua, West Indies Privateer. When Taken: 1 Mar 1813. Where Taken: off St. Bartholomew, West Indies. Prize Name: *Calmar*. Ship Type: Merchant Vessel. Discharged on 5 Jan 1814 and sent to Chatham on HMS *Poictiers*. Prison Depot: Chatham, Prisoner of War #3234. Received: 3 Jan 1814 from HM Ship-of-the-Line *Prince*. Died on 9 May 1814 from fever. (Johnson's Database, 2019)

Rose, Aquilla, served as a Private in Capt. Edward Orrick's Co., 41st Regiment, Baltimore Co. Militia, from 25 Aug 1814 and reported as "sick absent since 14 Aug" 1814 (Wright Vol. 2, p. 70)

Rose, Jonathan, served as a Private in Capt. Samuel Lane's Co., 14th U.S. Inf., enlisted 28 Jun 1812 for 18 months at the age of 27, 5' 11" tall, and was later captured, probably at Beaver Dams, Upper Canada on 24 Jun 1813. Prisoner of War #3967 at Halifax, interned 24 Jun 1813, discharged for exchange on 3 Feb 1814 and discharged from the service at Plattsburgh, NY on 5 Jul 1814 (Johnson and Christou, p. 321; Baker Vol. 2, p. 347)

Rose, Nathaniel, served as a Private in Capt. William McIlvane's Co., 14th U.S. Infantry, enlisted 7 Feb 1813 for 18 months and was captured at Beaver Dams, Upper Canada on 24 Jun 1813. Prisoner of War #3754 at Halifax, interned 24 Jun 1813, discharged for exchange on 3 Feb 1814, exchanged on 15 Apr 1814, returned to service and was discharged at Plattsburgh, NY on 6 Aug 1814 (Johnson and Christou, p. 321; Baker Vol. 2, p. 347)

Rosepaugh, Cornelius, served as a Private in Capt. Nathan Towson's Co., 2nd U.S. Artillery, enlisted 2 May 1812 for 5 years in Baltimore at the age of 32 or 38 (both ages were given), 5' 6" tall, born in New Jersey, captured at Battle of Stoney Creek, Upper Canada in June 1813, was later released and served until discharged at Fort Niagara, NY on 1 May 1817 (Johnson and Christou, p. 322)

Rosignol, James, served as a First Mate and was born in Maryland. Age: 34. Prison Depot: Chatham, Prisoner of War #1105. Captured by *Lion*, British Privateer. When Taken: 15 Feb 1813. Where Taken: Bay of Biscayne. Prize Name: *Tom Thumb*. Ship Type: Merchant Vessel. Received: 14 Mar 1813 from Portsmouth on HMS *Beagle*. Discharged on 23 Mar 1813 and released to the Cartel *Robinson Potter*. (Johnson's Database, 2019)

Ross, David, served as a Private in the 14th U.S. Infantry and was captured, probably at Beaver Dams, Upper Canada, on 24 Jun 1813. Prisoner of War #3861 at Halifax, NS, interned 24 Jun 1813 and died there on 17 Oct 1813 of smallpox (Johnson and Christou, p. 322; Baker, Vol. 2, p. 347)

Ross, David, served as a Private in the 22nd U.S. Infantry and died 25 Jul 1814, place and cause not stated; heirs received half pay for 5 years in lieu of bounty land (Johnson and Christou, p. 322)

Ross, James, served as a Private in the 14th U.S. Infantry, enlistment date not stated, and was later captured. Prisoner of War, date and place not stated, and was exchanged on 15 Apr 1814 (Johnson and Christou, p. 322)

Ross, Joseph, served as a Private in the 14th U.S. Infantry, enlistment date not stated, and was captured, probably at Beaver Dams, Upper Canada. Prisoner of War #4092 at Halifax, interned 24 Jun 1813 and was discharged for exchange on 3 Feb 1814 (Johnson and Christou, p. 322; Baker Vol. 2, p. 348)

Ross, Joseph N., served as a Private in Capt. Richard Arell's Co., 14th U.S. Infantry, enlisted 8 Jun 1812 in Allegany Co., MD, age 25, 5' 7½" tall, blue eyes, dark hair, light complexion, born in Allegany Co., MD, mustered at Greenbush, NY on 1 Mar and 30 Apr 1815, "left sick at Portland since 21 Jun 1814 (as of 28 Jun 1815)" and was discharged at Greenbush, NY on 29 May 1815 for disability; wife Elizabeth Ross received a pension (Johnson and Christou, p. 322; Pension WO-1178; Old War File IF-4130 and Old War File CF-627; BLW# 5709-160-12; however, Wright Vol. 10, p. 11, stated he deserted on 11 Mar 1815)

Rotch, David, served as a Seaman and was born in Baltimore. Age: 22. Prison Depot: Chatham, Prisoner of War #2031. How Taken: Gave himself up off MV *Clive*. When Taken: 14 Jul 1812. Where Taken: London. Received: 24 Jul 1813. From what ship: HMS *Raisonable*. Discharged on 21 Jan 1814 and released to HMS *Ceres*. (Johnson's Database, 2019)

Rowe (Roe), Michael, served as a Private in Capt. Nathan Towson's Co., 2nd U.S. Artillery, enlistment date not stated, age 30, and was captured at the Battle of Stoney Creek, Upper Canada on 12 Jun 1813. Prisoner of War #5075 at Halifax, NS, interned 28 Dec 1813 and was discharged for exchange on 31 May 1814 (Johnson and Christou, p. 320; Baker Vol. 2, p. 349)

Rowe, Noah (1787-1815), served as a Private in Capt. Charles Stansbury's Co. of the 38th U.S. Infantry, enlisted 12 Aug 1814 in Annapolis, age 27, 5' 5" tall, born in Baldwin, MA and died on 8 Feb 1815 (Johnson and Christou, p. 323)

Ruddock, John, served as a Corporal in the U.S. Marine Corps, enlisted 18 Apr 1811, and was taken from the barracks and admitted to the Naval Hospital in Washington, DC as Patient No. 87 on 28 Dec 1814 with typhoid fever and was discharged on 1 Jan 1815 and sent to the barracks (Sharp's Database, 2018)

Ruff, Henry (African American), served as Cabin Boy to 1st Lt. James P. Wilmer on U.S.S. frigate *Essex* and "was probably the 'Henry Ruff' listed as 'Boy,' crew member no. 61 in the crew list made when the *Essex* sailed from Delaware Bay on 28 Oct 1812" and was most likely from Harford County. After the action off Valparaiso, Chile on 28 Mar 1814 "Ruff" asked what had become of his master and when he received the news of Wilmer's death he deliberately jumped into the sea and drowned. ("Harford County in the War of 1812," by Christopher T. George, *Harford Historical Bulletin* No. 76, Spring 1998, pp. 8-9; *Niles Weekly Register*, 16 Jul 1814, reported a list of the men who served on the *Essex* and were lost during that action in Chile in 1814, including "Henry Ruff, boy," but misspelled his name as Henry Buff)

Rumsey, Joseph, served as a Private in Capt. Isaac Barnard's Co., 14th U.S. Inf., enlisted 5 Mar 1813 and was later captured. Prisoner of War #3819 at Halifax, NS, interned 6 Jun 1813, discharged 19 Nov 1813, sent to England and later released; wife Jeanette Rumsey also received a pension (SO-30121, SC-21658, WO-24790, WC-26410; Johnson and Christou, pp. 323-324; Baker Vol. 2, p. 350)

Rush, Samuel, served as a Seaman and was born in Baltimore. Age: 24. Prison Depot: Dartmoor, Prisoner of War #5777. Captured by HM Sloop *Acorn*. When Taken: 27 Oct 1812. Where Taken: Lat 14. Prize Name: *William Penn*. Ship Type: Merchant Vessel. Date Received: 26 Dec 1814. From what ship: HMT *Argo*. Discharged on 27 Apr 1815. (Johnson's Database, 2019)

Russell, Thomas, served as a Lieutenant in Capt. Charles Pennington's Artillery Co. and was slightly wounded on 13 Sep 1814 at Fort McHenry with "a severe contusion in the heel notwithstanding which he remained at his post during the whole of the bombardment." (Marine p. 169 listed him as Lieutenant Russel, p. 173 listed him as 3rd Lieutenant and p.425 listed him as 1st Lieutenant); also served as 2nd Lieutenant in Matthew McLaughlin's Artillery Co., Baltimore City, between 27 Apr and 4 Jul 1813 and 1st Lieutenant in Capt. Charles Pennington's Artillery Co., 1st Artillery Regt., from 19 Aug to 30 Nov 1814, but no mention was made of his wound (Wright Vol. 2, pp. 42, 47)

Rust, Charles, served as a Private in Capt. John Montgomery's Artillery Co., Baltimore City, joined 28 Aug 1814 and was wounded on 12 Sep 1814 at North Point (Wright Vol. 2, p. 46; Marine p. 170 did not give his name)

Rust, John, served as a Seaman and was born in Baltimore. Age: 29. Prison Depot: Portsmouth, Prisoner of War #154. Captured by HM Frigate *Orpheus*. When Taken: 3 Sep 1812. Where Taken: at sea. Prize Name: *Lydia*. Ship Type: Merchant Vessel. Date Received: 29 Oct 1812. From what ship: HM Ship-of-the-Line *Ardent*. Discharged on 19 Feb 1813 and sent to Chatham on HM Store Ship *Dromedary*. Prison Depot: Chatham, Prisoner of War #523. Captured by HM Frigate *Orpheus*. When Taken: 3 Sep 1812. Where Taken: at sea. Prize Name: *Lydia*. Ship Type: Merchant Vessel. Received: 23 Feb 1813 from Portsmouth on HMS *Dromedary*. Discharged on 10 May 1813 and was released to the Cartel *Admittance*. (Johnson's Database, 2019)

Rutherford, James (1786-1812), served as a Private in Capt. Samuel Lane's Co., 14th U.S. Infantry, enlisted 8 Jun 1812 for 5 years in Shepherdstown, VA at the age of 26, 5' 8" tall, born in Virginia and died at Black Rock, NY on 8 Dec 1812 (BLW# 27895-160-42; Johnson and Christou, p. 325)

Rutter, Thomas, served as a Sailing Master and was born in Baltimore. Age: 27. Prison Depot: Dartmoor, Prisoner of War #6131. Captured by British gunboats. When Taken: 6 Sep 1814. Where Taken: Lake Huron. Prize Name: U.S. Schooner *Scorpion*. Ship Type: Warship. Date Received: 17 Jan 1815. From what ship: HMT *Impregnable*. Discharged and sent on 22 Jan 1815 to Ashburton on parole. (Johnson's Database, 2019)

Ryan, John, served as a Private in Capt. Conrad Hook's Co., 2nd Regiment, 11th Brigade, Baltimore County, was stationed at Camp Hampstead in Baltimore from

25 Jul 1814 and reported "sick in hospital Sep 3, absent sick Oct 20" 1814 on the muster roll dated 25 Jul – 1 Dec 1814 (Wright Vol. 2, p. 81)

Ryan, John, served as a Private in the 19th U.S. Infantry, enlisted 24 Mar 1813 in Ohio at age of 30, 5' 10" tall, born in Maryland, transferred to Capt. Benjamin Watson's Co., 25th U.S. Infantry and was discharged on 20 Mar 1815 at Sackett's Harbor, NY because of scrotal hernia (Johnson and Christou, p. 325)

Ryan, Thomas, served as a Corporal in Capt. Jasper M. Jackson's Co., 34th Regt., Prince George's Co. Militia, from 21 Aug 1814 and was furloughed on 29 Aug 1814 for indisposition (Wright Vol. 6, p. 22)

Rye, Thomas, served as a Private in the 24th U.S. Infantry, later served in 7th U.S Infantry, enlisted 12 Jun 1813, age 30, 5' 8½" tall, born in Maryland and was captured, date and place not stated. Prisoner of War at Montreal, Canada until exchanged on 28 Apr 1814 and was discharged from service on 1 Dec 1815 on a Surgeon's Certificate, medical cause not stated (Johnson and Christou, p. 325)

Ryland, William (1793-1815), served as a Private in Capt. Samuel Raisin's Co., 36th U.S. Infantry, enlisted 5 Oct 1813 for 1 year at the age of 20, 5' 3" tall, born in Kent Co., MD and died in hospital on 29 Jan 1815, place not stated; bounty land issued to his brother Henry Ryland and other heirs at law (BLW# 26563-160-12; Johnson and Christou, p. 325)

Rynehart, Daniel, see Daniel Rinehart, q.v.

S

Sager, John, served as a Private in Capt. George Shryock's Co., Hagerstown, Washington Co. Militia, from 28 Sep 1814 and was discharged by a Surgeon in Dec 1814, but the medical reason was not stated (Wright Vol. 9, p. 8)

Sandbach, Richard, served as a Seaman and was born in Maryland. Age: 26. Prison Depot: Portsmouth, Prisoner of War #497. Captured by HM Ship-of-the-Line *Elephant*. When Taken: 28 Dec 1812. Where Taken: off Azores. Prize Name: *Sword Fish*. Home Port: Gloucester. Ship Type: Privateer. Date Received: 14 Jan 1813. From what ship: HMS *Elephant*. Discharged on 11 Mar 1813 and sent to Chatham on HM Store Ship *Abundance*. (Johnson's Database, 2019)

Sanders, William G. (1791-1845), served as a 2nd Lieutenant in the 14th U.S. Inf., at the age of 21, commissioned an Ensign on 12 Mar 1812, promoted to 3rd Lieutenant on 13 Mar 1813, promoted to 2nd Lieutenant on 13 May 1813. Prisoner of War (Dartmouth), released on 31 May 1814, resigned on 5 Aug 1814 and died on 1 Sep 1845 (Widow Caroline E. Sanders' Pension WO-42217 and BLW# 22922-160-50; Johnson and Christou, p. 327)

Sanderson, Francis, served as a Private in Capt. Andrew Smith's Co., 51st Regt., Baltimore City Militia, from 23 Aug to 30 Aug 1813 and from 22 Aug 1814 until his death on 16 Sep 1814 (Wright Vol. 2, pp. 31, 38)

Sanderson, William, of Maryland, served as a Seaman on the ship *Christian* and was reported by Capt. Jeduthan Upton, Jr. in 1814 as having been impressed into service and was being held as a Prisoner of War on the prison ship *San Antonio* at Chatham, England (*Niles Weekly Register,* 26 Feb 1814)

Sansbury, Edward, served as a Private in Capt. Gavin Hamilton's Co., 17th Regt., Prince George's Co. Militia, having entered service as substitute for his brother Middleton Sansbury who was drafted about 1 Jun 1813; he served until 1 Sep 1813 when he was taken sick and remained sick until camp was dispersed; he volunteered again on 1 Aug 1814 at Long Old Fields, served in the Battle of Bladensburg and was discharged in Oct or Nov 1814 "at Tee bee" in Prince George's Co.; he was also stationed at Accokeek Church and Tanyard Spring. In 1855 Edward Sandsbury, age 64, was living in Anne Arundel County. (Wright Vol. 6, pp. 5, 12, 47; BLW# 55-120-4366)

Sansbury, John, served as a Private in Capt. William Jett's Co., 20th U.S. Inf., enlisted 20 Apr 1812, age 40, 5' 6½" tall, born in Prince George's Co. and was discharged at Plattsburgh, NY on Surgeon's Certificte, date and medical cause not stated (Johnson and Christou, p. 327)

Sapp, Daniel, served as a Private in Capt. Isaac Raven's Co., Baltimore Co., 2nd Regt., 11th Brigade, stationed in Baltimore from 27 Jul 1814 and was reported "wounded in the service," but no date was given (Wright Vol. 2, p. 84)

Sargant, Thomas, served as a Private in the 5th U.S. Infantry, enlisted 6 May 1813 in Baltimore, age 43, 5' 8" tall, born in Baltimore and discharged on 1 Jun 1814 for disability (Johnson and Christou, p. 327)

Satterfield, Elijah, served as Captain of his own company in the 19th Regiment, Caroline Co., from 15 Aug to 19 Aug 1813 at St. Michaels and he, along with a few of his men, were discharged on account of disability (causes not stated) on 19 Aug 1813 and his company was divided between Capt. Peter Willis and Capt. James Rich (Wright Vol. 1, pp. 80, 106)

Saul, Emanuel, was a Seaman who was wounded on 24 Aug 1814 on the field of battle at Bladensburg, was admitted to the Naval Hospital in Washington, DC as Patient No. 12, was discharged on 28 Sep 1814 and sent to the Navy Yard (Sharp's Database, 2018)

Saunderson, William, served as a Seaman and was born in Baltimore. Age: 25. Prison Depot: Portsmouth, Prisoner of War #645. How Taken: Gave himself up off HM Guard Ship *Royal William*. Date Received: 3 Feb 1813. From what ship:

HMS *Royal William*. Discharged on 11 Mar 1813 and sent to Chatham on HM Store Ship *Abundance*. Prison Depot: Chatham, Prisoner of War #1311. Date Received: 16 Mar 1813 from Portsmouth on HMS *Abundance*. Discharged on 4 Aug 1814 and sent to Dartmoor on HMS *Alpheus*. Prison Depot: Dartmoor, Prisoner of War #2748 [name spelled Sanderson]. Date Received: 24 Aug 1814. From what ship: HMT *Liverpool* from Chatham. Discharged on 19 May 1815. (Johnson's Database, 2019)

Schaeman, Frederick, served as a Seaman and was born in Baltimore. Age: 19. Prison Depot: Plymouth 1, Prisoner of War #490. Captured by HM Brig *Reindeer*. When Taken: 3 Feb 1813. Where Taken: Bay of Biscayne. Prize Name: *Cashiere*. Home Port: Baltimore. Ship Type: Letter of Marque. Date Received: 12 Feb 1813. From what ship: HMS *Reindeer*. Discharged and sent to Dartmoor on 2 Apr 1813. Prison Depot: Dartmoor, Prisoner of War #7. Date Received: 2 Apr 1813 from Plymouth. Discharged and sent to Dartmouth on 10 Jul 1813. He was also listed at Prison Depot: Plymouth 1, Prisoner of War #1742. Date Received: 10 Jul 1813 from Dartmoor Prison. Discharged on 10 Jul 1813 and released to HMS *Salvador del Mundo*. (Johnson's Database, 2019)

Scheiltz, John, served as a Private in the 14th U.S. Infantry and was captured, probably at Beaver Dams, Upper Canada. Prisoner of War #4151 at Halifax, NS, interned on 24 Jun 1813 and discharged for exchange on 3 Feb 1814 (Johnson and Christou, p. 328; Baker Vol. 2, p. 356)

Schriver, Jacob, served as a Private in Capt. John H. Rodgers' Co., 51st Regt., Baltimore Militia, from 23 Aug 1814 and was discharged by the doctor on 26 Aug 1814, but no reason was given (Wright Vol. 2, p. 31)

Schultz, John, served as a Private in Capt. Dominic Bader's Co., 1st Rifle Bttn., Baltimore Militia, joined on 1 Sep 1814 and was discharged on 13 Sep 1814 by a Surgeon as unfit for duty (Wright Vol. 2, p. 54)

Schunck, John, served as a Private in Capt. Michael Peters' Co., 51st Regt., Baltimore Militia, from 19 Aug 1814 and was reported "sick absent since 8 Oct" 1814 (Wright Vol. 2, p. 36)

Schwickardt, George, served as a Steward of the U.S. Chesapeake Flotilla, entered service on 10 Sep 1813, was on board on 7 Apr 1814, reported sick (date not stated) and died 23 Apr 1814 (Shomette, p. 379)

Scott, Evan R. (c1790-1814), served as a Private in Capt. R. Holmes' Co., joined service at Nottingham around Jul or Aug 1814 and died at Montgomery Co. on 18 Aug 1814 (unknown cause, but probably service connected). His widow Elizabeth (Lewis) Scott, age 74, applied for bounty land in 1856 but was rejected.

They were married in Ann Arundel Co. on 26 Oct 1806 by Rev. John Welch. (Wright Vol. 7, p. 42; BLW# 55-rej-233082)

Scott, Henry (1785-1814), served as a Seaman and was born in Maryland. Age: 28. Prison Depot: Chatham, Prisoner of War #3015. Captured by HM Frigate *Barrosa*. When Taken: 1 Jul 1813. Where Taken: off Cape Virginia. Prize Name: *Go' On*. Ship Type: Merchant Vessel. Died on 3 Apr 1814 from fever. (Johnson's Database, 2019)

Scott, James, served as a Private in Capt. Kenneth McKenzie's Co., 14th U.S. Infantry, enlisted on 6 Jan 1813 in Baltimore at the age of 43, 5' 7" tall, born in Connecticut; a leg was shot off by a cannon ball in the attack on Fort Erie, Canada and he was captured. Prisoner of War #4166 at Halifax, interned 24 Jun 1813, discharged 27 Aug 1813 and sent to England on HMS *Regulus* (Johnson and Christou, p. 329; Baker Vol. 2, p. 357)

Scott, John, served as a Private in Capt. Robert Kent's Co., 14th U.S. Infantry, enlisted 24 Jul 1812 for 5 years in Baltimore at the age of 32, 5' 10½" tall, born in Baltimore and was captured at Beaver Dams, Upper Canada on 24 Jun 1813. Prisoner of War #3775 at Halifax, NS, interned 24 Jun 1813, discharged on 9 Nov 1813 and sent to England Prison Depot: Chatham, Prisoner of War #3115. Date Received: 7 Jan 1814 from Halifax, NS. Age 34. Discharged on 10 Oct 1814 and sent to U.S. on the Cartel *St. Philip*. Transferred to Ordnance Department as an artificer and was discharged at Richmond, VA on 24 Jul 1817 (Johnson and Christou, p. 329; Baker Vol. 2, p. 357; Johnson's Database, 2019)

Scott, William, served as a Private in Capt. Thomas Kearney's Co., 14th U.S. Infantry, enlisted 25 Jul 1812 and was discharged on 11 Jun 1814 for wounds received in service (Johnson and Christou, p. 329; Pension Old War IF-3861)

Scribble, Henry, served as a Seaman and was born in Baltimore. Age: 25. Prison Depot: Dartmoor, Prisoner of War #2431. Captured by HM Frigate *Orpheus*. When Taken: 20 Apr 1814. Where Taken: off Matanzas, Cuba. Prize Name: U.S. Sloop-of-War *Frolic*. Ship Type: Warship. Date Received: 16 Aug 1814. From what ship: HMT *Queen* from Halifax, NS. Discharged on 3 May 1815. (Johnson's Database, 2019)

Scriven, Richard, served as a Private in the 14th U.S. Infantry and was captured at Beaver Dams, Upper Canada on 24 Jun 1813, Prisoner of War #3806 at Halifax, NS, interned 27 Aug 1813, discharged 9 Nov 1813 and sent to England on HMS *Success* (Johnson and Christou, p. 330; Baker Vol. 2, p. 358; Johnson's Database, 2019, did not list him)

Sears, Abraham, served as a Private in the 14th U.S. Infantry and was captured at Beaver Dams, Upper Canada, on 24 Jun 1813. Prisoner of War #4666 at Halifax,

NS, interned 15 Nov 1813 and was discharged 19 Nov 1813 and sent to England (Johnson and Christou, p. 330; Baker Vol. 2, p. 359)

Sears, James, served as a Private in the 42nd Regiment, Harford Co. Militia, was captured when the British attacked and burned Havre de Grace on 3 May 1813, was taken onboard the ship *Maidstone* and released two days later through the valiant effort of a town delegation led by Miss Matilda O'Neill, daughter of Lt. John O'Neill who was also captured. "The elder, Mr. Levy, was taken about this time, as was also Capt. Barnes, and one or two men. John O'Neill, Christopher Levy, James Sears, eldest son of Mrs. Sears, Capt. Whitefoot [Whiteford] and Ensign Hare were also made prisoners, as was one Whitloe, an aged citizen. Most of the Prisoners they released while on shore, but John O'Neill, Christopher Levy and James Sears they carried on board the fleet." (*Narrative Respecting the Conduct of the British From Their First Landing on Spesutia Island Till Their Progress to Havre de Grace*, by James Jones Wilmer, 1814, p. 13; *Concord Point Lighthouse Station at Havre de Grace*, by Jack L. Shagena, Jr. and Henry C. Peden, Jr., 2017, p. 35; "Harford County in the War of 1812," by Christopher T. George, *Harford Historical Bulletin* No. 76, Spring 1998, p. 33)

Sears, John, served as a Private in Capt. Samuel Lane's Co., 14th U.S. Infantry, enlisted 19 May 1812 in Westminster, MD, age 38, 5' 7" tall, born in Frederick, MD and was captured, probably ay Beaver Dams, Upper Canada in 24 Jun 1813. Prisoner of War #4076 at Halifax, NS, interned 24 Jun 1813 and discharged for exchange on 3 Feb 1814, returned to service and was discharged at Greenbush, NY on 23 Jun 1814 (Johnson and Christou, o. 330; Baker Vol. 2, p. 359)

Selby, Hezekiah, served as a Private in the 14th U.S. Infantry (company and captain not named), enlisted 15 Apr 1812, age 31, 6' tall, born in Maryland and was discharged at Washington, DC on 15 Apr 1814 on a Surgeon's Certificate (Johnson and Christou, p. 331)

Selby, James, served as a Captain and was born in Maryland. Age: 39. Prison Depot: Chatham, Prisoner of War #759. Captured by HM Ship-of-the-Line *San Juan*. When Taken: 8 May 1812. Where Taken: Gibraltar Bay. Prize Name: *Margaret*. Ship Type: Merchant Vessel. Date Received: 25 Feb 1813. From what ship: HMS *Brazen*. Discharged on 23 Mar 1813 and was released to the Cartel *Robinson Potter*. (Johnson's Database, 2019)

Seth, John, served as a Seaman and was born in Maryland. Age: 25. Prison Depot: Chatham, Prisoner of War #2755. Captured by HM Frigate *Spartan*. When Taken: 13 Jun 1813. Where Taken: off Delaware. Prize Name: *Globe*. Ship Type: Privateer. Received: 7 Jan 1814 from Halifax, NS. Discharged on 25 Sep 1814 and sent to Dartmoor on HMS *Leyden*. (Johnson's Database, 2019)

Seth, William E., was a doctor who served as Surgeon for the 26th Regiment, Talbot Co. Militia, under Lt. Col. Hugh Auld, and was appointed 6 Nov 1797 and listed as dead, but the date and cause of death were not stated; he obviously died during the war since his replacement was appointed on 13 Sep 1814. (Wright Vol. 1, p. iv)

Sevier, Alexander, was commissioned a 2nd Lieutenant on 22 Apr 1810, a 1st Lieutenant on 17 Apr 1812 and a Captain on 18 Jun 1814. "Capt. Sevier of the Marine Corps who was wounded (although not dangerously so) in the neck by a musket ball, is now in this city." (*National Intelligencer*, Washington, DC, 2 Sep 1814) He was treated as an outpatient at the Naval Hospital in Washington, DC, was Brevet Major in 1814 and Major Sevier resigned on 3 Apr 1816. (Sharp's Database, 2018)

Sevier, William, served as a Seaman and was born in Maryland. Age: 20. Prison Depot: Dartmoor, Prisoner of War #6076. Captured by HM Frigate *Niemen*. When Taken: 18 Sep 1814. Where Taken: off Delaware. Prize Name: *Daedalus*. Home Port: Baltimore. Ship Type: Letter of Marque (Privateer). Date Received: 28 Dec 1814. From what ship: HMT *Penelope*. Discharged on 3 Jul 1815. (Johnson's Database, 2019)

Sewell, John, served as a Seaman and was born in Baltimore. Age: 26. Prison Depot: Dartmoor, Prisoner of War #6545. How Taken: Gave himself up off HM Frigate *Orlando*. When Taken: 7 May 1813. Received: 7 Mar 1815 from HMT *Ganges* from Plymouth. Discharged on 11 Jul 1815. (Johnson's Database, 2019)

Sewell, Lot, served as a Seaman and was born in Baltimore. Age: 26. Prison Depot: Dartmoor, Prisoner of War #3491. How Taken: Gave himself up off HM Brig *Prospero*. When Taken: 12 Sep 1814. Received: 19 Sep 1814 from HMT *Salvador del Mundo*. Discharged on 4 Jun 1815. (Johnson's Database, 2019)

Seyle, Frederick, served as a Private in Capt. Samuel Sterett's Co., 5th Regiment, Baltimore Militia, from 19 Aug 1814, was taken prisoner on 12 Sep at North Point and exchanged on 6 Nov 1814 (Wright Vol. 2, p. 6)

Shaffer, Valentine (1769-1817), served as a Private in Capt. Richard Arell's Co., 14th U.S. Infantry, enlisted 12 Dec 1812 in Lancaster, PA for 5 years at the age of 43, 5' 7" tall, born in Germany and was captured, but date and place were not mentioned. Prisoner of War, exchanged on 15 Apr 1814 and died in hospital on 15 Sep 1817, place and cause of death not given (Johnson and Christou, p. 332)

Shamtan, Samuel, served as a Seaman and was born in Baltimore. Age: 35. Prison Depot: Plymouth 1, Prisoner of War #585. Captured by HM Brig *Reindeer*. When Taken: 3 Feb 1813. Where Taken: Bay of Biscayne. Prize Name: *Cashiere*. Home Port: Baltimore. Ship Type: Letter of Marque. Date Received: 23 Feb 1813.

From what ship: HMS *Surveillante*. Discharged and was sent to Dartmoor on 2 Apr 1813. Prison Depot: Dartmoor, Prisoner of War #92. Date Received: 2 Apr 1813 from Plymouth. Discharged and was sent to Dartmouth on 2 Aug 1813. (Johnson's Database, 2019)

Shane, Daniel (c1794-1824), served as a Private in Capt. John Skrim's Co., 5th Regiment, Baltimore Militia, from 19 Aug to 18 Nov 1814 and was wounded during the Battle of North Point on 12 Sep 1814 (Wright Vol. 2, p. 9, did not mention being wounded) In Baltimore on 14 Mar 1823 Daniel Shane, former private in Capt. Shrim's (sic) Co. of Volunteers, 5th Regt., Maryland Militia, in the late war when disabled, and a lifelong resident of this city, collected his own $48.00 pension due from 4 Sep 1822 to 4 Mar 1823. (Pierce, p. 163). He died on 13 Jul 1824 and was buried in Baltimore's Green Mount Cemetery.

Shanks, William, served as a Mate and was born in Maryland. Age: 36. Prison Depot: Dartmoor, Prisoner of War #3893. Captured by HM Ship-of-the-Line *Saturn* & HM Frigate *Narcissus*. When Taken: 13 Jul 1814. Where Taken: off Long Island, NY. Prize Name: *Governor Shelby*. Home Port: Baltimore. Ship Type: Merchant Vessel. Received: 5 Oct 1814. From what ship: HMT *Orpheus* from Halifax, NS. Discharged on 9 Jun 1815. (Johnson's Database, 2019)

Sharp, Francis H. (1780-1815), served as a Private in Capt. Samuel Raisin's Co., 36th U.S. Infantry, enlisted 18 Jun 1814 at the age of 34, 5' 11" tall, born in Norfolk, VA and died in hospital on 31 Jan 1815; bounty land issued to brother William Sharp and others (BLW# 25185-160-12; Johnson and Christou, p. 333)

Sharpless, Robert, served as a Seaman and was born in Maryland. Age: 28. Prison Depot: Dartmoor, Prisoner of War #5039. Captured by HM Sloop *Pylades*. When Taken: 7 Sep 1814. Where Taken: Canton. Prize Name: *Betsy*, prize of the Privateer *Ayder Alley*. Ship Type: Letter of Marque. Date Received: 28 Oct 1814. From what ship: HMT *Alkbar* from Halifax, NS. Discharged on 11 Jul 1815. (Johnson's Database, 2019)

Shaver, George (c1783-1813) served as a Private in the 14th U.S. Infantry, at the age of 30, born Palatine Co., NY. Prisoner of War #137 at Quebec, interned on 8 Jul 1813 and died there on 25 Jul or 26 Jul 1813 of dysentery (Johnson and Christou, p. 333, states 25 Jul 1813; Johnson, pp. 138-139, states 26 Jul 1813)

Shaw, Edward, served as a 1st Mate and was born in Baltimore. Age: 29. Prison Depot: Dartmoor, Prisoner of War #2728. Captured by HM Frigate *Hotspur* & HM Frigate *Pyramus*. When Taken: 26 Oct 1813. Where Taken: off Nantes, France. Prize Name: *Chesapeake*. Ship Type: Letter of Marque. Date Received: 24 Aug 1814. From what ship: HMT *Liverpool* from Chatham. Discharged on 11 May 1815. (Johnson's Database, 2019)

Shaw, Richard, served as a Seaman and was born in Maryland. Age: 26. Prison Depot: Plymouth 1, Prisoner of War #1527. Captured by HM Frigate *Andromache*. When Taken: 14 Mar 1813. Where Taken: off Nantes, France. Prize Name: *Courier*. Home Port: Baltimore. Ship Type: Letter of Marque. Date Received: 29 May 1813. From what ship: HMS *Hannibal*. Discharged on 30 Jun 1813 and sent to Stapleton. Prison Depot: Stapleton, Prisoner of War #89. Date Received: 8 Jul 1813 from Plymouth. Discharged on 13 Jun 1814 and sent to Dartmoor. Prison Depot: Dartmoor, Prisoner of War #1382. Received: 19 Jun 1814 from Stapleton. Discharged on 28 Apr 1815. (Johnson's Database, 2019)

Shaw, Richard, served as a Private in Capt. Thomas F. W. Vinson's Co., 32nd Regt., Montgomery Co., Extra Battalion, from 1 Aug 1814 and was reported missing in action on 24 Aug 1814 at Bladensburg (Wright Vol. 7, p. 5)

Shaw, Thomas, served as a Private in Capt. James Dorman's Co., 5th U.S. Inf., enlisted 23 Jun 1812 at Baltimore, age 24, 6' 2½" tall, born in Baltimore and discharged on 25 Jun 1815 on Surgeon's Certificate for paralysis of the bladder (Johnson and Christou, p. 333)

Sheavers (Shivers), Thomas, served as a Private in Capt. Isaac Barnard's Co., 14th U.S. Infantry, enlisted 23 Oct 1812 and was captured, probably at Beaver Dams, Upper Canada. Prisoner of War #4053 at Halifax, NS, interned on 24 Jun 1813 and discharged for exchange on 3 Feb 1814 (Johnson and Christou, p. 334 spelled his name Sheaves, p. 335 spelled it Shivers, and Baker Vol. 2, p. 362 spelled it Sheaver, but neither source stated where he was captured)

Shepherd, Henry, served as a Seaman and was born in Maryland. Age: 28. Prison Depot: Chatham, Prisoner of War #3852. Captured by HM Brig *Harpy*. When Taken: 16 Dec 1812. Where Taken: off Isle de France, Mauritius. Prize Name: *James*. Ship Type: Merchant Vessel. Date Received: 22 Aug 1814 from Gravesend. Discharged on 22 Oct 1814 and sent to Dartmoor on HMS *Leyden*. Prison Depot: Dartmoor, Prisoner of War #5374. Date Received: 31 Oct 1814. From what ship: HMT *Leyden* from Chatham. Discharged on 27 Apr 1815. (Johnson's Database, 2019)

Sheppard, Yankee, served as a Cabin Boy on the privateer (armed brigantine) *Chasseur* of Baltimore commanded by Capt. Thomas Boyle and was severely wounded in action on 26 Feb 1815 (*Niles Weekly Register*, 25 Mar 1815)

Shepperd, Absolom, served as a Private in Capt. Edward Orrick's Co., 41st Regt., Baltimore Co. Militia, from 25 Aug 1814 and was discharged by the doctor on 30 Aug 1814 (Wright Vol. 2, p. 70)

Shepperd, James (1785-1815), served as a Private in Capt. Joseph Marshall's Co., 14th U.S. Infantry, enlisted 18 Jul 1814 in Baltimore at the age of 29, 5' 4" tall, born in Anne Arundel Co., MD and died at Greenbush, NY on 22 Jan 1815 from diarrhea (Johnson and Christou, p. 334)

Sherington, Ezekiel, served as a Private in the 14th U.S. Infantry and was later captured, probably at Beaver Dams, Upper Canada. Prisoner of War #3987 at Halifax, NS, interned 24 Jun 1813 and was discharged on 19 Nov 1813 and sent to England (Johnson and Christou, p. 335; Baker Vol. 2, p. 362)

Shields, Thomas, served as a Private in Capt. Amos Hale's Co., 4th Regiment, Mechanics Company of Easton, Talbot Co., from 14 Apr to 2 Jun 1813 and died some time before 19 Apr 1814 at which time militia pay was due to members of Capt. Hale's Co. and "Th. Shields" was reported dead. (Wright Vol. 1, p. 87; *Republican Star*, Talbot Co., MD, 19 Apr 1814)

Shlife (Schlife, Slife), John, served as a Private in Capt. George Washington Magee's Co., Frederick County Militia in the 1st Regiment, New Windsor area, from 22 Jul 1814, engaged in the Battle of Bladensburg and in the defense of Baltimore, was reported "sick absent 18 Sep" 1814 and "deserted" on 20 Nov 1814, yet his widow Mary Shlife (whom he married in 1810 in Frederick County) was issued bounty land in 1855 in Fairfield Co., OH. John died there on 21 Jan 1845 or 22 Jan 1844. (BLW# 55-160-36476; Mallick and Wright, pp. 267, 342)

Shinnick, Jacob, served as Quartermaster and Orderly Sergeant in Capt. John Hanna's Co., 5th Cavalry Regiment, Baltimore City, from 19 Aug 1814 and was wounded on 12 Sep 1814 at North Point. The family records of descendant Lawrence Webster Shinnick III indicates full name is Johan Jacob Shinnick and he lost a limb at the Battle of North Point. He was born on 22 Jan 1777, was married 1st to Elizabeth Knorr in 1799, moved to Baltimore, married 2nd to Harriett Divers in 1808, married 3rd to Barbara (Lammatt) Bowser, and died in Manchester, Carroll Co, MD, on 23 Jul 1842. "The gunfire in the east drew closer; the number of British ships hovering off Fort McHenry grew to 16, plus numerous gigs, cutters and barges. Convinced that the final assault was about to begin, General Foreman ordered the great ropewalk of Messrs. Calief and Shinnick set afire to keep it from falling into enemy hands. Shortly after 4:00 flames and smoke rolled skyward, consuming the hemp and cordage for the new frigate *Java* and throwing the city into even greater consternation." (Wright Vol. 2, p. 55; Walter Lord's "The Dawn's Early Light", p. 273; Society of War of 1812 Application of Lawrence Webster Shinnick III, Approved in 2019)

Shipley, Ezekiel served as a Private in 1st Lt. John Weer's Co., 36th Regiment, Baltimore Co., from 26 Aug 1814 and died on 9 Oct 1814 (Wright Vol. 2, p. 60)

Shipley, Lloyd, served as a Private in 1st Lt. John Thomas 3rd's Co., 32nd Regt., Anne Arundel Co. Militia, joined 6 Sep 1814 and reported "sick in town at his mothers" on the muster roll dated 24 Aug – 27 Sep 1814 (Wright Vol. 4, p. 43)

Shivers, Thomas, see Thomas Sheavers, q.v.

Shockley, David (1787-1815), served as a Private in Capt. Samuel Raisin's Co., 36th U.S. Infantry, enlisted 11 Jul 1814 at age 27, 5' 6" tall, born in Dunenbury, VA and died in barracks on 24 Feb 1815 (Johnson and Christou, p. 336)

Shockley, James, served as a Private in Capt. Clement Sullivan's Co., 14th U.S. Infantry, enlisted 20 Nov and died 26 Nov 1812; bounty land issued to his sister Sarah Coale and others (BLW# 25389-160-12; Johnson and Christou, p. 336)

Shockley, Perkins, served as a Private in Capt. Clement Sullivan's Co., 14th U.S. Infantry, enlisted 25 May and died 25 Dec 1812; bounty land issued to his sister Sarah Coale and others (BLW# 25388-160-12; Johnson and Christou, p. 336)

Shrotes, John, served as a Private in Capt. Samuel Dawson's Co., Frederick County Militia, from 26 Jul 1814, engaged in the Battle of Bladensburg and the defense of Baltimore City and was reported as sick in Baltimore, but date was not given (Mallick and Wright, p. 338)

Sickless, Michael, served as a Private in the 14th U.S. Infantry and was captured at Beaver Dams, Upper Canada on 24 Jun 1813. Prisoner of War #3814 at Halifax, NS, interned 27 Aug 1813, was discharged for exchange on 3 Feb 1814, returned to service and deserted on 19 Jun 1814 (Johnson and Christou, p. 337; Baker Vol. 2, p. 365)

Sidebottom, John, served as a Seaman and was born in Baltimore. Age: 28. Prison Depot: Dartmoor, Prisoner of War #1916. How Taken: Gave himself up off HM Guard Ship *Royal William*. When Taken: 3 Feb 1813. Date Received: 3 Aug 1814. From what ship: HMS *Alceste* from Chatham Depot. Discharged on 2 May 1815. (Johnson's Database, 2019)

Silence, Nicholas, served as a Private in Capt. Isaac Barnard's Co., 14th U.S. Infantry, enlisted 5 Jan 1813 for 5 years and was captured, probably at Beaver Dams, Upper Canada on 24 Jun 1813. Prisoner of War #3916 at Halifax, NS, interned 27 Aug 1813 and was discharged for exchange on 3 Feb 1814 (Johnson and Christou, p. 337, listed two other men with this name; Baker Vol. 2, p. 365)

Silkes, Peter, served as a Seaman and was born in Baltimore. Age: 39. Prison Depot: Dartmoor, Prisoner of War #6168. Captured by HM Frigate *Grancius*. When Taken: 2 Dec 1814. Where Taken: off Lisbon, Portugal. Prize Name: *Leo*. Home Port: Baltimore. Ship Type: Privateer. Received: 18 Jan 1815. From what ship: HMT *Impregnable*. Discharged on 5 Jul 1815. (Johnson's Database, 2019)

Simmons, Simon, served as a Seaman on the privateer *Surprise* of Baltimore and drowned in a shipwreck on 5 Apr 1815 (Marine p. 437; *Niles Weekly Register*, 15 Apr 1815)

Simms, Francis, served as a Private in Capt. James Forrest's Co., 4th Regimental Cavalry District, for 17 days between 10 Feb and 24 Jun 1814. On 2 Sep 1852, age 75, he applied for bounty land and stated he had volunteered at Chaptico, served as Quartermaster in Capt. Forrest's Co. and was discharged at Cedar Point in Charles Co. on account of sickness; his application was rejected. (Wright Vol. 5, pp. 47, 87; BLW# 50-rej-153590)

Simpson, Benjamin, served as a Private in Capt. John Fonsten's Co., Frederick Co. Militia, from 2 Sep 1814, marched to Baltimore, engaged in the defense of the city, and was reported "sick absent" on 14 Oct 1814. Benjamin was born in 1774 and was residing in Washington Co., MD in 1855. (Wright Vol. 8, p. 364; Mallick and Wright, p. 265; BLW# 55-120-15419)

Simpson, John, served as a Private in Capt. Hugh Deneale's Co., 36th Regt., U.S. Inf., enlisted 26 Mar 1814 in Annapolis for the duration of the war at the age of 21, 5' 9" tall, born in Prince George's Co., and was discharged at Washington, DC on 27 Nov 1815 (Johnson and Christou, p. 339, did not mention being wounded). In Baltimore City on 16 Mar 1831 John Simpson, former private in Capt. H. Deneale's Co. of Infantry, 36th U.S. Infantry, in the late war when disabled, and a resident of Prince George's Co. nearly all his life, collected his own $48.00 pension due from 4 Mar 1830 to 4 Mar 1831. (Pierce, p. 166)

Simpson, Mark, served as Sergeant Major in the 14th U.S. Infantry, enlisted 27 Jun 1812 for 18 months and was captured at Beaver Dams, Upper Canada on 24 Jun 1813. Prisoner of War #3807 at Halifax, NS, interned 15 Nov 1813, was discharged on 19 Nov 1813 and sent to England, was later released, returned to service and discharged on 31 Mar 1815 (Johnson and Christou, p. 339, listed him as Sergeant Major; Baker Vol. 2, p. 367, listed him as Sergeant)

Simpson, Thomas, served as a Seaman and was born in Maryland. Age: 36. Prison Depot: Stapleton, Prisoner of War #291. Captured by HM Frigate *Iris*. When Taken: 10 Mar 1813. Where Taken: off Cape Ortegal, Spain. Prize Name: *Messenger*. Ship Type: Merchant Vessel. Date Received: 11 Jul 1813 from Plymouth. Discharged on 16 Jun 1814 and sent to Dartmoor. Prison Depot: Dartmoor, Prisoner of War #1572. Age 37. Date Received: 23 Jun 1814 from Stapleton. Discharged on 1 May 1815. (Johnson's Database, 2019)

Sims, Clement (African American), served as a Seaman and was born in Baltimore. Age: 30. Prison Depot: Portsmouth, Prisoner of War #778. How Taken: Gave himself up off HM Frigate *Mermaid*. Date Received: 1 Apr 1813. From what ship: HM Ship-of-the-Line *Blake*. Discharged on 3 Apr 1813 and sent to Chatham on HM Transport *Chatham*. Prison Depot: Chatham, Prisoner of War #1525. Date Received: 8 Apr 1813 from Portsmouth on an admiral's tender. Discharged on 4 Aug 1814 and sent to Dartmoor on HMS *Alpheus*. Prison Depot: Dartmoor,

Prisoner of War #2765. Date Received: 24 Aug 1814. From what ship: HMT *Liverpool* from Chatham. Discharged on 19 May 1815. (Johnson's Database, 2019)

Sinner, James (1791-1815), served as a Private in Capt. William Bezeau's Co., 26th U.S. Infantry, enlisted 28 Oct 1814 in Baltimore at age 23, 5' 6" tall, born in Lancaster Co., PA, and later died in January 1815, cause unknown, but possibly service connected (Johnson and Christou, p. 339)

Skinner, James A. (1788-1814), served as Sergeant in Capt. Charles Crawford's Co., 8th U.S. Infantry, enlisted 29 Jun 1813 for 1 year in Lexington, GA at the age of 25, 5' 10¾" tall, born in Maryland and died on 30 Oct 1814, cause was not stated, but it was probably service connected (Johnson and Christou, p. 340)

Skinner, John S., see Francis Scott Key, q.v.

Slade, Ezekiel, served as a Private in Capt. Edward Orrick's Co., 41st Regiment, Baltimore County Militia, from 25 Aug 1814 and was reported as "sick-absent since Oct 27" 1814 (Wright Vol. 2, p. 70)

Slifer, Ezra, served as a Private in Capt. E. G. Williams' Co., 1st Cavalry Regt., Washington Co., from 11 Aug 1814 and was reported "absent, sick," but no date was given (Wright Vol. 9, p. 1)

Slaine, William, served as a Private in the 14th U.S. Infantry and was captured later, probably at Beaver Dams, Upper Canada on 24 Jun 1813. Prisoner of War #4189 at Halifax, NS, interned on 24 Jun 1813 and was discharged on 27 Aug 1813 and sent to England (Johnson and Christou, p. 340; Baker Vol. 2, p. 368)

Sloan, William, served as a Private in Capt. David Cummings' Co., 14th U.S. Inf., enlisted on 1 Feb 1813 and later captured, date and place not stated. Prisoner of War, sent to England, later released and was discharged from the service on 20 Apr 1815 on a Surgeon's Certificate (Johnson and Christou, p. 340). There was a William Sloane who served as Prize-Master on the privateer *Dolphin*, a merchant vessel out of Baltimore, and was captured at sea on 1 Feb 1813, sent to Halifax, NS from the prison ship *Magnet* on 17 Jan 1814 and later discharged on 11 Jul 1814 (Baker Vol. 2, p. 368). These were probably two different men.

Sly, Thomas, served as Drum Major in the 14th U.S. Infantry, enlisted 10 Oct 1812 for 18 mos. and was captured, probably at Beaver Dams, Upper Canada on 24 Jun 1813. Prisoner of War #3932 at Halifax, NS, interned 24 Jun 1813, discharged for exchange on 3 Feb 1814, exchanged on 15 Apr 1814, returned to service and was discharged 2 Jun 1814; wife Margaret Sly received bounty land (BLW# 68783-160-55; Johnson and Christou, pp. 340-341; Baker Vol. 2, p. 368)

Small, Richard, served as a Seaman and was born in Baltimore. Age: 18. Prison Depot: Plymouth 1, Prisoner of War #1124. Captured by HM Ship-of-the-Line *Superb*. When Taken: 15 Apr 1813. Where Taken: Bay of Biscayne. Prize Name: *Viper*. Home Port: New York. Ship Type: Privateer. Date Received: 22 Apr 1813. From what ship: HMS *Superb*. Discharged and sent to Dartmoor on 1 Jul 1813. Prison Depot: Dartmoor, Prisoner of War #427. Date Received: 1 Jul 1813 from Plymouth. Discharged on 20 Apr 1815. (Johnson's Database, 2019)

Smeethe, Peter, served as a Private in Capt. John Fonsten's Co., Frederick Co. Militia, from 2 Sep 1814, marched to Baltimore, engaged in the defense of the city on 12 Sep 1814 and was "discharged by certificate" [from a surgeon] on 8 Oct 1814 (Wright Vol. 8, p. 364; Mallick and Wright, p. 267)

Smick, Peter, (c1783-1813), served as a Private in Capt. Slicer's Co. and died on 14 Oct 1813 in Annapolis allegedly due to service connected problems; he had married Elizabeth Warner (7 Mar 1789, Harford Co. – 3 Aug 1890, Baltimore) in 1805, but she never filed for a pension. (Notes from Brig. Gen. Edward G. Jones, Jr., of Baltimore, a descendant, to genealogist Henry C. Peden, Jr., of Bel Air, MD, in 1992; Society of the War of 1812 Application National No. 3771 in 1975)

Smiley, John (1776-1817), served as a Private in Capt. Samuel Lane's Co., 14th U.S. Infantry, enlisting 14 May 1812 in Gettysburg, PA for 5 years at the age of 36, 6' tall, born in Ireland. Prisoner of War #3957 at Halifax, NS, interned 24 Jun 1813, was sent to England on HMS *Regulus* and discharged for exchange on 17 Aug 1813; he returned to service and drowned in Alabama on 8 May 1817. (Johnson and Christou, p. 341; Baker Vol. 2, p. 369)

Smith, Abijah, served as a Private in Capt. Richard Arell's Co., 14th U.S. Infantry, enlisted 26 Feb 1813 in Elkton, MD, age 19, 5' 7½" tall, born in Cumberland, NY and was captured, probably at Beaver Dams, Upper Canada. Prisoner of War #3973 at Halifax, NS, interned 24 Jun 1813, discharged for exchange on 3 Feb 1814, exchanged on 15 Apr 1814 and discharged from service at Greenbush, NY on 3 May 1815 (Johnson and Christou, p. 341; Baker Vol. 2, p. 369)

Smith, Adam, served as a Private in Capt. Andrew Smith's Co., 51st Regiment, Baltimore Militia, from 19 Aug 1814 and died 12 Sep 1814 (Wright Vol. 2, p. 38)

Smith, Alexander, served as Quartermaster, 11th Regiment, Dorchester Co. Militia, under Lt. Co. Joseph Daffin, appointed 3 Oct 1807 and listed as dead, but the date and cause of death were not stated; it was most probably in late 1813 since his replacement was appointed on 25 Jan 1814 (Wright Vol. 1, p. iii)

Smith, Andrew (1789-1815), served as a Seaman and was born in Maryland. Age: 23. Prison Depot: Plymouth 1, Prisoner of War #1378. Captured by HM Frigate *Surveillante*. When Taken: 27 Apr 1813. Where Taken: Bay of Biscayne. Prize

Name: *Tom*. Home Port: Baltimore. Ship Type: Letter of Marque. Date Received: 15 May 1813. From what ship: HMS *Foxhound*. Discharged on 3 Jul 1813 and sent to Stapleton Prison. Prison Depot: Stapleton, Prisoner of War #373. Date Received: 11 Jul 1813 from Plymouth. Discharged on 16 Jun 1814 and sent to Dartmoor. Prison Depot: Dartmoor, Prisoner of War #1624. Date Received: 23 Jun 1814. Died on 5 Mar 1815 from variola (smallpox). (Johnson's Database, 2019; Centennial Trails, United States Daughters of 1812, online at www.war1812trails.com/Dartmoor)

Smith, B., served as a Seaman and was born in Baltimore. Age: 20. Prison Depot: Plymouth 2, Prisoner of War #552. Captured by HM Frigate *Pique*. When Taken: 16 Dec 1814. Where Taken: off Porto Rico, West Indies. Prize Name: *Hera*. Ship Type: Merchant Vessel. Date Received: 16 Apr 1815. From what ship: HMS *Swiftsure*. Discharged on 2 Jun 1815 and was released to the Cartel *Soverign*. (Johnson's Database, 2019)

Smith, Benjamin B. (1786-1833), served as a Master's Mate on the privateer *Joseph and Mary* and was wounded in action in October 1812; later served as a Private in Capt. George Stiles' Co., Marine Artillery, from 19 Aug 1814 to 30 Nov 1814 and was at the Battle of North Point on 12 Sep 1814 (Marine p. 439; Society of the War of 1812 Application National No. 13 in 1889 stated Benjamin B. Smith married Ann Thompson, but did not mention his privateer service)

Smith, Charles, served as a Private (company not stated) and was captured at the Battle of Bladensburg on 24 Aug 1814 (Marine, p. 175)

Smith, Charles (African American), served as a Seaman and was born in Baltimore. Age: 34. Prison Depot: Dartmoor, Prisoner of War #5207. Captured by HM Frigate *Acasta* & HM Brig *Wasp*. When Taken: 17 Jun 1813. Where Taken: off Cape Sable, NS. Prize Name: *Porcupine*. Home Port: Boston. Ship Type: Letter of Marque. Date Received: 31 Oct 1814. From what ship: HMT *Mermaid* from Chatham. Discharged on 29 Jun 1815. Prison Depot: Chatham, Prisoner of War #3329. Date Received: 23 Feb 1814 from Halifax, NS on HMT *Malabar*. Discharged on 10 Oct 1814 and sent to Dartmoor on HMS *Mermaid*. (Johnson's Database, 2019)

Smith, David, served as a Private in Capt. Thomas Montgomery's Co., 14th U.S. Infantry, enlisted 5 Jan 1813 and died at Plattsburgh, NY in March 1814 from sickness; bounty land issued to his brother John Smith and other heirs at law (BLW# 25228-160-12; Johnson and Christou, p. 342)

Smith, George, served as a Seaman and was born in Maryland. Age: 35. Prison Depot: Dartmoor, Prisoner of War #3498. How Taken: Gave himself up in a boat of the *Fox*. Date Received: 24 Sep 1814. From what ship: HMT *Salvador del Mundo*. Discharged on 20 Mar 1815. (Johnson's Database, 2019)

Smith, Henry, served as a Private in Capt. Richard Arell's Co., 14th U.S. Infantry, enlisted 19 Nov 1812 in Baltimore, age 19, 5' 6" tall, born in Baltimore and was captured, probably at Beaver Dams, Upper Canada. Prisoner of War #3940, interned 24 Jun 1813, discharged for exchange on 3 Feb 1814, exchanged on 15 Apr 1814, returned to service and deserted at Fort Severn, MD on 15 Jul 1815 (Johnson and Christou, p. 342, stated 14th U.S. Infantry, new 4th U.S. Infantry, but Baker Vol. 2, p. 371, stated 23rd U.S. Regiment)

Smith, Isaac, served as a Seaman and was born in Baltimore. Age: 26. Prison Depot: Dartmoor, Prisoner of War #2457. Captured by HM Frigate *Orpheus*. When Taken: 20 Apr 1814. Where Taken: off Matanzas, Cuba. Prize Name: U.S. Sloop-of-War *Frolic*. Ship Type: Warship. Date Received: 16 Aug 1814. From what ship: HMT *Queen* from Halifax, NS. Discharged on 3 May 1815. (Johnson's Database, 2019)

Smith, Jacob (1768-1813), served as a Private in Capt. Samuel Lane's Co., 14th U.S. Infantry, enlisted 31 Aug 1812 at age 44, 5' 4½" tall, born in Germany and was captured, probably at Beaver Dams, Upper Canada. Prisoner of War #3852 at Halifax, NS, interned on 24 Jun 1813 and died there on 14 Sep 1813 from dysentery (Johnson and Christou, p. 343; Baker Vol. 2, p. 371)

Smith, John, served as a Seaman and was born in Maryland. Age: 24. Prison Depot: Plymouth 2, Prisoner of War #481. Captured by HM Brig *Barbadoes*. When Taken: 11 Jan 1815. Where Taken: off St. Bartholomew, West Indies. Prize Name: *Fox*. Home Port: Baltimore. Ship Type: Privateer. Date Received: 16 Apr 1815. From what ship: HMS *Swiftsure*. Discharged on 2 Jun 1815 and released to the Cartel *Soverign*. (Johnson's Database, 2019)

Smith, John, served as a Seaman and was born in Maryland. Age: 29. Prison Depot: Dartmoor, Prisoner of War #3822. Captured by HM Frigate *Niemen*. When Taken: 28 Jan 1814. Where Taken: off Delaware. Prize Name: *Bordeaux Packet*. Home Port: Baltimore. Ship Type: Letter of Marque. Date Received: 5 Oct 1814. From what ship: HMT *Orpheus* from Halifax, NS. Discharged on 9 Jun 1815. (Johnson's Database, 2019)

Smith, John, served as a Seaman and was born in Baltimore. Age: 19. Prison Depot: Dartmoor, Prisoner of War #6429. How Taken: Gave himself up off a drogger. When Taken: 12 Apr 1814. Prize Name: --?--, prize of the Privateer *Saucy Jack*. Ship Type: Privateer. Received: 3 Mar 1815. From what ship: HMT *Ganges* from Plymouth. Discharged 19 May 1815. (Johnson's Database, 2019)

Smith, John, served as 2nd Lieutenant on the privateer *Globe* and was killed in action on 1 Nov 1813 (Marine p. 441; *Niles Weekly Register*, 19 Feb 1814)

Smith, John, served as a Private in Capt. John Bond's Co., 41st Regt., Baltimore Co. Militia, stationed at Kelley's Field from 25 Aug 1814 and discharged by a Surgeon, but the date and reason were not stated (Wright Vol. 2, p. 67)

Smith, John, served as a Private in the 14th U.S. Infantry (company and captain not named) and was captured at Beaver Dams, Upper Canada on 24 Jun 1813. Prisoner of War #4025 at Halifax, NS, interned 24 Jun 1813 and discharged for exchange on 3 Feb 1814. (Johnson and Christou, p. 344; Baker Vol. 2, p. 373)

Smith, John, served as a Private in Capt. Samuel Lane's Co., 14th U.S. Infantry, enlisted 28 Jul 1812, age 29, 5' 6½" tall, born in Ireland. Prisoner of War #3958 at Halifax, NS, interned 24 Jun 1813, discharged on 27 Aug 1813 and sent to England, later released and was discharged from the service on 31 Mar 1815 (Johnson and Christou, p. 344, Baker Vol. 2, p. 373)

Smith, John, served as a Marine and was taken from the barracks and admitted to the Naval Hospital in Washington, DC as Patient No. 90 on 30 Dec 1814 with typhoid fever and died on 3 Jan 1815 (Sharp's Database, 2018)

Smith, Joseph, served as a Marine and was wounded on 24 Aug 1814 in the field of battle at Bladensburg, admitted to the Naval Hospital in Washington, DC as Patient No. 8, was discharged on 13 Dec 1814 and returned to barracks (Sharp's Database, 2018)

Smith, Joseph E. (1790-1813), served as a Lieutenant, U.S. Navy, and died on 1 Dec 1813 in his 24th year, eldest son of Capt. Joseph Smith of Baltimore, and was buried in Pittsburgh, PA with military honors. (*Baltimore Patriot*, 15 Dec 1813, but *Niles Weekly Register* did not report his death until 12 Aug 1815)

Smith, Michael, served as a Private in 2nd U.S. Infantry (company and captain not named), enlisted 1 Feb 1813 at the advanced age of 56, 5' 5" tall, born in Fredericktown, MD and was discharged at Sackett's Harbor, NY on a Surgeon's Certificate due to old age (Johnson and Christou, p. 345)

Smith, Nathaniel, served as a Private in Capt. William Littlejohn's Co., 2nd U.S. Light Dragoons, enlisted 27 Apr 1814 in Baltimore, age 25, 5' 9" tall, born in Franklin Co., PA, was captured at Bladensburg on 24 Aug 1814 and a Prisoner of War, paroled on 25 Aug 1814 and discharged from service at Carlisle Barracks, PA on 4 May 1815 (Johnson and Christou, pp. 345-346; Marine, p. 175)

Smith, Peter, served as a Seaman under Sailing Master Simmones Bunbury, U.S. Sea Fencibles, enlisted 29 Jan 1814 for 1 year and died at Baltimore on 27 Feb 1814, cause was not stated, but was possibly service connected; however, pension Navy Widow File 1413 was rejected (Johnson and Christou, p. 346)

Smith, Richard, served as a Private in Capt. William Bradford's Co., 17th U.S. Infantry, enlisted 18 Jul 1812 in St. Clairsville, OH, age 21, 5' 5" tall, born in Queen Anne's Co., MD and captured at Sackett's Harbor, NY on 12 Jun 1813. Prisoner of War #4959 at Halifax, NS, interned 15 Dec 1813, discharged for exchange on 31 May 1814 and discharged from the service at Fort Howard, WI on 17 Jul 1817 (Johnson and Christou, p. 346; Baker Vol. 2, p. 374)

Smith, Robert, served as a Private in Capt. Stephen Gill's Co., 41st Regiment, Baltimore Co., from 25 Aug 1814 and was reported as "sick-absent since Oct 10" 1814 (Wright Vol. 2, p. 68)

Smith, Robert, served as a Private in Capt. John McKane's Co., 27th Regiment, Baltimore Militia, from 19 Aug 1814 and was wounded on 12 Sep 1814 at North Point (Huntsberry, p. 92, but Wright Vol. 2, p. 18, and Marine p. 441, both did not mention being wounded and none of them indicated that he was captured) Dr. James H. McCulloh, Jr. wrote this note soon after the battle to the British commander: "In consequence of the humanity shown the following American prisoners of war, I do promise upon honor that they shall not directly or indirectly serve against the British until regularly exchanged." Robert Smith was on his list of prisoners of war. (Marine, p. 171)

Smith, Samuel D., served as a Seaman on the privateer *Globe* and was killed in action on 1 Nov 1813 (Maine p. 441; *Niles Weekly Register*, 19 Feb 1814)

Smith, Shapley, served as a Passenger and was born in Baltimore. Age: 29. Prison Depot: Dartmoor, Prisoner of War #1198. Captured by HM Brig *Achates*. When Taken: 14 Jun 1810. Where Taken: English Channel. Prize Name: *Ocean*. Ship Type: Privateer. Date Received: 4 Jun 1814 from Dartmouth. Escaped on 8 Aug 1814. (Johnson's Database, 2019)

Smith, Thomas, served as a Seaman and was born in Maryland. Age: 22. Prison Depot: Plymouth 1, Prisoner of War #117. Captured by HM Ship-Sloop *Jalouse*. When Taken: 1 Dec 1812. Where Taken: off Cape St. Vincent, Portugal. Prize Name: *Otter*. Ship Type: Merchant Vessel. Date Received: 30 Dec 1812. From what ship: HMS *Leonidas*. Discharged and sent to Portsmouth on 4 Jan 1813 on HMS *Revolutionnaire*. (Johnson's Database, 2019)

Smith, William (African American), served as a Seaman and was born in Baltimore. Age: 30. Prison Depot: Plymouth 1, Prisoner of War #1012. How Taken: Gave himself up. When Taken: Oct 1812. Where Taken: Gibraltar. Date Received: 20 Apr 1813. From what ship: HMS *Libria*. Discharged and sent to Dartmoor on 8 Sep 1813. Prison Depot: Dartmoor, Prisoner of War #459. Date Received: 8 Sep 1813 from Plymouth. Discharged on 26 Apr 1815. (Johnson's Database, 2019)

Smith, William (1789-1814), served as a Private in 14th U.S. Infantry and was born in Maryland. Age: 24. Prison Depot: Quebec, Prisoner of War #500. When Taken: 24 Jun 1813. Where Taken: Beaver Dams, Upper Canada. Died on 16 Jul 1813 from dysentery. (Johnson's Database, 2019)

Smith, William, served as a Private in Capt. James McConkey's Co., 27th Regt., Baltimore Militia, was wounded on 12 Sep 1814 at North Point and discharged on 29 Oct1814. (Huntsberry, p. 91, but Wright Vol. 2, p. 19, and Marine p. 442, both did not mention being wounded)

Smith, William (1777-1813), served as a Private in the 14th U.S. Infantry at the age of 36 and was captured at Beaver Dams, Upper Canada on 24 Jun 1813. Prisoner of War #502 at Quebec, interned 7 Jul 1813 and died on 16 Jul 1813 from dysentery (Johnson and Christou, p. 348; Johnson's Quebec book, p. 143)

Smith, William, served as a Private in Capt. Thomas Kearney's Co., 14th U.S. Infantry, enlisted 5 Jun 1812 for 5 years and died on or about 15 Aug 1813; bounty land was issued to his daughter Elizabeth Smith and other heirs at law (BLW# 18234-160-12; Johnson and Christou, p. 347)

Smith, William, served as a Private in Capt. D. McFarland's Co., 22nd U.S. Inf., enlisted 13 Aug 1812 at Fayette, PA by Capt. Foster for 5 years, age 25, 5' 7½" tall, blue eyes, black hair, dark complexion, born in Frederick Co., MD, was on extra duty at Niagara, NY from 11 to 24 Dec 1812, discharged at Burlington, VT on 19 Apr 1814 by Surgeon's Certificate for asthma (Mallick and Wright, p. 272)

Smith, William (c1777-1813), served as a Private in 14th U.S. Inf., enlistment date not stated, age 36, and was captured at Beaver Dams, Upper Canada on 24 Jun 1813. Prisoner of War #502 at Quebec, interned 7 Jul 1813 and died on 16 Jul 1813 (Johnson and Christou, p. 348; Johnson's Quebec book, p. 143)

Sneeds, Abraham C., served as a Private in the 14th U.S. Infantry, enlisted 23 May 1812 at Bladensburg, MD at the age of 30, 5' 8" tall, born in Orange Co., NY and was captured at Beaver Dams, Upper Canada on 24 Jun 1813. Prisoner of War at Halifax, NS, discharged for exchange on 3 Feb 1815 and deserted at Fort Severn, MD on 16 Jul 1815 (Johnson and Christou, p. 349)

Snow, Robert, served as a private in Capt. Trueman Duvall's Co., 34th Regt., Prince George's Co., and was listed as "dead" on the muster roll of 5 Aug – 2 Sep 1813, but no date or location were given. He was also noted as serving as a substitute for Edward Magruder. (Wright Vol. 6, p. 17)

Snyder, Frederick, served as a Private in Capt. Roderick Burgess' Co., Anne Arundel Co. Militia, and stated in 1851 that he was drafted around 15 Jul 1814 and was discharged at Montgomery County Courthouse on 20 Aug 1814 on account of sickness; however, muster roll dated 22 Jul – 19 Sep 1814 reported

"Frederick Snider deserted Aug 30" and his bounty land application in 1851 in Guersney Co., OH, filed at age 57, was rejected for that reason. (Wright Vol. 4, pp. 42, 122; BLW# 50-rej-71468; Smith's Database, 2019)

Snyder, George, served as a Private in the 14th U.S. Infantry, enlisted 6 Dec 1812 and was captured, probably at Beaver Dams, Upper Canada. Prisoner of War #3917, interned 24 Jun 1813, discharged for exchange on 3 Feb 1814 and exchanged on 15 Apr 1814 (Johnson and Christou, p. 349; Baker Vol. 2, p. 377)

Snyder, William, served as a Seaman and was born in Maryland. Age: 32. Prison Depot: Plymouth 1, Prisoner of War #2691. How Taken: Gave himself up off HM Brig *Barracouta*. Date Received: 7 Jun 1814. From what ship: *Inap*. Discharged on 14 Jun 1814 and sent to Dartmoor. Prison Depot: Dartmoor, Prisoner of War #1315. How Taken: Gave himself up off HM Brig *Barracouta*. Received: 14 Jun 1814 from Mill Prison. Discharged on 28 Apr 1815. (Johnson's Database, 2019)

Somerville, Charles, served as a Seaman and was born in Baltimore. Age: 17. Prison Depot: Dartmoor, Prisoner of War #354. Captured by HM Frigate *Magiciene*. When Taken: 17 Jan 1813. Where Taken: off Western Islands, Scotland. Prize Name: *Thrasher*. Home Port: Gloucester. Ship Type: Privateer. Date Received: 1 Jul 1813 from Plymouth. Discharged and sent to Dartmouth on 30 Jul 1813. (Johnson's Database, 2019)

Soran (Soren), Thomas, served as a Private in Capt. Reuben Gilder's Co., 14th U.S. Infantry, enlisted 26 Jan 1813 in Baltimore at age 42, 5' 8¼" tall, born in Dublin, Ireland and captured at Stoney Creek, Upper Canada on 12 Jun 1813. Prisoner of War #5085 at Halifax, NS, interned 28 Dec 1813 and discharged for exchange on 31 May 1814 (Johnson and Christou, p. 350; Baker Vol. 2, p. 378)

Southcomb, John, served as Captain of the privateer schooner *Lottery* that was attacked by nine boats of the British on 8 Feb 1813 and he was killed and the boat captured. (Marine, p. 444; *History of Harford County, Maryland*, by Walter W. Preston, 1901, p. 240)

Sowders, Valentine, served as a Musician in Capt. Daniel McFarland's Co., 22nd U.S. Infantry, enlisted 1 Jul 1812 in Allegany Co., MD at the advanced age of 56, 5' 8¼" tall, born in Prince George's Co. and was discharged on 19 Apr 1814 on a Surgeon's Certificate due to old age (Johnson and Christou, p. 350)

Spahn, Elias, served as a Private in Capt. Nicholas Turbutt's Co., Frederick County Militia, Fredericktown area, from 1 Sep 1814, marched to Baltimore, was stationed at Hampstead Hill and discharged by a Surgeon, but the cause and date were not given (Mallick and Wright, p. 358)

Spaldings, William, served as a Private in the 14th U.S. Infantry, enlisted 22 May 1812 for 18 months and was captured at Beaver Dams, Upper Canada on 24 Jun

1813. Prisoner of War #3788 at Halifax, NS, interned 24 Jun 1813 and was discharged on 9 Nov 1813, sent to England. Prison Depot: Chatham, Prisoner of War #3118. Age 22. Born in Maryland.. Date Received: 7 Jan 1814 from Halifax, NS. Discharged on 10 Oct 1814 and was sent to U.S. on the Cartel *St. Philip*. Returned to service and discharged on 31 Mar 1815. (Johnson and Christou, p. 350, listed him as Spalding; Baker Vol. 2, p. 378; Johnson's Database, 2019)

Sparks, John B., served as 2nd Lieutenant in the 14th U.S. Infantry (company not stated), commissioned on 12 Mar 1812 and died on 15 Jul 1813. (Johnson and Christou, p. 350, spelled his name Sparkes) J. B. Sparks, a native of Maryland and an officer in the U.S. Army, died at Sackett's Harbor, NY on 16 Jul 1813. (*Baltimore American*, 6 Aug 1813)

Sparks, Samuel, served as a Private in Capt. Simon Wickes, Jr.'s Co., 21st Regt., Maryland Militia, paid for 15 days service and died sometime between 16 Apr and 12 May 1813 (Wright Vol. 1, p. 11)

Sparks, Thomas, served as a Private in Capt. Edward Orrick's Co., 41st Regt., Baltimore Co. Militia, from 25 Aug 1814 and was discharged by a doctor on 28 Aug 1814, but the medical reason was not stated (Wright Vol. 2, p. 70)

Speelman (Spellman), Andrew, served as a Private in Capt. George Washington Magee's Co., Frederick County Militia, 1st Regiment, New Windsor area, joined 22 Jul 1814, was "sick on furlough on 1 Oct 1814, three weeks sick" and was discharged in Baltimore on 1 Dec 1814 by a Surgeon, but the medical reason was not stated (Mallick and Wright, pp. 274, 342, 343)

Spencer, Robert, served as a Gunner's Mate and was born in Maryland. Age: 42. Prison Depot: Dartmoor, Prisoner of War #2380. Captured by HM Frigate *Orpheus*. When Taken: 20 Apr 1814. Where Taken: off Matanzas, Cuba. Prize Name: U.S. Sloop-of-War *Frolic*. Ship Type: Warship. Received: 16 Aug 1814 on HMT *Queen* from Halifax, NS. Discharged and was sent to Dartmouth on 19 Oct 1814. (Johnson's Database, 2019)

Spicer, Abraham (1796-1873), served as a Private in Capt. John B. Bayless' Co., 42nd Regiment, Harford Co. Militia, joined on 7 Sep 1814 and "went home for 4 or 5 days later sick," as noted on the muster roll dated 27 Aug – 26 Sep 1814 (Wright Vol. 3, p. 28; *Harford Democrat*, 16 Jan 1874, did not mention service)

Spick, John H., served as a Passenger and was born in Baltimore. Age: 18. Prison Depot: Chatham, Prisoner of War #3353. Captured by HM Ship-of-the-Line *Victorious*. When Taken: 8 Jan 1813. Where Taken: off Halifax, NS. Prize Name: *Rolla*. Ship Type: Privateer. Date Received: 23 Feb 1814 from Halifax, NS on HMT *Malabar*. Discharged on 10 Oct 1814 and sent to Dartmoor on HMS *Mermaid*. Prison Depot: Dartmoor, Prisoner of War #5218. Date Received: 31 Oct 1814.

From what ship: HMT *Mermaid* from Chatham. Discharged on 29 Jun 1815. (Johnson's Database, 2019)

Sponseller, Jacob (c1792-1873), served as a Private in Capt. Fonsten's Co., joined 2 Sep 1814 and "sick absent" on 7 Oct 1814 (Mallick and Wright, p. 274, spelled his name Sponsaler). Jacob Sponseller died 23 Nov 1873, but his grave stone is broken so his age is not known. He was buried in Mt. Olivet Cemetery beside his wife Catherine who died on 1 Sep 1870, aged 77 years, 6 months and 20 days. (*Names In Stone*, by Jacob M. Holdcraft, 1966, Vol. 2, p. 1078)

Sponseller, John, served as a Private in Capt. Nicholas Turbutt's Co., Frederick County Militia, Fredericktown area, from 1 Sep 1814, marched to Baltimore, stationed at Hampstead Hill and was reported "sick absent without leave," but the cause and date of death were not given (Mallick and Wright, p. 358)

Sponseller (Sponsler), William (c1794-1841), served as a Private in Capt. Samuel Duvall's Co. between 3 Aug and 3 Oct 1814 and his widow "Elizabeth Sponsler" later moved to Ohio and subsequently stated William was discharged on account of sickness (Mallick and Wright, p. 274; BLW# 55-160-60089)

Spurrier, Lancelot (Lot), served as a Private in Capt. Samuel Lane's Co., 14th U.S. Infantry, enlisted 21 May 1812 at Westminster, MD, age 21, 5' 11" tall, born in Frederick and was captured at Beaver Dams, Canada on 24 Jun 1813. Prisoner of War #3808 at Halifax, NS, interned 27 Aug 1813 and was discharged for exchange on 3 Feb 1814, exchanged on 15 Apr 1814; re-enlisted at Boston on 30 Apr 1814 for the war in the Light Artillery, but was discharged on 6 Jan 1815, reason not stated (Johnson and Christou, p. 352, listed him as "Lot Spunie" and Lancelot Spurrier; Baker Vol. 2, p. 381, also listed him as "Lot Spunie")

Stacy, Perry (Mulatto), served as a Seaman and was born in Baltimore. Age: 23 or 28. Prison Depot: Portsmouth, Prisoner of War #760. How Taken: Gave himself up off HM Ship-of-the-Line *Blake*. When Taken: 10 Dec 1812. Date Received: 1 Apr 1813. From what ship: HMS *Blake*. Discharged on 3 Apr 1813 and sent to Chatham on HM Trandport *Chatham*. Prison Depot: Chatham, Prisoner of War #1507. Date Received: 8 Apr 1813 from Portsmouth on an admiral's tender. Discharged on 4 Aug 1814 and sent to Dartmoor on HMS *Alpheus*. Prison Depot: Dartmoor, Prisoner of War #2755. Date Received: 24 Aug 1814. From what ship: HMT *Liverpool* from Chatham. Discharged on 26 Apr 1815. (Johnson's Database, 2019)

Stacker, Jesse L., see Jesse L. Stocker, q.v.

Stafford, William S., served as Captain of the privateer *Dolphin* and it was captured in the Rappahannock River [Virginia] after a fierce engagement with boats of the British squadron (Marine p. 446, did not give the date of battle)

Staggs, Henry, served as a Seaman and was born in Harford Co., MD. Age: 32. Prison Depot: Portsmouth, Prisoner of War #514. How Taken: Gave himself up off HMS *Romulus*. Date Received: 22 Jan 1813. Discharged on 11 Mar 1813 and sent to Chatham on HM Store Ship *Abundance*. Prison Depot: Chatham, Prisoner of War #1193. Date Received: 16 Mar 1813 from Portsmouth on HMS *Abundance*. Discharged on 11 Aug 1814 and sent to Dartmoor on HMS *Freya*. Prison Depot: Dartmoor, Prisoner of War #2614. Date Received: 21 Aug 1814. From what ship: HMT *Freya* from Chatham. Discharged on 26 Apr 1815. (Johnson's Database, 2019)

Stake, Andrew (1787-1813), served as a Sergeant in Capt. Simon Owens' Co., 1st U.S. Infantry, enlisted 8 Jan 1810 in Newport, KY at the age of 23, 5' 7½" tall, born in Washington Co., MD and died at Belle Fontaine, MO on 20 Oct 1813 (Johnson and Christou, p. 353)

Staley, John, served as a Private in 14th U.S. Infantry and was born in Maryland. Age: 21. Prison Depot: Chatham, Prisoner of War #3073. When Taken: 24 Jun 1813. Where Taken: Beaver Dams, Upper Canada. Date Received: 7 Jan 1814 from Halifax, NS. Discharged on 10 Oct 1814 and sent to U.S. on the Cartel *St. Philip*. (Johnson's Database, 2019)

Stall, Andrew, served as a Private under Capt. James F. Huston and Capt. Lewis Weaver in the Frederick Co. Militia and was "sick in Baltimore since 20 Sep" 1814 (Mallick and Wright, p. 345)

Stallings, Charles T., was a native of Frederick and entered the U.S. Navy circa 1810 as a Midshipman, served as a Lieutenant during the War of 1812 and "fell victim to the yellow fever, contracted at Cuba" (Mallick and Wright, p. 276)

Standiford, Abraham, served as a Private and was listed as "dead" on roster of 27 Aug – 31 Dec 1812 for Capt. William Hitchcock's Co., Small's Regiment, Baltimore Militia. Along with Lt. James Almony he was under arrest on 30 Nov and dismissed from service 10 Dec "for pitching coins." (See full article about Col. James Almony's dismissal and return to service in *Maryland Genealogical Society Bulletin* Vol. 53, No. 1, and Vol. 55, p. 215-232; Wright Vol. 2, p. 59)

Stanforth, Levin, served as a Private, mustered into service in Calvert County when the British were in Patuxent River and he was wounded in action near St. Leonard's Creek in June 1814, stating he served under Capt. Griffith (sic) and Capt. Freeland (per his BLW# 55-160-85145 as cited in Wright Vol. 4, p. 123). He served in Capt. Alfred Freeland's Co. in June 1814 and Capt. Joseph Griffiss' Co., under Lieut. Clare, led by Major Stephen Johns, in July 1814, the captain of the camp being absent; Levin was wounded in the engagement at St. Leonard's Creek (per Isaac Smith, BLW# 55-rej-146361) and William Stallings' declaration who served with Captains Griffiss, Clare and Hungerford and was in the Battle of

St. Leonard's Creek. Levin was age 60 in 1855 and was still living in Calvert Co. in 1858. (BLW# 55-160-27288; Wright Vol. 4, pp. 53, 56, 58, 121, 123)

Stansberry, James, served as a Chief Mate and was born in Maryland. Age: 27. Prison Depot: Plymouth 1, Prisoner of War #2017. Captured by HM Brig *Royalist*. When Taken: 6 Sep 1812. Where Taken: coast of France. Prize Name: *Ned*. Home Port: Baltimore. Ship Type: Letter of Marque (Privateer). Date Received: 30 Sep 1813. From what ship: HMS *Royalist*. Discharged on 30 Sep 1813 and sent to Ashburton on parole. (Johnson's Database, 2019)

Stansbury, John (1788-1814), son of Gen. Tobias Stansbury, was a Lieutenant under Capt. Steven Decatur, fought in the Battle of Plattsburgh, NY; served on the *Macedonian*, died in battle on 11 Sep 1814 and was buried in Riverside Cemetery in Plattsburgh, Clinton Co., NY. (Johnson and Christou, p. 353)

Stansbury, Josias, served as a Private in Capt. John Hanna's Co., 5th Cavalry Regt., Baltimore City, from 19 Aug 1814 and was "unfit for duty since 12 Sep 1814 and not considered a trooper since" (Wright Vol. 2, p. 55)

Stansbury, Samuel, served as a Private in Capt. Nathan Towson's Co., 2nd U.S. Artillery, enlistment date not given, age 25, and captured during the Battle of Stoney Creek, Upper Canada in June 1813. Prisoner of War #285 at Quebec, interned 28 Jun 1813 and released 31 Oct 1813; bounty land issued to brother John Stansbury (Johnson and Christou, p. 354; Johnson's Quebec book, p. 146)

Stansbury, William, served as a Private in Capt. Joseph Marshall's Co., 14th U.S. Infantry, enlisted 25 Jun 1812 in Annapolis at the age of 16, 5' 4" tall, born in Annapolis and was discharged at Greenbush, NY on 4 May 1816 for inability (Johnson and Christou, p. 354)

Stanton, James, served as a Seaman and was born in Baltimore. Age: 24. Prison Depot: Portsmouth, Prisoner of War #1131. How Taken: Gave himself up off HM Ship-of-the-Line *Achille*. Date Received: 5 Oct 1813. From what ship: HM Ship-of-the-Line *Achille*. Discharged on 17 Oct 1813 and sent to Chatham on HMT *Malabar No. 352*. Prison Depot: Chatham, Prisoner of War #2392. Date Received: 20 Oct 1813 from Portsmouth on an admiral's tender. Discharged on 4 Sep 1814 and sent to Dartmoor on HMS *Freya*. Prison Depot: Dartmoor, Prisoner of War #3211. Received: 11 Sep 1814. From what ship: HMT *Freya* from Chatham. Discharged on 28 May 1815. (Johnson's Database, 2019)

Statt, F., served as a Seaman on the privateer *Globe* and was wounded in action on 1 Nov 1813 (Marine p. 447)

Steeds, John (c1785-1814), served as a Sergeant in Capt. Nathan Towson's Co., 2nd U.S. Artillery, enlisted on 12 Apr 1812 and was killed at Chippewa, Upper Canada on 15 Oct 1814 (Johnson and Christou, p. 354)

Steel, Charles, served as a Marine, probably at Bladensburg, was admitted to the Naval Hospital in Washington, DC as Patient No. 40 on 8 Sep 1814 (ulcer), was discharged on 7 Jan 1815 and sent to barracks (Sharp's Database, 2018)

Steel, James (1763-1851), served as a Private in Capt. William Whiteford's Co., Harford Co. Militia, Extra Battalion, from 26 Apr to 3 May 1813 and was present when the British attacked and burned the town of Havre de Grace on 3 May 1813, but an article in 1887 stated James Steele was an Ensign in Capt. James McComas' Co. in 1813. (Wright Vol. 3, p. 33, spelled his name Steal, but does not mention Ensign James Steel or Capt. James McComas' Co.; *The Aegis and Intelligencer*, 16 Dec 1887). "The James Steel of 1813 was a well educated and refined gentleman ... My father employed him to make a number of surveys for him, the first being as early as 1822. At that time he was probably between 35 and 40 years of age ... He had a great aversion to the British. When speaking of them you could observe his profound dislike to the whole nation. Hence his readiness to fire upon the British officer [and wound him] when called on to surrender. Probably his father, or near relatives, had been harshly treated by them in the Revolutionary [War] struggle. Signed: B. Silver, Sr." James Steel was possibly captured and made a prisoner of war for a day or two and was released along with others who had been detained on 3 May 1813. (*The Aegis and Intelligencer*, 16 Dec and 30 Dec 1887) "The elder, Mr. Levy, was taken [by the British] about this time, as was also Capt. Barnes, and one or two men ... Most of the Prisoners they released while on shore." One of those men could have been James Steel. (*Narrative Respecting the Conduct of the British From the First Landing on Spesutie Island Till Their Progress to Havre de Grace*, by James Jones Wilmer, 1814, p. 13; 1850 Harford Co. Census; 1851 Will)

Steel, John (1787-1815) served as a Seaman and was born in Maryland. Age: 26. Prison Depot: Plymouth 1, Prisoner of War #771. Captured by HM Ship-of-the-Line *Warspite*. When Taken: 3 Mar 1813. Where Taken: Bay of Biscayne. Prize Name: *William Bayard*. Ship Type: Merchant Vessel. Date Received: 19 Mar 1813. From what ship: HMS *Warspite*. Discharged and sent to Dartmoor on 28 Jun 1813. Prison Depot: Dartmoor, Prisoner of War #263. Date Received: 28 Jun 1813 from Plymouth. Died on 15 Dec 1814 from pneumonia. (Johnson's Database, 2019; Centennial Trails, United States Daughters of 1812, online at www.war1812trails.com/Dartmoor)

Steel, John, served as a Seaman and was born in Maryland. Age: 39. Prison Depot: Dartmoor, Prisoner of War #5863. Captured by HM Frigate *Grancius*. When Taken: 2 Dec 1814. Where Taken: off Lisbon, Portugal. Prize Name: *Leo*. Home Port: Baltimore. Ship Type: Privateer. Received: 26 Dec 1814. From what ship: HMT *Impregnable*. Discharged on 3 Jul 1815. (Johnson's Database, 2019)

Steel, Samuel H., served as a Private in Capt. Henry Fleming's Co., 14th U.S. Infantry, enlisted 26 Jan 1813 at the age of 28, 5' 8" tall, born in Cheshire Co., NH and discharged at Washington, DC on 23 Sep 1814 on Surgeon's Certificate due to gunshot wound received on 24 Jun 1813 (BLW# 2853-160-12; Johnson and Christou, pp. 354-355)

Steers, John, served as a Private in Capt. Jacob Alexander's Co., Frederick Co. Militia, from 22 Jul 1814 and was reported "sick on furlough," but the date was not stated (Mallick and Wright, p. 277)

Stenchcombe, George, served as a Mate and was born in Maryland. Age: 24. Prison Depot: Portsmouth, Prisoner of War #825. Captured by HM Frigate *Iris*. When Taken: 13 Apr 1813. Where Taken: Bay of Biscayne. Prize Name: *Price*. Home Port: New York. Ship Type: Letter of Marque (Privateer). Date Received: 13 May 1813. From what ship: HM Frigate *Revolutionnaire*. Discharged on 17 May 1813 and sent to Chatham on HMS *Impeleux*. Prison Depot: Chatham, Prisoner of War #1719. Date Received: 25 May 1813 from Portsmouth on HMS *Impetius*. Discharged on 24 Jul 1814 and sent to Dartmoor on HMS *Lyffey*. Prison Depot: Dartmoor, Prisoner of War #2014. Date Received: 3 Aug 1814. From what ship: HMS *Lyffey* from Chatham Depot. Discharged on 2 May 1815. (Johnson's Database, 2019)

Stephens, James (1774-1814), served as a Private in Capt. John Foster's Co., 22nd U.S. Infantry, enlisted 18 Nov 1812 at age of 38, 5' 6" tall, born in Prince George's Co., MD and died at French Mills, NY on 15 Jan 1814 from dysentery (Johnson and Christou, p. 355)

Stephens, John, served as a Private in Capt. Clement Sullivan's Co., 14th U.S. Infantry, enlisted 11 May 1812 in Annapolis and died at Black Rock, NY on 2 Dec 1812; bounty land issued to his son James M. Stephens and other heirs at law (BLW# 26390-160-12; Johnson and Christou, p. 355)

Stephens, John, served as a Private in the 14th U.S. Infantry and was captured, probably at Beaver Dams, Upper Canada. Prisoner of War #4087 at Halifax, NS, interned 24 Jun 1813 and was discharged for exchange on 3 Feb 1814 (Johnson and Christou, p. 355; Baker Vol. 2, p. 385)

Stephens, Michael, served as a Private in Capt. William Allen's Co., 24th U.S. Infantry, enlisted 7 Mar 1813 in St. Genevieve, MO at the age of 22, 5' 7" tall, born in Maryland, was wounded at Mackinaw Island, MI on 4 Aug 1814 and was discharged on 5 Mar 1815 (BLW# 2538-160-12; Pension Old War IF-25850; Johnson and Christou, pp. 355-356)

Stephens, William (1790-1814), served as a Private in Capt. James McDonald's Co., 14th U.S. Infantry, enlisted 10 Feb 1814 at age 24, 5' 5" tall, born in Caroline

Co., MD and died at Burlington, VT on 29 Sep 1814 from wounds received at Crab Island (Johnson and Christou, p. 356)

Stephens, William, served as a Private in Capt. Thomas F. W. Vinson's Co., 32nd Regt., Montgomery Co., Extra Battalion, from 1 Aug 1814 was reported missing in action on 24 Aug 1814 at Bladensburg (Wright Vol. 7, p. 5)

Stephenson, William (1790-1815), served as a Private in the 14th U.S. Infantry, Capt. Joseph Marshall's Co., enlisted 5 Mar 1814 in Baltimore at the age of 24, 5' 8" tall, born in Delaware, re-enlisted and died at Utica, NY on 17 Jan 1815 from diarrhea; bounty land issued to his nephew James Cochrane and other heirs at law (BLW# 14287-160-12; Johnson and Christou, p. 356)

Sterett, Samuel, served as Captain of his own company in Baltimore, 5th Regt., Baltimore Militia, from 19 Aug 1812, was wounded 24 Aug 1814 and promoted to the rank of Major on 20 Dec 1814 (Wright Vol. 2, pp. 6, 58; Marine p. 448)

Sterling, Elijah, a native of Dorchester Co., MD, petitioned for release from imprisonment from the British vessel *Decouverte* and stated he has served more than two years on board (*Niles Weekly Register*, 5 Dec 1812)

Steuart, George H. (1790-1867), served as a Captain under Lt. Col. James Biays in the 5th Regiment, Baltimore Militia, Washington Blues, and was wounded on 12 Sep 1814 during the Battle of North Point (Marine pp. 170, 449; Wright Vol. 2, p. 6) He was buried in Green Mount Cemetery.

Stevens, George, served as a Private in Capt. Henry Grindage's Co. of the 14th U.S. Infantry, enlisted 24 Jul 1812 and died on 30 Dec 1812 (BLW# 24486-160-12; Johnson and Christou, p. 357)

Stevens, John, served as a Marine and was admitted from the barracks to the Naval Hospital in Washington, DC as Patient No. 45 on 18 Sep 1814 in pain, was discharged on 7 Jan 1815 and returned to barracks (Sharp's Database, 2018)

Stevens, William (1793-1880), served as a Private in Captain Thomas F. W. Vinson's Co., 44th Regiment, Montgomery County Militia, from 1 Aug 1814 and William Stephens (sic) was reported "missing 24 Aug" on the company muster roll; however, in May 1856, age 63, Vinton Co., OH, he stated he was drafted in July 1814 under Capt. Eli Brashears and on same day was attached to Capt. Vinson; they marched to Annapolis, then to Bladensburg, then to Washington City, then to Montgomery Court House and then to Baltimore; he became sick for 2 to 3 months and most of the time was unable to help himself and for a considerable time he was not expected to live and never rejoined his company. Stevens also stated William Hornblower was a member of the same company and they were sick at the same time, but Hornblower never recovered and died about 6 weeks after he got home; however, William Hornblower is not listed in any muster roll in 1814. On 6 Dec 1879 William Stevens, age 86, of Allenville, Vinton Co., OH, stated at enlistment in 1814 he had brown hair, was 6' tall and weighed 186 lbs. On 20 Nov 1931 Finley B. Campbell stated William Stevens was born in Baltimore, probably in 1790, served in the War of 1812, came to Belmont Co., OH, married Elizabeth Camp in 1818, later went to Vinton Co., OH and died in the autumn of 1880. (Wright Vol. 7, pp. 5, 44; Pension SO-34456)

Stevenson, John, served as a Private in Capt. James Dorman's Co., 5th U.S. Infantry, enlisted 14 May 1812 in Baltimore, age 20, 5' 9" tall, born in Harford Co., MD, and was discharged at Buffalo, NY on 21 Jun 1814 due to disabilty (Johnson and Christou, p. 357)

Stevenson, Thaddeus, served as a Seaman and was born in Baltimore. Age: 30. Prison Depot: Portsmouth, Prisoner of War #565. Captured by HM Frigate *Dryad*. When Taken: 7 Jan 1813. Where Taken: at sea. Prize Name: *Rossie*. Ship Type: Merchant Vessel. Date Received: 25 Jan 1813. From what ship: HM Ship-of-the-Line *Queen*. Discharged on 11 Mar 1813 and sent to Chatham on HM Store Ship *Abundance*. Prison Depot: Chatham, Prisoner of War #1238. Date Received: 16 Mar 1813 from Portsmouth on HMS *Abundance*. Discharged on 24 Jul 1813 and released to the Cartel *Hoffning*. (Johnson's Database, 2019)

Stevenson, Thomas, served as a Seaman and was born in Havre de Grace, MD. Age: 19. Prison Depot: Portsmouth, Prisoner of War #164. Captured by HM Transport *Diadem*. When Taken: 7 Oct 1812. Where Taken: S. Andera (St. Andrews, Scotland). Prize Name: *Baltimore*. Home Port: Baltimore. Ship Type: Privateer. Received: 3 Nov 1812 San Antonio. From what ship: HMS *Diadem*. Discharged on 19 Feb 1813 and sent to Chatham on HM Store Ship *Dromedary*. Prison Depot: Chatham, Prisoner of War #533. Received: 23 Feb 1813 from Portsmouth on HMS *Dromedary*. Discharged on 8 Jun 1813 and released to the Cartel *Rodrigo*. (Johnson's Database, 2019)

Stevenson, Thomas, was a Seaman from Harford County who was imprisoned at Chatham aftrer the privateer (letter-of-marque ship) *Baltimore,* under Capt. Edward Veasey, was captured; taken into custody at Chatham on 23 Feb 1813 and released to go home aboard the Cartel *Rodrigo* four months later on 8 Jun 1813. ("Harford County in the War of 1812," by Christopher T. George, *Harford Historical Bulletin* No. 76, Spring 1998, pp. 17, 18, 20, citing *The Fatal Cruise of the Argus*, by Ira Dye, pp. 294-296, and *Records Relating to American Prisoners of War, 1812-1815, in the Public Record Office, London*, Admiralty Papers)

Steward, John, served as a Private in Capt. Nathan Towson's Co., 2nd U.S. Artillery, enlistment date not stated, and was killed during the Battle of Chippewa, Canada in July 1814 (Johnson and Christou, p. 357)

Stewart (Steward), Isaac (African American), served as a Seaman and was born in Baltimore. Age: 29. Prison Depot: Plymouth 1, Prisoner of War #2033. Captured by HM Schooner *Helicon* & HM Schooner *Whiting*. When Taken: 25 Oct 1813. Where Taken: Bay of Biscayne. Prize Name: *Friendship West*, prize of the Privateer *True Blooded Yankee*. Ship Type: Privateer. Date Received: 31 Oct 1813. From what ship: HMS *Whiting*. Discharged on 3 Nov 1813 and sent to Dartmoor. Prison Depot: Dartmoor, Prisoner of War #804. Received: 3 Nov 1813 from Plymouth. Discharged on 26 Apr 1815. (Johnson's Database, 2019)

Stewart, James, served as a Private in Capt. Edward Orrick's Co., 41st Regiment, Baltimore Co. Militia, from 25 Aug 1814 and reported as "sick-absent since Oct 14" 1814 (Wright Vol. 2, p. 70)

Stewart, John, served as a Captain in Lt. Col. Amey's 51st Regiment from 28 Jul 1813 and was wounded 12 Sep 1814 at North Point (Huntsberry, p. 108; Wright Vol. 2, pp. 31, 32, and Marine p. 450, last two did not mention being wounded)

Stewart, John, served as a Private in Capt. Thomas Sangster's Co., 12th U.S. Infantry, enlisted 26 Jun 1812 in Baltimore at the age of 43, 5' 8" tall, born in Maryland and was discharged on 1 Sep 1813, incapable to perform the duties of a soldier (Johnson and Christou, p. 358)

Stewart, John N., served as a Private in Capt. John McKane's Co., 27th Regt., Baltimore Militia, from 19 Aug to 18 Nov 1814 (Wright Vol. 2, p. 18, listed him as "John N/C Stewart" and did not mention he was wounded). In Anne Arundel Co. on 30 Mar 1821 John N. Stewart, former private in Capt. Kane's (sic) Co. of Foot, 27th Regt., Maryland Militia, in the late war when disabled, and a resident of Annapolis for 5 years and 6 months and previously of Baltimore, appointed Henry Slicer as his attorney to collect his $16.00 pension due from 4 Sep 1820 to 4 Mar 1821 (Peirce, p. 177)

Stewart, Thomas, served as a Private in Capt. Henry Lowrey's Co., Allegany Co. Militia, joined after 14 Oct 1814 and died on 30 Dec 1814 (Wright Vol. 9, p. 7)

Stiles, William, served as a 1st Lieutenant and was born in Baltimore. Age: 24. Prison Depot: Plymouth 1, Prisoner of War #505. Captured by HM Brig *Reindeer*. When Taken: 3 Feb 1813. Where Taken: Bay of Biscayne. Prize Name: *Cashiere*. Home Port: Baltimore. Ship Type: Letter of Marque. Date Received: 15 Feb 1813. From what ship: *Cashiere*, Privateer. Discharged and sent on 18 Feb 1813 to Ashburton on parole. He was captured again as a 1st Lieutenant, age 25, born in Baltimore and imprisoned at Prison Depot: Plymouth 1, Prisoner of War #2317. Captured by HM Brig *Pelican*. When Taken: 13 Jan 1814. Where Taken: at sea. Prize Name: *Siro*. Home Port: Baltimore. Ship Type: Letter of Marque. Date Received: 25 Jan 1814. From what ship: HMS *Pelican*. Discharged on 25 Jan 1814 and sent to Ashburton on parole. (Johnson's Database, 2019)

Stilts, William, served as a Private in Capt. Cuddy Lawson's Co., 5th Regiment, Baltimore City Militia, was wounded in the hand at Patapsco Point and was discharged on 3 Oct 1814 (Wright Vol. 2, p. 5)

Stinchcomb, George, see George Stencombe, q.v.

Stinchcomb, Vachel, of Frederick Town, served as 4th Sergeant in Capt. Joseph Green's Co. and Capt. James F. Huston's Co., Frederick Co. Militia, from 23 Jul 1814 until discharged in Baltimore City on 6 Dec 1814 by a Surgeon (Mallick and Wright, pp. 279, 345, also spelled his name Stinchacomb)

Stirrell, George (African American), served as a Seaman and was born in Baltimore. Age: 21. Prison Depot: Dartmoor, Prisoner of War #3000. Captured by HM Frigate *Aquilon*. When Taken: 9 Aug 1814. Where Taken: off Western Islands, Scotland. Prize Name: *St. Lawrence*, prize of the Privateer *Whig*. Ship Type: Privateer. Date Received: 29 Aug 1814. From what ship: HMT *Bittern*. Discharged on 28 May 1815. (Johnson's Database, 2019)

Stocker, Jesse L., served as a Sergeant in Capt. Isaac Barnard's Co., 14th U.S Infantry, enlisted 12 Jan 1813, age 27, 5' 10½" tall, born in Talbot Co., MD and captured at Beaver Dams, Upper Canada on 24 Jun 1813 by Commodore Yeo. Prisoner of War #7522 at Halifax, NS, interned 27 Oct 1814, discharged on 5 Mar 1815 for Salem and discharged from service at Baltimore on 30 Apr 1815 (Johnson and Christou, p. 359; Baker Vol. 2, p. 382 spelled his name Stacker)

Stoden, Henry, served as a Private in the 14th U.S Infantry, enlisted 26 Nov 1812 for 5 years and was later captured, probably at Beaver Falls, Upper Canada. Prisoner of War #4055 at Halifax, interned 24 Jun 1813 and discharged for exchange on 3 Feb 1814, exchanged on 15 Apr 184, returned to service and deserted at Schenectady, NY on 19 Jan 1819 (Johnson and Christou, p. 359; Baker Vol. 2, p. 389 spelled his name Stoding)

Stokes, John, served as a Private in Capt. Charles Randolph's Co., 36th U.S. Inf., enlisted 21 Aug 1812 for 1 year at the age of 30, 5' 4" tall, born in Delaware; re-enlisted at Annapolis on 8 Mar 1814 and was captured near Washington, DC on 24 Aug 1814. Prisoner of War at Halifax, NS, later released and discharged on 12 May 1815 at Washington, DC (Johnson and Christou, p. 360; Baker Vol. 2, p. 389, did not list him, but mentioned John Stokes, Prisoner of War #7359, who was a Private in the Volunteer Corps captured at sea on 19 Aug 1814 and was interned on 1 Oct 1814 and discharged on 24 Nov 1814)

Stone, Samuel, served as a Private in Capt. Clement Sullivan's Co., 14th U.S. Infantry, enlisted 29 May 1812 and died on 29 Nov 1812 (cause unknown, but likely service connected) (BLW# 10020-160-12; Johnson and Christou, p. 360)

Stoner, John (1768-1815), served as a Musician in Capt. Hugh Martin's Co., 13th U.S. Infantry, enlisted 30 Jun 1812 in Johnstown, PA at the age of 44, 5′ 11″ tall, born in Maryland and died on 28 Feb 1815, plce and cause were not stated, but possibly service connected (Johnson and Christou, p. 360)

Stoner, John, served as a Private in Capt. John Whistler's Co., 1st U.S. Infantry, enlisted 5 Jun 1807 in Lancaster, PA at age 21, 5′ 10″ tall, born in Baltimore, re-enlisted at Detroit on 5 Mar 1812 for 5 years and was captured, date and place not stated. Prisoner of War on parole and discharged at Detroit on 9 Jun 1816 on Surgeon's Certificate due to wound in foot (Johnson and Christou, p. 360)

Stottlemyer, David, served as a Private in Capt. Samuel Dawson's Co., Frederick Co. Militia, from 1 May to 5 Jul 1813 as a substitute for Christian Harshman, and then served as 1st Corporal in Capt. Jacob Alexander's Co. of Volunteers at Middletown Valley; they left for Annapolis after 22 Jul 1814 and later arrived on the field 15 minutes before the British arrived; he was wounded during the Battle of Bladensburg on 24 Aug 1814. David Stottlemyer, Jr. was born circa 1795, married Margaret Magruter and was residing near Middletown in 1855. (BLW# 55-80-23718; Wright Vol. 8, p. 11, 12, 340; Mallick and Wright, p. 281)

Stout, Peter, served as a Private in Capt. William McIlvane's Co., 14th U.S. Inf., enlisted 2 Jun 1812 for 5 years at the age of 40, 4′ 8″ tall, born in Northampton Co., PA. Prisoner of War, captured at Stoney Creek in June 1813, wounded in shoulder blade; also wounded in left knee at La Cole Mill, Canada; and was discharged at Burlington, VT on 18 Jan 1815 on a Surgeon's Certificate (BLW# 24997-160-12; Johnson and Christou, pp. 360-361)

Straghan, David, served as a Private in Capt. James Almoney's Co., 41st Regt., Baltimore Co., from 25 Aug 1814 and reported "sick in hospital" some time before 1 Nov 1814, exact date not stated (Wright Vol. 2, p. 66)

Stranghorn, Hugh, served as a Seaman on the privateer *High Flyer* and was killed in action in December 1812 (Marine p. 452)

Straye, George L., served as a Seaman and was born in Baltimore. Age: 30. Prison Depot: Dartmoor, Prisoner of War #5388. Captured by HM Frigate *Unicorn*. When Taken: 3 Jul 1814. Where Taken: off Christian *Land*. Prize Name: Sister. Ship Type: Merchant Vessel. Date Received: 31 Oct 1814. From what ship: HMT *Leyden* from Chatham. Discharged and released on 1 Jul 1815. (Johnson's Database, 2019)

Street, Ishmael, served as a Private in Capt. Reuben Gilder's Co., 14th U.S. Infantry, enlisted 18 May 1812 for 5 years in [probably Baltimore] Maryland, age 22, 6′ tall and was captured at Beaver Dams, Upper Canada on 24 Jun 1813. Prisoner of War #424 at Quebec, interned on 7 Jul 1813, discharged on 10 Nov

1814 and discharged from the service on 17 May 1817 (Johnson and Christou, p. 361, stated Ishmael Streets was in prison at Halifax, NS; Johnson, p. 148, stated Ishemail Street was in prison in Quebec)

Strong, Samuel, served as a Private in Capt. Roderick Burgess' Co., 32nd Regiment, Anne Arundel Co. Militia, from 22 Jul 1814 and was "sick on furlough since 10 Sep" 1814 as reported on the muster roll dated 22 Jul 1814 – 19 Sep 1814 (Wright Vol. 4, p. 42)

Strowd, John, served as a Private in Capt. Charles Page's Co., 12th U.S. Infantry, enlisted 30 Jun 1812 at the age of 30, 5' 7" tall, born in Harford Co. and was discharged at Pittsburgh on 19 Aug 1815 on a Surgeon's Certificate because of an injury to his side (Johnson and Christou, p. 362; BLW# 9409-160-12)

Stuart, David, served as a Private in the 14th U.S. Infantry (company not stated) and was captured, probably at Beaver Dams, Upper Canada. Prisoner of War #3838, interned 24 Jun 1813 and was discharged for exchange on 3 Feb 1814 (Johnson and Christou, p. 362; Baker Vol. 2, p. 391)

Study, David, served as a Private in Capt. George Shryock's Co., Hagerstown, Washington Co. Militia, joined after 14 Oct 1814 and reported as "sick in hospital in Baltimore," but no date was given (Wright Vol. 9, p. 9)

Sturdevant, Thomas, served as a Private in the 14th U.S. Infantry and was captured, probably at Beaver Dams, Upper Canada. Prisoner of War #4071 interned 24 Jun 1813 and discharged for exchange on 3 Feb 1814 (Johnson and Christou, p. 363; Baker Vol. 2, p. 391)

Sturgess, Major, served as a Seaman and was born in Maryland. Age: 30. Prison Depot: Dartmoor, Prisoner of War #5049. Captured by HM Ship-of-the-Line *Newcastle*. When Taken: 9 Aug 1814. Where Taken: at sea. Prize Name: *Ida*. Home Port: Boston. Ship Type: Letter of Marque. Date Received: 28 Oct 1814. From what ship: HMT *Alkbar* from Halifax, NS. Discharged on 29 Jun 1815. (Johnson's Database, 2019)

Sturgus, John, served as a Seaman and was born in Baltimore. Age: 34. Prison Depot: Chatham, Prisoner of War #1724. Captured by HMS Horatio. When Taken: 13 Dec 1812. Where Taken: Bay of Biscayne. Prize Name: *Powhattan*. Ship Type: Merchant Vessel. Date Received: 25 May 1813 from Portsmouth on HMS Impetius. Discharged on 24 Jul 1813 and released to the Cartel *Hoffning*. (Johnson's Database, 2019)

Suit, Nathaniel, served as a Sergeant in Capt. Thomas Montgomery's Co., 14th U.S. Infantry, enlisted 28 May 1812 for 5 years and was killed during the Battle of La Cole Mill, Canada on 30 Mar 1814; bounty land issued to his brother John Smith Suit and other heirs (BLW# 26697-160-12; Johnson and Christou, p. 363)

Suit, Philip C., served as a Private in Capt. Jasper M. Jackson's Co., 34th Regt., Prince George's Co. Militia, from 21 Aug 1814 and was furloughed on 2 Sep 1814 for indisposition. On 15 May 1871, Philip C. Suit, age 80, of Marion Co., IA, applied for pension and stated he participated in the Battle of Bladensburg, was discharged at Annapolis around 28 Aug 1814 and married Jamima Barrett on 17 Oct 1815 in Prince George's Co., MD. (Wright Vol. 6, pp. 22, 67; Pension SO-16394, SC-20382; Prince George's Co. Marriage License dated 14 Oct 1815)

Sullivan, Abraham, served as a Private in Capt. William Durbin's Co., Frederick Co. Militia, from 24 Aug 1814, marched off for Baltimore and was discharged for inability on 3 Sep 1814 (Mallick and Wright, p. 353, stated he was a Private and p. 283 mistakenly stated he was a Lieutenant; bounty land claim rejected)

Sullivan, Clement, served as a Captain in the 14th U.S. Infantry, commissioned on 28 Mar 1812 and died on 14 Dec 1812 (Johnson and Christou, p. 363)

Sullivan, John, served as a Seaman and was born in Annapolis. Age: 18. Prison Depot: Dartmoor, Prisoner of War #5133. Captured by HM Brig *Castilian*. When Taken: 29 Sep 1814. Where Taken: off Ireland. Prize Name: *Calabria*. Ship Type: Merchant Vessel. Date Received: 31 Oct 181 on HMT *Castilian*. Discharged on 29 Jun 1815. (Johnson's Database, 2019)

Sullivan, Laurence, served as a Seaman and was born in Baltimore. Age: 36. Prison Depot: Dartmoor, Prisoner of War #4114. Captured by HM Frigate *Niemen*. When Taken: 28 Jun 1814. Where Taken: off Delaware. Prize Name: *Bordeaux Packet*. Home Port: Baltimore. Ship Type: Letter of Marque. Date Received: 6 Oct 1814 on HMT *Chesapeake* from Halifax, NS. Discharged on 13 Jun 1815. (Johnson's Database, 2019)

Suman, Isaac (1794-1825), served as a Private in Capt. Andrew Madison's Co., 12th U.S. Inf., enlisted 5 Feb 1814 in Hagerstown, age 19, 5' 7" tall, gray eyes, brown hair, light complexion, born in Frederick Co., MD and later a Private under Capt. Post, left sick at Lake George on 5 Sep 1814, entered hospital on 7 Sep 1814, discharged from same on 28 Oct 1814 and discharged from service at Buffalo, NY on 6 Jun 1815 due to an injury of his right thigh received before enlistment (Johnson and Christou, pp. 363-364; Mallick and Wright, pp. 283-284) He was buried beside his wife Margaret Suman (1793-1860) in Mt. Olivet Cemetery in Frederick. (*Names In Stone*, by Jacob M. Holdcraft, 1966, p. 1123)

Summerville, Charles, served as a Boy onboard a ship and was born in Baltimore. Age: 17. Prison Depot: Plymouth 1, Prisoner of War #1014. Captured by HM Frigate *Magiciene*. When Taken: 17 Jan 1813. Where Taken: off Western Islands, Scotland. Prize Name: *Thrasher*. Home Port: Gloucester. Ship Type: Privateer. Date Received: 20 Apr 1813. From what ship: HMS Libria. Discharged and was sent to Dartmoor on 1 Jul 1813. (Johnson's Database, 2019)

Sumwalt, John Thornburg (1791-1868), served as 4th Corporal in Capt. John Berry's Co., Washington Artillery, 1st Artillery Regiment, from 5 Aug to 25 Aug 1813 and from 19 Aug 1814 and was wounded at the 6-gun Battery on 13 Sep 1814 at Fort McHenry. (Marine, p. 453; Wright Vol. 2, p. 43, 44, 49, did not mention his wound) He died on 20 Aug 1868 and was buried in Green Mount Cemetery (*The [Baltimore] Sun*, 21 Aug 1868; Society of the War of 1812 Application National No. 185 in 1894 stated he married Rachel Sparks, as also did *1812 Ancestor Index Volume I, 1892-1970*, National Society United States Daughters of 1812, 2005, p. 489, that stated he was born in 1791)

Surrat, John, served as a Private in Capt. Joseph Veitch's Co., 34th Regt., Prince George's Co. Militia, from 20 Jul 1814 and was "sent home sick at Nottingham" on 24 Jul 1814 (Wright Vol. 6, p. 20)

Surrell, William, served as 2nd Sergeant in Capt. John Montgomery's Artillery Co., Baltimore City, joined on 28 Aug 1814 and was wounded on 12 Sep 1814 at North Point (Wright Vol. 2, p. 46; Marine p. 170 did not give his name)

Suter, Henry, served as a Private in Capt. John Skrim's Co., 5th Regt., Baltimore Militia, from 19 Aug 1814, captured at North Point on 12 Sep 1814 and shown on muster roll of 19 Aug – 18 Nov 1814 as "in captivity" (Wright Vol. 2, p. 9)

Sutherly, Joseph, served as a Private in the 14th U.S. Infantry and was captured, probably at Beaver Dams, Upper Canada. Prisoner of War #4015, interned 24 Jun 1813 and discharged for exchange on 3 Feb 1814 (Johnson and Christou, p. 364; Baker Vol. 2, p. 393)

Swain, Paul, served as a Private in Capt. Samuel Lane's Co., 14th U.S. Infantry, enlisted 18 May 1812 and killed 28 Nov 1812 at Black Rock, NY; heirs received half pay for 5 years in lieu of bounty land (Johnson and Christou, p. 364)

Swann, John E., served as a Private in Capt. David Warfield's Co., 5th Regiment, Baltimore United Volunteers, from 19 Aug and was wounded 12 Sep 1814 at North Point (Marine, pp. 172, 454; Wright Vol. 2, p. 8 did not mention wound)

Swann, Samuel, served as a Private in Capt. Richard Arell's Co., 14th U.S. Inf., enlisted 12 Jun 1812 at Bladensburg, age 39, 5' 9" tall, born in Cumberland and captured at Beaver Dams, Upper Canada on 24 Jun 1813. Prisoner of War at Halifax, discharged from Halifax on 3 Feb 1813, exchanged on 15 Apr 1814 and discharged from the service at Annapolis on 18 Oct 1815 for inability (Johnson and Christou, p. 365; Baker Vol. 2, p. 393 did not mention him)

Swarthwood, Joseph, served as a Private in Capt. Thomas Montgomery's Co., 14th U.S. Infantry, enlisted 13 Jun 1812 for 5 years in Lewistown, Pa at the age of 18, 5' 6" tall, born in New Jersey and discharged at Greenbush, NY on 24 Aug

1815; was wounded in the right leg by a musket ball (BLW# 26584-160-12; Johnson and Christou, p. 365; Pension Old War IF-25869)

Sweeney (Sweney), Dennis, served as a Private in Capt. William H. Wilson's Co., 34th Regt., Prince George's Co. Militia, between 4 Aug and 18 Aug 1813 and was "sent home sick," but no date was give (Wright Vol. 6, p. 16)

Sweeney, James (1778-1815), served as a Private in Capt. James Charlton's Co., 12th U.S. Infantry, enlisted 11 May 1812 in Maryland at the age of 34, 5' 7¼" tall, born in Ireland and died on 21 Aug 1815; bounty land issued to son John Sweeney and other heirs (BLW# 23993-160-12; Johnson and Christou, p. 365)

Sweeting, James, served as a Private in Capt. Henry Grindage's Co., 14th U.S. Infantry, enlisted 22 Jun 1812 and died in Oct 1814; bounty land to his sister Ann Sweeting and others (BLW# 15860-160-12; Johnson and Christou, p. 366)

Swigget, Ralph, served as a Private in Capt. David Cummings' Co., 14th U.S. Infantry, enlisted 9 Nov 1814 and died on 15 Feb 1815; bounty land issued to brother Peter C. Swigget (BLW# 23972-160-12; Johnson and Christou, p. 366)

Switzer, John, served as a Musician in Capt. James McDonald's Co., 14th U.S. Inf., enlisted 28 Feb 1814 at the age of 42, 5' 6" tall, born in Lancaster, PA and was discharged at Greenbush, NY on 1 May 1815 on a Surgeon's Certificate (Johnson and Christou, p. 367)

Syder, John, served as a Seaman and was born in Baltimore. Age: 32. Prison Depot: Chatham, Prisoner of War #1725. Captured by HMS *Horatio*. When Taken: 13 Dec 1812. Where Taken: Bay of Biscayne. Prize Name: *Powhattan*. Ship Type: Merchant Vessel. Date Received: 25 May 1813 from Portsmouth on HMS Impetius. Discharged on 24 Jul 1813 and released to the Cartel *Hoffning*. (Johnson's Database, 2019)

T

Taggart, Archibald, served as a Private in Capt. Samuel Lane's Co., 14th U.S. Infantry, enlisted 17 May 1812 at Shepherdstown, VA at the age of 36, 5' 11" tall, born in Maryland and captured at Beaver Dams, Upper Canada on 26 Jun 1813. Prisoner of War #893 at Quebec, interned on 7 Jul 1813. (Johnson and Christou, p. 367, stated he was sent to England, but Johnson's Quebec book, p. 150, misspelled his name as Taggent and stated he was discharged on 10 Aug 1813, not indicating whether he was exchanged or sent to England)

Taggart, Thomas, served as a Corporal in the 14th U.S. Infantry (company not stated), enlisted 6 Jul 1812 and captured at Fort Erie, Canada on 17 Sep 1814. Prisoner of War #1863 at Quebec, interned 8 Nov 1814 (Johnson and Christou, p. 368, stated Private Taggart was sent to England, later released and was discharged from the service on 31 Mar 1815; Johnson, p. 150, stated CorporalTaggart was sent to Halifax, NS)

Talbot, Benjamin, served as a Private in Capt. Isaac Barnard's Co., 14th U.S. Infantry, enlisted 9 Nov 1812 and was captured, probably at Beaver Dams, Upper Canada. Prisoner of War #3849 at Halifax, NS, interned 24 Jun 1813, was discharged for exchange on 3 Feb 1814, exchanged on 15 Apr 1814 and was discharged from the service at Greenbush, NY on 23 Jun 1814 (Johnson and Christou, p. 368; Baker Vol. 2, p. 396, spelled his name Talbat)

Talbot, Elijah, served as a Private in Capt. William McIlvane's Co., 14th U.S. Inf., enlisted 21 Jan 1813, age 21, 5' 10" tall, born in Maryland and was captured at Beaver Dams, Upper Canada on 24 Jun 1813. Prisoner of War #3781 at Halifax, NS, interned 24 Jun 1813 and was discharged for exchange on 3 Feb 1814, exchanged 15 Apr 1814 and discharged from service at Plattsburgh, NY on 20 Jul 1814 (Johnson and Christou, p. 368; Baker Vol. 2, p. 396)

Talbot, John H., served as a Private in Capt. William McIlvane's Co., 14th U.S. Inf., enlisted 3 Feb 1813 and captured at Beaver Dams, Upper Canada on 24 Jun 1813. Prisoner of War #3780 at Halifax, NS, interned 24 Jun 1813, discharged for exchange on 3 Feb 1814, exchanged on 15 Apr 1814 and discharged from service at Plattsburgh, NY on 2 Aug 1814 (Johnson and Christou, p. 368, spelled his name Talbott; Baker Vol. 2, p. 396, spelled it Talbot)

Tall, Walter, served as a Private (company not stated) and was captured at the Battle of Bladensburg on 24 Aug 1814 (Marine, p. 175)

Taney, Augustus (1787-1823), served as a Private in Capt. John Heeter's Co., 44th Regiment, Montgomery Co. Militia, and was reported "sick absent" on the muster roll dated 4 Aug – 27 Sep 1814. On 11 Nov 1851 Catherine Taney, age 56, widow of Augustus Taney, resided in Montgomery Co. and stated they were married in Philadelphia, PA on 1 Feb 1821. She was the daughter of the late Thomas Hurley, of Philadelphia. Augustus Taney, Esq., died at Georgetown, DC on 21 Oct 1823, age 36. (Wright Vol. 7, pp. 4, 45; BLW# 50-40-54854; *Baltimore Patriot*, 8 Feb 1821 and 24 Oct 1823; *Baltimore American*, 24 Oct 1823)

Tanner, P. L., served as a Private in Capt. Samuel Sterett's Co., 5th Regiment, Baltimore Militia, from 19 Aug 1814, was taken prisoner on 24 Aug 1814 and later paroled, but the date was not given (Wright Vol. 2, p. 6)

Tap, William, served as a Private in Capt. Clement Sullivan's Co., 14th U.S. Infantry, enlisted 6 May 1812 for 5 years and died on 1 Dec 1812, but the place and cause of death were not stated (Johnson and Christou, p. 369)

Tarman, Joshua, served as a Private in Capt. Samuel Lane's Co., 14th U.S. Inf., enlisted 11 Jun 1812 at Shepherdstown, VA at the age of 20, 5' 9½" tall, born in

Maryland and was captured, date and place not stated. Prisoner of War sent to England (Johnson and Christou, p. 369)

Tarr, Daniel, served as a Private in Capt. Joseph Marshall's Co., 14th U.S. Inf., enlisted 27 Jul 1814 for durarion of the war and died at Greenbush, NY on 19 Jan 1815 (Johnson and Christou, p. 369)

Tarr, Levi, reportedly served as a Private in Capt. Cuyler's Co., 6th MD Regiment, U.S. Infantry, but he is not listed in War of 1812 books by Johnson and Christou, Wright, and Marine, yet he received a pension for having been wounded while serving in said company, but service dates and location were not given. On 7 Jun 1823, In Washington Co., KY, Levi stated he was wounded in the late war and appointed Basil S. Elder as his attorney to collect his $24.00 pension due from 4 Sep 1821 to 4 Mar 1822; he was paid on 27 Jan 1823. (Pierce, p. 179)

Taylor, Abraham S., served as a Private in Capt. Arthur Hayne's Co., 1st U.S. Light Dragoons, enlisted 4 Jan 1812 at Carlisle, PA at age 25, 5' 9" tall, born in Baltimore and was discharged an invalid on 21 Jul 1815, but place and medical specifics were not given (Johnson and Christou, p. 334)

Taylor, Andrew (1790-1814), served as a Private in Capt. Willis Foulk's Co., 22nd U.S. Infantry, enlisted 24 May 1814 for the war at the age of 24, 5' 10½" tall, was born in Maryland and died at Fort Erie, Upper Canada on 1 Sep 1814 from camp disease; bounty land was issued to his father Andrew Taylor and other heirs at law (BLW# 26381-160-12; Johnson and Christou, p. 369)

Taylor, Benjamin, served as a Private in Capt. Thomas F. W. Vinson's Co., 32nd Regiment, Montgomery Co. Militia, Extra Battalion, from 1 Aug 1814, was taken prisoner at the Battle of Bladensburg on 24 Aug 1814 and later exchanged. He moved to Washington Co., KY by 1820 and was age 62 in 1850, age 73 in 1860 and died before 1870. (Wright Vol. 7, pp. 5, 45; BLW# 55-160-37371; Censuses)

Taylor, James, served as a Seaman and was born in Maryland. Age: 30. Prison Depot: Plymouth 1, Prisoner of War #2163. How Taken: Gave himself up off MV *Princess*. When Taken: 1 Nov 1813. Where Taken: Liverpool, UK. Date Received: 13 Dec 1813. From what ship: HMS *Bittern*. Discharged on 31 Jan 1814 and sent to Dartmoor. Prison Depot: Dartmoor, Prisoner of War #879. Received: 31 Jan 1814 from Plymouth. Discharged on 27 Apr 1815. (Johnson's Database, 2019)

Taylor, John, served as a Seaman and was born in Annapolis. Age: 29. Prison Depot: Plymouth 2, Prisoner of War #133. How Taken: Gave himself up. When Taken: 7 Feb 1815. Where Taken: Portsmouth, UK. Date Received: 21 Feb 1815. From what ship: HMS *Slaney*. Discharged on 24 Feb 1815 and sent to Dartmoor. Prison Depot: Dartmoor, Prisoner of War #6387. Date Received: 24 Feb 1815.

From what ship: HMT *Ganges* from Plymouth. Discharged on 11 Jul 1815. (Johnson's Database, 2019)

Taylor, John (1769-1813), served as a Private in Capt. Joseph Marshall's Co., 14th U.S. Infantry, enlisted 4 Aug 1812 for 5 years at the age of 43, 5' 9" tall, born in Jersey and died at Black Rock, NY on 21 Feb 1813, cause not stated; widow Deborah Taylor received half pay for 5 years in lieu of bounty land (Old War CF-1068; BLW# 26779-160-12; Johnson and Christou, pp. 369-370)

Taylor, John (1792-1814), served as a Private in Capt. Abraham Hawkins' Co., 4th U.S. Infantry, enlisted 2 May 1814 for the war at the age of 22, 5' 5½" tall, born in Annapolis and died at Plattsburgh, NY in 1814; cause of death was not stated, but most probably service connected (Johnson and Christou, p. 370)

Taylor, John, served as a Private in Capt. James McDonald's Co., 14th U.S. Infantry, enlisted 1 Apr 1814 for 5 years at Williamsport, MD at the age of 35, 5' 6" tall, dark eyes, dark hair, dark complexion, born in Frederick, MD, was sick at Plattsburg, NY and discharged at Greenbush, NY on 1 Jun 1815 due to disability (Johnson and Christou, p. 370; Mallick and Wright, p. 287)

Taylor, John N. (1783-1815), served as a Private in Capt. George Goodman's Co., 32nd U.S. Infantry, enlisted 20 Jan 1814 for 1 year at Shippensburg, PA at the age of 31, 5' 8" tall, born in Maryland, re-enlisted on 16 Feb 1814 and died on 14 Feb 1815, but the cause was not stated (Johnson and Christou, p. 370)

Taylor, Joseph (1773-1829), served as a Private in Capt. Caleb Holder's Co., 17th U.S. Inf., enlisted 23 Sep 1814 at Dayton, OH at the age of 41, 5' 8" tall, born in Washington Co., MD and discharged on 9 Jun 1816 on a Surgeon's Certificate, but the place and medical reason were not stated (Johnson and Christou, p. 370). "Died at the house of Mrs. Kendal in this place [Hagerstown] ... Joseph Taylor, Esq. ... Washington City, in the 56th year of his [age] ... He arrived here about 2 weeks ago, with his Lady on his way to Bedford Springs for the benefit of his health, but his journey was arrested in consequence of his illness, which ended in his death after several days of severe suffering." (*The Torchlight and Public Advertiser*, Hagerstown, 4 Jun 1829)

Taylor, Joshua, served as a Private in Capt. T. Wheeler's Co., Montgomery Co. Militia, enrolled on 30 Apr 1813 and died on 30 May 1813 (Wright Vol. 7, p. 7)

Taylor, Richard, served as a Private in Capt. Reuben Gilder's Co., 14th U.S. Infantry, enlisted 1 May 1812 at Havre de Grace [Harford Co.], MD, age 26, 5' 8" tall, born in Juniata Co., PA and was captured at Beaver Dams, Upper Canada on 24 Jun 1813 by Commander Yeo. Prisoner of War #7526, interned 27 Oct 1814, discharged for exchange on 5 Mar 1815, exchanged on 11 May 1815, returned to service and reportedly deserted on 1 Jun 1816, yet Richard and his widow Ann

M. Taylor both received a pension (SO-2946, SC-5817, WO-20589, WC-27867; Johnson and Christou, p. 370; Baker Vol. 2, p. 399)

Taylor, Thomas, served as a Private in Capt. John Berry's Co., 1st Artillery Regiment, Baltimore City, in service at Fort McHenry from 19 Aug to 25 Aug 1813 and from 19 Aug 1814 until listed as "deceased Oct 5" on the muster roll dated 19 Aug – 30 Nov 1814 (Wright Vol. 2, pp. 44, 49)

Taylor, Thomas, served as a Private in Capt. William McIlvane's Co., 14th U.S. Infantry, enlisted 23 Mar 1813, age 35, 5' 8" tall, born in Ireland and discharged at Greenbush, NY on 4 May 1815 from a rupture (Johnson and Christou, p. 371)

Taylor, Thomas H., served as a Private in Capt. Reuben Gilder's Co., 14th U.S. Infantry, enlisted 5 Feb 1813 in Baltimore, age 28, 5' 6" tall, born in Bleturbet, County Cavan, Ireland and was captured, date and place not stated. Prisoner of War, exchanged on 11 May 1814; the soldier and his widow Elizabeth Taylor both received pensions (SO-23364, WO-27116; Johnson and Christou, p. 371)

Taylor, William (1772-1813), served as a Private in Capt. Reuben Gilder's Co., 14th U.S. Infantry, enlisted 12 Aug 1812, age 40, 5' 11" tall, born on the Eastern Shore of Maryland and died at Sackett's Harbor, NY in 1813, exact date was not given; bounty land was issued to his daughter and only heir Esther Denston (BLW# 26010-160-12; Johnson and Christou, p. 371)

Taylor, William, served as a Seaman and was born in Maryland. Age: 22. Prison Depot: Dartmoor, Prisoner of War #3658. Captured by HM Frigate *Spartan*. When Taken: 13 Jun 1813. Where Taken: off Delaware. Prize Name: *Globe*. Ship Type: Privateer. Date Received: 30 Sep 1814 on HMT *President*. Discharged on 4 Jun 1815. (Johnson's Database, 2019)

Teller, Aquila, served as a Private in Capt. Denton Darby's Co., Frederick Co. Militia, from 3 Aug 1814 and was wounded in action on 24 Aug 1814 during the Battle of Bladensburg (Wright Vol. 8, pp. 12, 287; Mallick and Wright, pp. 287, 348); see Aquilla Tulley, q.v.

Templeton, William (1793-1865), served as a Private in Capt. Adam Barnes' Co., Watkins' Regiment, Anne Arundel Co., from 16 Apr to 31 Jul 1813 and he stated in 1851, age 58, that he was drafted at Elk Ridge in September 1812 and was discharged at Annapolis around mid-October 1813 "in consequence of sickness." William Templeton lived in Orbisonia, Cromwell Twp., Huntington Co., PA before 1851, applied for bounty land in 1855, age 61, and died on 8 Mar 1865, age 72. His tombstone in Orbisonia Cemetery is inscribed "A Soldier of the War of 1812" and his wife was Anna Templeton (1797-1868). (BLW# 55-80-41219; Wright Vol. 4, pp. 41, 126; www.findagrave.com)

Terney, John, served as a Private in the 14th U.S. Infantry (company not stated) and was captured, probably at Beaver Dams, Upper Canada on 24 Jun 1813. Prisoner of War #3962 at Halifax, NS, interned 24 Jun 1813, discharged 24 Aug 1813 and sent to England (Johnson and Christou, p. 371; Baker Vol. 2, p. 400)

Tevis (Tivis), Peter (1780-1815), served as a Corporal in the 17th U.S. Infantry, enlisted on 24 or 28 Feb 1814 for duration of the war, age 34, 5' 10" tall, born in Maryland and died on 10 Jan 1815, but cause was not stated; heirs received half pay for 5 years in lieu of bounty land (Johnson and Christou, pp. 371, 376)

Thelis, James, served as a Seaman on the privateer *Globe* and was killed in action on 1 Nov 1813 (*Niles Weekly Register*, 19 Feb 1814)

Thistlewood, Charles, served as a Private in Capt. Henry Fleming's Co., 14th U.S. Infantry, enlisted 24 Dec 1812, age 25, 5' tall, born in Kent Co., DE and was captured, probably at Beaver Dams, Upper Canada. Prisoner of War #4812 at Halifax, NS, interned 24 Jun 1813, discharged 19 Nov 1813 and sent to England, later released and was discharged from the service on 31 Mar 1815 (Johnson and Christou, pp. 371-372; Baker Vol. 2, p. 400, also inexplicably listed Charles as Prisoner of War #3824 with slightly different dates for intern and discharge)

Thomas, Henry (African American), served as a Seaman and was born in Baltimore. Age: 23. Prison Depot: Plymouth 1, Prisoner of War #462. Captured by HM Ship-of-the-Line *Colossus*. When Taken: 5 Jan 1813. Where Taken: off Western Islands, Scotland. Prize Name: *Dolphin*. Home Port: Philadelphia. Ship Type: Letter of Marque. Date Received: 6 Feb 1813. From what ship: HMS *Rhin*. Discharged and sent to Chatham on 29 Mar 1813 on HMS *Braham*. Prison Depot: Chatham, Prisoner of War #1564. Age 25. Date Received: 8 Apr 1813 from Plymouth on HMS *Olympia*. Discharged on 18 Oct 1813 and released to HMS *Ceres*. (Johnson's Database, 2019)

Thomas, John (Mulatto), served as a Steward and was born in Maryland. Age: 29. Prison Depot: Portsmouth, Prisoner of War #1387. Captured by *Vittoria*, Guernsey Privateer. When Taken: 28 Jan 1814. Where Taken: off Bordeaux, France. Prize Name: *Pilot*. Home Port: Baltimore. Ship Type: Letter of Marque. Date Received: 7 Feb 1814. From what ship: *Mary* from Guernsey. Discharged on 13 Feb 1814 and sent to Chatham on HMT *Malabar No. 352*. Prison Depot: Chatham, Prisoner of War #3516. Date Received: 23 Feb 1814 from Portsmouth on HMT *Malabar*. Discharged on 25 Sep 1814 and sent to Dartmoor on HMS *Niobe*. Prison Depot: Dartmoor, Prisoner of War #4284. Date Received: 7 Oct 1814. From what ship: HMT *Niobe* from Chatham. Discharged on 14 Jun 1815. (Johnson's Database, 2019)

Thomas, John (African American), served as a Seaman and was born in Maryland. Age: 29. Prison Depot: Dartmoor, Prisoner of War #4186. Captured by *Vittoria*,

Guernsey Privateer. When Taken: 28 Jan 1814. Where Taken: off Bordeaux, France. Prize Name: *Pilot*. Home Port: Baltimore. Ship Type: Letter of Marque (Privateer). Date Received: 7 Oct 1814. From what ship: HMT *Niobe* from Chatham. Discharged on 11 Jul 1815. (Johnson's Database, 2019)

Thomas, John (African American), served as a Seaman and was born in Baltimore. Age: 20. Prison Depot: Dartmoor, Prisoner of War #5224. Captured by HM Transport *Dover*. When Taken: 27 Jun 1813. Where Taken: off Newfoundland. Prize Name: *Whig*. Home Port: Baltimore. Ship Type: Privateer. Date Received: 31 Oct 1814 on HMT *Mermaid* from Chatham. Discharged on 14 Jun 1815. (Johnson's Database, 2019)

Thomas, John, served as a Seaman and was born in Havre de Grace, MD. Age: 19. Prison Depot: Dartmoor, Prisoner of War #4116. Captured by HM Frigate *Niemen*. When Taken: 28 Jun 1814. Where Taken: off Delaware. Prize Name: *Bordeaux Packet*. Home Port: Baltimore. Ship Type: Letter of Marque. Date Received: 6 Oct 1814. From what ship: HMT *Chesapeake* from Halifax, NS. Discharged on 13 Jun 1815. (Johnson's Database, 2019) Prisoner of War at Dartmoor in Devon, England for 250 days from 6 Oct 1814 to 13 Jun 1815. ("Harford County in the War of 1812," by Christopher T. George, *Harford Historical Bulletin* No. 76, Spring 1998, p. 21 footnote)

Thomas, John, served as a Seaman and was born in Maryland. Age: 19. Prison Depot: Dartmoor, Prisoner of War #5806. Captured by British gunboats. When Taken: 26 Aug 1814. Where Taken: Lake Ontario. Prize Name: U.S. Frigate *Superior* (ship's gigg). Ship Type: Warship. Date Received: 26 Dec 1814. From what ship: HMT *Argo*. Discharged on 3 Jul 1815. (Johnson's Database, 2019)

Thomas, John, served as a Private in Capt. Thomas T. Simmons' Co., 2nd Regt., Anne Arundel Co. Militia, from 28 Sep 1814 and was reported "absent sick" on the muster roster dated 18 Oct – 1 Dec 1814 (Wright Vol. 4, p. 29)

Thomas, Josiah, served as a Private in Capt. Richard Clarke's Co., 12th Regiment, St. Mary's Co. Militia, from 23 Aug to 31 Aug 1813 and "still on duty on board a N. Caroline Schooner captured on the 29th inst. on suspicion of having been treading with the British." (Wright Vol. 5, p. 13)

Thomas, Samuel, served as a Captain of the Talbot Co. Volunteers Artillery Co., attached to the 12th Brigade, stationed at Easton Point, and the muster roll dated 14 Apr – 1 Jun 1813 reported, "Captain Thomas was sick and unable to attend during the whole time of the service of this company. We had volunteer guards for several days previously in which Capt. Thomas was very active day and night & I think it probably was the cause of his disability …" Signed by "Clement Vickars," 1st Lieutenant (Wright Vol. 1, p. 102)

Thomas, Terry (African American), served as a Seaman and was born in Talbot Co., MD. Age: 31. Prison Depot: Chatham, Prisoner of War #274. How Taken: Gave himself up. When Taken: 10 Dec 1812. Where Taken: London, UK. Date Received: 23 Dec 1812. From what ship: HMS *Raisonable*. Discharged on 24 Jul 1813 and released to the Cartel *Hoffning*. (Johnson's Database, 2019)

Thomas, William, served as a Seaman and was born in Maryland. Age: 21. Prison Depot: Dartmoor, Prisoner of War #2206. Captured by HM Ship-of-the-Line *Saturn*. When Taken: 25 May 1814. Where Taken: off Sandy Hook, NJ. Prize Name: *Hussar*. Home Port: New York. Ship Type: Privateer. Date Received: 16 Aug 1814. From what ship: HMS *Dublin* from Halifax, NS. Discharged on 2 May 1815. (Johnson's Database, 2019)

Thomas, William, served as Surgeon under Lt. Col. James Brown in 35th Regt., Queen Anne's Co., appointed 7 Nov 1810 and "now dead;" no date and cause noted, but his replacement was appointed on 4 Jul 1813 (Wright Vol. 1, p. ii)

Thomas, William, served as a Private in Capt. Thomas Montgomery's Co., 14th U.S. Infantry, enlisted 10 Dec 1812 at Hagerstown at the age of 42, 5' 5" tall, born in Warwick, England and discharged at Greenbush, NY on 4 May 1815 on Surgeon's Certificate, medical reason not stated (Johnson and Christou, p. 372)

Thomas, William, served as a Private in Capt. William McIlvane's Co., 14th U.S. Infantry, enlisted 30 Jan 1813, age 22, 5' 5" tall, born in Pennsylvania and was captured, probably at Beaver Dams, Upper Canada. Prisoner of War #3983 at Halifax, NS, interned 24 Jun 1813, was discharged for exchange on 3 Feb 1814, exchanged 15 Apr 1814, returned to service and was discharged at Plattsburgh, NY on 28 Jul 1814 (Johnson and Christou, p. 372; Baker Vol. 2, p. 402)

Thompson, Amos, served as a Private in Capt. Reuben Gilder's Co., 14th U.S. Infantry, enlisted 7 Oct 1812 and died on 29 Dec 1813, medical reason was not stated; bounty land issued to brother William Thompson and other heirs at law (BLW# 25557-160-12; Johnson and Christou, p. 373)

Thompson, Barnard, served as a Private (company not stated) and was captured at the Battle of Bladensburg on 24 Aug 1814 (Marine, p. 175)

Thompson, Henry, served as a Seaman and was born in Tunsbug, MD. Age: 27. Prison Depot: Chatham, Prisoner of War #352. Captured by HM Sloop *Helena*. When Taken: 31 Dec 1813. Where Taken: off Azores. Prize Name: *Postsea*, prize of the Privateer *Thrasher*. Ship Type: Privateer. Date Received: 19 Jan 1813. From what ship: HMS *Raisonable*. Discharged on 28 Apr 1813 and released to the *David Scott*. (Johnson's Database, 2019)

Thompson, John, served as a Seaman and was born in Baltimore. Age: 30. Prison Depot: Dartmoor, Prisoner of War #3525. Captured by HM Ship-of-the-Line

Conquestador. When Taken: 3 Aug 1814. Where Taken: off Grand Banks. Prize Name: *Sabine*. Prize. Ship Type: Privateer. Date Received: 28 Sep 1814. From what ship: HMT *Salvador del Mundo*. Discharged on 4 Jun 1815. (Johnson's Database, 2019)

Thompson, John, served as a Seaman and was born in Baltimore. Age: 16. Prison Depot: Portsmouth, Prisoner of War #549. Captured by HM Frigate *Dryad*. When Taken: 7 Jan 1813. Where Taken: at sea. Prize Name: *Rossie*. Ship Type: Merchant Vessel. Received: 25 Jan 1813. From what ship: HM Ship-of-the-Line *Queen*. Discharged on 11 Mar 1813 and sent to Chatham on HM Store Ship *Abundance*. (Johnson's Database, 2019)

Thompson, John, served as a Private in Capt. Reuben Gilder's Co., 14th U.S. Infantry, enlisted on 17 Sep 1812 for 5 years and was discharged on 23 Jul 1815 for inability (Johnson and Christou, p. 373)

Thompson, Jonathan, served as a Private in Capt. Richard Arell's Co., 14th U.S. Infantry, enlisted 29 Apr 1812 at Hagerstown, MD, age 40, 5' 8" tall, born in Lancaster, PA and was later captured, probably at Beaver Dams, Upper Canada. Prisoner of War #4074 at Halifax, NS, interned 24 Jun 1813, was discharged for exchange on 3 Feb 1814, exchanged on 15 Apr 1814, returned to service and discharged on 29 Apr 1817 (Johnson and Christou, p. 374; Baker Vol. 2, p. 403)

Thompson, Peter, served as a Seaman and was born in Maryland. Age: 26. Prison Depot: Plymouth 1, Prisoner of War #2251. Captured by HM Frigate *Belle Poule*. When Taken: 14 Dec 1813. Where Taken: Bay of Biscayne. Prize Name: *Squirrel*. Ship Type: Merchant Vessel. Date Received: 15 Jan 1814. From what ship: HMS *Teazer*. Discharged on 31 Jan 1814 and was sent to Dartmoor. Prison Depot: Dartmoor, Prisoner of War #917. Date Received: 31 Jan 1814 from Plymouth. Discharged on 27 Apr 1815. (Johnson's Database, 2019)

Thompson, Robert, served as a Private in Capt. Francis Thompson's Co., 43rd Regiment, Charles Co. Militia, from 22 Jul 1814 and was furloughed sick on 6 Aug 1814 (Wright Vol. 5, p. 42)

Thompson, Thomas (Mulatto), served as a Seaman and was born in Maryland. Age: 39. Prison Depot: Plymouth 1, Prisoner of War #1400. Captured by HM Brig *Orestes*. When Taken: 13 Apr 1813. Where Taken: Bay of Biscayne. Prize Name: *Henry Clements*. Ship Type: Merchant Vessel. Date Received: 15 May 1813. From what ship: HMS *Salvador del Mundo*. Discharged on 23 May 1813. (Johnson's Database, 2019)

Thompson, William, served as a Seaman on the privateer *Surprise* of Baltimore and drowned in a shipwreck on 5 Apr 1815 (Marine p. 461; *Niles Weekly Register*, 15 Apr 1815)

Thomson, Hugh (c1788-1852), served as Ensign under Capt. William Farquhar and as 2nd Lieutenant under Capt. Henry Lowrey, was called into service from Taneytown on 26 Jul 1814, was wounded at Bladensburg on 24 Aug 1814 and discharged at Annapolis. He married Elizabeth Sponsellar on 5 Feb 1811 and died in Taneytown, Carroll Co., MD on 18 Dec 1852. (BLW# 50-80-8833, BLW# 55-80-7718; Pension WO-397; Wright, Vol. 9, p.4; Mallick and Wright, p. 288)

Thorn, Ephraim (1784-1815), served as a Private in Capt. Hopley Yeaton's Co., 1st U.S. Artillery, enlisted 8 Dec 1810 for 5 years in Washington, DC at the age of 26, 6' 1½" tall, born in Prince George's Co., MD and died at Fort Nelson, VA on 22 Mar 1815, cause of death was not stated (Johnson and Christou, p. 375)

Thornell, William, served as a Private in Capt. Reuben Gilder's Co., 14th U.S. Infantry, enlisted 22 Jul 1813 in Baltimore at age 23, 5' 7" tall, born in Baltimore and discharged at Greenbush, NY on 4 May 1815 because of wounds (BLW# 6549-160-12; Johnson and Christou, p. 375)

Thrasher, John, served as a Seaman and was born in Maryland. Age: 24. Prison Depot: Chatham, Prisoner of War #2749. Captured by HM Schooner *Bream*. When Taken: 9 Jun 1813. Where Taken: off Halifax, NS. Prize Name: *Wasp*. Home Port: Salem. Ship Type: Privateer. Date Received: 7 Jan 1814 from Halifax, NS. Discharged on 8 Sep 1814 and sent to Dartmoor on HMS *Niobe*. Prison Depot: Dartmoor, Prisoner of War #3392. Date Received: 13 Sep 1814. From what ship: HMT *Niobe* from Chatham. Discharged on 28 May 1815. (Johnson's Database, 2019)

Thrush, George, served as a Private in Capt. Shepperd Leakin's Co., 38th U.S. Infantry, enlistment date not given, age 40, 5' 10" tall, born in Baltimore and was discharged on 11 Jan 1815 due to old age (Johnson and Christou, p. 375)

Tilden, William D., served as a Surgeon in Lt. Col. William Spencer's 33rd Regt., Kent Co., appointed 20 Aug 1813, now dead (no date and no cause of death), but his replacement was appointed on 13 Oct 1814. (Wright Vol. 1, p. ii)

Tilkins, John, served as a Private in the 14th U.S. Infantry (company not stated) and was captured, probably at Beaver Dams, Upper Canada. Prisoner of War #3844 at Halifax, NS, interned 24 Jun 1813 and discharged for exchange on 3 Feb 1814 (Johnson and Christou, p. 376; Baker Vol. 2, p. 406)

Timms, James R. (1786-1813), served as a Sergeant in Capt. John Stanard's Co., 20th U.S. Inf., enlisted 26 Jul 1812 at the age of 26, 5' 8" tall, born in Charles Co., MD and died on 3 Mar 1813 at Williamsport, NY, cause of death not stated; bounty land was issued to his father and only heir Joseph Timms (BLW# 25190-160-12; Johnson and Christou, p. 376)

Tingstrum, Peter, served as a Private under Capt. James F. Huston and Capt. Lewis Weaver in the Frederick Co. Militia and was sick in Fredericktown since 30 Sep 1814 (Mallick and Wright, p. 345)

Tinnus, John, served as a Private in Capt. John Whistler's Co., 1st U.S. Infantry, enlisted 7 Mar 1810 in Detroit or 5 years, at the age of 34, 5' 7½" tall, born Charles Co., MD and was captured, place and date not stated. Prisoner of War on parole, place and date not stated, and died at Greenbush, NY on 17 May 1815 (Johnson and Christou, p. 376)

Tipton, Solomon, served as a Seaman and was born in Baltimore. Age: 53 (sic). Prison Depot: Plymouth 1, Prisoner of War #372. Captured by HM Brig *Achates*. When Taken: 29 Jan 1813. Where Taken: Lat 44N Long 13W. Prize Name: *Orbit*. Ship Type: Merchant Vessel. Date Received: 4 Feb 1813. From what ship: HMS Achates. Discharged and sent to Chatham on 29 Mar 1813 on HMS *Braham*. Prison Depot: Chatham, Prisoner of War #1446. Date Received: 6 Apr 1813 from Plymouth on HMS *Decoy*. Discharged on 24 Jul 1814 and was sent to Dartmoor. Prison Depot: Dartmoor, Prisoner of War #1973. [Tipton was mistakenly copied as Ripton by the compiler.] Date Received: 3 Aug 1814. From what ship: HMS *Lyffey* from Chatham Depot. Discharged on 2 May 1815. (Johnson's Database, 2019)

Titus, John (African American), served as a Seaman and was born in Baltimore. Age: 31. Prison Depot: Dartmoor, Prisoner of War #3641. Captured by HM Frigate *Niemen*. When Taken: 28 Jan 1814. Where Taken: off Delaware. Prize Name: *Bordeaux Packet*. Home Port: Baltimore. Ship Type: Letter of Marque. Date Received: 30 Sep 1814. From what ship: HMT *Sybella*. Discharged on 4 Jun 1815. (Johnson's Database, 2019)

Todd, John, served as a Private in Capt. David Cummings' Co., 14th U.S. Infantry, enlisted on 14 May 1812 and was captured at Beaver Dams, Upper Canada, ten miles west of Niagara Falls, on 24 Jun 1813. Prisoner of War #3953 at Halifax, NS, interned 24 Jun 1813, discharged on 27 Aug 1813 and sent to England on HMS *Regulus*. Prison Depot: Chatham, Prisoner of War #2619. Age 40. Born in Maryland. Date Received: 5 Nov 1813. From what ship: HMS *Hindostan*. Discharged on 10 Oct 1814 and sent to U.S. on the Cartel *St. Philip*, returned to service and was discharged on 30 Apr 1815 on a Surgeon's Certificate (Johnson and Christou, p. 377; Baker Vol. 2, p. 407; Johnson's Database, 201.; *Baltimore American and Commercial Advertiser*, 19 Nov 1813; *Niles Weekly Register*, 20 Nov 1813 reported that John Todd, of Prince George's Co., was "impressed from a prison ship at Quebec")

Toland, Aquila (1793-1866), served as a Private, then as 3rd Corporal, in Capt. James Rampley's Co., Harford Co. Militia, 42nd Regiment, and was called out or enrolled around 28 Aug 1814 at Cook's Tavern and continued in service for two months except for what time he was sick with the measles and taken to the hospital which was about the time of the attack on Baltimore on 12 Sep 1814. He was a corporal when discharged at Baltimore on 27 Oct 1814 and moved to London, OH after the war. On 23 Jan 1854, age 60, he applied for bounty land in Medina Co., OH and died in 1866. His wife was Elizabeth Lewis. (Wright Vol. 3, pp. 31, 69; BLW# 55-160-13029; *1812 Ancestor Index Volume I, 1892-1970*, National Society United States Daughters of 1812, 2005, p. 504)

Tomlin, George (1783-1813), served as Commander of U.S. Navy *Gunboat No. 153* and died on 22 Aug 1813, age 30, formerly of Baltimore. "Savannah paper." (*Baltimore Patriot*, 8 Sep 1813)

Tonlinson, John, served as a Private in 14th U.S. Infantry (company not stated) and was captured at Beaver Dams, Upper Canada on 24 Jun 1813. Prisoner of War #4014 at Halifax, NS, interned 24 Jun 1813, discharged on 9 Nov 1813 and sent to England (Johnson and Christou, p. 377; Baker Vol. 2, p. 408)

Totten, Edmond, served as a Private in Capt. Adam Barnes' Co., Watkins' Regt. Anne Arundel Co. Militia, between 16 Apr and 31 Jul 1813 and was reported on that muster roll as sick in hospital, but no date was given (Wright Vol. 4, p. 41)

Tottman, John, served as a Private in Capt. Benjamin Thomas' Co., 49th Regt., Cecil Co. Militia, for 14 days between 18 Apr 1813 and 16 May 1813 and was "discharged on account of health" (Wright Vol. 3, p. 13)

Towers, James, served as Captain and late Sailing Master of the *Comet*, dates of service not stated, and died on 8 Apr 1813, a resident of 71 Albemarle St. in Baltimore (*Baltimore Federal Gazette*, 8 Apr 1813)

Townsend, Marshal (1788-1816), served as a Private in Capt. Walter Overton's Co., 7th U.S. Infantry, enlisted 11 Oct 1808 at the age of 20, 5' 9" tall, born in Maryland, re-enlisted at Fort Claiborne on 26 Oct 1813 for five years and died in New Orleans on 24 Jul 1816, cause not stated (Johnson and Christou, p. 377)

Townsend, Samuel, served as a Corporal under Lt. Col. George Armistead in the 1st U.S Artillery, enlisted 22 Feb 1812 at Fort McHenry at age 26, 5' 6¼" tall, born in Maryland and was discharged as an invalid in New York City on 21 Jul 1814 (Johnson and Christou, p. 377)

Towson, Benjamin (1770-1814), served as a Private in Capt. William Adair's Co., 17th U.S. Infantry, enlisted 8 Feb 1814 for the duration of the war at the age of 44, 5' 10" tall, born in Maryland and died on 13 Dec 1814; heirs received half pay for 5 years in lieu of bounty land (Johnson and Christou, pp. 377-378)

Towson, William, served as a Musician in Capt. William Henshaw's Co., 5th U.S. Infantry, enlisted 19 Apr 1813 in Baltimore at the age of 21, 5' 8¼" tall, born in Towsontown, MD and discharged at Buffalo, NY on 21 Jan 1815 on a Surgeon's Certificate due to diseased lungs (Johnson and Christou, p. 377)

Towson, William, served as a ship's Carpenter and was born in Maryland. Age: 26. Prison Depot: Dartmoor, Prisoner of War #2565. Captured by HM Frigate *Hyperion*. When Taken: 25 Jun 1814. Where Taken: off Cape Finisterre, Spain. Prize Name: *Rattlesnake*. Home Port: Philadelphia. Ship Type: Privateer. Date Received: 21 Aug 1814. From what ship: HMS *Hyperion*. Discharged on 3 May 1815. (Johnson's Database, 2019)

Towson, William, served as a Second Mate and was born in Maryland. Age: 25. Prison Depot: Plymouth 1, Prisoner of War #957. Captured by HM Frigate *Andromache*. When Taken: 14 Mar 1813. Where Taken: off Nantes, France. Prize Name: *Courier*. Home Port: Baltimore. Ship Type: Letter of Marque (Privateer). Date Received: 7 Apr 1813. From what ship: HMS *Sea Lark*. Discharged and sent to Dartmoor on 28 Jun 1813. Prison Depot: Dartmoor, Prisoner of War #350. Date Received: 28 Jun 1813 from Plymouth. Discharged on 20 Apr 1815. (Johnson's Database, 2019)

Tracey, John, served as a Private in Capt. Conrad Hook's Co., Baltimore Co., 2nd Regt., 11th Brigade, stationed at Camp Hampstead in Baltimore from 25 Jul 1814 and was listed as "sick absent Aug 24 – Oct 14 & Oct 29 – Dec 1" 1814 (Wright Vol. 2, p. 81)

Tracey, Richard (1784-1814), served as a Private in Capt. John Rothrock's Co., 38th U.S. Infantry, enlisted 13 Jan 1814 at the age of 30, 5' 7" tall, born in Baltimore and died on 2 Oct 1814; bounty land to his sister Amelia Tracey and other heirs at law (BLW# 23228-160-12; Johnson and Christou, p. 378)

Tracey, William, served as a Private in Capt. Stephen H. Moore's Co., Balti-more Volunteers Infantry Co., from 8 Sep 1812 for 1 year and was discharged at Baltimore on 24 Sep 1812 as unfit for service (Wright Vol. 2, p. 57)

Tracy, Garrard, served as a Private in Capt. John Rochester's Co., 29th U.S. Inf., enlisted 8 Mar 1814 for 5 years at Sackett's Harbor, NY at the age of 27, 5' 7½" tall, born in Baltimore and discharged at Plattsburgh, NY on 20 Oct 1818 due to disability (Johnson and Christou, p. 378)

Tracy, Isaiah (1788-1872), served as a Private in Capt. Lawson Cuddy's Co., Nace's Regiment, Baltimore Co. Militia, from 17 Aug to 10 Sep 1813, was a Private in Capt. James Almoney's Co., 41st Regiment, Baltimore Co., from 25 Aug 1814 and was "sick-absent from Oct 10" 1814 (Wright Vol. 2, p. 66). He died on

22 Mar 1872 in his 84th year and was buried in Wiseburg Cemetery at White Hall, Baltimore Co. (Smith's Database, 2019; www.findagrave.com)

Tracy, William, served as a Private in Capt. William McIlvane's Co., 14th U.S. Infantry, enlisted 21 Dec 1812 for 5 years and captured at Beaver Dams, Upper Canada, ten miles west of Niagara Falls, on 24 Jun 1813. Prisoner of War #3784 at Halifax, was discharged for exchange on 3 Feb 1814 and died at Whitehall in 1814; bounty land was issued to Caroline Tracy, his daughter and only heir (BLW# 26905-160-12; Johnson and Christou, p. 379; Baker, Vol. 2, p. 409)

Trainor, James, served as a Private in Capt. Nathan Towson's Co., 2nd U.S. Artillery, enlisted 12 Apr 1812 in Baltimore, age 18, 5' 5" tall, born in Baltimore and captured during the Battle of Stoney Creek [in June 1813]. Prisoner of War, place not named, later released, returned to service and was discharged at Fort Niagara, NY on 12 Apr 1817 (Johnson and Christou, p. 379)

Trapin, Joseph (1782-1815), served as a Private in Capt. Richard Bell's Co., 5th U.S. Infantry, enlisted 4 Mar 1814 for 5 years in Harrisburg, PA at the age of 32, 5' 10" tall, born in Baltimore and died at Buffalo, NY on 13 Feb 1815, cause of death not stated (Johnson and Christou, p. 379)

Travers, Thomas (African American), served as a Seaman and was born in Maryland. Age: 28. Prison Depot: Chatham, Prisoner of War #3244. How Taken: Gave himself up off HMS *Conqueror*. When Taken: 26 Dec 1813. Where Taken: Gravesend, UK. Date Received: 14 Feb 1814. From what ship: HMS *Raisonable*. Discharged on 26 Sep 1814. Sent to Dartmoor on HMS *Leyden*. Prison Depot: Dartmoor, Prisoner of War #4711. Date Received: 9 Oct 1814 from HMT *Freya* from Chatham. Discharged on 11 Jul 1815. (Johnson's Database, 2019)

Troth, George, served as a Master's Mate and was born in Maryland. Age: 23. Prison Depot: Dartmoor, Prisoner of War #3520. Captured by HM Sloop *Martin*. When Taken: 30 Jun 1814. Where Taken: off Halifax, NS. Prize Name: *Snap Dragon*. Ship Type: Privateer. Received: 28 Sep 1814. From what ship: HMT *Salvador del Mundo*. Discharged on 3 May 1815. (Johnson's Database, 2019)

Trott, Sabret (1786-1858), served as a Private in Capt. William S. Tillard's Co., 2nd Regiment, Anne Arundel Co. Militia, for 2 days between 18 Aug and 27 Aug 1814 and in Capt. Thomas T. Simmons' Co. from 28 Sep to 17 Oct 1814 and was discharged on 1 Dec 1814 at Baltimore, 45 miles from home; earlier, "Sabut Trott Jr." was a private in Capt. William S. Tillard's Co. for 16 days between 1 Aug and 30 Aug 1813. On 12 Jul 1853 Sabret Trott, age 67, stated he enrolled at Tracy's Landing as a private in the company commanded by Capt. Simmons, a company of drafted men from the 22nd Regiment, and marched from Tracy's Landing to Bladensburg and thence to Baltimore; on the march to Baltimore Capt. Simmons was taken sick and he was detailed to remain with and attend on the captain;

while engaged in that duty he was taken sick himself, but he and the captain both recovered and were at their posts at Baltimore with their company on the 12th, 13th and 14th of September 1814. Sometime after the battle and the British fleet having moved down the Bay he learned that the enemy had landed and plundered his family of everything, leaving them in great distress. He applied for and obtained a furlough for a few days to go home and arriving there he found the report to be true, for they had not even left a fowl or a vegetable. He returned to Baltimore in accordance with his furlough and was discharged. As to his Christian name, to the best of his recollection he was often called Gabret or Gabriel and why it was so he cannot tell, but one thing he is certain of – there was no other person of the name of Trott in the company under the command of Capt. Simmons but himself. In 1853, age 67, he was living in Baltimore County and in 1855, age 69, he was living in Baltimore. "Sabriet Trott" died 4 Sep 1858, age 74 (sic). (Wright Vol. 4, pp. 28, 29, 30, 127; BLW# 55-120-46902; *The [Baltimore] Sun*, 15 Sep 1858)

Tucker, Benjamin, served as a Private in Capt. William McIlvane's Co., 14th U.S. Infantry, enlisted 25 Aug 1812 for 5 years at the age of 38, 5' 7" tall, born in Calvert Co., MD and captured at Beaver Dams, Upper Canada on 24 Jun 1813. Prisoner of War #3765 at Halifax, NS, interned 24 Jun 1813, was discharged for exchange on 3 Feb 1813, exchanged on 15 Apr 1814, returned to service and was discharged at Fort Crawford, GA on 17 Nov 1816 on a Surgeon's Certificate (Johnson and Christou, p. 381; Baker Vol. 2, p. 411)

Tucker, Joseph, served as a Private in Capt. William McIlvane's Co., 14th U.S. Infantry, enlisted 8 Jan 1813 for 5 years and was captured, probably at Beaver Dams, Upper Canada. Prisoner of War #3947, interned 24 Jun 1813, discharged for exchange on 3 Feb 1814, exchanged on 15 Apr 1814, returned to service and deserted at Greenbush, NY on 17 Jun 1814 (Johnson and Christou, p. 381; Baker Vol. 2, p. 411)

Tuel, Abner A., served as a Private in Capt. Thomas Blair's Co. and serving under Lt. Col. John Ragan, Jr. from Allegany Co. from 2 Sep to 28 Oct 1814 and listed as dead, but the date and cause were not stated (Wright Vol. 10, p. 6)

Tull, John, served as a Seaman and was born in St. Michaels, MD. Age: 27. Prison Depot: Portsmouth, Prisoner of War #177. Captured by HM Transport *Diadem*. When Taken: 7 Oct 1812. Where Taken: S. Andera (St. Andrews, Scotland). Prize Name: *Baltimore*. Home Port: Baltimore. Ship Type: Privateer. Date Received: 3 Nov 1812 San Antonio. From what ship: HMS *Diadem*. Discharged on 19 Feb 1813 and sent to Chatham on HM Store Ship *Dromedary*. (Johnson's Database, 2019)

Tulley, Aquila, served as a Private in Capt. Denton Darby's Co., Frederick Co. Militia, and stated in a letter on 3 Jan 1818 that he was drafted into service of the United States in the fall of 1814, marched from Fredericktown and near the beginning of August 1814 was severely wounded in the left arm by a musket ball by which his arm was broken so as to disable him from performing manual labor. Dr. John Wooton, of Montgomery Co., in letters on 6 Feb 1818 and 7 Feb 1818, 5th Military District, Washington, stated a gunshot wound in his left arm has weakened and partly disabled him. Aquila Tulley married Mrs. Margaret Glisan or Gleson on 30 Dec 1821. (Pension SO-25892; Mallick and Wright p. 291, citing *Republican Gazette*, 5 Jan 1822); see Aquila Teller, q.v.

Turner, Daniel, served as a Seaman and was born in Maryland. Age: 44. Prison Depot: Plymouth 1, Prisoner of War #2451. How Taken: Gave himself up off a Russian ship. When Taken: 28 Jan 1814. Where Taken: Cove of Cork, Ireland. Date Received: 15 Feb 1814. From what ship: HMS *Zealous*. Discharged on 10 May 1814 and sent to Dartmoor. Prison Depot: Dartmoor, Prisoner of War #1057. Date Received: 10 May 1814 from Plymouth. Discharged on 27 Apr 1815. (Johnson's Database, 2019)

Turner, Walter, served as a Private in Capt. Richard Arell's Co., 14th U.S. Inf., enlisted 23 May 1812 at Salisbury, MD, age 25, 5' 10½" tall, born in Worcester Co., MD and was captured, probably at Beaver Dams, Upper Canada. Prisoner of War #4057 at Halifax, NS, interned 24 Jun 1814, discharged for exchange on 3 Feb 1814, exchanged on 15 Apr 1814 and deserted at Fort Severn, MD on 15 Jul 1815 (Johnson and Christou, p. 383; Baker Vol. 2, p. 413)

Turner, William (African American), served as a Seaman and was born in Maryland. Age: 28. Prison Depot: Dartmoor, Prisoner of War #2111. How Taken: Gave himself up off HM Transport *Alkbar*. When Taken: 20 Jun 1814. Date Received: 5 Aug 1814. From what ship: *Bristol*. Discharged on 2 May 1815. (Johnson's Database, 2019)

Turner, William, served as a Surgeon on the Staff of the 8th Military District, born in Maryland. Garrison Surgeon's Mate from 9 Jul 1810. Prisoner of War, captured at Detroit, date was not given; served as a Surgeon's Mate in the 1st U.S. Artillery, as a Surgeon in the 17th U.S. Infantry from 7 Apr 1813 and was discharged from the service on 31 Jan 1815 (Johnson and Christou, p. 383)

Turpin, William S., served as a Private in Capt. Josiah W. Heath's Co., 23rd Regiment, Somerset Co. Militia, for 4 days and then reported as "sick, paroled by Major" on the muster roll dated April 1814. (Wright Vol. 1, p. 55) Alfred B. Turpin, merchant, Kingston, Somerset Co., stated he was the son of John whose father William had served in the War of 1812 and was a farmer in this county. (*Sketches of Maryland Eastern Shoreman*, by F. Edward Wright, 1985, p. 41)

U

Underwood, John, was a Seaman who sustained a concussion on 24 Aug 1814 on the field of battle at Bladensburg, was admitted to the Naval Hospital in Washington, DC as Patient No. 17 and was discharged on 5 Sep 1814 and sent to Baltimore by order of Col. Carberry (Sharp's Database, 2018)

Upcraft, Thomas (1786-1815), served as a Private in Capt. Shepperd Leakin's Co., 38th U.S. Infantry, enlisted 9 Apr 1814 at the age of 28, 5' 11½" tall, born in Frederick, MD and died in the regimental hospital on 27 Jan 1815; bounty land issued to his sister Margaret Cochran and other heirs (BLW# 23500-160-12; Johnson and Christou, p. 384)

Updegraff, David (1784-1814), served as a Private in Capt. Joseph Marshall's Co., 14th U.S. Infantry, enlisted 30 May 1814 in Sharpsburg, MD at the age of 30, 5' 10½" tall, born in Frederick, MD and died at Manlins, NY on 7 Nov 1814 of flux (Johnson and Christou, p. 384; Mallick and Wright, p. 293)

Updegraft, Jesse, served as a Corporal in Capt. Clement Sullivan's Co., 14th U.S. Infantry, enlisted 23 Jul 1812 and was captured, probably at Beaver Dams, Upper Canada. Prisoner of War #3812 at Halifax, NS, interned 27 Aug 1813, was discharged for exchange on 3 Feb 1814 and was exchanged on 15 Apr 1815 (Johnson and Christou, p. 384; Baker Vol. 2, p. 414)

Urie, Zacharias, served as a Private in Capt. Nathan Towson's Co., 2nd U.S. Artillery, enlisted 12 Apr 1812 at the age of 43, 6' tall, born in Pennsylvania, wounded at Black Rock, NY on 17 Mar 1814 and was discharged at Buffalo, NY on 2 Aug 1815 (Johnson and Christou, p. 384)

Usher, Edward, served as a Private in Capt. Isaac Banard's Co., 14th U.S. Inf., enlisted 13 Jan 1813 and was captured at Beaver Dams, Upper Canada on 24 Jun 1813. Prisoner of War #3764 at Halifax, NS, interned 24 Jun 1813, was discharged for exchange on 3 Feb 1814, was exchanged on 15 Apr 1814 and returned to service and was discharged from the service at Greenbush, NY on 14 Jul 1815 (Johnson and Christou, p. 384; Baker Vol. 2, p. 414)

V

Valiant, George, served as a Private in Capt. Isaac Raven's Co., Baltimore Co., 2nd Regiment, 11th Brigade, stationed in Baltimore from 25 Jul 1814 and was "discharged sick Aug 2" 1814 (Wright Vol. 2, p. 84)

Valiant (Valient), Richard, served as a Seaman and was born in Maryland. Age: 26. Prison Depot: Plymouth 1, Prisoner of War #2106. Captured by HM Frigate *Hotspur* & HM Frigate *Pyramus*. When Taken: 26 Oct 1813. Where Taken: Bay of Biscayne. Prize Name: *Chesapeake*. Ship Type: Letter of Marque (Privateer). Date

Received: 22 Nov 1813. From what ship: HMS *Pyramus*. Discharged on 29 Nov 1813 and sent to Dartmoor. Prison Depot: Dartmoor, Prisoner of War #827. Date Received: 29 Nov 1813 from Plymouth. Escaped on 5 Sep 1814. (Johnson's Database, 2019)

Valiant, William (1789-1813), served as a Private in Capt. Thomas Kearney's Co., 14th U.S. Infantry, enlisted 19 May 1812, captured at Beaver Dams, Upper Canada, ten miles west of Niagara Falls, on 24 Jun 1813, age 24. Born in Maryland. Prisoner of War #3884 at Halifax, NS, interned 24 Jun 1813 and died there on 26 Sep or 28 Sep 1813 from smallpox; bounty land issued to his mother Margaret Perry (BLW# 24594-160-12; Johnson and Christou, p. 385; Baker, Vol. 2, p. 415; Johnson's Database, 2019)

Van Bibber, Isaac (1780-1825), served as a Private in Capt. Samuel Lane's Co., 14th U.S. Infantry, enlisted 8 Oct 1812 in Baltimore at the age of 32, 5' 7" tall, born in Baltimore and was captured, probably at Beaver Dams, Upper Canada on 24 Jun 1813. Prisoner of War at Halifax, NS, exchanged on 15 Apr 1814 and discharged at Greenbush, NY on 17 Mar 1815 (Johnson and Christou, p. 385; Baker Vol. 2, p. 415, stated he was Prisoner #3915, interned 24 Jun 1813 and sent to England on 9 Nov 1813 and also Prisoner #4641, interned 24 Jun 1813 and discharged on 15 Nov 1813; Baltimore County Will Book 12, pp. 125-126)

Van Blake, Isaac, served as a Gunner of the U.S. Chesapeake Flotilla on a barge under Commodore Joshua Barney, entered service on 28 Sep 1813, on board on 7 Apr 1814 and was killed at Bladensburg on 24 Aug 1814 (Shomette, p. 361)

Van Horn (Vanhorn), Thomas, served as a Private in Capt. Adam Barnes' Co., 32nd Regt., Anne Arundel Co. Militia, from 23 Aug 1814 and "sick on furlough" as reported on muster roll dated 23 Aug – 27 Sep 1814 (Wright Vol. 4, p. 43)

Vanlamp, Henry, served as a Seaman on the privateer *Surprise* of Baltimore and drowned in a shipwreck on 5 Apr 1815 (Marine p. 468; *Niles Weekly Register*, 15 Apr 1815)

Van Wyck, Stedman R., served as a Private in Capt. David Warfield's Co., 5th Regiment, Baltimore Union Volunteers, from 19 Aug 1814 and was wounded twice on 12 Sep 1814 at North Point. He was the son of W. Van Wyck, Esq. (North Point dead and wounded Article 4 Oct 1814 Columbian Register CT Vol. III 97, p. 4; Wright Vol. 2, p. 8; Marine, pp. 172, 468)

Varden, Robert B. (1796-1878), served as 1st Corporal in Capt. Peter Pinney's Co., 27th Regt., Baltimore Militia, from 19 Aug to 18 Nov 1814 (Wright Vol. 2, pp. 19-20, did not mention being wounded; *The [Baltimore] Sun*, 8 May 1878). In Baltimore on 4 Oct 1842 Robert B. Varden, former private in Capt. Penny's (sic) Co., 27th Regt., Maryland Militia, a resident of Baltimore for 29 years and previously of Washington, DC, collected his own $16 pension due from 4 Mar to 4 Sep 1842. (Pierce, p. 186). Robert received Pension IF-25467 (Old War) and Pension SC-4651 and his widow Susan C. S. Varden received Pension WC-27785 (*Index to War of 1812 Pension Files*, by Virgil D. White, Vol. 2, p. 1757)

Varner, Robert, served as a Private in Capt. Nicholas Burke's Co., 6th Regt., Baltimore Militia, from 19 Aug 1814 and was discharged because of age some time before 18 Nov 1814 (Wright Vol. 2, p. 10)

Vaughn, James, served as a Private in Capt. William McIlvane's Co., 14th U.S. Infantry, enlisted 25 Feb 1813 at the age of 31, 5' 7" tall, born in Lancaster, PA and captured, date and place not stated. Prisoner of War #3952 at Halifax, NS, interned 24 Jun 1813, discharged from Halifax on 3 Feb 1814, exchanged on 15 Apr 1814 and discharged from the service at Washington, DC on 28 Jul 1815 for inability (Johnson and Christou, p. 386; Baker Vol. 2, p. 416)

Veverlan, John, see John Weaverling, q.v.

Vincent, Alfred, served as a Ship Steward on the privateer (armed brigantine) *Chasseur* of Baltimore commanded by Capt. Thomas Boyle and was slightly wounded in action on 26 Feb 1815 (*Niles Weekly Register*, 25 Mar 1815)

Vinemiller, Michael, served as a Private (company not stated) and was captured at the Battle of Bladensburg on 24 Aug 1814 (Marine, p. 175)

Vinton, Samuel, served as a Seaman of the U.S. Chesapeake Flotilla, entered service on 6 Mar 1814, was on board on 7 Apr 1814 and died on 4 Jan 1815 (Shomette p. 371)

Vlach, Thomas (1785-1815), served as a Private in Capt. James Belsche's Co., 35th U.S. Infantry, enlisted 20 Nov 1814 in Norfolk, VA at the age of 29, 5' 10" tall, born in Prince George's Co., MD and died at Camp Defiance, VA on 4 Feb 1815 (Johnson and Christou, p. 387)

Von Harten (Van Harten), Gerrard, served as a Private in Capt. John Stewart's Co., 51st Regiment, Baltimore City, from 23 Aug 1813 to 30 Aug 1813 and as a Private in Capt. Dominic Bader's Co., 1st Rifle Bttn., Baltimore City, from 19 Aug 1814, captured at Bladensburg on 24 Aug 1814, later exchanged and died from his wounds on 14 Sep 1814 (Wright Vol. 2, pp. 31, 54; see Von Hasten below)

Von Hasten, G., served as a Lieutenant in Capt. Dominic Bader's Co. and was captured at Bladensburg on 24 Aug 1814 (Marine, p. 174, may have his rank wrong because this could actually be the Pvt. Gerrard Vonharten cited above)

Vorge, James (African American), served as a Seaman and was born in Harford Co., MD. Age: 24. Prison Depot: Portsmouth, Prisoner of War #567. Captured by HM Frigate *Dryad* on 7 Jan 1813. Where Taken: at sea. Prize Name: *Rossie*. Ship

Type: Merchant Vessel. Date Received: 25 Jan 1813. From what ship: HM Ship-of-the-Line *Queen*. Discharged on 11 Mar 1813 and sent to Chatham on HM Store Ship *Abundance*. Prison Depot: Chatham, Prisoner of War #1240. Date Received: 16 Mar 1813 from Portsmouth on HMS *Abundance*. Discharged on 24 Jul 1813 and released to the Cartel *Hoffning*. (Johnson's Database, 2019)

W

Waddell, John, served as a Seaman of the U.S. Chesapeake Flotilla, entered service on 24 Feb 1814, was on board on 7 Apr 1814 and died on 26 Apr 1814 (Shomette p. 371)

Waddle, Leonard, served as a Private in Capt. Richard Arell's Co., 14th U.S. Infantry, enlisted 1 Jul 1812 in Baltimore, age 22, 5' 3" tall, born in Baltimore and was captured, probably at Beaver Dams, Upper Canada on 24 Jun 1813. Prisoner of War at Halifax., NS, was discharged for exchange on 3 Feb 1814, exchanged on 15 Apr 1814, returned to service and was discharged on 23 Mar 1821 {Johnson and Christou, p. 387; Baker Vol. 2, p. 417, did not mention him)

Waldron, Richard, served as a Private in Capt. Richard Whartenby's Co., 5th U.S. Infantry, enlisted 20 Apr 1813 for 5 years at Baltimore, born in Prince George's Co., transferred to the Corps of Artillery at Plattsburgh, NY on 1 Aug 1814 and discharged there on 9 Nov 1814 on a Surgeon's Certificate for injury in line of duty, but date and medical details were not given (Johnson and Christou, p. 88)

Walker, Andrew, served as a Private in Capt. Reuben Gilder's Co., 14th U.S. Inf., enlisted 23 Mar 1813 for 5 years in Baltimore at age 30, 5' 11¾" tall, born in Donegal, Ireland and discharged at Annapolis on 16 Oct 1816 for varicose veins and rheumatism (Johnson and Christou, p. 388)

Walker, Armstrong, served as a Seaman and was born in Baltimore. Age: 16. Prison Depot: Plymouth 1, Prisoner of War #1526. Captured by HM Frigate *Andromache*. When Taken: 14 Mar 1813. Where Taken: off Nantes, France. Prize Name: *Courier*. Home Port: Baltimore. Ship Type: Letter of Marque. Date Received: 29 May 1813. From what ship: HMS *Hannibal*. Discharged on 30 Jun 1813 and sent to Stapleton. Prison Depot: Stapleton, Prisoner of War #88. Date Received: 8 Jul 1813 from Plymouth. Discharged on 13 Jun 1814 and sent to Dartmoor. Prison Depot: Dartmoor, Prisoner of War #1381. Received: 19 Jun 1814 from Stapleton. Discharged on 28 Apr 1815. (Johnson's Database, 2019)

Walker, Benjamin (Mulatto), served as a Seaman and was born in Maryland. Age: 27. Prison Depot: Portsmouth, Prisoner of War #1157. How Taken: Gave himself up off HM Store Ship *Woolwich*. Received: 7 Oct 1813. From what ship: HM Frigate *Spartan*. Discharged on 17 Oct 1813 and sent to Chatham on HMT *Malabar No. 352*. Prison Depot: Chatham, Prisoner of War #2404. Received: 21

Oct 1813 from Portsmouth on HMT *Malabar*. Discharged on 4 Sep 1814 and sent to Dartmoor on HMS *Freya*. Prison Depot: Dartmoor, Prisoner of War #3221. Received: 11 Sep 1814 on HMT *Freya* from Chatham. Discharged on 28 May 1815. (Johnson's Database, 2019)

Walker, Christopher, served as a Private in Capt. Lawson Cuddy's Co., 41st Regiment, Baltimore Co., from 25 Aug 1814 and was reported "sick – absent since Oct 11" 1814 (Wright Vol. 2, p. 68)

Walker, Daniel (African American), served as a Seaman and was born in Baltimore. Age: 25. Prison Depot: Dartmoor, Prisoner of War #6445. Captured by HM Frigate *Rhin*. When Taken: 28 May 1814. Where Taken: off Bermuda. Prize Name: *Sennett*, Swedish brig. Ship Type: Merchant Vessel. Date Received: 3 Mar 1815. From what ship: HMT *Ganges* from Plymouth. Discharged on 11 Jul 1815. (Johnson's Database, 2019)

Walker, Francis, served as a Seaman and was born in Baltimore. Age: 25. Prison Depot: Plymouth 1, Prisoner of War #1204. Captured by HM Frigate *Pyramus*. When Taken: 20 Apr 1813. Where Taken: Bay of Biscayne. Prize Name: *Zebra*. Home Port: New York. Ship Type: Letter of Marque (Privateer). Date Received: 9 May 1813. From what ship: HMS *Andromache*. Discharged and sent on 3 Jul 1813 to Stapleton prison. Prison Depot: Stapleton, Prisoner of War #255. Date Received: 11 Jul 1813 from Plymouth. Discharged on 16 Jun 1814 and sent to Dartmoor. (Johnson's Database, 2019)

Walker, Sater T., served as a Private in Capt. James Horton's Co., 5th Cavalry Regiment, Baltimore, from 19 Aug 1814 and was "discharged sick Sep 30" 1814 (Wright Vol. 2, p. 56)

Wallace, James, served as a Private in Capt. Alexander Crook's Co., 27th Regt., Baltimore Militia, from 9 Aug 1813 and in Capt. Peter Pinney's Co., 27th Regt., and Capt. George J. Brown from 23 Aug 1814 and was killed on 12 Sep 1814 at North Point. His name is on the Baltimore Battle Monument. (Wright Vol. 2, pp. 20, 48; NARA; CMSR; *Baltimore American*, 12 Jun 1819)

Wallace, Thomas, served as a Private in Capt. Benjamin Edes' Co., 27th Regt., Baltimore Militia, and was allegedly killed on 12 Sep 1814 at North Point. His name is <u>not</u> on the Baltimore Battle Monument. (Huntsberry, p. 90; Wright Vol. 2, p. 17, and Marine p. 470, both did not mention his death)

Wallace, William, served as a Caulker and was born in Baltimore. Age: 38. Prison Depot: Chatham, Prisoner of War #401. How Taken: Gave himself up off HM Gunpowder Hulk *Alexander*. When Taken: 1 Feb 1813. Received: 13 Feb 1813. From what ship: HMS *Raisonable*. Discharged on 25 Sep 1814 and sent to Dartmoor on HMS *Freya*. Prison Depot: Dartmoor, Prisoner of War #4169. Date

Received: 7 Oct 1814. From what ship: HMT *Niobe* from Chatham. Discharged on 13 Jun 1815. (Johnson's Database, 2019)

Waller (Walter), George, served as a Seaman and was born in River Neck, MD. Age: 24. Prison Depot: Portsmouth, Prisoner of War #160. Captured by HM Transport *Diadem*. When Taken: 7 Oct 1812. Where Taken: S. Andera (St. Andrews, Scotland). Prize Name: Baltimore. Home Port: Baltimore. Ship Type: Privateer. Received: 3 Nov 1812 San Antonio. From what ship: HMS *Diadem*. Discharged on 19 Feb 1813 and sent to Chatham on HM Store Ship *Dromedary*. Prison Depot: Chatham, Prisoner of War #529. Date Received: 23 Feb 1813 from Portsmouth on HMS *Dromedary*. Discharged on 8 Jun 1813 and released to the Cartel *Rodrigo*. (Johnson's Database, 2019)

Walters, Henry, served as a Musician in Capt. Wilson Elliott's Co. of the 19th U.S. Infantry, enlisted 30 Jul 1812 in Warren, Trumbull Co., OH at the age of 24, born in Maryland; wounded at Mississinewa, IN on 18 Dec 1812; discharged on 27 Jul 1817 (Johnson and Christou, p. 390)

Walters, Philip (African American), served as a Seaman and was born in Baltimore. Age: 25. Prison Depot: Plymouth 1, Prisoner of War #2640. Captured by HM Frigate *Magiciene*. When Taken: 14 Mar 1814. Where Taken: off Cape Finisterre, Spain. Prize Name: *Adeline*. Ship Type: Letter of Marque. Date Received: 17 May 1814. From what ship: HMS *Tortois*. Discharged on 14 Jun 1814 and sent to Dartmoor. Prison Depot: Dartmoor, Prisoner of War #1266. Date Received: 14 Jun 1814 from Mill Prison. Discharged on 28 Apr 1815. (Johnson's Database, 2019)

Walton, Edward, served as a Private in Capt. Henry Fleming's Co., 14th U.S. Inf., enlisted 3 Feb 1813 at age 22, 5' 2¼" tall and was captured in Upper Canada. Prisoner of War #731 at Quebec, interned 7 Jul 1813, discharged for exchange on 31 Oct 1813, returned to service and discharged on 7 Aug 1814 (Johnson and Christou, p. 390, stated he was captured at Stoney Creek, Upper Canada, but Johnson, p. 161, stated it was at Beaver Dams, Upper Canada)

Waples, Burton, served as a Private in Capt. Henry Fleming's Co., 14th U.S. Inf., enlisted 7 Nov 1812 and captured at Beaver Dams, Upper Canada on 24 Jun 1813. Prisoner of War #3375 at Halifax, NS, interned 24 Jun 1813, discharged for exchange on 3 Feb 1814, exchanged on 15 Apr 1814 and discharged from the service at Greenbush, NY on 23 Jun 1814 (Johnson and Christou, p. 390; Baker Vol. 2, p. 421, misspelled his name as Bweton Wapley)

Ward, Edward, served as a Private in Capt. Nicholas Turbutt's Co., joined 1 Sep 1814, enlisted in regular army by Lt. Cochran at Baltimore on 5 Sep 1814, age 22, 5' 11" tall, grey eyes, dark hair, fair complexion, born in Ireland, served in Capt. Samuel C. Leakin's Co. at Fort McHenry, reported as "sick absent" in the General

Hospital on 31 Dec 1814 and deserted from that hospital on 1 Jan 1815 (Mallick and Wright, pp. 295-296)

Ward, Richard, served as a Private in Capt. Adam Shower's Co., Baltimore Co., 2nd Regiment, 11th Brigade, was stationed in Baltimore from 26 Jul 1814 and was "discharged by doctor Aug 11" 1814 (Wright Vol. 2, p. 84)

Ward, Thomas, served as a Prize Master and was born in Baltimore. Age: 39. Prison Depot: Portsmouth, Prisoner of War #1271. Captured by HM Frigate *Ethalion.* When Taken: 14 Dec 1813. Where Taken: at sea. Prize Name: *Pomona,* prize of Privateer *Princede Neuchaftel.* Ship Type: Privateer. Date Received: 22 Dec 1813. From what ship: HMS *Ethalion.* Discharged on 26 Dec 1813 and sent to Chatham on HMS *Diomede.* Prison Depot: Chatham, Prisoner of War #2910. Date Received: 7 Jan 1814 from Portsmouth. Discharged on 25 Sep 1814 and sent to Dartmoor on HMS *Leyden.* Prison Depot: Dartmoor, Prisoner of War #4451. Received: 8 Oct 1814. From what ship: HMT *Leyden* from Chatham. Discharged on 1 May 1815. (Johnson's Database, 2019)

Ware, John, served as a Seaman and was born in Baltimore. Age: 38. Prison Depot: Dartmoor, Prisoner of War #3928. Captured by HM Frigate *Loire.* When Taken: 10 Dec 1813. Where Taken: off Block Island, RI. Prize Name: *Rolla.* Home Port: Baltimore. Ship Type: Privateer. Date Received: 5 Oct 1814. From what ship: HMT *President* from Halifax, NS. Discharged on 9 Jun 1815. (Johnson's Database, 2019)

Warfield, William W., served as a Private in Capt. Thomas T. Simmons' Co., 2nd Regiment, Anne Arundel Co. Militia, from 28 Sep 1814 and was reported "sick on furlough Nov 18" 1814 on the muster roster dated 18 Oct – 1 Dec 1814 (Wright Vol. 4, p. 29)

Warner, Andrew E. (1786-1870), served as a Captain in Lt. Col. Fowler's 39th Regiment and reported "mortally wounded at North Point" (Marine p. 473); however, he survived and served as President of the Association of Defenders (Veterans of 1812), now Society of the War of 1812 in the State of Maryland, from 1852 to 1870. (Society Records; *The [Baltimore] Sun,* 17 Jan 1870) In June 1812 Andrew E. Warner, of Baltimore, married Dorothy Litzinger, of Baltimore Co. (*Baltimore Whig,* 27 Jun 1812; Society of the War of 1812 Application National No. 209 in 1892 stated he married Elizabeth Lands)

Warner, John, served as a Sailing Master of the U.S. Chesapeake Flotilla on a barge under Commodore Joshua Barney, entered service on 22 Sep 1813 and was killed at the Battle of Bladensburg on 24 Aug 1814 (Shomette pp. 6, 325; 1853 recollections of Naval Capt. John Adams Webster; Marine p. 178, did not give his first name) He was buried in Green Mount Cemetery, Area I, Lot 131.

Warner, Samuel (Mulatto), served as a Seaman and was born in Baltimore. Age: 20. Prison Depot: Plymouth 1, Prisoner of War #2602. How Taken: Gave himself up off HM Frigate *Furieuse*. When Taken: 23 Sep 1812. Date Received: 16 May 1814. From what ship: HMS *Repulse*. Discharged on 14 Jun 1814 and sent to Dartmoor. (Johnson's Database, 2019)

Warren, John (African American), served as a Seaman and was born in Baltimore. Age: 40. Prison Depot: Plymouth 1, Prisoner of War #344. How Taken: Gave himself up. When Taken: 25 Jan 1813. Where Taken: Plymouth, UK. Date Received: 25 Jan 1813. From what ship: HMS *Salvador del Monde*. Discharged and sent to Chatham on 29 Mar 1813 on HMS *Braham*. Prison Depot: Chatham, Prisoner of War #1421. Date Received: 5 Apr 1813 from Plymouth on HMS *Dwarf*. Discharged on 27 Jul 1813 and released to the Cartel *Hoffning*. (Johnson's Database, 2019)

Warren, Thomas, served as a Private in Capt. Joseph Talbott's Co., 19th Regt. Caroline Co. Militia, from 10 May to 18 May 1813 and died some time before 19 Apr 1814 at which time militia pay was due to members of Capt. George Parrott's Co. and Thomas was reported dead; however, his name does not appear on any extant muster roll of Capt. Parrott's Company (Wright Vol. 1, p. 80; *Republican Star*, 19 Apr 1814)

Washington, John, served as a Private in Capt. Woodburn's Co., 45th Regiment, St. Mary's Co. Militia, from 29 Jul 1813 for 3 days and was "furlowed till he gets well." (Wright Vol. 5, p. 32)

Waterfield, William (1789-1814), served as a Private in Capt. Joseph Marshall's Co., 14th U.S. Infantry, enlisted 4 Jul 1814 in Snow Hill, MD at the age of 25, 5' 7" tall, born in Accomack Co., VA and died at Buffalo, NY on 20 Dec 1814; bounty land was issued to his brother John Waterfield and other heirs at law (BLW# 15974-160-12; Johnson and Christou, p. 392)

Waters, John, served as a Captain in the 34th U.S. Regiment and died in 1814 (Marine p. 473)

Waters, Louis (African American), served as a Steward and was born in Maryland. Age: 22. Prison Depot: Plymouth 2, Prisoner of War #197. Captured by HM Frigate *Statira*. When Taken: 1 Apr 1814. Where Taken: Lat 38 Long 24. Prize Name: *Chance*. Home Port: Virginia. Ship Type: Privateer. Date Received: 2 Mar 1815. From what ship: HMS *Dannemark*. Discharged on 3 Mar 1815 and sent to Dartmoor. Prison Depot: Dartmoor, Prisoner of War #6441. Received: 3 Mar 1815. From what ship: HMT *Ganges* from Plymouth. Discharged on 11 Jul 1815. (Johnson's Database, 2019)

Waters, Philip (African American), served as a Seaman and was born in Baltimore. Age: 29. Prison Depot: Plymouth 1, Prisoner of War #477. How Taken: Gave himself up. When Taken: 27 Nov 1812. Where Taken: Greenock, Scotland. Date Received: 10 Feb 1813. From what ship: HMS *Frederick*. Discharged and sent on 20 Feb 1813 to Ashburton on parole. Prison Depot: Chatham, Prisoner of War #1572. Date Received: 8 Apr 1813 from Plymouth von HMS *Olympia*. Discharged on 27 Jul 1813 and was released to the Cartel *Hoffning*. (Johnson's Database, 2019)

Waters, William G., served as Paymaster, 23rd Regiment, Somerset Co. Militia, appointed on 2 Sep 1811 and was later listed as dead, but the date and cause of death were not stated; he obviously died soon after being appointed since his replacement was appointed on 9 Dec 1813 (Wright Vol. 1, p. ii)

Wathen, Faben, served as a Private in Capt. James Walker's Co., 45th Regiment, St. Mary's Co. Militia, for 4 days between 14 Jul and 26 Jul 1813 and was furloughed sick (Wright Vol. 5, p. 29)

Watkins, Gassaway, served as 2nd Lieutenant, 38th U.S. Infantry; commissioned an Ensign on 20 May 1813; promoted to 3rd Lieutenant on 31 Dec 1813; promoted to 2nd Lieutenant on 20 May 1814 and died on 8 Sep 1814 (Johnson and Christou, p. 392)

Watkins, Gassaway (1787-1851), served as a Private in Capt. Thomas F. W. Vinson's Co., 32nd Regt., Montgomery Co., Extra Battalion, from 1 Aug 1814 was reported as missing in action on 24 Aug 1814 at Bladensburg. On 21 Dec 1850 Gassaway Watkins, age 63, stated he was drafted at Damascus at the last of July 1814 and was discharged near Washington City in 1814. On 21 Apr 1855 Arianna Watkins, age 66, widow, stated her maiden name was Norwood and she married Gassaway Watkins on 9 Apr 1813 in Montgomery County and he died on 1 Oct 1851. (Wright Vol. 7, p. 5. BLW# 55-160-98560)

Watkins, William, served as a Private in Capt. Stephen H. Moore's Co., Baltimore Volunteers Inf. Co., from 8 Sep 1812 for 1 year, was sick at 18 Mile Creek, survived and was promoted to 5th Corporal in May 1813 (Wright Vol. 2, p. 57)

Watson, Jesse, served as a Private in Capt. Horatio Stark's Co., 1st U.S. Infantry, enlisted 24 Dec 1811 at Fort Madison, IA at the age of 38, 5' 8" tall, was born in Maryland and discharged at Sackett's Harbor, NY on 5 Jul 1815 for disability (Johnson and Christou, p. 393)

Watson, Joshua, served as a Private in Capt. Joshua Naylor Jr.'s Co., 17th Regiment, Prince George's Co. Militia, was stationed at Milltown between 17 Jul and 2 Aug 1814 (listed as Josiah Watson). On 10 Jan 1851 Joshua Watson, age

68, stated he was called out in 1813 or 1814 and discharged at Piscataway on account of sickness. (Wright Vol. 6, pp. 9, 44, 53; BLW# 50-rej-68526)

Watson, Mathew, served as a Corporal in Capt. Nathan Towson's Co., 2nd U.S. Artillery, enlisted on 16 Oct 1812 and died on 27 Aug 1813, place and cause of death not stated (Johnson and Christou, p. 393)

Watson, William, served as a Private in 14th U.S. Infantry and was born in Baltimore. Age: 27. Prison Depot: Chatham, Prisoner of War #3067. When Taken: 24 Jun 1813. Where Taken: Beaver Dams, Upper Canada. Date Received: 7 Jan 1814 from Halifax, NS. Discharged on 10 Oct 1814 and sent to U.S. on the Cartel *St. Philip*. (Johnson's Database, 2019)

Watts, Robert, served as a Private in Capt. John Rothrock's Co., 38th U.S. Infantry, enlistment date not stated, and died on 5 Jan 1815, place and cause of death were not stated; heirs received half pay for 5 years in lieu of bounty land (Pension Old War MC-878; Johnson and Christou, p. 394)

Watts, Saybert W., served as a Private in Capt. Clement Guiton's Co., 2nd Regt., 11th Brigade, Baltimore, from 27 Jul 1814 and reported "sick on furlough since Sep 26" 1814 (Wright Vol. 2, p. 87)

Wavernce, James (Mulatto) served as a Seaman and was born in Baltimore. Age: 20. Prison Depot: Dartmoor, Prisoner of War #1229. How Taken: Gave himself up off HM Frigate *Furieuse*. When Taken: 23 Sep 1812. Received: 14 Jun 1814 from Mill Prison. Discharged on 26 Apr 1815. (Johnson's Database, 2019)

Way, John, served as a Mate and was born in Baltimore. Age: 26. Prison Depot: Plymouth 1, Prisoner of War #1099. Captured by HM Frigate *Andromache*. When Taken: 14 Mar 1813. Where Taken: off Nantes, France. Prize Name: *Courier*. Home Port: Baltimore. Ship Type: Letter of Marque. Date Received: 22 Apr 1813. From what ship: HMS *Superb*. Discharged and sent on 25 Apr 1813 to Ashburton on parole. (Johnson's Database, 2019)

Wayne, John, served as a Private in the 14th U.S. Infantry (company and captain were not stated), enlisted at the age of 38, born in Virginia. Prisoner of War at Quebec and died there on 6 Oct 1813, cause was not stated (Johnson and Christou, p. 394; Johnson's Quebec book, p. 163, did not mention him)

Wayne, Joseph, served as a Private in Capt. Henry Fleming's Co., 14th U.S. Infantry, enlisted 23 Jan 1813, place was not stated. Prisoner of War and died about 1 Aug 1813; bounty land was issued to John L. Wirt, his sole heir (BLW# 26945-160-12; Johnson and Christou, p. 394)

Wayne, Michael, served as a Private in the 14th U.S. Infantry (company and captain were not stated) and was captured probably at Beaver Dams, Upper

Canada. Prisoner of War #4174 at Halifax, NS, interned 24 Jun 1813, discharged 27 Aug 1813 and sent to England on HMS *Regulus* (Johnson and Christou, p. 394; Baker Vol. 2, p. 424)

Ways, William, served as a Private in Capt. Christian Adreon's Co., 39th Regt., Baltimore Militia, from 16 Aug to 23 Aug 1813 and in Capt. Thomas Warner's Co., 39th Regt., from 19 Aug 1814 until killed in action on 12 Sep 1814 at North Point. His name is on the Baltimore Battle Monument. (Wright Vol. 2, pp. 21, 28; *Baltimore American*, 12 Jun 1819; CMSR; Marine, p. 476)

Weaver, Aquilla, served as a Marine on board the privateer (armed brigantine) *Chasseur* of Baltimore commanded by Capt. Thomas Boyle and was severely wounded in action on 26 Feb 1815 (*Niles Weekly Register*, 25 Mar 1815)

Weaverling, John (1783-1813), served as a Private in Capt. John Burd's Co., 2nd U.S. Light Dragoons, enlisted 25 Aug 1812 at the age of 29, 5' 9" tall, born in Washington, MD and captured at Beaver Dams, Upper Canada, ten miles west of Niagara Falls. Prisoner of War #4022, interned on 24 Jun 1813, and died at Halifax, NS on 10 Sep 1813 of dysentery; bounty land was issued to his brother Jacob Weaverling and other heirs at law (BLW# 26895-160-12; Johnson and Christou, p. 394; Baker, Vol. 2, p. 416, misspelled his name as Veverlan)

Webb, Elisha, served as a Private in Capt. Reuben Gilder's Co., 14th U.S. Inf., enlisted 15 Aug 1812 for 5 years at the age of 33, 6' 1" tall, born in Snow Hill, MD and was discharged at Greenbush, NY on 24 May 1814 on a Surgeon's Certificate for rheumatism (Johnson and Christou, p. 394)

Webb, Lambert (1794-1815), served as a Corporal in Capt. John Buck's Co., 38th U.S. Infantry, enlisted 1 Jul 1813 at the age of 19, 5' 8" tall, born in Harford Co., MD, re-enlisted at Baltimore on 28 Feb 1814 for the war and died in regimental hospital on 23 Feb 1815; bounty land issued to his brother William Webb and other heirs at law (BLW# 16720-160-12; Johnson and Christou, p. 395)

Webb, Stephen, served as a Seaman and was born in Baltimore. Age: 31. Prison Depot: Portsmouth, Prisoner of War #165. Captured by HM Transport *Diadem*. When Taken: 7 Oct 1812. Where Taken: S. Andera (St. Andrews, Scotland). Prize Name: *Baltimore*. Home Port: Baltimore. Ship Type: Privateer. Date Received: 3 Nov 1812 San Antonio. From what ship: HMS *Diadem*. Discharged on 19 Feb 1813 and sent to Chatham on HM Store Ship *Dromedary*. Prison Depot: Chatham, Prisoner of War #534. Date Received: 23 Feb 1813 from Portsmouth on HMS *Dromedary*. Discharged 11 Aug 1814. Sent to Dartmoor on HMS *Freya*. (Johnson's Database, 2019)

Webster, John Adams (1787-1877), of Harford Co., "began life as a sailor when fourteen years old. In 1812 he served as Captain under Commodore Barney; also in the flotilla on the Chesapeake in 1813 and 1814; and was in the same command at the battle of Bladensburg Aug. 24, 1814 in which his horse was shot under him. After the battle he marched to Baltimore with his sailors and by Gen. Smith's order took command of the SIX GUN BATTERY from which on the night of the 13th of September 1814 he attached the enemy's barges and defeated them with great loss, thus rendering most efficient service in the defense of Baltimore. On Nov 22, 1819 he was commissioned Captain in the U. S. R. N. and in May 1846 commanded a fleet of eight vessels in cooperation with the army and navy in the War with Mexico. He took part in twenty engagements by land and sea, was twice wounded and at the time of his death was senior Captain in the Revenue Service. In every position he served his country faithfully, gallantly and efficiently. And died a Christian." (Inscription on the back of his tombstone in the Webster-Dallam family cemetery situated on the *Broom's Bloom* land tract located between Bel Air and Creswell, adjoining *Mt. Adams*, the homestead of Capt. Webster) During the battle in Baltimore "Webster stayed in command of his battery despite being in severe pain from a broken shoulder. He explained, 'I had my right shoulder broken by a handspike, and subsequently broken again, which rendered me a complete invalid. During the right, one of my seamen, an obstinate Englishman, attempted to lay a train of powder to the magazine; without thought, I laid him out for dead with a handspike.'" ("Harford County in the War of 1812," by Christopher T. George, *Harford Historical Bulletin* No. 76, Spring 1998, p. 55) Capt. John A. Wenster and Miss Rachel Biays, daughter of Col. Joseph Biays, were married in Baltimore on 8 Feb 1816 by Rev. James Inglis at the First Presbyterian Church. (*Baltimore Telegraphe*, 10 Feb 1816; *Presbyterian Records of Baltimore City, Maryland, 1765-1840*, by Henry C. Peden, Jr., 1995, p. 88) On Defenders Day 2014 The Society of the War of 1812 in the State of Maryland and invited guests met at the home of John Adams Webster. Local historian James E. Chrismer discussed the life of John Adams Webster and his wife Rachel Biays Webster's search for

her wounded husband after the war. Historical architect James T. Wollon, Jr. talked about their beautiful home that still remains in the family. Compatriots attending the celebration paused for a group photograph on the steps of the historic home and were given a tour by Katie Dallam, a family member who lives there. (Information and photographs are contained in *The Society of the War of 1812 2014 Yearbook*, pp. 10-11)

Webster, Michael, served as a Seaman and was born in Annapolis. Age: 18. Prison Depot: Plymouth 2, Prisoner of War #183. Captured by HM Ship-of-the-Line *Leviathan*. When Taken: 20 Mar 1814. Where Taken: at sea. Prize Name: *Farmer's Daughter*. Ship Type: Merchant Vessel. Date Received: 2 Mar 1815. From what ship: HMS Dannemark. Discharged on 3 Mar 1815 and sent to Dartmoor. Another record stated Michael Webster served as a Seaman and was born in Annapolis. Age: 32 (sic). Prison Depot: Dartmoor, Prisoner of War #6426. Captured by HM Ship-of-the-Line *Leviathan*. When Taken: 29 May 1814. Where Taken: Cape --?--. Prize Name: *Farmer's Daughter*. Ship Type: Merchant Vessel. Date Received: 3 Mar 1815. From what ship: HMT *Ganges* from Plymouth. Discharged on 11 Jul 1815. (Johnson's Database, 2019)

Webster, William, served as a Private under Capt. Stephen Moore in the U.S. Volunteers, enlisted on 8 Sep 1812 and discharged on 31 May 1813 for inability (Johnson and Christou, p. 395)

Wedding, John, served as a Private in Capt. Thomas Kearney's Co., 14th U.S. Infantry, enlisted 9 Jun 1812 and died on 7 Dec 1812; bounty land issued to son Frederick Wedding and other heirs at law (BLW# 23830-160-12; Johnson and Christou, p. 395)

Weeks, James (African American), served as a Seaman and was born in Maryland. Age: 32. Prison Depot: Stapleton, Prisoner of War #7. Captured by Naval *Rendezvous Bristol*. When Taken: 14 May 1813. Date Received: 14 May 1813. From what ship: *Bristol*. Discharged on 13 Jun 1814 and sent to Dartmoor. Prison Depot: Dartmoor, Prisoner of War #1321. Date Received: 19 Jun 1814 from Stapleton. Discharged 28 Apr 1815. (Johnson's Database, 2019)

Weems, Daniel, served as a Private in Capt. Reuben Gilder's Co., 14th U.S. Infantry, enlisted on 12 Dec 1812 and was killed during the Battle of Lyon's Creek on 19 Oct 1814 (Johnson and Christou, p. 396)

Weiser, John, served as a Private in 20th U.S. Infantry (company not stated) and died on 5 Jan 1815; heirs received half pay for 5 years in lieu of bounty land (Johnson and Christou, p. 396)

Welch (Welsh), Henry, served as a Private in Capt. John Burd's Co., 2nd U.S. Light Dragoons, under Lt. Col. Charles C. Boerstler, enlisted on 1 Jun 1812 at Bedford, PA at the age of 22, 5' 11" tall, born in Harford Co., MD and was captured at Beaver Dams, Upper Canada, ten miles west of Niagara Falls, on 24 Jun 1813. Prisoner of War #4635 at Halifax, NS, interned on 15 Nov 1813, discharged on 19 Nov 1813 and sent to England. Prison Depot: Chatham, Prisoner of War #3162. Date Received: 7 Jan 1814 from Halifax, NS. Age 24. Discharged on 10 Oct 1814 and sent to U.S. on the Cartel *St. Philip* and arrived in Norfolk, VA on 26 Feb 1815. Discharged from the service on 31 Mar 1815 (Johnson and Christou, p. 396; Baker Vol. 2, p. 427; Johnson's Database, 2019; "Harford County in the War of 1812," by Christopher T. George, *Harford Historical Bulletin* No. 76, Spring 1998, p. 19, citing *Encyclopedia of the War of 1812*, by Heidler and Heidler, pp. 45-46, 58-59); however, this same source in a footnote on page 20 stated, "Among a list of the American prisoners of war in Ottawa, Canada ... 'Welsh, Henry, Md.' listed as Prisoner 671. *Index to Certified Copy of List of American Prisoners of War 1812-1815 as Recorded in General Entry Book, Ottawa, Canada,* compiled by Mrs. Henry James Carr (Washington, DC: National Society, United Daughters of 1812 (1923); reprinted 1986)."

Welch, John, served as a Quartermaster and was born in Baltimore. Age: 25. Prison Depot: Dartmoor, Prisoner of War #4889. How Taken: Gave himself up off HM Ship-of-the-Line *Centaur*. When Taken: 16 Oct 1814. Date Received: 24 Oct 1814. From what ship: HMT *Salvador del Mundo*. Discharged on 19 May 1815. (Johnson's Database, 2019)

Welch, Richard, served as a Private in Capt. Adam Barnes' Co., Watkins' Regiment, Anne Arundel Co. Militia, from 16 Apr 1813 and died on 7 Jul 1813 (Wright Vol. 4, p. 41)

Welch, Samuel, served as a Seaman and was born in Baltimore. Age: 24. Prison Depot: Chatham, Prisoner of War #1333. Captured by HM Brig *Thrasher*. When Taken: 4 Mar 1813. Where Taken: off River Jade (Germany). Prize Name: *Sea Nymphe*. Ship Type: Merchant Vessel. Date Received: 22 Mar 1813. From what ship: HMS *Thrasher*. Discharged on 23 Jul 1814 and sent to Dartmoor. Prison Depot: Dartmoor, Prisoner of War #2539. Date Received: 16 Aug 1814. From what ship: HMT *Salvador del Mundo*. Discharged on 3 May 1815. (Johnson's Database, 2019)

Welion, Thomas C., served as a Marine and was taken from the barracks and admitted to the Naval Hospital in Washington, DC as Patient No. 60 on 18 Jul 1814 (injury or illness was not specified) and was discharged on 23 Jul 1814 and sent to the barracks (Sharp's Database, 2018)

Wells, Daniel, served as a Private in Capt. Joseph Perrigo's Co., 41st Regiment, Baltimore Co. Militia, from 25 Aug 1814 and was taken prisoner on 12 Sep 1814 at North Point (Wright Vol. 2, p. 70)

Wells, Daniel (1794-1814), served as a Private in Capt. Edward Aisquith's Co. of Riflemen, 1st Rifle Battalion, Maryland Militia, from 19 Aug and was killed in the advance of 12 Sep 1814. "Annapolis, 16th Dec 1814: I do hereby certify that Mr. Daniel Wells of this City is the legal representative of Daniel Wells Jr. who fell in the Battle at North Point in Sep last witness my hand Robert Welch of Ben. Sir please to pay unto Richard Wells the sum due to the within deceased Daniel Wells Jr. and his receipts shall be good against yours. Respectfully Daniel Wells his father. (NARA; CMSR) August 13, 1813 newspaper: Daniel Wells, an infant, by George Mackenzie vs. John Kennedy. The petitioner was an infant under the age of 21, and above the age of 18, and he was also an apprentice to George Mackenzie. On the 10th of August, he was arrested by a file of soldiers, under the orders of the defendant, John Kennedy, and forcibly carried to Camp, near this city. The above application being made, a Habeas Corpus was issued by his Honor Judge Bland, returnable at the court on Wednesday, the 11th August at 10 o'clock, at which time, Capt. Kennedy appeared, with the infant in his custody. In consequence of a defect in the return, for want of certain papers, the petitioner was remanded to the custody of the defendant until this day at 10 o'clock and the case stood adjourned. This day 10 o'clock, the petitioner appeared, in custody of the defendant who made a return in substance as follows: The said Daniel Wells resided in his district and was of the

legal age to do duty as a militia man, that in virtue of division orders from Major-General Samuel Smith dated 6th Aug. and of brigade orders, dated 7th Aug., he, the said John Kennedy, a captain in the 27th Regiment was ordered by Lt. Col. Long, commanding said regt. to call out the militia men in his district on a tour of duty for a week, in order to repel a threatened invasion of the state; that in compliance with said orders, he the said John Kennedy, did duly notify the said Wells (the petitioner) so liable as a militia man, to do the said tour of duty and as a member of his militia Co. to attend at the usual place; that the said Wells did not attend according to said notice ... by the articles of War, by act of Assembly passed at Nov. session 1811, Capt. 182, sect 31 - He is therefore in legal custody, and must be remanded to his officer and conducted to camp." (NARA; CMSR; Wright Vol. 2, p. 53; *Baltimore American*, 12 Jun 1819; see information at Henry Gough McComas herein about burial and re-burial)

Wells, James, served as a Private in Capt. George Steele's Co., 16th U.S. Inf., enlisted on 14 Mar 1814 at Lancaster, PA for 5 years, age 27, 5' 10½" tall, born in Harford Co., and was discharged at Sackett's Harbor, NY on 4 Apr 1816 for rheumatism (Johnson and Christou, p. 397). In Baltimore on 9 Mar 1822 James Wells, former sergeant in Lt. Brant's Co., 2nd Regt., U.S. Infantry, in the late war when disabled, a resident of this city about 4 years and previously of Frederick Co., collected his $48 pension from 4 Sep 1821 to 4 Mar 1822. (Pierce, p. 192)

Wellsbarger, Jacob, served as a Private in Capt. Gerrard Wilson's Co., 6th Regt., Baltimore Militia, from 19 Aug 1814 and was discharged by the doctor on 19 Oct 1814 as unfit for service (Wright Vol. 2, p. 11)

Welsh, Daniel (1786-1814), served as a Corporal in Capt. Samuel Lane's Co., 14th U.S. Infantry, enlisted 19 Sep 1812 for 5 years at the age of 26, 5' 7" tall, born in Maryland and died at French Mills, NY in Jan 1814; bounty land issued to brother Robert A. Welsh (BLW# 13143-160-12; Johnson and Christou, p. 397)

Welsh, Henry, see Henry Welch, q.v.

Welsh, John, served as a Private in Capt. Thomas Montgomery's Co., 14th U.S. Infantry, enlisted 11 Jun 1812 and died on 24 Jun 1813 (BLW# 13323-160-12; Johnson and Christou, p. 397)

Welsh, John (1795-1814), served as a Seaman under Sailing Master Simmones Bunbury, U.S. Sea Fencibles, enlisted 3 Jan 1814 at the age of 19, 5' 7½" tall, born in Baltimore City and died on 24 Nov 1814 (Johnson and Christou, p. 397)

Wertz, Samuel, served as a Private in Capt. John Buck's Co., 38th U.S. Infantry, enlisted 6 Mar 1814 in Hagerstown, MD at age 22, 5' 6½" tall, born in Bedford, PA and discharged at Baltimore on 8 Feb 1815 from an accidental hand wound (BLW# 877-160-12; Pension Old War IF-3515; Johnson and Christou, p. 398)

Wescott, William, served as Captain of the privateer *Joseph and Mary* and was captured by the frigate *Narcissus* on 25 Nov 1812 and sent to Jamaica (Marine, p. 478; *American Prisoners of War Paroled at Dartmouth, Halifax, Jamaica and Odiham during the War of 1812*, by Eric Eugene Johnson, did not mention him)

Wesley, William, served as a Private in Capt. Roderick Burgess' Co., Watkins' Regiment, Anne Arundel Co. Militia, from 22 Jul 1814, deserted on 1 Aug 1814, returned on 11 Aug 1814 and sick on furlough since 22 Aug 1814 as reported on the muster roll dated 22 Jul – 19 Sep 1814 (Wright Vol. 4, p. 42)

West, Abraham, served as a Private in Capt. George Washington Magee's Co., Frederick Co. Militia, 1st Regt., New Windsor area, from 22 Jul 1814, engaged in the Battle of Bladensburg and in the defense of Baltimore and was reported "sick absent 1 Sep" 1814 and discharged on 26 Dec 1814 by a Surgeon (Mallick and Wright, pp. 298, 342, 343)

West, Charles, served as a Sergeant in Capt. David Cummings' Co., 14th U.S. Infantry. Enlisted 20 May 1812 for 5 years at the age of 21, 5' 7½" tall, born in Dorchester Co., MD and was captured at Beaver Dams, Upper Canada on 24 Jun 1813 by Commander Yeo. Prisoner of War #7520 at Halifax, NS, interned 24 Oct 1813, discharged 5 Mar 1815, returned to service and was discharged at Raleigh, NC on 19 May 1817 (Johnson and Christou, p. 398; Baker Vol. 2, p. 428; Johnson,

p. 164, stated he was first imprisoned at Quebec on 7 Jul 1813 as Prisoner of War #409 and was discharged for transport on 31 Oct 1813)

West, George (1789-1815), served as a Seaman and was born in Baltimore. Age: 24. Prison Depot: Portsmouth, Prisoner of War #843. How Taken: Gave himself up off HM Ship-of-the-Line *Malta*. Date Received: 15 Jun 1813. From what ship: HM Sloop *Helena*. Discharged on 2 Jul 1813 and sent to Chatham on HMS *Tribune*. Prison Depot: Chatham, Prisoner of War #1851. Date Received: 7 Jul 1813 from Portsmouth on HMS *Tribune*. Discharged on 25 Jul 1814 and sent to Dartmoor on HMS *Bittern*. Prison Depot: Dartmoor, Prisoner of War #2094. Received: 3 Aug 1814 on HMS *Bittern* from Chatham Depot. Died on 27 Jan 1815 from gastritis. (Johnson's Database, 2019)

West, Hugh S., served as a Private in Capt. Nathan Towson's Co., 2nd U.S. Artillery, enlisted 20 Apr 1812 in Baltimore, age 30, 5' 9" tall, born in Virginia and was captured at Beaver Dams, Upper Canada on 2 4 Jun 1813. Prisoner of War #5240 at Halifax, NS, interned 28 Dec 1813, discharged for exchange on 31 May 1814 and discharged from service on 28 Sep 1815 (Johnson and Christou, p. 398; however, Johnson, p. 164, stated Hugh West was captured at the Battle of Stoney Creek, Upper Canada on 6 Jun 1813, was Prisoner of War #289 at Quebec, interned 28 Jun 1813 and discharged for transport on 31 Oct 1813)

West, Jonathan, of Baltimore Co., served as a Private in Capt. Adam Shower's Co., 2nd Regt., stationed in Baltimore and died 1 Oct 1814, cause not stated, but it was probably service connected. His name is not on the Baltimore Battle Monument. (Wright Vol. 2, p. 85)

West, Thomas (1778-1815), served as a Private in Capt. David Espy's Co., 22nd U.S. Infantry, enlisted 27 Oct 1813 in Gettysburg, PA at the age of 35, 5' 8" tall, born in Maryland and died at Sackett's Harbor, NY on 5 Jan 1815 (Johnson and Christou, p. 399)

Westbrook, Nicholas, served as a Private in Capt. Samuel Lane's Co., 14th U.S. Infantry, date not stated, and was wounded at Black Rock, NY on 28 Nov 1812 and died from his wounds on 29 Nov 1812 (Johnson and Christou, p. 399)

Westcott, William, served as a 1st Lieutenant and was born in Baltimore. Age: 45. Prison Depot: Plymouth 2, Prisoner of War #218. Captured by HM Frigate *Rhin*. When Taken: 5 Jun 1814. Where Taken: off San Domingo (Haiti). Prize Name: *Decatur*. Home Port: Charleston. Ship Type: Privateer. Date Received: 2 Mar 1815. From what ship: HMS *Dannemark*. Discharged on 3 Mar 1815 and sent to Dartmoor. Prison Depot: Dartmoor, Prisoner of War #6457. Captured by HM Frigate *Rhin*. When Taken: 5 Jun 1814. Date Received: 3 Mar 1815. From what ship: HMT *Ganges* from Plymouth. Discharged on 11 Jul 1815. (Johnson's Database, 2019)

Westlake, Josiah, served as a Private in Capt. William M. Littlejohn's Co., commanded by Electus Baccus, transferred to Lt. Stephenson's Co., U.S. Corps of Artillery, in the War of 1812 and was disabled, but no dates were given. On 7 Sep 1826 in Mercer Co., PA Josiah stated he was a resident of this county for about 7 years and previously of Baltimore, and appointed John White to collect his $96.00 pension due from 4 Sep 1824 to 4 Sep 1826. On 25 Sep 1826 Dr. Jeremiah Gage and Dr. James S. Cossite, of Mercer Co., PA, certified that his disability continues, that being a scrofula of the thorax. (Pierce, pp. 193-194)

Weston, David, served as a Seaman and was born in Baltimore. Age: 27. Prison Depot: Plymouth 1, Prisoner of War #1600. Captured by HM Brig *Royalist*. When Taken: 31 May 1813. Where Taken: Bay of Biscayne. Prize Name: *Governor Gerry*. Home Port: New Haven. Ship Type: Merchant Vessel. Date Received: 14 Jun 1813. From what ship: HMS *Royalist*. Discharged on 30 Jun 1813 and sent to Stapleton. Prison Depot: Stapleton, Prisoner of War #140. Date Received: 8 Jul 1813 from Plymouth. Discharged on 16 Jun 1814 and sent to Dartmoor. Prison Depot: Dartmoor, Prisoner of War #1516. Received: 23 Jun 1814 from Stapleton. Discharged on 1 May 1815. (Johnson's Database, 2019)

Whaler, Caleb, served as a Private in the 14th U.S. Infantry (company and captain not named) and died at French Mills, NY on 18 Jan 1814 from sickness (Johnson and Christou, p. 399)

Whalin, William, served as a Private in Capt. Thomas Ramsey's Co., 1st U.S. Rifles, enlisted 10 Feb 1814 at Louisville, KY at the age of 17, 5' 4" tall, born in Maryland and discharged at Detroit on 23 Sep 1815 on a Surgeon's Certificate (Johnson and Christou, pp. 399-400)

Wheatley, William (1784-183), served as a Private in Capt. William Smtih's Co., 16th U.S. Infantry, enlisted 6 May 1813 at the age of 29, 5' 4" tall, born in Maryland and died on 11 Dec 1813 (Johnson and Christou, p. 400)

Wheatly, James, served as a Private in Capt. Clement Sullivan's Co., 14th U.S. Infantry, enlisted 30 May 1812 and died 7 Dec 1812; bounty land issued to his brother Joseph Wheatley (BLW# 13552-160-12; Johnson and Christou, p. 400)

Wheedon, Horace, served as a Private in Capt. Samuel Sterett's Co., 5th Regt., Baltimore Militia, from 19 Aug 1814 and was wounded at North Point on 12 Sep 1814 (Wright Vol. 2, p. 6)

Wheeler, Anthony, served as a Private in Capt. David Cummings' Co., 14th U.S. Infantry, enlisted 17 Jun 1812 for 5 years, age 21, 5' 8½" tall, born in Dorchester Co., MD and was captured at Beaver Dams, Upper Canada on 24 Jun 1813. Prisoner of War #3854 at Halifax, NS, interned 24 Jun 1813, discharged 9 Nov 1813, sent to England on the HSM *Success*. Prison Depot: Chatham, Prisoner of

War #3147. Received on 7 Jan 1814 from Halifax. Age 23. Discharged on 10 Oct 1814 and sent to U.S. on the Cartel *St. Philip*. Transferred to the Ordnance Department on 21 Jun 1815 and was discharged at Baltimore on 14 Jun 1817. (Johnson and Christou, p. 400; Baker Vol. 2, p. 430; Johnson's Database, 2019)

Wheeler, Greenbury (1793-1814), served as a Private in Capt. Benjamin Sanders' Co., 17th U.S. Inf., enlisted on 28 Apr 1814, age 21, 5' 9" tall, born in Maryland and died at Buffalo on 22 Nov 1814 from fever; bounty land issued to brother William Wheeler (BLW# 25731-160-12; Johnson and Christou, p. 401)

Wheeler, Solomon, served as 2nd Sergeant in Capt. Walter S. Hunt's, 41st Regiment, Baltimore Co., from 25 Aug 1814 and was reported as "sick-absent since Sep 8" 1814 (Wright Vol. 2, p. 68)

Wheeler, William, served as a Private at age 24 and an Artificer at age 25 in Capt. Nathan Towson's Co., 2nd U.S. Artillery, enlisted 25 Jun 1812 for 5 years in Baltimore at the age of 24, 5' 7½" tall, born in Baltimore and was captured at the Battle of Stoney Creek, Upper Canada [in June 1813], age 25. Prisoner of War #288 at Quebec, interned 28 Jun 1813, released for transport on 31 Oct 1813. Prisoner of War at Halifax, NS (sic), later released and discharged from service at Fort Niagara, NY on 24 Jun 1817 (Johnson and Christou, p. 401, but Baker Vol. 2, p. 430, did not list him and Johnson, p. 164, listed him at Quebec)

Wheelock, James, served as a Private in the 14th U.S. Infantry (company not stated), enlisted 23 Sep 1812 in Baltimore, age 48, 5' 5½" tall, born in Dublin, Ireland and captured at Stoney Creek Upper Canada on 12 Jun 1813. Prisoner of War #5101 at Halifax, NS, interned 28 Dec 1813, discharged for exchange on 31 May 1814, returned to service and deserted on 16 Jul 1815 (Johnson and Christou, pp. 401-402; Baker Vol. 2, p. 431, spelled his name Whelock)

Whetman, Stephen, served as a Private in the 14th U.S. Infantry (company not stated) and was captured, probably at Beaver Dams, Upper Canada. Prisoner of War #3853 at Halifax, NS, interned 24 Jun 1813, discharged 9 Nov 1813 and sent to England (Johnson and Christou, p. 402; Baker Vol. 2, p. 431)

Whetton, John, served as a Private in the 14th U.S. Infantry (company not stated) and was captured, probably at Beaver Dams, Upper Canada. Prisoner of War #4016 at Halifax, NS, interned 24 Jun 1813, discharged 19 Nov 1813 and sent to England (Johnson and Christou, p. 402; Baker Vol. 2, p. 431)

Whipps (Whips), Benjamin (1759-1831), served as a Private in Capt. Jasper M. Jackson's Co., 34th Regiment, Prince George's Co. Militia, from 21 Aug 1814, at the advanced age of 55, and was furloughed on 4 Sep 1814 for "indisposition" (Wright Vol. 6 p. 22; *1812 Ancestor Index Volume I, 1892-1970*, National Society United States Daughters of 1812, 2005, p. 540)

Whistler, John Jr., served as a 1st Lieutenant in Capt. Harris Hickman's Co., 19th U.S. Infantry, born in Maryland, commissioned as an Ensign on 12 Mar 1812, promoted to 2nd Lieutenant on 30 Mar 1813, promoted to 1st Lieutenant on 20 Nov 1813, wounded at Brownstown, MI on 9 Aug 1812 and captured at Detroit on 16 Aug 1812. Prisoner of War on parole and died in Dec 1813 (Johnson and Christou, p. 402)

White, Alexander, P., served as a Carpenter's Mate on the privateer (armed brigantine) *Chasseur* of Baltimore, commanded by Capt. Thomas Boyle, and was killed in action on 26 Feb 1815 (*Niles Weekly Register*, 25 Mar 1815)

White, David (1785-1815), served as a Private in Capt. John Buck's Co., 38th U.S. Inf., enlisted 3 Jan 1814 in Cumberland, age 29, 5' 3" tall, born in Connecticut and died at Baltimore on 15 Jan 1815 (Johnson and Christou, p. 403)

White, David, served as a Boy onboard a ship and was born in Baltimore. Prison Depot: Plymouth 1, Prisoner of War #1531. Captured by HM Frigate *Andromache* on 14 Mar 1813. Age 15. Where Taken: off Nantes, France. Prize Name: *Courier*. Home Port: Baltimore. Ship Type: Letter of Marque. Date Received: 29 May 1813. From what ship: HMS *Hannibal*. Discharged on 30 Jun 1813 and sent to Stapleton. Prison Depot: Stapleton, Prisoner of War #95. Date Received: 8 Jul 1813 from Plymouth. Discharged on 13 Jun 1814 and sent to Dartmoor. Prison Depot: Dartmoor, Prisoner of War #1385. Date Received: 19 Jun 1814 from Stapleton. Discharged 28 Apr 1815. (Johnson's Database, 2019)

White, George, served as a Private in Capt. Stanton Sholes' Co., 2nd U.S. Artillery, enlisted on 16 Jan 1815 at Beaver Co., PA at the age of 24, 5' 6" tall, born in Maryland and discharged on 16 Oct 1815 because of blindness of the left eye and loss of the left great toe (Johnson and Christou, p. 403)

White, Henry, served as a Seaman and was born in Maryland. Age: 21. Prison Depot: Plymouth 1, Prisoner of War #720. Captured by HM Frigate *Belle Poule*. When Taken: 14 Feb 1813. Where Taken: Bay of Biscayne. Prize Name: *Criterion*. Ship Type: Merchant Vessel. Date Received: 19 Mar 1813. From what ship: HMS *Warspite*. Discharged and sent to Dartmoor on 2 Apr 1813. Prison Depot: Dartmoor, Prisoner of War #209. Captured by HM Frigate *Belle Poule*. Date Received: 2 Apr 1813 from Plymouth. Discharged on 20 Apr 1815. (Johnson's Database, 2019)

White, Jacob, served as a Private in Capt. Henry Grindage's Co., 14th U.S. Inf., enlisted 22 Aug 1812 and died on 9 Apr 1813; bounty land issued to his father Joseph W. White (BLW# 24888-160-12; Johnson and Christou, p. 401)

White, John, served as a Private in Capt. George Howard's Co., 25th U.S. Inf., enlisted 12 Aug 1813 for 5 years at Greenwich, NY, at the age of 25, 5' 6" tall, born in Baltimore and discharged at Sackett's Harbor, NY on 21 Mar 1816 on a Surgeon's Certificate (Johnson and Christou, p. 404)

White, John, served as a Private in Capt. David Cummings' Co., 14th U.S. Inf., born in Baltimore, enlisted on 21 Jun 1812 and was captured at Beaver Dams, Upper Canada on 24 Jun 1813. Prisoner of War #3749 at Halifax, NS, interned 24 Jun 1813, discharged on 9 Nov 1813 and sent to England on HMS *Success*. Prison Depot: Chatham, Prisoner of War #3103. Age 24. Received: 7 Jan 1814 from Halifax, NS. Discharged 10 Oct 1814, sent to U.S. on the Cartel *St. Philip*. (Johnson's Database, 2019.; Johnson and Christou, p. 404; Baker Vol. 2, p. 433)

White, Joseph, served as an Ordinary Seaman of the U.S. Chesapeake Flotilla, entered service on 5 Aug 1814 and died on 12 May 1814 (Shomette, p. 399)

Whiteford, William Hugh (1769-1849), served as Captain in the Extra Battalion of Harford Co. Militia under Lt. Col. William Smith for "9 days plus 4 days more a prisoner" as noted on the muster roll dated 26 Apr – 3 May 1813 (Wright Vol. 3, p. 33; *Whiteford Genealogy*, by Hazel Whiteford Baldwin, pp. 87-88). "Mr. Levy, was taken [by the British] about this time [3 May 1813], as was also Capt. Barnes, and one or two men. John O'Neill, Christopher Levy, James Sears, eldest son of Mrs. Sears, Capt. Whitefoot [Whiteford] and Ensign Hare were also made prisoners, as was one Whitloe, an aged citizen. Most of the Prisoners they released while on shore, but John O'Neill, Christopher Levy and James Sears they carried on board the fleet." (*Narrative Respecting the Conduct of the British From Their First Landing on Spesutia Island Till Their Progress to Havre de Grace*, by James Jones Wilmer, 1814, pp. 19-20; *Concord Point Lighthouse Station at Havre de Grace*, by Jack L. Shagena, Jr. and Henry C. Peden, Jr., 2017, p. 35; "Harford County in the War of 1812," by Christopher T. George, *Harford Historical Bulletin No. 76*, Spring 1998, p. 33)

Whiteley (Whitley), David R., served as a Private in Capt. Nathan Towson's Co., 2nd U.S. Artillery, enlisted 11 Apr 1812 in Baltimore at the age of 34, 5' 10" tall, born in Baltimore and captured at the Battle of Stoney Creek, Upper Canada on 12 Jun 1813. Prisoner of War #5074 at Halifax, NS, interned 28 Dec 1813 as David Whitley. Prisoner of War #374 at Quebec, interned as David R. Whitley, discharged on 31 Oct 1813 (sic), returned to service and was discharged at Fort Niagara, NY on 2 Jan 1817 (Johnson and Christou, p. 405, listed him twice as David R. Whiteley; Baker Vol. 2, p. 434, and Johnson's Quebec book, p. 166, spelled his name Whitley)

Whitloe, Mr., was not a soldier, but a citizen captured when the British burned Havre de Grace on 3 May 1813. "The elder, Mr. Levy, was taken about this time, as was also Capt. Barnes, and one or two men. John O'Neill, Christopher Levy, James Sears, eldest son of Mrs. Sears, Capt. Whitefoot [Whiteford] and Ensign

Hare were also made prisoners, as was one Whitloe, an aged citizen. Most of the Prisoners they released while on shore, but John O'Neill, Christopher Levy and James Sears they carried on board the fleet." (*Narrative Respecting the Conduct of the British From Their First Landing on Spesutia Island Till Their Progress to Havre de Grace*, by James Jones Wilmer, 1814, p. 13; *Concord Point Lighthouse Station at Havre de Grace*, by Jack L. Shagena, Jr. and Henry C. Peden, Jr., 2017, p. 35; "Harford County in the War of 1812," by Christopher T. George, *Harford Historical Bulletin* No. 76, Spring 1998, p. 33)

Whitmore, Humphrey (1774-1814), served as a Private in the 14th U.S. Infantry (company and captain not stated), enlisted on 1 Jun 1814 in Alexandria, DC at the age of 40, 5' 8" tall, born in Prince George's Co. and died on 31 Jul 1814; bounty land issued to son Humphrey Whitmore and other heirs at law (Johnson and Christou, p. 405; BLW# 18667-16-12)

Whitney, Joseph G., served as a Private in Capt. Isaac Raven's Co., Baltimore Co., 2nd Regiment, 11th Brigade, stationed in Baltimore from 27 Jul 1814 and was reported to b a "prisoner of war 12 Sep" 1814 (Wright Vol. 2, p. 84)

Whittington, Edward, served as a Private in Capt. Benjamin Leitch's Co., 31st Regiment, Calvert Co. Militia, for 3 days as shown on the muster roll dated 2 Aug – 17 Aug 1814 and was reported sick, but the exact date and cause were not stated (Wright Vol. 4, p. 51)

Whitton, William, served as a Private in Capt. William McIlvane's Co., 14th U.S. Infantry, enlisted on 7 Sep 1812 for 5 years at the age of 47, 5' 8" tall, born in Maryland and was discharged at Greenbush, NY on 1 May 1815 due to a hernia (Johnson and Christou, p. 403)

Whittington, Joshua, see Joshua Wittington, q.v.

Wickham, David, served as a Private in Capt. Joseph Nelson's Co., 36th U.S. Infantry, enlisted 20 Jun 1814 and died 17 Nov 1814; bounty land issued to his brother Levi A. Wickham (BLW# 22881-160-12; Johnson and Christou, p. 406)

Wickware, John (1791-1815), served as a Private in Capt. Isaac Baker's Co., 44th U.S. Infantry, enlisted 2 Jun 1814 in Gallatin, TN at age 23, 6' 1 ½" tall, born in Caroline Co., MD and died on 12 Mar 1815 (Johnson and Christou, p. 406)

Widafell, Mathias, served as a Private in Capt. Roderick Burgess' Co., 32nd Regt., Anne Arundel Co. Militia, from 22 Jul 1814 and reported as "missing Aug 24, believed to be kild (sic) on the field of battle" (Wright Vol. 4, p. 42)

Wilcoxon, Tbomas C., served as a Sergeant in Capt. Jasper M. Jackson's Co., 34th Regt., Prince George's Co. Militia, from 21 Aug 1814 and was "furloughed for indisposition" on 28 Aug 1814 (Wright Vol. 6, p. 22). Thomas C. Wilcoxen died by 25 Mar 1822. (Prince George's Co. Administration Accounts Index)

Wilkins, Elisha, served as a Private in Capt. Henry Grindage's Co., 14th U.S. Infantry, enlisted on 22 Aug 1812 and died on 8 Apr 1813; bounty land issued to his sister Sarah Wilkins (BLW# 27558-160-42; Johnson and Christou, p. 407)

Wilkins, James (1791-1813), served as a Private in Capt. Henry Grindage's Co., 14th U.S. Infantry, enlisted on 15 Aug 1812 for 5 years and was captured at Beaver Dams, Upper Canada on 26 Jun 1813. Prisoner of War #783 at Quebec, interned 7 Jul 1813, discharged on 10 Aug 1813 and died on 1 Nov 1813 from fever; bounty land was issued to his sister Sarah Wilkins (BLW# 27559-160-42; Johnson and Christou, p. 407; Johnson's Quebec book, p. 168; Johnson's Database, 2019, states he was age 22, served as a Private in the 6th U.S. Infantry and was Prisoner of War #4000 at Halifax, NS)

Wilkins, John, served as a Private in 14th U.S. Infantry (company not stated) and was captured, probably at Beaver Dams, Upper Canada. Prisoner of War #3859 at Halifax, NS, interned 24 Jun 1813 and was discharged for exchange on 3 Feb 1814 (Johnson and Christou, p. 407; Baker Vol. 2, p. 436)

Wilkins, William, served as a Private in Capt. Thomas Montgomery's Co., 14th U.S. Infantry, enlisted 15 Aug 1812 In Snow Hill, MD at the age of 24, 5' 8" tall, born in Snow Hill, MD and captured at Stoney Creek, Upper Canada on 12 Jun 1813. Prisoner of War #5125 at Halifax, NS, interned 28 Dec 1813 and was discharged for exchange on 31 May 1814 (Johnson and Christou, pp. 407-408, listed him as William Wilkins; Baker Vol. 2, p. 436, listed him as Will Wilkins)

Wilkinson, James, served as a Private in Capt. William McIlvane's Co., 14th U.S. Infantry, enlisted 1 Mar 1813 and was captured at Beaver Dams, Upper Canada on 24 Jun 1813. Prisoner of War #3736 at Halifax, NS, interned 24 Jun 1813, discharged for exchange on 3 Feb 1814, exchanged on 15 Apr 1814 (Johnson and Christou, p. 408; Baker Vol. 2, p. 436)

Wilkinson, James Biddle, served as a 2nd Lieutenant in Capt. James Wilkinson's Co., 2nd U.S. Infantry, was born in Maryland and commissioned a 2nd Lieutenant, 4th U.S. Infantry, on 16 Feb 1801, transferred to 2nd U.S. Infantry on 1 Apr 1802, promoted to 1st Lieutenant on 30 Sep 1803, promoted to Captain on 8 Oct 1808 and died on 7 Sep 1813 (Johnson and Christou, p. 408)

Wilkinson, Mr., served as an officer on the privateer *Nonsuch* of Baltimore under Capt. Levely and was killed in action on 28 Sep 1812 during a battle with a British schooner off Martinique (*Niles Weekly Register*, 14 Nov 1812; J. Thomas Scharf's *The Chronicles of Baltimore*, Vol. 1, p. 359)

Wilkison, Thomas, served as a Private in Capt. Adam Shower's Co., Baltimore Co., 2nd Regiment, 11th Brigade, was stationed in Baltimore from 26 Jul 1814 and reported "sick absent since Oct 20" 1814 (Wright Vol. 2, p. 84)

Wilkson, John, served as a Seaman and was born in Baltimore. Age: 23. Prison Depot: Plymouth 1, Prisoner of War #2666. Captured by HM Schooner *Canso*. When Taken: 11 May 1814. Where Taken: off Cape Clear, Ireland. Prize Name: *Traveler*, prize of the Privateer *Surprise*. Home Port: Baltimore. Ship Type: Privateer. Received: 5 Jun 1814. From what ship: HMS *Gronville*. Discharged on 14 Jun 1814 and sent to Dartmoor. (Johnson's Database, 2019)

Willelmi, Charles, served as a Private in 14th U.S. Infantry (company not stated) and was captured at Beaver Dams, Upper Canada on 24 Jun 1813. Prisoner of War #3801 at Halifax, NS, interned on 27 Aug 1813 and was discharged for exchange on 3 Feb 1814 (Johnson and Christou, p. 408; Baker Vol. 2, p. 436)

Willen, Littleton (c1792-1814), served as a Private in Capt. John Brookes' Co., 38th U.S. Infantry, enlisted on 27 Jul 1812, age was not given, 5' 9" tall, born in Maryland, re-enlisted at Craney Island, VA on 17 Apr 1814 for the duration of the war and died on 9 May 1814 (Johnson and Christou, p. 408)

Willer, William, served as a Corporal in the U.S. Marine Corps and was taken from the barracks and admitted to the Naval Hospital in Washington, DC as Patient No. 79 on 16 Dec 1814 with Prussian typhoid and died on 19 Dec 1814 (Sharp's Database, 2018)

Willett, John, served as a Seaman and was born in Baltimore. Age: 28. Prison Depot: Chatham, Prisoner of War #2020. How Taken: Gave himself up off HM Sloop-Brig *Rosario*. Received: 15 Jul 1813 from Plymouth. Discharged on 17 Jun 1814 and sent to Dartmoor on HMS *Pincher*. (Johnson's Database, 2019)

Williams, Amos A. (1776-1861), served as a Private in Capt. Samuel Sterett's Co., 5th Regiment, Baltimore Militia, from 19 Aug 1814 and was wounded on 12 Sep 1814 during the Battle of North Point. "Amos A. Williams, lawyer, senator in the state legislature, private, 5th regt. Wounded." (North Point dead and wounded Article 4 Oct 1814 Columbian Register CT Vol. III 97, p. 4; Wright Vol. 2, p. 6; J. Thomas Scharf's *History of Baltimore City and County*, p. 192) Amos A. Williams was born in Massachusetts and became an iron manufacturer in Baltimore (1850 Maryland Census). He was buried in Green Mount Cemetery.

Williams, Andrew, served as a Private in the 14th U.S. Infantry (company not stated) and was captured at Beaver Dams, Upper Canada on 24 Jun 1813. Prisoner of War #3811 at Halifax, NS, interned 27 Aug 1813 and was discharged on 9 Nov 1814 and sent to England on HMS *Success* (Johnson and Christou, p. 408; Baker Vol. 2, p. 436)

Williams, Barton, served as a Private in Capt. Archibald Sneed's Co., 1st U.S. Light Dragoons, enlisted 11 Aug 1812 in Virginia at the age of 45, 5' 9" tall, born in Prince George's Co., MD and discharged at Fort Hawkins, GA on 9 Aug 1815 on general debility (Johnson and Christou, p. 409)

Williams, Benjamin, served as a Boy onboard a ship and was born in Baltimore. Age: 14. Prison Depot: Portsmouth, Prisoner of War #560. Captured by HM Frigate *Dryad*. When Taken: 7 Jan 1813. Where Taken: at sea. Prize Name: *Rossie*. Ship Type: Merchant Vessel. Date Received: 25 Jan 1813. From what ship: HM Ship-of-the-Line *Queen*. Discharged on 11 Mar 1813 and sent to Chatham on HM Store Ship *Abundance*. Prison Depot: Chatham, Prisoner of War #1233. Received: 16 Mar 1813 from Portsmouth on HMS *Abundance*. Discharged on 24 Jul 1813 and was released to the Cartel *Hoffning*. (Johnson's Database, 2019)

Williams, George (African American), served as a Seaman and was born in Maryland. Age: 24. Prison Depot: Plymouth 1, Prisoner of War #752. Captured by HM Ship-of-the-Line *Warspite*. When Taken: 3 Mar 1813. Where Taken: Bay of Biscayne. Prize Name: *Charlotte*. Ship Type: Merchant Vessel. Date Received: 19 Mar 1813. From what ship: HMS *Warspite*. Discharged and sent to Dartmoor on 2 Apr 1813. Prison Depot: Dartmoor, Prisoner of War #239. Date Received: 2 Apr 1813 from Plymouth. Discharged and sent to Mill Prison on 10 Jul 1813. Prison Depot: Plymouth 1, Prisoner of War #1737. Received 10 Jul 1813 from Dartmoor Prison, discharged on same day and released to HMS *Salvador del Mundo*. (Johnson's Database, 2019)

Williams, George (African American), served as a Seaman and was born in Queen Anne's Co., MD. Age: 23. Prison Depot: Plymouth 1, Prisoner of War #29. Captured by HM Frigate *Leonidas*. When Taken: 31 Jul 1812. Where Taken: off Ireland. Prize Name: *Catherine*. Ship Type: Merchant Vessel. Date Received: 23 Nov 1812. From what ship: HMS *Stork*. Discharged and sent to Portsmouth on 29 Dec 1812 on HMS *Northumberland*. Prison Depot: Portsmouth, Prisoner of War #306. Date Received: 31 Dec 1812. From what ship: HM Ship-of-the-Line *Northumberland*. Discharged on 4 Mar 1813 and sent to Chatham on HMS *Queen*. Prison Depot: Chatham, Prisoner of War #1037. Date Received: 11 Mar 1813 from Yarmouth on HMS *Tenders*. Discharged on 26 Jul 1813 and released to the Cartel *Hoffning*. (Johnson's Database, 2019)

Williams, George (African American), served as a Seaman and was born in Baltimore. Age: 26. Prison Depot: Plymouth 1, Prisoner of War #30. Captured by HM Frigate *Leonidas*. When Taken: 31 Jul 1812. Where Taken: off Ireland. Prize Name: *Catherine*. Ship Type: Merchant Vessel. Date Received: 23 Nov 1812. From what ship: HMS Stork. Discharged and sent to Portsmouth on 29 Dec 1812 on HMS *Northumberland*. Prison Depot: Portsmouth, Prisoner of War #307. Date Received: 31 Dec 1812. From what ship: HM Ship-of-the-Line *Northumberland*.

Discharged on 4 Mar 1813 and sent to Chatham on HMS *Queen*. Prison Depot: Chatham, Prisoner of War #1038. Date Received: 11 Mar 1813 from Yarmouth on HMS *Tenders*. Discharged on 26 Jul 1813 and released to the Cartel *Hoffning* (Johnson's Database, 2019)

Williams, George, served as a Private in Capt. Frederick Evans' Co., Corps of Artillery, enlisted 4 Apr 1814 at Fort McHenry at the age of 18, 5' 8" tall, born in Pennsylvania and was discharged on 22 Apr 1815 for deafness (Johnson and Christou, p. 409) He was buried in Green Mount Cemetery.

Williams, Hendrick, served as a Seaman and was born in Maryland. Age: 16. Prison Depot: Plymouth 1, Prisoner of War #2127. Captured by HM Frigate *Hotspur* & HM Frigate *Pyramus*. When Taken: 26 Oct 1813. Where Taken: Bay of Biscayne. Prize Name: *Chesapeake*. Ship Type: Letter of Marque. Date Received: 22 Nov 1813. From what ship: HMS *Pyramus*. Discharged on 29 Nov 1813 and sent to Dartmoor. (Johnson's Database, 2019)

Williams, Henry, served as a Boy onboard a ship and was born in Maryland. Age: 16. Prison Depot: Dartmoor, Prisoner of War #848. Captured by HM Frigate *Hotspur* & HM Frigate *Pyramus*. When Taken: 26 Oct 1813. Where Taken: at sea off Nantes, France. Prize Name: *Chesapeake*. Ship Type: Letter of Marque. Date Received: 29 Nov 1813 from Plymouth. Discharged on 26 Apr 1815. (Johnson's Database, 2019)

Williams, Henry Lee, served as a Private in Capt. Samuel Sterett's Co., 1st Baltimore Hussars, 5th Cavalry Regiment, from 19 Aug 1814 and was wounded on 12 Sep 1814 at North Point (Huntsberry, p. 63, but Wright Vol. 2, p. 57, and Marine p. 483, both did not mention his wound)

Williams, Jacques (African American), served as a Seaman and was born in Baltimore. Age: 18. Prison Depot: Plymouth 1, Prisoner of War #1996. Captured by HM Brig *Royalist*. When Taken: 6 Sep 1812. Where Taken: coast of France. Prize Name: *Ned*. Home Port: Baltimore. Ship Type: Letter of Marque. Date Received: 22 Sep 1813. From what ship: HMS *Royalist*. Discharged on 27 Sep 1813 and sent to Dartmoor. Prison Depot: Dartmoor, Prisoner of War #715. Date Received: 27 Sep 1813 from Plymouth. Discharged on 26 Apr 1815. (Johnson's Database, 2019)

Williams, James (African American), served as a Seaman and was born in Baltimore. Age: 21. Prison Depot: Chatham, Prisoner of War #3773. Captured by HM Ship-of-the-Line *San Domingo*. When Taken: 1 Mar 1814. Where Taken: off Savannah, GA. Prize Name: *Argus*. Ship Type: Privateer. Date Received: 26 May 1814. From what ship: HMS *Hindostan*. Discharged on 25 Sep 1814 and sent to Dartmoor on HMS *Niobe*. Prison Depot: Dartmoor, Prisoner of War #4622. Date

Received: 9 Oct 1814. From what ship: HMT *Leyden* from Chatham. Discharged on 15 Jun 1815. (Johnson's Database, 2019)

Williams, James, served as a Seaman and was born in Baltimore. Age: 46. Prison Depot: Dartmoor, Prisoner of War #1759. How Taken: Gave himself up off HM Brig *Badger*. When Taken: 15 Nov 1812. Date Received: 20 Jul 1814. From what ship: HMS *Milford* from Plymouth. Discharged on 26 Apr 1815. (Johnson's Database, 2019)

Williams, Jeremiah (1786-1813), served as a Private in Capt. Joseph Hook's Co., 36th U.S. Infantry, enlisted 5 May 1813 in Baltimore at the age of 27, 5' 6" tall, born in Virginia and died on 14 Jul 1813 (Johnson and Christou, p. 410)

Williams, John, served as a Marine, was taken from the barracks and admitted to the Naval Hospital in Washington, DC as Patient No. 68 on 3 Aug 1814 (injury or illness was not specified) and died on 4 Sep 1814 (Sharp's Database, 2018)

Williams, John, served as a Private in Capt. Walter S. Hunt's, 41st Regiment, Baltimore Co., from 25 Aug 1814 and reported as "sick-absent since Sep 10" 1814 (Wright Vol. 2, p. 69)

Williams, John, served as a Private in Capt. Lawson Cuddy's Co., 41st Regiment, Baltimore Co., from 25 Aug 1814 and was reported "sick – absent since Sep 17" 1814 (Wright Vol. 2, p. 68)

Williams, John (African American), served as a Seaman and was born in Baltimore. Age: 25. Prison Depot: Dartmoor, Prisoner of War #6122. Captured by HM Ship-of-the-Line *Bellerophon*. When Taken: 2 Nov 1814. Where Taken: Long 61. Prize Name: *Betsy*, prize of the Privateer *Grand Turk*. Ship Type: Privateer. Date Received: 6 Jan 1814. From what ship: HMT *Impregnable*. Discharged on 5 Jul 1815. (Johnson's Database, 2019)

Williams, John (African American), served as a Seaman and was born in Baltimore. Age: 26. Prison Depot: Dartmoor, Prisoner of War #4338. Captured by HM Frigate *Loire*. When Taken: 18 Feb 1814. Where Taken: off St. Thomas, West Indies. Prize Name: *Venus*, prize of the Privateer *Nonsuch*. Ship Type: Letter of Marque. Received: 7 Oct 1814. From what ship: HMT *Salvador del Mundo* from Halifax, NS. Discharged 14 Jun 1815. (Johnson's Database, 2019)

Williams, John, served as a Seaman and was born in Baltimore. Age: 27. Prison Depot: Plymouth 1, Prisoner of War #1998. Captured by HM Brig *Royalist*. When Taken: 6 Sep 1812. Where Taken: coast of France. Prize Name: *Ned*. Home Port: Baltimore. Ship Type: Letter of Marque. Date Received: 22 Sep 1813. From what ship: HMS *Royalist*. Discharged on 27 Sep 1813 and sent to Dartmoor. Prison Depot: Dartmoor, Prisoner of War #717. Age 26. Date Received: 27 Sep 1813 from Plymouth. Discharged and released on 7 May 1814. (Johnson's Database, 2019)

Williams, John, served as a Seaman and was born in Baltimore. Age: 38. Prison Depot: Dartmoor, Prisoner of War #5972. Captured by HM Ship-of-the-Line *Bulwark*. When Taken: 22 Sep 1814. Where Taken: Georges Bank. Prize Name: *Halifax Packet*, prize of the Privateer *Harpy*. Home Port: Baltimore. Ship Type: Privateer. Received: 27 Dec 1814. From what ship: HMT *Penelope*. Discharged on 3 Jul 1815. (Johnson's Database, 2019)

Williams, John, served as a Seaman and was born in Baltimore. Age: 19. Prison Depot: Dartmoor, Prisoner of War #4910. Captured by HM Ship-of-the-Line *Saturn*. When Taken: 25 May 1814. Where Taken: off Sandy Hook, NJ. Prize Name: *Hussar*. Home Port: New York. Ship Type: Privateer. Date Received: 28 Oct 1814. From what ship: HMT *Alkbar* from Halifax, NS. Discharged on 21 Jun 1815. (Johnson's Database, 2019)

Williams, John, served as a Seaman and was born in Baltimore. Age: 25. Prison Depot: Plymouth 1, Prisoner of War #763. Captured by HM Ship-of-the-Line *Warspite*. When Taken: 3 Mar 1813. Where Taken: Bay of Biscayne. Prize Name: *William Bayard*. Ship Type: Merchant Vessel. Date Received: 19 Mar 1813. From what ship: HMS *Warspite*. Discharged and was sent to Dartmoor on 28 Jun 1813. Prison Depot: Dartmoor, Prisoner of War #256. Date Received: 28 Jun 1813 from Plymouth. Discharged and then enlisted on 13 Sep 1813 in the British service. (Johnson's Database, 2019)

Williams, Joseph (c1790-1815), served as Captain of his own company in the 12th Regiment, St. Mary's Co. Militia, stationed at Point Lookout from 13 Apr to 18 Apr 1813 and at Leonard Town from 24 Jul to 26 Jul 1814 and died in March 1815 in St. Mary's Co. On 13 Mar 1851 Clara Medley, age 67, widow of Joseph Williams, stated she married him on 27 Dec 1813 and her former name was Greenwell; she later married a Medley, applied for bounty land in 1855, age 71, and was granted 80 acres. (Wright Vol. 5, pp. 17, 91; BLW# 55-80-49304)

Williams, Lancelot, served as a Private in Capt. Frederick Evans' Co., Light Dragoons, enlisted 12 Feb 1814, age 44, 5' 8½" tall, born in Maryland and was discharged on 19 Aug 1815 as unfit for service (Johnson and Christou, p. 410)

Williams, Lot, served as a Private in the U.S. Light Dragoons and died **on** 24 Nov 1814 (Johnson and Christou, p. 410)

Williams, Mr., served as an officer on the privateer *Nonsuch* of Baltimore and was killed on 28 Sep 1812 (*Niles Weekly Register*, 14 Nov 1812)

Williams, Nathaniel (1782-1864), served as a Private in Capt. Samuel Sterett's Co., 5th Regt., Baltimore Militia, and was wounded on 12 Sep 1814 at North Point.

(Huntsberry, p. 68, but Wright Vol. 2, p. 6, and Marine p. 485, both did not mention his wound) He died on 10 Sep 1864 in his 83rd year and was buried in Green Mount Cemetery. (*The [Baltimore] Sun*, 12 Sep 1864) He married Maria Dalrymple. (*1812 Ancestor Index Volume I, 1892-1970*, National Society United States Daughters of 1812, 2005, p. 549)

Williams, Richard, served as a Private in Capt. Nathan Towson's Co., 2nd U.S Artillery, and was killed during the Battle of Stoney Creek, Upper Canada [in June 1813] (Johnson and Christou, p. 411)

Williams, Thomas, served as a Private in Capt. William McIlvane's Co., 14th U.S. Infantry, and was captured, probably at Beaver Dams, Upper Canada. Prisoner of War #4062 at Halifax, NS, interned 24 Jun 1813 and discharged for exchange on 3 Feb 1814 (Johnson and Christou, p. 411; Baker Vol. 2, p. 440)

Williams, Thomas (Mulatto), served as a Seaman and was born in Maryland. Age: 27. Prison Depot: Portsmouth, Prisoner of War #970. How Taken: Gave himself up off HM Ship-of-the-Line *Leviathan*. Date Received: 31 Jul 1813. From what ship: HMS *Leviathan*. Discharged on 7 Aug 1813 and sent to Chatham on HMS *Rinaldo*. Prison Depot: Chatham, Prisoner of War #2185. Received: 16 Aug 1813 from Portsmouth on an admiral's tender. Discharged on 11 Aug 1814 and sent to Dartmoor on HMS *Freya*. Prison Depot: Dartmoor, Prisoner of War #2636. Received: 21 Aug 1814 on HMT *Freya* from Chatham. Discharged on 3 May 1815. (Johnson's Database, 2019)

Williams, Thomas, served as a Seaman and was born in Baltimore. Age: 40. Prison Depot: Portsmouth, Prisoner of War #1140. Captured by HM Brig *Zenobia*. When Taken: 22 Jun 1813. Where Taken: off Lisbon, Portugal. Prize Name: *Hepsey*. Ship Type: Merchant Vessel. Date Received: 6 Oct 1813. From what ship: HM Sloop *Kingfisher*. Discharged on 17 Oct 1813 and sent to Chatham on HMT *Malabar No. 352*. Prison Depot: Chatham, Prisoner of War #2431. Date Received: 21 Oct 1813 from Portsmouth on HMT *Malabar*. Discharged on 4 Sep 1814 and sent to Dartmoor on HMS *Freya*. Prison Depot: Dartmoor, Prisoner of War #3240. Date Received: 11 Sep 1814. From what ship: HMT *Freya* from Chatham. Discharged on 28 May 1815. (Johnson's Database, 2019)

Williams, Thomas G., served as a Private in Capt. William Jett's Co., 20th U.S. Infantry, enlisted 25 Jul 1813 at Alexandria, DC at the advanced age of 50, 5' 11" tall, born in St. Mary's Co., transferred to 35th U.S. Infantry on 20 Mar 1815 and was discharged at Norfolk, VA on 26 Jul 1815 on a Surgeon's Certificate for old age and rheumatism (Johnson and Christou, p. 411)

Williams, William, (African-American runaway slave), served as a Private in the 38th U.S. Artillery and was in the battle of Bladensburg, at Hampstead Hill and at Fort McHenry where he was wounded on 13 Sep 1814 (lost a leg when hit by a cannon ball) and died two weeks later in a Baltimore Hospital. Name is <u>not</u> on the Baltimore Battle Monument. His actual name was Frederick Hall and he was Maj. Benjamin Oden's slave who ran away from the Bellefields Plantation and on April 14, 1814, enlisted in the 38th U.S. Infantry as a private under the name of William Williams. He also received his $50 enlistment bounty plus a private's wage of $8 per month. Hall served with the rest of his Co. in the dry moat of Fort McHenry during the bombardment of September 13-14, 1814, where his leg was blown off by a cannon ball. He died two months later in the Baltimore Public Hospital. His story is known because Major Oden later tried to claim the bounty of 160 acres of land to which Williams' heirs were entitled for his military service. Congress denied the claim, saying that Oden had not tried hard enough to get his former slave back, even although he had advertised for his return. *"Forty Dollars Reward, For apprehending and securing in jail so that I can get him again, NEGRO FREDERICK; Sometimes calls himself FREDERICK HALL a bright mulatto; straight and well made; 21 years old; 5 feet 7 or 8 inches high, with a short chub nose and so fair as to show freckles; he has no scars or marks of any kind that is recollected; his clothing when he left home, two months since, was home made cotton shirts, jacket, and Pantaloons of cotton and yarn twilled, all white. It is probable he may be in Baltimore, having a relation there, a house servant to a Mr. Williams, by the name of Frank, who is also a mulatto, but not so fair as Frederick. Benjamin Oden, Prince George's County, May 12th"* (*Baltimore American*, May 18, 1814; also, *Washington Daily National Intelligencer*, June 30, 1814, carried an advertisement by Benjamin Oden, but the reward was only $20; date on the advertisement was April 25, 1814 suggesting Oden later upped the reward). William Williams was a mulatto who also used the name Frederick Hall and served as a Corporal in Capt. Shepperd Leakin's Co., 38th U.S. Infantry, having enlisted on 5 Apr 1814 at the age of 22, 5' 8" tall, and was born in Baltimore (Johnson and Christou, p. 411, In Full Glory Reflected, Eshelman and Kummerow p 83)

Williams, William, served as a Private in the 14th U.S. Infantry (company and captain not named) and died at Sackett's Harbor, NY on 16 Jan 1814 (Johnson and Christou, pp. 411-412)

Williams, William, served as a Private in Capt. David Warfield's Co., 5th Regt., Baltimore United Volunteers, from 19 Aug and was wounded at Bladensburg on 24 Aug 1814 (Marine p. 485). He served as a Private in Capt. William Cooke, Jr.'s Co., formerly Capt. Warfield's Co., from 18 Oct 1814 to 18 Nov 1814 and was reported "sick in quarters" (CMSR), but he was listed on the muster roll dated 19 Aug – 18 Nov 1814 as wounded. (Wright Vol. 2, p. 8). Pension #34203 on 14 Mar 1879 he stated he was age 83 and was wounded and later sick in the war. He was born in Kingston, Somerset Co., MD, enlisted in Baltimore City on 5 Mar 1813 when about age 18 and was discharged in Nov 1813. No statement was made regarding service in 1814 so this may be another William Williams. (Note: Pension Application SC-25192, however, was filed by William Williams for alleged service in Capt. Warfield's Co. and in Capt. William Cook's Co.)

Williams, William J., served as a Private in the 38th U.S. Infantry, enlisted 21 Apr 1814 at the age of 21, 5' 4½" tall, dark hair, sallow complexion, born in England. D.R. [roster] dated Baltimore 1 Jun 1814, J.R. [roster] of Capt. J.H. Hook, near Port Covington, dated 31 Dec 1814, discharged 9 Dec 1814, wounded at Fort McHenry on 12 Sep 1814 and his left leg was amputated; he was discharged as a sergeant at Baltimore. (Johnson and Christou, p. 412)

Williamson, Charles, served as a Seaman and was born in Maryland. Age: 27. Prison Depot: Plymouth 1, Prisoner of War #93. Captured by HM Brig *Rover*. When Taken: 21 Oct 1812. Where Taken: off Bordeaux, France. Prize Name: *Experiment*. Ship Type: Merchant Vessel. Date Received: 25 Dec 1812. From what ship: HMS *Northumberland*. Discharged and sent to Portsmouth on 29 Dec 1812 on HMS *Northumberland*. Prison Depot: Portsmouth, Prisoner of War #347. Date Received: 31 Dec 1812. From what ship: HM Ship-of-the-Line *Northumberland*. Discharged on 4 Mar 1813 and sent to Chatham on HMS *Queen*. Prison Depot: Chatham, Prisoner of War #924. Date Received: 10 Mar 1813. From what ship: HMS *Tigress*. Discharged on 8 Jun 1813 and released to the Cartel *Rodrigo*. (Johnson's Database, 2019)

Williamson, Charles, served as a Seaman and was born in Maryland. Age: 29. Prison Depot: Dartmoor, Prisoner of War #2377. Captured by HM Frigate *Orpheus*. When Taken: 20 Apr 1814. Where Taken: off Matanzas, Cuba. Prize Name: U.S. Sloop-of-War *Frolic*. Ship Type: Warship. Date Received: 16 Aug 1814 on HMT *Queen* from Halifax, NS. Discharged and was sent to Dartmouth on 19 Oct 1814. (Johnson's Database, 2019)

Williamson, Frederick, was a Seaman who was wounded on 24 Aug 1814 on the field of battle at Bladensburg and was admitted to the Naval Hospital in Washington, DC as Patient No. 9; he was discharged on 10 Oct 1814 and sent to Baltimore (Sharp's Database, 2018)

Willimea, John N., served as a Private in Capt. William McIlvane's Co., 14th U.S. Infantry, enlisted on 8 Oct 1812 and was captured, probably at Beaver Dams, Upper Canada. Prisoner of War #4072 at Halifax, NS, interned 24 Jun 1813, discharged for exchange on 3 Feb 1814, exchanged on 15 Apr 1814 and discharged at Greenbush, NY on 29 Mar 1815 (Johnson and Christou, p. 412, spelled his name John N. Willimea and also listed John Williner, both in the 14th U.S. Infantry and both captured; Baker Vol. 2, p. 441, spelled it John Williner)

Willin, Loudor, served as a Private in Capt. Thomas Montgomery's Co., 14th U.S. Infantry, enlisted 10 May 1813 and died on 29 Dec 1813; bounty land issued to his sister Nancy Westcoat (BLW# 27031-160-12; Johnson and Christou, p. 412)

Williner, John, see John Willimea, q.v.

Willing, Samuel (1792-1814), served as a Private in Capt. Joseph Hook's Co., 36th U.S. Infantry, enlisted 23 May 1813 for 1 year in Baltimore at the age of 21, 5' 10" tall, was born on the Eastern Shore of Maryland and died on 6 Apr 1814 (Johnson and Christou, p. 412)

Willingham, William (1782-1815), served as a Private in the 3rd U.S. Rifle Co. under Capt. Edward Carrington, enlisted 14 Jun 1814 in Truerty (Liberty?) Town at the age of 32, 5' 9½" tall, born in West Liberty, MD and died on 12 Feb 1815; bounty land was issued to James Willingham, his only heir at law (BLW# 27132-160-42; Johnson and Christou, p. 412)

Willis, John, served as a Sergeant in Capt. William McIlvane's Co., 14th U.S. Infantry, enlisted 3 Jun 1812 for 5 years at the age of 51, 5' 9" tall, born in Baltimore, and was wounded at Beaver Dams, Upper Canada, ten miles west of Niagara Falls, with a gunshot wound in his arm. Prisoner of War, exchanged on 15 Apr 1814 and discharged from the service at Greenbush, NY on 24 May 1815 (Johnson and Christou, p. 412)

Willis, Stephen, served as a Private in the 14th U.S. Infantry (company not stated) and was captured at Beaver Dams, Upper Canada on 24 Jun 1813. Prisoner of War #3813 at Halifax, NS, interned 27 Aug 1813, discharged 9 Nov 1814 and sent to England (Johnson and Christou, p. 413; Baker Vol. 2, p. 441)

Willoughby, George, served as a Corporal in Capt. Richard Whartenby's Co., 5th U.S. Infantry, enlisted on 17 Jul 1811 at Eastown [Easton, MD] at the age of 24, 5' 9" tall, born in Caroline Co., MD and was captured at Stoney Creek, Upper Canada on 12 Jun 1813. Prisoner of War #5064 at Halifax, NS, interned 28 Dec 1813 and discharged for exchange on 31 May 1814 (Johnson and Christou, p. 413; Baker Vol. 2, p. 442)

Willson, John, served as a Seaman and was born in Maryland. Age: 30. Prison Depot: Chatham, Prisoner of War #900. Captured by HM Brig *Papillon*. When Taken: 17 Aug 1812. Where Taken: off Cadiz, Spain. Prize Name: *Pallas*. Home Port: Boston. Ship Type: Merchant Vessel. Date Received: 1 Mar 1813 from Plymouth on HMS *Namur*. Discharged on 23 Mar 1813 and was released to the Cartel *Robinson Potter*. (Johnson's Database, 2019)

Willson, Nicholas, served as a Private in Capt. Henry Fowler's Co., Randall's Rifle Bttn., Baltimore Co., from 26 Aug 1814 and reported as "in captivity from Oct 13" 1814 (Wright Vol. 2, p. 74)

Willy, John, served as a Seaman and was born in Baltimore. Age: 25. Prison Depot: Chatham, Prisoner of War #3272. Captured by HM Ship-of-the-Line *Valiant* & HM Brig *Curlew*. When Taken: 26 Mar 1813. Where Taken: Georges Bank. Prize Name: *Volant*. Ship Type: Letter of Marque. Date Received: 23 Feb 1814 from Halifax, NS on HMT *Malabar*. Discharged on 21 Jul 1814 and sent to Dartmoor on HMS *Portia*. Prison Depot: Dartmoor, Prisoner of War #1860. Date Received: 29 Jul 1814 on HMS *Ville de Paris* from Chatham Depot. Discharged on 2 May 1815. (Johnson's Database, 2019)

Wilmer, Isaac (Mulatto), served as a Seaman and was born in Rock Hall, MD. Age: 27. Prison Depot: Portsmouth, Prisoner of War #167. Captured by HM Transport *Diadem*. When Taken: 7 Oct 1812. Where Taken: S. Andera (St. Andrews, Scotland). Prize Name: *Baltimore*. Home Port: Baltimore. Ship Type: Privateer. Received: 3 Nov 1812 San Antonio. From what ship: HMS *Diadem*. Discharged on 19 Feb 1813 and sent to Chatham on HM Store Ship *Dromedary*. Prison Depot: Chatham, Prisoner of War #536. Date Received: 23 Feb 1813 from Portsmouth on HMS *Dromedary*. Discharged on 8 Jun 1813 and released to the Cartel *Rodrigo*. (Johnson's Database, 2019)

Wilmer, James P. (c1782-1814), of Harford Co., served as 1st Lieutenant on Capt. David Porter's frigate U.S.S. *Essex* during the War of 1812 (he had been appointed a Midshipman on 27 Dec 1802). "For months the *Essex* had been preying on the British whaling fleet off the west coast of South America. The British sent the frigate *Phoebe* (36 guns) and sloop-of-war *Cherub* (18 guns) to terminate the career of the Yankee raider ... [and] during the frantic engagement" Wilmer was "knocked overboard by a splinter while getting the sheet anchor from the bows, and was drowned" on 28 Mar 1814 off Valparaiso, Chile. ("Harford County in the War of 1812," by Christopher T. George, *Harford Historical Bulletin* No. 76, Spring 1998, pp. 8-9; *Niles Weekly Register*, 16 Jul 1814, reported a list of the men of the *Essex* who were lost during that action)

Wilson, Alexander, served as a Private in Capt. Henry Grindage's Co., 14th U.S. Infantry, enlistment date not given, age 26, and was captured at the Battle of Stoney Creek, Upper Canada [June 1813] (Johnson and Christou, p. 413, listed two Alexanders, both were captured, but Baker Vol. 2, p. 442, listed only one)

Wilson, Alexander, served as a Sergeant in Capt. Richard Arell's Co., 14th U.S. Infantry, enlisted 6 Oct 1812 in Baltimore, age 27, 5' 4" tall, born in Hunterdon Co., NJ and was captured, probably at Beaver Dams, Upper Canada. Prisoner of War #4109 at Halifax, NS, interned on 24 Jun 1813 and was discharged for exchange on 3 Feb 1814 (Johnson and Christou, p. 413; Baker Vol. 2, p. 442)

Wilson, Andrew, served as a Private in Capt. Denton Darby's Co., Frederick Co. Militia, was wounded in action at Bladensburg on 24 Aug 1814 and died on 5 Sep 1814 (Wright Vol. 8, pp. 12, 349; Mallick and Wright, pp. 304, 349)

Wilson, Azariah, served as a Private in the 14th U.S. Infantry, enlisted 20 Oct 1812 for 5 years and died on 7 Jan 1814; bounty land issued to Samuel Wilson, heir at law (BLW# 3231-160-12; Johnson and Christou, pp. 413-414)

Wilson, Charles (African American), served as a Seaman and was born in Baltimore. Age: 19. Prison Depot: Plymouth 1, Prisoner of War #2311. Captured by HM Brig *Pelican*. When Taken: 13 Jan 1814. Where Taken: at sea. Prize Name: *Siro*. Home Port: Baltimore. Ship Type: Letter of Marque (Privateer). Date Received: 23 Jan 1814. From what ship: HMS *Pelican*. Discharged on 31 Jan 1814 and sent to Dartmoor. Prison Depot: Dartmoor, Prisoner of War #974. Date Received: 31 Jan 1814 from Plymouth. Discharged on 27 Apr 1815. (Johnson's Database, 2019)

Wilson, Daniel (1776-1842), served as a Private in Capt. Samuel Lane's Co., 14th U.S. Infantry, enlisted 1 Aug 1812 at age 36, 5' 8" tall, born in Marlborough, MD, severely wounded in the leg and captured at Beaver Dams, Upper Canada, ten miles west of Niagara Falls, on 24 Jun 1813. Prisoner of War #3993 at Halifax, NS, discharged and exchanged on 3 Feb or 15 Apr 1814, and discharged from the service at Greenbush, NY on 20 Jun 1814 on a Surgeon's Certificate (BLW# 7932-160-12; Johnson and Christou, p. 414; Baker, Vol. 2, p. 442). In Baltimore on 11 Oct 1842 Delila Wilson, widow of Daniel Wilson, late invalid pensioner, a former private in Capt. Cummings' Co., 14th Regt. U.S. Infantry, who resided in Calvert Co. for eight years and previously of Baltimore, collected her own $20.40 pension arrears due from 4 Mar 1842 to 16 Jan 1842, the date of Daniel's death. (Pierce, p. 200)

Wilson, James, served as a Private in Capt. Michael Peters' Co., 51st Regiment, Baltimore Militia, from 19 Aug 1814 and was reported "sick absent, 29 days in actual service" (Wright Vol. 2, p. 36)

Wilson, James (African American), served as a Seaman and was born in Maryland. Age: 38. Prison Depot: Chatham, Prisoner of War #2600. How Taken: Gave himself up off HM Ship-of-the-Line *Berwick*. When Taken: 27 May 1813. Date Received: 5 Nov 1813. From what ship: HMS *Hindostan*. Discharged on 12 Aug 1814 and sent to Dartmoor on HMS *Alpheus*. Prison Depot: Dartmoor, Prisoner of War #2934. Date Received: 24 Aug 1814. From what ship: HMT *Alpheus* from Chatham. Discharged 19 May 1815. (Johnson's Database, 2019)

Wilson, John, served as a Seaman and was born in Baltimore. Age: 23. Prison Depot: Portsmouth, Prisoner of War #1495. Captured by HM Schooner *Canso*. When Taken: 11 May 1814. Where Taken: off Cape Clear, Ireland. Prize Name:

Traveler, prize of the Privateer *Surprise*. Home Port: Baltimore. Ship Type: Privateer. Received: 1 Jun 1814. From what ship: HMS HMS *Canso*. Discharged on 2 Jun 1814 and sent to Plymouth on HMS *Growler*. Prison Depot: Dartmoor, Prisoner of War #1290. Received 14 Jun 1814 from Mill Prison. Discharged on 28 Apr 1815. (Johnson's Database, 2019)

Wilson, John, of Alexander, served as a Private in Capt. Joseph Green's Co. and Capt. James F. Huston's Co., Frederick County Militia, from 23 Jul 1814 and was discharged in Baltimore on 6 Dec 1814 by a Surgeon, but the medical reason was not stated; he lived in Frederick Town. (Mallick and Wright, pp. 304, 346)

Wilson, Johnzey, served as a Private in Capt. Conrad Hook's Co., Baltimore Co., 2nd Regt., 11th Brigade, stationed at Camp Hampstead in Baltimore from 25 Jul 1814 and was listed as "sick absent since Aug 24" 1814 (Wright Vol. 2, p. 81)

Wilson, Nicholas, see Nicholas Willson, q.v.

Wilson, Robert M., served as a Private in Capt. John Symmes' Co., 1st U.S. Infantry, enlisted 6 Mar 1813 in Nashville, TN at the age of 41, 5' 10" tall, born in Maryland, wounded at Chippewa, Upper Canada on 25 Jul 1814, discharged at Sackett's Harbor, NY on 10 Jun 1815 (Johnson and Christou, p. 415)

Wilson, Stephen, served as a Private in Capt. Lawson Cuddy's Co., 41st Regt., Baltimore Co., from 25 Aug 1814 and was reported "sick-absent since Sep 25" 1814 (Wright Vol. 2, p. 68)

Wilson, Thomas (African American), served as a Seaman and was born in Baltimore. Age: 35. Prison Depot: Plymouth 1, Prisoner of War #2622. Captured by HM Ship-of-the-Line *Edinburgh*. When Taken: 28 Oct 1812. Date Received: 16 May 1814. From what ship: HMS *Repulse*. Discharged on 14 Jun 1814 and sent to Dartmoor. (Johnson's Database, 2019)

Wilson, Thomas, served as a Seaman and was born in Baltimore. Age: 26. Prison Depot: Dartmoor, Prisoner of War #3533. Captured by HM Ship-of-the-Line *Conquestador*. When Taken: 22 Aug 1814. Where Taken: Long 19 Lat 107. Prize Name: *Rover*, prize of the Privateer *York*. Home Port: Baltimore. Ship Type: Privateer. Date Received: 28 Sep 1814. From what ship: HMT *Salvador del Mundo*. Discharged on 4 Jun 1815. (Johnson's Database, 2019)

Wilson, William, served as a Seaman and was born in Baltimore, MD. Age: 26. Prison Depot: Chatham, Prisoner of War #43. Captured by HM Brig *Recruit*. When Taken: 11 Jun 1812. Where Taken: off Rhode Island. Prize Name: *General Blake*. Ship Type: Merchant Vessel. Date Received: 3 Nov 1812. From what ship: HMS *Plover*. Discharged on 23 Mar 1813 and released to the Cartel *Robinson Potter*. (Johnson's Database, 2019)

Wilson, William W., served as a Private in Capt. Thomas Montgomery's Co., 14th U.S. Infantry, enlisted 1 Dec 1812 and died at Burlington, VT, in April 1814 from sickness (Johnson and Christou, p. 416)

Winder, William Henry (1775-1824), served as Brigadier General of the 14th U.S. Infantry; commissioned a Lieutenant Colonel on 16 Mar 1812, promoted to Colonel on 6 Jul 1812, promoted to Brigadier General on 12 Mar 1813 and was captured at the Battle of Stoney Creek, Upper Canada on 12 Jun 1813. Prisoner of War #255 at Quebec, interned 24 Jun 1813 and discharged 3 Apr 1814; yet, he was also listed as Prisoner of War #1426, captured at Fort Niagara, interned 29 Jan 1814; born in Maryland and died on 24 May 1824; bounty land was issued to his widow Gertrude Winder (BLW# 14081-160-50. There is an obvious conflict in the dates of his imprisonment published in Johnson's Quebec book, p. 171, while Johnson and Christou, p. 416, stated he was discharged on 15 Jun 1815 and only that he was captured at Stoney Creek). The following might help clarify matters somewhat: 'William Henry Winder was born in Somerset Co., Maryland on February 18, 1775. After being graduated at the University of Pennsylvania, he studied law under Judge Gabriel Davis and in 1789 settled in Baltimore. In March, 1812, he was commissioned lieutenant-colonel of the 14th U.S. Infantry; on July 6 was placed in command, and on November 28 let a successful expedition from Black Rock, near Buffalo, NY to the Canadian shore below Fort Erie. On March 12, 1813, Winder was promoted [to] brigadier-general. At the battle of Stony (sic) Creek, June 1, 1813, he was taken prisoner and held as a hostage until some time in the year 1814. In May 1814 he was appointed adjutant-general and placed in command of a newly created military district embracing Maryland and Virginia, the actual force consisting of 400 men. General Winder was court-martialed for the defeat at Bladensburgh [Aug 1814], but the trial resulted in a report of 'commendation' for having heroically done his duty under circumstances beyond his control. The court found that Winder showed great zeal and energy, but in a misdirected manner; that the loss of the battle was not due to a lack of energy on the part of the commanding officer, but to his lack of skill and ability to handle troops properly! He was again sent to the Niagara frontier, and at the close of the war returned to Baltimore, broken in health and fortune. On the reduction of the army in June, 1815, he was retired and resumed the practice of law in Baltimore, where he died May 24, 1824." (Marine, p. 71) Gen. William H. Winder, former State Senator and Grand Master of Masons in Maryland, died 24 May 1824 in his 49th year; buried with honors. (*Niles Weekly Register*, 29 May 1824; *Baltimore Federal Gazette*, 24 May 1824; *Marriages and Deaths from Baltimore Newspapers, 1817-1824*, by Henry C. Peden, Jr., 2010, p. 248) He was buried in Baltimore's Green Mount Cemetery. (www.findagrave.com)

Winebrenner, Peter, served as a Private in Capt. Isaac F. Preston's Co., enlisted 10 Aug 1813 for 1 year at Richmond, age 20, born in Frederick Co., MD and reported sick in hospital on 6 Mar 1814 (Mallick and Wright, p. 305)

Winn, Clement, served as a Private in 14th U.S. Infantry and was born in Maryland. Age: 21. Prison Depot: Chatham, Prisoner of War #3114. When Taken: 24 Jun 1813. Where Taken: Beaver Dams, Upper Canada. Date Received: 7 Jan 1814 from Halifax, NS. Discharged on 10 Oct 1814 and sent to U.S. on the Cartel *St. Philip*. (Johnson's Database, 2019)

Wisbaugh, Martin (1786-1850), served as a Private in Capt. George Steever's Co., 27th Regiment, Baltimore Militia, from 19 Aug 1814 and was wounded on 12 Sep 1814 at North Point (Wright Vol. 2, p. 15). In Baltimore County on 5 Mar 1851 the Court was satisfied that Martin Wisbaugh was a pensioner and former private in the 27th Regiment, Maryland Militia, who resided in Baltimore at his death on 8 Oct 1850, leaving a widow Harriet Wisbaugh. On that same day she collected her own $9.07 arrears due from 4 Sep 1850 to 8 Oct 1850 (Pierce, p. 202); however, this date of death was incorrect as noted in his obituary: "Died, on Wednesday, the 2nd instant, of consumption, Martin Wisebraught (sic) in the 65th year of his age, leaving a wife and five children to mourn the loss of a kind and affectionate husband and father. His friends and relatives, and the Old Defenders, are respectfully invited to attend his funeral, this (Friday) afternoon, at three o'clock, from his late residence, 126 Orleans Street, without further notice." (*The [Baltimore] Sun*, 4 Oct 1850)

Wise, Jacob, served as a Private (company not stated) and was captured at the Battle of Bladensburg on 24 Aug 1814 (Marine, p. 175)

Wise, John, served as a Private in Capt. Samuel McDonald's Co., 6th Regiment, Baltimore Militia, from 19 Aug 1814 and was discharged by the Surgeon on 21 Aug 1814, but the medical reason was not stated (Wright Vol. 2, p. 13)

Wiseman, William, served as a Private in Capt. David Twiggs' Co., 8th U.S. Inf., enlisted 3 Sep 1813 in Georgia at the age of 22, 5' 7½" tall, born in Washington, MD and discharged on 21 Aug 1815 for debility (Johnson and Christou, p. 418)

Wittington, Joshua (African American), served as a Seaman and was born in Baltimore. Age: 33. Prison Depot: Plymouth 1, Prisoner of War #1140. Captured by HM Ship-of-the-Line *Superb*. When Taken: 15 Apr 1813. Where Taken: off Belle Isle. Prize Name: *Magdalen*. Ship Type: Merchant Vessel. Date Received: 22 Apr 1813. From what ship: HMS *Superb*. Discharged and sent on 21 Jun 1813 to the U.S. ship *Hope*. (Johnson's Database, 2019)

Witzell, Frederick, served as a Marine and was taken from the barracks and admitted to the Naval Hospital in Washington, DC as Patient No. 64 on 25 Jul 1814 (injury or illness was not specified) and was discharged on 19 Aug 1814 and sent to the barracks (Sharp's Database, 2018)

Wolf (Woolf), Isaac (1791-1814), served as a Private in Capt. James McConkey's Co., 27th Regiment, Baltimore Militia, from 19 Aug 1814 and was reported "Dead Oct 15, 1814." (CMSR, but Huntsberry p. 91, and Marine p. 489, both did not mention his death; Wright Vol. 2, p. 19 states "Woolf" was discharged on 29 Oct 1814, yet the *Baltimore American*, 12 Jun 1819, stated "Woolf" was killed in the defense of Baltimore). Name is on the Baltimore Battle Monument.

Wolfe (Woolf), Andrew, served as a Seaman and was born in Baltimore. Age: 28. Prison Depot: Portsmouth, Prisoner of War #591. How Taken: Gave himself up off HM Ship-of-the-Line *Mars*. Date Received: 31 Jan 1813. From what ship: HMS *Mars*. Discharged on 11 Mar 1813 and sent to Chatham on HM Store Ship *Abundance*. Prison Depot: Chatham, Prisoner of War #1260. Date Received: 16 Mar 1813 from Portsmouth on HMS *Abundance*. Discharged on 23 Jul 1814 and sent to Dartmoor. Prison Depot: Dartmoor, Prisoner of War #1913. Date Received: 3 Aug 1814. From what ship: HMS *Alceste* from Chatham Depot. Discharged on 26 Apr 1815. (Johnson's Database, 2019) Andrew Wolfe, of Maryland, served as a Seaman on the ship *Mars* and was reported by Capt. Jeduthan Upton, Jr. in 1814 as having been impressed into service and was being held as a Prisoner of War on the prison ship *San Antonio* at Chatham, England. (*Niles Weekly Register*, 26 Feb 1814)

Wolfe, William, served as a Seaman and was born in Baltimore. Age: 20. Prison Depot: Plymouth 1, Prisoner of War #1999. Captured by HM Brig *Royalist*. When Taken: 6 Sep 1812. Where Taken: coast of France. Prize Name: *Ned*. Home Port: Baltimore. Ship Type: Letter of Marque. Received: 22 Sep 1813. From what ship:

HMS *Royalist*. Discharged 27 Sep 1813 and sent to Dartmoor. Prison Depot: Dartmoor, Prisoner of War #718. Received: 27 Sep 1813 from Plymouth. Discharged on 26 Apr 1815. (Johnson's Database, 2019)

Wolfrom, William, served as a Private in the 14th U.S. Infantry (company not stated) and captured at Stoney Point, Upper Canada on 24 Jun 1813. Prisoner of War #3869 at Halifax, NS, interned 7 Jul 1813, discharged for exchange on 3 Feb 1814 (Johnson and Christou, p. 418; Baker Vol. 2, p. 446; Johnson, p. 172, stated he was Prisoner of War #628 at Quebec, discharged on 10 Aug 1813 and spelled his name Wolffrom)

Wood, Bennet, served as a Private in Capt. Fonsten's Co., joined 2 Sep 1814 and reported as deserted on 28 Sep 1814, but he stated he was taken sick near Baltimore and was sent home on furlough; he moved to Ohio before 1850 and filed for bounty land, but his claim was rejected (Mallick and Wright, p. 308)

Wood, John, served as a Seaman and was born in Baltimore. Age: 24. Prison Depot: Dartmoor, Prisoner of War #5449. Captured by HM Ship-of-the-Line *Glasgow*. When Taken: 2 Nov 1814. Where Taken: English Channel. Prize Name: --?--, prize of Privateer *Lawrence*. Home Port: Baltimore. Ship Type: Privateer. Date Received: 10 Dec 1814. From what ship: HMT *Impregnable*. Discharged on 11 Jul 1815. (Johnson's Database, 2019)

Wood, Joseph, served as a Seaman and was born in Baltimore. Age: 27. Prison Depot: Chatham, Prisoner of War #2457. Captured by HM Frigate *Shannon*. When Taken: 11 Oct 1812. Where Taken: off Halifax, NS. Prize Name: *Wiley Reynard*. Home Port: Boston. Ship Type: Privateer. Date Received: 21 Oct 1813 from Portsmouth on HMT *Malabar*. Discharged on 4 Sep 1814 and sent to Dartmoor on HMS *Freya*. Prison Depot: Dartmoor, Prisoner of War #3254. Date Received: 11 Sep 1814. From what ship: HMT *Freya* from Chatham. Discharged on 27 Apr 1815. (Johnson's Database, 2019)

Wood, Moses, served as a Private in Capt. Nathan Towson's Co., 2nd U.S. Artillery, enlisted 3 Jun 1812 and died in 1812, exact date and cause of death not stated; bounty land issued to Elisha Wood and Mary Riley, his children and only heirs at law (BLW# 27929-160-42; Johnson and Christou, p. 418)

Wood, Nicholas (1767-1814), served as a Private in Capt. Mortimer Hall's Co., 36th U.S. Infantry, enlisted 29 Aug 1813 in Baltimore at the age of 46, 5' 8" tall, born in Holland and died on 10 Feb 1814 (Johnson and Christou, p. 418)

Wood, Pratt, served as a Private in the 14th U.S. Infantry (company not stated) and was later captured. Prisoner of War #3829 at Halifax, NS, interned on 6 Jun 1813 and was discharged for exchange on 3 Feb 1814 (Johnson and Christou, p. 419; Baker Vol. 2, p. 447)

Wood, Thomas (African American), served as a Seaman and was born in Prince George's Co., MD. Age: 21. Prison Depot: Dartmoor, Prisoner of War #647. Captured by HM Brig *Pelican*. When Taken: 14 Aug 1813. Where Taken: off St. David's Head, Wales. Prize Name: U.S. Brig *Argus*. Ship Type: Warship. Date Received: 8 Sep 1813 from Plymouth. Discharged and sent to Dartmouth on 30 Jul 1813. (Johnson's Database, 2019)

Wood, Thomas, served as a Seaman and was born in Prince George's Co., MD. Age: 21. Prison Depot: Plymouth 1, Prisoner of War #491. Captured by HM Brig *Reindeer*. When Taken: 3 Feb 1813. Where Taken: Bay of Biscayne. Prize Name: *Cashiere*. Home Port: Baltimore. Ship Type: Letter of Marque. Date Received: 12 Feb 1813. From what ship: HMS *Reindeer*. Discharged and sent to Dartmoor on 2 Apr 1813. Prison Depot: Dartmoor, Prisoner of War #8. Date Received: 2 Apr 1813 from Plymouth. Discharged and sent to Dartmouth on 30 Jul 1813. (Johnson's Database, 2019)

Wood, Thomas, served as a Seaman and was born in Baltimore. Age: 22. Prison Depot: Dartmoor, Prisoner of War #5020. Captured by HM Brig *Wasp*. When Taken: 27 Jul 1814. Where Taken: Georges Bank. Prize Name: HM Schooner *Landrail*, prize of the Privateer *Syren*. Home Port: Baltimore. Ship Type: Privateer. Date Received: 28 Oct 1814. From what ship: HMT *Alkbar* from Halifax, NS. Discharged on 21 Jun 1815. (Johnson's Database, 2019)

Wooden, John, served as a Private in Capt. James Almoney's Co., 41st Regt., Baltimore County, from 25 Aug 1814 and was reported "sick-absent 20 Oct" 1814 (Wright Vol. 2, p. 66)

Woodford, James, served as a Seaman and was born in Baltimore. Age: 19. Prison Depot: Chatham, Prisoner of War #2848. Captured by HM Brig *Recruit*. When Taken: 17 Aug 1813. Where Taken: coast of U.S. Prize Name: *Blockade*. Ship Type: Privateer. Date Received: 7 Jan 1814 from Halifax, NS. Discharged on 26 Sep 1814 and sent to Dartmoor on HMS *Leyden*. Prison Depot: Dartmoor, Prisoner of War #4678. Date Received: 9 Oct 1814. From what ship: HMT *Leyden* from Chatham. Discharged on 15 Jun 1815. (Johnson's Database, 2019)

Woodland, Samuel (1771-1814), served as a Private in the 36th U.S. Infantry (company and captain not named), enlisted 19 Mar 1814 at Sandy Point, VA at the age of 43, 5' 9" tall, born in Kent Co., MD and died in 1814 (Johnson and Christou, p. 419)

Woodland, William, served as a Private in Capt. William McIlvane's Co., 14th U.S. Infantry, enlisted 15 May 1812 at the age of 37, 5' 5" tall, born in Maryland and was captured at Beaver Dams, Upper Canada on 24 Jun 1813. Prisoner of War #3748 at Halifax, discharged on 3 Feb 1813, exchanged 15 Apr 1814 and discharged from the service on 4 May 1814 at Greenbush, NY on a Surgeon's Certificate for rheumatism (Johnson and Christou, p. 419; Baker Vol. 2, p. 448)

Woodland, Zebediah, served as a Private in Capt. Isaac Barnard's Co., 14th U.S. infantry, enlisted 20 Nov 1812, age 25, 5' 5" tall, and was captured at Stoney Creek, Upper Canada on 12 Jun 1813. Prisoner of War # at Halifax, NS, interned 28 Dec 1813, was discharged for exchanged on 31 May 1814 and discharged on 7 Aug 1814 (Johnson and Christou, pp. 419-420; Baker Vol. 2, p. 448, misspelled his first name Lebediah)

Woodward, Brinton (1790-1815), served as a Private in Capt. George W. Ent's Co., Frederick Co. Militia, 3rd Maryland Regiment, from 24 Aug to 30 Sep 1814 (Mallick and Wright, p. 308, spelled his name Branton). Brinton Woodward died 6 Aug 1815, in his 26th year, after a long and severe illness "contracted in Camp last Autumn" and was buried with military honors (*Fredericktown Herald*, 12 Aug 1815, did not state where he was buried)

Wooker, Henry (1773-1812), served as a Private in Capt. John Bowyer's Co., 2nd U.S. Infantry, enlisted 23 Feb 1808 in Fredericktown, MD at the age of 35, 5' 6" tall, born in Germany and died in 1812 (Johnson and Christou, p. 420)

Woolfred, John, served as a Private in the 14th U.S. Infantry (company not stated) and was later captured. Prisoner of War #4041 at Halifax, NS, interned on 24 Jun 1813 and was discharged for exchange on 3 Feb 1814 (Johnson and Christou, p. 420; Baker Vol. 2, p. 448)

Wooters, David (1794-1813), served as a Private in Capt. Samuel Raisin's Co., 36th U.S. Infantry, enlisted 11 May 1813 for 1 year in Cambridge, MD at age 19, 5' 6½" tall, born in Talbot Co. and died 15 May 1813 (Johnson and Christou, p. 421; *1812 Ancestor Index Volume I, 1892-1970*, National Society United States Daughters of 1812, 2005, p. 561, spelled his name Wootters and stated his wife was named Ann, but gave no last name and no dates of birth and death)

Worrowell, William, served as a Private in Capt. Joshua Naylor's Co., 17th Regt., Prince George's Co. Militia, for six days between 17 Jul and 2 Aug 1814, was stationed at Milltown and was taken ill on the march from Milltown to Port Tobacco, but no date was given (Wright Vol. 6, p. 9)

Worthington, John H. (1793-1858), served as a Private in Capt. Thomas F. W. Vinson's Co., 32nd Regiment, Montgomery Co. Militia, from 1 Aug 1814 to 27 Sep 1814 (company muster roll dates) after volunteering in the 21st Regiment (sic) in the latter part of July at a place called Long Old Fields and continued in service except for a few days on furlough for sickness and was discharged at Baltimore. By 1852 John H. Worthington, age 59, lived in Frederick Co. and died on 18 Apr 1855, age 65 years, 3 months, 10 days. He was buried in Mt. Olivet Cemetery in

Frederick, MD next to his wife Ann H. Worthington (25 Jul 1791 – 26 Dec 1866). (Wright Vol. 7, pp. 5, 50; BLW# 55-120-24832; *Names In Stone*, by Jacob M. Holdcraft, 1966, p. 1263)

Wright, Clinton (c1783-1818), served as a 2nd Lieutenant in the Light Dragoons of the U.S. Army; born in Maryland, commissioned a Coronet on 19 Jan 1813, transferred to 2nd Light Dragoons on 29 Jan 1813, promoted to 3rd Lieutenant on 29 Apr 1813, promoted to 2nd Lieutenant on 19 Apr 1814, transferred to Light Dragoons on 12 May 1814 and transferred to 4th Infantry on 17 May 1815. Maj. Clinton Wright, the assistant adjutant-general assigned to the staff of Maj. Gen. Edmund Pendleton Gainesand, died on 24 Feb 1818 when a keelboat struck a sawyer and piled into the rocks of the Flint River near today's Newton, Georgia. "Genl. Gains ... lost his Asst. Adjt. Genl. & two soldiers drowned..." Clinton, third son of Gov. Robert Wright, was a very brave and fearless man, priding himself upon his military skill. He had charge of a recruiting station at Centreville for the U.S. Army. On 4th of September 1812, he left Centreville for Niagara in full uniform, at the head of 30 dragoons. He fought a duel with a French officer during the Canadian War. Friends tried to reconcile them but Wright insisted that the fight should go on. On the second fire the Frenchman was killed. Mr. Wright boasted that he would "die with his armor on,",which he did in endeavoring to swim the St. Lawrence River. All of his brothers served in the War of 1812 except for one brother who was too young. (Johnson and Christou, p. 421, Seminole War History in The Papers of Andrew Jackson 1816-1820; A Sketch of the Adjutant General's Department: U. S. Army, from 1775 to 1875, p. 70, *Colonial Families and Their Descendants*, by Mary Emory, p. 122)

Three new plaques were placed at the Centreville War Memorial in 2014 that included Major Clinton Wright (above at right) who died on February 24, 1818.

Wright, John (1789-1875), served as a Private in 14th U.S. Infantry (company not stated) and was later captured, probably at Beaver Dams, Upper Canada. Prisoner of War #4044 at Halifax, NS, interned 24 Jun 1813, discharged for exchange on 3 Feb 1814 and was exchanged on 15 Apr 1814 (Johnson and

Christou, p. 422; Baker Vol. 2, p. 450) He died on 15 Jan 1875, age 86, and was buried in Green Mount Cemetery. (*The [Baltimore] Sun*, 16 Jan 1875; Society of the War of 1812 Application National No. 174 in 1892 stated he served as 2nd Corporal in Capt. Joseph Myers' Co., Franklin Artillery, and was at the Battle of North Point on 12 Sep 1814, but did not mention his service in the U.S. Infantry in 1813-1814. John Wright, of Baltimore, married Rebecca Leaf. Wright Vol. 2, p. 43 listed him as a Private in Capt. Joseph Myers Co. from 16 to 23 Aug 1813 and p. 47 as 2nd Corporal on the muster roll dated 19 Aug 1814 to 30 Nov 1814)

Wright, Lerick (Zerick, Zenick), served as a Private in the 14th U.S. Infantry (company not stated) and was later captured. Prisoner of War #4056 at Halifax, NS, interned 24 Jun 1813 and discharged for exchange on 3 Feb 1814 (Johnson and Christou, pp. 422, 423; Baker Vol. 2, p. 450)

Wright, Samuel, served as a Private in George Armistead's 1st U.S. Artillery, enlisted 27 Dec 1810 for 5 years at Fort McHenry at the age of 25, 5' 8" tall, born in Pennsyslvania and discharged at Fort Columbus, NY on 13 Mar 1815 for debility (Johnson and Christou, p. 422)

Wright, William (1792-1816), served as 3rd Lieutenant in Capt. Thomas Sangster's Co., 12th U.S. Infantry, enlisted 24 Jul 1812, as a Sergeant, age 20, 5' 8" tall, born in Maryland, commissioned an Ensign on 23 Oct 1813, promoted to 3rd Lieutenant on 5 Apr 1814, discharged on 15 Jun 1815 and died 4 Sep 1816, speculatively from service connected problems (Johnson and Christou, p. 422)

Wright, William, served as a Seaman and was born in Baltimore. Age: 37. Prison Depot: Plymouth 1, Prisoner of War #2283. Captured by HM Brig *Pelican*. When Taken: 13 Jan 1814. Where Taken: at sea. Prize Name: *Siro*. Home Port: Baltimore. Ship Type: Letter of Marque. Date Received: 23 Jan 1814. From what ship: HMS *Pelican*. Discharged on 31 Jan 1814 and sent to Dartmoor. Prison Depot: Dartmoor, Prisoner of War #947. Date Received: 31 Jan 1814 from Plymouth. Discharged on 27 Apr 1815. (Johnson's Database, 2019)

Wright, Zadock, served as a Sergeant in Capt. William McIlvane's Co., 14th U.S. Infantry, enlisted 23 May 1812 for 5 years and was killed during the Battle of Lyon's Creek on 19 Oct 1814; bounty land issued to William Wright, his brother and only heir at law (BLW# 27167-160-42; Johnson and Christou, pp. 422-423)

Wright, Zerick, see Lerick Wright, q.v.

Wroe, Everett, served as a Private in Capt. Michael Peters' Co., 51st Regiment, Baltimore Militia, from 19 Aug 1814 and was discharged on 26 Aug 1814 by a Surgeon, but the cause was not reported (Wright Vol. 2, p. 36)

Wroe, Richard, served as a Private in Capt. Michael Peters' Co., 51st Regiment, Baltimore Militia, from 19 Aug 1814 and was discharged on 24 Aug 1814 by a Surgeon, but the cause was not reported (Wright Vol. 2, p. 36)

Wyatt, Frederick, served as a Seaman and was born in Baltimore. Age: 25. Prison Depot: Plymouth 1, Prisoner of War #1835. Captured by HM Brig *Pelican*. When Taken: 14 Aug 1813. Where Taken: off St. David's Head, Wales. Prize Name: U.S. Brig *Argus*. Ship Type: Warship. Date Received: 17 Aug 1813. From what ship: USS *Argus*. Discharged on 8 Sep 1813 and sent to Dartmoor. Prison Depot: Dartmoor, Prisoner of War #575. Received: 8 Sep 1813 from Plymouth. Discharged and sent to Dartmouth on 2 Nov 1814. (Johnson's Database, 2019)

Wymes, David, served as a Private in Capt. Myndert Cox's Co., 13th U.S. Inf., enlisted 2 Jun 1812 at Canandaigua, NY, age 32, 5' 7½" tall, born in Annapolis and captured at Queenston Heights, Upper Canada on 3 Oct 1812, later paroled and discharged on 11 Mar 1814 (Johnson and Christou, p. 423)

Wynne, Aaron, served as a Private in Capt. Thomas Montgomery's Co., 14th U.S. Infantry, enlisted 20 Apr 1812 for 5 years and was killed on the Canadian shore on 27 Nov 1813 (Johnson and Christou, p. 423)

Wyvill (Wyville), Marmaduke, served as a Private in Capt. Charles Pennington's Co. of Baltimore's 1st Independent Artillery Regiment, from 12 to 19 Aug 1813 and from 19 Aug 1814 and was slightly wounded on 13 Sep 1814 at Fort McHenry while serving with Capt. Hughes' Baltimore Independent Artillerists (Marine pp. 173, 493; Wright Vol. 2, pp. 43, 47, did not mention his wound)

Wysham, Williams, served as a Private in Capt. Sands' Co., 22nd Regiment, was a Corporal in Capt. Chase's Co., 22nd Regiment, a Private in Ensign Brewer's Detachment, 36th Regiment, and was captured at Bladensburg on 24 Aug 1814 (Marine, pp. 175, 493)

Y

Yale, Nathaniel, served as a Cook and was born in Prince George's Co., MD. Age: 27. Prison Depot: Plymouth 1, Prisoner of War #128. Captured by HM Sloop *Pheasant*. When Taken: 13 Dec 1812. Where Taken: off Oporto, Portugal. Prize Name: *Hope*. Ship Type: Merchant Vessel. Date Received: 2 Jan 1813. From what ship: *Hope*. Discharged and sent to Portsmouth on 4 Jan 1813 on HMS *Revolutionnaire*. Prison Depot: Portsmouth, Prisoner of War #406. Date Received: 10 Jan 1813. From what ship: HM Guard Ship *Royal William*. Discharged on 6 Mar 1813 and sent to Chatham on HMS *Cornwall*. Prison Depot: Chatham, Prisoner of War #1125. Date Received: 14 Mar 1813 from Portsmouth on HMS *Beagle*. Discharged on 2 Jul 1813 and was released to the Cartel *Moses Brown*. (Johnson's Database, 2019)

Yates, Henry D., served as a Sergeant in Capt. David Cummings' Co., 14th U.S. Infantry, enlisted 23 Jun 1812 at age 25, 5' 8" tall, born in Charles Co., MD and was captured at Beaver Dams, Upper Canada on 24 Jun 1813. Prisoner of War #7521, interned 27 Oct 1814, released on 5 Mar 1815 and was discharged from the service in Baltimore on 20 Apr 1815. (Johnson and Christou, pp. 423-424; Baker Vol. 2, p. 451)

Yerk (Yirk), James, of Emmittsburg, served as a Private under Capt. James F. Huston, Capt. Lewis Weaver and Capt. Joseph Green, Frederick Co. Militia, from 23 Jul 1814 and was "sick in quarters since 2 Oct" 1814; he moved to Ohio and died circa August 1840. (Mallick and Wright, pp. 311, 345; BLW# 55-160-52544)

Yingling, Henry, served as a Private in Capt. Fonsten's Co., Frederick Co. Militia, joined 2 Sep 1814 and deserted 3 Oct 1814, but he said he was drafted by Adam Feiser in Sep 1814, "took sick and was discharged at Baltimore in Oct" 1814; he moved to Ohio before 1855 at which time his bounty land claim was rejected. (Mallick and Wright, pp. 311-312; BLW# 55-rej-162888)

Yingling, John (1785-1880), served as a Private in Capt. John Galt's Co., Frederick Co. Militia, from 31 Aug 1814 and was reported as "sick absent 15 Sep" 1814 in Baltimore; he resided within 5 miles of Taneytown (Mallick and Wright, pp. 312, 362) In 1818 Jacob Yingling was administrator of the estate of John Yingling, dec. (*Star of Federalism*, Frederick, MD, 25 Sep 1818). He was buried in Meadow Branch of the Brethren Cemetery, west of Westminster, MD.

Yohn, John (1779-1813), served as a Private in Capt. Colin Buckner's Co., 5th U.S. Infantry, enlisted 9 Mar 1813 in Baltimore at the age of 34, 5' 10" tall, born in Baltimore and died at Sackett's Harbor, NY on 10 Nov 1813; heirs received half pay for 5 years in lieu of bounty land (Johnson and Christou, p. 424)

Young, Benjamin, served as a Private in Capt. Isaac Barnard's Co., 14th U.S. Infantry, enlisted 2 Oct 1812 and died 30 Jun 1813; bounty land was issued to his son William B. Young (BLW# 27542-160-42; Johnson and Christou, p. 424)

Young, Cook (African American), served as a Seaman and was born in Baltimore. Age: 21. Prison Depot: Dartmoor, Prisoner of War #3905. Captured by HM Frigate *Loire*. When Taken: 10 Jun 1814. Where Taken: Chesapeake Bay. Prize Name: *Eliza*, packet. Ship Type: Merchant Vessel. Date Received: 5 Oct 1814. From what ship: HMT *Orpheus* from Halifax, NS. Discharged on 9 Jun 1815 (Johnson's Database, 2019)

Young, Jacob, served as a Private (company not stated) and was captured at the Battle of Bladensburg on 24 Aug 1814 (Marine, p. 175)

Young, John, served as a Private in Capt. Samuel Hopkins' Co., 2nd U.S. Light Dragoons, enlisted on 5 Sep 1812 at Carlisle, PA by Capt. Hayne for 5 years, age

33, 5' 6" tall, grey eyes, dark hair, dark complexion, born in Frederick Co., MD, joined Capt. S. Halsey's Co. on 15 Apr 1813, served in Capt. Hopkins' Co. at New York on 18 Nov 1813, was "absent sick at Schlasser," served in Capt. G. Haig's Co. on 16 Feb 1815 and 30 Apr 1815 and in a hospital report dated at New York Harbor on 11 Jul 1815 he was noted as unfit for service due to old age and infirmity at age 37 (Mallick and Wright, p. 313; Johnson and Christou, p. 424)

Young, Nathaniel (African American), served as a Seaman and was born in Baltimore. Age: 30. Prison Depot: Chatham, Prisoner of War #2277. Captured by HM Ship-of-the-Line *Elizabeth*. When Taken: 25 Jan 1813. Where Taken: off St. Bartholomew, West Indies. Prize Name: *Garter Wester*. Ship Type: Merchant Vessel. Received: 17 Sep 1813. From what ship: HMS *Raisonable*. Discharged on 4 Sep 1814 and sent to Dartmoor on HMS *Freya*. Prison Depot: Dartmoor, Prisoner of War #3128. Received: 11 Sep 1814. From what ship: HMT *Freya* from Chatham. Discharged on 28 May 1815. (Johnson's Database, 2019)

Young, Samuel, served as a Seaman and was born in Maryland. Age: 23. Prison Depot: Plymouth 2, Prisoner of War #466. Captured by HM Brig *Barbadoes*. When Taken: 11 Jan 1815. Where Taken: off St. Bartholomew, West Indies. Prize Name: *Fox*. Home Port: Baltimore. Ship Type: Privateer. Date Received: 16 Apr 1815. From what ship: HMS *Swiftsure*. Discharged on 2 Jun 1815 and released to the Cartel *Soverign*. (Johnson's Database, 2019)

Young, Thomas (1790-1814), served as a Private in Capt. Thomas Carbery's Co., 36th U.S. Infantry, enlisted 16 Apr 1814 in Washington, DC at age 24, 6' 1" tall, born in Maryland and died on 6 Dec 1814; bounty land issued to Eleanor Young and other heirs at law (BLW# 4118-160-12; Johnson and Christou, p. 425)

Young, William, served as a Private in Capt. E. G. Williams' Co., 1st Cavalry, Washington Co., from 11 Aug 1814 and died on 19 Aug 1814, but the place and cause of death were not stated (Wright Vol. 9, p. 3)

Young, William, served as a Private in Capt. William Oliver's Co., 5th U.S. Inf., enlisted 26 Aug 1813 in Philadelphia, age 26, 5' 6" tall, born in Princess Anne, MD, and was discharged at Greenbush, NY on 24 May 1815 for rheumatism and palsy (Johnson and Christou, p. 425)

Z

Zimmerman, Henry, served as a Private in Capt. Denton Darby's Co., joined on 3 Aug 1814 and was captured at the Battle of Bladensburg on 24 Aug 1814 (Mallick and Wright, p. 315; Marine, p. 175)

"Only the dead have seen the end of war."
Plato, *Greek philosopher and mathematician*

1812 Monuments to the Soldiers

Daniel Webster, *American politician*
"Although no sculptured marble should rise to their memory, nor engraved stone bear record of their deeds, yet will their remembrance be as lasting as the land they honored."

Although many of our fallen were not given a memorial to their memory, we have not forgotten their sacrifices. Maryland is fortunate to have many monuments dedicated to the deceased of 1812. Some of these went up almost immediately and some started but took years to complete. Many of these markers or signs were encouraged or supported by the War of 1812 Society from the earliest foundations before there even was a society just a group of soldiers who continued to remember the heroic deeds they and their comrades accomplished and those compatriots who gave their all for this nation. Our Society has over time dedicated or been involved in erecting grave markers for numerous heroes of the War including:

- Commodore Joshua Barney
- Private Thomas V. Beeson
- Drummer Henry Lightner
- Shipbuilder Thomas Kemp
- Gen. Anthony Kimmel
- Sgt. Timothy McNamara
- Private Thomas Owings
- Gen. Philip Reed
- Private Thomas Ruckle
- Corporal Richard Shaw
- Dragoon Bernard Todd

A few of the larger monuments and signages are noted on the following pages.

Aquila Randall Monument

– Built and Dedicated on July 21, 1817 at 3970 North Point Road in Dundalk, MD, just north of the intersection of Old Battle Grove Road.

The Aquila Randall Monument is the oldest military monument in the nation and the first one that was dedicated to a non-officer. Privates were rarely memorialized. Typically, officers' lives were counted as more important and often reports from the battlefield noted the officer's fate by name, but lower ranks were noted with count and left unnamed.

This monument was built by the men of Aquila Randall's company on July 21, 1817. Commander Benjamin C. Howard and his men marched from downtown Baltimore, carrying the materials to build it on a cart. Upon their arrival they constructed the monument, taking most of the day, and Captain Howard made a speech that was published in the papers of the time.

Benjamin C. Howard Speech July 21, 1817

"....I can picture to myself the sensation of those who in far distant days will contemplate this monument...and the melancholy event which has caused our assemblage at this spot...This monument which we are now erecting, will stand as a solemn expression of the feeling of us all...But I regret that the spot, which is made classic by the effusion of blood, the sport where the long line stood unappalled by the system and advances of an experienced and disciplined foe, has been suffered to remain unnoticed. It is here where her citizens stood arrayed soldier's garb that honors to a soldier's memory should have been paid. To mark the spot be then our care..."

This monument sits today in its original location despite it being moved and changed over the years. It is fortunate that so many loving hands cared for this monument over the last 200 years to ensure it survives and is remembered. At times it was fenced in, and placed upon several larger pedestals, and finally returned to its original state as it stands today.

As Historian Scott Sheads has said: "All too often we relocate our monuments (i.e., Armistead, Smith) for the name of progress and development. Would we not move the 1815 Battle Monument from its location downtown to improve traffic flow for the transitions of modern life? Our 1812 sites have not achieved the national popular notoriety of other military sites associated with the Revolution and Civil War – and yet this monument (believed to be the third oldest martial monument in the nation) should be respected at the original birth site."

On the 200thanniversary of this monument (July 21, 2017), a celebration was held with numerous attendees, including the 5th Regiment Armory, Dundalk-Patapsco Neck Historical Society, War of 1812 Society, Friends of Todd's Inheritance, and numerous VIPs and community members.

Alex Radius, Chris Christou, and Dave Embrey participated in period style uniform for the occasion.

For those who do not know, Aquila Randall is now buried at Green Mount Cemetery after he was removed from Potters field (next to the Baltimore Hospital – today Johns Hopkins Hospital parking lot) some time after 1837.

Armistead Statue Monument at Ft. McHenry
– Dedicated September 12, 1914 at Ft. McHenry National Park and Historic Shrine in Baltimore, MD

This 8-foot tall bronze monument is dedicated to Col. George Armistead who commanded Fort McHenry during the bombardment. He is also remembered for being the one who ordered the large flags that flew over the fort from Mary Young Pickersgill. In an 1813 report to General Smith, he wrote *"We, Sir, are ready at Fort McHenry to defend Baltimore against invading by the enemy. That is to say, we are ready except that we have no suitable ensign to display over the Star Fort, and it is my desire to have a flag so large that the British will have no difficulty in seeing it from a distance"*. This flag would later inspire the song by Francis Scott Key that became the Star Spangled Banner National Anthem.

ARMISTEAD
ERECTED SEPT. 12, 1914
BY THE CITY OF BALTIMORE
SOC. WAR OF 1812 CONTRIBUTING
IN COMMEMORATION OF THE GALLANT
DEFENSE OF FORT McHENRY
UNDER THE COMMAND OF
COL. GEORGE ARMISTEAD
WHICH WAS THE INSPIRATION
OF THE
NATIONAL ANTHEM
THE STAR SPANGLED BANNER
TO
COL. GEORGE ARMISTEAD
APRIL 10 1779 APRIL 25 1818
COMMANDER OF THIS FORT
DURING THE BOMBARDMENT
BY THE BRITISH FLEET

COMMISSION
JAMES H. PRESTON MAYOR
PRESIDENT OF THE SAR SPANGLED BANNER CENTENNIAL COMMISSION

ARTHUR B. BIBBINS
CHAIRMAN

DR. JAMES D. IGLEHART
PRES. MD SOC. OF THE WAR OF 1812

JOHN A. WILSON
GEORGE ARMISTEAD
RICHARD H. SPENCER

EDWARD BERGE
SCULPTOR

The Sculptor Edward Henry Berge was a Baltimore born native known for his traditional style works in bronze, having studied at the Maryland Institute of Art and for a time studied in Paris under Rodin. He sculpted numerous works of arts including Calvert County World War I Monument in Prince Frederick, Calvert County. He is buried at Lorraine Park.

During the War of 1812 Bicentennial President General Larry Casey and Daughters of 1812 President National Ginger Apyar rededicated the monument with attendees from the State Society and General Society as Maryland Society President Christos Christou, Jr. hosted the General Society's visit to Baltimore and conducted the Cavalcade, just prior to the visit of the President of the United States.

Armistead Monument at Federal Hill
- Dedicated September 12, 1882 at Federal Hill, Baltimore, MD

The City of Baltimore erected the Colonel George Armistead Monument on Eutaw Place on September 12, 1882 to him as the commander of Fort McHenry during the British attack of September 13-14, 1814. The architectural firm of G. Metzger designed this monument that features the outline of Armistead's career in the inscription on the shaft. The marble block of fourteen feet rests on a base one foot and a half high. This monument was commissioned as a "substitute" for an earlier circa 1828 tablet of commemoration that became defaced and destroyed by time. Initially installed on Eutaw Place, the monument was moved to Federal Hill after residents protested that its height did not harmonize with the loftiness of their homes.

In 2013, CHAP hired Conservator of Fine Art, Steven Tatti, to conserve the monument. The monument and the ornamental fence were gently washed. The projected was funded by the City of Baltimore, through CHAP's Monument Restoration Program in the Department of Planning, with the additional contributions of the Maryland Military Monument's Commission and the City-wide Adopt A Monument Fund.

Battle Monument

– Cornerstone Dedicated September 12, 1815, Baltimore, MD

The Battle Monument was erected by Defenders themselves, members of our earliest society from 1815 to 1825, to honor all of those who lost their lives in the defense of Baltimore at the Battle of North Point on 12 September 1814 and the British bombardment of Fort McHenry on 13 and 14 September 1814.

The architect was Maximilian Godefroy who emigrated from France about 1805 and also designed the chapel at the original Saint Mary's Seminary and Mother Seton House, both located on North Paca Street, and the Unitarian Church on Franklin Street at North Charles Street in Baltimore. He later worked with Benjamin Henry Latrobe and In 1819 left America to live in England. Eventually he returned to France and died there prior to 1840.

The monument is constructed of marble and stands 39 feet in height. The base is unusual in that it resembles an Egyptian cenotaph or tomb. There are eighteen rows of marble at the base representing the states of the Union as of the time of the War of 1812. The column is carved like that of a Roman fasces – a bundle of rods having among them an ax with the blade projecting outward, borne before Roman magistrates as a badge of authority. The rods are bound with cords listing the names of the soldiers who died during the battle. The officers who died are listed at the top.

Atop the monument is a marble statue of a female, representing the City of Baltimore, "Lady Baltimore". The figure was sculpted by an Italian, Antonio Capellano. He, also, created the plaques displayed on the face of Old Saint Paul's on North Charles Street and the statue of George Washington atop the Washington Monument in Mount Vernon Place. In addition, he did work on the U.S. Capitol. On her head "Lady Baltimore" wears a crown of victory. In her hands she holds a laurel wreath and a ship's rudder.

The monument is located in the heart of the financial and government district on North Calvert Street just north of East Baltimore Street and just south of East Fayette Street in the City of Baltimore, Maryland. When it was built, this was the most fashionable, residential part of town, and the square was lined with lovely and elegant townhouses. Governor Charles Carnan Ridgely. of "Hampton" (who served as governor from 1815 to 1818), was responsible for the acquisition of the land for the monument.

The Seal of the City of Baltimore adopted in 1827 prominently features the monument. Since early in the 20th Century, the monument has been featured on the city's flag.

The Battle Monument was placed on the National Register of Historic Places, 4 June 1973.

A subscription book of the members and their donations is at the Maryland Historical Society and within its pages are listed the names of those shown on the monument, as illustrated on the following pages.

List of those Citizens who fell in the defence of
the City of Baltimore in the attack of the 12th & 13th Sept.
1814. or who have since died of the wounds then rec'd

James L. Donaldson   Adjutant 27th Reg'n M. M.
Levi   Claggett & Lieut Cap't J. Nicholson Fencibles
John — Clemm 2 Serg)
Thomas V Beeson   of the Washington artillerish
Jacob Haubert Mat [Cap't Wheyofields Co.] 5th Reg't
John Jephson   Cap't Kennedy's Co.   27 D°
James Wallace — Cap't Pennis Co.   Ditto Ditto
James H. Merriot   Cap't Adreons Co. —   5th Ditto
David Davis   Ditto   Ditto
Jacob Meraken   Ditto   Ditto
William Ways   Cap't Warners Co.   39th Reg't
Joshua Armstrong   Ditto   D°   Ditto
Gregorius Andre in Cap't Warden D°   Rifle Batt'n
James Richardson   Cap't Kennedy's D°   27. Reg't
Benjamin Bond   Cap't Haubert D°   51. Ditto
Clement Cox   Ditto   D°   d°

440

Names of those who fell &c. Continued —

Cecilius Belt — Cap.ᵗ Haubert Comp.ᵈ — 51.ˢᵗ Reg.ᵗ

John Garrett — Cap.ᵗ Deemes D.ᵒ — D.ᵒ D.ᵒ

Henry G. McComas, Cap.ᵗ Asquith's D.ᵒ Sharp Shooters

~~Daniel Wells~~ — ~~D.ᵒ~~ — ~~D.ᵒ~~

William McClellan ⎫ Balt.ᵒ United Volunteers ⎫ 5.ᵗʰ Reg.ᵗ
John Carter Byrd ⎭ then Cap.ᵗ Littlefield's Co ⎭

Daniel Wells Jr. — Cap.ᵗ Asquith's Sharp Shooters

John K. Cox — Cap.ᵗ Herbert — 51.ˢᵗ Reg.ᵗ

Benjamin Neal — Cap.ᵗ John McKane — 27.ᵗʰ D.ᵒ

Bryan Reynolds Cap.ᵗ Montgomery's Artillery

David Howard D.ᵒ D.ᵒ D.ᵒ

Uriah Prosper — 4.ᵗʰ Company — 27 Reg.ᵗ m. M.

Aquila Randall Cap.ᵗ Howard's Comp.ᵗ 5 Reg.ᵗ m.

Rich.ᵈ K Coakse

BATTLE MONUMENT.

Erected in Commemoration of those who fell in defence of this City on the 12th of Sept. 1814 at the Battle of North Point, and on 13th at the Bombardment of Fort McHenry.

J.L. Donaldson	Gregorius Andre
Levi Clagett	Dan.l Wells Jun.r
Jn.º Clemm	Jn.º K. Cox
T.V. Beeston	Benj.n Neal
J. Haubert	B. Reynolds
Jn.º Jephson	B. Howard
J. Wallace	Uriah Prosser
J.H. Marriot of Jn.º	A. Randall
E. Marriot	R.K. Cooksey
David Davis	J. Gregg
J. Merrikin	J. Evans
Wm Ways	A. Maas
J. Armstrong	J. Woolfe
J. Richardson	G. Jenkins
Benj Bond	W. Alexander
Clement Cox	G. Fauer
Cecilius Belt	T. Burneston
Jn.º Garrett	J. Dunn
J.G. McComas	P. Byard
Wm McClellan	J. Craig
Jn.º C. Byrd	M. Desk

The Corner stone of which was laid at the Solemnity of the 12th September 1815.
Estimated Cost 40,000 Dollars.

The 42 names as they appear on the monument.

W. Alexander	R. K. Cooksey	T. Garrett	H. G. McComas
Gregorius Andre	C. Cox	J. Gregg	J. Merriken
J. Armstrong	J. K. Cox	J. Haubert	B. Neale
T. V. Beeston	J. Craig	D. Howard	U. Prosser
C. Bell	D. Davis	G. Jenkins	A. Randall
B. Bond	M. Desk	J. Jephson	B. Reynols
J. Burneston	James Lowry	A. Maas	J. Richardson
P. Byard	Donaldson	E. Marriot	J. Wallace
J. C. Byrd	J. Dunn	J. H. Marriot of	W. Ways
Levi Clagett	J. Evans	John	D. Wells
J. Clemm	G. Fallier	W. McClellan	I. Woolf

The killed at North Point fall into 6 regiment under Stricker and it shows which regiments were in the thickest part of the battle. Three officers' names (Andre, Clagget, and Donaldson) appear at the top of Monument and 39 names are on ribbons on the lower pillar. Research has proven out their full names and units they served in.

3rd Division Maryland Militia under MGen Sam Smith
(3rd Brigade under BGen John Stricker)

5th Regiment (Lt. Col. Richard K. Heath):

John Carter Byrd

Richard Cooksey

David Davis

John Gregg

Jacob Haubert

George Jenkins

James H. Marriot

William McClellan

Jacob Merriken

Aquila Randall

27th Regiment (Lt. Col. Kennedy Long):

James Lowry Donaldson, Adjutant

Joseph Burneston Jr.

James Craig
Michael Desk
John Evans
John Jephson
Benjamin Neale
Uriah Prosser
James Richardson
James Wallace
Isaac Woolf (DOW Oct 15th)

39th Regiment (Lt. Col. Benjamin Fowler):
William Alexander
Joshua Armstrong
Peter Byard
George Fallier
Andrew Maas (MIA, presumed dead)
William Ways

51st Regiment (Lt. Col. Henry Arney):
Cornelius Bell
Benjamin Bond
John Kempson Cox
Thomas Garrett (DOW Sep 17th)

1st Rifle Battalion:
Lt. Gregorius André
Henry Gough McComas
Daniel Wells Jr.

1st Artillery Regiment:
David Howard
Brian Reynolds

Battle Acre Park
– Dedicated September 12, 1839. Monument erected 1914. Dundalk MD

On the eve of the 25th Anniversary of the Battle of North Point, a prominent merchant of Frederick County, Jacob Houck, gave to the State of Maryland an acre of land on the battlefield for the princely sum of one dollar. His gift today is known as Battle Acre and is along the North Point Road in Baltimore County.

In 1839 he purchased the land called "Swan Harbour" and soon thereafter built "one of the most splendid hotels in the vicinity" that became known as "Houck's Pavilion." For years thereafter served it as a prominent annual commemorative gathering site for the Old Defenders' of Baltimore. Jacob Houck, Sr. died in 1850 and is buried in Mount Olivet Cemetery in West Baltimore.

"Know all men by these presents, that I Jacob Houck of the city and county of Baltimore in the State of Maryland am held and firmly bound unto the State of Maryland in the full and just sum of one Dollar lawful money to be paid to the said state, or to its attorney to the payment whereof. I bind myself, my heirs Executors and Administrators firmly by these presents, sealed with my seal, and dated this eleventh day of September in the year of our Lord one thousand eight hundred and thirty nine.

Whereas the said Jacob Houck in consideration of the sum of one dollar to him paid at or before the sealing and delivery hereof, the receipt whereof is hereby acknowledged and also delivered good causes and valuable considerations herein thereunto moving, hath contracted to give grant and convey or to cause and procure to be granted and conveyed unto the said state this or part of a tract, piece or parcel of herein after described the same constituting a part of the North Point Battle Ground "for the purpose of erecting a Monument thereon." Now the Condition of the foregoing obligation is such, that the said Jacob Houck, or his heirs do and shall within six months next ensuing the date hereof, grant and convey, or cause and procure to be granted and conveyed to the State of Maryland aforesaid, to be held by the said State forever, for the use and purpose aforesaid. All that Lot or parcel of Land situated and lying in Baltimore County aforesaid being part of a tract called "Swan Harbour" which is contained within the meter and bounds, courses and distances following, that is to say; Beginning for the same part at a stone standing in the ground on the southwestern most side of the road leaving from the City of Baltimore to North Point..." *Excerpted from the deed of land conveyed to the State of Maryland.* [Baltimore County Court (Land Records) TK 292, pp. 246-247, Jacob Houck, "Swan Harbor," 11 September 1839, MSA CE 66-342].

For 75 years no monument was erected, despite the elaborated ceremonies held on September 12, 1839. A granite monument was finally dedicated in 1914 on the centennial of the battle.

Jacob Houck's son Dr. Jacob Wever Houck (1822-1888) was the father of Ella Virginia Houck (1862-1940) who married Reuben Ross Holloway and she was often described as the "number one patriot in Baltimore." She consistently and persistently advocated for the making of :The Star-Spangled Banner" as the official national anthem and other patriotic causes. She ultimately succeeded.

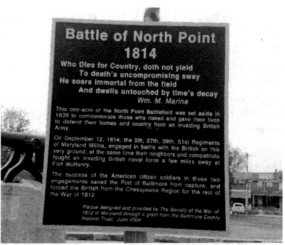

In 2004, a new Battle of North Point plaque was dedicated at the site by the War of 1812 Society commemorating the events of the day. Young and old attended the event including members of our Society, the Color Guard as well as community members. This exciting rededication of the park ensured continuous recognition of the often forgotten battle.

In 2014, for the Bicentennial ,the Park was cleaned up and rededicated for the Bicentennial celebrations. It received a major facelift that had been advocated for years by our society including new fencing, walkways, and paving.The front gates were replaced by the generosity of a community member after the originals were stolen. A mural was painted on the adjacent wall of the business shopping center depicting the events of that great time. Wayside markers were placed to educate visitors to the Park.

The bronze plaque was also replaced.

Bladensburg Monument

- Dedicated August 23, 2014, Bladensburg, Prince Georges Co., MD

The Battle of Bladensburg Memorial depicts Commodore Joshua Barney being assisted by Charles Ball (a former slave who served in his flotilla) and an unnamed marine helping the Commodore who had been wounded severely during the battle.

The Bicentennial of The Battle of Bladensburg during the War of 1812 was a perfect time for the commemoration of the battle, where Prince George's County hosted the "Undaunted Weekend" August 23-24. The event kick-off with the Marine Band performing patriotic music for the dedication of the "Undaunted in Battle" monument at 11 a.m., Saturday, Aug. 23 at Monument Park, located at 4100 Baltimore Ave. and Upshur Street in Bladensburg, Md.

Joanna Campbell Blake, the sculptor, designed a memorial to Americans who fought at the Battle of Bladensburg during the War of 1812 with the challenge of how to create a scene that commemorates a defeat, but a defeat that would prove to be a significant turning point in an eventual U.S. victory. "It galvanized the nation," Blake said of the August 1814 battle. The outcome was a major setback — it opened the door for the British to sack Washington — but it also alerted the country that its independence was tenuous and that a more sophisticated battle plan and military were needed. Nearly three weeks after the battle at Bladensburg, the Americans were victorious in Baltimore, where Francis Scott Key wrote the poem that became the fledgling nation's anthem, "The Star-Spangled Banner." "The Americans might not have had the victory at Baltimore if not for the Battle of Bladensburg," said Blake, a Cottage City resident who worked on the National World War II Memorial in Washington before taking on the job of creating the Bladensburg memorial. The sculptor died shortly after on May 22, 2016 in Toscana, Italy in a motorcycle crash and is buried in Magnolia Cemetery in Mobile, Alabama, where she was born.

The defeat of the American troops by the British at the Battle of Bladensburg unfortunately left the road to Washington open as the city had been left relatively unguarded since American leaders did not think the small capital would be a target. The British entered the city and burned several government buildings including the U.S. Capitol, the White House, and the Library of Congress. Historic Marine Barracks and the Home of the Commandants were left untouched, however. According to legend, this was due to British respect for the Marines and their fighting during the Battle of Bladensburg. Assistant Drum Major Staff Sgt. Steven Williams led the band during the concert and ceremony dedicating the monument. "I'm excited that we are a part of this event," Williams said. "The Marines from Marine Barracks Washington fought at that battle, including some members of the Marine Band."

While there may have been many members of the Marine Band that fought in the battle, historical records only confirm the names of four musicians: Fife Major Venerando Pulizzi, bugler George Woolgar, and musicians John Goldie and James Kale.

At the 2018 Old Defenders' Day a memorial was conducted at the monument.

Caulk's Field Monument
– Dedicated 1901 by Rev. Christopher T. Denroche and Capt. Columbus A. Leary
near Chestertown, Kent Co., MD

Address of Capt. Columbus A. Leary

Captain Columbus A. Leary, of Kent County, being introduced by President Denroche, spoke as follows: LADIES AND GENTLEMEN: - I must first comfort you with the assurance that you will not be called upon to endure what I may inflict upon you for but a few minutes, as at the end of that time I must make room for something more interesting and more instructive, indeed, it is circumstances and not my own presumption which bring me before you at all. The sub-committee appointed to procure, inscribe and erect a monument or slab at the grave of General Reed and a "Marker" on this field, have to explain that they have given much more attention to stability and durability than to ornamentation. In reference to the inscription on the slab (for such it really is) at General Reed's grave, they have simply briefly recited his public services, the ability with which they were executed and the good fortune to his fellow-countrymen which attended them, and concluded that they could not easily invent a much higher compliment. In reference to the inscription on the Marker on this field the committee deliberately determined to free it from clumsiness and to leave it abounding in charity. This sentiment was suggested by the recollection that our ancestor abundantly proved themselves worthy of the valor of a manly and chivalrous people in time of war, and this laid upon us the more agreeable but no less binding duty of showing by our magnanimity that we were worthy the friendship of that same people in time of peace. But our action in this regard was principally inspired by obedience to a law which governed man long before he had learned to temper the steel, weave the cloth, or to write the parchment, and is as potent to-day as it was when the Pyramids first cast their shadows across the blue Nile, or when Jacob was a young herdsman guarding the flocks of Laban

451

on the hills of Padanaram. ... the men and boys who confronted each other on this field eighty-eight years ago, we find that the Americans were chiefly, indeed, almost altogether sons of Revolutionary soldiers who had heard much of the follies and vices of men who ruled by hereditary and sometimes claimed to rule by divine right. Who was there to tell them that society had suffered nearly, or quite as many ills, from the schemes and machinations of irresponsible demagogues as it ever had by the vices and follies of kings? ...

THE BRITISH, COMMANDED BY
SIR PETER PARKER, BARONET,
AND THE AMERICANS, COMMANDED BY
COL. PHILIP REED,
MET IN ENGAGEMENT ON THIS FIELD,
AUGUST 31ST, 1814.
THE BRITISH WERE DEFEATED
AND
SIR PETER PARKER KILLED.
ERECTED A. D. 1902,
BY MARYLANDERS,
TO COMMEMORATE THE PATRIOTISM
AND FORTITUDE
OF THE VICTOR AND VANQUISHED.

(At the Caulk's Field Memorial dedication in 1902 and Gen. Reed's Gravemarker)

Address by Percy Granger Skirven

In 1914 at the remembrances stated: The war had been in progress nearly two years and neither country had been able to force its conclusion. Wearying of the rather desultory fighting at last Great Britain determined to make a final effort to terminate the struggle with the United States. In August 1814, she directed her war vessels to again enter the Chesapeake Bay. The "Annual Register" of 1814, a British publication, says: "The operations of the British Armaments on the coast of the southern American States had hitherto been on a small scale and calculated rather to alarm and irritate than to produce any considerable effect, - but in this year the resolution was taken of striking some important blow in these quarters." Tactics in that war were similar to those of earlier date and England's policy of burning the defenceless shore towns and villages, as well as the pillaging of farms that laid along the watercourses, was expected by the American citizens and soldiers at that time. The previous year the British had burned Havre-de-Grace and Frenchtown at the bead of Chesapeake Bay. They then went into the Sassafras River and burned both Georgetown and Fredericktown - bringing to light the heroism of Kitty Knight.

452

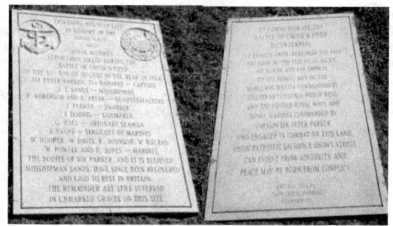

New slabs erected by Tulip Forest Farming Corporation of Chestertown, MD

Gen. James Adkins held a 200th Anniversary celebration on August 31, 2014 honoring the Battle on this field and invited the Birtish Commander Lt. Col. Colby Corrin to join in the celebration of 200 years of peace between our two countries.

Front row: Rededicated by Gen. James A. Adkins, William Leonard, Robert J. Ayres, Gen. Hall Worthington, Virginia "Ginger" Apyar, President National of Daughters of 1812, British Lt. Col. Colby Corrin, Royal Marine liaison officer to the U.S. Marine Corps Combat Development Command; Back Row: Kayleigh Gott, Junior Member Daughters of 1812, and Christos Christou, Jr., President War of 1812 Society in the State of Maryland.

Fort McHenry Wayside Marker
– Dedicated September 12, 2014, Fort McHenry, Baltimore, MD

In 2014, The Maryland Society worked hard to have a wayside marker erected at Fort McHenry to mark the location of the founding of our society at a former tavern near the wall of the fort.

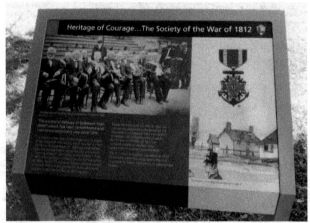

President Christos Christou dedicated the marker during the visit of the General Society for the Bicentennial with the leaders unveiling the marker including Past President Hall Worthington, President General Lawrence Casey, President General Thomas Jacks, Robert Cummins, and President National Ginger Apyar.

North Point Battlefield Park
— Dedicated September 12, 2015, Dundalk, MD

In 2015, North Point State Battlefield preserves nine acres of open land which represent the last undeveloped parcel from the site of the Battle of North Point, a turning point in the Defense of Baltimore during the War of 1812. On September 12, 1814, 3,000 citizen soldiers of the Maryland militia deployed across this field and fought invading British regulars from behind a fence line along its eastern edge. American Brigadier General Stricker, the hero of North Point, commanded his forces from within the borders of the State Battlefield.

President Christou attended the morning dedication prior to the Cavalcade tour with politicians and speakers including Christopher George. Later during the afternoon formal dedication with the War of 1812 Society Cavalcade, 1812 President Christou and SAR President William P. Smithson posed for pictures under the flag poles. 1812 President J. Patrick Warner and Daughters of 1812 President Sally Johnston gave remarks. Despite the pouring rain, the event was well attended and celebrated.

The park was dedicated to the soldiers who died on this field.

Sam Smith Statue Monument

- Dedicated July 4, 1918, Federal Hill, Baltimore, MD

At Federal Hill overlooking the Baltimore Harbor stands the monumental statue of Sam Smith who heroically established the defenses of Baltimore that saved the city. The statue, funded by the city's 1914 centennial celebration of the Battle of Baltimore, is the design of sculptor Hans Schuler (1874-1951) who studied at the Maryland Institute College of Art. The statue was first erected at Wyman Park Dell at North Charles and 29th Streets in 1917 and dedicated on July 4, 1918. Mr. Schuler is buried at Loudon Park Cemetery.

Hans Schuler received three commissions during the Centennial of the War of 1812, including the General Smith monument. Schuler's sculpture represents the General in his military uniform. This monument has been relocated twice and was originally on the edge of Wyman Park. In 1953, the monument moved to a park named for Samuel Smith at the corner of Pratt and Light Streets. In 1970, it was moved to its current location, overlooking the grand view of Baltimore's harbor and skylinewhere in 1814 a gun battery had been erected and the citizens of Baltimore witnessed the fiery bombardment of Fort McHenry.The inscriptions on the monument read: MAJOR-GENERAL SAMUEL SMITH, 1752-1839 / UNDER HIS COMMAND THE ATTACK OF THE BRITISH UPON BALTIMORE BY LAND AND SEA SEPTEMBER 12-14, / 1814 WAS REPULSED. MEMBER OF CONGRESS FORTY SUCCESSIVE YEARS, / PRESIDENT U.S. SENATE, SECRETARY OF THE NAVY, MAYOR OF BALTIMORE. /HERO OF BOTH WARS FOR AMERICAN INDEPENDENCE – LONG ISLAND – WHITE / PLAINS – BRANDYWINE – DEFENDER OF FORT MIFFLIN – VALLEY FORGE – / MONMOUTH – BALTIMORE. /
ERECTED BY THE NATIONAL STAR-SPANGLED BANNER CENTENNIAL

456

Wells and McComas Monument
- Dedicated 10 Sep 1858, Baltimore, MD
-

Folklore holds that on September 12, 1814, two teenaged militiamen, Daniel Wells and Henry G. McComas, (of Capt. Edward Aisquith's Sharpshooters, 1st Rifle Battalion, Maryland Militia) shot British Major General Robert Ross during the Battle of North Point. Though they were killed in the resulting action, Ross's death ultimately may have spared Baltimore from ransom and destruction.

On 10 September 1858, the bodies of Wells and McComas were exhumed from Green Mount Cemetery and placed in the Maryland Institute Building above the central market on Baltimore Street, for public viewing, then transferred to their final resting place, then below the monument's foundation, at the present-day monument at Ashland Square on 12 September 1858. The Wells and McComas Funeral and Monument Song was sung to the tune of the "Star-Spangled Banner" (but not the same words) in a play performed at the Holiday Street Theatre about Wells and McComas as martyrs, after which, there was the funeral procession to the monument. For those interested in the entire Maryland and Baltimore City funeral entourage see the *Baltimore American and Commercial Advertiser of 13 September 1858* on the following page.

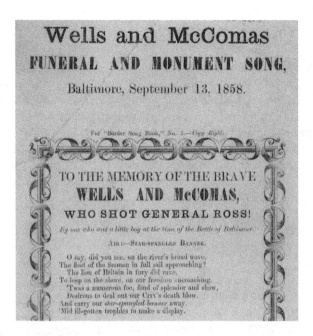

Wells and McComas

FUNERAL AND MONUMENT SONG,

Baltimore, September 13, 1858.

For "Border Song Book," No. 2.—Copy Right.

TO THE MEMORY OF THE BRAVE
WELLS AND McCOMAS,
WHO SHOT GENERAL ROSS!

By one who was a little boy at the time of the Battle of Baltimore.

AIR:—STAR-SPANGLED BANNER.

O say, did you see, on the river's broad wave,
The fleet of the fooman in full sail approaching?
The lion of Britain in fury did rave,
To leap on the shore, on our freedom encroaching.
'Twas a numerous foe, fond of splendor and show,
Desirous to deal out our City's death blow,
And carry our *star-spangled banner* away,
'Mid ill-gotten trophies to make a display.

The monument (an obelisk) was completed in 1872." It is located at Aisquith and Gay Streets in Old Town, an area just west of Johns Hopkins Hospital in Baltimore City. The monument was donated through private subscription and by the City of Baltimore. The inscription reads:

- *Daniel Wells, born December 30th, 1794 Killed September 12, 1814 at the Battle of North Point. Aged 19 years, 8 months, 13 days*
- *Henry G. McComas, born September 20, 1795 Killed September 12, 1814 at the Battle of North Point. Aged 18 yrs, 11 months, and 22 days.*

General Ross was killed on September 12, transported to *HMS Surprize*, placed in a hogshead of Jamaican rum, and further transported to Halifax, Nova Scotia, arriving September 28, where he was buried at St Paul's Church cemetery.

Battle of North Point –Americans Died

As with all wars, casualty lists vary as to the dead, wounded, and prisoners of war depending on the date of the report. The 1812 Battle Monument has the names of 42 men on it which was the best they could confirm at that time. Several inquiries to the public in early newspaper articles helped build this list [*The American Commercial Daily Advertiser* dated Sep 12, 1817, *Baltimore Patriot* dated June 15, 1819 courtesy of Robert Cummins Jr.]. Later stories and other publications such our own *"The British Invasion of Maryland 1812-1815"* authored by William Marine in 1914 expand on this list of participants. The number of dead at North Point however appears to be 36 with a few extra names who died at Ft. McHenry and at Bladensburg.

The official British Army casualty report, signed by Major Henry Debbeig, gives 39 killed and 251 wounded. Of these, 28 killed and 217 wounded belonged to the British Army; 6 killed and 20 wounded belonged to the 2nd and 3rd Battalions of the Royal Marines; 4 killed and 11 wounded belonged to the contingents of Royal Marines detached from Cockburn's fleet; and 1 killed and 3 wounded belonged to the Royal Marine Artillery. As was normal, the Royal Navy submitted a separate casualty return for the engagement, signed by Rear-Admiral George Cockburn, which gives 4 sailors killed and 28 wounded but contradicts the British Army casualty report by giving 3 killed and 15 wounded for the Royal Marines detached from the ships of the Naval fleet. The total British losses, as officially reported, were either 43 killed and 279 wounded or 42 killed and 283 wounded, depending on which of the two casualty returns was accurate. Historian Franklin R. Mullaly gives still another version of the British casualties: 46 killed and 295 wounded.

B.

STATEMENT, *showing the Widows and Orphans who are inscribed on the books of this office, as half-pay pensioners, for five years, conformably to the laws of the United States, especially the first section of the act of April the 16th, 1816, "the sum annually paid to each, and the states or territories in which the said pensioners are respectively paid;" made in obedience to a resolution of the Senate of the United States, passed under date of February the 22d, 1818.*

MARYLAND.

No.	Names of decedents, &c.	Rank or grade.	Original commencement of pension.	Pension per month.	Pension per annum.	Remarks, &c.
380	Atwell, James, *widow*	Private	30th March, 1814	84 00	$48 00	
581	Addison, William H. do.	Captain.	18th Dec. -	20	240	
382	Andre Gregorius, *widow and children*	1st lieutenant	12th Sept. -	15	180	Widow intermarried 8th Feb. 1817.
383	Bond, Benjamin, *widow*	Private	12th Sept. -	4	48	
384	Bowers, Jacob, do.	Do.	28th Nov. 1812	2 50	30	
385	Cres, Hugh, do.	Do.	15th Sept. 1814	4	48	
386	Davis, David, do.	Do.	16th Oct. -	4	48	
587	Dillon, James, do.	Captain	2d Oct. -	20	240	
588	Desk, Michael, do.	Private	12th Sept. -	4	48	
. 589	Donaldson,James L. do.	Lieut. and adj't.	12th Sept. -	20	240	
590	Evans, John, do.	Private	12th Sept. -	4	48	
591	Earnest, Charles, *widow and children*	Private	31st Aug. 1816	84 00	$ 48 00	Died of wounds. Widow intermarried, 20th January, 1817.
592	English,Marshall, *widow*	2d lieutenant	21st April, 1815	12 50	150	
593	Garrett, Thomas, do.	Private	13th Sept. 1814	4	48	
594	Green, John, do.	Do.	23d Oct. 1814	4	48	
595	Grant, John, do.	Do.	28th April, 1815	4	48	
596	Hull, Edward, do.	Do.	24th Aug. 1814	4	48	
597	Haney, Thomas, do.	Do.	16th Aug. 1815	4	48	
598	Kithcart, Robert, do.	Do.	24th Sept. 1814	4	48	
599	Latham, Edward, do.	Do.	1st May, 1814	4	48	
400	Lee, James, do.	Do.	9th Nov. 1813	4	48	
401	Marrott, Elisha, do.	Sergeant	24th Aug. 1814	5 50	66	
402	Morgan,Loderwick, *child*	Major	12th Aug.	25	500	
403	Mathews,Edward *widow*	Private	6th Sept. 1814	8 4	$ 48 00	
404	M'Lean, Roger or Rhoddy, *widow*	Do.	8th April, 1815	4	48	
405	Mills, George, *widow*	Do.	26th June, 1815	4	48	
406	Martin, Anthony, do.	Do.	21st Oct. 1814	4	48	
407	M'Kenny, Philip, *widow and children*	Do.	1st Oct. -	4	48	Widow intermarried, Dec. 14, 1815.
408	Prosser Uriah, *widow*	Do.	12th Sept. -	4	48	
409	Prince, John, do.	Do.	2d Dec. 1813	4	48	
410	Routzong, John, do.	Do.	31st Jan. 1815	4	48	
					$ 2,550 00	

252

153

[170]

254

British Dead or Wounded in Maryland

Most people know of the death of Gen. Robert Ross at the Battle of North Point supposedly shot from his white horse by two sharpshooters Wells and McComas or one of Howard's Mechanical Volunteers, and the death of Sir Peter Parker who was shot at the Battle of Caulk's Field and taken from the field and expired in a few minutes, but no comprehensive list has been put together of the dead and wounded on the British side and it may be impossible to do so. The lives of privates for example were not valued as many of them were left behind to be buried here in Maryland. Only the life of an officer was considered of value and might be transported back to England.

By Christopher T. George

There are several reports listing the number of British soldiers, sailors and marines who became casualties of the Battle of North Point. A consolidated list of casualties did not exist and there are discrepancies in the records as to the actual numbers. It is generally agreed that the British suffered as many as 295 wounded and 46 dead in the Battles of North Point and Baltimore.

Colonel Arthur Brooke, commander of the ground forces at the Battle of North Point, reported in a letter to Lord Bathurst, dated September 17, 1814, that the British Army losses were one general staff officer (Major General Robert Ross), one subaltern (Lieutenant Gracie of the 21st Foot), 2 sergeants and 35 rank and file soldiers killed, and 251 wounded.

Vice Admiral Cochrane, in his letter to John Wilson Croker, First Secretary of the Admiralty, dated September 22, 1814, reported the Royal Navy losses were one petty officer, 3 seamen and 3 Royal Marines killed and 32 seamen and 16 Royal Marines wounded, and one missing seaman.

By John McCavitt

I have been following up on the British casualties with my friend Kevin Chambers who works at the National Archives in London. See below details to date from the 21st Regiment. As Chris pointed out in earlier correspondence a lot of the British troops were Irish, and many of them were Scottish. I am happy to try to work away at finding as definitive a list as possible, while recognizing that there may be some gaps. If the names were ever to feature on a monument I suggest that the places the men came from should feature - the common assumption often being that for British read English.

Just to clarify regarding the British casualty list: Maj. Henry DeBieg listed 39 killed in action and 251 wounded as part of Brooke's after action report for North Point. Of the casualties, 4 rank and file killed and 1 officer; 10 rank and file wounded were Royal Marines detached from the fleet as part of the provisional battalion of Marines under Captain Robyns and those attached to the 2nd Battalion. Captain Robyns is also listed as the wounded officer.

There's three lists of Royal Navy personnel: one states losses "with the Army under Major-General Ross, September 12, 1814" and signed off by Cockburn; the second is a list of casualties of the Naval Brigade under Captain Crofton for 12 Sept 1814; and, the third is a list of Royal Marine casualties under Captain Robyns, again for September 12, 1814. It appears that Cochrane sent the first list on to Croker, but states it was casualties of Naval personnel between the 12th and 14th.

The first list has 1 Petty Officer, 3 seamen and 3 marines as being killed and 1 officer, 6 petty officers, 22 seamen and 15 marines as wounded. That's a total of 7 killed and 44 wounded which when added to DeBieg's list gives a total of 46 killed and 295 wounded.

The second list actually names each individual and has 6 killed, 32 wounded and 1 missing. This is 2 killed, 4 wounded and 1 missing more than the first list states.

The third list, again with names, has 1 killed and 15 wounded. The end tally states 1 killed and 16 wounded(?). Captain Robyns is listed as one of the wounded and the tally is 2 killed and 1 wounded below the first list results. By the way, the one marine killed is listed as dying of fatigue!

In summation: Robyns is listed on the Army list and the Navy list; The Royal Marine list did not tally up with the Army list; and, both the Navy and Marine lists do not tally up with Cockburn's list. DeBieg may not have counted those who eventually died of wounds.

August 1814

Effectives	Effectives as %	Sick present	Sick absent	Totals Sick	Sick as %	On Command	Total ORs	Dead since last retur
470	96.11	18	1	19	3.89	0	489	0
55	74.32	0	1	1	1.35	18	74	0
59	98.33	1	0	1	1.67	0	60	0
592	73.72	93	103	196	24.41	15	803	23
984	88.09	31	58	89	7.97	44	1117	2
574	64.42	45	234	279	31.31	38	891	19
670	76.31	73	8	81	9.23	127	878	5
398	78.97	0	106	106	21.03	0	504	13
3802	78.95	261	511	772	16.03	242	4816	62

ectives	Effectives as %	Sick present	Sick absent	Sick Total	Sick as %	On Command	Total ORs	Dead, since last return	De
)	88.64	31	3	34	7.02	21	484	5	0
	60.81	6	5	11	14.86	18	74	0	0
	93.33	2	2	4	6.67	0	60	0	0
)	79.44	29	113	142	18.96	12	749	7	4
	81.95	60	67	127	12.52	56	1014	26	2
	55.96	58	281	339	38.88	45	872	19	0
	68.11	89	16	105	17.53	86	599	5	1
	85.75	32	29	61	14.02	1	435	11	0
!5	75.23	307	516	823	19.20	239	4287	73	7

21st Regiment

Sgt. Francis Treacy, Culmory, Culmony

Pvt. Andrew Blair, Paisley, Scotland

Pvt. James Carland, Cappo

Pvt. Archibald Graham, Ballinreach, Scotland

Pvt. Thomas Thompson, Limerick, Ireland

Pvt. Charles Scaffan, Stafford, England

Pvt. Bernard McFadden, Newry, Ireland

Pvt. John Boyd, Glasgow, Scotland

Pvt. John Frawly, Limerick, Ireland

Pvt. James Russell, Swords, Ireland

Pvt. Hugh McDonald, Ferns, Ireland

Pvt. Walter Little, Gilborrough

Pvt. Roger Courlay, Everaugh(?)

Pvt. John Moffatt, Ayr, Scotland, died of wounds 14th September received in action on 12th September

Pvt. Peter McAllister, Leck,Ireland, died 14th September of wounds received in action on 12th September

Pvt. John McGrath, Kilmarnock, Scotland, died 16th September of wounds received in action on 12th September

Pvt. George McKenzie, died of wounds received in action on 17th September (does not specify when the action took place – looks like 12th September)

Pvt. James Hall, Mansfield, England, died 17th September of wounds received in action on 12th September

Pvt. James Orr, Paisley, Scotland, died 18th September of wounds received in action 12th September

Pvt. William Mooney, Rossmore, died 18th September of wounds received in action on 12th September

Cpl. Adam Geddes, Loughbrickland, died 26th September of wounds received in action at Bladensburg

Pvt. John Dougherty, Donegal, Ireland, died 2nd October of wounds received in action at Bladensburg

Pvt. Thomas Leacock, Longford, Ireland, died 6th October of wounds received in action at Bladensburg

Pvt. William Hood, Tetborough, England, died 7th October of wounds received in action at Bladensburg

RN of the Non-Commissioned Officers, Drummers, Fifers, and Privates of the _____ Regiment of _____ ,
...th, Desertion, &c. has been ascertained, but whose Accounts are not yet made up, from 25th _____ to 24th _____ ,

Rank	Regiments	Christian Names	Place of Birth	Trade when Enlisted	How become Non-effective	Date on which

Signature of Commanding Officer _____
Rank _____
Station _____

Additional Sources:

Baltimore Monumental Subscription Book, 19 Sep 1815

Baltimore Patriot newspaper, various dates, 1815-1819

Hickman, Nathaniel, *Citizen Soldiers at North Point and Fort McHenry* (1858)

Huntsberry, Thomas V. and Joanne M., *North Point, War of 1812* (1985)

Huntsberry, Thomas Vincent, *Western Maryland, Pennsylvania, Virginia Militia in Defense of Maryland, 1805 to 1815* (1983)

Johnson's Database, 2019 (Records relating to American Prisoners of War 1812-1815, British Admiralty, Microfilm BRAAM ADM 103 series, reels 1 through 11, Public Records Office, London, Great Britain), compiled by Eric E. Johnson

Mallick, Sallie A. and Wright, F. Edward, *Frederick County Militia in the War of 1812* (1992)

Marine, William M., *The British Invasion of Maryland, 1812-1815* (1913)

Peterson, Clarence S., *Known Military Dead during the War of 1812* (1955)

Pierce, Alycon Trubey, *Selected Final Pension Payment Vouchers 1818-1864 Maryland: Baltimore* (1997)

Scharf, J. Thomas, *History of Baltimore City and County* (1881)

Sharp's Database, 2018 (Patients at Naval Hospital, Washington, DC in 1814, transcribed with notes by John G. Sharp and contributed by Ralph Eshelman)

Sheads, Scott S., *The Chesapeake Campaign of 1813-1815* (2014)

Shomette, Donald G., *Flotilla: The Patuxent Naval Campaign in the War of 1812* (2009)

Smith's Database, 2019 (Grave Information for Maryland Soldiers compiled by Samuel Y. Smith, Jr., a member of the Maryland Society of the War of 1812 through research of cemeteries, tombstones and Findagrave records)

Heritage Books by Christos Christou, Jr. and Henry C. Peden, Jr.:

Maryland Casualties in the War of 1812
Christos Christou, Jr. and Henry C. Peden, Jr.

Heritage Books by Christos Christou, Jr.:

Abstracts of Kent County, Maryland Wills, Volume 1: 1777–1816
Christos Christou, Jr. and John Anthony Barnhouser

Abstracts of Kent County, Maryland Wills. Volume 2: 1816–1867
Christos Christou, Jr. and John Anthony Barnhouser

Colonial Families of the Eastern Shore of Maryland, Volume 4
Christos Christou, Jr. and F. Edward Wright

Maryland Regulars in the War of 1812
Eric Eugene Johnson and Christos Christou, Jr.

Heritage Books by Henry C. Peden, Jr.:

*A Closer Look at St. John's Parish Registers
[Baltimore County, Maryland], 1701–1801*

A Collection of Maryland Church Records

*A Guide to Genealogical Research in Maryland:
5th Edition, Revised and Enlarged*

*Abstracts of Marriages and Deaths in Harford County,
Maryland, Newspapers, 1837–1871*

Abstracts of the Ledgers and Accounts of the Bush Store and Rock Run Store, 1759–1771

Abstracts of the Orphans Court Proceedings of Harford County, 1778–1800

Abstracts of Wills, Harford County, Maryland, 1800–1805

Anne Arundel County, Maryland, Marriage References 1658–1800
Henry C. Peden, Jr. and Veronica Clarke Peden

Baltimore City [Maryland] Deaths and Burials, 1834–1840

Baltimore County, Maryland, Overseers of Roads, 1693–1793

Bastardy Cases in Baltimore County, Maryland, 1673–1783

Bastardy Cases in Harford County, Maryland, 1774–1844

Bible and Family Records of Harford County, Maryland, Families: Volume V

Cecil County, Maryland Marriage References, 1674–1824
Henry C. Peden, Jr. and Veronica Clarke Peden

Children of Harford County: Indentures and Guardianships, 1801–1830

Colonial Delaware Soldiers and Sailors, 1638–1776

*Colonial Families of the Eastern Shore of Maryland
Volumes 5, 6, 7, 8, 9, 11, 12, 13, 14, 16, and 19*
Henry C. Peden, Jr. and F. Edward Wright

*Colonial Families of the Eastern Shore of Maryland
Volume 21 and Volume 23*

Colonial Maryland Soldiers and Sailors, 1634–1734

Colonial Tavern Keepers of Maryland and Delaware, 1634–1776

Dorchester County, Maryland, Marriage References, 1669–1800
Henry C. Peden, Jr. and Veronica Clarke Peden

Dr. John Archer's First Medical Ledger, 1767–1769, Annotated Abstracts

Early Anglican Records of Cecil County

*Early Harford Countians, Individuals Living in
Harford County, Maryland in Its Formative Years
Volume 1: A to K, Volume 2: L to Z, and Volume 3: Supplement*

Family Cemeteries and Grave Sites in Harford County, Maryland

First Presbyterian Church Records, Baltimore, Maryland, 1840–1879

*Frederick County, Maryland, Marriage References
and Family Relationships, 1748–1800*
Henry C. Peden, Jr. and Veronica Clarke Peden

*Genealogical Gleanings from Harford County,
Maryland, Medical Records, 1772–1852*
Winner of the Norris Harris Prize from MHS for
the best genealogical reference book in 2016!

Harford (Maryland) Homicides

Harford County Taxpayers in 1870, 1872 and 1883

Harford County, Maryland Death Records, 1849–1899

Harford County, Maryland Deponents, 1775–1835

Harford County, Maryland Divorces and Separations, 1823–1923

Harford County, Maryland, Death Certificates, 1898–1918: An Annotated Index

Harford County, Maryland, Divorce Cases, 1827–1912: An Annotated Index

Harford County, Maryland, Inventories, 1774–1804

*Harford County, Maryland, Marriage References
and Family Relationships, 1774–1824*
Henry C. Peden, Jr. and Veronica Clarke Peden

*Harford County, Maryland, Marriage References
and Family Relationships, 1825–1850*

*Harford County, Maryland, Marriage References
and Family Relationships, 1851–1860*
Henry C. Peden, Jr. and Veronica Clarke Peden

*Harford County, Maryland, Marriage References
and Family Relationships, 1861–1870*
Henry C. Peden, Jr. and Veronica Clarke Peden

*Harford County, Maryland, Marriage References
and Family Relationships, 1871–1875*

*Harford (Old Brick Baptist) Church, Harford County, Maryland,
Records and Members (1742–1974), Tombstones, Burials (1775–2009)
and Family Relationships*

Heirs and Legatees of Harford County, Maryland, 1774–1802

Heirs and Legatees of Harford County, Maryland, 1802–1846

Inhabitants of Baltimore County, Maryland, 1763–1774

Inhabitants of Cecil County, Maryland 1774–1800

Inhabitants of Cecil County, Maryland, 1649–1774

Inhabitants of Harford County, Maryland, 1791–1800

Inhabitants of Kent County, Maryland, 1637–1787

Joseph A. Pennington & Co., Havre De Grace, Maryland, Funeral Home Records: Volume II, 1877–1882, 1893–1900

Kent County, Maryland Marriage References, 1642–1800
Henry C. Peden, Jr. and Veronica Clarke Peden

Marriages and Deaths from Baltimore Newspapers, 1817–1824

Maryland Bible Records, Volume 1: Baltimore and Harford Counties

Maryland Bible Records, Volume 2: Baltimore and Harford Counties

Maryland Bible Records, Volume 3: Carroll County

Maryland Bible Records, Volume 4: Eastern Shore

Maryland Bible Records, Volume 5: Harford, Baltimore and Carroll Counties

Maryland Bible Records, Volume 7: Baltimore, Harford and Frederick Counties

Maryland Deponents, 1634–1799

Maryland Deponents: Volume 3, 1634–1776

Maryland Prisoners Languishing in Goal, Volume 1: 1635–1765

Maryland Prisoners Languishing in Goal, Volume 2: 1766–1800

Maryland Public Service Records, 1775–1783: A Compendium of Men and Women of Maryland Who Rendered Aid in Support of the American Cause against Great Britain during the Revolutionary War

Marylanders and Delawareans in the French and Indian War, 1756–1763

Marylanders to Carolina: Migration of Marylanders to North Carolina and South Carolina prior to 1800

Marylanders to Kentucky, 1775–1825

Marylanders to Ohio and Indiana, Migration Prior to 1835

Marylanders to Tennessee

Methodist Records of Baltimore City, Maryland: Volume 1, 1799–1829

Methodist Records of Baltimore City, Maryland: Volume 2, 1830–1839

Methodist Records of Baltimore City, Maryland: Volume 3, 1840–1850 (East City Station)

More Maryland Deponents, 1716–1799

More Marylanders to Carolina: Migration of Marylanders to North Carolina and South Carolina prior to 1800

More Marylanders to Kentucky, 1778–1828

More Marylanders to Ohio and Indiana: Migrations Prior to 1835

Orphans and Indentured Children of Baltimore County, Maryland, 1777–1797

Outpensioners of Harford County, Maryland, 1856–1896

Presbyterian Records of Baltimore City, Maryland, 1765–1840

Quaker Records of Baltimore and Harford Counties, Maryland, 1801–1825

Quaker Records of Northern Maryland, 1716–1800

Quaker Records of Southern Maryland, 1658–1800

Revolutionary Patriots of Anne Arundel County, Maryland, 1775–1783

Revolutionary Patriots of Baltimore Town and Baltimore County, 1775–1783

*Revolutionary Patriots of Calvert
and St. Mary's Counties, Maryland, 1775–1783*

Revolutionary Patriots of Caroline County, Maryland, 1775–1783

Revolutionary Patriots of Cecil County, Maryland, 1775–1783

Revolutionary Patriots of Charles County, Maryland, 1775–1783

Revolutionary Patriots of Delaware, 1775–1783

Revolutionary Patriots of Dorchester County, Maryland, 1775–1783

Revolutionary Patriots of Frederick County, Maryland, 1775–1783

Revolutionary Patriots of Harford County, Maryland, 1775–1783

Revolutionary Patriots of Kent and Queen Anne's Counties, 1775–1783

Revolutionary Patriots of Lancaster County, Pennsylvania, 1775–1783

Revolutionary Patriots of Maryland, 1775–1783: A Supplement

Revolutionary Patriots of Maryland, 1775–1783: Second Supplement

Revolutionary Patriots of Montgomery County, Maryland, 1776–1783

Revolutionary Patriots of Prince George's County, Maryland, 1775–1783

Revolutionary Patriots of Talbot County, Maryland, 1775–1783

Revolutionary Patriots of Washington County, Maryland, 1776–1783

*Revolutionary Patriots of Worcester
and Somerset Counties, Maryland, 1775–1783*

*St. George's (Old Spesutia) Parish, Harford County, Maryland
Church and Cemetery Records, 1820–1920*

St. John's and St. George's Parish Registers, 1696–1851

*Survey Field Book of David and William Clark
in Harford County, Maryland, 1770–1812*

Talbot County, Maryland Marriage References, 1662–1800
Henry C. Peden, Jr. and Veronica Clarke Peden

The Crenshaws of Kentucky, 1800–1995

The Delaware Militia in the War of 1812

*Union Chapel United Methodist Church Cemetery
Tombstone Inscriptions, Wilna, Harford County, Maryland*